"This ambitious book is nothing less than a complete re-imagining of the human condition. Existing ways of thinking and practices, rooted in political realism where countries pursue national security through balance-of-power policies, have brought the world to a perilous stage. Johansen outlines an alternative grand strategy rooted in 'empirical realism' where national capabilities are harnessed to achieve human security in a new global governance architecture that implements correlates of peace to reduce human suffering and universalize human dignity. An invaluable guide on the shared journey to a more perfect global community."

—**Ramesh Thakur**, United Nations University;
Australian National University

"An urgent, ambitious, deeply thoughtful, and clear-eyed search for principles and strategies of peace-building and conflict resolution for a troubled world. Reflecting a lifetime of thinking and writing, Johansen ranges widely across literatures, debates, and contemporary world politics to distill core insights and offer an agenda for action. An extraordinary achievement!"

—**G. John Ikenberry**, Princeton University

"With lucidity, astounding breadth of knowledge, conceptual mastery, and social scientific rigor, Robert Johansen proposes an innovative foreign policy paradigm called 'empirical realism,' which if actualized would enhance human security and help governments meet the seemingly overwhelming challenges of our time. Not only a masterwork culminating a distinguished career, but a hopeful and persuasive assessment of the contemporary human predicament."

—**Richard Falk**, Princeton University, Emeritus

"This is a profoundly important book that offers critical insight into the false premises and misguided thinking that lie at the heart of US foreign and security policy. For those seeking an explanation for why US military policy has failed in Vietnam, Afghanistan, Iraq and beyond, here is the answer. Essential reading for those seeking realistic approaches for advancing international peace and human rights."

—**David Cortright**, University of Notre Dame

"In this unique synthesis of 60 years of research, teaching, and current scholarly evidence, Johansen demonstrates the need for a global strategy of peace with security that includes equity, rule of law, and democratic global governance. This book validates the significance of transnational civil society in necessary change. Johansen has produced a thorough, thought-provoking, and insightful volume that should leave no reader untouched."

—**Peter Wallensteen**, University of Uppsala

"Peace is an elusive goal and those who advocate for it are dreamers who do not have their feet firmly grounded in the world of reality. In this clear and compelling book, Johansen explodes both of these clichés. In a state-of-the-art analysis of social science research and the direction of empirical data findings, he recommends much-needed changes in policy directions for sustainable peace. His recommendations, if embraced by policy makers, will go a long way in making the world a far more peaceful and flourishing place. This is essential reading for anyone interested in sustainable peacebuilding."

—**A. Rashied Omar**, Claremont Main Road Mosque, Cape Town; University of Notre Dame

"Johansen's attention to the role local struggles play to help rein in the 'hyper-independent' 'realist' states that have created the existential threats we confront today should advance new thinking in international relations theory and inspire more people to think in imaginative ways about how to realize a just peace."

—**Jackie Smith**, University of Pittsburgh

"*Where the Evidence Leads* is a cogent critique of political realism. It demonstrates the damage done by an ideology narrowly based on belief in military power alone as the ultimate arbitrator of international relations. Political realism has dominated American foreign policy for a generation and played a role in endless war, climate collapse, the pandemic, and vast human rights atrocities. Johansen provides a blueprint to escape this dominance. He argues for a return to ideas repressed by political realism and for the creation of new concepts and practices to meet the needs of a suffering world."

—**Mary Ellen O'Connell**, University of Notre Dame

"The good old days are gone for good, and they were not so good for many of the planet's poorest citizens. What has not yet disappeared is the antiquated conviction that borders and walls can protect us from disease, pollution, and desperate people. Johansen pushes us to set aside our tired thinking, taken-for-granted assumptions, and received wisdom. He asks readers to imagine the ethical, prudent, and non-zero-sum policies required for a better world. That is 'where the evidence leads.'"

—**Thomas G. Weiss**, CUNY Graduate Center

"A courageous book which states in no uncertain terms that all the evidence we have proves that (international) politics-as-usual does not work. Narrow conceptions of national interest have time and again led to policy failures and away from a better, safer life for all. Johansen asks us to look anew at what we already know: that national security will only happen when we see and develop strategies for global and human security. Global governance in the human interest works better than military might and only old habits and assumptions prevent us from actualizing peace on this earth."

—**Catia Cecilia Confortini**, Wellesley College

WHERE THE EVIDENCE LEADS

STUDIES IN STRATEGIC PEACEBUILDING

Series Editors
R. Scott Appleby, John Paul Lederach, and Daniel Philpott
The Joan B. Kroc Institute for International Peace Studies
University of Notre Dame

STRATEGIES OF PEACE
Edited by Daniel Philpott and Gerard F. Powers

UNIONISTS, LOYALISTS, AND CONFLICT TRANSFORMATION IN NORTHERN
IRELAND
Lee A. Smithey

JUST AND UNJUST PEACE
An Ethic of Political Reconciliation
Daniel Philpott

COUNTING CIVILIAN CASUALTIES
An Introduction to Recording and Estimating Nonmilitary Deaths in Conflict
Edited by Taylor B. Seybolt, Jay D. Aronson, and Baruch Fischhoff

RESTORATIVE JUSTICE, RECONCILIATION, AND PEACEBUILDING
Edited by Jennifer J. Llewellyn and Daniel Philpott

QUALITY PEACE
Peacebuilding, Victory and World Order
Peter Wallensteen

THE PEACE CONTINUUM
What It Is and How to Study It
Christian Davenport, Erik Melander, and Patrick M. Regan

WHEN POLITICAL TRANSITIONS WORK
Reconciliation as Interdependence
Fanie Du Toit

EVERYDAY PEACE
How So-called Ordinary People Can Disrupt Violent Conflict
Roger Mac Ginty

Where the Evidence Leads

A REALISTIC STRATEGY FOR PEACE AND HUMAN SECURITY

Robert C. Johansen

For Jane,
Whose scholarship, embodied
values, personal example, and
friendship have deeply moved
me and Ruthann and
contributed to the highest
message of this book,

Bob

OXFORD
UNIVERSITY PRESS

OXFORD
UNIVERSITY PRESS

Oxford University Press is a department of the University of Oxford. It furthers the University's objective of excellence in research, scholarship, and education by publishing worldwide. Oxford is a registered trade mark of Oxford University Press in the UK and certain other countries.

Published in the United States of America by Oxford University Press
198 Madison Avenue, New York, NY 10016, United States of America.

Library of Congress Cataloging-in-Publication Data
Names: Johansen, Robert C., author.
Title: Where the evidence leads : a realistic strategy for peace and human security / Robert C. Johansen.
Other titles: Realistic strategy for peace and human security
Description: New York : Oxford University Press, 2021. |
Series: Studies in strategic peacebuilding | Includes bibliographical references and index. |
Identifiers: LCCN 2021027071 (print) | LCCN 2021027072 (ebook) |
ISBN 9780197586655 (paperback) | ISBN 9780197586648 (hardback) |
ISBN 9780197586679 (epub) | ISBN 9780197586662 (updf) | ISBN 9780197586686 (oso)
Subjects: LCSH: National security—United States. | United States—Foreign relations—2017– |
Human security—Government policy—United States. | Peace.
Classification: LCC UA23 .J544 2021 (print) | LCC UA23 (ebook) | DDC 355/.033573—dc23
LC record available at https://lccn.loc.gov/2021027071
LC ebook record available at https://lccn.loc.gov/2021027072

DOI: 10.1093/oso/9780197586648.001.0001

1 3 5 7 9 8 6 4 2

Paperback printed by LSC Communications, United States of America
Hardback printed by Bridgeport National Bindery, Inc., United States of America

For Ruthann, Erik, and Sonia,
Who have taught me the foundation of the world
And for students,
Whose hopes and fears shape the world that is yet to be

Contents

Figure

Tables

Acknowledgments

<hr/>

THIS BOOK HAS grown from a lifetime of research, teaching, and scholarship during which many people have contributed professional insights and personal experiences that have deepened my understanding of the questions examined here. Many people have shaped significant parts of this analysis, but of course none is responsible for its weaknesses. I am grateful for what each person named in these acknowledgments has contributed to this analysis.

For their intellectual contributions over the years and their willingness to read and comment on the manuscript in whole or in part, I especially thank the Marilyn Keough Dean of the Keough School of Global Affairs, R. Scott Appleby, who strongly supported and advised me on the writing; John Paul Lederach, an inspiration in all seasons; Peter Wallensteen, who has exuded exemplary peace research over the four decades I have known him; and these other esteemed colleagues: David Cortright, George Lopez, Mary Ellen O'Connell, Daniel Philpott, Jackie Smith, Alexander Dukalskis, and two excellent anonymous reviewers chosen by Oxford University Press.

This book has also been influenced by much intellectual stimulation and growth that have occurred in conversations at the Kroc Institute for International Peace Studies since we together founded it more than three decades ago. It has been an exciting intellectual community of interactions with thoughtful and committed students, visiting fellows, and faculty colleagues—the most frequent interlocuters I mention here: Catherine Bolton, Erin Corcoran, Gary Goertz, Dennis Goulet, Anne Hayner, David Hooker, Douglass Cassel, Emmanuel Katongole, Asher Kaufman, Gil Loescher, Laura Miller-Graff, Juan Mendez, Mahan Mirza, Ann Mische, Ebrahim Moosa, Laurie

Nathan, Rashied Omar, Atalia Omer, Jerry Powers, Jason Springs, Susan St. Ville, Raimo Vayrynen, Ernesto Verdeja, John Howard Yoder, and, of course, those named previously as readers of this manuscript.

I also am grateful for help from the Kroc Institute's excellent staff who have always been supportive, tireless, efficient, and friendly, especially including our Institute's founding director, John J. Gilligan, who inspired me and others to join this pioneering initiative at the University of Notre Dame, Hal Culbertson, Barbara Lockwood, Joan Fallon, Anna Van Overberghe, Andre Ratassep, Cathy Laake, Rosemarie Green, Rita Kopczynski, Jennifer Betz, Hannah Heinzekehr, and Michele Talos.

I first learned the value of transnational, comparative analysis of the structure of world order by examining "preferred worlds" with insightful participants from all the major cultural regions of the world in the World Order Models Project. From among many participants in that project and for their pathbreaking and extraordinarily stimulating research I especially thank Saul Mendlovitz, Richard Falk, Johan Galtung, Ali Mazrui, Yoshikazu Sakamoto, Mary Kaldor, Rajni Kothari, Mohamed Sid-Ahmed, Georgi Arbatov, Georges Abi-Saab, David Held, Elise Boulding, Rob Walker, and Lester Ruiz.

This book is a personal response to Mrs. Joan Kroc's earnest concerns about ending unnecessary violence and her generous philanthropy without which the Kroc Institute for International Peace Studies and the Hesburgh Center for International Studies would not have been possible, nor would have the research and educational experiences of the 640 MA and 27 PhD graduates who have entered our halls from 109 countries to earn advanced degrees. Without wanting to call attention to herself, she sought the highest possible quality of peace studies education for international and US students in order to reduce violence throughout the world.

Of course it was university president Father Theodore M. Hesburgh, C.S.C.'s prophetic vision of a world freed from the threat of nuclear weapons with the help of young people coming from adversarial great powers to study together at the University of Notre Dame that inspired Mrs. Kroc's interest in supporting the new initiatives here, and it is to him that heartfelt thanks go for his farsighted commitment at the institute's creation and for his continuous leadership and strong support thereafter.

In addition, this analysis is a partial response to questions that lingered from many international and US students after our classes were over and they went off to use their peacebuilding skills to reduce human suffering, which has always been our overall goal. As individual students come and go, they change my life forever in ways that leave me profoundly grateful for the meaning, noble quality, and seriousness of purpose that they contribute to the student-teacher learning process.

I personally and the Kroc Institute for International Peace Studies have benefited from the insight, leadership, and financial and moral support of exceptionally dedicated board members. I note here only those who have personally contributed to this project, including John R. Mullen, our gifted, long-time chairman, Richard Starmann, Steven Pepe, Michael Heisler, J. Patrick Danahy, Judy Scully, John Scully, Janna Hunter-Bowman, and Landrum Bolling.

I am also indebted and deeply grateful to excellent teachers who laid the first foundation for this book, only four of whom I can mention here: Ken Brown, who inspired me as a college student to explore how ethics apply to war and peace; Richard Falk, who demonstrated to me as a graduate student and many times thereafter how international law and ethics can advance the values of human dignity; Tim Rieman, whose social conscience made clear that a moral issue lay behind every major political issue; and Paul Keller, a teacher's teacher, who unveiled how our habits of language and thought determine whom we turn into friends or "enemies" and how we choose to relate to each.

Others who have influenced the contents of this book through panel presentations and interpersonal conversations, often at professional meetings, include John Ikenberry, John Mearsheimer, Daniel Deudney, Mary Kaldor, Chad Alger, Gareth Porter, David Forsythe, Thomas Weiss, Ramesh Thakur, Cecelia Lynch, Paul Wapner, Catia Confortini, and Joseph Schwartzberg.

I am grateful for the help of professionals at Oxford University Press, including David McBride, Editor-in-in-Chief, Social Sciences; Holly Mitchell, Assistant Editor; Haripriya Ravichandran, Project Manager; and copy editor Patterson Lamb.

My earliest debts and deepest gratitude go to my first teacher and personal "counselor," Vera Emmert Johansen, and to my politically astute, example-setting, immigrant father, Martinus Charles Johansen. They helped me understand that I should treat all people the way I want to be treated and that the nation-state is not the highest authority in life. I am grateful to members of our extended family on both sides of the Atlantic for reinforcing these understandings.

Above all, I warmly thank Ruthann Knechel Johansen, my wife and soul-mate forever, who read the entire manuscript at three different stages and parts of it even more, for her substantive insights, spiritual inspiration, constant support, and uplifting love that arise from lifelong work together on projects rooted in shared values and the experience of daily striving, despite failings, to live faithfully into our growing value commitments. I cherish her partnership in all things. Among other joys, the manuscript kept our minds focused on important issues over dinners while confined at home because of Covid-19.

I thank our two adult children, Erik Christopher Johansen and Sonia Lisbeth Johansen, for their lifelong acceptance, patient understanding, intellectual stimulation, and unique commitments to human dignity and human security. The ways that each of their lives have unfolded and intertwined with mine helped me understand the lives of others in ways that I would not have known without them. Our shared life experiences gave birth to this project and brought forth the energy necessary to bring it to completion. I thank our son-in-law, Andrew Volckens, for his friendship, unwavering support, and focused concentration and faith which have contributed to my life far beyond this project. Finally, I thank our grandchildren, Demetria, Daria, and Doren Johansen and Vera Volckens for teaching me some of life's most precious qualities related to human security that I would never have fathomed except for their relationships with me.

I express joyful appreciation to each person who has contributed to this book while keenly aware that, in spite of their good help, some of my own limitations doubtless remain evident in these pages. Despite the many policy criticisms voiced here, this is a book of hope for human possibilities. My analysis constitutes an authentic synthesis of evidence and theory that describe an open-ended, truth-seeking, life-enhancing path for people to walk together in the quest for a more perfect global community. This book will succeed whenever it brings teachers, students, policymakers, and citizens, along with scholars from security studies and peace studies, into conversation to learn from one another.

* * * * *

None of my previous publications have been included in this book but some sections draw on these earlier publications: "Peace *and* Justice? The Contribution of International Judicial Processes to Peacebuilding," in *Strategies of Peace: Transforming Conflict in a Violent World*, ed. Daniel Philpott and Gerard F. Powers (New York: Oxford University Press, 2010), 189–230; "Developing a Grand Strategy for Peace and Human Security: Guidelines from Research, Theory, and Experience," *Global Governance* 23, no. 4 (2017): 525–536; *The National Interest and the Human Interest* (Princeton, NJ: Princeton University Press, 1980); "The Impact of U.S. Policy toward the International Criminal Court on the Prevention of Genocide, War Crimes, and Crimes against Humanity," *Human Rights Quarterly* 28 (May 2006): 301–331; "Proposal for a United Nations Emergency Peace Service," in *A United Nations Emergency Peace Service*, ed. Robert C. Johansen (New York: Global Action to Prevent War, Nuclear Age Peace Foundation, and World Federalist Movement, 2006), 23–42; "The Future of United Nations Peacekeeping and Enforcement: A Framework for Policymaking," *Global Governance* 2, no. 3 (September–December 1996): 299–333; and "The E-Parliament: Global Governance to Serve the Human Interest," *Widener Law Review* 13 (2007): 319–427.

Robert C. Johansen
Kroc Institute for International Peace Studies
Keough School of Global Affairs
University of Notre Dame
Notre Dame, IN 46556

Abbreviations

ATT	Arms Trade Treaty
CEDAW	Convention on the Elimination of all Forms of Discrimination Against Women
CTBT	Comprehensive Nuclear-Test-Ban Treaty
EPA	Environmental Protection Agency
FMCT	Fissile Material Cutoff Treaty
ICC	International Criminal Court
ICCPR	International Covenant on Civil and Political Rights
ICJ	International Court of Justice
ICs	international courts
IAEA	International Atomic Energy Agency
IGO	International Governmental Organizations
ILC	International Law Commission
IMF	International Monetary Fund
INGO	International Non-Governmental Organization
IR	international relations
ISIS	Islamic State of Iraq and al-Sham, or Islamic State of Iraq and Syria
MP	Member of Parliament
NATO	North Atlantic Treaty Organization
NGO	non-governmental organization
NPT	(Nuclear) Non-Proliferation Treaty
OECD	Organization for Economic Cooperation and Development
SIPRI	Stockholm International Peace Research Institute

TNC	transnational corporation
UDHR	Universal Declaration of Human Rights
UNDP	United Nations Development Program
UNAMIR	United Nations Assistance Mission in Rwanda
WHO	World Health Organization
WTO	World Trade Organization

Introduction

TO EMPOWER PEOPLE to stop unnecessary violence and human suffering is my reason for writing this book. As a professor of international relations and scholar of peace
research I have taught many US and international students who have never allowed
me, even for one class period, to forget why we have gathered. Some have witnessed a
family member or friend being killed for no reason other than his or her identity. Many
have suffered violent oppression. A few have experienced arbitrary imprisonment and
torture. Nearly all have seen children victimized by poverty that has left them permanently maimed in body and mind. Some, like a Muslim Bosnian and an Orthodox Serb
who animated our class one year, have been on opposite sides of all-out fighting but
lived to become respectful of and even friendly toward one another. These students,
who have known oppression and violence firsthand, also know that a more positive,
mutually respectful future is possible.

Indeed, all want to leave the world a better place than they found it. Yet they are
not sure they will be able to do so, because the odds against constructive change are
so long. I recall a female student activist from China at the time of demonstrations in
Tiananmen Square whose friends and mentors at home confidentially told her that it
would not be safe for her to return home at the end of the semester. Some years later,
a youth leader from South Sudan received the same counsel from back home. "Take
these warnings seriously," fellow students in each respective class advised. Yet what
were these endangered students to do if they wanted to honor their inner calling to
help their families and societies? Over the years, many of my international students
have spoken frankly about discouragement with their own governments' misguided
priorities and corruption, the cruel ostracizing they face at home, the disappointing

prejudices they face in the United States, and the doors that close in their faces because of unfair institutional structures. How can they implement their values of compassion and justice when these are not respected by their own governments?

Somewhat surprisingly at first, I discovered that I shared this question with them. As a US citizen and taxpayer, how can I be a good citizen of the world when my own government does not always respect human dignity? Given the immediacy of my students' life-and-death issues and their families' sacrifices—whether they have suffered war, ethnic cleansing, racism, oppression, malnutrition, or chronic unemployment—my own feeble response is troubling. For me to cast a ballot once every few years for a member of Congress or the US president, while paying taxes that fund some US policies that violate my conscience, seems a woefully inadequate expression of my values and disrespect for my own conscience. Surely there must be more that I could do to uphold universal human rights and dignity even though my own government, relatively wealthy and enlightened, often has other priorities. Could I speak more effectively to my government and my fellow citizens, and more clearly to other members of the human race, to communicate my commitment to human dignity and my willingness to join hands with like-minded people around the world? If it is clear that many of the violent deaths and acts of human suffering occurring each day could be prevented, my students keep asking, why do they continue? What more can we do to stop them?

Informed by my experience over 60 years of studying, teaching, and conducting transnational research with people from more than 100 countries representing all the major cultural regions of the world, this book attempts to answer those questions by providing, first of all, a disciplined analysis of the threats to US national security and human security. By critiquing the findings of peace research and security studies while scrutinizing US diplomacy, this synthesis tries to explain what we know about why major problems persist and why solutions remain beyond our grasp.

Second, this synthesis shapes a comprehensive argument that the days are over for reaping success by following traditional ways of thinking. These ways have failed us, because the world has entered a new era of security challenges, with its own dramatic dangers and opportunities. This book goes to press at an extraordinary, pivotal moment in national and world history, when societies are locked down, with billions sheltering in place in response to the coronavirus pandemic and economies in desperate straits. Previous assumptions about health, national and cyber security, human migration, and economic prosperity are in question. Yes, "the old days" are gone for good, making an alternative paradigm and reformed international system necessary to achieve sustainable peace and human security in the new era.

To be sure, there is much to build on in traditional thinking, still referred to as "political realism," but continued denial of its inadequacies will only speed the coming peril for US citizens. As a result, this book has a third goal, namely, to develop and test proposed changes in worldview, by presenting specific policy proposals that together construct a new global architecture able to take full advantage of opportunities that traditional thinking has scoffed at and passed over, inexcusably since the end of the Cold War. The strategy proposed here also draws on philosophical and religious insights and on deep commitment to human dignity that can enliven motivation to make the changes called for.

The limits of one book do not allow sufficient space to answer or even anticipate all criticisms of the proposed paradigm change, yet this analysis tries to lay out a compelling vision of a better way to live by recommending policies that challenge and in some respects overturn entrenched attitudes and behaviors that perpetuate the status quo. Although they refuse many opportunities for change, our policymakers generally have not been malevolent people. Out of habit and custom they do things that impede peace and justice even though they believe that they personally favor these ideals. In any case, if we are to end unnecessary human suffering, to build sustainable peace, and to advance freedom and justice, all of us will need to change some of our thinking and acting. For that reason, there is something for everyone in this book. No one has all the answers, but by listening deeply and inclusively to one another, we together can find ways to end unnecessary suffering and secure the values of human dignity for future generations.

If we step back for a moment to reflect on our world, which seems constantly in crisis, we can see how poorly our policies and institutions are serving us: Some people in other countries whom we do not trust are interested in developing weapons of mass destruction. Others, who already have them, cannot realistically be expected forever to avoid using them even as they pour billions of dollars into remodeling their own arsenals. More hands are now capable of firing missiles that go higher and faster or are harder to stop than ever before. Profit-seeking corporations have developed drone attack systems to go under the radar and evade detection, sometimes selling these to almost anyone who will pay, no matter how irresponsible the buyer. Before long a drone will likely fly to haunt those who first made them. The United States now sets the technological pace for moving attack weapons into space so that the entire earth can be brought within the purview of Washington's attempts to maintain military primacy. Yet the advantage will be short-lived as others are likely to follow Washington's preparation to weaponize space.[1] China's huge economic power is growing and almost irresistibly pulling others, including some US-based corporations, along with it. Russia destabilizes politics where it can with sophisticated cyber attacks that persist for months without detection and without targets knowing what has happened after detection, while spreading authoritarianism worldwide and supporting violent repression in Syria and elsewhere. Where authoritarian governments exist in the Middle East, they trade in the currencies of prejudice, oppression, and violence. Many societies in Africa have been unable to remove predatory, authoritarian governments. Violent conflict and oppression have generated nearly 80 million refugees and displaced persons, the most in history.[2]

---

[1] For the dangers these measures may bring, see Daniel Deudney, *Dark Skies: Space Expansionism, Planetary Geopolitics, and the Ends of Humanity* (New York: Oxford University Press, 2020).

[2] See United Nations High Commissioner for Refugees, "Figures at a Glance," https://www.unhcr.org/en-us/figures-at-a-glance.html#:~:text=How%20many%20refugees%20are%20there,under%20the%20age%20of%2018.

The European Union (EU), once an unquestioned home of democracy, human rights, and open-mindedness, has been lurching from crisis to crisis arising from bureaucratic insensitivity, economic mismanagement, and populist challenges to refugees, migratory pressures, and democratic values. Poverty engulfs half of the human species with indescribable heartache, gross violation of human rights, and pressures for polarization and extremism. As billions of people stand by, drastic environmental deterioration occurs with untold imminent disasters for the human and most other species. Even when those using terrorist violence face military losses, their violent ideologies have not stopped making political gains. The United States spends trillions on military preparedness but in return reaps no sustainable peace. People fleeing poverty and violence appeal at many countries' closed gates. If governments act constructively in the international arena, often they seem to do too little, too late.

People throughout world society do not need to accept this agenda of violence and suffering, just as no national society needs to submit to an agenda fueled by domestic violence. Human knowledge provides for us the ways and means to reduce violence and to build respect for all. Societies exist now, and have in the past, that are quite peaceful, where people respect one another. We know how to build such societies, although it is true that building them is not easy and too often people do not insist on building them. The point is that whatever has existed can happen. It is possible. We need to think more seriously about why peace and mutual respect are not more widely practiced in world society and what could be done to spread such practices to the point that they become the rule, not the exception.

Although there is much that we do not know about how to halt or prevent specific wars, there is much that we do know about how to build peace over the long run.[3] If many governments earnestly tried to implement the insights of peace and security

---

[3] A synthesis of research findings can be drawn from diplomatic practitioners, political realists, liberal internationalists, constructivists, cosmopolitans, peace researchers, economists, historians, philosophers, evolutionary sociologists and psychologists, and international relations and securities studies scholars, including Seyom Brown, *The Causes and Prevention of War* (New York: St. Martin's Press, 1994); John Mearsheimer, *The Tragedy of Great Power Politics* (New York: W.W. Norton, 2014); Chester Crocker, Pamela Aall, and Fen Hampson, eds., *Leashing the Dogs of War: Conflict Management in a Divided World* (Washington, DC: US Institute of Peace Press, 2007); Chester Crocker, Fen Osler Hampson, and Pamela Aall, eds., *Turbulent Peace: The Challenges of Managing International Conflict* (Washington, DC: United States Institute of Peace Press, 2001); Michael W. Doyle and Nicholas Sambanis, *Making War and Building Peace: United Nations Peace Operations* (Princeton, NJ: Princeton University Press, 2006); G. John Ikenberry, *Liberal Leviathan: The Origins, Crisis, and Transformation of the American World Order* (Princeton, NJ: Princeton University Press, 2011); G. John Ikenberry, *A World Safe for Democracy: Liberal Internationalism and the Crises of Global Order* (New Haven, CT: Yale University Press, 2020); Daniel Philpott, *Revolutions in Sovereignty: How Ideas Shaped Modern International Relations* (Princeton, NJ: Princeton University Press, 2008); Charles A. Kupchan, *How Enemies Become Friends: The Sources of Stable Peace* (Princeton, NJ: Princeton University Press, 2010); James N. Rosenau, "Governance in the Twenty-first Century," *Global Governance* 1, no. 1 (Winter 1995): 13–43; Bruce M. Russett, *Grasping the Democratic Peace: Principles for a Post–Cold War World* (Princeton, NJ: Princeton University Press, 1993); Bruce M. Russett and John R. Oneal, *Triangulating Peace: Democracy, Interdependence, and International Organizations* (New York: W.W. Norton, 2001); Bruce Russett, John Oneal, and Michael Berbaum, "Causes of Peace: Democracy, Interdependence, and International Organizations, 1886–1992," *International Studies Quarterly* 47, no. 3 (September 2003): 371–393; Mary Kaldor, *New and Old Wars*

research, the human species probably could prevent most wars and build sustainable peace with enhanced justice, human rights, and economic well-being for all, as well as avert catastrophic environmental destruction. In brief, we could have peace and security if we implemented what we know about peacebuilding.[4] But many governments and their citizens do not. Why?

Answering that question leads us to look at the fears, outmoded ways of thinking, and familiar yet ineffective institutional structures that discourage desirable change. These impediments are maintained almost as articles of faith in prevailing US national-security thinking, which is based on assumptions about how states will behave and whether they can change. These fundamental assumptions are not reviewed or periodically reexamined. Some fears are irrational and some ways of thinking are maintained by ideology rather than by empirical observation.

(Stanford, CA: Stanford University Press, 2012); Esref Asku and Joseph A. Camilleri, eds., *Democratizing Global Governance* (New York: Palgrave, 2002); Patrick Haydn, *Cosmopolitan Global Politics* (Aldershot, UK: Ashgate, 2005); David Held, *Cosmopolitanism: Ideals and Realities* (Cambridge: Polity Press, 2010); David Held, *Global Covenant: The Social Democratic Alternative to the Washington Consensus* (Cambridge: Polity, 2004); Alexander Wendt, "Why a World State Is Inevitable," *European Journal of International Relations* 9, no. 4 (December 2003): 491–542; Thomas Weiss, *Global Governance: Why? What? Whither?* (Cambridge: Polity Press, 2013); Johan Galtung, *Peace by Peaceful Means: Peace and Conflict, Development and Civilization* (London: Sage, 1996); John Paul Lederach and R. Scott Appleby, "Strategic Peacebuilding: An Overview," in *Strategies of Peace: Transforming Conflict in a Violent World*, ed. Daniel Philpott and Gerard F. Powers (New York: Oxford University Press, 2010), 19–44; Peter Wallensteen, "War in Peace Research," *Peace Research: Theory and Practice* (New York: Routledge, 2011); Peter Wallensteen, ed., *Preventing Violent Conflicts: Past Record and Future Challenges* (Uppsala: Uppsala University Department of Peace and Conflict Research, 1998); Peter Wallensteen, *Quality Peace: Peacebuilding, Victory, and World Order* (New York: Oxford University Press, 2015); Peter Wallensteen, *Understanding Conflict Resolution: War, Peace and the Global System* (London: Sage, 2015); Paul Collier, *The Bottom Billion: Why the Poorest Countries Are Failing and What Can Be Done About It* (Oxford University Press, 2007); Paul Collier, Lani Elliott, Havard Hegre, Anke Hoeffler, Marta Reynal-Querol, and Nicholas Sambanis, *Breaking the Conflict Trap: Civil War and Development Policy* (Washington, DC: World Bank, 2003); Thomas C. Schelling, *The Strategy of Conflict* (New York: Oxford University Press, 1963); Kenneth E. Boulding, *Three Faces of Power* (Newbury Park: Sage, 1989); Paul Kennedy, *The Rise and Fall of the Great Powers: Economic Change and Military Conflict from 1500 to 2000* (New York: Vintage, 1987); Thomas Pogge, *World Poverty and Human Rights* (Cambridge: Polity, 2008); Joshua S. Goldstein, *Winning the War on War: The Decline of Armed Conflict Worldwide* (New York: Dutton, 2011); John A. Vasquez, "The Steps to War: Toward a Scientific Explanation of Correlates of War Findings," *World Politics* 40, no. 1 (1987): 108–145; Paul D. Senese and John A. Vasquez, *The Steps to War: An Empirical Study* (Princeton, NJ: Princeton University Press, 2008); John A. Vasquez, *What Do We Know About War?* (Lanham, MD: Rowan & Littlefield, 2012); World Commission on Environment and Development, *Our Common Future* (Oxford: Oxford University Press, 1987); Quincy Wright, *A Study of War* (Chicago: University of Chicago Press, 1965); Robert Wright, *Nonzero: The Logic of Human Destiny* (New York: Vintage Books, 2001); Douglas P. Fry, *Beyond War: The Human Potential for Peace* (New York: Oxford University Press, 2007); Douglas P. Fry, ed., *War, Peace and Human Nature: The Convergence of Evolutionary and Cultural Views* (New York: Oxford University Press, 2013); Augusto Lopez-Claros, Arthur L. Dahl, and Maja Groff, *Global Governance and the Emergence of Global Institutions for the 21st Century* (Cambridge: Cambridge University Press, 2020); National Intelligence Council, *Global Trends 2040: A More Contested World*, March 2021, https://www.dni.gov/index.php/global-trends-home.

[4] For a clear exposition of the concept of strategic peacebuilding, see Lederach and Appleby, "Strategic Peacebuilding," 19–44. An early synthesis of scientific and experiential knowledge about peacemaking appeared in the work of the Commission on Global Governance, *Our Global Neighbourhood: The Report of the Commission on Global Governance* (Oxford: Oxford University Press, 1995).

Many policymakers and national institutions perpetuate behavior that they have an interest in changing, but they seem unaware that making changes to protect human dignity would serve their own long-term interests. Of course, lack of awareness is a reason that other species have become extinct rather than adapt to new conditions. As a result of inertia, many national security decisions have become counter-productive, fostering insecurity rather than security. Yet they are maintained because they are familiar. Diplomatic habits continue even though they interfere with reasonable measures for finding common ground among nations and building regional and global institutions actually capable of implementing peace and justice.

Insecurity for nations and the ineffectiveness of diplomacy in alleviating human suffering arise, not only from widely acknowledged human selfishness,[5] but also from the limited focus of current national security thinking about "grand strategy," especially in the United States and the other great powers. This book argues that following a grand strategy limited to conceived national interests is responsible for keeping us mired in an increasingly ineffective set of policies and institutions. Accordingly, it is urgent that we carefully reexamine our current grand strategy and devise a new, more comprehensive one.

If we accept historian John Lewis Gaddis's definition of strategy "as the alignment of potentially unlimited aspirations with necessarily limited capabilities,"[6] we have a basis for examining global needs and nationally limited capabilities. Grand strategy provides an overview of everything that should be done after considering diverse specific strategies in policymakers' attempt to align capacities to meet goals. It should be an integrated set of ideas that spell out the purpose of a country's relationships with the rest of the world. This should include an examination of the global context in which relationships occur, a prioritizing of national interests and values, and an honest recognition of the threats to and opportunities for realizing US goals. Grand strategy "is a country's guiding conception of where it wants to go and how it seeks to get there."[7] In part to make US diplomacy more effective and in part to advance justice, this book shifts the focus for grand strategy from serving one country, the United States, to advancing sustainable peace with justice for all human beings. This wider focus also best serves the interests of US citizens in the long run. Available resources, opportunities, and the limits posed by human beings' reluctant willingness to sacrifice selfish gain for the common good are all realistically aligned with the goal of sustainable peace and justice for all.

To achieve a just, sustainable peace in the future, past ways of pursuing more limited peace and security goals must change. Yet many people resist change or, without thinking, obstruct it. Even before the Donald Trump administration, US national security planners were not coming to grips with the need to initiate a *global* grand strategy

---

[5] Of course, the same human selfishness is managed reasonably well within exemplary national societies.

[6] John Lewis Gaddis, *On Grand Strategy* (New York: Penguin, 2018), 21.

[7] Hal Brands, *American Grand Strategy in the Age of Trump* (Washington, DC: Brookings Institution Press, 2018), ix.

for peace and human security rather than continuing a *national* grand strategy focused on one country's security. Among the major powers today, policymakers are not considering a grand strategy to change the international system[8] or to construct policies capable of building lasting peace and sustainable security for all the world's people.[9] Yet without such a strategy, every nation's security is, from now on, forever in danger.

Even though building peace is exceedingly complex, a synthesis of findings from diverse studies of war and peace reveals correlates of peace that, if nurtured, could build sustainable world peace.[10] The theory arising from this synthesis of findings, discussed in Chapter 2, is a distillation of current research findings, past human experience, and philosophical and religious inquiry. Gaddis notes that one of the most celebrated grand strategists, Carl von Clausewitz, valued strategic training because it prepares minds for "being able to draw upon principles extending across time and space, so that you'll have a sense of what's worked before and what hasn't."[11] A strategic understanding enables policymakers to develop an effective plan to achieve a major goal such as victory in war or, as in this book, sustainable peace and human security.

Security threats from terrorism,[12] prolonged wars, proliferation of weapons of mass destruction, possibilities for orbiting attack satellites, alarming weather extremes,

---

[8] In this analysis, "international system" means the body of intertwined customs, agreements, laws, and institutions that constitute the environment in which countries engage one another and that govern how countries relate to one another. A crude balancing of power among sovereign states operates because there is no reliable, effective overarching law or central authority that governs interstate behavior. Shifting alliances may prevent any one power from dominating all the rest. In practice, the system usually maintains some independence for the units in the system. Unlike most domestic political systems, the international system is sub-system dominant; the most powerful units within the system are more powerful than the central system itself. Therein lies the reality of international anarchy and the collective action problem of enforcing international law.

[9] See Barry R. Posen and Andrew L. Ross, "Competing Visions for U.S. Grand Strategy," *International Security* 21, no. 3 (Winter 1996–1997): 5–53; Stephen Brooks, John Ikenberry, and William Wohlforth, "Lean Forward: In Defense of American Engagement," *Foreign Affairs* 92, no. 1 (January–February 2013): 130–142; I. William Zartman, ed., *Peacemaking in International Conflict: Methods and Techniques* (US Institute of Peace Press, 2007); Ho-Won Jeong, *Peacebuilding in Postconflict Societies: Strategy and Process* (Boulder, CO: L. Rienner, 2005); Thomas Weiss and Rorden Wilkinson, *International Organization and Global Governance* (New York: Routledge, 2014); Brands, *American Grand Strategy in the Age of Trump*; Hal Brands, *American Grand Strategy and the Liberal Order: Continuity, Change, and Options for the Future* (Santa Monica, CA: Rand Corporation, 2016). An exception to the widespread inattention to remodeling the global system is Daniel Deudney and G. John Ikenberry, "Democratic Internationalism: An American Grand Strategy for a Post-Exceptionalist Era," Council on Foreign Relations, *Working Paper* (2012), ttps:// cdn.cfr.org/sites/default/files/pdf/2012/11/IIGG_WorkingPaper11_Deudney_Ikenberry.pdf.

[10] To illustrate this point, if democratic elements of governance, economic intercourse among states, and participation in international organizations all increase, the likelihood of violent conflicts decreases by more than 70 percent. Moreover, if all three factors remain at relatively high levels, "the incidence of fatal disputes drops by 95 percent." See Russett and Oneal, *Triangulating Peace*, 282, 388.

[11] Gaddis, *Grand Strategy*, 24. See Carl von Clausewitz, *On War*, ed. and trans. Michael Howard and Peter Paret (Princeton, NJ: Princeton University Press, 1976).

[12] Because political overtones of the terms "terrorist" and "terrorism" may obscure rather than clarify, I prefer to define terrorist acts empirically by the targets selected and the means used, rather than by who the actors are or the goals or causes that actors espouse. Terrorism can be defined as the use of violence or violent threats against civilians. This means that governments, depending on their targets and tactics, may be terrorists as well as individuals and non-state actors.

climate devastation and polar meltdowns, desperate human migrations, massive extinctions of species, cyber lawlessness, global pandemics, populist me-first nationalisms and other political polarizations animated by extremism and greed—all these underscore the urgent need to implement what we know about building peace worldwide. To do this would be preferable to ignoring existing knowledge, which we now do primarily because implementing it would require an uphill political struggle and sufficient courage to take reasonable short-term risks in order to obtain long-term, dependable increases in peace and human security.[13]

Why have policymakers been missing a policy boat that could take us all toward greater peace and human well-being? Part of the answer lies in the usually dismissive judgmentalism toward innovative policy alternatives by policymaking elites who simply say "those recommendations lack credibility" before really examining their possibilities. To expand understanding of what may be possible, the analytic perspective taken throughout this study draws on a wide range of social science disciplines and the study of law, particularly the discipline of political science, the sub-discipline of international relations, and the multidisciplinary findings of peace research. The analysis also cautiously notes some resonances between research conclusions and virtues expounded in relevant philosophical and religious traditions. In addition, the prospects for change are examined in the light of the long history of human evolution, both biological and cultural, because evolutionary history provides some scientific insights into human possibilities that many policymakers ignore.

The failures of the dominant policymaking communities of the great powers, which continue to rely on "political realism" in resisting more cooperative international structures, call forth in this book an analytic search for a more "empirical realism." My commitment to empirical analysis pays attention to the ways in which more peaceful and just institutional and behavioral changes could be constructed if those with deeper understanding of new structural possibilities were able to generate the insight, courage, and support to build them.

With this in mind, the chapters that follow question one of the hallmarks of political realist theory, namely, a tendency to reify the nation-state, a human construct, treating it as if its existence and current conduct express a law of nature.[14] In fact, some adherents of political realism are messengers of a self-fulfilling prophecy in which a self-perpetuating, political-ideological belief prevents the idea of a more cooperative, legally managed international system capable of transforming and, to a limited degree, transcending separate national identities from coming into being, not for

---

[13] See, for example, Kaldor, *New and Old Wars*; Charles W. Kegley Jr. and Greg Raymond, *How Nations Make Peace* (New York: St. Martin's, 1999); John Darby and Roger MacGinty, *Contemporary Peacemaking: Conflict, Violence and Peace Processes* (New York: Palgrave, 2003); Doyle and Sambanis, *Making War and Building Peace*; and Roland Paris, "International Peacebuilding and the 'Mission Civilisatrice,'"*Review of International Studies* 28, no. 4 (2002): 637–656.

[14] Mearsheimer, *Tragedy of Great Power Politics*.

the purpose of eliminating states but to defang them enough to make them safe for human flourishing.

Massive-reach destructive technology now threatens every nation; in this context, an overblown reification of nation-statism could pose a threat to humanity. Wiser use of planet-encompassing technology can tame virulent nation-statism and help to liberate every nation. We know that even a strong, well-established species can become extinct if their members are unable to adapt swiftly enough to arising new conditions that threaten them. Albert Einstein recognized this immediately after the US bombing of Hiroshima and Nagasaki, when he said: "The unleashed power of the atom has changed everything save our modes of thinking, and thus we drift toward unparalleled catastrophe."[15]

We may need to question certain modes of thinking and taken-for-granted assumptions undergirding political realism as currently understood. Ideas, beliefs, values, and behaviors that are mutually reinforced within political culture may become internalized as "natural" articles of faith or truth. Even if they are not empirically warranted (e.g., the idea of pure races or ethnicities, or of the moral exceptionalism of certain nations, or that the present international system cannot be changed), they can impede cooperative interstate action necessary for survival.

Obviously, some almost automatically held political beliefs are constructive, such as the principle that people should have equal rights, but other beliefs might be self-destructive. As in biological evolution, an otherwise healthy species and culture may become extinct because of a failure to adapt rapidly enough to new conditions because of widespread belief in a popular idea whose useful time may have passed, such as that the Westphalian state is "given."[16] Virulent nationalism and negative stereotyping and fear of outgroups, wedded to new military technologies, pose a possibly life-threatening danger.[17] As Einstein correctly recognized, "Our world faces a crisis as yet *unperceived by those possessing power* to make great decisions for good or evil. . . . A new type of thinking is essential if mankind is to survive and move toward higher levels."[18] This study examines whether "a new type of thinking" is occurring or instead if familiar beliefs about military power's utility continue to thrive long after Hiroshima and to replicate themselves in US policies even as the nuclear, ecologically fragile age deepens.

The following analysis identifies peacebuilding paths that the United States and other powerful governments have not taken because many policymakers (and their

---

[15] Albert Einstein said this in a telegram circulated widely to educate political leaders and the public about the dangers of nuclear weapons, reported in "Atomic Education Urged by Einstein," *New York Times*, May 25, 1946, 11.

[16] I use "Westphalian" as a label referring to the origin of the modern state in Europe after the Peace of Westphalia in 1648.

[17] Early in human evolution when roving bands of hunters and gatherers felt fear of out-groups, this habit was often species preserving. Natural selection rewarded those hosting this belief. Now, when conditioned fears and hostilities toward out-groups interfere with developing cooperative means to enhance security, this belief not only undermines security in the short run but also threatens the extinction of the species in the long run.

[18] "Atomic Education Urged by Einstein." Italics added.

constituents) believed that they would not lead in a desirable direction. I make the case that certain paths *could have* brought us to a safer and fairer place than the precarious position in which we now find ourselves. Unless we take more collaborative and mutually beneficial paths in order to capitalize on existing cooperative possibilities, we will deepen our own and everyone else's insecurities, as Einstein and others with long-range vision anticipated.

The argument that follows also suggests that we can learn something about social and political integration by synthesizing research and by examining recent historical experience with an eye on how, to use admittedly awkward language, "non-zero-sumness"[19] may advance human civilization at this stage of history. In common parlance, a non-zero-sum relationship may be understood as a cooperative one in which mutually beneficial or win-win outcomes are possible for all the adversaries in a conflict. All parties may gain a benefit from a cooperative arrangement without any party suffering an overall loss. In contrast, "zero-sum" relations may be understood as competitive: In a two-party zero-sum relationship any gain made by X comes at an equal expense to Y. Although I use both "cooperative" and "non-zero-sum" in this book, the latter more accurately describes a relationship in which cooperation is not yet occurring, but if it *did* occur, all parties would benefit with a positive sum. In one regard, non-zero-sumness is like potential energy in physics. People may tap it or ignore it. Meaningful arms control in space, for example, would seem likely to generate a non-zero-sum arrangement because all countries on earth would benefit simultaneously from keeping immediate destruction more than 10 minutes away. Although the non-zero-sum potential in an armed relationship may exist now, without an actual agreement to constrain adversaries' arms, a positive sum outcome is lost. So far, the new US Space Command appears to be a product of zero-sum thinking.

Both serious crises and opportunities face US citizens. Many people believe the political realist dogma that "anarchy is here to stay" in the international system and that military preparedness is the primary source of security.[20] Alternatively, others see promise in a gradually expanding collection of nations seeking to exploit non-zero-sum possibilities, such as manifested by those who genuinely supported the Paris

---

[19] In game theory and economic theory, a zero-sum game is a mathematical way of depicting a relationship in which one party's gain is equal to loss suffered by the other parties in the relationship. The sum of their utilities remains constant. Non-zero-sum refers to positive sum or mutually beneficial interactions that result in a win for all parties at the same time. Zero-sum depicts competitive relationships and non-zero-sum cooperative relationships.

   The founders of game theory, John von Neumann and Oskar Morgenstern, coined this terminology to provide a mathematical way of representing relative utilities gained or lost by parties in conflict. Oskar Morgenstern and John Von Neumann, *Theory of Games and Economic Behavior* (Princeton, NJ: Princeton University Press, 1957). Robert Wright explains the usefulness of this concept in Appendix 1, "On Non-zero-sumness," in Wright, *Nonzero*, 337–343.

[20] John J. Mearsheimer, *The Great Delusion* (New Haven, CT: Yale University Press, 2018), Kindle, 2330. International anarchy in this context means the absence of a central international authority capable of enforcing rules and punishing aggressive states that violate the rules. In other words, it is the lack of a central authority to govern state conduct.

climate agreement or the highly successful Montreal Protocol of 1987 to halt future emissions of chlorofluorocarbons.

Although the dominant approach to policymaking in all the great powers remains political realism, this analysis shows its lack of both empirical precision and imagination in assessing the need for global thinking and structural changes. The most promising opportunities will not be seized unless many people take a fresh look at their worldviews, tilting them mindfully from national security toward human security, from state sovereignty toward popular sovereignty rooted in human rights, and from exclusive identities toward inclusive identities. The concept of US "foreign policy" might benefit if it were approached more as "world policy," because the latter would be more likely to encourage the attitudes needed in policymaking.

Although this book focuses primarily on the United States because its people and policies are capable, when at their best, of exerting enormous positive influence throughout the world, it seeks to engage readers and their most thoughtful ideas from around the world. It must do this to remain true to its purpose, and imaginative opportunities will be most fruitful when non-US citizens help shape and implement the world policies that the United States and other countries should together embrace to maximize human security.

Cultivating an empirically accurate worldview open to policy and institutional innovations tries to take seriously possibilities that traditional thinking has dismissed without serious study. This does not mean that all of these possibilities will work, of course, but in temporarily suspending judgment against an alternative view, readers can consider creative ways to enable them to succeed. Readers also need to imagine how, after a significant change occurs, follow-on changes may have an easier time to become reality than would be assumed when viewing things from the short-term alone. When observing German-French animosity in the late 1930s, for example, would any person have anticipated that Germany, France, and four other European states would voluntarily join a cooperative political and economic community within the next 15 years? Did political scientists predict the end of the Cold War, the Soviet Union, and the Warsaw pact before these things happened?

Some discussions in this book suggest that a new initiative can be taken immediately, and that second and third steps are desirable, while recognizing that they cannot be taken at once because political conditions are not right. Because they are not politically feasible today does not mean that they are not politically desirable and worthy of attention now, even though they remain aspirational until conditions are right for their realization. To illustrate: For many generations people knew it would be desirable to hold political leaders accountable *as individuals* to laws that prohibited aggressive war, war crimes, and crimes against humanity. But for centuries this simply did not seem possible. At the end of World War II, it became politically possible to implement this idea by putting top German and Japanese officials on trial. That was a positive precedent even though it was flawed by being "victors' justice." Political conditions were right to place Germans and Japanese on trial, but they were not yet right for a globally impartial process of holding officials of all nationalities internationally responsible for crimes. Yet in the opening statement at the Nuremberg trial of Nazi leaders in 1945, the chief counsel for the United States, Robert H. Jackson, acknowledged that the ideal for future justice was to hold all officials of all nationalities individually responsible for honoring the law.[21] A half-century later the international community[22] came much closer to that ideal with the creation of the permanent International Criminal Court (ICC), but we are not yet fully able to hold leaders accountable. Even though there is a significant distance still to travel, holding an itinerary that identifies the destination helps travelers realize the destination. Most of the 123 countries that have become members of the ICC believe that the journey is headed in the right direction. Having the institutional destination in mind is useful as long as the impossibility of arriving at the destination today is not used to discredit the early steps on the journey.

When aspirational proposals are mentioned in this analysis, even though they will remain aspirational until the political conditions are right for implementing them, their aspirational quality should not be taken as evidence that, because they will not happen today, the earlier steps leading toward them necessarily lack credibility. Long-range vision ought not to be used by critics of it to discredit short-term credibility.

Because some aspects of globalization and the worldwide dimensions of many problems are here to stay, this analysis puts substantial weight on multilateral processes and international organizations for the formulation, implementation, and enforcement of initiatives. The international community today lacks the collective wherewithal to do some of what is needed, but with reasonable intentionality its institutions and rules can be strengthened. Because cooperative actions by the international community, such as limiting greenhouse gas emissions, potentially may serve the interests of most states (i.e., a situation of abundant non-zero-sumness), the international community possesses enormous unrealized power and enforcement capabilities. Although it was admittedly far from perfect collective action, the United Nation's removal of Iraq from Kuwait after Iraq invaded and annexed it in 1990 illustrates one form of potential in collective enforcement action.[23] If rudimentary ways and means of successful

---

[21] Jackson said "the record on which we judge these defendants today is the record on which history will judge us tomorrow. To pass these defendants a poisoned chalice is to put it to our own lips as well. We must summon such detachment and intellectual integrity to our task that this Trial will commend itself to posterity as fulfilling humanity's aspirations to do justice." Robert H. Jackson, "Opening Statement before the International Military Tribunal, Nuremberg," https://www.roberthjackson.org/speech-and-writing/opening-statement-before-the-international-military-tribunal/.

[22] By "international community" I mean all the countries of the world considered collectively, including both governments and peoples, mindful that they are connected by modern telecommunications and are economically, socially, politically, environmentally, and militarily interdependent.

[23] For further analysis of this and other examples of collective action, see Joseph E. Schwartzberg, *Transforming the United Nations System: Designs for a Workable World* (Tokyo: United Nations University Press, 2013), 225–271.

international enforcement become institutionalized, they open the door to further collective action as long as initiatives serve most or all of the international community's common needs and interests.[24]

Although it does not happen frequently, significant improvements in worldview can occur with surprising speed after many years have passed without change. José Alvarez has noted that significant legal changes, such as re-thinking sovereignty as conditional rather than absolute, can occur quickly, with the concurrence of a majority of the international community, when political conditions are right.[25]

Readers of this book can nurture such conditions to usher in the future. The international community plays a significant role in this analysis, keeping in mind that the institutions it creates can change. The League of Nations can be understood as the first generation of a worldwide general-purpose political organization seeking to discourage war. The United Nations is a second-generation organization with a similar but expanded sense of purpose, moving colonial territories toward independence. It also helped spawn the International Criminal Court, a halfway house on the third-generation path toward enforcing laws on individuals who hold governmental powers, not simply on governments or states themselves. Obviously, no generation has been successful preventing all wars, but, despite its disappointments and failures, the UN has prevented some wars, shortened others, and kept the peace in still other contexts. This analysis emphasizes that humanity should now design and implement a full-fledged third generation, while also thinking about a fourth. When this analysis assigns important functions to the international community, it has in mind not only the easily criticized first- and second-generation institutions, but also the potential power in the third and fourth generations.

Before describing a new grand strategy designed to bring more of what we know into what we do, it is useful to examine the changing empirical realities that must inform national security policies if they are to succeed. These include the low utility of war for achieving desired political outcomes, the increase of non-state actors' access to destructive technologies, the rise of non-military threats to security, and the underutilized potentials in nonviolent action, strengthened international law, and more effective global governance (Chapter 1).

Although dangerous security consequences now flow from failing to take these changes into account and from following theories and diplomatic habits appropriate for earlier times, the new realities can be addressed more effectively by developing

---

[24] The international community's ability to enforce constructive international laws will become more reliable as it gradually develops independent police and quasi-military enforcement capability as discussed below.

[25] José Alvarez, who is past president of the American Society of International Law and former counselor to the US Department of State, commented: "Traditional descriptions of the requisites of custom—the need for the passage of a considerable period of time and the accumulation of evidence of the diplomatic practices between sets of states reacting to one another's acts—appear increasingly passé." José E. Alvarez, *International Organizations as Law-Makers* (Oxford: Oxford University Press, 2005), 591.

an empirically more accurate theoretical framework to find a path toward increased security (Chapter 2).

A largely static vision of the international system has led Washington officials repeatedly to reject new strategic thinking and promising multilateral initiatives, especially since the end of the Cold War in 1989, when many new opportunities arose. Simply stated, to continue old diplomatic habits in the face of new international realities produces repeated policy failures, perhaps best described as mindless misalignment of national power with aspirations for global peace and security (Chapter 3).

Because security policies have remained rooted in strategic thinking confined to seeking *national* security rather than *global* security, there has been little creative space in official minds for developing policies or institutional architecture that could provide dependable peace and security. US policies have failed to achieve stable peace abroad while other governmental failures have animated rapid populist gains at home.[26] Upon reflection, it becomes clear that the policy failures observed in Chapter 3 rose directly out of policymakers' tendency to deny new empirical realities and to operate with theoretical and philosophical flaws in their thinking and policy planning. Most of all, they have ignored the near impossibility of succeeding with policies based on their traditional assumptions, such as that sovereignty and the international system are unchanging and that international lawmaking institutions are unhelpful in the new age (Chapter 4).

The advent of the Trump administration made the consequences of narrowly nationalistic, self-centered policymaking even more obvious than before, but problematic tendencies were present already in the Ronald Reagan and George W. Bush administrations, and to lesser degrees in other administrations and Congresses, particularly in their dismissiveness toward multilateralism and international law. Because US policies were failing well before President Trump appeared on the scene, they will be unlikely to succeed just because he has left Washington—unless the US government, Congress, and supporting citizens commit to making some fundamental changes. US policies are failing because they place faith primarily in maximizing US military power when what an interdependent world needs is sufficient global governance to institutionalize peace. A synthesis of peace research and security studies shows what is needed to achieve peace and security. To implement the primary correlates of peace holds more promise than maximizing US military power. The correlates can be fused in a global grand strategy for human security (Chapter 5).

---

[26] Populist thinking became more popular because US officials of both parties were incapable of solving problems arising from globalization. As a result of "weak and ineffective" US government, "problems have intensified, people have grown angry, and populist appeals have found a receptive audience." Howell and Moe conclude: "The socioeconomic forces driving populism cannot be stopped, and they will continue long after Trump has left the scene." William G. Howell and Terry M. Moe, *Presidents, Populism, and the Crisis of Democracy* (Chicago: University of Chicago Press, 2020), 2, 4, 14, 17.

Most US national security problems, ranging from terrorism to the spread of weapons of mass destruction, from environmental destruction to life-threatening poverty, and from unwanted migration to gross violations of human rights, can be more effectively addressed if they are viewed as problems of global governance rather than as problems to be solved by deploying US military power. The United States, as well as humanity, needs internationally agreed-on and enforceable rules that specify appropriate conduct and enable reliable enforcement of international laws—in short, more effective governance with some changes in the international system (Chapter 6).

To implement a preferred design requires new institutional architecture capable of limiting weapons of mass destruction, reducing terrorism, salvaging environmental health, abolishing poverty, and strengthening the enforcement of international law. Arising from the correlates of peace, numerous practical, institutional initiatives can be built to advance human security and gradually to change the international system enough to provide sustainable peace (Chapter 7).

To enable taking these steps while achieving security for US citizens and all people everywhere requires building grassroots support locally and transnationally to construct laws, economic policies, and international institutions in support of the values of democracy and human dignity, sustained by a broadening understanding of US nationalism that is welcoming to *human* identity. Citizens need to press for several major reforms in US democracy to ensure a future for US democracy and to uphold human rights as well as to enable effective US participation in transnational social movement initiatives to implement the correlates of peace (Chapter 8).

To employ wiser policies in the future requires citizens and policymakers to make choices now between whether they intend to follow traditional security policies or instead to commit themselves to a path attuned more closely to today's changing empirical realities and research findings. Facing squarely the ethical harms and dangerous impracticalities of the present international system also brings to the foreground for many people some wisdom from the major religious traditions and encourages the moral imagination and more inclusive human identities necessary for shaping a global grand strategy for human security—a strategy that is capable of building transnational political support for sufficient global governance to sustain peace with enhanced justice, human rights, economic well-being, and environmental health for the entire human family. Such a strategy could be realized if many citizens participate in public education and action, working with like-minded people elsewhere in a transnational movement constituted by women as well as men, young and old, from every culture and religious tradition on Earth, to carry the banners upholding human dignity for all (Chapter 9).

The inertia in US thinking and misalignment of means and ends, particularly since the opening of the Berlin wall in 1989, make clear that informed citizens need not wait, indeed dare not wait, for their own US government to initiate wiser policies aimed at global structural change. Instead, citizens themselves are called, by their own best values and ethical commitment to human dignity, as well as by their desire to do what is prudent for US security, to press for new policies and institutions in the Biden administration and thereafter.

With this roadmap in mind, we explore in Chapter 1 seven changes in international relations that have rendered old ways of thinking and acting politically unwise and ethically undesirable. The first four of these are moving in extremely dangerous directions. The last three offer hope and suggest a fruitful direction for the future.

1

Understanding New Global Realities

MANY US CITIZENS vaguely sense that recent changes in international relations, which arise largely from new technologies applied to modes of communication and destruction, should change calculations about how to achieve security. Although they are not sure about what the changes may eventually mean in their lives, four of the changes reported below threaten security so severely that they call for a complete re-examination of security policies. At the same time, other changes bring new opportunities made possible by the ease and speed of communication and observation, by evolving international institutions and arising transnational influences, and by broader awareness of human rights. These suggest a more promising utility for international law and institutions—if new thought and action rise to seize the opportunities to deliver this promise. These three hold promise for a more hopeful direction. We now look in turn at all seven major changes.

1.1 WAR: DECLINING UTILITY

First, the utility of war has become extremely low for producing desirable political outcomes.[1]

---

[1] Karl von Clausewitz, Rupert Smith, and others say that "the utility of force should be judged not by its destructive capacity but by its ability to achieve intended political purposes." David Cortright, Conor Seyle, and Kristen Wall, *Governance for Peace: How Inclusive, Participatory and Accountable Institutions Promote Peace and Prosperity* (New York: Cambridge University Press, 2017); Rupert Smith, *The Utility of Force: The Art of War in the Modern World* (London: Penguin, 2006). Joshua S. Goldstein, in *Winning the*

To be sure, military power has high utility for destroying, but it provides only low utility for achieving peace and democracy that can be sustained. Indeed, peace research shows that violence frequently begets more violence,[2] that armed conflicts exacerbate conditions, such as fear and hatred, that cause wars in the first place,[3] that countries that have experienced war bear a higher risk of another war,[4] and that terrorists usually are motivated by a sense of grievance over violence inflicted on them or on people with whom they identify.[5] Mediation is a more effective means for preventing the recurrence of violent conflict than are military victories.[6]

Another sign of low military utility is that although the United States spends as much on military purposes as all the other major military powers combined,[7] US officials still expect unending wars. Growing evidence suggests that *military* primacy in itself does not pay positive dividends.[8]

The one area in which military means succeed is in combat with other national military organizations. Yet year-in, year-out military competition between states leads almost inevitably to less security because each side's increase in its own military strength increases the threat felt by the other side, leading it to respond with more armaments of its own, resulting in the familiar "security dilemma."[9]

War on War: The Decline of Armed Conflict Worldwide (New York: Dutton, 2011), documents that war is both less frequent and less productive than earlier in history. Steven Pinker, in *The Better Angels of Our Nature: Why Violence Has Declined* (New York: Viking, 2011), corroborates a decline in the number and utility of wars but offers a somewhat different explanation. For the past 10 years, however, the Uppsala Conflict Data Program (UCDP) has reported an uneven yet upward trend of international armed conflicts. Therése Pettersson and Peter Wallensteen, "Armed Conflicts, 1946–2014," *Journal of Peace Research* 52, no. 4 (2015): 536. Of all US military interventions since 1946, roughly 80 percent have taken place after 1991. Stephen Wertheim, "The Only Way to End 'Endless War,'" *New York Times*, September 14, 2019.

[2] One form of contagion is that "in a globalized world, the brutalization of a society, with daily experience of high levels of violence and the cheapening of human life, is bound to affect other societies." Marlies Glasius and Mary Kaldor, "A Human Security Vision for Europe and Beyond," in *A Human Security Doctrine for Europe: Project, Principles, Practicalities*, ed. Marlies Glasius and Mary Kaldor (London: Routledge, 2006), 10.

[3] Human Security Report Project, *Human Security Report 2009/2010: The Causes of Peace and the Shrinking Costs of War* (New York: Oxford University Press, 2011), 36, 58, http://www.hsrgroup.org/human-security-reports/20092010/text.aspx.

[4] Human Security Report Project, *Causes of Peace*, 38.

[5] Robert Pape, *Dying to Win: The Strategic Logic of Suicide Terrorism* (New York: Random House, 2005).

[6] Peter Wallensteen and Isak Svensson, "Talking Peace: International Mediation in Armed Conflicts," *Journal of Peace Research* 51, no. 2 (2014): 323.

[7] Christopher Preble, "Adapting to American Decline," *New York Times*, April 22, 2018, IV: 6.

[8] Daniel W. Drezner, "Military Primacy Doesn't Pay (Nearly as Much as You Think)," *International Security* 38, no 1 (Summer 2013): 56; Christopher Preble, *The Power Problem: How American Military Dominance Makes Us Less Safe, Less Prosperous, and Less Free* (Ithaca, NY: Cornell University Press, 2009).

[9] See John H. Herz, "Idealist Internationalism and the Security Dilemma," *World Politics* 2, no. 2 (1950): 157. The security dilemma is a "structural" feature of the balance-of-power system "in which the self-help attempts of states to look after their [own] security needs tend, regardless of intention, to lead to rising insecurity for others as each interprets its own measures as defensive and measures of others as potentially threatening." See also John H. Herz, *Political Realism and Political Idealism* (Chicago: University of Chicago, 1951). Ken Booth and Nicholas J. Wheeler describe the possibility of transcending or transforming the balance of power as the only way to escape the dangers of the security dilemma, in *The Security Dilemma: Fear, Cooperation and Trust in World Politics* (New York: Palgrave Macmillan, 2008).

Despite the misguided veneration of military primacy, it cannot be counted on to pay dividends in today's new realities because maintaining primacy tempts policymakers to choose war and strong-arm diplomacy when it is unlikely to be successful and exacts huge amounts of resources from more productive economic uses for US citizens.[10] Historian Paul Kennedy's research, published in the *Rise and Fall of the Great Powers*, shows that throughout history leading great powers eventually have declined because they overextended themselves in projecting military power.[11] In so doing they sap their economic strength that enabled them to become a leading power in the first place.

The US attack on Iraq in 2003 illustrates how maintaining a high degree of military preparedness can tempt a country to launch an unnecessary, eventually self-harming attack. It also shows that a country can win a war only to discover that military victory produced what the initiator of the war, although victorious, did *not* want: more violence than before the war. Far more US casualties occurred after the fall of Baghdad than before,[12] confirming that military power often has been a poor instrument for reducing violence and bringing peace, and that relying on military strength to replace even a widely opposed government may cost far more lives after its defeat than terminating the government in military victory in the first place. Although military strength led to quick victory over Iraq, it also caused the defeat of peace;[13] Iraqis have not had stable peace since the US victory many years ago.

More than 20 years of wars in southwest Asia and the Middle East have cost the United States more than $6 trillion and more than 7,000 military and 8,000 contractors' lives, killed more than 800,000 people of all nationalities, generated more than 37 million refugees and displaced persons, caused hundreds of thousands of US soldiers and contractors lifelong disabilities,[14] and fed virulent nationalisms, militarism, and violent bigotry in the Middle East, Europe, and the United States. Interest on the money borrowed to fight these wars may cost the United States another $8 trillion by mid-century.[15] Yet, the world has not gained any lasting security in return for these

---

[10] Drezner, "Military Primacy Doesn't Pay," 56.

[11] Kennedy, *The Rise and Fall of the Great Powers*. Drezner concludes: "Military supremacy on its own is insufficient to prevent the renewal of great power tensions in the world; full spectrum unipolarity is necessary. Without a sufficient amount of economic power, the pacifying effects of military supremacy will eventually erode." Drezner, "Military Primacy Doesn't Pay," 77.

[12] Reuters and Iraq News, "Casualties by Country and Year," http://www.icasualties.org/.

[13] For example, by mindlessly disbanding the Iraqi army, the United States was "laying the foundations for a deadly insurgency" because for hundreds of thousands of Sunni young men who were trained in the military arts, the United States was taking away their jobs, their income, their self-respect, and their personal and professional security. Ronan Farrow, *War on Peace: The End of Diplomacy and the Decline of American Influence* (New York: Norton, 2018), xxv.

[14] Payments to veterans over the four decades following the wars could cost $4 trillion. Daniel Trotta, "Iraq War Costs U.S. More Than $2 Trillion," Reuters, https://www.reuters.com/article/us-iraq-war-anniversary-idUSBRE92D0PG20130314.

[15] All data are from the Watson Institute, "Costs of War," http://watson.brown.edu/costsofwar/costs/human or /economic; https://www.stripes.com/news/us/the-cost-of-post-9-11-wars-hit-5-9-trillion-480-000-lives-lost-study-says-1.556646 (January 2, 2019). See also Daniel Trotta, "Iraq War Costs U.S. More than $2 Trillion," Reuters (March 14, 2013), http://www.reuters.com/article/

massive expenditures, particularly if one takes account of the extent to which the US economy was weakened by rising deficits, rising oil prices, and then deep recession, all of which were made worse by the country's borrowing money to buy war.

The result of large-scale violence and destruction is that the Middle East is less stable and more violent after US victory than before the US invasion. The US attack on Iraq resulted in far-reaching destabilization that led to a spike in suicide bombings of civilians and civil wars in Afghanistan, Iraq, and Syria; huge refugee flows that destabilized the Middle East and Europe and caused political and economic havoc in the European Union (EU) and the domestic politics of most members; and complicated life for Israel. Another consequence of US military victory in Iraq and the disempowerment of Sunni Muslims led directly to the growth of Al-Qaeda in Iraq and to the creation of ISIS, the "Islamic State," in Iraq and Syria.[16] ISIS did not exist before the US invasion. The US war and its aftermath contributed to the rise of nativist populism in Europe; the weakening of Angela Merkel's stable democratic leadership in Germany; many difficulties for all members of the European Union on economic, political, and human rights issues; and the narrow decision by Britain to leave the EU. The U.S. attack on Iraq also caused heartbreaking moral consequences in terms of lives lost and political options for peace and justice closed off. This was a war of choice, not a war of necessity. Those who died perished because of someone else's unnecessary choice.

Despite the good intentions, similar inutility of war has occurred elsewhere. The US military victory in Afghanistan did not lead to peace or stability there.[17] Instead, it has become the United States' longest war in history.[18] Earlier, for nine years during the 1980s, the Soviet Union also fought a bloody war in Afghanistan, with no positive outcome. Years of French and later US fighting in Vietnam also failed to produce desirable outcomes. Even the proponents of a US missile strike against suspected Syrian chemical weapons sites said that the attack was unlikely to accomplish much more than express US strong disapproval of Syrian uses of poison gas.[19] If one reflects on the utility of even larger wars in which nuclear weapons might be used, US society could suffer irretrievable disaster and the earth undergo "nuclear winter" even while Washington claimed military victory.

Some experts conclude that recent US wars "have caused far more harm than good."[20] Whether or not one agrees with that assessment, military power has low utility for achieving desirable political outcomes in other people's societies, even when a

---

us-iraq-war-anniversary-idUSBRE92DoPG20130314. See also https://watson.brown.edu/costsofwar/costs/human. Already in 2014, Neta Crawford estimated that total costs of US warfare, including care of veterans after returning home, totaled $5.9 trillion.

[16] It is sometimes referred to as ISIL, the Islamic State in Iraq and Levant.

[17] At times, the failure of war to produce desired outcomes becomes clear when a military power ends its fighting in defeat, not for lack of firepower but for lack of wisdom, taking the side against history, as illustrated by the United States in Vietnam in the 1960s and 1970s.

[18] The United States first attacked in October 2001.

[19] Preble, "Adapting," 6.

[20] William D. Hartung, "The Costs of War," The Nation 307, no. 15 (December 17/24, 2018): 3.

militarily superior superpower tries to control a smaller state in one-sided fighting. Yet US policymakers persist in thinking that military power is the key to international security because their worldview is rooted in one version or another of increasingly outmoded forms of what is called "political realism."

Of course, today's inutilities of war were not as obvious when political realism,[21] nurtured by fears of the other, took hold of people's minds, from the life-experiences of Niccolo Machiavelli and Thomas Hobbes to the present, and formed the foundation for existing security policies. Yet many of our security problems appear unsolvable to us because we and much of the human species learned to respond to insecurity in a way that may have been useful earlier in history and which relied on violence in a militarized balance-of-power system,[22] but no longer pays sufficient security dividends to warrant discarding the growth of international law and institutions.

The political cultures of the great powers take the legitimacy of war for granted. Policymakers seldom evaluate the utility of war. They assume that occasional war is inevitable and a "natural expression of aggressive human nature." Although most leaders and citizens are sad about the destructiveness of war, they believe that it is "effective" and that its "costs . . . can be offset by gains." These unexamined implicit assumptions and ancient beliefs shape attitudes toward war and decisions about war. They remain "the essential foundation for decision-making, action and institutionalized practices."[23]

Studies in both democratic and authoritarian states show that political elites believe (1) that war works and that more violence will often work more quickly, and (2) that threats to other leaders and harsh treatment of them will generate fears that make them more likely to cooperate or capitulate.[24] However, research also shows that this outcome is seldom likely because threats trigger defensive egoistic drives in other leaders and more often than not lead citizens, who feel threatened, to a rally-around-the-flag effect for their leaders. This often generates stonewalling opposition to diplomatic initiatives, counter-threats, and counter-violence by the society first threatened in order to "pacify" it.[25]

Political leaders also tend to believe (3) that "it is possible to use military force discriminately, with exactness, and to do so with few unwanted side effects."[26] Of course,

---

[21] As explained further below, I use "political realism" to refer to nearly all schools of thought sharing political realism, except "empirical realism" which I clearly differentiate from other realist theories.

[22] States push each other around to the extent that their power enables them to do so. In the existing balance-of-power system, military power is considered the ultimate arbiter of conflicts. Such a militarized balance-of-power system could be gradually demilitarized if governments would be pressed to do so while establishing political-legal processes to resolve conflicts.

[23] Neta Crawford, "What Is War Good For? Background Ideas and Assumptions about the Legitimacy, Utility, and Costs of Offensive War," *British Journal of Politics and International Relations* 18, no. 2 (May 1, 2016): 283, 285–286.

[24] Crawford, "What Is War Good For?," 288.

[25] This is evident in US threats against Iran in 2019 and attempts to bully US allies seeking a more sophisticated diplomacy. Also, see Crawford, "What Is War Good For?," 290.

[26] Crawford, "What Is War Good For?," 291.

this is problematic in practice, given the economic costs and high percentage of civilian casualties in modern war-fighting. While overestimating the utility of war, national security managers usually underestimate the costs of war. The costs normally are figured for the duration of the war, but in fact they extend far beyond the formal conflict period. These indirect costs of war are hidden and usually paid over many years, even decades, after the initiation of war, both by the victor and the vanquished societies. In the United States, no leaders want to pay for the costs of a war that they start, so they use deficit spending and obtain huge loans to defer war costs until later, often burdening political leaders and citizens long after those spending for war have left office. This "credit-card" fighting often results in finance costs that exceed the initial spending on the war itself. The *interest* payments on the wars following 9/11, for example, could total $7.9 trillion by 2053.[27]

Even calculating the added costs of borrowing the money to fight does not cover huge macro-economic negative economic consequences of war. There are incalculable opportunity costs of using trillions of dollars for war-fighting when they could have been spent for more useful purposes such as research or development and productive investment, to strengthen health delivery, to educate more citizens, or to abolish poverty domestically and worldwide. Moreover, the vast and far-reaching inutility of unwanted inflation or possible recession resulting from war spending can hardly be estimated.

Why do governments continue to rely on war and vast expenditures for military preparedness despite their low utility and their often producing more war, more fears in others, and more insecurity? In a hostile world without reliable law enforcement, people understandably fear the consequences of lowering their military guard. In addition, many people and corporations who benefit economically from high levels of military preparedness keep encouraging more spending by sustaining fears of adversaries even when the fears may be exaggerated. Yet the very same factors that stimulate preparations for war and willingness to kill in combat—fear and economic self-interest—could also lead to peace—if fears and self-interest would be addressed with reason and mature, insightful perception.

To move onto a more promising path requires recognizing and taking seriously that the purpose of all politics, both domestic and international, regardless of culture, geography, or time in history, can be summed up in only five words: "Don't hurt me. Help me." There are two components: First, people fear that others will hurt them, so they and other citizens with whom they identify build their destructive capabilities and military strength. Second, because they need security and do not want others to gang up on them, they seek cooperation and assistance from allies. Because fears of insecurity may arise almost anywhere, even at home, and because people need help from almost everyone, both friends and foes, at home and worldwide, to be secure, the costs of security maintenance through military preparedness have become nearly

---

[27] Brown University, "Costs of War Project," http://watson.brown.edu/costsofwar/costs/economic.

intolerable and the prospects for success through primarily self-help have become extremely low. If security cooperation is sought from only some others, rather than all others, that cooperation will inevitably frighten those not included, generate their fears, and spur their armament, a process commonly known as the security dilemma, but not seriously addressed in existing grand strategies. To transcend the horns of this dilemma, people in one country need to reach out for assistance from people else-where to build a world system of peace based on law and justice, turning the universal motivation for survival arising from fear of insecurity away from excessive reliance on self-help of military preparedness and toward legal-institutional "peace preparedness" with ironclad security guarantees.

If all politics, including all political conflict, boil down to "don't hurt me; help me," it is relatively easy to figure out how to succeed at conflict transformation. While refus-ing to enable an adversary's illegitimate claims, one should try not to hurt an adver-sary's enjoyment of legitimate rights and even to help an adversary feel a legitimate sense of security, thereby making it possible for an adversary, eventually, to identify with a gradually more inclusive international community able to respond to an adver-sary's desire for "help me."

If enforcement of international norms seems to require armed force, it could be employed cautiously and it can, in good hands, be molded less by maximizing kill-ing and exacting advantages than by enforcing law and rights as humanely as pos-sible. The purpose of armed coercion is then transformed from fighting that seeks to overwhelm others through killing, while seldom acknowledging their rights, into using armed personnel to carry out policing functions of law enforcement.[28] In today's world, even if war is viewed as politics by other means, those means are sufficiently counter-productive that prudence requires them to be replaced by more effective use of law and peacebuilding politics.

Consistent with this policy direction, Christopher Preble has concluded that US military primacy is a handicap for US security because it takes money away from more pressing economic and security needs, it encourages the United States to use military force when it should not, and it invites friendly countries to expect US military bail-outs and unfriendly ones to hate the United States even more because of its forward-based military deployments. In brief, "We should reduce our military power to be more secure."[29]

Given the enormous security problems throughout the world—whether oppos-ing aggressive use of military force, terrorism, the structural violence of poverty, or environmental destruction—problems of national and international security are too important to be left to unreliable balancing of military rivalries. These are admittedly

---

[28] Of course, military personnel often do not have training for police enforcement and do not prefer doing it. As explained below, whenever I talk about "police enforcement," I mean police who act to preserve life rather than act as predators. In any case, thinking about war as violent politics may encourage human-izing or domesticating the war context rather than militarizing politics.

[29] Preble, *The Power Problem*, 3.

extremely difficult and complicated problems, but the serious US policy failures of the past four decades, discussed in Chapter 3, and inability to provide even reasonable reliability for future security call for deeper examination of why trillions of dollars and the best thinking of the US national security community cannot provide a dependable peace. The first explanation is that great military power has low utility for producing desirable political outcomes. A second is that non-state actors wield new power while states' territories enjoy less impermeability than heretofore, issues to which we now turn.

1.2 NON-STATE ACTORS: RISING POWER

A second change in international relations arises from non-state actors possessing more destructive power than ever before. Nineteen people inflicted horrendous death and destruction in New York and Washington on September 11, 2001, using box cutters to hijack civilian airliners. They caused death or injury to 9,000 others, destroyed the World Trade Center, and burned part of the Pentagon.

The violence reported in Table 1.1 demonstrates that non-state actors have a significant impact on national and human security. Bombings continue because of insufficient international governance to enable and encourage effective sharing of information and better enforcement of law across borders.[30] Armies and war-fighting strategies are not highly effective in addressing these threats, but more effective policing among most nations could be. The more than 182,000 terrorist acts that occurred in 103 countries from 1970 to 2019[31] show not only the alarming destructive capacity of people who feel alienated from national or global society and are willing to use violence to express their grievances, but also the widespread multilateral interest in finding effective ways to address terrorism,[32] including nearly all societies throughout the world. Addressing this problem in ways that people of all cultures and religions can readily support could be a significant cohesive force in generating a political coalition for the common good. Because of the inutilities of competing military powers and

---

[30] By "law" I refer to both international law and domestic law. These often intertwine and may reinforce or undermine each other.

[31] The Institute for Economics & Peace's annual report, *Global Terrorism Index 2020* and *Global Terrorism Index 2019*, 2. http://visionofhumanity.org/app/uploads/2019/11/GTI-2019web.pdf.

[32] The UN High-Level Panel carefully defined terrorism as "any action . . . intended to cause death or serious bodily harm to civilians or non-combatants, when the purpose of such an act, by its nature or context, is to intimidate a population, or to compel a Government or an international organization to do or to abstain from doing any act." United Nations High-Level Panel On Threats, Challenges, and Change, *A More Secure World: Our Shared Responsibility: Report of the High-Level Panel on Threats, Challenges, and Change* (New York: United Nations, 2004), 49, para 164, https://documents-dds-ny.un.org/doc/UNDOC/GEN/N04/602/31/PDF/N0460231.pdf?OpenElement. This definition usefully enables the international community to move beyond its past rationalization for doing almost nothing because "one person's terrorist is another person's freedom fighter." It also makes clear that states as well as non-state actors may engage in terrorist acts. I use this definition in this book, recognizing that when others use the term they may refer only to non-state actors being their target in a "war on terrorism."

TABLE 1.1

Terrorist Incidents Worldwide

Year	Number of incidents	Deaths	Injuries
1970	651	174	212
1971	471	173	82
1972	568	566	409
1973	473	370	495
1974	581	539	865
1975	740	617	617
1976	923	674	756
1977	1,319	456	518
1978	1,526	1,459	1,600
1979	2,662	2,100	2,506
1980	2,662	4,400	3,645
1981	2,586	4,851	3,337
1982	2,544	5,136	3,342
1983	2,870	9,444	4,047
1984	3,495	10,450	5,291
1985	2,915	7,094	5,130
1986	2,860	4,976	5,814
1987	3,183	6,482	5,775
1988	3,721	7,208	6,960
1989	4,324	8,152	5,539
1990	3,887	7,148	6,128
1991	4,683	8,429	7,591
1992	5,071	9,742	9,915
1993	746	2,665	5,607
1994	3,456	7,690	7,569
1995	3,081	6,103	14,292
1996	3,058	6,966	10,795
1997	3,197	10,924	9,072
1998	934	4,688	8,183
1999	1,395	3,393	5,341
2000	1,814	4,403	5,869
2001	1,906	7,729	22,774
2002	1,333	4,805	7,162
2003	1,278	3,317	7,384
2004	1,166	5,743	12,022
2005	2,017	6,331	12,784
2006	2,758	9,380	15,550
2007	3,242	12,824	22,524
2008	4,805	9,157	18,998

(*continued*)

Table 1.1   Continued

Year	Number of incidents	Deaths	Injuries
2009	4,721	9,273	19,138
2010	4,826	7,827	15,947
2011	5,076	8,246	14,659
2012	8,522	15,497	25,445
2013	12,036	22,273	37,688
2014	16,903	44,490	41,128
2015	14,965	38,853	44,043
2016	13,587	34,871	40,001
2017	10,900	26,445	24,927
2018	9,600	22,980	?
2019	8,473	20,309	?
Total	182,437	414,533	529,476

Sources: "Terrorist Incidents Worldwide," https://en.wikipedia.org/wiki/Number_of_terrorist_incidents_by_country#Worldwide; https://en.wikipedia.org/wiki/List_of_terrorist_incidents; National Consortium for the Study of Terrorism and Responses to Terrorism, *Global Terrorism Database*, https://www.start.umd.edu/pubs/START_GTD_TerrorismIn2018_Oct2018.pdf.; https://ourworldindata.org/terrorism

the political objections that military responses to terrorism usually generate in one region of the world or another, more individually focused, less combative methods of law enforcement could be employed with prospects of greater success. Governments are not likely to stop the recruitment of future terrorists by drone attacks or by waging war in other people's countries, because locally unwanted bombings usually create more than one future terrorist to take the place of each one killed.

Terrorists now seek chemical, biological, and nuclear weapons of mass destruction, with potential for delivering them with drones to inflict even more surprising harm. Indeed, "cheap new technologies allow even minor militant groups to inflict serious damage on major powers."[33] Because state boundaries are quite permeable today compared to the ability of states to keep threats at a distance in the past, non-state actors using terrorist tactics operate relatively easily across national borders. They cannot be effectively controlled by any state acting alone or in the absence of broad international cooperation. Those who attacked the United States on 9/11 did not send an army across any borders. If they had tried, the US military would have stopped them. Because they did not, US military preparedness did not prevent the devastation.

The operations of the existing international system are dysfunctional in part because they are based on the simplistic assumption that states are the primary cause of security problems and states will supply the solutions, especially through self-help. Yet states in this relatively anarchic international system fail to manage well the

---

[33] Palko Karasz, "Saudi Facilities Are Set Ablaze in Drone Strike," *New York Times*, September 15, 2019, 1.

TABLE 1.2

Number of International Non-Governmental Organizations (INGOs) and
International Governmental Organizations (IGOs) Founded by Decade

Years	# INGOs founded	# IGOs founded	Ratio of INGOs to IGOs
1900–09	445	118	3.77
1910–19	492	118	4.17
1920–29	845	215	3.93
1930–39	731	208	3.51
1940–49	1244	317	3.92
1950–59	2580	523	4.93
1960–69	3822	775	4.93
1970–79	5645	1219	4.63
1980–89	7839	924	8.48
1990–99	8988	1299	6.92
2000–09	3505	500	7.01

Source: Weiss, Seyle, and Coolidge, *Rise of Non-State Actors*, 7

threats posed by non-state actors, as demonstrated by non-state bombings in states that are otherwise relatively secure, such as Belgium, France, Germany, Spain, Sweden, the United Kingdom, and the United States, as well as numerous other societies.

The existing balance-of-power system's failures, as we have seen, are demonstrated in the rise and spread of Al-Qaeda, the establishment and growth of ISIS, the killings and abductions by Boko Haram, the attacks by al-Shabab, thousands of deaths and abductions in South Sudan, and 800,000 civilians killed in Rwanda. Of course, the rise in disruptive violence caused by non-state actors does not encompass the many diverse and often positive influences exercised by the dramatic growth of non-state actors, both private- and public-sector international governmental organizations (IGOs) participating in global governance. Among these are transnational corporations (TNCs), which are private for-profit organizations usually not included in the category of non-governmental organizations (NGOs) or international non-governmental organizations (INGOs), which are private, generally non-profit organizations of civil society. These have all increased in number, financial assets, and power since 1945. Over the 20th century, more than 38,000 IGOs and INGOs were founded,[34] primarily the latter, as Table 1.2 shows.

Taken together, non-state actors have greatly expanded the reach and capacity of global governance over the past century, enabling more extensive legal and institutional initiatives than have ever been utilized to counter some of the negative consequences

---

[34] Thomas G. Weiss, D. Conor Seyle, and Kelsey Coolidge, *The Rise of Non-State Actors in Global Governance: Opportunities and Limitations* (Broomfield, CO: One Earth Future Foundation, 2013), 7, https://acuns.org/wp-content/uploads/2013/11/gg-weiss.pdf; www.oneearthfuture.org.

of non-state violent actors.[35] For example, in the sphere of human rights, influence has shifted "away from a system in which states make the rules to a more cosmopolitan order in which IGOs and NGOs play central roles as well."[36] One benefit before the rise of nativist forces was the establishment of a major institution like the International Criminal Court with the purpose of curtailing violence and insecurity. If non-state human rights actors had not been present in the UN's life, "it is unlikely that the world organization's record would be as good as it is."[37] In sum, the rising influence of non-state actors carries important implications both for increasing insecurity for people as well as increasing opportunities for good governance that will enhance security. To remain focused mainly on how states can use military power to counter violent non-state actors is of little help in either addressing violence or utilizing positive governing opportunities.

1.3 NON-MILITARY THREATS: INCREASING INSECURITY

In a third change in international relations, non-military threats to human security have grown enormously, posing far greater threats than the early exponents of political realism could have imagined. Threats to millions of people steadily mount from environmental dangers, poverty, and cyberattacks in the face of woefully inadequate responses by separate states and their feeble efforts to act decisively and cooperatively to address these non-military security threats.

The Earth's biosphere has begun collapsing as industrial growth and expansive human consumption overwhelm ecosystems and alter the delicate balance that maintains Earth's biosphere. When environmental stability is threatened, it often causes political conflict as people compete for possession of tillable land, fresh water, clean air, petroleum, and other scarce resources.

Climate change poses a physical threat to the security of millions of people who face losing their homes and fields to rising seas. The Ecological Threat Register reports that "the total number of natural disasters has tripled in the last four decades." Their economic impact has risen "from $50 billion in the 1980s to $200 billion per year in the last [2010–2020] decade." In addition, "more than two billion people [now] . . . live in countries experiencing high water stress." Four billion people suffer severe water scarcity for at least one month of the year.[38] Experts, including the Intergovernmental Panel on Climate Change, estimate that the number of climate-change refugees will

---

[35] Craig N. Murphy, "The Last Two Centuries of Global Governance," *Global Governance* 21, no. 2 (2015): 189–196.

[36] Thomas Weiss, David Forsythe, Roger Coate, and Kelly-Kate Pease, *The United Nations and Changing World Politics* (Boulder, CO: Westview, 2014), 243.

[37] Weiss et al., *The United Nations and Changing World Politics*, 245.

[38] Institute for Economics and Peace, *Global Peace Index 2020: Measuring Peace in a Complex World* (Sidney: Institute for Economics and Peace, 2020), 3.

rise to 100 million by 2025 and to 150 million to 200 million by 2050.[39] Some estimates predict that 1 billion people will be displaced by climate change.[40]

Weather extremes disrupt agricultural output and cause rising seas which in turn reduce the earth's livable space and tillable cropland. Food and water shortages exacerbate ethnic tensions, civil and international unrest,[41] and migration pressures. Food insecurity and water shortages harm development projects. Many dwindling fisheries that are not contained within a single country's territory have become sources of international conflict, such as that adjudicated by Chile and Peru before the International Court of Justice.[42] Food shortages, disappearing forests, spreading deserts, polluted seas, inadequate fresh water, and migration pressures also depress public revenue available to meet human needs.

Environmental issues, which confirm the interconnectedness of life-support systems of water and atmosphere for every person on Earth, make clear that security can no longer be based mainly on national territory and military power alone. The rain needed for crops and life itself, and the air carrying fresh oxygen, as well as toxic chemicals and diseases from neighbors, are influenced by every country of the world. Interdependence and common security threats, such as burning rainforests that previously absorbed carbon dioxide, narrow the options for separate states while environmental degradation makes violent conflict more likely.

Collective, international measures are required to address common environmental problems. The environmental stresses that US political leaders have sought to avoid undermine the economic prosperity on which great power status depends. Income and employment in agriculture, forestry, fishing, and other services are adversely affected by denial of environmental changes. Eroding natural capital often undermines other elements of strength and well-being. The seriousness of environmental insecurity has become even graver because the speed of its progression allows inertia-bound minds to dismiss it. Many scientific findings about climate change are not taken seriously by government leaders because to do so would bring inconvenient challenges to many people's minds and investments. Yet the global scale of the problem requires global solutions that are not welcome to traditional nationalist thinking.

Although most informed people understand that only global solidarity underpinning limits on greenhouse gas emissions can save humanity from a climate-changing

---

[39] International Organization for Migration, *Migration and Climate Change* (Geneva: International Organization for Migration, 2008), 9–11. Approximately 86 million additional migrants will come from sub-Saharan Africa, 40 million from South Asia, and 17 million from Latin America. Institute for Economics and Peace, *Global Peace Index 2020: Measuring Peace*, 3

[40] Jeremy Lovell, "Climate Change to Make One Billion Refugees," Reuters, May 13, 2007, http://www.reuters.com/article/latestCrisis/idUSL10710325.

[41] Elizabeth Chalecki, *Environmental Security: A Case Study of Climate Change* (Oakland: Pacific Institute for Studies of Development, Environment, and Security, 2002).

[42] Adriana Leon and Chris Kraul, "Peru Wins Maritime Border Dispute with Chile over Key Fishing Grounds," *Los Angeles Times*, January 14, 2014, https://www.latimes.com/world/la-xpm-2014-jan-27-la-fg-wn-peru-territorial-dispute-chile-20140127-story.html.

doomsday, many conservative[43] economic and political forces in Washington continue to deny extensive scientific evidence. In 2015, 189 nations of the world came together in Paris to craft and later ratify a document in which each signatory adopted its own "nationally determined contribution" for curtailing climate-changing greenhouse-gas emissions; in 2017, the United States, with the support of most US conservatives, withdrew from the agreement, shocking most of the rest of the world. The United States faces a supreme legislative test to determine whether Congress will support re-joining the agreement and pursuing serious US efforts to limit temperature rise to 1.5 C degrees.

For years before Donald Trump became president, many leading conservatives and fossil fuel corporations cavalierly dismissed scientific evidence that documented the disasters that human beings have been bringing on. Yet those who have eyes can easily see the tragedy of the commons being lived out day after disastrous day by those who ignore evidence that is inconvenient for their wasteful lifestyles. They continue "enjoying" overconsumption while they kill the biosphere, vandalize the homesteads of those living in low areas, and continue to assume that their own security can be maintained through ever more military preparedness. Yet if the relatively wealthy European and North American states do not solidly back compulsory standards to limit greenhouse gas emissions, what states can be expected to shoulder the required burdens?

Until obligations to save the climate from massive destruction can be made legally binding and incentivized worldwide, threats to the livelihoods, food and drink, and homes of millions of human beings and the extinction of hundreds of species will continue.[44] This non-military threat to security will grow as destruction of the commons deepens.

World poverty is another serious non-military security threat because it causes more than a million unnecessary deaths each month, deepens political polarization, generates unmanageable immigration pressures, and triggers violence arising from chronic mistreatment. "Poverty" means lacking the means to acquire sufficient food, water, shelter, healthcare, and education for a life of dignity and opportunity to realize one's capabilities. In the midst of huge inequities among countries, even well-intentioned governments find it difficult to develop the sense of shared purposes among diverse cultures that is needed to achieve common security. Yet, as Peter Singer has pointed out, "in the global village, someone else's poverty very soon becomes one's own problem: of lack of markets for one's products, illegal immigration, pollution, contagious disease, insecurity, fanaticism, terrorism."[45] US actions, as well as those of many other

---

[43] I use "conservative" to refer to those who call themselves conservatives even if they do not hold beliefs that have been associated with classic conservativism in the past.

[44] John Vidal, "UN Environment Programme: 200 Species Extinct Every Day, Unlike Anything Since Dinosaurs Disappeared 65 Million Years Ago," http://www.huffingtonpost.com/2010/08/17/un-environment-programme-_n_684562.html, accessed March 10, 2017. With the exit of the United Kingdom from the European Union, even the usual expectation of European solidarity on the climate issue cannot be assured.

[45] Peter Singer, *One World: The Ethics of Globalization* (New Haven, CT: Yale University Press, 2002), 7.

well-off governments, ignore this reality to such an extent that poverty "kills one-third of all human beings born into our world." Yet, "its eradication would require no more than 1 percent of the global product."[46]

Economic instability arising from countries' interdependency is another threat that can be a life-and-death matter that traditional international relations and its attendant international system have not effectively addressed. Destabilizing threats arise when national societies become dependent on each other but their economic decision-making remains largely individual and independent of the other's. Wall Street affects markets in Shanghai, London, Frankfurt, and Tokyo, and vice versa, yet no national government has reliable influence in other countries' economic decisions or global financial matters. National mismanagement of one large economy can cause a global economic downturn, yet such crises cannot be managed satisfactorily as long as decision-making remains fragmented in national capitals operating separately even though the international economy functions as a single interdependent system. The US financial crisis of 2008, for example, spread quickly throughout the world's financial system. It caused bank losses of $4.1 trillion and "drove global unemployment up by thirty million."[47]

Many national security planners believe that the world's international economic system, hungry for more energy and raw materials, requires relying on the existing international military balance to keep order and protect their corporations' and consumers' interests. Often raw materials are purchased by making international payments to governments whose officials are corrupt and dictatorial, thereby giving oppressive national governments the money they need to stay in power. As a result, the international system and many predatory domestic systems seem locked in dysfunctional embrace, making it impossible to build local democratic institutions and effective international institutions capable of gradually replacing military influences with the rule of law, poverty with greater equity, and denial of human rights with human dignity.

The existing international system has encouraged the holders of capital in one nation to advance their own interests while ignoring the interests of other stakeholders. This is especially likely to happen if the other stakeholders, whether workers, consumers, or owners of natural resources, live outside the national boundaries of the homeland of the capital exporters. Over time, advanced capitalism has pulled people, especially in many Western cultures, away from their earlier acceptance of community life that instilled some sense of broader human solidarity into daily productivity to earn money. Many citizens have lost a sense of human solidarity even at home,

---

[46] Pogge, *World Poverty*, 264, 26.

[47] Institute for Economics and Peace, *Global Peace Index 2020: Measuring Peace in a Complex World* (Sydney: June 2020), http://visionofhumanity.org/reports; Commission on Global Security Justice and Governance, *Confronting the Crisis of Global Governance: Report of the Commission on Global Security, Justice and Governance* (The Hague: The Hague Institute for Global Justice and Stimson Center, 2015), xvii.

and they are further from it outside their own nationality. The existing international economic system enables markets and profits to be global but allows responsibility to remain national or less than national. Most benefits go to an economic elite even within only a single national society. In recent years, the self-centeredness of major actors in the marketplace and tailor-made, predatory advertising have displaced the human solidarity that had been encouraged by earlier religious beliefs and institutions. The market has become so powerful that it, not scriptures or human concerns, shapes both the economies of the world and new versions of religious and personal ethics. Some believers in the market emphasize that God rewards the faithful with material acquisition and individual accumulation of wealth rather than rewards those who help the poor, build justice, eschew killing, or respect nature. Harvey Cox, for example, has concluded that modern capitalism in the United States "ultimately marks a break from the communitarian and egalitarian impulses of Christianity" and that the economic and political norms of capitalism have displaced religion as an organizing principle in society. Yet, to underscore that this selfishness is not inevitable, Cox notes, "We as human beings constructed [the market] and we can renovate, dismantle, or transform it if we want to."[48]

Unbridled capitalism can encourage authoritarianism because it provides incentives justifying inequality and paying workers, where possible, less than the value of their labor. On the other hand, appropriately bridled capitalism can serve human needs efficiently. Ideally it could be guided in part by social democratic principles and political processes rather than by market mechanisms alone, thereby addressing economic injustices that threaten security at home and abroad.

Cyberspace poses another enormous set of security problems that cannot be managed by today's militarized international system. Unlike the great powers that number a mere score of major actors, there are thousands of actors in cyberspace. They are usually out of sight and out of control. Multiple dangers arise from beyond national jurisdiction yet they secretly move within the most trusted and secretive US governmental and corporate offices. Attacks can be carried out in ways that make deterrence almost impossible. "Cyber weapons are so cheap to develop and so easy to hide that they have proven irresistible."[49] Indeed, "cyberspace increasingly resembles nothing so much as the old American Wild West with no real sheriff."[50] There are few rules and few means for enforcing any rule that might exist. There are, of course, some governing initiatives, such as the Internet Corporation for Assigned Names and Numbers and the Safe Harbor agreement embracing the United States and the European Union. Nonetheless, manipulating elections; exacerbating racial and religious hostilities in

---

[48] Harvey Cox, *The Market as God* (Cambridge, MA: Harvard University Press, 2016) quoted by Elizabeth Bruenig, "Harvey Cox's Radicalism," *The Nation* (January 30, 2017), 36, https://www.thenation.com/article/a-moral-bulwark/.

[49] David E. Sanger, *The Perfect Weapon: War, Sabotage, and Fear in the Cyber Age* (New York: Broadway Books, 2019), xii, https://ebookcentral.proquest.com/lib/[SITE_ID]/detail.action?docID=5425144.

[50] Richard Haass, *A World in Disarray: American Foreign Policy and the Crisis of the Old Order* (New York: Penguin Press, 2017), 142.

another country; practicing espionage and sabotage; and stealing identities, intellectual property, and financial resources are common. In cyberwar, destruction of national power grids, databases, control of one's weapons systems, and national democratic processes can be paralyzed, and the means of providing security for corporate life and civilians' work, healthcare, and basic needs are also. In 2020, while United States security experts were watching for Russian attacks on presidential electoral processes, Russian cyber experts and officials enjoyed access to hundreds of top-secret government and corporate offices, including labs engaged in modernizing nuclear weapons, for eight or nine months before being discovered. Even after discovery, there was no way of knowing exactly what happened or whether US systems were secure.[51]

The international governance gap for the internet is huge and getting larger, with no prospect that the traditional balance-of-power system will come to grips with the needed creation of legally binding decisions that can be enforced. US cyber weapons have been created by the intelligence community who want to keep them shrouded in secrecy in the hope of retaining some advantage over other cyberattackers. US officials "often argue that public discussion of how we might want to use or control these weapons imperils their utility."[52] Because US officials discourage public discussion of how to address the cyber security threat, democratic control of decision-making about high-tech warfare does not exist and is unlikely to be established in the foreseeable future.

In *The Perfect Weapon*, David Sanger warns that, unlike claims in the nuclear sphere, "deterrence is not working in the cyber realm." Even after spending billions of dollars, "the United States has still failed to create a deterrent against cyberattacks."[53] One of the most promising developments is that private leaders like Brad Smith, president of Microsoft, have strongly advocated a "Digital Geneva Convention" in which companies take leadership to establish rules for cyber because governmental "arms control" in cyber is too slow and those who know the most will talk the least about it in public. National governments, once again, are falling down in their responsibilities to protect their own people, largely for reasons of insufficient urgency but also because of limited imaginations about what is needed. Microsoft, Facebook, Intel, and other companies have agreed to a basic set of principles, including a "vow that the signatories would refuse to help any government, including the United States, mount cyber attacks against 'innocent civilians and enterprises from anywhere.'" Sensibly, the companies also promised to aid any nation that was attacked, "whether the motive for the attack is 'criminal or geopolitical.'"[54] As Brad Smith pointed out, "We're going to need laws passed that make clear that certain principles need to be respected around the world, that governments need to refrain from attacking critical infrastructure in times of peace or war, or even when it's unclear whether we're at a time of peace or war"[55]—in

[51] David E. Sanger, Nicole Perlroth, and Julian E. Barnes, "As Understanding of Russian Hacking Grows, So Does Alarm," *New York Times,* January 2, 2021, A1.

[52] Sanger, *Perfect Weapon,* xxii.

[53] Sanger, *Perfect Weapon,* 297–298.

[54] Sanger, *Perfect Weapon,* 306.

[55] Quoted by Sanger, *Perfect Weapon,* 307.

other words, at *all* times. Yet no companies from China or Russia participated in these initiatives, and the initiatives that companies did take are grossly inadequate to provide genuine security in the fast-moving technological area. Citizens who leave these initiatives to voluntary efforts of private corporations are exposing themselves to heavy risks of major and recurring catastrophes in the near future.

What is needed to address this non-military threat is a unified worldwide initiative to encourage responsible uses of the internet, including ability to enforce global law against offenders launching cyberattacks from anywhere on the planet and to discourage other misuses. Because many national governments are not well equipped to enforce law on perpetrators of cybercrimes even occurring within their own territory, international or supranational government is needed for effective law enforcement and provision of minimal security. A worldwide arrangement is needed to maintain a single, integrated system to allow free flow of information and communication while preventing espionage of commercial information, theft of intellectual property, and interference with civilian and military systems on which life and security depend. For example, cyber enforcement by a global authority is necessary in the service of laws prohibiting terrorism and proliferation or use of nuclear, biological, and chemical weapons of mass destruction. Of course, any global authority would need to work closely with national governments to ensure that prohibited actions would not occur from within each national government's territory.

1.4 NATIONAL MILITARY COMPETITION: GROWING VULNERABILITIES

Innovation and spread of new destructive technologies occur not simply in the domain of cyber weapons, of course, but also in all categories of conventional weapons as well as chemical, biological, nuclear, and environmental weapons. Although national arsenals are certainly not new, when changing intensities of nationalism are wedded with newly destructive technologies, they together may produce increasingly dangerous offspring. These require looking more closely at nationalism itself to uncover more hopeful means for coping with new dangers.

The Merriam-Webster Dictionary defines nationalism as "loyalty and devotion to a nation." This part of nationalism does not present a problem. However, the definition continues, "especially a sense of national consciousness exalting one nation above all others and placing primary emphasis on promotion of its culture and interests as opposed to those of other nations or supranational groups."[56] This part of nationalism's meaning calls attention to contemporary problems with nationalism. Although loyalty and devotion to a nation are no problem, they become problematic if they lead to exaltation that places one's own nation above others in terms of moral worth or above the interests of the human species that might be expressed through international or supranational organizations. This definition, which no doubt encompasses

---

[56] Merriam-Webster Dictionary, https://www.merriam-webster.com/dictionary/nationalism.

most conventional usages and ways of thinking about nationalism, contains normative ambiguities that enable practitioners of nationalism to become confused about
or even unfaithful to their own values. Moderate forms of nationalism, here called
"healthy" or "civil" nationalism, can be consistent with human dignity, but intense,
virulent, exclusionary, or narrow nationalism contradicts human dignity because it
does not leave much psycho-political space for reciprocity and nonviolent modes of
conflict transformation.

Intense or virulent nationalism is "narrow" in the sense that its practitioners' identities and sense of solidarity include only people in their national group rather than
opening to a more inclusive group of humanity. Their sense of oneness excludes large
parts of the human race. Insofar as they deny that other nationalities may be equal
to their own exalted nation, they also remain narrow-minded. Although nationalism usually encourages a wide spectrum of favorable attitudes toward diverse people
within the national group with which one identifies, it also often harbors unfavorable
attitudes toward other groups and the remainder of species as a whole. In contrast
to exclusionary nationalism, a more cosmopolitan version of nationalism, discussed
below, would fit more prudently with contemporary political, economic, and environmental realities.

Although 19th-century nationalism could be virulent, it could not come close to
destroying as much as it can today. If US national security managers and citizens justify security policies that include the possibility of nuclear war, as they do, they in
effect are exalting their own national identity above that of the human species itself,
because nuclear war risks irreversible harm to the human species and other species as
well. No previous military technology even came close to that.

Old-time nationalism might be less than sane when expressed through 21st-century
technologies for the clinically relevant reason that it can invite national suicide. If
nuclear war-fighting led to nuclear winter, it might cause the end of human civilization.
Privileging one's own national group at the expense of another national group could
and did have serious consequences in the 19th and early 20th centuries. But today it
can bring genocidal, even suicidal consequences. Only two decades ago, a small, distant, poor country like North Korea could not significantly threaten the United States,
but today it can. Nowadays nationalism can kill hundreds of thousands overnight and
tens or hundreds of millions over the weekend. An imprudent act by a great power like
the United States, Russia, or China, or even a small power like North Korea, could be
cataclysmic. Narrow nationalism can bring far more dangerous consequences in the
21st century than ever before.

Policymakers have come to take these forms of nationalism for granted as "normal"
public support for continually advancing weapons' technologies and arms races, but
the new dangers are not normal. Throughout the past century, the destructiveness of
ever-evolving technologies and new attack weapons, products of nationalism's habit,
has outpaced national governments' capacity to constrain it. Old hands with weapons
of mass destruction, such as the United States and Russia, are now, again, developing
more destructive, less-centrally controlled, more likely-to-be-used nuclear weapons.

The United States plans to spend $400 billion from 2017 to 2026 and $1.2 trillion over the next three decades[57] to modernize and expand its nuclear arsenal, including plans to make nuclear weapons both larger and smaller, some more destructive and able to penetrate the earth, others smaller and easier to use in battle.

President Trump established a new space command with the possibility of deploying attack weapons in satellites orbiting the earth, and this is only the most recent manifestation of mindless, militarized nationalism. If implemented, there is high likelihood that it will be deeply regretted later on. It could put every community on Earth under constant threat of immediate destruction, with no satisfactory defense even remotely possible. Attack drones flying close to the Earth and under radar also will be able to threaten any person anywhere with sudden destruction.

The plans for newly destructive technologies need not be detailed here since they are available elsewhere,[58] but it is important to emphasize that the militarized balance-of-power system does not provide adequate means for controlling these technologies any more than it was able to control the spread of COVID 19. The balance-of-power system allows—and even encourages—weapons programs to advance, no matter how deadly and irrational strategies may be, while providing a boomeranging competitive ethos that stimulates other countries' weapons development as they try not to fall behind their military competitors. Today's US military primacy will encourage and justify other countries' obtaining similar systems to threaten the United States only a few years after US weapons development has threatened them. The existing international system acts as a permissive cause of destructive technologies, stimulated by economic benefits to their manufacturers, but it does not equally encourage developing institutional architecture to limit destructive instruments or mitigate the dangers they bring. Narrow and often self-congratulatory forms of nationalism drive these destructive technologies. The anti-internationalist administrations of Ronald Reagan, George W. Bush, and Donald Trump have expressed these attitudes, which have also been advanced by many members of Congress. Plans for arms buildups were present also, to somewhat lesser degrees, in the governments of Bill Clinton, Barack Obama, and Joe Biden.

Many independent observers would agree that the US president and the supporting congressional majorities that took office in 2017 expressed a dangerous nationalism in declaring that all US decisions would put "America first" and that the United States would become "great again" by spending more for military preparedness and less for abolishing poverty, upholding human rights, and sustaining a healthy environment.

---

[57] Brad Jones, "The US Plans to Spend $1.2 Trillion on Nuclear Weapons over the Next 30 Years," https://futurism.com/us-plans-spend-trillion-nuclear-weapons-years.

[58] See, for example, Michael E. O'Hanlon, "Forecasting Change in Military Technology, 2020–2040," September 2018, https://www.brookings.edu/research/forecasting-change-in-military-technology-2020-2040/; National Intelligence Council, *Global Trends 2040: A More Contested World*, March 2021, https://www.dni.gov/index.php/global-trends-home/.

Dangerous militarization exists not only in the United States. The Global Peace Index reported that 79 countries had increased their military spending as a percentage of GDP in 2019–2020. "The average level of global peacefulness . . . deteriorated by 2.5 per cent since 2008," with the average level of country peacefulness declining during 9 of the past 12 years.[59] No less daunting for human dignity, exclusionary nationalisms are on the rise in many democracies, while authoritarian governments, which usually employ narrow nationalism and seek autocratic colleagues on the world stage, support the ascent of authoritarian leaders in semi-authoritarian or quasi-democratic societies.[60] In addition to encouraging reliance on new military technologies, narrow nationalisms threaten human security because they reinforce the false impression that the balance of military power is the only security game in town.

Given the high stakes of military competition, even during peacetime, the new destructive technologies seem to justify down-playing the importance of human dignity, because privileging one's own nation, sacrificing democracy and human rights at home and abroad to maintain military secrecy and manipulate public opinion in support of an arms buildup, disrupting open trading relationships, justifying self-serving impediments to economic equity, and turning a blind eye to environmental destruction—all these seem to be justified in order to maintain US national security. What could be more important, national security managers understandably ask? Yet when military competition and international insecurities intensify national feelings in the 21st century, they may threaten one's way of life even without war, if they narrow national identities and impede common security goals.

Fortunately, not all changes in international relations have a predominantly threatening nature. We move now to examine three more hopeful developments.

1.5 NONVIOLENT CAMPAIGNS: OFFERING POSSIBILITIES

A fifth change in international relations arises from growing understanding that nonviolent direct action can do more to protect human security and enable civilians to exert influence on political decision-making than has been commonly recognized in the past.[61] Research examining all 323 resistance campaigns that have occurred in the world since 1900, both violent and nonviolent, which have sought to oust dictators or resist external military aggression, shows that nonviolent campaigns have succeeded

---

[59] Institute for Economics and Peace, *Global Peace Index 2020: Measuring Peace in a Complex World* (Sidney: Institute for Economics and Peace, 2020), 4.

[60] "It is the combination of authoritarian values disguised by populist rhetoric which we regard as potentially the most dangerous threat to liberal democracy," Howell and Moe, *Crisis of Democracy*, 11.

[61] See Erica Chenoweth and Maria J. Stephan, *Why Civil Resistance Works: The Strategic Logic of Nonviolent Conflict* (New York: Columbia University Press, 2011); David Cortright, *Gandhi and Beyond: Nonviolence for a New Political Age* (Boulder, CO: Paradigm, 2009); Sharon Erickson Nepstad, *Nonviolent Struggle: Theories, Strategies, and Dynamics* (Oxford: Oxford University Press, 2015). For an excellent introduction to classic writings on the power and nature of nonviolent action, see David Cortright, *Truth Seekers: Voices of Peace and Nonviolence from Gandhi to Pope Francis* (Maryknoll: Orbis Books, 2020).

more often than violent efforts.[62] Neither violence nor nonviolence works 100 percent of the time, of course, but nonviolent campaigns are more likely than violent campaigns to result in peace and to ensure that peace is sustained after a campaign has ended.[63]

Remarkably, nonviolent campaigns are also more likely than are violent ones to result in democracy being established one or two decades later—even if a nonviolent campaign fails to take power[64] and even if a violent campaign succeeds in its immediate goal of taking power. Similarly, if there is a violent campaign or, in effect, a civil war, the long-term prospects for obtaining democracy and for preventing recurrence of violence are both increased if there is a negotiated settlement to the fighting rather than if one side obtains outright victory.[65] "Victorious governments tend to become more authoritarian" and more "[averse] to international insight."[66] Societies suffering from civil war are also more likely to develop democratic customs and institutions if they end fighting with a negotiated agreement that is supported by international diplomatic missions, and that uses UN peacekeeping forces rather than intervention by a great power to reinforce the peace.[67]

A growing body of research shows that nonviolent means for overcoming an authoritarian government or resisting a foreign occupation, although no panacea, are more likely than violent means to succeed and far more likely to lead to democratic government after an anti-government campaign, even against authoritarian governments;[68] unfortunately, these are not utilized in traditional balance-of-power thinking because political realists believe that what goes on inside a state is largely insignificant in determining what goes on between states.

If given additional study and support, nonviolent initiatives could become more widely and successfully used as preferred forms of conflict transformation.[69] Whether embraced as a realistic strategy for social change, as described above, or as a

---

[62] Chenoweth and Stephan, *Why Civil Resistance Works*, 3–29.

[63] Chenoweth and Stephan, *Why Civil Resistance Works*, 201–231.

[64] "The long-term effects of failed nonviolent campaigns are more favorable to democracy and civil peace than the long-term effects of successful violent campaigns." Chenoweth and Stephan, *Why Civil Resistance Works*, 202.

[65] Wallensteen, *Quality Peace*, 206–207.

[66] Wallensteen, *Quality Peace*, 207.

[67] Wallensteen, *Quality Peace*, 50, 205–208; Jeffrey Pickering and Mark Peceny, "Forging Democracy at Gunpoint," *International Studies Quarterly* 50, no. 3 (September 1, 2006): 552–553, https://www.jstor.org/stable/4092792; Virginia Page Fortna, *Does Peacekeeping Work? Shaping Belligerents' Choices After Civil War* (Princeton, NJ: Princeton University Press, 2008), https://www.jstor.org/stable/j.ctt7sv7j; Cortright, Seyle, and Wall, *Governance for Peace*, 237–240.

[68] Erica Chenoweth and Maria Stephan, "Why Civil Resistance Works," *International Security* 33, no. 1 (2008): 7–44; Erica Chenoweth and Maria Stephan, "Drop Your Weapons: When and Why Civil Resistance Works," *Foreign Affairs* 93, no. 4 (July/August 2014): 94–106; Chenoweth and Stephan, *Why Civil Resistance Works*. See also Mel Duncan, "Greater Than the Tread of Mighty Armies: Unarmed Civilian Protection Gaining Momentum Worldwide," *Courier*, no. 91 (Fall 2017): 3–7; Cortright, *Gandhi and Beyond*.

[69] See especially the work of Gene Sharp, *The Politics of Nonviolent Action* (Boston: P. Sargent, 1973).

commitment to nonviolence as a way of life, as exemplified by Mohandas Gandhi, both groups of citizens can play useful roles in transforming conflicts through negotiation, advancing legislation for justice, and reforming law enforcement. Pope Francis has taken interest in expanding education about the utility of nonviolent action, cultivating a culture of nonviolence, and recommending its use by governments and activists, arising from awareness that violent responses often lead to more violence, including unjustifiable killings, refugees and displaced persons, forced migrations, terrorism, and devastation of the environment. In poor societies violence benefits warlords but not others. In noting the power of nonviolence in diverse cultural contexts, the pope has cited the work of Gandhi, Martin Luther King Jr., and Mother Teresa.[70] He also has noted the Islamic Pashtun leader, Abdul Ghaffar Khan, and the interfaith peace activist, Leymah Gbowee of Liberia, for their commitments to nonviolent transformations, pointing out that "no religion is terrorist."[71]

The surprisingly high utility of nonviolent resistance and low utility of war-fighting are in part due to a dematerialization of some forms of power that is poorly understood and seldom accepted. For example, the superior firepower of France and later of the United States in fighting against Vietnamese and of the Soviet Union and later of the United States in fighting against Afghans never led to victory for the French, Russian, or US military organizations in these cases. Superior firepower failed. In these conflicts, local resistance to apparently stronger military power gained an upper hand in the long run, despite suffering enormous costs. Similarly, nonviolent resistance freed India from British rule and has successfully challenged oppressive forces in a number of countries: Brazil, 1984–86; Chile, 1983–89; Czechoslovakia, 1989; East Germany, 1989; Estonia, 1988; India, 1930–47; Iran, 1978–79; Lebanon, 2005; Liberia, 2003; Nigeria, 1993–99; Palestinian First Intifada, 1987–92; Philippines, 1983–86; Poland, 1980–89; Serbia, 2000; South Africa, 1985; Tunisia, 2010–2011; Ukraine, 2004–05; and United States, 1960s.[72]

The dematerialization of power often leaves oppressors less strong, even though they command the most guns, and activists more powerful if they can communicate effectively about victimization by oppressors and empower a unified, resolute public. It would be blind overstatement, of course, to say that non-material power usually wins over material power, yet when used wisely it does show great strength in some contexts and often does make gains in the long run. Some military technology has become self-paralyzing because of its destructiveness, while citizen-based monitoring of misdeeds, communicated widely with the help of smart phones, helps to empower

---

[70] Carol Glatz, "Pope: World Needs Nonviolent Responses to Social, Political Problems," Catholic News Service, December 15, 2016, https://www.ncronline.org/blogs/francis-chronicles/pope-world-needs-nonviolent-responses-social-political-problems; https://www.catholicnewsagency.com/news/pope-tells-ambassadors-to-make-courageous-choice-for-nonviolence-33375.

[71] He also emphasized that "God cannot be used to justify violence." Pope Francis, "Nonviolence: A Style of Politics for Peace," January 1, 2017, http://www.vatican.va/content/francesco/en/messages/peace/documents/papa-francesco_20161208_messaggio-l-giornata-mondiale-pace-2017.html.

[72] Chenoweth and Stephan, *Why Civil Resistance Works*; Nepstad, *Nonviolent Struggle*.

activists who have no guns, and often broadens their appeal if they choose not to get any.

Because a wider segment of people in almost every society may more willingly join a nonviolent movement than a violent one, the potential for exerting influence is enormous in any context where a large number of people are committed to a cause such as to stop oppression or war. In some cases nonviolence can even replace a violent campaign and become more effective at the same time that it is becoming less violent. Much of the promise of nonviolent action has yet to be explored, systematically applied, and broadly supported. National governments and the international community could do much more to provide training, logistical help, and diplomatic protection for nonviolent activists who may be eager to organize and work for peace, justice, and human rights in their own societies and around the world. Perhaps the greatest genius of nonviolent action is that it forever keeps open the possibility that adversaries eventually may come to accept or respect the other, and in the meantime they have not killed the other. They have kept the other alive just in case. It is a startling commitment to non-zero sumness. That a more inclusive identity, possibly including a former adversary, always remains a possibility can attract supporters and encourage respect from others.

1.6 THE RULE OF LAW: SEEKING TRACTION

A sixth change, accompanied by both positive and negative consequences, has grown out of the rise of global interdependence and vast increases in the speed and frequency of communication among billions of people. This makes effective global governance[73] an ever more realistic possibility. An expanding web of cross-border influences, international laws, and organizations enables the international level to "join directly with the local, private, or individual level without a state or public intermediary."[74] This enables an incipient process of cosmopolitan democracy "where individuals may have direct access to international activities and may even be able to assert rights and

---

[73] In this analysis, I use "governance" in the same way as did the Commission on Global Governance. The Commission defined it as "the sum of many ways individuals and institutions, public and private, manage their common affairs. It is a continuing process through which conflicting or diverse interests may be accommodated and co-operative action taken. It includes formal institutions and regimes empowered to enforce compliance, as well as informal arrangements that people and institutions either have agreed to or perceive to be in their interest." Commission on Global Governance, *Our Global Neighbourhood*, 2.

Peter Hägel explains that to include in one's calculus individuals, private agencies and organizations, informal arrangements, and people's movements—not simply states—"indicates that an equal amount of attention is paid to nongovernmental actors and noninstitutionalized practices—which is why the term *governance* is preferred over *government*." See Peter Hägel, "Global Governance," *Oxford Bibliographies*, http://www.oxfordbibliographies.com.proxy.library.nd.edu/view/document/obo-9780199743292/obo-9780199743292-0015.xml?rskey=5hn11f&result=19&q=kant+perpetual+peace#firstMatch.

[74] Charlotte Ku, "The Evolution of International Law," in *International Organization and Global Governance*, ed. Thomas Weiss and Rorden Wilkinson (London: Routledge, 2014), 39.

challenge their own government's actions either in court or through institutions like the World Bank Inspection Panels."[75] As UN Secretary-General Kofi Annan wrote on the eve of the new millennium, post–World War II institutions "were built for an inter-*national* world, but we now live in a *global* world."[76] Global, transnational politics will not work magic, but even in the absence of deliberate efforts to legislate positive law, they are generating support for a larger role for international law, a rule of law that applies to all equally, not just a law of the powerful to protect and serve them.[77] Indeed, "international lawmaking and implementation have become more generally accessible and participatory than at any other time since the advent of international political institutions, and the process is ongoing."[78]

It would be possible to establish a much more effective rule of law in the world today—*if* enough people would insist on it. Karen Alter's research shows that an influential minority of people around the world "share many of the goals inscribed in international law and agree that powerful governments must respect international law and the rule of law."[79] We now are able to see much of what is happening through-out the world as it happens,[80] which makes gross cheating on laws difficult to con-ceal. International currency transactions of roughly $6.6 trillion each *day* occur with unquestioned reliability.[81] The politico-legal processes that precede and follow deci-sions made by two dozen permanent international courts established by states affect many more actors than the number directly participating in the judicial proceedings themselves. These processes have developed new cross-border, transnational political allies and expanding coalitions of interests.[82]

Where small changes in the practice of sovereignty have occurred, they usually have happened without highly visible campaigns or hotly contested political conflicts. They have arisen from a desire to conduct commerce more efficiently and to protect human rights. Despite some populist opposition, the long-term rising influence of international law and international adjudicatory bodies over the past several decades

---

[75] Ku, "Evolution of International Law," 39.

[76] Quoted by Ku, "Evolution of International Law," 40. Italics in original.

[77] Stephen Gill, "Reimagining the Future: Some Critical Reflections," in *Critical Perspectives on the Crisis of Global Governance: Reimagining the Future*, ed. Stephen Gill (New York: Palgrave Macmillan, 2016), 17.

[78] Ku, "Evolution of International Law," 43.

[79] Karen J. Alter, *The New Terrain of International Law: Courts, Politics, Rights* (Princeton, NJ: Princeton University Press, 2014), 18, 340–344.

[80] Chief-of-Staff General Ronald Fogelman explained Air Force strategic planning: "Our goal is to find, fix, track, and target everything that moves on the face of the earth. We can do it now, but not in real time." This ability to observe has been improved since the speech was delivered in 1996. It could be used con-structively for law enforcement. His speech at the Heritage Foundation, Washington, DC, December 13, 1996, was quoted by Glenn D. Paige, *Nonkilling Global Political Science* (Bloomington, IN: Xlibris, 2007), 9, http://www.xlibris.com/LP02F10C007.aspx?cat=PPC&ls=Search+Engine&src=Google&gkw=Brand+Search&kw=Xlibris&gclid=CLyR7MqDh9ICFcUlgQod-LUKdA.

[81] Bank for International Settlements, "Triennial Central Bank Survey: Foreign Exchange Turnover in April 2019," https://www.bis.org/statistics/rpfx19_fx.pdf.

[82] Alter, *New Terrain*, 4–5, 6–31.

demonstrates the possibility of building a post-balance-of-military-power world where legality would shape more of international security policy and govern economic relations.[83]

The prospects for more effective international law are increased by the rising number and influence of non-state actors not only in courts but also in other governing relationships. Growth in international intergovernmental organizations, international non-governmental organizations, multinational corporations, regional organizations, and transnational and international networks of actors share varying degrees of different common interests across borders. The traditionally sharp distinction between what goes on inside a state and what goes on outside a state, between intra-national relations and international relations, no longer applies. In the past, citizens felt morally responsible for caring for other citizens within their society, but almost no responsibility for citizens who lived outside the borders of their own state. Traditionally, the state has exercised sovereignty internally by relating to individuals and groups within its boundaries, but it has expressed its external sovereignty by relating mainly to other states. Other state governments in turn expressed internal sovereignty by dealing with their own citizens. Now many traditional views of "us" and "them" are eroding as people and sometimes the government in one state support the law upholding human rights of people in other states even though they live beyond their own national government's internal jurisdiction.

The growth of transnational corporations, non-governmental organizations, international governmental organizations, and multilateral and supranational organizations, combined with the rising influence of international law, transnational rules, and customary practices, also deeply influence domestic societies. These interactions stimulate what in this book are called "legalization processes"[84] or "judicialization processes," which bring specific political or military actions under the influence of

---

[83] See Alter, *New Terrain*, 342. This possibility opens the door to using international policing in new ways that run parallel to new uses of transnational and supranational judicial institutions.

[84] For "legalization" to occur means that an act that was formerly seen as a political or military matter falling *outside* the law is increasingly seen as a legal matter falling *within* legal constraints. The scope of law may expand as a result of evolving customs, writing new treaty law, consolidating informal practices, or adjudicating a dispute in an international tribunal. An example is the historical transformation of an act of aggressive war, which was once accepted as the political and military right of any sovereign government, into an act that now is clearly prohibited by law in the Kellogg-Briand pact and the United Nations Charter. Confirmation of the evolving law against aggression occurred in the Nuremberg precedent, with clarification that government officials accused of crimes against the peace are not allowed to use as a defense argument that they were merely following orders or were justified in making a war of aggression for *raison d'etat* or "reason of state."

Legalization in international relations also may be understood as partial "depoliticization" or "demilitarization" of conduct as it is brought into the sphere of legal guidance. Similarly, "judicialization processes" may be understood as movement of an act that previously was understood as primarily political in nature into a courtroom for judicial determination of what is legal or illegal, just or unjust.

Another meaning of "legalization," totally different from the one embraced here, refers to accepting certain conduct as legal even though it was previously criminal, such as state laws legalizing uses of marijuana that were previously illegal. In these two contrasting meanings, legalization processes may either "criminalize" or "decriminalize" conduct.

international law, thereby expanding international law to render decisions more predictable and safe at home and abroad. Many lines of communication and legal action cross US borders without going through the US capital and its formal diplomatic relations with other states. In some areas of life there are institutions with complicated systems of practices and rules accompanied by legal enforcement mechanisms crossing borders. These actors and laws exert extensive influence on the lives of US citizens. Of course, many cross-border influences are not well governed, but they are beginning to be recognized as needing better governance. These include rules affecting pollution and climate change, diseases and epidemics, culture and information, new technologies such as the internet, weapons such as drones and space-based attack vehicles, market forces and currency exchange, import and export of raw materials, agricultural products, and manufactured goods, standards for labor and environmental practices, and much more.

Although populist movements oppose transnationalizing forces (except where boundary-transcendence strengthens populist movements), these will not go away. The unpopularity of some elements of interdependence will not erase it. Anti-EU populists found themselves reversing their earlier opposition to holding the elections for the European Parliament in 2019, in order to enable themselves to campaign for election to the Parliament and build cross-border alliances with other populist parties from other countries in Europe. Despite populist opposition, astute use of new international law and understandings of moral obligation can help generate positive change that will, in fact, help address some populist grievances about being left behind by globalization.

Some traditional national security policies and the national identities on which they have been based simply lack wisdom any longer because they no longer provide security. Nor are national policies morally desirable if they fail to acknowledge every person's connection with people outside their national borders. Simply by breathing oxygen from Earth's atmosphere or drinking water drawn from the Earth's universally shared reservoir, every person is connected with other person on Earth. Every person either remains indifferent to, tacitly supports, or actively seeks to institute legal reforms to the existing militarized balance-of-power system and the interwoven international economic-environmental system.

In sum, the interdependence of national societies and the permeability of their borders makes national governing unsuccessful when it stops at the water's edge or any national boundary. At the same time, this interdependence increases the prospects for a global rule of law *if* people build transnational networks and create global structures capable of becoming increasingly representative and effective because they nurture impartial legalization processes. Yet without increased pressure from a worldwide coalition of civil society groups explicitly seeking to change the international system, sufficiently effective forms of governance, based on inclusive identities, are unlikely to flourish in the face of existing vested interests opposing them.[85]

---

[85] Indeed, reversals are possible in the absence of an awakened international civil society, as suggested in the popular rejection of the peace agreement in Colombia in 2016; the popular vote for withdrawal of Britain from the EU in 2016; and popular support for Donald Trump's narrow nationalism.

1.7 GLOBAL GOVERNANCE: NEEDING NURTURE

An imaginative use of global governance holds more promise for addressing the afore-mentioned destabilizing international realities than does the traditional national security approach expressed through the existing, militarized balance-of-power system. Similarly, the positive new developments noted above cannot be fully utilized while limiting national governmental operations within the old international system. Indeed, the human species has reached the historical turning point in which some global governance, structured as democratically as possible, will be necessary to produce the security people need. To be sure, whether any international system is nationally fragmented or more globally integrated, it will be imperfect and not without risk. But some choice is needed now between an old system incapable of managing new problems and a newly buttressed rule-of-law system designed to nurture specific globally shared decision-making,[86] referred to here as democratic global governance.

International law shows some of its potential governing colors in small, vertical dispersals of national sovereignty that have occurred in international legal institutions like the World Trade Organization, the International Atomic Energy Agency, the United Nations Law of the Sea Convention, and two dozen functioning international courts. More fulsome illustrations of regional or global governance exist in the European Community, the Antarctic Treaty System, and the UN Security Council decision to remove Iraq from Kuwait in 1990. These demonstrate incipient global governance.

The most effective way to build support for constructive global governance and to address populism is to establish effective political institutions capable of addressing citizens' serious grievances. In the past, that could be done within a single country like the United States, but today it also requires new international legal norms to govern international relations. Without more effective global governance, populism will be likely to fester while support for needed global initiatives will plummet. Rather than simply speaking against populist movements that resist globalization, internationalists and cosmopolitans should foreground the question "Who benefits?" in discussing every major international decision.[87] This will encourage learning about how to yield more political and economic justice for the aggrieved, regardless of whether the locus of a decision or operation is local or global. Achieving justice should be the standard for deciding where governance is needed. In the long run, this strategy will enable more people to support and benefit from cultivating useful global governance.

---

[86] As Thomas Weiss and Ramesh Thakur document, "The evolution of intergovernmental institutions to facilitate robust international responses lags well behind the emergence of collective problems with trans-border, especially global, dimensions." Thomas G. Weiss and Ramesh Thakur, *Global Governance and the UN: An Unfinished Journey* (Bloomington: Indiana University Press, 2010), 4.

[87] Cosmopolitans emphasize that human dignity belongs to every person regardless of origin. They attribute less moral significance to national boundaries than internationalists. A cosmopolitan can be considered a "citizen of the world."

Although narrow nationalism, militarism, bigotry, and authoritarianism may be on the rise in parts of the United States, Europe, Russia, and elsewhere, such trends will not halt the rise of interdependence nor will they diminish the need for global governance. Indeed, they increase it. Primarily voluntary, international arrangements can no longer protect people within a particular nation-state. Increasingly, if a nation wants to flourish, prudence requires it to pay attention to the common good and imposes on it the need to incentivize others' conduct to make it more responsible and fair. To encourage global compliance with desirable conduct, global governance could take a page from the US system, and from other federal systems as well, in which a substantial amount of the federal government's power over states is not direct coercion, mandated by the Constitution. It is made up of incentives or conditions attached to federal subsidies.

Throughout human history, the development of new information technologies, from writing to bookkeeping to the printing press to the computer, have unlocked additional opportunities for mutually beneficial (non-zero-sum) governing relationships, because it enables separate groups to successfully address the communication barrier and the trust barrier, which are the two main barriers to separate groups living peacefully with one another. Recent advances in communication technologies made possible by micro-computers, smart phones, and the internet enable cooperation in global governance if they are used wisely.[88]

In concluding this exploration of changing global realities, four of these—declining utility and increasing costs of military power, rising threats from non-state actors, growing non-military threats to security, and narrowing nationalism wielding ever more destructive technologies—worsen all the traditional security problems that arise in the existing international system. They amplify the failings of today's militarily oriented international system, poorly equipped to sustain peace and security. Indeed, the newly destabilizing realities, when added to the old familiar difficulties of "anarchic balancing" for peace and security, produce an absolutely unsettling consequence: the existing balance-of-power system, the one that national security managers and publics have grown to know and love and consider "natural," has become so ineffective that it cannot be relied on for security *regardless* of how much military power the United States or another state may accumulate and how shrewdly their national security policies are implemented.

Three more promising evolving realities—rising potential in nonviolent direct action for increasing non-zero sumness, expanding the rule of law internationally, and increasing potential in global governance—provide a foundation for improved human security and justice. Taken together, the seven changing processes in international relations indicate that serious changes in security policies and institutions are necessary to address the most dangerous trends and take advantage of the most promising

---

[88] Wright, *Nonzero*, 98–100; 198–208.

opportunities in order to make national government, once again, and global governance, for the first time, truly effective.

New military technology cannot be "balanced" in the old balance-of-power system as reliably as earlier forms of military strength were managed—and that management was never very good. The possibilities for basing attack weapons in earth orbits, above national security radar, and of sending attack drones and cruise missiles under radar threaten to reduce secure control of national airspace and national boundaries. Dangerous technological innovations, often spawned by unconstrained, private actors who draw on information widely available, are coming at a more rapid rate than separate national governments can manage. Weapons using artificial intelligence can easily cross borders and attack on a moment's notice. Cyber weapons are unstoppable at this time. Environmental stresses threaten security while rendering national boundaries less significant. Unmanaged pandemics threaten hundreds of thousands of lives and every national economy, not for weeks but for years. To address these problems creates a need for more effective and more democratic global institutions to monitor and address in legally binding ways the implications of emerging technologies for human security.[89]

To address these deepening realities successfully will require drawing a new, less ideological, more pragmatic and normative roadmap, to which we now turn.

---

[89] See, for example, Anja Kaspersen, "Security by Design: Emerging Technologies Require New Approach to Oversight, Governance," *Courier*, Summer (Muscatine, IA: Stanley Foundation, 2017).

2

Conceiving a Security-Enhancing Theory

IN FACING NEW global realities while relying on old national habits, the US government inadvertently produces one national security tragedy after another for its citizens. When other great powers follow similar patterns, they together produce tragedy for the human species and for many other species. Policymakers are not aligning US power and resources to meet security needs. Most nations are not receiving a good security bargain from each other or from the existing international system. National military means are simply not up to the global governing ends that must be met.

As policies of the United States and other great powers demonstrate their ineffectiveness, people's frustrations and fears deepen, generating a heedless populism that forestalls constructive innovations. As policymakers continue to rely heavily on military means to increase security, despite the declining effectiveness of these means, US security policy becomes a fool's errand, especially because strengthening international law and multilateral institutions *is* possible. Overemphasizing military "solutions" makes it more difficult to abolish poverty, promote international economic integration, protect the environment, and strengthen international law and institutions. Yet progress toward these ends must occur to enhance security.

2.1 RESPECTING EMPIRICAL REALITY

The main problem is that US policymakers focus too much on national interests and too little on human interests, too much on military threats and coercion of others and too little on positive incentives, too much on the short term and too little on the long run. They promote US "independence" at the expense of international law and human rights, and prefer tinkering with national policies at the expense of cooperative institution-building and global structural change.

Respecting empirical reality would encourage a shift in priorities. This change of direction would *enhance* national security, but requires adopting a new paradigm for thinking and acting. The new way of perceiving and acting should be rigorously empirical, eschewing hyper-nationalism and doctrinaire ways of perceiving the international system in order to see the full scale of both crises and opportunities. Underlying this recommendation, which stands at the heart of this book, is the theory proposed here, which I call "empirical realism." Like any useful theory, it interprets and accounts for the world in a way that "fits the facts." Empirical realism invites a richer, more penetrating, complex view of reality—in this case, the reality of global interdependence and human dignity —than do the theories that have motivated and sometimes blinkered US policymakers in recent decades.

This study builds the theory of empirical realism inductively on evidence accrued and examined through diverse research disciplines in order to identify how to achieve sustainable security and peace, which is the dependent variable in this analysis, or what we want to achieve. The prime correlates of security and peace, elaborated in Chapter 5, represent mutually reinforcing independent variables, or what we can vary to bring more peace and security. This theory substantiates the claim that the path to sustainable security and peace requires addressing all nations' security fears, focusing on human security, honoring positive reciprocity, implementing equity, strengthening international law, and building global governance. Those measures that respect fundamental human rights and correlate with security and peace over time should be considered for inclusion in a global grand strategy for human security. Empirical realist analysis finds US national security inseparable from human security, and human security inseparable from sustainable peace. It sees more complexity than does political realism. It rejects dogmatism and doctrinaire thinking and remains forever open to new insights, which always are tentative and hypothetical in the sense that they might be modified by superior understanding arising in a later day.

Empirical realism invites bridge-building conversation among (1) international relations scholars of realism, liberalism, and constructivism; (2) theorists of peace research; and (3) experts from related fields such as national security studies. In building a dynamic new framing of the world, empirical realism draws on and synthesizes relevant insights from related disciplines. From traditional political realism, empirical realists draw insight about the tendency of independent states to maximize their military power in an anarchic international system lacking central authority, but this is not treated as an iron law. From liberal internationalism, empirical realism integrates the security benefits, in the long run, of cooperative efforts to build international institutions, integrate economic interests, and peacefully nurture democratic values. Peacebuilding theory adds the benefits of adversaries deliberately collaborating as equals rather than acting unilaterally from separate spheres with one group trying to impose expectations on another. Cosmopolitan and feminist political theories undergird empirical realism's emphasis on fostering respect for equal human rights for all. Evolutionary psychology sheds light on how relationships between conflicting groups, when historical conditions allowed or dictated, have been restructured into larger units of cooperation to enable them to survive.[1] Additional fields of learning will provide yet other insights for shaping this theory as the analysis unfolds.

It is especially important to understand how *empirical* realism differs from traditional *political* realism because the latter has been the dominant theory or ideology informing policymakers in the United States and other great powers throughout the post–World War II period. Most political realists believe that great powers have no choice but to maximize their military power in the balance-of-power system, except during a rare moment when there may be only a single superpower, making it unnecessary for it to compete "normally."[2] In any case, "almost all governments continue to be led by political realists who view their role as serving short-term national interests." They are "privately dismissive of any encroachment on these priorities that derive from notions of 'world community,' even if based on international law and morality."[3]

For the sake of clarity in this analysis, I refer to policymakers and scholars who embrace "political realism," "neo-realism," "structural realism," "defensive realism," "offensive realism," and other sub-strands of realism as simply "political realists" or "traditional realists." I use the latter two labels interchangeably. Although significant differences exist among the various strands of realism, they all share fundamental assumptions,[4] enabling us to treat them collectively as the main intellectual force driving US foreign policy. Traditional realism has become so pervasive that its assumptions about the nature of the balance-of-power system are widely shared by most policymakers and citizens, even if not all are familiar with the theory of political realism itself.

Empirical realists see the main flaw in political realism as its automatic, unrelenting justification of and demand for a never-ending maximizing of power, particularly military power, by the national governments of the competing great powers. John Mearsheimer, a leading political realist, justifies this sweeping maximization of military power in political realism this way: "States understand that the best way to survive in an anarchic system in which they can never be certain about the intentions of other states is to be as powerful as possible relative to their competitors. States therefore aim to maximize the military assets they control and make sure other states do not gain power at their expense, while also looking for opportunities to shift the balance of power in their favor. This zero-sum competition for power, which sometimes

---

[1] For evidence on the possibilities for cross-cultural cooperation and an analysis of human possibilities for cooperative relationships from an evolutionary perspective, see Nicholas A. Christakis, *Blueprint: The Evolutionary Origins of a Good Society* (New York: Little, Brown, 2019); and Wright, *Nonzero*.

[2] "As long as liberal states operate in either bipolarity or multipolarity, they have no choice but to act toward each other according to realist logic." Mearsheimer, *Delusion*, Kindle, 146, 2319.

[3] Richard Falk, *Power Shift: On the New Global Order* (London: Zed Books, 2016), 241.

[4] Mearsheimer indicates that when "there is no higher authority in the international system . . . liberalism devolves into realism." Also, "As long as the international system is anarchic, liberalism is no different from realism in that realm." Mearsheimer, *Delusion*, Kindle, 2480, 2602.

leads to war, is what makes international politics a ruthless and treacherous business."[5] Empirical realists do not share with political realists the belief that this approach is the only way or the best way to achieve national security or to institutionalize international peace, let alone to reach human security, all three of which empirical realists strive to achieve.

Some further clarification is needed of the term "liberal," often used among decision makers in discussing "liberal internationalism," "liberal hegemony," and "liberal democracy." A useful anchor is the Latin origin, *liber*, meaning a free person. I follow a familiar definition of "liberalism" to mean the philosophy that emphasizes respect for individual human rights and a full range of political liberties, such as freedom of speech, religion, assembly, and other democratic values, including selecting one's governing officials while protecting minority rights against majoritarian rule that might otherwise result in illiberal domination of minorities or individuals in whom rights inhere.[6] Historically, the United States has been strongly committed to liberal values even though it has never been a perfect liberal democracy.

"Liberal internationalism," which an eminent proponent says could be "best understood as an ongoing project to make the world safe for democracy,"[7] can easily be distinguished from political realism, in part because of its interest in human rights, liberal democracy, international rules, and multilateral institutions.[8] But "liberal hegemony" is less clear. Well-known political realists, Mearsheimer, Barry Posen, and Stephen Walt, for example, describe liberal hegemony as an activist US policy aimed at maintaining US military dominance as a superpower while advancing liberalism overseas and US national security worldwide,[9] especially following the end of the Cold War in 1989.

At that time, Mearsheimer notes, the United States had no strategic rival so it could undertake military adventures to implant liberal values overseas. In his words, "No recent president embraced the mission of spreading liberalism more enthusiastically than George W. Bush."[10] According to this view, the Bush administration's invasion of Iraq in 2003 to overthrow Saddam Hussein's authoritarian government and install democratic rule represents a clear example of "liberal interventionism" or "liberal hegemony." "Restrained" political realists persuasively argue that US policies of "liberal hegemony," in which the United States has been engaged in nearly constant fighting since 2001, have been a huge failure.[11] These wars, which embody US officials' imperial

---

[5] *Delusion*, Kindle 2524–2529.

[6] For discussion of liberalism in international relations, see Michael W. Doyle, "Kant, Liberal Legacies, and Foreign Affairs," *Philosophy & Public Affairs*, Part 1, 12, no. 3 (1983): 205–235.

[7] Ikenberry, *A World Safe for Democracy*, 287.

[8] "Realists do not assign much importance to the so-called international community, which is based on a deep respect for inalienable rights." Mearsheimer, *Delusion*, Kindle, 2577.

[9] See Barry R. Posen, *Restraint, A New Foundation for U.S. Grand Strategy* (Ithaca, NY: Cornell University Press, 2015); William Ruger, "A Realist's Guide to Grand Strategy," *The American Conservative*, August 26, 2014, https://www.theamericanconservative.com/articles/a-realists-guide-to-grand-strategy/.

[10] Mearsheimer, *Delusion*, Kindle, 168.

[11] Mearsheimer had warned before the attack that major US policy failures would occur if the United States invaded. Mearsheimer, *Delusion*.

ambitions, have been unnecessary, unwise, and a tragic waste of human lives and money. They have undermined US security throughout the world and US democracy at home.[12]

Although assessing these US policies as failures seems convincing, the definitional characterization of them as a product of liberalism makes sense only to a limited degree. On the one hand, Bush's rhetoric justifying the US attack on Iraq did express a crusading spirit to bring democracy to the Middle East. On the other hand, these recent US wars have not been primarily geared to advancing liberal democracy. The invasion of Iraq arose from US officials' imperial ambition and desire to have forward-based deployment of US military power in the Middle East.[13] The attack was conceived and pressed for by neo-conservatives, Vice-President Dick Cheney, Secretary of Defense Donald Rumsfeld, and Deputy Secretary of Defense Paul Wolfowitz, who were not known for pursuing genuinely liberal goals. They chose to launch a war of aggression without respect for prudential or international legal restraints and against UN Security Council resolutions, hardly characteristic of liberal internationalists. Although, in theory, moral or ideological crusades should not be favored by political realists, in policymaking practice they often are. Ideology provides an easy way to justify hegemonic military postures. Secretary of State Henry Kissinger, another well-known political realist, also carried on a crusade for the US war in Vietnam because of his anti-communist ideology of falling dominoes. Secretary of Defense Robert McNamara, a political realist of a different political party, also crusaded for the war in Vietnam.[14]

To be sure, if the United States attacks another country to try to impose liberal democracy there, elements of both political realism and liberalism are represented. Yet if military hegemony constitutes a primary goal, it fits more naturally with political realism.[15] In any case, to separate US hegemonic policies from political realism, mainly because they are justified with liberal rhetoric for advancing democracy, may go too far in reducing the responsibility of political realism for many of the failures in US foreign policy. Those failures seem to flow more from policymakers' commitment to hegemony and narrow nationalism than to classical liberalism. These US policies are rooted in political realism and bolstered by imperial ambition, even though they lack

---

[12] Mearsheimer, *Delusion*; Posen, *Restraint*; Stephen M. Walt, *The Hell of Good Intentions: America's Foreign Policy Elite and the Decline of U.S.* Primacy (New York: Farrar, Straus and Giroux, 2018).

[13] G. John Ikenberry, "America's Imperial Ambition," *Foreign Affairs* 81, no. 5 (2002): 44–60; Andrew J. Bacevich, *America's War for the Greater Middle East: A Military History* (New York: Random House, 2016); Andrew J. Bacevich, *American Empire: The Realities and Consequences of U.S. Diplomacy* (Cambridge, MA: Harvard University Press, 2002).

[14] See *The Fog of War: Eleven Lessons from the Life of Robert S. McNamara*, https://movie.douban.com/review/5822451/#:~:text=Until%20then%2C%20we%20still%20can%20assert%20that%20McNamara%20was%20a%20realist.&text=But%20in%20the%20film%2C%20when,force%20in%20restricting%20the%20Military.

[15] Political realist Barry Posen confirms that the policies of some exponents of liberal hegemony and political realism "are nearly indistinguishable." Barry R. Posen, *Restraint: A New Foundation for U.S. Grand Strategy* (Ithaca: Cornell University Press, 2014), 170.

the military restraint desired by the more restrained political realists. Policy differences exist among those who together share traditional realist assumptions.[16]

Certainly, significant arguments differentiate the restraint of Mearsheimer, Posen, and Walt from the crusading, poorly thought-out ambitions of the Bush administration to impose US expectations on Iraq through a military invasion. They strongly criticized these US policies even before they were implemented. Nonetheless, political realists favor maintaining US military primacy as part of *normal* national security policy;[17] it is not surprising if this priority becomes entangled with and justified by liberal ideological rhetoric. In contrast to empirical realism, maximizing military power is an expected prescription from political realism, so it easily embraces hegemonic military goals, which may be defended with rhetoric claiming that such capabilities are necessary to protect liberal democracy at home or advance it abroad.

No matter how one labels the US policymakers and policies in question over recent decades, Republican or Democratic, realist or liberal, they in general are characterized by the same underlying, traditional political realist assumptions, including

- primary reliance on national self-help and on maximizing military power as the main guarantor of security;
- the desire to maintain US military primacy and dominance throughout the world;
- the existence of a fundamentally unchanging, anarchic, militarized balance-of-power system; and
- little or no emphasis on increased roles for international law and global institutions in promoting structural change for security internationally.

One difference has been the degree to which some US officials have emphasized liberal values as a rhetorical justification for wars and forward-based US military deployments,[18] while more restrained political realists have strongly criticized these ideological justifications and the unnecessary wars that they enabled.

My theory of empirical realism begins by acknowledging the power-maximizing tendencies of great powers competing in an international balance-of-power system of relative anarchy,[19] but it quickly moves beyond this political realist mindset because it recognizes that these conditions are not the full picture, are not written in stone, and are not totally beyond human ingenuity to change. The new paradigm's empiricism

---

[16] Mearsheimer unequivocally believes that "States . . . ultimately seek hegemony." Again, "No great power can pursue liberal hegemony when there is at least one other great power in the system, which there typically is. As long as the system is either bipolar or multipolar, a powerful state must act according to realist principles." Mearsheimer, *Delusion*, Kindle 226, 2472.

[17] "The best way to survive in an anarchic system in which they [states] can never be certain about the intentions of other states is to be as powerful as possible relative to their competitors." Mearsheimer, *Delusion*, Kindle, 2535.

[18] In his first run for the presidency, Barack Obama campaigned against traditional realist assumptions that a great power is limited to power-maximization, but after he was in office he succumbed to those assumptions that pervaded the policy community and relevant congressional committees.

[19] Mearsheimer, *Delusion*, Kindle, 2484–2543.

pays attention to diverse factors that may affect state conduct, including the influence of culture and ideas about human freedom, human rights, sovereign rights, and human survival, all of which are now in flux; the possibility that anarchy is neither the totality of the international system nor beyond human re-design; the integrative political potential in economic intercourse; the profound importance of environmental and other non-military security threats; the mobilizing capacities of non-state actors, social movements, and transnational society; and the prospects for more effective use of international legal processes, international institutions, soft power, and nonviolent resistance.

Empirical realists also take more seriously than traditional realists the diverse dangers threatening US society. Although eminent political realists believe that "the United States is the most secure great power in recorded history,"[20] that conclusion turns a blind eye to a broad range of security threats. It reveals the tendency of political realists to assume that military power *is* security. Military power does not equal security. The United States surely has more destructive military power than any nation in history, but it is far from the most secure in history. That power does little to protect against environmental insecurity, pandemics, or germ warfare, to say nothing of cyberattacks and the corruption of US democracy that has occurred from foreign predators. The United States itself was probably more secure when it did not have a regular standing army in the late 19th century than it is today.

The value added by empirical realist theory, especially in terms of explanatory and predictive power, arises not only from including presently underutilized evidence, such as the impact of ideas, laws, and culture or the depth and diversity of security problems. It also invites creative moral imagination to help re-think how to make adversarial relations less dangerous and intractable. Empirical realists see pragmatic politics and universal ethics as fraternal twins, both nourished by impartial international law, capable of growing to serve the human interest.

Empirical realists share with traditional political realists and liberal internationalists a foundational focus on survival, yet they widen the horizon to identify the *best* means for ensuring survival by engaging a variety of potential partners. When empirical realists focus on *survival with dignity for all*, they chart a fundamentally different course for international conflict management and for increasing the prospects for human survival. The new paradigm necessarily draws attention to possibilities for promoting structural change in the international balance-of-power system, expanding analytic focus from national interests to encompass human interests, and tailoring peacebuilding theory drawn from domestic contexts so as to apply it globally.

An emphasis on human security naturally arises, because it contributes more strongly to sustainable peace and security than a focus on national security alone, especially given two fundamental factors, the first prudential and the second normative: (1) in this era of history, national security in one state cannot be achieved,

---

[20] Mearsheimer, *Delusion*, Kindle, 4321.

let alone sustained, if it ignores security for other societies, and (2) all human beings have equal moral worth, a belief that, as we will see, animates the identities and behaviors needed to achieve security and peace.[21]

Striving for both national survival and human security leads directly to concern for fundamental human rights, without which peace is neither real nor sustainable. Human rights, deeply understood, include economic and environmental rights as well as civil and political rights. These constitute the correlates of peace. Additionally, advancing human security naturally encourages a paradigm shift from national grand strategy to global grand strategy, along with a deliberate effort to domesticate international relations.

In seeking the spread of human freedom and democratic values and institutions, empirical realists recognize a basic tenet: that the same human conditions and aspirations that make political liberalism attractive for those already living with various forms of democracy in Europe, North America, northeast Asia, and parts of Latin America and Africa also make it of interest for people in all nations, as already expressed in the Universal Declaration of Human Rights.[22] But unlike liberal hegemonists, empirical realists would not try to impose liberal values on others through military means or paternalistic interventions. Spreading the correlates of peace should be mediated within the cultural contexts of the people interested in them. Empirical realists seek ways to nurture an international society in which there must be some enforceable agreements for maintaining security, yet with abundant room for moral argument and persuasion directed at empowering citizens in struggles for justice within their own nations.[23]

In summary, five factors differentiate empirical realism from political realism and the prevailing practices of the US policymaking community. First, empirical realists take pains to avoid reifying the state and the international system. They recognize that human beings have created the state and the post-1648 Westphalian interstate system. If created, these can be changed. In resisting common reifications, empirical realists are less likely to build policies based on political realists' ideological assumption of the unchanging nature of the international system and state conduct within it, such as that "anarchy is here to stay."[24]

Empirical realists emphasize that government officials need not feel straitjacketed by political realism or bureaucratic inertia. Policymakers are not required by the international system to follow short-term power-seeking policies in all circumstances. They may choose some of what they do.[25] As Alexander Wendt famously said, "Anarchy is

---

[21] Peace studies, like medical studies, combine empirical research with philosophical analysis, recognizing that one can be sensibly prescriptive only by first being accurately descriptive.

[22] For a cosmopolitan formulation of a similar idea, see Martha C. Nussbaum, *The Cosmopolitan Tradition: A Noble but Flawed Ideal* (Cambridge, MA: Belknap Press of Harvard University Press, 2019), 247.

[23] Nussbaum, *Cosmopolitan Tradition*, 246.

[24] Mearsheimer, *Delusion*, Kindle, 2853. For discussion of how international anarchy may give way to international society, see Kupchan, *How Enemies Become Friends*, 116–172.

[25] Mikhail Gorbachev undeniably demonstrated this when he embraced *glasnost* and *perestroika* and ended the Cold War.

what states make of it."[26] State conduct is influenced by the international system of relative anarchy, lacking a central authority over member states, but it is not totally determined by it.

Second, empirical realists study influences at work *within* states. They are not satisfied with the assumption that billiard-ball interactions fully capture relationships between states, whereas traditional realists believe that "states are like balls on a billiard table"[27] or that "great powers are like billiard balls that vary only in size."[28] Looking inside states enables assessing more readily what changes may be possible in both the state and the interstate system and thinking creatively about how to induce changes in both. To illustrate, the structure of interstate relations in Europe did change, regardless of current difficulties, because of the political support generated within six countries for creating the European Coal and Steel Community in 1952.

Third, empirical realists pay attention to ideas, customs, international laws and institutions, ethics, religion, and culture as well as to economic and political interactions, because these all influence international peacebuilding and even shape the nature and workings of sovereignty.[29] In contrast, it has been difficult for national security managers in the United States and Russia overseeing their nations' interventions in places such as Vietnam, Iraq, and Afghanistan, to learn that non-material influences may be so strong in some contexts that the militarily weaker side may win a war because great military power did not heed the power of ideas.[30] Better awareness of non-material factors, such as different varieties of nationalism and internationalism, in conjunction with changing verification technologies, could enable policymakers to employ them more readily for constructive changes in the role of international institutions. Empirical realists do not share the conviction of political realists that international institutions "have no independent effect on state behavior." Mearsheimer's "central conclusion" after studying international institutions is that they "hold little promise for promoting stability in the post-Cold War world."[31]

Fourth, empirical realists understand the importance of looking at the good of the whole rather than mainly at the good of the parts, particularly only "my" part. The

---

[26] Alexander Wendt, *Social Theory of International Politics* (Cambridge: Cambridge University Press, 1999), 377.

[27] Mearsheimer, *Delusion*, Kindle, 2483.

[28] Mearsheimer, quoted by Robert D. Kaplan, "Why John J. Mearsheimer Is Right (About Some Things)," *The Atlantic*, January/February 2012, https://www.theatlantic.com/magazine/archive/2012/01/why-john-j-mearsheimer-is-right-about-some-things/308839/.

[29] For how ideas have changed the practices of sovereignty, see Philpott, *Revolutions in Sovereignty*.

[30] As Richard Falk observes, "It has been difficult for the opinion makers of the world to absorb the shocking news that global history was increasingly being shaped by the weaker side militarily." Falk, *Power Shift*, 14.

[31] John J. Mearsheimer, "The False Promise of International Institutions," *International Security* 19, no. 3 (1994): 5–49. Yet substantial empirical work shows that participation in international organizations dampens violent conflict over the long run and that "a dense network of IGOs does reduce the incidence of conflict." See Russett and Oneal, *Triangulating Peace*, 281; Edward D. Mansfield and Jon C. Pevehouse, "Trade Blocs, Trade Blows, and International Conflict," *International Organization* 54 (2000): 775–808.

whole human species affects US national security. The planet's resource limits, such as its carbon reservoir, matter for everyone's future security, not simply for US military power. The state and the present interstate system are simply inadequate for addressing today's security problems, no matter how resilient they may appear to political realists. Perspectives should move from primarily nation-state centric to increasingly global geo-centric.

Fifth, although empirical realists agree with political realists that survival is the most fundamental human motivation animating international relations, they understand the history of cultural evolution to show that changes in political organization are possible, even likely. In contrast, political realists seem content with believing that biological evolution has set humanity on a competitive nation-state track from which it cannot escape. Yet the history of cultural evolution shows repeated, if irregular, changes that make non-zero-sum relationships possible between ever larger units of political organization.[32]

The evolutionary record does not promise any political inevitabilities, but it does suggest the high likelihood that cooperative processes in the international community will grow in number and importance and that the human societies employing them will continue to increase in size, accompanied by abundant pluralism. Cooperative processes or non-zero-sum relationships will be likely to continue the growth that they have manifested throughout human history—*if* the human species is not devastated in the meantime because of its inability to adapt to changed conditions that humans themselves have created, such as hazardous climate changes, fresh water shortages, or the possibility of a nuclear winter after nuclear war.

Many people misconstrue biological evolutionary understandings to suggest that human beings are hardwired to be fiercely competitive and aggressive in a never-ending struggle for survival.[33] They downplay evidence of human cooperation in both biological and cultural evolution and pay little attention to Charles Darwin's observation that "as man advances in civilization, and small tribes are united into larger communities, the simplest reason would tell each individual that he ought to extend his social instincts and sympathies to all the members of the same nation, though personally unknown to him. This point being once reached, there is only an *artificial barrier* to prevent his sympathies extending to the men [and women] of *all* nations and races."[34] Indeed, there is substantial evolutionary evidence that human groups are capable of mutually beneficial relationships with others—all others.[35] When the

---

[32] Wright, *Nonzero*; Christakis, *Blueprint: Evolutionary Origins*.

[33] For explication of this tendency, see Richard Ned Lebow, "You Can't Keep a Bad Idea Down: Evolutionary Biology and International Relations," *International Politics Reviews* no. 1 (2013): 2–10, https://doi.org/10.1057/ipr.2013.2.

An example of this misleading tendency is Brad Thayer, *Darwinism and International Relations: On the Evolutionary Origins of War and Ethnic Conflict* (Lexington: University of Kentucky Press, 2004).

[34] Charles Darwin, *The Descent of Man, and Selection in Relation to Sex* (New York: Appleton, 1878), 122–123. Italics added.

[35] Christakis, *Blueprint: Evolutionary Origins*, xv–xxiii, 389–419.

evidence is carefully examined, the evolution of both human genetic makeup and its cultural content demonstrates at least as many possibilities for increasing cooperation as for hostile competition and war-fighting.[36]

Future human decisions can influence the outcome of some cultural evolutionary forces. An examination of new technologies of destruction and irresponsible actors' access to these, plus prospects for environmental insecurities, suggests that the desire for survival may now require an end to violent-power maximization within an anarchical system. Empirical realists encourage exploring ways of designing sufficient global governing hierarchy to bridle the most dangerous elements of anarchy. They recognize the utility of a system of international law to nurture a sustainable world community and establish reliable bonds of global citizenship[37] that are necessary to erect new political architecture.

By interrupting the inertia of past ways of thinking about security policy, identifying the main correlates of sustainable peace, and implementing these by following a global grand strategy through the maze of current crises, the theoretical framework proposed here can empower political decision makers and citizens to build sustainable peace and greater justice for US citizens and all people. A cautionary comment is useful here. References to evolutionary psychologists' and sociologists' observations about the history of human group interactions are useful for opening our eyes to possibilities, but *explanations* for *why* this evolutionary history has happened need to be taken cautiously to avoid confusing conjecture with more certain explanation. Our analysis does not rely on evolutionary interpretations to predict future human interactions or to suggest any inevitability in future human organization. Like Ebenezer Scrooge, it is important for us to differentiate future images of what *may* be from what *will* be.

2.2 RESPECTING HUMAN DIGNITY

Pursuing national security carries a noble quality, especially when one's pursuit focuses on security for one's own group. It seems less noble if it involves secret killings or torture of others; indifference to killing civilians; deliberate bombing of people's homes, hospitals, or vegetable gardens; or advancing the interests of one's own group at the severe, life-shortening expense of another group. Not surprisingly, research shows that war-fighting for security is more likely between conflicting groups if one perceives the other as less worthy. Moreover, peaceful relations are more likely to be maintained or newly established if some degree of mutual respect between groups can be nurtured and maintained. With these findings in mind, it is empirically realistic to ground security theory in part on the value of human dignity and efforts to institutionalize widespread respect for it. The centrality of human dignity keeps the pursuit of security noble. Dislodging its centrality makes the pursuit ignoble.

---

[36] Wright, *Nonzero*, 243–336; Christakis, *Blueprint: Evolutionary Origins*.
[37] See Falk, *Power Shift*, 243.

"Human dignity" refers to the unconditional worth inherent in every person from birth to death (as attested to in many legal, philosophical, and religious traditions). Dignity is inalienable and independent of any state. Entitlement to dignity does not need to be earned, nor can it be taken away—although of course it can be violated. This analysis operationalizes human dignity primarily through implementing people's basic human rights as recognized in the international bill of human rights,[38] but the concept of human dignity also has been described in the work of the United Nations Development Program and its *Human Development Reports*. This has been inspired in part by the "capabilities approach" developed by economist Amartya Sen as an alternative to welfare economics. The central focus is on what individuals are capable of doing and on ensuring that they are enabled to realize their full potential.

Human dignity is further elaborated in Martha Nussbaum's analysis of the cosmopolitan tradition and its recognition of a universal moral obligation to enable all people to develop their "central human capabilities." These include "being able to live to the end of a human life of normal length; possessing good bodily health; being secure in bodily integrity; using one's senses, imagination, and thought with adequate education and freedom of choice in religion, art, expression, and political identity; being able to express emotions without fear; engaging in practical reason with protection for liberty of conscience and religious observance; freedom of affiliation with others and opportunity to enjoy self-respect and non-humiliation; being able to enjoy recreational activities; and participating in [constructive] control over one's political and material environments."[39] These 10 capabilities, in Nussbaum's view, "must be secured up to a minimum threshold level, if a nation is to have any claim to justice."[40] A central argument advanced in the present book is that a fundamental minimum threshold also must be achieved for every person on Earth if the world order is to have any claim to justice, and if, indeed, it is to become more capable of building sustainable peace, human security,[41] and environmental health. Advancing toward this threshold for all would also enable everyone to experience greater human freedom.

Human dignity is the foundation for human rights, and many values of human dignity are expressed in the articles of the Universal Declaration of Human Rights (UDHR). Foremost among these is, as officials from many nations wrote in Article 1: "All human beings are born free and equal in dignity and rights." The values of human dignity, which have worldwide roots,[42] also include basic duties: Every right

---

[38] The "international bill of human rights" includes the Universal Declaration of Human Rights, the International Covenant on Civil and Political Rights and its Optional Protocols, and the International Covenant on Economic, Social, and Cultural Rights. See Tom J. Farer, "Introduction," *The International Bill of Human Rights* (Glen Ellen, CA: Entwhistle Books, 1981), xiii–xxi.

[39] Nussbaum, *Cosmopolitan Tradition*, 241–243.

[40] Nussbaum, *Cosmopolitan Tradition*, 240.

[41] "Human security" is used here to mean access of all human beings to the right to peace and to basic necessities for a life of dignity. This concept is elaborated in Chapter 5.

[42] Nussbaum, *Cosmopolitan Tradition*, 3–4.

in the Universal Declaration includes a duty to respect that right for others: human beings "should act towards one another in a spirit of brotherhood [and sisterhood]."[43]

2.3 EXPANDING PEACEBUILDING THEORY

Peacebuilding theory and practice generate some promising insights and tools for addressing conflicts successfully. Although peacebuilding theory originally focused on conflicts within war-torn societies, empirical realists are tailoring it more broadly for conflict transformation *internationally*.[44] Political realists pay little heed to such possibilities, given their belief that there is no need to look inside states to understand how they relate to each other in the international system.[45]

In any case, "peacebuilding" is used in this analysis generally to mean "social integration," regardless of whether it works to strengthen peace in national or international society.[46] Much, although of course not all, peacebuilding theory can be applied seamlessly from municipal to global contexts. It need not be limited to either an in-country application or a post-conflict situation. Its measures may apply to diverse contexts and any phase of evolving conflicts. Empirical realists can use peacebuilding theory to lay a foundation for more cooperative international relations. Even though peacebuilding may not constitute an entire security policy for the United States, US policy would benefit from decision makers' drawing some inspiration from the idea that "at its core, peacebuilding nurtures constructive human relationships," in the words of John Paul Lederach and R. Scott Appleby.[47]

Peacebuilding can play a strategically vital role at any level when it "draws intentionally and shrewdly on the overlapping and imperfectly coordinated presences, activities, and resources of various international, transnational, national, regional, and local institutions, agencies, and movements that influence the causes, expressions, and outcomes of conflict."[48] The purpose is not only to reduce violence but also to alleviate, continuously, its underlying causes. Peacebuilders encourage "deeper and more frequent convergence of mission, resources, expertise, insight, and benevolent self-interest" among formerly hostile adversaries. Peacebuilders aim to build constructive relationships, undergirded by developing customs, laws, and institutions that encourage positive forms of interdependence as useful processes for pursuing human rights,

---

[43] Universal Declaration of Human Rights, Article 1.

[44] Cortright, Seyle, and Wall, *Governance for Peace*, 244–246.

[45] "Realpolitik is blind to the existence of social spaces, relationships, ideas, and processes that do not fit its preexisting definition of what counts. . . . It completely misses some of the most significant elements of social process capable of generating new relational patterns and structures." John Paul Lederach, *The Moral Imagination: The Art and Soul of Building Peace* (Oxford: Oxford University Press, 2005), 59–60.

[46] Robert C. Johansen, "Peace *and* Justice? The Contribution of International Judicial Processes to Peacebuilding," in *Strategies of Peace: Transforming Conflict in a Violent World*, ed. Daniel Philpott and Gerard F. Powers (New York: Oxford University Press, 2010), 191.

[47] Lederach and Appleby, "Strategic Peacebuilding," 22.

[48] Lederach and Appleby, "Strategic Peacebuilding," 22.

uncorrupt governance, economic prosperity, environmental health, and "the promotion of transparent communication across sectors and levels of society in the service of including as many voices and actors as possible in the reform of institutions and the repair or creation of partnerships conducive to the common good." In addition, they expand coordination and wherever possible "integration of resources, programs, practices, and processes." Peacebuilding theory upholds an end goal best expressed in the idea of "*justpeace*, a dynamic state of affairs in which the reduction and management of violence and the achievement of social and economic justice are undertaken as mutual, reinforcing dimensions of constructive change,"[49] especially when achievements can be institutionalized.

Empirical realists recognize the importance of parties exercising moral imagination with the capacity "to understand that the welfare of my community is directly related to the welfare of your community." This theory's attention to structural change to implement human security recognizes that imagining human security "does not just think outside the box; it is willing to take the risk to live outside the box."[50]

These ideas, although formed in the context of addressing conflicts within fragmented countries, can help internationally because sustainable peace requires much more than conventional diplomatic friendliness. It also requires "the redress of legitimate grievances" among nations and "the establishment of new relations characterized by equality and fairness according to the dictates of human dignity and the common good." Of course, peace, once established, can be dependably sustained only when ways and means of justice "become routinized" and institutionalized in international society. If effective institutions for more participatory global governance are established, they, like domestic institutions, will "require continual oversight, nurturing, and renewal." Moreover, initiatives to prevent violence "must unfold at every stage of conflict." Building constructive political relationships, after all, "is perpetual.[51]"

Empirical realists know that particular acts of violence often may be understood as part of a larger cycle of violence, with a history of actions and counter-actions. Odds for making peace sustainable can be increased by shaping one's world "less by our divisions than by our cooperation, more by our ability to meet fundamental human needs than by the . . . denigration of human dignity and rights."[52] Lederach and Appleby have concluded that greater peacebuilding potential "can be realized by envisioning peacebuilding as a holistic enterprise, a comprehensive and coherent set of actions and operations that can be improved by greater levels of collaboration, complementarity, coordination, and where possible, integration across levels of society."[53] Again, much of this can apply internationally as well as domestically.

---

[49] Lederach and Appleby, "Strategic Peacebuilding," 23.
[50] Lederach, *Moral Imagination*, 62.
[51] Lederach and Appleby, "Strategic Peacebuilding," 24.
[52] Lederach, *Moral Imagination*, 25, 21.
[53] Lederach and Appleby, "Strategic Peacebuilding," 24.

Empirical realists try to take a broader perspective on what transforms conflicts,[54] and also a deeper look at what makes conflicts intractable. This means being sensitive to all parties, including those who feel repeatedly marginalized. This approach facilitates the transformation of conflicts within states, which often must be addressed to achieve sustainable world peace, as well as the adjustment of equity conflicts between states.[55] In both domains, two problems should be avoided insofar as possible: (1) premature or false conflict resolution, which occurs when serious underlying conflicts or structural defects remain unaddressed or hidden; and (2) failure to differentiate unhealthy conflict, in which opponents treat each other as enemies, from healthy conflict, in which opponents see each other as adversaries in strong disagreement yet who also bear human dignity. In the latter, even when conflicts appear intractable, parties relate to one another with a sense of minimal human respect, reciprocity, and forbearance. In contrast, one party treats another as an enemy if it tries to impose "a permanent and intentionally insurmountable disadvantage," trying to maintain political control "by whatever means one can get away with."[56] Not all international conflicts enable moving away from an enemy relationship, because this is not totally within one's control, but the more desirable standard should be kept in mind. In domestic conflicts, democratic processes cannot be sustained unless both of the preceding problems are avoided.[57] Empirical realists encourage more effective deliberative democracy at all levels of governance because this form of governance correlates most closely with violence prevention and promotion of "life, liberty, and security of person."[58]

---

[54] For conflict transformation, see John Paul Lederach, *Building Peace: Sustainable Reconciliation in Divided Societies* (Washington, DC: United States Institute of Peace Press, 1997), and Elise Boulding, *Cultures of Peace: The Hidden Side of History* (Syracuse, NY: Syracuse University Press, 2000).

[55] By drawing on the American pragmatist tradition of democratic social transformation, agonistic democratic theory, and conflict transformation in peace research, Jason Springs has expanded our understanding of how it may be possible, even in intractable conflicts, to initiate or invigorate democratic values by waging *healthy* conflict within deeply conflictual settings. Although his work explores domestic conflicts over racial injustice in the United States, because these conflicts express extreme polarization, some of his findings can be applied to international conflicts as well. Jason A. Springs, *Healthy Conflict in Contemporary American Society: From Enemy to Adversary* (Cambridge: Cambridge University Press, 2018).

[56] Springs's explication of "healthy conflict" includes some "efforts that might be transformational even with self-declared enemies who appear to be most intransigent and apparently most beyond the possibilities of engagement and repair." Jason A. Springs, "Healthy Conflict in an Era of Intractability: Reply to Four Critical Responses," *Journal of Religious Ethics* 48, no. 2 (2020): 335–336.

[57] Jason Springs and other peace researchers studying agonistic democracy have shown benefits from empowering disadvantaged groups to wage conflicts safely and constructively through democratic processes even when consensus remains beyond adversaries' grasp. This research suggests that weaving a global social fabric can occur if conflict can be waged in healthy, as opposed to unhealthy ways, even when agreement among adversaries remains beyond reach, as often is the case. Nurturing the ingredients for healthy conflict can increase the prospects for developing future democratic systems where none exist and for strengthening them where they do. Springs, "Era of Intractability," 316–341.

[58] Universal Declaration of Human Rights, Article 3.

In paying attention to psychological influences and the impact of culture on conflict, peacebuilders aim to address what British historian Herbert Butterfield a half century ago called the "tragic element" of modern intractable conflicts: Each side fails to comprehend and attend to the full range of motivations driving its counterpart.[59] Often the opponent's underlying worldview is not understood or explored, thereby blinding officials to existing opportunities for non-zero-sum outcomes that are not even seen, rendering efforts to resolve conflicts unsuccessful.

Partial blindness has afflicted many US responses in what has naively been called "the war on terrorism." US policymakers have been slow to understand and take account of what motivates people to engage in terrorist acts. New interdisciplinary research that follows a sociotheological epistemology illustrates some of what may be helpful in dealing with mass killings. This scholarship provides an "insider-oriented attempt to understand the reality of a particular worldview" and "to transcend the walls between facts and perceptions, between scientific reasoning and empathetic understanding" of how religious worldviews may motivate violent (or nonviolent) acts.[60]

Such research has shown, for example, that there can be an understandable, "rational logic behind religious acts of violence, instead of their being seen as mere irrational acts" by observers who use only "secular criteria for what counts as evidence."[61] To take an example, trying to deal with members of Hamas by marginalizing and humiliating them should be expected to be counter-productive, to fuel anger, and to strengthen their cause among adherents. In many cases, violence should not be addressed as a strategic act but instead as a symbolic one, requiring a different response.[62]

To uncover partly hidden or seldom tried peacebuilding ways of addressing political conflicts more effectively, the empirical realist's first task is one of understanding, not of judgment. Judgment may come later; if and when it does, it should be based on upholding international norms of respect for civilian lives rather than on imposing a nationally partisan point of view. Unless policymakers deliberately take on some aspects of the more holistic approach of peacebuilding, it may be difficult to resist the tendency to make nationalism the dominant driver of polices toward many international conflicts. Resisting this tendency becomes more likely if they come to see a narrow nationalism as being at cross purposes with peace and security.

---

[59] Herbert Butterfield, "The Tragic Element in Modern International Conflict," *Review of Politics* 12, no. 2 (1950): 147–164.

[60] Mark Jurgensmeyer and Mona Kanwal Sheikh, "A Sociotheological Approach to Understanding Religious Violence," in *The Oxford Handbook of Religion and Violence*, ed. Michael Jerryson, Mark Juergensmeyer, and Margo Kitts (Oxford: Oxford University Press, 2013), 624; Mona K. Sheikh, "Guardians of God: Understanding the Religious Violence of Pakistan's Taliban," PhD dissertation, University of Copenhagen, Department of Political Science, 2011.

[61] Jurgensmeyer and Sheikh, "A Sociotheological Approach," 639.

[62] Jurgensmeyer and Sheikh, "A Sociotheological Approach," 636, 639–642.

2.4 RECOGNIZING NATIONALISM'S HELP AND HINDRANCE

Nationalism, one of the most potent forces in the world, can be enormously helpful or terribly dangerous. Relevant for typical citizens is the formation and expression of one's political identity with one's own nation and perceptions of other nations, which sometimes generate fears. New fears arise whenever US policies fail to address the destabilizing changes in international relations noted in Chapter 1. Chronically ineffective policies have aroused some US hyper-nationalism[63] and populism, which eventually exacerbate conflict and become self-defeating.

Nationalism has many faces, two of which we note here: One generates in-group national solidarity based on an inclusive identity that encourages people to care about human dignity for all people inside their nation, even if others are somewhat different from oneself. By extension, this kind of nationalism encourages also caring about dignity for other people who live outside one's own country and enjoy their own nationalities. This version limits the exaltation of one's own nationhood sufficiently to recognize similar rights for people of other nations.

A second face of nationalism expresses an identity more exclusively focused on an exaltation of one's own nation, deepened by emphasizing differences between "us" and "them," and inclined to foster feelings among outgroups of being excluded. This form of nationalism usually incites fears in others because national exaltation is unrestrained. Citizens' degree of inclusiveness and openness to others influence their perceptions, shape their behavior, and guide their leaning toward the first or the second face. Their orientation emanates from automatic psychological processes in which people naturally seek confirmation that the meaning of their behavior lines up with the meaning of their identity.[64] If their identity is pejoratively limited to one national group of humanity, their caring will be limited primarily to their own nation. On the other hand, in their most open-hearted manifestations, nationalism and patriotism can contribute to international justice and peace and be quite inclusive in caring for people regardless of their race, religion, language, class, or national origin.

Indian nationalism illustrates both faces. Loyalty to India includes over a billion people with diverse subnational identities, using 22 official languages and more than 150 languages with sizable populations, with 1,652 different mother tongues. It includes believers of every major religious tradition. This inclusivity suggests that even a worldwide, all-inclusive human identity might be possible.[65] Yet rising prejudice and discrimination against Muslims, a large minority in India, demonstrate how easily

---

[63] These are intense beliefs that one's own group is superior and one or more out-groups are inferior, dangerous, and must be dealt with harshly.

[64] Jan E. Stets and Michael J. Carter, "A Theory of the Self for the Sociology of Morality," *American Sociological Review* 77, no. 1 (2012): 120–140; Jan E. Stets and Michael J. Carter, "The Moral Self: Applying Identity Theory," *Social Psychology Quarterly*, 74, no. 2 (2011): 192–215.

[65] As Nussbaum concludes, "There is nothing about India or Argentina that makes the arguments for political liberalism work differently from the way they work in Germany or Spain." Nussbaum, *Cosmopolitan Tradition*, 248.

a potentially inclusive identity can become predatory if identities slide down the slippery slope toward less inclusivity. Although the first form of national identity includes respect for all Indians with a potential of respect for all people, the second does not. It exalts Hindu nationalism and distorts Indian identity.

Nationalism may readily encourage nationalists to be two-faced: if some Hindus (or Muslims) claim that they are not prejudiced against Muslims (or Hindus) but they actually are, then their claims about identity are false. They may be deceiving others and even themselves. Because nationalism's ambiguous, fluid identity structures enable it to be practiced in multiple disguises, some of which are healthy and some of which are predatory, it is resilient. It can accommodate many different kinds of people and obscure what the "real" motivations are for a war, a tax, a torture, a lynching, or a law. It can be used by demagogues and by democrats.

Empirical realists try to differentiate nationalism's egoistic excesses from its genuine respect for others by identifying nationalism's possible weaknesses, which can be its narrow identity or exclusivity, sense of superiority, and virulence, as well as its possible strengths, which can be its inclusivity, moderation, and sense of solidarity with people across racial, religious, or other boundaries. They try to retain nationalism's boundary-transcending cohesive qualities while correcting historical error and chauvinistic mythmaking, which contribute to attitudes of superiority.

Nationalists whose identity has narrowed to the point that people outside of their nationality, race, or religion are not equally valued, suffer from two difficulties. The first is *moral and ethical*: excessive exaltation of one's own national identity obstructs welcoming others to a condition of genuine peace and well-being. The second difficulty is *practical and prudential*: preferential treatment of one's own nationality interferes with smart and effective strategies for managing conflict in today's world, which require treating others respectfully and as morally equivalent. US Senator John McCain appeared to have this in mind when he observed in 2017 that the US government was expressing "spurious nationalism": "To fear the world we have organized and led for three-quarters of a century, to abandon the ideals we have advanced around the globe, to refuse the obligations of international leadership and our duty to remain 'the last best hope of earth' for the sake of some half-baked, spurious nationalism cooked up by people who would rather find scapegoats than solve problems is as unpatriotic as an attachment to any other tired dogma of the past that Americans consigned to the ash heap of history."[66] To "abandon ideals" is not helpful in serving US. interests because it rejects the legitimate rights of others and torpedoes the sense of common cause essential for sustainable peace and justice.

Differentiating the nature and utility of various expressions of nationalism, which is necessary to foster identities capable of supporting wise inter-nation policies, begins by assessing the degree to which nationalism either does or does not serve the

---

[66] Edward-Isaac Dovere, "McCain, in Speech, Denounces 'Spurious Nationalism,'" *Politico*, October 16, 2017, https://www.politico.com/story/2017/10/16/john-mccain-nationalism-constitution-243848.

common good. According to the psychoanalyst Erich Fromm, a "loving interest in one's own nation, which is the concern with the nation's spiritual as much as with its material welfare [and] never with its power over other nations" is much healthier and more useful than nationalism that puts one's own nation "above humanity, above the principles of truth and justice." Fromm's key distinction between healthy and unhealthy nationalism is clear: "Just as love for one individual which excludes love for others is not love, love for one's country which is not part of one's love for humanity is not love, but idolatrous worship."[67] He cautioned against the possibility that "nationalism is our form of incest, is our idolatry, is our insanity."[68] In contrast, when functioning as "civic solidarity,"[69] national feelings can open the door to appreciating people in other nations and to understanding other people's identity with *their* nation.

To align US nationalism with security purposes, it is useful to ask: When is national identity, which citizens understandably cherish, held at the expense of others and when does it encourage respect for others? When does it justify harm toward another nationality and when does it build inclusive human solidarity? Making matters even more complicated, national feelings may be relatively inclusive in one context and exclusive in another, with these differences sometimes arising in the same person at nearly the same times. National pride may lead one to support giving generously to help people of another nationality when they are hit by a tsunami, only to bomb people of that nationality if its government is perceived as threatening one's interests, even though the moral worth and the guilt or innocence of the civilian population may not have changed in the two circumstances.

Of course, nationalism at times has been helpful in fighting against imperialism and for human rights, democracy, and national security, because it has encouraged people of different heritages or tribes to work together to lift the burden of domination imposed by imperial powers or local tyrants. Nationalism can strengthen people's sense of identity about who they are. Although it can be cohesive glue to bind diverse groups into one, it also can divisively pit one group against another. Although developing an exemplary form of nationalism responsive to the new international realities by upholding human dignity and generating empathy for people bearing other nationalities is not easy, conflict research shows that it is prudent and wisdom literature suggests that it is morally desirable.[70] An inclusive identity contributes to building world peace and justice through nonviolent means, recognizing that wars between national identities may be seen as "civil" wars when viewed from within a universal identity.[71]

---

[67] Erich Fromm, *The Sane Society* (New York: Fawcett World Library, 1955), 60.

[68] Fromm, *Sane Society*, 60.

[69] Jürgen Habermas, "A Political Constitution for the Pluralist World Society?" in *The Cosmopolitanism Reader*, ed. Garrett.W. Brown and David Held (Cambridge: Polity Press, 2010), 273.

[70] Some psychologists see the golden rule as "actually a scientific psychological rule. It is a formula for harmony." Izzy Kalman, "The Golden Rule," *Psychology Today*, May 11, 2011, https://www.psychology-today.com/us/blog/resilience-bullying/201105/principle-number-three-the-golden-rule; Neil Duxbury, "Golden Rule Reasoning, Moral Judgment, and Law," *Notre Dame Law Review* 84, no. 4 (2009): 1529–1606, http://ndlawreview.org/wp-content/uploads/2013/07/Duxbury.pdf.

[71] Historians note that what some called the "U.S. Civil War" others called the "War Between the States."

In contrast, a narrow, exclusive identity might characterize immigrants as "animals" who "aren't people"[72] and threaten adversaries "with fire and fury like the world has never seen."[73] Mature psychological expressions of nationalism discourage such attitudes because they easily generate fear and trigger ancient fight or flight responses that prevent creative thinking about conflict management.

2.5 COSMOPOLITANIZING NATIONALISM

Because nationalism can be both useful and dangerous, empirical realists emphasize that it can be safely tempered when, and only when, it serves the value of human dignity. "Cosmopolitan nationalism" constitutes a conceptual hybrid expressing the personal identity likely to be most useful for a successful security strategy, which is one informed by human dignity. Nussbaum has described cosmopolitanism as the ability to "recognize humanity wherever it occurs" and the willingness to "give its fundamental ingredients, reason and moral capacity, our first allegiance and respect."[74] It starts with the autonomous individual, posits the equal moral worth of all people, and universalizes the principle that the dignity and rights of all should be the goal of political, economic, and educational decisions. "If one imagines the nation as itself striving toward justice and human rights, and built on a commitment to human dignity . . . [then] loving the country is easy to extend outward."[75] Research has confirmed that the inclusivity of a person's identity turns out to be the most critical component for explaining altruistic behavior toward strangers,[76] and that such behavior is possible even when people feel a strong sense of nationhood at the same time as expressing concern about people not part of their nation.[77]

---

[72] The words of Donald Trump, quoted by Robert Cohen, "The Moral Rot Threatening America," *New York Times*, May 19, 2018, A 21.

[73] "President Trump Threatening North Korea," reported by the Associated Press, August 8, 2017, https://www.google.com/search?source=hp&ei=jOSIXZ-hNKHR9APB_46oBQ&q=fire+and+fury+trump&oq=fire+and+fury&gs_l=psy-ab.1.2.0l10.3068.6133..9084...0.0..0.165.1809.0j13......0....1..gws-wiz.......0i131.haRVRhr11OY.

[74] Martha Nussbaum, "Patriotism and Cosmopolitanism," in *For Love of Country: The New Democracy Forum on the Limits of Patriotism*, ed. J. Cohen (Boston: Beacon Press, 2002), 7.

[75] Nussbaum, *Cosmopolitan Tradition*, 5.

[76] Adam Martin and Kristen Renwick Monroe, "Identity, Moral Choice, and the Moral Imagination: Is there a Neuroscientific Foundation for Altruism?" in *Morality, Ethics, and Gifted Minds*, ed. Don Ambrose and Tracy Cross (New York: Springer, 2009), 73–88.

[77] Research also confirms that when a person "feels strongly connected to others through the bonds of a common humanity," the bond is "surprisingly constant" over time. Martin and Monroe, "Identity," 74; Kristen Renwick Monroe, *The Heart of Altruism: Perceptions of a Common Humanity* (Princeton, NJ: Princeton University Press, 1996), 235.

The possibility for connection appears to be "universal, available to everyone merely by virtue of their existence." Indeed, "the potential for altruism exists in all people." Monroe, *Heart of Altruism*, 233–234.

The moral process examined here is a "relational one, one that all people have in actuality or potentiality." This relational identity differs fundamentally from ethics, whether deontological, virtue, or consequentialist. Martin and Monroe, "Identity," 75.

Astute leaders from Abraham Lincoln to Franklin Roosevelt, from Mahatma Gandhi to Martin Luther King Jr., and from Jawaharlal Nehru to Nelson Mandela, have refashioned "patriotic national loyalty into a loyalty to values that are also keys to a just global order."[78] Doing this is central to the theoretical framework proposed here. Cosmopolitan nationalism fosters a sense of community and caring about citizens outside one's country that is analogous to nationalism's healthy, familiar role inside one's home country. Although a challenge, this possibility can become easier in time as elements of central world authority grow, moderating international anarchy's near-requirement today to deny affirmation of all persons' inherent worth. In seeking enough international central authority to diminish the most dangerous parts of international anarchy, empirical realism differs fundamentally from both political realism and liberal hegemony. It anticipates building more inclusive regional and global institutions that gradually reduce strands of international anarchy in a mutually reinforcing relationship with cosmopolitan nationalism.

By way of contrast, in-grown nationalism, which apparently lives comfortably with political realists and liberal hegemonists, embodies an exclusive group consciousness that both subordinates individual worth to the benefit of one's own nation and exalts the worth of one's own national group above other parts of the human species. Political, economic, and educational goals become nationalized rather than universalized.

People dwelling at the extreme ends of an identity spectrum stretching from the broadly cosmopolitan to the narrowly national are likely to favor policies that are simply incompatible. But by moving away from the extremes, cosmopolitan nationalist policies are possible. Cosmopolitanism can be combined with healthy nationalism because neither nationalism nor cosmopolitanism needs to constitute a person's *only* or absolute allegiance. One's affection for people in one's own nation can inspire understanding of other nationalities and similar respect, affection, and concern for all who are part of the human family, sharing the same air, water, and from now on, security fate. This is a cosmopolitan analogue of intermingled identities that are already experienced by many US citizens whose families may have immigrated from England, Germany, Ireland, Italy, Sweden, Mexico, and many other countries throughout Europe, Asia, Africa, and Latin America. These citizens simultaneously appreciate their family's earlier ethnic and national heritages while being devoted citizens actively engaged in US nationalism today.

Cosmopolitanism's worldwide inclusiveness traces roots back at least as far as the Stoics (third century BCE), but it is no longer limited to being a philosophical perspective. The idea that all human beings, regardless of their political affiliations, may be citizens in an Earth-encompassing community, has moved to an empirically observable degree of social, political, economic, and psychological reality. In the words of Ulrich Beck, "The human condition has itself become cosmopolitan."[79] Terrorist acts,

---

[78] Nussbaum, *Cosmopolitan Tradition*, 211.
[79] Ulrich Beck, *The Cosmopolitan Vision* (Cambridge: Polity Press, 2006), 2.

like pandemics, "know no borders."[80] The melting of polar icecaps and permafrost harms everyone on Earth. In early 2003, public demonstrations against US plans to attack Iraq occurred in 3,000 different protests, carried out by 36 million people around the world, including 3 million in Rome alone.[81] These largest peace demonstrations in world history emanated spontaneously from something we might call cosmopolitan empathy, an awareness that human suffering other than one's own should still be opposed by oneself. Beck calls this the "globalization of emotions." Even populist "resistance against globalization itself produces political globalization."[82]

Cosmopolitanism has become a defining feature of current reality, yielding a reflexive modernity in which the meaning of national boundaries and national differences is changing. These new meanings constitute a reason that security policy, if it is to be successful into the future, must arise from a more-than-national vantage point. The old nationalism of self-centered narcissism, to which President Trump, a supreme narcissist, called Americans in 2016–2020, gave him domestic political success and his followers' good feelings, but it can never give US citizens genuine security.

Yet to try to move fully from nationalism to cosmopolitanism would be mindless and fruitless, because a cosmopolitanism deprived of all nationalism and provincialism would feel empty and rootless for many people, while a nationalism without any cosmopolitan understanding would be blind.[83] Empirical realists do not intend to replace national empathy with cosmopolitan empathy. With some of each co-existing, they animate one another. A healthy national feeling introduces beyond-national empathy and makes cosmopolitanism more comprehensible. Emotions may become more inclusive and global in reach, as many religious traditions have long affirmed. One benefit of cosmopolitan leaven in a nationalist loaf is the rising of a new ethical and methodological mindfulness that enables people to distance themselves from their traditional national, religious, and ethnic loyalties without rejecting them, enabling people to reflect critically on other cultures as well as their own.[84]

By being broadly intercultural, empirical realists seek to free international relations scholarship and US security policy from any historical influences of white supremacy and imperial thinking. The age of colonialism did legitimize oppression, dehumanization, and in some cases genocidal practices by colonizers who viewed themselves as representing superior cultures.[85] Robert Vitalis argues that implicit assumptions of white superiority and imperial ambition have motivated some US and European foreign policies, shaping foreign policy and strategic studies even into the 1950s and

---

[80] Beck, *Cosmopolitan Vision*, 2.

[81] Patrick Tyler, "A New Power in the Streets," *New York Times*, February 17, 2003; Alex Callinicos, "Anti-War Protests Do Make a Difference," *Socialist Worker*, March 19, 2005.

[82] Beck, *Cosmopolitan Vision*, 2, 5–6.

[83] See Beck, *Cosmopolitan Vision*, 2.

[84] Brian Turner, "Cosmopolitan Virtue, Globalization and Patriotism," *Theory, Culture and Society* 19 (1–2), 2002: 45–63; Beck, *Cosmopolitan Vision*.

[85] Walter D. Mignolo, "The Making and Closing of Eurocentric International Law: The Opening of a Multipolar World Order," *Comparative Studies of South Asia, Africa and the Middle East* 36, no. 1 (2016): 193.

1960s. In his view, US policy "was and arguably still is hegemonic" toward non-white societies, with attitudes of racial and cultural superiority that have had significant influence on both US policies and the profession of international relations in the academy.[86] Because the foundation of international law and the Eurocentric system of international relations had historical roots in racism and imperialism, deliberate efforts are needed to promote policies that are genuinely emancipatory for all people. Care certainly must be exercised when advocating strengthened international law, as the following chapters do, to ensure that it is, in fact, "good" or impartial law rather than law that maintains implicit cultural superiority or imperial ambition.[87]

Empirical realism recognizes that cosmopolitanism and globalization are not the same energy, the former being more of a fragile personal attitude and the latter more of a relentless socioeconomic force. In some cases, cosmopolitanism may need to be rescued from elitist pretensions if it is to temper both nationalism and globalization. This would enable it to counter hyper-nationalism, to humanize globalization, and to become "a vehicle of freedom and opportunity for most, not just a privileged few."[88] The theoretical framework of empirical realism anticipates that security strategies of the future, to succeed, will need to employ national identities that extend respect for others, heed anti-war warnings of restrained political realists and others, avoid temptations for military interventions favored at times by liberal hegemonists, and adopt an attitude of worldwide support for justice for people in other societies, while showing that advances in human security also serve the survival interests of people in the United States and every country of the world.

2.6 OPEN QUESTIONS

The logic underlying this theory is that individuals (in all countries) are entitled to have their basic rights respected by others, and their national group is similarly entitled to have its rights respected by other nations. Yet neither an individual citizen nor a nation-state has a right to engage in conduct that threatens the survival and basic rights of others. That is a reasonable limit on every person's and every nation's conduct.[89] That limit can be insisted upon and maintained while liberal democratic values

---

[86] Robert Vitalis, *White World Order, Black Power Politics: The Birth of American International Relations* (Ithaca, NY: Cornell University Press, 2015), 174, 179.

[87] International law constituted itself on the foundation of Eurocentrism and at first saw many different cultures as barbaric, uncivilized, primitive, and, more recently, underdeveloped and a source of terrorism. Mignolo, "Eurocentric International Law," 186.

   "The colonized invested the war-time ideals of the allies—human solidarity, international friendship, and global goodwill—with new meaning and new norms, opening doors to international justice, equality, and peace." Siba N'Zatioula Grovogui, *Beyond Eurocentrism and Anarchy: Memories of International Order and Institutions* (New York: Palgrave Macmillan, 2006), 233.

[88] Gianpiero Petriglieri, "In Defense of Cosmopolitanism," *Harvard Business Review* (December 15, 2016), https://hbr.org/2016/12/in-defense-of-cosmopolitanism.

[89] See Nussbaum, *Cosmopolitan Tradition*, 215.

are still honored. In fact, it *must* be achieved to enjoy those values. This limit is already expressed in the international community's existing international laws and declarations, although the means for upholding these laws are not. Constructing the means is what this book is about.

In reflecting on the influence of liberal values on the conduct of international relations, Michael Doyle concludes that the "conventions of mutual respect have formed a cooperative foundation for relations among liberal democracies of a remarkably effective kind."[90] Those "remarkably effective" past successes for democracies, empirical realists claim, suggest attractive future possibilities, both for further institutionalizing the conventions and expanding participation to include all states. Yet several serious questions remain open for empirical realism. What about so-called "bad" states, "bad" international institutions, and "bad" human nature? Each set of problems presents huge challenges to what is proposed here. Each could throw key aspirations off track. Yet for each of these three questions there is at least a reasonable possibility that it can be dealt with.

First, people understandably fear what bad actors, rogue states, or illiberal governments might do during a transition toward establishing a sufficient governing hierarchy in world affairs to neutralize the violence-inducing elements of international anarchy and the war-making elements of national sovereignty. To what extent can "conventions of mutual respect" be institutionalized, expanded to include all states, and enforced?

Although growing a rules-based international society seems to work best among liberal democracies,[91] regime type does not limit who cooperates in much of international relations, including war prevention, arms control, alliances, upholding laws against mass killings, facilitating trade and economic cooperation, pandemic disease prevention, environmental protection, and management of the global commons, such as Antarctica and space. Of course, enforcement becomes more difficult when any system of rules is open to a diversity of regime types.

Yet illiberal states can also see benefits from enforcing stable interstate relations, especially if they encounter incentives from other states to become full members of a more cooperative community of nations. At times, it has been possible to bring foot-dragging governments into constructive institution-building processes. The World Trade Organization, for example, grew out of community-building among US-led democracies, yet both Russia and China eventually became eager to join and willing to accept its rules and enforcement procedures for trade practices to gain the overall benefits of membership. If liberal states wisely construct incentives and opportunities for them, illiberal states might be moved over time.[92] Unprincipled conduct by rogue

---

[90] Doyle, "Kant," 213.

[91] Ikenberry, *A World Safe for Democracy*, 299.

[92] Russett and Oneal's research confirms the likelihood that non-threatening U.S. diplomacy toward Russia, China, and possibly other illiberal states could integrate them in a global system of trade and international organizations. See *Triangulating Peace*, especially 282–297.

states can be improved if most other states impose strict limits on undesirable conduct and open opportunities to principled conduct. Moreover, the enforcement difficulty may be more successfully addressed if the goal of US grand strategy moved away from national advantage, where it now resides, to embrace human security, at a time when survival hangs in the balance for every nation.

Second, what about the danger that multilateral institutions, such as the United Nations, may fail to respect and uphold all nations' rights? On the one hand, this has been a problem all along, in part because the powers of the permanent members far exceed that of other states and enable them to be quite irresponsible in vetoing resolutions, even those designed to protect human rights. As a result, the United Nations may not intervene when it should. On the other hand, when empirical realists emphasize strong connections between human rights, democratic governance, impartial rule of law, and sustainable peace, their efforts to nurture and spread these values could be misunderstood as simply another form of "liberal imperialism," forcing ways of thinking on those who do not want them. As a result, the United Nations may intervene when it should not.

Although empirical realism promises no panacea for improving international organizations, its "God's-eye" perspective offers some hope. For example, the strategy proposed here for spreading preferred values of democracy and human rights strictly avoids military interventions for such a purpose. The values themselves should never be implemented as abstract principles. The people likely to be affected by their possible implementation should discuss their meaning and actively shape any application in their communities. This approach is eminently anti-imperialist. As for the earlier problem, if cataclysmic threats recede sufficiently in the international security equation for the permanent members, pressures to stop vetoing resolutions to uphold human rights resolutions might be more likely to be heeded.

Third, is empirical realism simply too idealistic about human nature and humanity's ability to construct cooperative arrangements to shape international politics? Even if its proposals seem desirable in theory, are they feasible in practice? This theory is wedded to constantly evolving assessments of what influences human and state behavior. It adjusts to facts on the ground while searching for peacebuilding opportunities that others may miss. Its ends are crystal clear, but its means are tentative and experimental. The latter change when needed. The strategy of implementation never proceeds faster than verifiable checks and balances can be martialed to guard against the abuse of power by states or individuals, even as strategy aims to demilitarize balancing processes as much as possible and as soon as prudent. It emphasizes monitoring and reducing political corruption and predatory economic forces. It recognizes both the need for more reliable enforcement of law, which at times must be coercive, and the opportunity to do more of it without military combat.

Although the new paradigm certainly does not solve all problems, it does offer an approach for maximizing the possibilities to address as many as can be at this time. Critics may demand too much if they ask for assurances that all risks will be eliminated. It is enough to show that the proposed theory will produce and institutionalize more non-zero-sum relationships among nations, without falsely claiming that it will immediately control all violent dangers, because after more cooperative webs have been spun, engaging the remaining recklessly predatory powers will have become much more feasible.

All that empirical realists need to show is that risking major war arising out of an anarchic balance-of-power system constitutes a bigger threat to human survival than the risks of arranging new institutions to prevent such a war. When the risks of maintaining the existing anarchic system exceed the risks of making the changes proposed in the following chapters, as they surely will if they have not already reached that point, the motivation for survival, if clear-headed, will itself encourage the creation of international institutions capable of increasing the chances for survival by reliably preventing major war and environmental devastation. The needed institutions can be deliberately grown over time. They do not need to be created all at once to justify taking strong steps toward their creation now, before it is too late.

Is human nature too self-interested to build global institutions truly sensitive to the common good? In many times and places human beings have demonstrated a sense of concern for and solidarity with others, especially raised around interests held in common, even though they have not shared genetic, linguistic, national, or religious heritages. The common US experience is a partial illustration of this, although the common interest at first tragically abused African Americans and indigenous Americans. For many years inclusivity did not encompass women. Prejudices toward southern Europeans, Asians, Catholics, Irish, and others fluctuated over time. The UN Charter and the South African constitution, as later examples expressing common concern, were more inclusive from their origins.

A weakness of empirical realism is not, as some critics at first suggest, that it overlooks societies' tendency to be self-interested. It is based on the idea that societies do serve self-interest and that if they served their self-interest over the long term, they would, as empirical realism recommends, constrain the war-making function of sovereignty, because it promises catastrophe if not suicide. As the following chapters show, the problem lies in societies' conduct that is less wise than enlightened self-interest.

Empirical realism is in accord with human nature's capacity for serving both self-interest and altruistic goals. Political realists and entire academic disciplines, such as economics and political science, which are based on assumptions of self-interest as the main human motivation worthy of attention, find it difficult to incorporate elements of altruism in a more complex understanding of human behavior. Yet dichotomizing human motivation into two exclusive categories, either egoism or altruism, misses ways that altruistic seasoning may mix with self-interest,[93] and it glosses over differences between short- and long-term self-interest, of great importance in both interpersonal and interstate conduct. Empirical realists recognize that theories of self-interest have great explanatory power, but they are empirically limited. They omit

---

[93] Monroe, *Heart of Altruism*, 234.

some possibilities for bringing out the best in human behavior and governance. The more broadly one identifies, of course, the more self-interest expands and overlaps other-interest.

With all the aforementioned understandings, limitations, and opportunities, the theoretical framework proposed here offers to sketch a realistic political architecture, based solidly on empirical foundations, for effective and sustainable efforts to achieve human security. On the way toward that goal, the proposed theory also guides the analysis of the threats arising from following political realism (Chapter 3) and their implications and consequences (Chapter 4).

3

Watching National Policies Fail

DESPITE BEING THE world's sole military superpower, the United States has implemented policies that have failed to deliver genuine security and sustainable peace because US assets have been concentrated on military means rather than on all ways and means of achieving security. Means have not been well aligned with the desired ends of peace and security. As a result, US strategy has failed in five areas: Policies have maximized US military power rather than aiming to minimize all states' military influences in the international system; policies have maximized economic gain for the well-off rather than aiming to eliminate poverty for all; policies have emphasized economic nationalism more than international economic integration; policies have put off rather than quickly seized initiatives for environmental balance; and policies have expressed indifference toward or even disrespect for international law rather than aiming to enhance a global rule of law.

3.1 MISALIGNING MILITARY POWER AND SECURITY

Heavy emphasis on US military power may align well with advancing narrow nationalistic or hegemonic goals but not well with the purpose of maximizing security, whether for the United States or others. Yet the most powerful and consistent influence exercised by the United States internationally for decades has been its pursuit of high levels of military preparedness. These preparations are for fighting and winning war; they are not preparedness for building peace—a quite different goal. Constant reliance on ever-advancing military power, on nuclear weapons, and on adversarial, often unilateralist, foreign policies pulls the United States away from working with other countries to rein in global military spending and military preparedness.[1] For more than half a century, the highly militarized US security agenda has ignored or undermined many peaceful norms and multilateral initiatives.[2] Backed by roughly 800 military bases and outposts in more than 70 countries, US officials have wielded so much military power that they have been tempted to over-use it, as in Vietnam, Iraq, and Afghanistan.

A comprehensive understanding of violence reveals that it often is part of a violence cycle that continues until it is deliberately interrupted. To most US citizens, the violence of September 11, 2001, was a horrible shot out of the blue, as it was. Yet it also was part of a history of other people facing other acts of violence that provided some motivation, however unjustified, for 9/11. No less important, the violence of 9/11 would, if allowed to do so, generate a responsive wave of violence, as it did. The United States launched two wars, one of which turned out to be the longest war in US history. Neither contributed much to long-term US security or peace. Both continued the cycle of generating additional violence. A perceptive understanding of the tragedies on September 11, 2001, acknowledges its cyclical nature, which the United States and US adversaries in the Middle East have perpetuated rather than interrupted.

Of course, to decrease the role of military power and international violence while increasing the role of international law is not easy, nor is it likely to occur quickly. Still, some deliberate efforts to move in that direction could have been undertaken safely, without any serious risk, especially after the Cold War ended in 1989. Even after President Eisenhower identified the increasing power of the US military-industrial complex as a dangerous trend because it threatened the functioning of US democracy and the content of its diplomacy, there has never been a sustained US effort to limit its influence or to advance the role of international law and to demilitarize international relations. Despite his warning, which specified real threats to US citizens and their democratic practices even in the absence of any war, the power of the military-industrial complex has grown enormously and now encompasses many segments of the economy and indirectly influences electoral processes and public values in favor of candidates who favor more arms spending.[3] This nucleus of political power and

---

[1] See the Stockholm International Peace Research Institute, "SIPRI Military Expenditure Database," for country by country military expenditures, https://www.sipri.org/databases/milex. https://www.sipri.org/research/armament-and-disarmament/arms-transfers-and-military-spending/military-expenditure.

[2] G. John Ikenberry, "America's Imperial Ambition," *Foreign Affairs* 80, no. 5 (2002): 44–60; Andrew Bacevich, *The New American Militarism: How Americans Are Seduced by War* (Oxford: Oxford University Press, 2013). David Held, "Reframing Global Governance: Apocalypse Soon or Reform!," in *The Cosmopolitan Reader*, ed. Garrett Wallace Brown and David Held (Cambridge: Polity, 2010), 297.

[3] Dwight D. Eisenhower, "Farewell Address," *Public Papers of the Presidents of the United States* (Washington, DC: Government Printing Office, 1960), 1035–1040; William D. Hartung, "Eisenhower's Warning: The Military-Industrial Complex Forty Years Later," *World Policy Journal* 18, no. 1 (Spring 2001): 39–44; Andrew Cockburn, "The Military-Industrial Virus: How Bloated Budgets Gut Our Defenses," *Harper's Magazine* 338, no. 2029 (June 2019): 61–67; Gordon Adams, *The Iron Triangle: The Politics of Defense Contracting* (New York: Council on Economic Priorities, 1981).

economic strength has shaped contemporary political culture, public influence on the economy, and the national budget. The informal alliance between the US military and the industries, workforce, lobbyists, researchers, and congressional leaders that supply it constitutes the most powerful vested interest currently shaping public policy in the United States.

As Eisenhower feared, many members of Congress have become, almost like automatons, a predictable part of what now might be called the military-industrial-congressional-electoral complex, so vast is the spread and influence of those individuals and groups that are part of it. Huge corporations reaping lavish profits from military production offer large contributions to campaign chests for re-electing members of Congress who chair and serve on the armed services and appropriations committees. While in office, members generally vote for big spending for the military. The availability of military power and the economic and political power of lobbyists, both in Washington and in electoral districts across the nation, working with congressional allies happy for military contracts in every congressional district in America, dwarf and overwhelm comparatively weak efforts to foreground non-military means to keep the peace.

A striking illustration of coalescence around familiar yet fruitless aspirations occurred in the competition to become the Republican nominee for US president in 2016. Although one of the most pressing problems for the world's sole superpower was *not* lack of military firepower, 16 of the 17 hopefuls to be nominated for president argued strongly that US military power must be substantially *increased* to make the United States great again. It mattered little to their ideology that US military spending and strength exceeded that of the next eight of the world's greatest powers *combined* (China, Russia, Saudi Arabia, France, India, United Kingdom, Germany, and Japan), five of whom are US allies.[4] Some critics have argued that the United States today "is the only advanced democracy where public figures glorify and exalt the military."[5] Thomas Weiss and Ramesh Thakur believe that the US leadership's advocacy for military power partially explains "the UN's failures to bring human warfare to an end. Its most powerful member state, which has virtual control over many security issues, believes in the efficacy and morality of the use of force."[6]

---

[4] The Stockholm International Peace Research Institute has carefully examined world military spending and developed reliable comparisons of spending equivalencies. The world's nine largest military spenders in 2016, measured in 2015 US dollars, showed the United States spending $606 billion, while the total of the next eight countries came to $603 billion: China $226; Russia $70; Saudi Arabia $61; France $55; India $55; United Kingdom $54; Germany $41; and Japan $41, https://www.sipri.org/sites/default/files/Milex-constant-2015-USD.pdf, accessed July 5, 2017; https://www.sipri.org/research/armament-and-disarmament/arms-transfers-and-military-spending/military-expenditure. Also see Peter Wallensteen, Michel Wieviorka, Itty Abraham, Karin Aggestam, et al., "Violence, Wars, Peace, Security," in *Rethinking Society for the 21st Century: Report of the International Panel on Social Progress: Political Regulation, Governance, and Societal Transformations* 2 (2018): 411–456.

[5] Tony Judt, "What Have We Learned, if Anything?," *New York Review of Books*, May 1, 2008, http://www.nybooks.com/articles/21311.

[6] Weiss and Thakur, *Global Governance and the UN*, 60.

When Donald Trump took office, US military expenditures had averaged $561 billion per year since 2001.[7] The Trump administration projected spending nearly $200 billion more per year or $3.78 trillion from 2019 to 2023—$757 billion per year.[8] The National Defense Strategy Commission called for an increase in military spending of 3 to 5 percent above inflation each year for the following five or more years, which would bring Pentagon spending to $972 billion by 2024.[9] Over the next three decades, the United States intends to spend $1.2 trillion alone on a new generation of nuclear weapons.[10] The United States spends 275 times as much for national military operations as for UN peacekeeping operations, about 3.3 percent of GDP compared to 0.012 percent respectively.[11]

In addition to maintaining a level of military spending that stimulates adversaries to arm more, the United States also pursues an unhelpful, pace-setting emphasis on developing new technologies of destruction, such as attack drones and missiles, often using them first in combat, thereby setting destabilizing, violent precedents. Although the United States sees itself as an influence for peace, it has led the militarization of international relations since the late 1940s with its own conduct, thereby seeming to justify other countries' military expansions, in practice encouraging other countries, with but few exceptions, to reject initiatives for reducing the role of armaments. The United States also leads the way in exporting arms to other countries. Between 2010 and 2014, the Obama administration exported more weapons to more states than any other country in the world.[12] The Trump administration expanded sales further, delivering 76 percent more material than runner-up Russia, to a total of 96 different countries.[13] With very few exceptions, US officials have chosen not to de-emphasize military power or to align US military means with the goals of peacebuilding. They have had no plan for institution-building to delegitimize violent conflict or for legally apprehending and trying those who wrongfully engage in violence, other than to threaten ever greater violence against those whose violence they oppose, which is quite different from a principled delegitimation of violence. If an alternative plan were constructed and implemented, one that aligned military and non-military means with peacebuilding ends, the United States could help minimize the role of military power and encourage similar policies by others.

---

[7] Preble, "Adapting," 6.

[8] Preble, "Adapting," 6.

[9] Hartung, "Costs of War," 3–4.

[10] Hartung, "Costs of War," 3.

[11] Wallensteen et al., "Violence, Wars, Peace," 448.

[12] The five biggest exporters were the United States, Russia, China, Germany, and France, selling 16 percent more in this period than in 2005–2009. Stockholm International Peace Research Institute, *Trends in International Arms Transfer*, 2014. www.sipri.org; and https://www.sipri.org/research/armament-and-disarmament/arms-transfers-and-military-spending/international-arms-transfers.

[13] Stockholm International Peace Research Institute, "USA and France Dramatically Increase Major Arms Exports," March 9, 2020, https://www.sipri.org/media/press-release/2020/usa-and-france-dramatically-increase-major-arms-exports-saudi-arabia-largest-arms-importer-says.

The next section of this chapter looks at initiatives, advanced by other governments and progressive US citizens, that *could* have aided de-militarization. The United States chose to reject them, even though the measures, if implemented, probably would have increased US security and opened the door to nudging the international system from a war-fighting system toward a law-enforcing system.

3.1.1 *Failing to Constrain Conventional Arms*

The US failure to work more creatively and intensely to constrain destabilizing armaments, despite their declining utility for achieving positive political ends, is one of the most negative and consequential US policies over the past half century. Continuous development and production of enormously destructive conventional arms, many of which are capable of offensive use, and its heavy traffic in conventional arms exports legitimate these horrendous weapons. These policies underscore the main US security problem of preparing for war, but not for peace.

Most people who die in most wars are killed by conventional arms, and many of these arms are sold or given by arms-exporting governments to warring governments, warlords, criminals, illegal militias, and terrorist groups who together slaughter tens of thousands every year. The fighting in Afghanistan, Congo, Iraq, Libya, Mali, Myanmar, Sierra Leone, Sudan, Syria, Yemen, and elsewhere in recent years underscores the need for common-sense rules restricting the international transfer of weapons. Yet arms exporters moved $2.2 billion worth of arms and ammunition to war zones between 2000 and 2012. Many of these were imported by countries operating under 26 UN, regional, or multilateral arms embargoes that were supposed to be in force during the period of the arms transfers,[14] but they were not followed by arms merchants. Total arms exports, including those to countries not at war, totaled about $100 billion annually, with the United States expanding its lead over other exporters in recent years.[15]

An enforceable treaty restricting trade in conventional arms could be a good first step toward reducing the number of civilians killed worldwide by requiring all governments who sell weapons to abide by a code of conduct that the United States and other Western democracies have endorsed. The purpose of such a treaty is to reduce the flow of weapons and ammunition that often fuel wars and abuse civilians' human rights. An existing Arms Trade Treaty (ATT) seeks to establish legal prohibitions on arms and ammunition transfers that may contribute to war crimes; requires that all states establish national regulations on international arms transfers; and sets forth common international standards for approval of and reporting on arms transfers. Ninety-two

---

[14] Daryl G. Kimball, "Closing the Deal on a Robust Arms Trade Treaty," *Arms Control Association Issue Briefs* 4, no. 3 (March 13, 2013), https://www.armscontrol.org/issuebriefs/Closing-the-Deal-on-a-Robust-Global-Arms-Trade-Treaty.

[15] Tim Bowler, "Which Country Dominates the Global Arms Trade?," BBC report on SIPRI data, May 9, 2018, https://www.bbc.com/news/business-43873518#:~:text=And%20unsurprisingly%20it%20is%20a,Sipri)%2C%20tells%20the%20BBC.

countries have ratified this treaty and 40 others have signed it. When the UN General Assembly voted on it, only North Korea, Syria, and Iran voted against it.[16] But it lacks legal clout because the United States has not ratified it or sought to implement it.

All Republican senators but one bitterly opposed the treaty when it was being negotiated during the Obama administration. They sent a letter to President Obama asking him to oppose the treaty while it was being negotiated, claiming that it was a huge threat to gun ownership that they and the National Rifle Association favored.[17] Independent arms experts, the American Bar Association Center for Human Rights, and the Obama administration all said this claim was simply not true because the treaty does not even govern internal arms purchases within a country.[18] Although the Obama administration worked effectively to negotiate this first-step treaty, conservatives in Congress, supported by the National Rifle Association, lied about its purpose and refused to ratify it, even though it was limited to curtailing illicit international trade in arms and to prevent international arms merchants from selling weapons to unstable and irresponsible international buyers such as warlords and terrorists. It is a modest arms-trade-regulating treaty, not a treaty to end arms exports, let alone sales within the United States. Much stronger verifiable and enforceable limits on transferring conventional arms and broader conventional arms control measures remain necessary to reduce war crimes, curtail human rights abuses, reinforce constraints on armed conflict, and generally help to institutionalize peace. Nonetheless, a majority of members of the US Senate and the Trump administration fiercely opposed developing international laws that could achieve these goals, help save lives, and demilitarize international relations.

The earlier, more general US interest in arms control also has not been pursued by recent administrations, even though the end of the Cold War in 1989 opened new possibilities for taking major steps forward. The United States, Russia, and China were outliers during negotiations leading to the Convention on the Prohibition of the Use, Stockpiling, Production and Transfer of Anti-Personnel Mines and on their Destruction, known simply as the "Mine Ban Treaty." Even though this has been signed by more than three-fourths of all countries around the world, the United States has rejected it and accompanying opportunities to build bridges of cooperation between military powers and militarily weak states, even though these are crucial for developing adequate monitoring and enforcement of many international arms control agreements.[19]

---

[16] Dennis Jett, "Republicans Are Blocking Ratification of Even the Most Reasonable International Treaties," *New Republic* (December 26, 2014), https://newrepublic.com/article/120646/ratification-arms-trade-treaty-others-blocked-republicans.

[17] Five Democratic senators joined the letter to the president opposing the treaty. Jett, "Republicans Are Blocking."

[18] Daryl G. Kimball, "Closing the Deal on a Robust Arms Trade Treaty," *Arms Control Association Issue Briefs* 4, no. 3 (March 13, 2013), https://www.armscontrol.org/issuebriefs/Closing-the-Deal-on-a-Robust-Global-Arms-Trade-Treaty.

[19] The UN High-Level Panel recommended that all states parties to the Biological and Toxin Weapons Convention "should without delay return to negotiations for a credible verification protocol, inviting

3.1.2 *Failing to Constrain Nuclear Weapons*

Although the United States in the 1950s, '60s, '70s, and '80s took many initiatives for arms control, during the three decades since the end of the Cold War, many US officials and influential congressional leaders have refused to support reasonable arms control measures for nuclear weapons. During the Trump presidency, the United States resisted arms control more fervently than at any time in US history, even opposing the 2010 Strategic Arms Reduction Treaty (New START) with Russia and pulling out of the Intermediate-Range Nuclear Forces Treaty after more than 30 years, terminating an agreement that abolished an entire class of nuclear weapons.[20]

Rather than attempting to reduce reliance on nuclear weapons while still retaining a minimum number during a transition toward nuclear disarmament, the United States instead has relied on nuclear weapons and favored upgrading them. Moreover, US policymakers insist on understanding the problem of nuclear weapons proliferation as one in which it will try to force non-proliferation on governments it dislikes rather than practice nuclear disarmament that could include itself and others. This approach actually increases the likelihood of nuclear proliferation because it encourages those governments that the United States attempts to push toward non-proliferation to become even more eager to acquire weapons. The US policy also weakens international law and the United Nations as it provides additional pretexts for US recourse to force, as it did against Iraq.[21]

Perhaps the most disappointing and self-defeating example of US opposition to limiting weapons of mass destruction has been the US Senate's refusal, since 1996, to ratify the Comprehensive Nuclear-Test-Ban Treaty (CTBT). If ratified, it would ban all nuclear explosions for both civilian and military purposes, whether underground, in the atmosphere, or in space. It would be an added influence to discourage testing by other states. Nonetheless, the US Senate has refused, under both Democratic and Republican leadership, to approve this treaty even though the United States has conducted 1,054 nuclear tests, far more than any other country.[22] Until recently, all US presidents had favored the test ban treaty. The Obama administration wanted to ratify it, but the Senate would not even bring it up for consideration. Secretary of State John Kerry told the UN Security Council that the United States supported the treaty's purposes: "to diminish our reliance on nuclear devices, to reduce competition among nuclear powers, and to promote responsible disarmament."[23] Yet the prospects

---

the active participation of the biotechnology industry." UN High-Level Panel, *A More Secure World*, 42, para 126.

[20] Arms Control Association, "The Trillion (and a half) Dollar Triad?," *Arms Control Today* 9, no. 6 (August 18, 2017), https://www.armscontrol.org/issue-briefs/2017-08/trillion-half-dollar-triad; Beatrice Fihn,"Women Against the Bomb," *The Nation* (December 3–10, 2018): 13–25.

[21] Richard Falk, "International Law and the Future," *Third World Quarterly* 27, no. 5 (2006): 727–737.

[22] The United States has conducted 1,054 nuclear weapons tests; the Soviet Union, 715; France, 210; United Kingdom, 45; and China, 45. See Wikipedia, "Nuclear Weapons Testing," https://en.wikipedia.org/wiki/Nuclear_weapons_testing.

[23] Michelle Nicoles, "U.N. Urges U.S., China, Others to Ratify Nuclear Test Ban Treaty," Reuters (September 23, 2016), http://www.reuters.com/article/us-un-nuclear-idUSKCN11T29J.

for Senate ratification of the treaty, which has been open for ratification since 1996, have been close to zero.

The CTBT has been approved by 166 other states, including Russia, France, and the United Kingdom. US ratification would help to discourage other countries from developing nuclear weapons and proliferating destructive technology. Although China, India, Pakistan, and North Korea are other nuclear-weapons countries that have not ratified the agreement, they would be more likely to do so if the United States ratified. US failure to do so for a quarter of a century has weakened the informal regime against testing and the persuasiveness of US arguments over the years that North Korea and other countries should not test. It is hardly realistic to insist that other states must not test even though the United States has conducted over a thousand tests and still refuses to ratify the treaty to halt testing, while also preaching that every national government should put its own national interest first.[24]

A second US rebuke to those seeking to restrain the international community's acceptance of nuclear weapons is US failure to honor its own treaty obligation to engage in multilateral negotiations to reduce all nuclear weapons. In this refusal, the United States has violated the promise that it made when it ratified the Nuclear Non-Proliferation Treaty. In Article 6, all nuclear-weapons states pledged "to pursue negotiations in good faith on effective measures relating to cessation of the nuclear arms race at an early date and to nuclear disarmament, and on a treaty on general and complete disarmament under strict and effective international control."[25] That pledge became legally binding in 1970, and still is, but it has been largely ignored by every US administration since then. This casts doubt on the integrity of US official commitments to other countries and to the people of the United States. All states of the world, except India, Israel, Pakistan, and South Sudan, have signed the treaty, so the failure to implement Article 6 has violated a promise made to most countries of the world even as Washington officials insist that other parties honor their obligations under this treaty not to proliferate.

A third security-eroding nuclear policy has been the US refusal, since the beginning of the George W. Bush administration, to pursue international limits on the future production of fissile materials required to make nuclear bombs, even though the United States clearly wants many other countries to eschew upgrading their nuclear materials to the point that they could be used for fission or fusion reactions capable of manufacturing weapons. When the United States quit negotiations for a treaty to stop further production of fissile materials,[26] officials indicated they were withdrawing because such a treaty could not be verified. Other countries and independent experts,

---

[24] Mark Landler, "President Reshapes Vision for US Role with Emphasis on One Word: Sovereignty," *New York Times*, September 20, 2017.

[25] Treaty on the Non-Proliferation of Nuclear Weapons, Article VI, https://www.un.org/disarmament/wmd/nuclear/npt/.

[26] This is formally called the Fissile Material Cutoff Treaty (FMCT), which forbids the production of highly enriched uranium and plutonium capable of fabricating nuclear weapons.

however, report that treaty obligations could be verified. The treaty would merely need to extend safeguards to nuclear-armed states, such as inspections and monitoring measures that already exist and are well known to be effective. The International Atomic Energy Agency (IAEA) already inspects the nuclear facilities of non-nuclear-weapon states under the Nuclear Nonproliferation Treaty. US national security planners refused to move forward with the fissile-ban treaty even though the United States, France, Russia, the United Kingdom, and possibly China have already halted fissile material production for weapons on their own, suggesting that the United States does not want more fissile material production for itself right now as much as it wants to *block an international agreement* that would (1) halt all production of fissile material and (2) start an effective system of international monitoring to verify a fissile materials ban because then the United States would be required to accept inspection.

In a speech early in his first administration (in Prague in April 2009), President Obama tried to re-open the door for negotiations on a fissile cutoff treaty by proposing it as one of his "concrete steps towards a world without nuclear weapons." He said that the United States should "seek a new treaty that verifiably ends the production of fissile materials intended for use in state nuclear weapons."[27] Nonetheless, US officials subsequently opposed negotiations halting fissile material production despite the recommendation of International Atomic Energy Agency Director-General Mohamed El Baradei to complete an internationally verifiable fissile material cutoff treaty (FMCT). The IAEA reported that "it is the IAEA Secretariat's assessment that verification of a treaty banning the production of fissile materials would be possible through a verification system quite similar to the one applied for the IAEA safeguards system."[28]

One benefit of a treaty would be to make irreversible the new material moratoria that the five major nuclear-weapon states have informally undertaken. Even more important, the value of a cutoff of production of new weapons material "could help prevent proliferation" and "jump-start nuclear disarmament."[29] The proposed treaty would end production in other states which became parties to the treaty. Moreover, it could strengthen resolve among many non-weapon states to take action against challenges posed by countries seeking nuclear capabilities, such as North Korea and Iran. Once a cutoff has been legally mandated, it would give all governments and political activists more solid ground for asking nuclear-armed states to reduce their weapons-grade materials. At the least, arms control advocates could ask that existing stockpiles not now fabricated in weapons should never be used for weapons.[30]

---

[27] President Barack Obama, quoted by Alexander Glaser, Zia Mian, and Frank N. von Hippel, "Time to Ban Production of Nuclear Weapons Material," *Scientific American* (January 13, 2010), https://www.scientificamerican.com/article/time-to-ban-production-of-nuclear-weapons-material/.

[28] Reported in Arms Control Association, "U.S. Fissile Material Ban Plan Fizzles," https://www.armscontrol.org/act/2004_10/Fissile_Material, accessed 3 August 2017. See also Glaser, Mian, and von Hippel, "Time to Ban."

[29] Glaser, Mian, and von Hippel, "Time to Ban."

[30] Glaser, Mian, and von Hippel, "Time to Ban." The authors report that Pakistan has made such a request because India possesses a substantial stockpile of plutonium that could be used for either civilian or military purposes.

However, despite the Obama administration's promising rhetoric and first initiatives for human security, which in a sense confirmed the wisdom of the approach recommended here, there was no progress because of widespread opposition in the US Congress, especially among conservatives, to taking constructive steps. The Obama presidency faced enormous criticism because it "sought to diminish its dependence on militarism by a pragmatic recourse to diplomacy."[31] Well before the Trump administration, US policymakers were unable to ratify constructive treaty constraints,[32] underscoring the need for citizen pressures.

A fourth example of blocking good prospects for systemic change[33] and security enhancement occurred in 2016–17, when many countries participated in negotiating a treaty to prohibit the use, threat of use, testing, development, production, possession, or transfer of nuclear weapons, or stationing of them in a different country.[34] The Obama administration opposed convening these negotiations, and the subsequent Republican administration strongly opposed the treaty. Rather than try to shape the treaty even if officials would later decide not to ratify it, the United States and other nuclear-weapons powers boycotted all the negotiations. Fifty-three UN member states signed the treaty. US officials said that "the treaty would do nothing to alleviate the possibility of nuclear conflict and might even increase it."[35]

The purpose of the Treaty on the Prohibition of Nuclear Weapons is to consolidate international opinion against the use and possession of nuclear weapons, encourage those who have them to negotiate reductions, and to discourage additional states from developing such weapons. As Peter Maurer, president of the International Committee of the Red Cross, explained: "Of course, adopting a treaty to prohibit nuclear weapons will not make them immediately disappear." But the treaty "will reinforce the stigma against their use, support commitments to nuclear risk reduction and be a disincentive for proliferation."[36] More than 50 countries have ratified the treaty which entered into force in January 2021.

To encourage the interest of nuclear-armed states in joining, the treaty outlined a process for destroying stockpiles and, significantly, for *enforcing* countries' promise to remain free of nuclear weapons. US officials' responses to the treaty showed no

---

[31] Falk, *Power Shift*, 17.

[32] John Mearsheimer notes that "Obama challenged liberal hegemony when he was a candidate, yet as president he was forced to stick to the Washington playbook." Mearsheimer, *Delusion*, Kindle, 4291.

[33] "System change" refers to changing the institutional structure or power relationships established among groups in a social or political system. Such change affects "fundamentals," as contrasted with more modest "policy changes," which occur without transforming a system or structure of relationships. For the United States to stop further stockpiling of fissile materials for nuclear weapons would be a policy change. To authorize the IAEA to monitor all countries' nuclear installations and enforce a universal ban on producing new nuclear weapons would be "system change" or "structural change."

[34] Rick Gladstone, "Nobel Peace Prize Goes to Group Opposing Nuclear Weapons," *New York Times*, October 6, 2017.

[35] Gladstone, "Nobel Peace Prize."

[36] Somini Sengupta and Rick Gladstone, "United States and Allies Protest U.N. Talks to Ban Nuclear Weapons," *New York Times*, March 27, 2017.

appreciation for the way that legalization processes occur in international relations, often beginning with gathering as much support for a norm as possible, even though not all governments can support it, delegitimizing the posture of those opposing it over the long run, and gradually building broader consensus for the norm. Flat opposition to negotiations aimed at delegitimizing nuclear weapons showed no inclination to educate the US or world publics about the need to ensure that these weapons will never be used. The standard argument, which US ambassador to the UN, Nicki Haley, and other conservatives considered a clinching argument against the treaty, was that, since North Korea had refused to prohibit nuclear weapons, the United States and other nuclear powers could not support such a treaty.

A more thoughtful position would have been to support the treaty without immediately ratifying it, while at the same time challenging all states to support it with a solemn pledge to participate in a nuclear disarmament process if and when it would include the entire world and contain strong verification and enforcement provisions to address all countries' fears about cheating. Under such conditions, the United States could have supported prohibition, thereby placing more worldwide pressure on North Korea and other states to curtail developing nuclear arsenals.

The four preceding US policies legitimize nuclear weapons, discourage international system change, and actually undermine US security. Taken together, they also highlight a fifth failure: the lack of a serious strategy to reduce the role of nuclear weapons in general and to discourage dissatisfied states from developing technology useful for developing nuclear weapons and delivery systems in the future. US officials have instead drawn up extensive plans to modernize and upgrade the US nuclear arsenal, even though the use of nuclear weapons is perceived by many objective observers to be illegal and immoral. The Departments of Defense and Energy requested approximately $27 billion in fiscal year 2017 alone to maintain and upgrade US nuclear weapons.[37] The US Arms Control Association projected the total cost of nuclear weapons over the next 30 years at between $1.25 trillion and $1.46 trillion.[38] These costs caused the late Senate Armed Services Committee chairman John McCain to say: "It's very, very, very expensive. . . . Do we really need the entire triad [land-based missiles, submarine-based cruise missiles, bombs on aircraft], given the situation?"[39] After taking office, President Trump indicated he wanted to expand the nuclear modernization program even more than President Obama had committed the US government to during his second term. Despite these emphases, independent

---

[37] US Arms Control and Disarmament Agency, "U.S. Nuclear Modernization Programs," *Arms Control Today* (August 2017), https://www.armscontrol.org/factsheets/USNuclearModernization, accessed October 10, 2017.

[38] See Arms Control Association, "The Trillion (and a half) Dollar Triad?" These calculations are in then-year dollars, meaning the figures include expected price increases due to inflation.

[39] John McCain, speaking at the Brookings Institution, May 19, 2016, US Arms Control and Disarmament Agency, "U.S. Nuclear Modernization Programs," *Arms Control Today* (August 2017), https://www.armscontrol.org/factsheets/USNuclearModernization, accessed October 10, 2017.

arms control experts have developed reliable plans to constrain nuclear weapons if intentions and resources were committed to that task.[40]

Rather than trying to diminish the appetite of other states for obtaining nuclear weapons by delegitimizing the possession and use of nuclear weapons, President Trump used US nuclear weapons to threaten attacks with "fire and fury like the world has never seen"[41] against weaker, poorer states like North Korea whose government professes interest in possessing nuclear weapons to use them as a deterrent to attack on North Korea. Every US nuclear threat probably whets the appetite of some state to have nuclear weapons to neutralize US threats.

In an earlier neo-conservative administration, President George W. Bush had singled out Iraq, Iran, and North Korea as an "axis of evil," and then attacked Iraq to terminate the Iraqi government under Hussein. In addition, a few years after persuading Libya not to develop nuclear weapons and to give up its nuclear research, the United States led efforts to attack Libya, resulting in the killing of its leader. The attack came soon after Libya's decision to de-nuclearize. To connect these two actions may be fortuitous, but they do reinforce the felt need of some national governments who might fear US attack to obtain as many nuclear weapons as possible as soon as possible. President Trump's belligerent rhetoric reinforced US threats to national governments already nursing an appetite for nuclear weapons, thereby increasing their desire to satisfy their appetite while making matters worse for non-proliferation.

Even when the Obama administration successfully negotiated a landmark multilateral deal that required Iran to give up its existing weapons-grade nuclear materials and to halt for 15 years its program for manufacturing fissile material for nuclear weapons, President Trump and a Republican Congress were eager to "tear it up."[42] In addition to requiring Iran to give up its nuclear materials capable of being made into bombs, the agreement strictly prohibited Iran from enriching new weapons-grade materials and other activities necessary to make nuclear weapons. The Joint Comprehensive Plan of Action also provided important first-time intrusive verification measures.[43]

Although the International Atomic Energy Agency repeatedly found that Iran had been complying with the agreement[44] and France, the United Kingdom, Russia,

---

[40] US Arms Control and Disarmament Agency, "U.S. Nuclear Modernization Programs."

[41] President Trump's threats to North Korea were reported by the Associated Press (August 8, 2017), https://www.youtube.com/watch?v=8p1JIgTuKQk, https://www.google.com/search?source=hp&ei=jOSIXZ-hNKHR9APB_46oBQ&q=fire+and+fury+trump&oq=fire+and+fury&gs_l=psy-ab.1.2.0l10.3068.6133..9084...0.0..0.165.1809.0j13......0....1..gws-wiz.......0i131.haRVRhr11OY.

[42] Julian Borger, Saeed Kamali Dehghan, and Peter Beaumont, "Trump Threatens to Rip Up Iran Nuclear Deal," *The Guardian*, October 13, 2017, https://www.theguardian.com/us-news/2017/oct/13/trump-iran-nuclear-deal-congress; William Spaniel, "Here's What Could Happen if a President Trump Tore Up the Iran Nuclear Deal," *Washington Post*, July 11, 2016, https://www.washingtonpost.com/news/monkey-cage/wp/2016/07/11/heres-what-could-happen-if-a-president-trump-tore-up-the-iran-nuclear-deal/; Mark Landler, "Trump Abandons Iran Nuclear Deal He Long Scorned," *New York Times*, May 8, 2018, https://www.nytimes.com/2018/05/08/world/middleeast/trump-iran-nuclear-deal.html.

[43] Rick Gladstone, "What Is the Iran Deal? Why Does Trump Hate It?," *New York Times*, October 5, 2017, A9.

[44] Gladstone, "What Is the Iran Deal?"

China, Germany, and the European Union all strongly supported the continuation of the agreement, and despite the unjustifiable threat by the United States to withdraw, President Trump refused to confirm Iranian compliance even while acknowledging that it might be "technically" in compliance. Iran said it would not feel bound by the agreement any longer if the United States withdrew and resumed sanctions against it or violated US obligations under the deal. Secretary of State Rex Tillerson confirmed that Iran was honoring its obligations under the agreement, as did all US intelligence agencies and the other countries that were party to the agreement and the IAEA which had inspectors on the ground in Iran.

Still, the US president did not like the agreement because it failed to require Iran to do what he wanted in fields that US negotiators had never intended that the agreement would be able to cover, such as missile development or support for groups accused of terrorism. During his campaign for president, Donald Trump said that it was a "terrible agreement" and that if elected he would immediately tear it up. In order to justify his desire to scuttle the agreement, he complained that Iran had violated "the spirit of the agreement" even if it was not in material breach. He also referred to the Iranian government's failure to respect human rights, which seemed a bit out of character after his occasionally effusive comments of admiration for authoritarian leaders in Russia, Turkey, Philippines, China, and Egypt, despite their human rights violations.[45]

Of course, Iranian officials have committed serious human rights violations for which they should be held accountable. But for the United States to torpedo an agreement that had constrained Iran's nuclear weapons programs and established reliable verification systems made no sense, as his own advisers and many members of Congress understood. At the least, US officials might have complimented Iran for abiding by the nuclear agreement and encourage that to continue. The success of the agreement would reinforce the international legal structure against proliferation and the IAEA's role in verifying it. US officials could still have sought additional agreements with Iran to limit missile development and respect human rights. At issue is the level of US interest in constraining nuclear development through multilateral diplomatic means even when the process included Iran and the five permanent members of the Security Council plus Germany and the EU.

For conservatives to cast doubt on the reliability of US commitments in general by withdrawing from an agreement being honored by Iran also encourages the spread of nuclear weapons to countries that have been time-honored close allies. President Trump suggested that countries like South Korea, Japan, Germany, and other NATO allies should do more for their own security and that, unless they did, they might not be able to count on the United States coming to their aid. Even though other members of the Trump administration at first rushed to reassure these allies of the constancy of US promises, President Trump with some congressional support repeatedly

---

[45] For a keen analysis of US policies toward Iran, see Kelsey Davenport, "Trump's Cynical Gambit on the Iran Nuclear Deal," Arms Control Association, *Issue Briefs* 10, no. 2, January 17, 2018, https://www.arms-control.org/issue-briefs/2018-01/trumps-cynical-iran-nuclear-deal.

undermined allied countries' belief in the reliability of US security promises, as well as adversaries' trust in agreements with Washington.

In brief, the US government and a majority of members of both houses of Congress have favored policies that increased the appetites of other governments for obtaining nuclear and conventional arms. To claim that such an outcome was not their intention hardly relieves them of responsibility for refusing to heed empirical evidence pointing to counter-productive outcomes. For officials and legislators to believe that US threats toward countries already fearing the United States will move them to do US bidding ignores the history of armed rivalries and the psychology of fear. The United States did not even try to address the Iranian nuclear appetite by following the recommendation of the UN High-Level Panel to attempt a nuclear-weapon-free zone in the Middle East region similar to those established for Latin America and the Caribbean, Africa, the South Pacific and South-East Asia.[46] Leaders in the White House and the Senate in recent years have repeatedly implemented policies expressing faith that US security issues could be best addressed by expanding and exerting US. military power forcefully, rather than by trying to constrain the role of military power with international regulations and institutions.

3.1.3 *Failing to Constrain Chemical and Biological Weapons*

Although US officials wisely oppose the use of chemical and biological weapons of mass destruction, they have not worked hard to establish adequate international monitoring and verification of constraints on such weapons. Chemical weapons, like nuclear and biological weapons, are considered weapons of mass destruction because they can easily kill thousands of people. Once deployed, there may be no effective defense against some of them. The Chemical Weapons Convention,[47] supported by the George W. Bush administration, may be something of an exception to US skepticism about arms control in recent years. Yet in shaping the treaty in ways that made it easier for US officials to accept, they have not pressed for strong verification and enforcement measures that would strengthen the constraints on toxic chemicals, because inspection would bring an international presence in US installations that the US government opposes.

Parties to the convention seek "to exclude completely the possibility of the use of chemical weapons."[48] They agreed "never under any circumstances: (a) To develop, produce, otherwise acquire, stockpile or retain chemical weapons, or transfer, directly or

---

[46] United Nations Secretary-General Kofi Annan, UN High-Level Panel, *In Larger Freedom: Towards Development, Security and Human Rights for All*, Report of the Secretary-General, UN Doc. A/59/2005 & annex (2005), http://www.un.org/largerfreedom/contents.htm, 41, para 124.

[47] The Chemical Weapons Convention entered into force on April 29, 1997, 98 years after chemical weapons were first outlawed in the Hague Convention of 1899. https://www.opcw.org/fileadmin/OPCW/CWC/CWC_en.pdf,

[48] Preamble, Chemical Weapons Convention, https://www.opcw.org/chemical-weapons-convention.

indirectly, chemical weapons to anyone; (b) To use chemical weapons; (c) To engage in any military preparations to use chemical weapons; (d) To assist, encourage or induce, in any way, anyone to engage in any activity prohibited to a State Party under this Convention."[49] States possessing chemical weapons agreed to destroy them and chemical weapons production facilities.[50] Yet because verification provisions focus more on destruction of weapons than on the capacity to produce or store them, there are large loopholes in the treaty despite its rather sweeping positive provisions.

US officials favored these obligations because the United States earlier had decided to destroy much of its poison gas stockpile because the agents and their aging storage containers were becoming unstable. The convention encouraged other states to destroy their stockpiles also and established measures to verify their destruction. Moreover, the pace of destruction could be decided independently by parties to the treaty, thereby softening its immediate impact. Although under way, the process of destruction has been uncompleted two decades after the treaty came into force. Moreover, small amounts of toxic chemical agents are allowed in order to continue manufacturing for research, developing antidotal agents, and using agents for medical purposes. Many countries maintain large stockpiles of chemical weapons, justifying them as a precaution or deterrent against use by others.

Although the prohibitions are not strictly enforced, the Organization for the Prohibition of Chemical Weapons, based in The Hague, has been established to observe destruction of chemical weapons and monitor chemical weapons stockpiles. It oversees the terms of the Chemical Weapons Convention, signed by 192 governments, representing 98 percent of the world's population. The Organization has conducted over 6,000 inspections at 235 chemical weapons sites and over 2,000 industrial sites, an impressive set of observations that prepare this organization to implement more strict adherence to chemical weapons prohibitions when the United States and other countries agree to its doing so.[51]

Similar enforcement problems arise with biological toxins or infectious agents that can be deployed with intent to kill or incapacitate humans, animals, or plants. A deterrent to their use in the past has been the difficulty of controlling who might be harmed and of ensuring that friendly forces are not hurt. However, some agents, such as anthrax, can be controlled and the possibility of employing other agents with precision when delivered by drones opens new doors to their use. Terrorists may also obtain and transport some agents at relatively low cost. Their use could result in massive civilian casualties as large as nuclear or chemical weapons. Yet they cost far less to develop and store.

The use of biological weapons in armed conflict would be a war crime, prohibited by customary international humanitarian law as well as specific treaties, including

---

[49] Chemical Weapons Convention, Article 1 (1).
[50] Chemical Weapons Convention, Article 1 (2)–1 (4).
[51] Organization for the Prohibition of Chemical Weapons, "OPCW by the Numbers," https://www.opcw. org/media-centre/opcw-numbers.

the Biological Weapons Convention of 1972. It outlawed mass production, stockpiling, and use of biological weapons. The United States, United Kingdom, Russia, and many other countries signed the ban on "development, production and stockpiling of microbes or their poisonous products except in amounts necessary for protective and peaceful research."[52] However, Russia and perhaps several other countries appear to have continued research and produced offensive weapons in apparent violation of the convention which, significantly, contained no monitoring or enforcement provisions.

In 2001, the United States "opposed and killed an effort dating back to 1995 to augment the Biological Weapons Convention with a legally binding verification protocol."[53] US officials claimed that legally binding inspection would be "too burdensome" for governments and interfere with the confidentiality of private corporations, yet might not be effective enough to stop deliberate, secret violations.[54] Yet, given their extreme danger if used or not securely stored, a worldwide monitoring capacity to verify and enforce regulations for them remains desirable, although it cannot happen without US backing. As a result, the maintenance of some arsenals that are not limited strictly to self-defense weapons stimulates fears and further military procurement in competing countries.

3.2 MISALIGNING ECONOMIC ASSETS AND ABOLITION OF POVERTY

Second, as the wealthiest and most powerful country of the world, citizens might reasonably expect the United States to lead the way in abolishing global poverty, not only because the poor, like all people, possess the right to a life of dignity, but also because chronic poverty and unemployment exacerbate many other problems, such as terrorism and unwanted migration, that harm US and human security. In appropriating $1.3 trillion for its military every two years, US officials might show sufficient concern for the poor to divert, say, $100 billion from the Pentagon budget to abolish poverty, thereby addressing causes of unrest and political-religious polarization that are the justification for high military expenditures. But this has not happened. Instead, international unrest leads to more military spending and less poverty reduction, thereby increasing the felt need for high military spending in subsequent years. The 15 biggest military spenders in the world allocate $1.7 trillion[55] annually for military purposes. Redirecting 10 percent of this annually could abolish global poverty in 20 years,[56] an achievement as likely to reduce violent threats to human security as putting that

---

[52] United Nations Office for Disarmament Affairs, "Biological Weapons Convention," https://www.un.org/disarmament/wmd/bio/.

[53] Arms Control Association, "Arms Control and Proliferation Profile: The United States," Profile, https://www.armscontrol.org/factsheets/unitedstatesprofile#bio.

[54] Arms Control Association, "Arms Control and Proliferation Profile: The United State."

[55] In 2015 dollars. Wallensteen et al., "Violence, Wars, Peace."

[56] Mark Anielski, "The Real Cost of Eliminating Poverty in 2016," http://www.anielski.com/real-cost-eliminating-poverty/, accessed June 1, 2019.

10 percent into more weapons. Or to make another comparison, the cost of the coffee consumed annually in the United States is "1.7 times the estimated cost of eliminating global extreme poverty."[57]

In the late 1960s and early 1970s, the Organization for European Cooperation and Development and several international commissions and UN development agencies agreed on a goal of designating 0.7 percent of industrialized countries' GNP for development assistance to flow from rich to poor countries every year.[58] During the more than half a century that has passed since then, the United States never has come close to meeting this widely agreed-on UN-specified amount to abolish poverty, even though US development assistance greatly exceeded that recommended percentage years earlier, during the Marshall plan, when US aid was going to Europe rather than Africa, the Middle East, Asia, and Latin America.[59] Outside the United States, most independent observers agree that the United States has actively opposed paying a fair share of the cost of abolishing poverty. The United States has ranked 23rd out of 27 of the wealthiest countries in the world measured by how its development aid compares with the rest of the world.[60] Many European countries, which have been criticized by the US president for not paying enough for military preparedness, have done far more than the United States to contribute to development assistance. The congressional appropriations policies that in practice perpetuate poverty are not a Republican or Democratic construct, although Republicans generally favor less aid than Democrats. Niggardly US policies are simply due to US officials expressing the attitudes of many, but of course not all, US citizens. People have not been encouraged by US leaders to understand the benefits of reducing poverty now, as they were led to understand the benefits during the years of assistance to Europe after World War II.

Poverty around the world is perpetuated by citizens who overstate the impediments to its abolition and who believe its continuation is morally acceptable—even though they may not think of themselves as favoring poverty and wish it would disappear. Yet the policies of the globally rich and powerful, which in practice perpetuate poverty, can accurately be considered "crimes against humanity" according to philosopher Thomas Pogge, a leading world expert on global poverty. He documents that "world poverty is actively perpetuated by our [developed states'] governments and officials." He shows that "citizens, too, have enough information to know what is going on, or at

---

[57] Anielski, "The Real Cost."

[58] Jan Tingbergen suggested this amount was needed to generate economies capable of abolishing poverty. In the 1950s, the agreed-on goal was 1.0 percent, including both public and private development assistance. "Financing for Sustainable Development," http://www.oecd.org/dac/stats/the070dagnitarget-ahistory.htm.

[59] This manifests a US nationalism, particularly in Congress, reluctant to extend its inclusivity much beyond European identity.

[60] The index is prepared by the Center for Global Development. Jesse Chase-Lubitz and Robbie Gramer, "Report: U.S. Ranks Near Bottom in Commitment to Global Development," Foreign Policy (September 6, 2017), https://foreignpolicy.com/2017/09/06/report-u-s-ranks-near-bottom-in-commitment-to-global-development-foreign-aid-diplomacy/.

least to find out easily, if we care."[61] Although many justifications are offered for the failure of the well-off to do more, "if we don't shut our eyes, we also know that our efforts against poverty abroad are tiny compared to our means and tiny also relative to the poverty we systematically produce through unjust policies and social institutions." People "are disregarding, trivializing, and condoning these crimes [against human-ity] in the vague belief that we are benefiting from them." US elites who formulate poverty-perpetuating policies may believe that they serve US interests, but in truth they do not. Pogge reports that "the lies and deceptions, the hypocrisy, the carefully made-up statistics . . . keep us comfortably ignorant of what we are doing."[62] Many US citizens believe that global poverty is a given that they cannot change, and they also think of themselves as exponents of human rights. Pogge documents in detail that chronic global poverty is the biggest human rights violation in the world today.

Because there is only one international economic system, all societies are part of it. As a result of US leadership and dominant influence in this economic system and its main institutions since 1945, the poorest 50 percent of the world's people now possess only 1 percent of the world's total wealth and earn only 3 percent of the world's house-hold income. The top 10 percent possess 85 percent of the world's wealth and take in 71 percent of humanity's annual income. The world's richest 10 percent of people have 387 times the per capita wealth of the bottom 50 percent and 119 times their per capita income.[63]

Pogge concludes that "the dominant Western countries are designing and uphold-ing global institutional arrangements, geared to their domestic economic elites, that foreseeably and avoidably produce massive deprivations in most of the much poorer regions of Asia, Africa, and Latin America." If these "global institutional arrangements" showed more concern for reducing poverty, the poorest half of the world's population might enjoy a global household income that "might well have sunk no lower than to 5 percent," rather than its current 3 percent, and this would be all that is required "to avoid life-threatening poverty."[64] The data show that "even if this protection of the poor had come entirely at the expense of the top tenth of the world's wealthiest peo-ple, the latter's share of global household income would still be . . . 69.1 times the per capita income of the poorest half." He asks: "Would this not have been good enough for us? Are we leading better, happier lives with those extra 2 percent of global household income?"[65]

US policies have largely ignored that world poverty is people's "greatest source of avoidable human misery."[66] As the Cold War ended and the United States faced no serious strategic competitors or threats, tens of billions of dollars could have been

---

[61] Thomas Pogge, *Politics as Usual* (London: Polity, 2010), 2.
[62] Pogge, *Politics as Usual*, 2.
[63] Pogge, *Politics as Usual*, 4–5.
[64] It is currently at 3 percent. Pogge, *Politics as Usual*, 3–5.
[65] Pogge, *Politics as Usual*, 5.
[66] Pogge, *Politics as Usual*, 11.

moved from annual military expenditures to ending poverty and in so doing could have enhanced world security enormously. Instead, approximately 18 million people have been allowed to die *each year* from hunger and remediable diseases, 360 million over the two decades following the end of the Cold War.[67] These poverty-related deaths could have been easily prevented through better nutrition, drinking water, sanitation, and existing, but not readily available, medicines and vaccines. Children under the age of 5 account for over half of the deaths. Over a billion human beings are chronically undernourished. Nearly that number do not have safe drinking water and lack adequate shelter. Over 2.5 billion lack basic sanitation;[68] 774 million unschooled adults remain unable to read.[69]

Because the lives of people everywhere on Earth are affected by the elaborate trade and tariff relationships, cross-border investments, currency manipulations, and use of natural resources in producing consumer goods, those who participate in the international economic system, which certainly includes everyone in the wealthy countries, are morally implicated in the influence that the system exerts in perpetuating poverty, because they and their governments are responsible for designing, imposing, and continuing to use this poverty-maintaining system. Wealthy countries eagerly buy oil, timber, copper, and other natural resources, paying authoritarian leaders large sums, who in turn pay large amounts back to wealthy countries willing to export weapons to them, which they use to keep themselves in power and to resist local initiatives for democracy and social justice. A simple, poverty-reducing alternative strategy would be for wealthy purchasers of raw materials to insist that some of the sales proceeds go to help the poor in the raw-material exporting country.

Over 3 billion people, approximately 45 percent of the world's population, live below the World Bank's poverty line, drawn at a consumption level below the purchasing power of $2.50 a day.[70] Despite the staggering numbers, the collective shortfall of these people's poverty line easily could be overcome by redirecting only 2 percent of global household income. This amount "could wholly eradicate the severe poverty that currently blights the lives of nearly half the human population."[71] Such a shift could be implemented without much cost to the rich but with enormous benefit to poor and rich alike, when one recognizes that 10 percent of the world's highest paid people take in 71.1 percent of global household income while the bottom 10 percent bring in only 0.26 percent, an incomprehensible inequality of 273 to 1. There simply is no prudential argument, let alone any moral or religious justification, for maintaining this grotesque

---

[67] Pogge, *Politics as Usual*, 11.

[68] Food and Agricultural Organization of the United Nations, "1.02 Billion People Hungry," June 19, 2009, www.fao.org/news/story/en/item/20568/icode/; WHO and UNICEF, *Progress on Drinking Water and Sanitation* (2017), 7, 30, https://www.unicef.org/reports/progress-on-drinking-water-sanitation-and-hygiene-2019; Pogge, *Politics as Usual*, 11.

[69] Pogge, *Politics as Usual*, 11; UNESCO, Institute for Statistics, "Literacy Topic," 1, 2008, www.uis.unesco.org/ev.php?.

[70] Based on what $2.50 would buy in the United States in 2005.

[71] Pogge, *Politics as Usual*, 12.

inequity. Yet US citizens are routinely asked by US officials to accept this morally and politically unacceptable equation and to amass sufficient military might to perpetuate this unfair international system.[72]

3.3 MISALIGNING ECONOMIC COMPETITION AND COOPERATION

Third, in recent years United States support has wavered for cooperative trade agreements encouraging free trade and economic integration regionally and globally. US policies have been lukewarm toward the European Union, negative toward the North American Free Trade Agreement (NAFTA), and hostile toward the Trans Pacific Partnership (TPP)[73] from which the United States withdrew. President Trump even declared an end to US negotiating multilateral trade agreements.

The trans-Pacific agreement, which was painstakingly negotiated during the Obama administration, represented what many objective experts thought was a reasonable set of US benefits in return for some necessary compromises. It was ready to begin working when President Trump and Republicans took control of the executive and legislative branches of government. Independent economic experts said the Pacific partnership would have contributed to US economic growth and enhanced US influence in Asia by reassuring friends and adversaries that the United States is a resident power in Asia and the Pacific. In withdrawing, US officials increased uncertainty among US corporations and caused allies to doubt the reliability of US commitments on foreign and economic matters. Most significantly, it abandoned an active US role in the hugely important Asian-Pacific area and left the field of influence wide open for others to exploit after the United States withdrew from the trade scene that it at one time had championed. As a result, the United States chose not to be a part of other trade agreements, including the EU-Japan Free Trade Agreement and the 16-nation trade agreement between East Asian countries, which provided preferential trading arrangements that the United States gave up. By abandoning the Asian Pacific venture Washington officials in practice turned over the reins of economic leadership in Asia to China. The US response to expanding Chinese power has been to demand that the United States spend more on military preparedness and try to counter China by making threats. Mild forms of broadly multilateral economic integration, engaging 16 countries, have been rejected while two-country militarily adversarial relations take center stage.

Although a new agreement has been worked out between the United States, Mexico, and Canada to replace NAFTA, stronger overall US support for cooperative trade practices throughout the world could encourage international cooperation, political

---

[72] See Branko Milanović, *Worlds Apart: Measuring International and Global Inequality* (Princeton, NJ: Princeton University Press, 2005), 107–108; Pogge, *Politics as Usual*, 205, note 15.

[73] The agreement included the United States, Japan, Mexico, Canada, Australia, New Zealand, Vietnam, Peru, Chile, Malaysia, Singapore, and Brunei.

understanding, and transnational politico-economic integration, while helping to build peace and security.[74]

3.4 MISALIGNING ENVIRONMENTAL ASSETS AND ENVIRONMENTAL NEEDS

A fourth set of misalignments between US power and its security interests has been the US refusal to take reasonable steps to ensure a healthy environment and respect for environmental human rights, steps that would reduce future threats from extreme temperatures and rising seas, changing climate, dwindling fresh water, and many species' tenuous health. Most notably, the United States refused to embrace the Kyoto limits on carbon emissions in 2001, and 16 years later US officials, with strong support from congressional Republicans, pulled out of the Paris agreement to protect people's right to a congenial climate and environmental health—an agreement that the United States had helped to write and previously accepted. With actions that were insulting and offensive to many US allies, US officials denigrated the efforts of supporters of the Paris accord to limit environmental destruction and to view the agreement as the best possible global initiative to avoid the worst dangers of climate change. Because the United States over time has been the biggest cumulative polluter in history, its withdrawal from this initiative, after never embracing Kyoto guidelines, caused a devastating impact on the collective environmental effort.

Re-joining the agreement is clearly a step forward. The challenge in the Biden administration is for the United States not only to meet but also to exceed its former goals in order to make up for lost time. John Kerry will face challenges from former US officials, corporate leaders, and citizens who oppose reasonable environmental protections because they fear these would interfere with their profits and economic advantages. Many had complained that the Kyoto guidelines were not fair because some developing countries were not participating, although the latter argued that they had not financed large-scale industrialization historically by ignoring its impact on the environment, as many industrialized countries had done. If the United States, the wealthiest economy in the world, which historically gained significant wealth by polluting freely, claims that it cannot afford to meet minimal goals specified by most of humanity, who can? If the United States can afford to cooperate more fully but chooses not to, who will feel they should sacrifice more than the United States?

The fluctuating nature of various presidents' values and identities helps explain the US record on the environment. Narrow nationalism led the George W. Bush

---

[74] See, for example, Håvard, Hegre, John R. Oneal, and Bruce Russett, "Trade Does Promote Peace: New Simultaneous Estimates of the Reciprocal Effects of Trade and Conflict," *Journal of Peace Research* 47, no. 6 (2010): 763–774; Russett and Oneal, *Triangulating Peace*; Jon Pevehouse and Bruce Russett, "Democratic International Governmental Organizations Promote Peace," *International Organization* 60, no. 4 (2006): 969–1000.

administration to reject the Kyoto guidelines for carbon emissions to which 192 other states agreed. Somewhat healthier nationalism led Barack Obama's administration to negotiate and commit to voluntary guidelines for carbon emissions in the Paris agreement of 2015. The Donald Trump administration, motivated by extremely narrow nationalism and wealth-aggrandizement, attacked the Paris agreement that 195 other countries had signed. The United States, with the active support of many conservatives in Congress, withdrew from the accord even though for the first time in history a single agreement had brought all countries into a common, cooperative effort to address climate change and assist developing countries to participate. This agreement charted a new direction in a unified global effort to protect the environment, yet the United States pulled out of it to allow US corporations the opportunity to make a bit more profit, to encourage them to re-finance and re-elect the political elite serving them, and to enable a narcissistic leader to feel the self-satisfaction of rejecting something his predecessor had favored.

Withdrawing from the painstakingly negotiated accord signed by all other countries of the world lacked rational foundation or moral justification. All commitments in the accord are voluntary anyway, so the United States could have remained within the accord while adjusting its own goals for carbon emission, if that turned out to be necessary. US policy appeared to teach other societies to try to amass as much wealth as they could as fast as they could without regard for how it harms others and ourselves, even when it causes irreversible disaster for the human race. Although the Paris agreement constituted a major positive achievement, its standards needed to be raised and probably made more obligatory to enable humanity to avoid major environmental destruction already under way. This remains the challenge for US citizens even after the United States has rejoined and all countries participate.

Serious long-term security costs often arise from short-sighted US environmental policies and failures to moderate profit motivation to ensure that it does not bring ecocide.[75] When under immediate pressure to address security problems that have arisen from environmental deterioration, national security managers understandably show more willingness to send US soldiers into harm's way than to address underlying environmental destruction that has precipitated violence. For example, the Obama and Trump administrations deployed US military personnel to Niger, where 71 died

---

[75] One unfortunate example is the way that profit-taking manufacturers of chemical insecticides and herbicides have spread them so pervasively that global food production has been harmed, poisoning organisms essential to food production, from bees to earthworms. To kill natural organisms that create healthy soils causes calamity for biodiversity, ecological sustainability, food security, and even human health. See Task Force on Systemic Pesticides, *Report: Worldwide Integrated Assessment of the Impact of Systemic Pesticides on Biodiversity and Ecosystems*, www.tfsp.info/worldwide-integrated-assessment; Springer Link, "Worldwide Integrated Assessment," https://link.springer.com/article/10.1007/s11356-014-3220-1https://oaq.qc.ca/wp-content/uploads/2016/03/TaskForce_Pesticide.pdf; Stephen Gill, "At the Historical Crossroads—Radical Imaginaries and the Crisis of Global Governance," in *Critical Perspectives on the Crisis of Global Governance: Reimagining the Future*, ed. Stephen Gill (New York: Palgrave Macmillan, 2016), 187–190.

in 2019,[76] because ISIS sympathizers were gathering there and violently intimidating those who grazed herds in the northern part of the country. Yet the underlying reason for violent conflict was the frightening expansion of desertification and the shocking reality, largely ignored in the United States, that climate change, accepted to expand profits, was permanently decreasing arable land and rainfall for use in farming and grazing. In addition, population growth, which is more common among the economically dispossessed throughout the world, puts more people pressure on less productive land. The decline of farming as the desert expands, combined with rising population, leads to violence along desert perimeters and to migration pressures on North Africa and Europe. In response to these and analogous circumstances throughout much of the world living on the margins of survival, the United States ignored the Kyoto guidelines and, until the Biden presidency, the Paris accord which together offered the last, best hope of slowing further desertification and climate change.

Parts of West Africa have already suffered a sharp decrease in rainfall and an increase in average temperature of 2 degrees Celsius, the ceiling set by the international community.[77] The Paris accord aimed to hold to 2 degrees Celsius the increase in average temperature for the entire planet by 2100. In addition, US officials callously slashed funding for family planning and birth control initiatives in Africa and have scarcely supported funding for public education in Africa, all of which reduce the rate of population growth. The bottom line: US decisions have given more priority to being prepared to fight the people whom it thinks threaten its economic and power interests than to serving human needs and environmental health which, if funded adequately, would be a more effective antidote to high fertility rates, immigration pressures, rising temperatures, polarization, and violence.

3.5 MISALIGNING THE POWER OF LAW AND GLOBAL SECURITY

A fifth area of misaligning power and purpose is a failure to use international law effectively to improve conduct. Although most US officials and citizens see themselves as law-abiding members of the international community and want other states to obey international law, for the past half century, following the US-led burst of institution-building in the immediate wake of World War II, the United States has not had any grand strategy to develop a more effective international legal system, to strengthen and democratize international intergovernmental organizations, or to buttress the work of the International Court of Justice and the International Criminal Court— the two leading judicial institutions that judge, respectively, conduct by states and conduct by individuals to distinguish legal from illegal behavior. In some areas, the United States has actively undermined rather than strengthened international law.

---

[76] NPR report, "71 Soldiers Killed in Attack on Army Camp in Niger, December 12, 2019," www.npr.org/2019/12/12/787415274/71-soldiers-killed-in-attack-on-army-camp-in-niger.

[77] Thomas L. Friedman, "Trump, Niger, and Connecting the Dots," *New York Times*, October 31, 2017.

Yet the United States clearly "benefits . . . by having a robust body of international legal rules—rules for promoting peace, human rights, the environment, and prosperity."[78] This is in part because "threats to human security cannot be cabined within the borders of any one nation"[79] or even several nations. International laws are necessary to guide, authorize, or constrain.

Although the United States played a leadership role in establishing the United Nations and many international organizations following World War II and has participated in shaping most positive international law, in recent decades it has given up its leading role and become a foot-dragging, negative influence. Washington's failure to enhance international enforcement of laws prohibiting genocide, crimes against humanity, war crimes, and crimes against the peace—the very crimes for which Washington led the world in prosecuting German officials at Nuremberg after World War II—has been damaging to US security. To their credit, US officials have tried to bolster several treaties against international terrorism.[80] Yet these have not been incorporated into an overall international program to address causes of terrorist acts and to strengthen international law generally and to honor strictly the laws prohibiting the killing of civilians. It is not realistic to believe that the United States will be effective in leading international progress in law enforcement against non-state terrorists if it refuses to obey the laws that prohibit states' misconduct, and if Washington continues its refusal to join the International Criminal Court and support its efforts to enforce laws impartially against terrorism by any person throughout the world.

At its heart, "international law is fundamentally an idea—a social construct—like all law. Its power lies in our belief in its power."[81] The dominance of political realism has undermined policymakers' thinking about the utility of law in international relations. Mary Ellen O'Connell recommends that political realists' opposition to lawmaking be reversed to "reestablish the rule of law as the definition of national security, including first and foremost respect for the prohibition on the use of force." She points out that political realism is based on a misunderstanding that power is only "material."[82] How a state chooses to use power in the material sense depends on the cultural and ideational context in which it is exercised, a reminder that impartial law must govern material power for democratic values and human rights to survive.

Because international law is in part ideational and heavily influenced by custom, an indifferent attitude toward the formation of international law from the world's

---

[78] Mary Ellen O'Connell, *The Power and Purpose of International Law* (Oxford: Oxford University Press, 2008), 7, 130–131.

[79] Anne-Marie Slaughter, "Security, Solidarity, and Sovereignty: The Grand Themes of UN Reform," *American Journal of International Law* 99, no. 3 (2005), 627.

[80] Some international conventions against terrorism were written and ratified with US support after 2001. David Cortright and George A. Lopez, eds., *Uniting Against Terror: Cooperative Nonmilitary Responses to the Global Terrorist Threat* (Cambridge, MA: MIT Press, 2007).

[81] O'Connell, *Power and Purpose*, 131; Mary Ellen O'Connell, "Reestablishing the Rule of Law as National Security," in *Reimagining the National Security State: Liberalism on the Brink*, ed. Karen J. Greenberg (New York: Cambridge University Press, 2019), 154–168.

[82] O'Connell, "Reestablishing the Rule of Law," 168.

most influential country has constituted a profound impediment to international rule-making and robust legalization processes. Many opportunities have been lost even though some could have enhanced security, especially after the end of the Soviet Union and simultaneous increase in Chinese interest in playing a somewhat more constructive role in the world system.

The negative consequences of weak US support for lawmaking processes are especially problematic when the United States declines to ratify some treaties, fails to honor some international laws, is indifferent toward the ICJ, and opposes the ICC.

3.5.1. Rejecting Treaties

Stunning US opposition to lawmaking progress has arisen in a surprising number of multilateral treaties that have been negotiated, painstakingly in many cases, but that the United States has refused to ratify. Many of these are listed in Table 3.1, with the more consequential treaties indicated by an asterisk. Taken together, these efforts to establish a strong network of treaty law embody an overall strategy by progressive governments and international lawyers for increasing an effective role for international law in international relations. Of course, opponents to these treaties have reasons for not accepting them. Detailed analyses of the objections cannot be provided here, but in most cases the overriding general interest in strengthening the rule of law in a situation where most other democratic states favor it should weigh at least as heavily as the more narrowly self-interested arguments against ratification. In some cases—for example, the treaty to ban land mines—the humanitarian benefits of ratification and the added pressures on additional governments to ratify would seem to outweigh the "benefits" of the United States retaining military license to use anti-personnel land mines. The surprising number of treaties that have been signed but not ratified often indicates that the US diplomatic community and Department of State favored the international governance added by a particular treaty, but the conservative members of the US Senate opposed it.[83] They have for years routinely opposed making treaties legally binding and giving treaty provisions the force of law in the United States, even when doing so would advance the rule of law worldwide and strengthen the legal obligations of other states to abide by treaty obligations. This often could be an enormous benefit to US security and to an international right to influence other states.

Looking a bit more closely at several of these treaties can clarify the opportunities, which the United States has not utilized, to expand the rule of law. Not to join a treaty is not merely a neutral stance in most cases. It may have a profoundly negative influence because omitting the United States from formal support for a norm calls the norm into question for others, not simply for the United States.[84] The cumulative

---

[83] In some cases, the weight of the military-industrial complex also opposed the preferences of the Department of State and the arms control community.

[84] Custom exerts influence on the strength of the obligation that other states feel to comply with a particular international law.

TABLE 3.1

Treaties Not Ratified by the United States

1948—Freedom of Association and Protection of the Right to Organise Convention, not signed or ratified

1949—Right to Organise and Collective Bargaining Convention, not signed or ratified

1950—Convention for the Suppression of the Traffic in Persons and of the Exploitation of the Prostitution of Others, not signed or ratified

1951—Convention relating to the Status of Refugees, not ratified except for the 1967 protocol

1951—Equal Remuneration Convention, not ratified

1954—Convention relating to the Status of Stateless Persons, not signed or ratified

1958—Discrimination (Employment and Occupation) Convention, not ratified

1960—Convention against Discrimination in Education, not ratified

1961—Convention on the Reduction of Statelessness, not signed or ratified

1962—Convention on Consent to Marriage, Minimum Age for Marriage and Registration of Marriages, signed but not ratified

1964—Employment Policy Convention, not ratified

1966—*International Covenant on Economic, Social and Cultural Rights, signed but not ratified

1966—*Optional Protocol to the International Covenant on Civil and Political Rights, not signed or ratified

1969—*Convention on the Non-Applicability of Statutory Limitations to War Crimes and Crimes against Humanity, not ratified

1969—*Vienna Convention on the Law of Treaties, signed but not ratified

1972—*Anti-Ballistic Missile Treaty, signed but later withdrew in 2002

1973—International Labor Organization Minimum Age Convention, not ratified

1977—*American Convention on Human Rights, signed but not ratified

1977—*Protocol I (an amendment protocol to the Geneva Conventions), not ratified

1977—*Protocol II (an amendment protocol to the Geneva Conventions), not ratified

1979—*Convention on the Elimination of All Forms of Discrimination against Women, signed but not ratified

1979—*The Agreement Governing the Activities of States on the Moon and Other Celestial Bodies, commonly known as the Moon Treaty, not signed or ratified

1981—Occupational Safety and Health Convention, not ratified

1989—*Second Optional Protocol to the International Covenant on Civil and Political Rights, not signed or ratified

1989—*Convention on the Rights of the Child, signed but not ratified

1989—Basel Convention, signed but not ratified

1990—*United Nations Convention on the Protection of the Rights of All Migrant Workers and Members of Their Families, not signed or ratified

1991—*United Nations Convention on the Law of the Sea, not signed or ratified

1992—*Convention on Biological Diversity, signed but not ratified

(*continued*)

Table 3.1   Continued

1994—*Convention on the Safety of United Nations and Associated Personnel, signed but
   not ratified

1996—*Comprehensive Test Ban Treaty, signed but not ratified

1997—*Kyoto Protocol (to limit greenhouse gas emissions), signed with no intention to
   ratify

1997—*Ottawa Treaty (to ban land mines), not signed or ratified

1998—*Rome Statute of the International Criminal Court, signed by the Clinton
   administration but later unsigned by the Bush administration, neither intending to
   ratify

1999—*Optional Protocol to the Convention on the Elimination of All Forms of
   Discrimination against Women, not signed or ratified

1999—*Criminal Law Convention on Corruption, signed but not ratified

1999—Civil Law Convention on Corruption, not signed or ratified

2002—*Optional Protocol to the Convention against Torture, not signed or ratified

2006—*International Convention for the Protection of All Persons from Enforced
   Disappearance, not signed or ratified

2007—Convention on the Rights of Persons with Disabilities, signed but not ratified

2008—*Convention on Cluster Munitions, not signed or ratified

2011—Anti-Counterfeiting Trade Agreement, signed but not ratified

2013—*Arms Trade Treaty, signed but not ratified

2016—*Trans-Pacific Partnership (trade agreement), signed but US withdrew

2017—*Paris Agreement (on climate protection), signed but US withdrew, then rejoined

Source: "List of treaties unsigned or unratified by the United States," https://en.wikipedia.org/wiki/
List_of_treaties_unsigned_or_unratified_by_the_United_States.

strengthening of treaty law, aided by US ratifications, is necessary both to reduce the range of issues that now lend themselves to military threats and to move state conduct generally toward less reliance on military power in resolving conflicts. US failure to seize legalization opportunities is due to intellectual inertia, narrow nationalism, and habitual opposition to the growth of international law grounded in unrealistic faith that unbridled separate sovereignties, relying on military self-help, is the preferred method for managing global problems.

Since 1991, the Law of the Sea Treaty has been working to bring the planet's first reliable order to using the world's oceans. It defines the extent of sovereignty of coastal states beyond their land territory and the rights of such states over the sea-bed and subsoil, aiming to lessen the chances for conflict on the high seas and the continental shelf, including places like the South China Sea. One hundred sixty-seven governments have ratified this constitutive treaty, but not the United States, even though the US Department of Defense, the oil industry, environmentalists, and past US presidents from both parties have supported the treaty. Senate Republicans have blocked its ratification,[85] thereby making nonviolent conflict resolution, specified in the treaty, more difficult and less likely. US refusal to ratify also reduces US leverage in disputes with China over rights in the South China Sea.

By not ratifying the treaty, the United States has refused legally binding support of treaty language that says it is committed to "the desire to settle, in a spirit of mutual understanding and cooperation, all issues relating to the law of the sea" and honors "the historic significance of this Convention as an important contribution to the main-tenance of peace, justice, and progress for all peoples of the world."[86] US rejection of treaty ratification undermines detailed dispute resolution provisions designed to but-tress "three basic principles: (1) the peaceful resolution of disputes, (2) a high degree of flexibility in choice of dispute resolution mechanisms and (3) compulsory dispute resolution where States are unable to settle a dispute on their own."[87] These are pre-cisely the principles that the United States should have been doing everything in its power to make part of an informal global "constitution." But it has not been able to align itself fully with this exemplary conduct. Another major disadvantage is that the United States is the only Arctic country that has not had its claims to the continental shelf vetted and approved by the relevant UN Law of the Sea commission.

To take a second example, the Comprehensive Nuclear-Test-Ban Treaty, noted above, aims at "constraining the development and qualitative improvement of nuclear weap-ons and ending the development of advanced new types of nuclear weapons."[88] It bans "any nuclear weapon test explosion."[89] Since 1996, conservative senators have blocked the ratification of this important treaty, even though it has been ratified by Russia, the United Kingdom, France, and 163 other states and would employ legal means, aided by effective inspection for verification of obligations, to deter additional states from developing nuclear weapons. Rather than turn this draft treaty into law to help deter other states from testing, the Department of Defense, Department of Energy, and Republican senators, usually with the help of a few conservative Democrats, want to spend between one and two trillion dollars to build a new generation of nuclear weap-ons and delivery systems.

Third, since 1989, the Convention on the Rights of the Child, one of the most widely respected and ratified human rights treaties in world history, has been trying to protect children around the world. Like the Law of the Sea treaty, it was negotiated with exten-sive input by US officials during the Reagan and George H. W. Bush administrations.

---

[85] Ratifying the United Nations Convention on the Law of the Sea might have little direct effect on the South China Sea dispute, but it would put the weight of the United States clearly on the side of legal management of the oceans and nonviolent settlement of any disputes that arise.

[86] United Nations Convention on the Law of the Sea, "Preamble," 1833 U.N.T.S. 397, http://www.un.org/depts/los/convention_agreements/texts/unclos/preamble.htm.

[87] See Part XV of the Convention, Fletcher School, Tufts University, *Law of the Sea*, "LOSC Dispute Resolution Provisions," https://sites.tufts.edu/lawofthesea/chapter-nine/.

[88] United Nations Convention on the Law of the Sea, "Preamble."

[89] United Nations Convention on the Law of the Sea, Article 1.

One hundred ninety-four countries have ratified it, but US conservatives have blocked its ratification because, in addition to opposing legal obligations on the United States in general, they claim it would harm the rights of parents, a claim that the rest of the world's societies have not found to be true.

Fourth, the Convention on the Elimination of all Forms of Discrimination against Women (CEDAW) is an international bill of rights for women, a treaty adopted in 1979 by the United Nations General Assembly. This treaty prohibits restrictions made on the basis of sex that impair the enjoyment by women, on a basis of equality with men, of human rights and fundamental freedoms in the political, economic, social, cultural, civil, or any other field. The treaty requires states to try to eliminate prejudices and customs based on the idea of the inferiority or the superiority of one sex or on stereotypical roles for women and men. It calls for an end to all forms of trafficking of women. It guarantees women equality in political and public life. It calls for equal opportunity in education for female students. The right to work is described as "an unalienable right of all human beings" and requires equal pay for equal work. It calls on states to grant women equal economic rights and to guarantee "women equality with men before the law."[90]

Conservatives have opposed the treaty by arguing that it would reduce US sovereignty by making women's human rights legally binding in the United States, undermine capitalism by asking equal pay for equal work, increase access to abortion, and call into question traditional roles for men and women. Although the treaty has been ratified by 189 other states, US opponents have blocked ratification for over 40 years, placing the United States in legal circles with three other opponents: Iran, Somalia, and Sudan. The United States is the only democracy in the world that has not ratified it. Several dozen states that did ratify the treaty have placed a reservation on enforcement Article 29 which explains various non-military means for settling disputes concerning the interpretation of the Convention. The United States could have adopted this reservation also, if it feared enforcement of norms against discrimination, but it has rejected this option also. In addition to losing the benefit that the treaty might have on human rights in the United States, there are significant losses in progress with international legalization processes because the United States cannot make a strong case for women's rights in other countries, given its own refusal to ratify this treaty.

Fifth, the Convention on the Rights of Persons with Disabilities applies many standards found in US law to other countries. Most veterans' groups and corporations support its ratification, as do 141 other countries that have ratified it. Conservative members of Congress have blocked its ratification, fearing that it would interfere with local control of education and somehow increase abortion.

Widespread US opposition to strengthening treaty law arises from fear that accepting reasonable legal constraints on US behavior in return for reciprocal constraints on

---

[90] "Convention on the Elimination of All Forms of Discrimination Against Women," www.ohchr.org/EN/ProfessionalInterest/Pages/CEDAW.aspx.

the misconduct of others would not be a good bargain. Opponents view placing state conduct in a legal framework, such as ratification of a treaty, as loss of US sovereignty,[91] as if sovereignty were an unchanging, quantitative attribute of a state, and that its constancy must be assured. This widespread faith in the virtue of sovereignty needs re-examination for three reasons. First, some aspects of sovereignty cannot be held constant simply because of technological changes, such as the extent of a country's airspace above its national territory. Whether wanted or not, US airspace has been reduced by the invention of earth satellites. Cyberattacks are another example of technological change placing a security threat simultaneously outside of US national jurisdiction and yet inside our most revered and secretive institutions. Second, although legal guidelines for international cooperation do exact some specification about how sovereignty should and should not be exercised, a positive specification for what a national sovereign may do, when written into a treaty on the rights of the child, for example, prohibiting children from being recruited into military activity before they reach age 15, does not need to be viewed as "undermining US sovereignty." It could be viewed as expanding US sovereign influence throughout the world in protecting children's human rights. It potentially extends an element of US sovereignty into the conduct of every other sovereignty in the world that ratifies the treaty on the rights of the child because it prohibits child soldiers. In one sense a treaty obligation may be a worldwide formal acceptance of a value that the United States holds dear for itself, combined with a confirmation that the same value will guide the conduct of others. It is like the formulation of a good law.

Of course, the treaties in Table 3.1 that the United States has not ratified lists only those legal innovations that made it into the form of a treaty ratified by a majority of countries. There have been many more legal initiatives than those listed there, ideas that progressive governments favored but that were never written into treaty language because of Washington's early opposition. A foot-dragging superpower quickly discourages smaller states from trying to take new legal initiatives.

In any case, the premature opposing of smaller states' efforts to establish positive legal agreements, as well as refusing to ratify already negotiated treaties, harms both the growth of international institutions' governing ability and the governability of world society. Non-ratification of a treaty is easier to mark, but preventing negotiations from moving forward and from ever bearing fruit can be no less harmful.

Another revealing example of US officials' obstructing universal enforcement of international law was the intense US pressure that Washington imposed on Belgium to rescind a law it adopted in 1993 to allow victims of gross violations of human rights from anywhere in the world to file their legal cases in Belgium. This was a Belgian effort to establish a legal foundation for *universal jurisdiction* to be exercised over especially egregious crimes that victims could not prosecute in their own countries or other venues, usually because of tyrannical governments. Under the Belgian law, such crimes

---

[91] Jett, "Republicans Are Blocking."

committed in other countries could be prosecuted in Belgium if circumstances enabled prosecution and defense to go forward there.

After a decade of intense US pressure,[92] aimed not at advancing the enforcement of international law but instead at rolling back what limited strength universal jurisdiction already had gained, Belgium rescinded its law. In contrast, the United States has had no problem with universal jurisdiction for maritime piracy. Yet presumably one reason for US pressure on Belgium was a concern that former US officials traveling there might be subject to legal inquiries into whether they had committed war crimes. However, if the price of eventually eliminating war crimes by officials of every country throughout the world would be for the United States to support legal processes establishing universal jurisdiction over crimes that the United States has always claimed not to be committing anyway, would it not be a price worth paying?

Overall, US conduct has been especially egregious, in terms of undermining possibilities for increasing the role of international law in order to reduce the role of military power, by refusing

- to accept the compulsory jurisdiction provisions of the International Court of Justice;
- to ratify the Rome Statute establishing the International Criminal Court;
- to ratify the Law of the Sea Treaty;
- to ratify the Comprehensive Nuclear Test Ban agreement;
- to accept a treaty ban on further production of weapons-grade nuclear material;
- to negotiate a ban on unrestricted modernization of nuclear weapons;
- to outlaw the first use of nuclear weapons;
- to negotiate mutual, verifiable nuclear arms reductions for all nuclear-weapons states (as required by Article VI of the Nuclear Non-Proliferation Treaty);[93]
- to seek strict limitations on the manufacture, possession, and use of attack drones;[94]
- to negotiate a ban on deploying weapons of mass destruction in space; and
- to ratify the convention banning anti-personnel land mines.[95]

---

[92] Richard W. Mansbach and Kirsten L. Rafferty, *Introduction to Global Politics* (New York: Routledge, 2008), 472.

[93] Treaty on the Non-Proliferation of Nuclear Weapons, Article VI, https://www.un.org/disarmament/wmd/nuclear/npt/.

[94] The Obama administration ordered more than 250 drone attacks in Pakistan from 2009 to 2012, during which more than 1,400 people were killed. Peter L. Bergen, "Warrior in Chief," *New York Times*, April 29, 2012, 4.

[95] The United States was a major world producer of land mines prior to the treaty banning them. Despite US opposition, those writing the Ottawa Treaty appeared to establish a new norm to constrain practice by the major military powers. Moreover, the process "would contradict the realist expectation, described by E. H. Carr, which characterizes international morality and law as the product of dominant nations or groups of nations." Matthew Evangelista, Henry Shue, and Tami Davis Biddle, *The American Way of Bombing: Changing Ethical and Legal Norms, from Flying Fortresses to Drones* (Ithaca, NY: Cornell University Press, 2014), 13. The reference to Carr is *The Twenty Years' Crisis* (New York: Perennial, 2001), 79. The norms prohibiting land mines were advanced by non-governmental organizations and small and medium-sized states, a good example of how legalization processes may sometimes "legislate" new norms.

One example of success from placing state conduct in an international legal framework, which suggests what could be done, has been the ratification of the Montreal Convention to limit chlorofluorocarbon emissions.[96] This has been ratified by all the world's major producers of the chemicals that it was designed to limit and has succeeded in countering the threatened destruction of the atmospheric ozone layer protecting humans, animals, and plants from excessive ultraviolent radiation. This innovation was aided by lawmaking initiatives that came from large corporations that developed a positive alternative to the use of chlorofluorocarbons.

3.5.2 *Violating Laws*

Another negative drag on the development of international law has occurred even where the United States has endorsed and ratified treaties, such as the United Nations Charter, the Geneva Conventions and their Additional Protocols, or the statute of the International Court of Justice, but later has failed to honor what it ratified. In some cases it deliberately has violated important norms, causing profoundly negative legal consequences, as the following examples illustrate.

First, at times the United States has violated perhaps the most important law of the international community, which is the prohibition of launching a war of aggression.[97] By invading Iraq in 2003, the United States violated its solemn obligation not to use force unless authorized by the Security Council or in a use that constitutes self-defense. Before the US attack, loyal allies like France and Germany warned that the UN Security Council had not endorsed the US proposal for war, nor would a US attack constitute an act of self-defense. US officials ignored these friendly evaluations of anticipated US behavior and the Security Council's refusal to endorse war. Even a preemptive US claim was not justifiable because there was no reasonable possibility of a surprise attack by Iraq against the United States. UN IAEA inspectors, who were in Iraq and reporting during the months that the United States prepared its invasion, could have reported any Iraqi preparations for attack. Also, Iraq lacked sufficient power projection capability to attack the United States.

The US violation of the prohibition against aggressive war not only has harmed US soldiers and Iraqis killed or injured in the US attack. It also has undermined the strength of the norm itself and reduces expectations that other countries will comply with the norm. No direct consequence can be shown to flow from US illegalities, but certainly subsequent criticisms of Russian aggression toward Ukraine and, more generally, of other governments' military misconduct have been weakened by US

---

[96] See Richard Elliot Benedick, *Ozone Diplomacy: New Directions in Safeguarding the Planet* (Cambridge, MA: Harvard University Press, 1991).

[97] United Nations Charter, Article 2 (4).

behavior.[98] US failure to uphold this norm will be discussed further below in the analysis of drone warfare.

Second, the Geneva Conventions and additional protocols define the rights of soldiers, civilians, and prisoners during wartime. They are the foundation of international law for humanitarian treatment in war. The United States had always sought to honor these until US compliance ended abruptly during the George W. Bush administration.[99] US officials in both the Bush and Trump administrations expressed willingness to use extreme methods that international observers have always considered torture, such as water boarding. President Bush asked the White House legal counsel to prepare lengthy legal memoranda justifying torture. The United States tortured prisoners in Iraq in violation of both international and domestic law. President Trump indicated willingness to do water boarding and what he called "much worse."[100]

Such conduct by US officials violates international humanitarian law and the right of US citizens to have a legal US foreign policy. It also takes away the US national security benefit of earlier times when soldiers of other countries more willingly surrendered to US armed forces than to any other country's army because they felt confident they would receive legal treatment as US prisoners of war.

Albert J. Mora, US Navy general counsel, has lamented the loss of a US moral consensus that the United States would never torture. Many people now "are of the view that cruel treatment, or even torture . . . should be applied against our enemies, or those who may possibly be our enemies." Indeed, "cruelty, once held in disrepute, has been astonishingly rehabilitated." Nonetheless, Mora argues "both as a matter of instinct and rational deliberation, we should be astonished that our nation has applied cruelty, . . . that such cruelty should have been authorized at the highest levels, by how easily this authorization was obtained, and by how completely those legal and policy safeguards that should have prevented this abuse failed." US citizens should also be moved "by how much acceptance and support there appears to be in our country for its use and how negligent and casual this acceptance has been both on the part of officials and citizens." In his view, "cruelty harms our nation's legal, foreign policy, and national security interests."[101]

Third, as indicated above, the United States has not acted in good faith to honor the nuclear Non-Proliferation Treaty, which calls on each of the parties to the treaty to negotiate a "cessation of the nuclear arms race" and to bring it "under strict and effective international control."[102] Although this treaty has been in force since 1968, the United States and other signatories have not moved toward nuclear arms reductions

---

[98] Weiss and Thakur, *Global Governance and the UN*, 88–89.

[99] David P. Forsythe, "United States Policy toward Enemy Detainees in the War on Terrorism," *Human Rights Quarterly* 28, no. 2 (2006): 465–491.

[100] Jenna Johnson, "Trump Says 'Torture Works,' Backs Waterboarding and 'Much Worse,'" *Washington Post*, February 17, 2016.

[101] Alberto J. Mora, *Ethical Considerations: Law, Foreign Policy, and the War on Terror* (New York: Carnegie Council for Ethics in International Affairs, 2007), 9.

[102] The text of the treaty may be accessed at https://www.un.org/disarmament/wmd/nuclear/npt/text.

even though this commitment was given by nuclear weapons states in return for a commitment from nonnuclear weapons states to refrain from developing nuclear weapons.

Fourth, beginning with the attack of an unmanned Predator in Afghanistan in 2002, US officials in the Bush, Obama, and Trump administrations have readily employed attack drones as a preferred counter-terrorism weapon because they are quick, relatively inexpensive, easily targeted in remote areas, and pose no direct threat to the lives of US commanders who sit hundreds of miles from combat zones. Drone warfare deserves careful attention because it illustrates so well how military preparedness, which officials and citizens seldom question, can inadvertently destroy vital legal fabric.[103] Often, what happens to US Predators and their prey occurs in secret, so there is not even any evaluation of these attacks until later when news may leak out about what actually happened. In some cases, US officials may not even know for sure.

Many people understandably feel proud of US technological virtuosity in developing drones and using them for constructive purposes such as aerial photography or humanitarian assistance. As attack vehicles, drones are valued because they enable the United States (or any attacker) to surveil disliked people in remote areas where it is impossible to place US military personnel directly and to move attack weapons undetected to any place on earth, easily crossing borders and difficult terrain to deliver explosives on any unsuspecting person that the attacker decides to kill. No permission is requested. No US soldiers will be killed. No post-attack investigation is likely to carry much weight.

Despite what appear to be the attractive qualities of these robotic killers, which their exponents believe do great harm to terrorists but no harm to the United States, in practice these weapons can desensitize their users' psyches and undermine security, because they have been destroying the rules specifying when it is legal to attack and the norms of right and wrong that have constrained the violence of war. US officials are deliberately using these versatile weapons in ways that dismantle most of the legal constraints on international violence that have been established over the past 150 years. Because the United States leads with technologies to develop these weapons and uses them frequently, it also leads in undermining international laws that US citizens and soldiers worked long and hard to establish to restrict international war and to protect civilians and soldiers. As the United States goes in violating rules, so goes much of the rest of the world. The United Kingdom, for example, moved to targeted killings by following the US example.[104]

---

[103] Rebecca Saunders, *Plausible Legality: Legal Culture and Political Imperative in the Global War on Terror* (New York: Oxford University Press, 2018).

[104] Mary Ellen O'Connell, "The Law on Lethal Force Begins with the Right to Life," *Journal on the Use of Force and International Law* 16, no. 2 (2016), 205–209.

Although drone attacks are not inherently illegal if used in conformity with usual expectations governing the cause and conduct of a justifiable war, the United States appears to have purposefully violated international norms in the following five areas.[105]

First, in addition to using drones in Afghanistan and Iraq where the United States has been formally at war, the United States has attacked people in countries with which the United States has been at peace. US drone strikes have killed or injured thousands of people in Iran, Libya, Pakistan, Somalia, Syria, and Yemen, "many of them civilians."[106] This kind of attack arguably violates the straightforward prohibition of aggressive war in the UN Charter.[107] The United States usually claims that its attacks are in self-defense, but an attack out of the blue on another country is not transformed into an act of self-defense simply because the attacking state suspects or accuses someone within that other country of harboring hostility toward US forward-based military deployments or Washington's support for disliked governments in the Middle East.[108]

Abandonment of the Charter standard defining the legitimate use of force represents a return to an ancient and essentially discretionary, lawless approach to uses of force and recourse to war. Some international lawyers have noted that "the world would be chaotic if what the United States is claiming is lawful for its undertakings . . . is undertaken by other states."[109] Indeed, the precedents being set by the United States are likely to be relied on both by aggressive states and by terrorist organizations to evade efforts to maintain any legal order at all.[110] A detailed study by the International Bar Association reported that "the massive unlawful use of dronesextraterritorially may constitute an act of aggression in manifest violation of the Charter of the UN, giving rise to individual criminal responsibility [of officials] for the crime of aggression."[111] Their uses of force could "produce the individual criminal responsibility of

---

[105] For a detailed discussion of the ethical, legal, and strategic consequences of these weapons, see David Cortright, Rachel Fairhurst, and Kristen Wall, eds., *Drones and the Future of Armed Conflict* (Chicago: University of Chicago Press, 2015).

[106] Ruth Blakeley, "Drones, State Terrorism and International Law," *Critical Studies on Terrorism* 11, no. 2 (2018): 322, https://www-tandfonline-com.proxy.library.nd.edu/doi/full/10.1080/17539153.2018.1456722; Marjorie Cohn, "Introduction: A Frightening New Way of War," in *Drones and Targeted Killing: Legal, Moral, and Geopolitical Issues*, ed. Marjorie Cohn (Northampton, MA: Olive Branch Press, 2015), 14.

[107] UN Charter, Article 2(4).

[108] The self-defense argument arises from the Authorization for the Use of Military Force Act drafted by the George W. Bush administration following the 9/11 attacks. It is very broad and authorizes the US military to attack any country or non-state actor involved in the 9/11 attacks. This national authorization should not automatically override the international laws in treaties, such as the UN Charter, that the Constitution declares are part of the supreme law of the land.

[109] Richard Falk, "Why Drones Are More Dangerous than Nuclear Weapons: Threats to International Law and World Order," in *Drones and Targeted Killing: Legal, Moral, and Geopolitical Issues*, ed. Marjorie Cohn (Northhampton, MA: Olive Branch Press, 2015), 43.

[110] Falk, *Power Shift*, 71.

[111] The International Bar Association, Human Rights Institute, "The Legality of Armed Drones Under International Law," *Background Paper* (May 25, 2017), 44, www.ibanet.org/Human_Rights_Institute/council-resolutions.aspx.

the perpetrators, who could be prosecuted before the ICC . . . or before a competent national jurisdiction."[112]

Recurring US violations of this basic rule in international relations will destroy it eventually. Such conduct undermines expectations that others must honor the rule against aggressive attacks, even though that is a necessity to maximize peace and security. US drone policies destroy the line between war and peace, making a surprise attack at any time and in any place on Earth the life that US officials are asking people to accept and that they too must accept. The United States is bending international law to make more legal space for what could be called "state terrorism."[113] For US officials to embrace state terror in a war against non-state terror "makes war into a species of terror, and tends toward making all limits on force seem arbitrary, if not absurd."[114]

Drone warfare decisions also are in practice beyond the reach of constitutional constraints. No declaration of war by Congress is expected. They are beyond the reach of domestic law also, because decisions to kill arise from the non-reviewable discretion of a closed circle of executive branch officials. Official justifications for their violent responses to subjective threat assessments boil down to "trust us." Because subjectivity surrounds most threat perceptions that officials use in drone warfare, such warfare undermines the centuries-long effort to limit uses of violence to objectively determined claims of self-defense that can be reviewed by friend and foe to determine their reasonableness.

Second, US drone attacks also do not differentiate carefully between (1) combatants, who could be legal targets if they live in a country with which the United States is at war, and nearby (2) civilians, who are not legal targets, thereby undermining the law of civilian immunity and seeming to endorse civilian killings. US policies have killed many civilians. Although reliable data are difficult to find, in part because the United States has at times considered any adult male who is killed to be a terrorist, the Bureau of Investigative Journalism estimates that since it began keeping records in 2002, a number ranging from 910 to 2,200 civilians have been killed in drone attacks, of which from 283 to 454 were children, of the total deaths of 8,858 to 16,901.[115] Air Wars estimated that the United States killed more than 6,238 civilians in drone strikes across Iraq and Syria alone.[116] A Council on Foreign Relations study reported that although some high profile leaders were killed in attacks, "most were low-level, anonymous

---

[112] International Bar Association, "Legality of Armed Drones," 40–41.

[113] Blakeley, "Drones," 84.

[114] Falk, *Power Shift*, 71.

[115] Bureau of Investigative Journalism, https://www.thebureauinvestigates.com/projects/drone-war. The time covered is from 2002 to 2020. Critics think the Bureau uses an expansive definition of combatants. The Bureau also reported that the United States has launched a minimum of 13,694 drone attacks since the Bureau began keeping records in 2002, with the range of total killed from 8,845 to 16,749 people. US Senator Lindsey Graham reported that 4,756 people had been killed by US unmanned vehicles up to February 2013. Amanda Terkel, "Lindsey Graham: Drone Strikes Have Killed 4,700 People," *New York Times*, February 21, 2013.

[116] "The Air Wars program tracks strikes in Iraq, Syria and Libya," https://airwars.org/. See also Blakeley, "Drones," 322.

suspected militants who were predominantly engaged in insurgent or terrorist operations against their governments, rather than in active international terrorist plots."[117]

Third, officials consider most drone attacks to be "targeted killings," which are, many
analysts agree, a euphemism for assassination by a state acting outside a battlefield or
judicial process. These extrajudicial executions are prohibited by both international
human rights law and the international law of war. Assassinations violate US law prescribed for soldiers in the US Army Field Manual.[118] The International Bar Association
notes that such killings also violate "the right to life."[119] The Bar Association also points
to the requirement of the Geneva Conventions that governments conduct an investigation into any of its citizens, including officials, who may have ordered or carried
out civilian killings that would amount to war crimes. Regardless of disagreement as
to numbers, there is no question that many civilians have been killed. Yet in 30 US
drone strikes in which civilians were killed or injured in Afghanistan, Gaza, Pakistan,
Somalia, and Yemen, "all . . . went without being investigated."[120]

Fourth, US policies do not enable any due process proceedings for those whose
names are placed on "kill lists." Although putting a notorious killer on the list of future
targets is not controversial, selection of other people is more subjective and less certain.[121] These extrajudicial processes have led to some decisions based on unreliable
evidence. Some people placed on target lists in the Obama administration apparently
were only "under suspicion" of wrongdoing, although they often were in the "wrong
places."[122]

Without in any way endorsing the horrendous violence done by perpetrators of terrorist acts against the United States or its allies, this process of deciding whom to kill in
countries with which the United States is not at war surely must cheapen the value of
life, because there is no process for reviewing kill decisions made by a very small number of people making the decision. Often there may be only one: the president. There is
no presumption of innocence for those under suspicion, no right of defense, no trial or

---

[117] Micah Zenko, *Reforming U.S. Drone Strike Policies*, Council Special Report no. 65, Council on Foreign
Relations (January 2013), i.cfr.org/content/publications/attachments/Drones_CSR65.pdf., 10. Italics
added. Also reported in Cohn, *Drones and Targeted Killing*, 20.

[118] The US Army's *Law of Land Warfare* quotes the 1907 Hague Convention and more recent executive
orders to declare that "This article is construed as prohibiting assassination." Field Manual 27–10: 85,
271, 378, A-5, A-24, A-41, A-70, A-118. https://web.archive.org/web/20041015013450/; http://www.afsc.
army.mil/gc/files/FM27-10.pdf.

[119] In those situations examined at the time of their study "in which the existence of an armed conflict is
not clear (Gaza, Pakistan, Somalia, Yemen, and possibly Libya), the use of drone strikes may be particularly problematic." International Bar Association, "Legality of Armed Drones," 35.

[120] International Bar Association, "Legality of Armed Drones," 38. Military documents leaked in 2015 suggest that a large majority of people killed have not been the intended targets. Approximately 13 percent
of those killed were intended targets, 81 percent were other suspected militants, and about 6 percent
were reported as civilians. *The Intercept* (October 15, 2015).

[121] Critics argue that to place any human being on a "kill" list outside the context of war is a questionable
decision because it is extra-judicial killing.

[122] Blakeley reports that individuals "appear to have been targeted on the basis of . . . patterns of suspect
behavior." Blakeley, "Drones," 329.

conviction. The time-honored human rights efforts to uphold civilian innocence and respect for the rule of law, especially in non-war settings, is completely disregarded.

There is also no systematic, impartial process to hold decision-making officials accountable for their actions or to follow up after attacks to investigate whether any of the killed met or did not meet what few selection criteria there were. Of course, there has been no process of appeal, even if a US citizen is targeted overseas. Strategies acceptable in war contexts may be too easily moved into situations where non-war processes should govern. As Georgetown University law professor Rosa Brooks testified before Congress: "When a government claims for itself the unreviewable power to kill anyone, anywhere on earth, at any time, based on secret criteria and secret information discussed in a secret process by largely unnamed individuals, it undermines the rule of law."[123]

Fifth, US drone policies undermine the purpose of the international bill of human rights to protect every person from cruel treatment.[124] A study by medical professionals of people living in communities familiar with drone attacks found that these strike deep fears into people. They frequently feel terrified, yet they are powerless to protect themselves. Many suffer post-traumatic stress disorder with hallucinations, emotional breakdowns, and insomnia.[125] They suffer anticipatory anxiety, fearing they could be the next victim killed or injured. On the basis of this report and additional evidence, the International Bar Association study of US drone policies concluded, "It is highly likely that drone use may amount to cruel, inhuman or degrading treatment or punishment" and therefore constitutes a fundamental violation of law.[126]

Treating civilians this way when they are living at home in non-war settings appears to constitute committing terrorist acts. Some critics report evidence that this terrifying effect on the population is intended by some US officials,[127] although of course not all. In order to disguise the probable lawlessness of US policy, the Bush, Obama, and Trump administrations have engaged in what their critics call "lawfare." This practice uses novel interpretations of law and "military necessity" to unravel the fabric of international humanitarian and human rights law to allow assassinations or targeted killings, attacking those only *suspected* of crimes, and accepting civilian killings, including the deaths of children. Critics say US officials have attempted "to conceal illicit actions, or in the event they are exposed, to shroud them in a veil of legitimacy."[128] Perhaps

---

[123] Rosa Brooks, "The Constitutional and Counterterrorism Implications of Targeted Killing," *Hearing Before the Senate Judiciary Subcommittee on the Constitution, Civil Rights, and Human Rights of the Senate Committee on the Judiciary*, 113th Congress (April 23, 2013), 19–20, www.judiciary.senate.gov/pdf/04-23-13BrooksTestimony.pdf. Also quoted by Cohn, *Drones and Targeted Killing*, 18.

[124] International Covenant on Civil and Political Rights, Article 7, https://www.ohchr.org/en/professionalinterest/pages/ccpr.aspx.

[125] International Human Rights and Conflict Resolution Clinic of Stanford Law School and Global Justice Clinic of New York University School of Law, *Living Under Drones: Death, Injury, and Trauma to Civilians from U.S. Drone Practices in Pakistan* (September 2012), 82–83.

[126] The International Bar Association, "Legality of Armed Drones," 35.

[127] Blakeley, "Drones," 324, 330.

[128] Blakeley, "Drones," 323.

recognizing that illegalities could be more easily practiced when the drone program was largely within the CIA, President Obama ended CIA involvement and placed drones under a single command within the Department of Defense. President Trump reversed that decision to enable drone attacks to occur without much oversight or accountability.

Despite the attractiveness of attack drones for exponents of a "war on terrorism," their corrosive effect on hard-earned legal limits on violence means that it would be desirable to find better ways to address acts of terror. To halt further unraveling of international laws that prohibit killing civilians, it would be useful to ground all attack drones and to address all terrorist acts of violence against civilians as crimes subject to international and national legal processes rather than as a "war against an 'ism,'" which is hardly ever winnable anyway. Tellingly, former US Ambassador Kurt Volker has concluded that "drone strikes . . . do not solve our terrorist problem." On the contrary, "drone use may prolong it. . . . In the long run the contributions to radicalization through drone use may put more American lives at risk."[129] A Council on Foreign Relations study noted a "strong correlation" between an increase in US drone attacks in Yemen, for example, and increased hostility there toward the United States.[130] Increases in drone attacks also correlated with increases in sympathy for and allegiance to Al-Qaeda in the Arabian Peninsula and led to ease of recruiting additional young people willing to attack the United States.[131] Many research studies show that drone strikes are often counter-productive and in fact exacerbate the conditions that spawn terrorism. Moreover, there are viable non-military means of countering violent extremism.[132]

A strong argument for shifting US focus away from drone attacks and toward reducing the causes of terrorist acts is that current US drone policies undermine the rule of laws on which the United States may someday want to lean. Current policies make it difficult for US officials effectively to object when other actors with drones begin to develop "kill lists" of persons those actors believe represent threats to them.[133] Prudence suggests changing policy from "no permission slip needed" to "permission

---

[129] Kurt Volker, "What the U.S. Risks by Relying on Drones," *Washington Post,* October 26, 2012, www. washingtonpost.com/opinions/we-need-a-rule-book-for-drones/2012/10/26/957312ae-1f8d-11e2-9cd5-b55c38388962_story.html.

[130] Cohn, *Drones and Targeted Killing,* 16.

[131] Micah Zenko, *Reforming U.S. Drone Strike Policies,* Council Special Report no. 65, Council on Foreign Relations Ctr. 14 (January 2013), i.cfr.org/content/publications/attachments/Drones_CSR65.pdf., 10; Cohn, *Drones and Targeted Killing,* 16; John Quigely in Cohn, *Drones and Targeted Killing,* 21, chapter 12.

[132] David Cortright and Rachel Fairhurst, "Winning Without War: Evaluating Military and Nonmilitary Strategies for Countering Terrorism," in *Drones and the Future of Armed Conflict,* ed. David Cortright, Rachel Fairhurst, and Kristen Wall (Chicago: University of Chicago Press, 2015).

[133] "The Constitutional and Counterterrorism Implications of Targeted Killing," *Hearing Before the Senate Judiciary Subcommittee on the Constitution, Civil Rights, and Human Rights of the Senate Committee on the Judiciary,* 113th Cong. 19–20 (April. 23, 2013), www.judiciary.senate.gov/pdf/04-23-13BrooksTestimony.pdf.

required." An international treaty banning attack drones could contribute to human security.[134]

3.5.3 *"Accepting" the International Court of Justice*

For more than 100 years, the international community has tried, half-heartedly much of the time, to expand the use of international judicial processes in settling disputes between national governments.[135] States created the Permanent Court of International Justice following World War I as a venue where governments might bring interstate disputes to be settled as a matter of law. The United States, held back by a conservative Senate, refused to join this court. Following World War II, the international community created the International Court of Justice (ICJ) as a second attempt to establish a more effective rule of international law. The court has the capacity to settle almost any legal dispute between any states *if* the parties are willing to let it do so. The United States joined the court this time, but rather than vigorously utilize legal settlement, the United States ratified the court's statute with a reservation that allowed the United States to decide whether the court has jurisdiction in any particular case. This in effect nullified the court's compulsory jurisdiction over any US cases.

The court's potential power lies in member states' acceptance of its legitimacy and compulsory jurisdiction over international legal disputes. Yet because many states have not accepted the court's compulsory jurisdiction, it seldom has the opportunity to resolve disputes that one party or another does not wish to bring to the court.[136]

Some countries, such as Norway, *have* accepted the "Optional Clause" of the court statute, which explicitly states that Norwegians recognize "as compulsory *ipso facto* and without special agreement, in relation to any other State accepting the same obligation, that is on condition of reciprocity, the jurisdiction of the International Court of Justice."[137] Norway does not appear to have suffered losses of its interests because of its acceptance of compulsory jurisdiction on the basis of reciprocity with other states. Similarly, it is unlikely that the United States or other countries would suffer negative consequences from also accepting reciprocal compulsory jurisdiction, because this action would strengthen the rule of law and give added weight to rulings of the court, thereby advancing the interests of all law-abiding states.[138]

---

[134] See Cohn, *Drones and Targeted Killing*, 20.

[135] Mary Ellen O'Connell and Lenore VanderZee, "The History of International Adjudication," in *The Oxford Handbook of International Adjudication*, ed. Cesare P. R. Romano, Karen J. Alter, and Yuval Shany (Oxford: Oxford University Press, 2013), DOI: 10.1093/law/9780199660681.003.0003.

[136] For a more comprehensive account, see O'Connell and VanderZee, "The History of International Adjudication."

[137] "Declarations Recognizing as Compulsory the Jurisdiction of the International Court of Justice under Article 36, paragraph 2, of the Statute of the Court," 12, https://treaties.un.org/doc/Publication/MTDSG/Volume%20I/Chapter%20I-4.en.pdf.

[138] Domestically, the consequences would be disastrous if courts did not have compulsory jurisdiction requiring disputing parties to settle in court.

To be sure, the International Court of Justice could not resolve some deeply politi-cized, polarized issues, because states would not perceive them as primarily legal in nature. Nonetheless, this acknowledgment is not a compelling reason to reject the court's compulsory jurisdiction in disputes that are primarily legal and with other states willing to accept the optional clause. The court can be genuinely useful in many disputes when states are willing to employ law to resolve differences. It could become more successful if enough citizens would insist that their governments accept com-pulsory jurisdiction and honor court decisions in order to settle disputes through legal means.

The US refusal to accept the court's compulsory jurisdiction in cases where the other party would also accept compulsory jurisdiction has been a negative legal force because the main problem in enhancing the role of international law is not the lack of adequate institutions and procedures for legal settlement. It is that there is no legal *duty* to use the court unless specific treaties call explicitly on parties to do so. If the United States had accepted the provision for compulsory jurisdiction and employed the court more frequently, the international community would almost certainly be at a different place now, with routinized uses of legal settlement, more legally binding guidelines on state conduct, and far less felt need to rely on military power for conflict resolution.

The United States has had an uneasy relationship with the court for decades. It has refused to comply with or respect court decisions and advisory opinions, including an important advisory opinion on the legal status of nuclear weapons. Although US soci-ety embraces the rule of law domestically and likes to view the United States as a law-abiding member of the international system, US practices toward the court have been at best equivocal and at times outside the law. Although the United States on occasion has participated in cases before the court, it "has never been willing to submit itself to the plenary authority of the Court, and has typically reacted negatively to decisions by the Court that are adverse to U.S. interests."[139]

A unilateral US rejection of the ICJ's jurisdiction in 1986 contradicted good legal process rather than fulfilled it. In *Republic of Nicaragua v. the United States of America*, the United States refused to accept the court's authority during a case already before it. Rather than honor whatever verdict the law brought forth, US officials withdrew from proceedings after the court rejected the US claim that the court lacked jurisdic-tion. Nicaragua had brought the case to stop illegal US conduct and obtain reparations for injuries when the United States mined Nicaraguan harbors in order to help the Contras overthrow the Nicaraguan government. The Reagan administration's action marked the first time the United States had walked out of a case being considered by the court. Some congressional Democrats, former officials, and independent interna-tional legal experts denounced the US action as "lawless," but without any effect.[140]

---

[139] Sean D. Murphy, *The United States and the International Court of Justice: Coping with Antinomies*, 1, http://scholarship.law.gwu.edu/cgi/viewcontent.cgi?article=1902&context=faculty_publications, accessed September 20, 2017.

[140] Stuart Taylor, "U.S. Plans to Quit World Court Case on Nicaragua Suit," *New York Times*, January 19, 1985.

The court later ruled that the United States had violated international law by supporting the Contras' violence against the Nicaraguan government and by mining Nicaragua's harbors. The United States was "in breach of its obligations under customary international law not to use force against another State," "not to intervene in its affairs," "not to violate its sovereignty," "not to interrupt peaceful maritime commerce," and "in breach of its obligations under Article XIX of the Treaty of Friendship, Commerce and Navigation between the Parties." The court called on the United States to "cease and to refrain" from its "unlawful use of force" against Nicaragua and ordered the United States to pay reparations.[141] The court also said that the United States had encouraged human rights violations by the Contras by providing them with training and a manual, *Psychological Operations in Guerrilla Warfare*. In addition to rejecting the court and the law, the United States also blocked the UN Security Council's mandate to enforce the court judgment. The United States never paid any reparations.

The United States also supported Israel's refusal to accept an ICJ advisory opinion to the UN General Assembly in which the court ruled that the "security fence" constructed by Israel on Palestinian land was illegal because in some places it annexed Palestinian territory and violated the human rights of Palestinians.

Because the ICJ is the world's only court established for the purpose of hearing general international law cases between states, dismissive US policies toward the court exert a deeply negative influence on the growth of international law and the practice of other states. To walk out of a court proceeding and flout a court judgment undermines the law and probably brings security consequences more grave than would have been incurred in paying reparations to Nicaragua. US political leaders gave no apparent weight to the lawlessness they encouraged, first, by violating the law against aggressive use of military force and, second, by preventing the Security Council from enforcing a duly authorized court decision.

3.5.4 *Rejecting the International Criminal Court*

In 2002 the international community created, for the first time in world history, a permanent International Criminal Court (ICC) to investigate and try individuals, including heads of government and military organizations, who are charged with the gravest of all crimes: genocide, war crimes, crimes against humanity, and crimes against the peace. In this treaty, commonly called the Rome Statute, 123 governments have sought to enforce laws prohibiting these crimes, typically of mass murder, and to deter future

---

[141] The Court found that the United States was "in breach of its obligations under customary international law not to use force against another State. . . , not to intervene in its affairs. . . , not to violate its sovereignty. . . , not to interrupt peaceful maritime commerce. . . ," and "in breach of its obligations under Article XIX of the Treaty of Friendship, Commerce and Navigation between the Parties signed at Managua on 21 January 1956." International Court of Justice, "Military and Paramilitary Activities in and against Nicaragua" (Nicaragua v. United States of America) Merits, Judgment, I.C.J. Reports (1986), 14; International Court of Justice, "Summary of the Judgment of 27 June 1986," retrieved September 5, 2006.

crimes by developing exemplary practices of international criminal justice. Because deterring gross violations of human rights and upholding justice are key ingredients of lasting peace, the work of the court can contribute also to long-term peace, stability, and equitable development, the foundation stones for building a future to protect human rights and maximize human freedom.

In the final round of negotiations to create a court, the United States joined China, Iraq, Israel, Libya, Qatar, and Yemen in voting against the treaty to establish the court.[142] From the court's beginning, the United States has undermined it, not only by refusing to participate but also by actively discouraging others from joining. Although the United States had signed the Rome Statute at the end of the Clinton administration to stay involved in deliberations, despite voting against the text, it made no effort to ratify the treaty because of deep hostility to it among conservatives in Congress. When the neo-conservatives of the George W. Bush administration took office in 2001, rather than try to amend the treaty to make it more acceptable to US officials, they said they would be delighted to "unsign" this foundational treaty. As John Bolton, President Bush's nominee for US ambassador to the United Nations, nullified the US signature on the treaty, he declared it "the happiest moment in my government service."[143] He said the United States would try to make the court "wither and collapse."[144] This intense attitude against aiding an expansion of the rule of law pervades the conservative mindset among US officials and supportive members of Congress and the public.

The international community's legal efforts to end impunity for officials of any nationality accused of mass murder could have been supported by the United States without harming any of its legitimate security interests. Instead, the United States has undermined the court because it opposes international enforcement of laws on US citizens. Conservatives do not want US military conduct to be subject to any external authority's examination. They fear that the mere existence of the court might have a cooling impact on US national security planners and soldiers for doing war-fighting if their strategies were to come under international scrutiny. Also, the Bush and Trump administrations did not want any additional international obligation to honor the Geneva Conventions against torture and mistreatment of prisoners of war, which the United States violated during the war with Iraq.

---

[142] The refusal of the United States to join the International Criminal Court and to accept fully the role of the International Court of Justice has done more to blunt the development of international enforcement than the similar refusals of China and Russia, which are less influential. The narrow nationalism of the United States also relieves China and Russia from international pressure to change their more authoritarian policies.

[143] Glenn Kessler and Colum Lynch, "Critic of U.N. Named Envoy," *Washington Post*, March 8, 2005; David Bosco, *Rough Justice: The International Criminal Court's Battle to Fix the World, One Prosecution at a Time* (Oxford: Oxford University Press, 2014), 73; Olivia Gazis, "In First Major Address, John Bolton Attacks Old Foes," *CBS News*, September 10, 2018, https://www.cbsnews.com/news/in-first-major-address-john-bolton-attacks-old-foe/; Susan E. Rice, "John Bolton: Tough Love or Tough Luck?," *Brookings*, March 8, 2005, https://www.brookings.edu/opinions/john-bolton-tough-love-or-tough-luck/.

[144] John R. Bolton, "No, No, No to the International Criminal Court," *Human Events* 54 (August 21, 1998), 2.

Even if external scrutiny of US military action occurred, of course, there would be nothing for anyone to fear if US conduct followed the international humanitarian and human rights laws that the United States has accepted as legally binding and instructs its soldiers to follow. In addition, the ICC would be unlikely to prosecute any US citizen because the ICC is a court of last resort, not first resort. It bears authority to try an accused person only if the accused's national courts are unable or unwilling to examine alleged crimes. The ICC simply does not prosecute citizens in any country where indigenous judicial processes are working.

In opposing this promising legal innovation, the United States did not merely refuse to join the world's first permanent court to try individuals for high crimes, which was the same initiative that it had vigorously led in prosecuting German officials of the Nazi government in the Nuremberg war crimes tribunal following World War II. The United States also worked intensely to discourage scores of states in Africa, Asia, and Latin America from supporting the ICC. It aggressively punished countries that moved toward ratifying the treaty, going to the extreme of cutting US assistance to countries that did ratify the Rome Statute. The Bush administration worked with anti-international law conservatives to design legislation, which Congress passed, to require the withdrawal of foreign assistance to countries refusing to do Washington's bidding that they not join the court. The legislation also stipulated that the United States would use military force to prevent any US nationals or US contract employees of other nationalities from ever being taken to The Hague for trial.[145]

The US record toward the court was especially pernicious in the first George W. Bush administration and again in the Trump administration because of intense hostility toward international enforcement of international law in general.[146] US officials who opposed making international law more effective inconsistently pointed in other contexts to the law's ineffectiveness in limiting misconduct to justify enormous military expenditures and quick resort to national military threats in international conflicts. Conservatives' opposition to the court was so strong and widespread that the Obama administration did not submit the treaty to the Senate for ratification even though the administration took a more positive attitude toward the court, recognizing that it could be used to prosecute officials accused of war crimes or crimes against humanity in Sudan, Libya, and Kenya.

After the ICC began collecting evidence of torture, rape and other possible crimes by people on all sides of the war in Afghanistan, the Trump administration took offense, since US forces were present in these war zones. The United States imposed economic and legal sanctions and travel restrictions on ICC staff looking into allegations. US Attorney-General William Barr reflected the breadth of US hostility to an impartial investigation of possible crimes in saying that US sanctions against ICC officials "are

---

[145] See Robert C. Johansen, "The Impact of U.S. Policy Toward the International Criminal Court on the Prevention of Genocide, War Crimes, and Crimes against Humanity," *Human Rights Quarterly* 28 (May 2006), 301–331.

[146] Johansen, "International Criminal Court," 310–331.

an important first step in holding the ICC accountable for exceeding its mandate and violating the sovereignty of the United States."[147]

The ICC indicated that such restrictions were "an unacceptable attempt to interfere with the rule of law and . . . an attack against the interests of victims of atrocity crimes, for many of whom the Court represents the last hope for justice."[148] Diego García-Sayán, UN special rapporteur speaking on behalf of 34 independent legal experts, said the US sanctions constituted a "direct attack" on "the institution's judicial independence." In their judgment, the US policy aimed to impede the ICC's effort "to seek justice against crimes of genocide, war crimes, [and] crimes against humanity." These efforts constituted "a further [US] step in pressuring the ICC and coercing its officials" to stop their "independent and objective investigations and impartial judicial proceedings."[149]

Another law-inhibiting consequence of US policies toward the ICC has been its implicit acceptance of impunity by officials from other countries who have been indicted by the court for alleged war crimes or crimes against humanity. More than a dozen indictees have evaded trial because the United States and the rest of the Security Council have not applied sufficient pressure to bring the accused to court or to apprehend the indicted.[150]

Every European democracy joined the ICC, including Britain and France, the other two democracies that are, along with the United States, permanent members of the Security Council. In contrast, the United States, like China and Russia, refused to join. US policies constitute significant opposition to the growth of legal processes in world affairs and raise a big impediment to efforts to deter war crimes by dictators and militarily aggressive or unprincipled governments. Overall, US policy toward the ICC "has had a profoundly negative effect on the prospects for effective, impartial enforcement of international humanitarian and human rights law."[151] The refusal of the United States to support a permanent international court for trying those accused of mass

[147] UN News, "U.S. Sanctions Against International Court Staff a 'Direct Attack' on Judicial Independence," UN News, June 25, 2020, https://news.un.org/en/story/2020/06/1067142.

[148] In 2017, the Court's chief prosecutor, Fatou Bensouda, concluded that there was enough information to prove that US forces had "committed acts of torture, cruel treatment, outrages upon personal dignity, rape and sexual violence" in Afghanistan in 2003 and 2004, and later at clandestine CIA facilities in Poland, Romania, and Lithuania. Lara Jakes and Michael Crowley, "U.S. to Penalize War Crimes Investigators Looking into American Troops," *New York Times,* June 11, 2020, https://www.nytimes.com/2020/06/11/us/politics/international-criminal-court-troops-trump.html?searchResultPosition=3.

[149] UN News, "U.S. Sanctions Against International Court Staff a 'Direct Attack' on Judicial Independence," UN News, 25 June, 2020, https://news.un.org/en/story/2020/06/1067142. Some international investigations of alleged crimes may have been warranted after several prosecutions of US troops accused of atrocities were dismissed by US judicial institutions and President Trump pardoned four Blackwater military contractors convicted of murder in Iraq and a Green Beret charged with murdering an Afghani in 2010. Maggie Haberman and Michael S. Schmidt, "Trump Pardons Two Russia Inquiry Figures and Blackwater Guards," *New York Times*, December 22, 2020.

[150] International Criminal Court, "Situations Under Investigation," https://www.icc-cpi.int/pages/situation.aspx; Interpol, "Wanted: International Criminal Court," https://www.interpol.int/Search-Page?search=international+criminal+court.

[151] Johansen, "International Criminal Court," 330.

murder "shows the extent to which the former standard-bearer for human rights has become a prominent delinquent or 'outlier.'"[152]

3.5.5 *Maintaining Structures that Enable Outlaws*

The preceding examples of maintaining an international system of largely unbridled separate sovereignties keeps many potentially security disrupting actions beyond the reach of international law. This produces consequences over time that negatively impact security and the spread of responsible democracies worldwide. Some enable outlaws, whether governmental officials, who may annex a neighbor's "Crimean territory," or non-state actors, bent on killing hated "others," to hide behind national boundaries, shielded from international legal scrutiny while they commit crimes or deny people's rights with impunity. These policies also indefinitely allow a strongman leader, no matter how corrupt, to sell natural resources from territories he controls to "earn" money to enrich himself and buy weapons to oppress others.

Policies that discourage legalization processes aimed at increasing governments' international responsibility also undermine initiatives to create incentives and sanctions for enforcing law. Weak support for law has facilitated killing countless people because of allowing impunity; it has enabled the extinction of thousands of species because of almost no legally binding environmental protection; and it has enabled the destruction of Earth's natural climate. No one will ever know the exact costs of US foot dragging, because other great powers have been dragging their feet also, but it is clear that unprecedented opportunities have been lost, year after time-wasting year. Many will never be repeated, because "me-first" nationalism itself has spread and impeded international enforcement of treaties in which compulsory law enforcement might have been established some years ago.

Aligning US military power, economic power, environmental power, and legal power more effectively to serve security needs would require major changes in each area. Preparing international law for a more forceful role in the future, for example, could happen if it were given a fraction of the resources assigned to military preparedness.

Given the negative impacts of the anarchic, existing international system on war prevention and on the prospects for constructive change, and the dominant role that the United States has played in maintaining this dysfunctional system while blocking the creation of more inclusive, worldwide legal processes, one might conclude that US policies too frequently contribute more to perpetuating major problems than to ushering in their solutions, whether this happens through inadvertence to governance needs or deliberate opposition to them. The United States has played a major role in preventing the world from progressing to a better place, even though other countries, such as China and Russia, have been strongly opposed to most positive changes also and deeply committed to irresponsible forms of national sovereignty as means

---

[152] Weiss and Thakur, *Global Governance and the UN*, 268.

for perpetuating their authoritarian-dictatorial systems. Despite these negative influences, many multilateral initiatives proposed by middle-range democracies around the world could have gone forward, even without support from China and Russia, especially in their first manifestations, if the United States had supported them. But they could not go forward without Washington's support. If the United States had played a more positive role, perhaps China or Russia might have responded with more cooperative interactions.[153]

The hour is likely to come—indeed is now approaching—when a majority of US citizens will wish that their government had blazed the rule-of-law path in the late 20th and early 21st centuries, because that path eventually will be understood to be more effective, despite its imperfections, than the military-threat path, especially when it comes to protecting the lives and well-being of innocent people from violence and from the huge costs of environmental destruction. Whether through deliberate opposition or inadvertence and lack of attention, the short-sightedness of staying on the military-threat path is encapsulated by the hypocrisy of US officials when they asked the International Criminal Court to enforce international law on violent leaders in Sudan, Libya, Kenya, and Syria while refusing to join the court and accept the same enforcement protocols for themselves. This double standard is not something that citizens of integrity will forever accept, nor should they. They may feel a need to clarify their support for the equal application of the law and for their willingness to abide by it. When they do, US policies will be less likely to fail in achieving human security.

---

[153] Joseph Nye has noted, for example, that, more than is widely appreciated, "China has tried not to overthrow the current order but rather to increase its influence within it." Joseph S. Nye, "Will the Liberal Order Survive?," *Foreign Affairs* 96 (January/February 2017), https://www.foreignaffairs.com/articles/2016-12-12/will-liberal-order-survive. Russett, Oneal, and Berbaum's research showed that, with astute diplomacy, the rising power of China might have been managed by drawing it into a system of rules and international organizations governing trade. "Causes of Peace," 388.

4

Recognizing Structural Breakdown

THE PREVIOUS CHAPTER demonstrates how US power and policies were not employed effectively to maximize prospects for peace, security, and long-term well-being. This chapter shows that the theory and philosophical assumptions undergirding US policies and purposes have also been faulty and misaligned: They have not squarely faced structural flaws in the international system.[1] Nationalist motivations for policy have narrowed while the policy outcomes required need to express *less* narrow nationalism and more engagement with interdependence. Following World War II, US nationalism, which underpins all US policies, was kept relatively healthy and inclusive with an abundant infusion of internationalism. This expressed an internationally cooperative humanitarian spirit in initiating multilateral legal processes to

(1) found the United Nations and its fifteen vital though imperfect associated agencies, including the World Bank and the International Monetary Fund;
(2) establish the Nuremberg and Tokyo war crimes trials to deal somewhat objectively with the crimes of the vanquished after World War II;

---

[1] The latest U.S. National Intelligence Council estimates of future global trends notes that a deep-seated mismatch exists between the scale of global problems and the weakness of institutions to address them. The intelligence experts predict that this mismatch will cause more disruptive conflicts and severe contestations at every level of societal organization over the next two decades. "Challenges are likely to manifest more frequently and intensely in almost every region and country." National Intelligence Council, *Global Trends* 2040, 1–3, 5.

(3) launch the Marshall Plan that generously helped European economies get back on their feet;

(4) co-author, promote, and publicize the Universal Declaration of Human Rights;

(5) establish and join the International Court of Justice;

(6) back economic integration in the European Coal and Steel Community (later the European Union) and its European peace project;

(7) promote free trade guidelines for private enterprise in the General Agreement on Tariffs and Trade (later the World Trade Organization);

(8) support movement toward national independence for many colonial territories; and

(9) advance numerous multilateral development plans and far-reaching arms control measures.

During this high moment for international cooperation, which had taken root during the traumatic war years, US officials skillfully built multilateral international institutions to protect US interests and to place some limits on dangerous national excesses that were likely as long as the Westphalian interstate system continued. US policies expressed sufficient magnanimity toward other countries that the United States successfully engaged many other governments, quite willingly, in upholding the main features of a rules-based international system in which both the United States and other countries would benefit. This open-handed nationalism, which wisely valued internationalism and multilateralism to enable national societies to flourish, was probably much more effective than a less generous, closed-fist nationalism would have been, as reflected in many US policy successes orchestrated by both US political parties over three decades.[2]

In contrast, since the 1980s, when new global initiatives have been advanced by progressive[3] national governments and by a series of important international commissions on issues ranging from environment to development to global governance,[4] US lack of support, more than any other impediment, has prevented many promising proposals from blossoming forth. With only a few exceptions (discussed below), policymakers and legislators in the twenty-first century have lost much of the far-sighted prudence and international magnanimity shown after World War II. They have not taken international initiatives to address directly the changing international realities

---

[2] See Ikenberry, *Liberal Leviathan*; and G. John Ikenberry, *After Victory: Institutions, Strategic Restraint, and the Rebuilding of Order After Major Wars* (Princeton, NJ: Princeton University Press, 2019). For criticism of the liberal order see Patrick Porter, "A World Imagined: Nostalgia and Liberal Order," *Policy Analysis*, CATO Institute, no. 843, June 5, 2018.

[3] By "progressive," I mean people interested in up-to-date empirical evidence to explore new opportunities and to support moderate political change and social improvement, sometimes by governmental action, including openings to address problems cooperatively and transnationally to implement the values of human dignity.

[4] See, for example, Commission on Global Governance, *Our Global Neighbourhood*. This report details other international commissions' examination of all pressing global issues, 377–394.

discussed in Chapter 1, and this inaction has been occurring at a time when the community of fate can no longer be located within the borders of a single nation-state, even one as large and powerful as the United States.

The US government has not skillfully aligned US nationalism and power to address security needs. Instead, many critics of internationalism have distorted and attacked the previous higher-mindedness that enabled US power to deliver valuable security assets. Although the US-led ethic of multilateral cooperation that had grown among allied countries during World War II did continue for long enough for a blossoming of new international institutions to help the victorious coalition and the defeated countries to gain strength after the war, President Roosevelt's allied legacy began to fade in the Truman administration as US officials understandably locked horns with Soviet policies to control Eastern Europe.

During the Johnson and Nixon administrations' conduct of fighting in Vietnam and Cambodia, the United States ignored the United Nations and broke international laws restricting bombing. Although some multilateral cooperation among US allies continued, it began to decline markedly by the Reagan presidency as US policies became more narrowly self-seeking economically and militarily. Policymakers in the Reagan administration scorned giving deference to UN agencies. During the Reagan years, the United States turned from being the biggest trading creditor nation into the biggest debtor. The United States violated international laws restricting the use of force in Nicaragua and walked out of the International Court of Justice when the court appeared about to call it to account. Negativity toward international law and multilateral institutions increased further in the George W. Bush administration, which broke long-standing international laws against aggressive use of force and torture. Opposition to international institutions became even more fierce among conservatives in Congress, as illustrated by passage of legislation promising US military action against the Netherlands, if necessary, to prevent any US nationals from coming before the ICC in The Hague.[5] Some members of Congress began to adopt anti-UN conspiracy theories and other arguments advanced by conservative radio talk shows after the Reagan administration ended fairness practices on public airwaves. During the Reagan presidency, the center of public debate generally moved far to the right. For a senator merely to favor paying the United States' legally required dues to the UN often subjected that member to the charge of being far to the left on the spectrum. This exclusionary nationalistic senatorial opposition to ratifying many treaties brought the progressive development of international law to a halt. Reagan campaigned against strategic arms control and détente with the Soviet Union, but after Mikhail Gorbachev radically changed Russian policies, he did support some arms control. Although Presidents Clinton and Obama supported treaties in the areas of arms control, international human rights, and the law of the sea, seldom could they obtain sufficient senatorial support to commit the United States to treaty ratification. Led by the George W. Bush administration,

---

[5] Johansen, "International Criminal Court," 305.

anti-UN feelings grew throughout the United States, especially after the UN refused to approve the US invasion of Iraq.

How could the United States so easily give up the multilateralism that had served it so well during and immediately following the Second World War? Many reasons help to explain this turn. First, US officials were informed primarily by political realism, which taught them not to value multilateral diplomacy or international institutions, and instead to value the maximization of national military power as the key to diplomatic success. This thinking fit with the narrowing of nationalism and the rise of the military-industrial complex. Neither supported expanding the rule of law internationally. Instead, they pushed international law into the background as US military and technological advantages grew to make the United States the sole superpower on the planet. Rising military power, including a first-use nuclear deterrence posture, spurred unilateralist thinking, encouraged decline in US magnanimity, and diminished people's sense of inclusivity. Interest in making other nationalities' representation in international institutions more equitable declined as the number of independent states increased. These trends were especially pronounced among conservative leaders during and after the Reagan administration, when the United States dropped much of the cooperative internationalism that had already been fading throughout the Cold War.

Moreover, during this entire period, the United States and other World War II victors refused to relax their unrepresentative veto-grip on the UN Security Council, thereby sapping its legitimacy and rendering it frequently unworkable (except to remove Iraq from Kuwait), despite the end of the Cold War, during recurring humanitarian crises in Rwanda, Kosovo, Sudan, Afghanistan, Iraq, Libya, Syria, Congo, Myanmar, Palestine, and elsewhere, and in UN geostrategic conflicts with Iran, Syria, Russia, China, the United States, and North Korea.

As more and more diplomacy proceeded without orchestrating multilateral cooperation, a populist segment of the public began to applaud, while another segment simply went along with rising unilateralism. These segments together constituted a majority of US citizens (approximately 55 percent) who held an "unfavorable" view of the UN.[6] For a small power to thumb its nose at the UN is one thing. For the leading internationalist power, which had been the single most important influence in establishing and funding the UN, to do that is quite another.

In addition, as the state system expanded to include the entire globe by the 1960s, the larger number of states and diverse economies complicated multilateral decision-making.[7] Favorable public opinion of the United States in Britain, France, and Germany sharply declined during the George W. Bush presidency,[8] apparently because of unhappiness with the decline of multilateralism in US foreign policy. Of course, this loss of favorable opinion nose-dived further during the Trump presidency. As US

---

[6] Roper Center for Public Opinion Research, "Seventy Years of US Public Opinion on the United Nations" (2015), https://ropercenter.cornell.edu/blog/seventy-years-us-public-opinion-united-nations.

[7] Ikenberry, *A World Safe for Democracy*, 294.

[8] Mansbach and Rafferty, *Global Politics*, 428.

approval ratings from other countries fell because of rising US unilateralism, that new attitudinal context made it more difficult still for US officials to succeed in leading a multilateral coalition in the direction they wanted because other states were already disgruntled.

In any case, policymakers gradually replaced the multilateral grand strategy that had been motivating US conduct after World War II with a pulling back on implementation of common values and expanding US unilateral economic and security advantages. More constructive efforts to democratize international decision-making might have enabled further multilateralism. Integrating the newcomers into the international system on a fair-minded basis would have encouraged them to play a more constructive role in democraticizing the international system. Instead, the well-off countries kept many of the newly independent countries as raw material suppliers. In many cases, the corrupt and autocratic leaders of the newly independent countries were helped to stay in power by purchases from the well-off countries.

Another influence against multilateralism was occurring within the United States. The hopes inspired among many disadvantaged citizens by the New Deal coalition[9] and an anticipated growth of human solidarity in the United States, although temporarily given new life by the civil rights movement of the Kennedy-Johnson years, gradually gave way to a more selfish focus on "what's in it for me" and acquisitive desires for more consumer goods. This more selfish attitude also contributed to suffocating multilateralism in US foreign policies. Moreover, an undying legacy of racism in America diminished support for multilateralism as the non-white profile of the world became more obvious. A part of the US body politic expressed negative reactions more loudly against the human rights movement of Martin Luther King Jr., the civil rights legislation successfully advanced by Lyndon Johnson, the elevation of a black man to the US presidency in 2009, and the fears that demographic changes would reduce the power of whites in the United States.

The meaning of US policies shifting away from multilateral initiatives can perhaps be better understood by reflecting on the parable of the tragedy of the commons, because it shows how strong group identity, if unwilling to open its boundaries beyond zero-sum calculations, can bring tragedy to all.

4.1. BRINGING THE TRAGEDY OF THE COMMONS

This parable, brought to US attention by Garret Hardin many years ago,[10] portrays a path that US national security planners and many citizens are taking today. Imagine living in a medieval village where every family owns some cattle or sheep. During the day each herd owner takes animals out to graze on land around the village that all share and hold in common, called simply "the commons." Each family owner can increase its

---

[9] Ikenberry, *A World Safe for Democracy*, 293.
[10] Garrett Hardin, "The Tragedy of the Commons," *Science* 162, no. 13 (December 1968): 1243–1248.

income by expanding its herd. Eventually the herds grow so large that they must compete for scarce grass. When they overgraze the pastures, grass becomes scarce and the land bare. Topsoil erodes, making plant recovery impossible in enlarging areas. Even though all producing units observe that the commons are being destroyed, unless each family can be assured that other families will constrain the size of *their* herds if one does so oneself, no one will cut back. All producers will try to profit as much as they can as fast as they can before the commons are completely destroyed. If each owner of a herd makes this decision, which seems individually rational, collectively all will suffer irreversible losses.

Herd owners could overcome their self-destructive behavior if they would simply establish an equitable rule of law, to bridle the short-term profit motive sufficiently to protect the grass in the environment—which also would protect some benefit from a profit motive reasonably constrained by governance. By establishing community rules to govern herd sizes and owners' relationships, they could agree to limit each family's herd to the size that, when added to others' herds, would enable them all to enjoy but not to destroy the common pastures. This is the functional equivalent of international law in the medieval setting, The families' belief that such legal innovations would not be practical or possible—the medieval functional equivalent of policymakers' belief in political realism in our day—prevented the governing innovation needed in this medieval parable. No doubt the largest family herders may not have been willing to cut back as far as the smaller herders would have preferred. Or perhaps almost no one thought an agreement would hold. The result was no deal, followed by tragedy for what they held in common. Yet system change in the form of more inclusive governance that included all who used the common pastures could have prevented tragedy in the commons.

When applied to contemporary issues, this parable suggests the need for taking a globally inclusive point of view and strengthening the collective rule of law to address security threats to the common environment. Instead, the United States has wielded great military power unilaterally in attempting to control world affairs while refusing to implement and now move beyond the Kyoto and Paris guidelines to constrain greenhouse gas emissions, in order to avoid any constraint on separate US wealth maximization and to protest the failure of some less industrialized countries to meet restrictions without assistance. Although all European democracies accepted the guidelines, one *could* argue that the US refusal would enable the United States to maximize economic gains in the short run, even if this contributed to destroying the environment in the long run, because other free riders would harm the environment anyway. But policymakers gave little weight to how US support of internationally prescribed guidelines might have helped move some other countries closer and more quickly to a global arrangement that eventually would bring all societies into some legally binding rules, thereby contributing to US economic benefits in the long run. So US conduct has encouraged the world's people to accept a tragedy in our commons because of insufficient support for using international law to protect the common good, even though achieving some short-sighted corporate profits increased risks of climatic catastrophe for the United States and everyone else. "Tragedy" applies.

Although the UN Climate Change Conference of 2015 produced some promising results, the guidelines were still voluntary, and precious time has been lost as environmental destruction proceeds. Earlier US compliance would have provided additional leverage to influence foot-draggers toward stronger legal standards. Without that, the United States has helped to accelerate tragedy for the commonly held environment. Meanwhile, US national security experts say that the world must have a high degree of environmental stability and sustainability over the next century if we are to avoid violent clashes that will increasingly erupt over water scarcity and other environmental stressors.[11]

Tragedies parallel to this one in the environment are looming in the political, economic, and security commons because of devaluing shared needs and rejecting benefits from cooperative action. Examples include dangerous precedents from using attack drones, no multilateral effort to constrain cyberwarfare, support for largely unguided neoliberal global economics, plans to drill for oil in fragile eco-systems, and, like the medieval parable, no plans to consider limits on consumerism or dubious aspects of economic growth.[12]

4.2 FORGETTING THE RECIPROCITY OF NUREMBERG

The United States could have chosen a more fruitful international path. Indeed, it was on such a path following US cooperative experiences with the Allied coalition working to win the Second World War. But the center of debate moved politically to the right and ushered back into play more exclusionary nationalistic values characteristic of a less bridled Westphalian interstate system at the time when more international governance was needed to enhance security. To appreciate the full extent of the damage done to US interests, it is useful to place declining US support for international institutions in the context of what one might call the global "constitution." Unlike a singular written constitutional document familiar in national societies, the global constitution is made up of many international customs and treaties, mutually agreed on and generally practiced by the members of international society. These "define the holders of authority," which are states, "and their prerogatives."[13] Even in our international society,[14] which lacks an overarching sovereign, there are rules and expectations

---

[11] National Intelligence Council, *Global Trends 2040*.

[12] See Falk, *Power Shift*, 135–138.

[13] Philpott, *Revolutions in Sovereignty*, 12.

[14] Hedley Bull and Adam Watson first developed the concept of international society to describe states that, although separate, agree on common rules and institutions. They "have established by dialogue and consent common rules and institutions for the conduct of their relations, and recognize their common interest in maintaining these arrangements." Hedley Bull and Adam Watson, *The Expansion of International Society* (Oxford: Oxford University Press, 1984), 1.

that define and govern legitimate actors. These norms, some of which constrain states against dangerous tendencies, may be strengthened or weakened by the actions of states and international society as a whole. It is the parts of this global constitution designed to reduce threats and increase cooperation that the United States has particularly undermined in recent decades even though it was a primary architect of these rules during and after World War II.

The United States launched a particularly promising initiative following the Second World War, by constructing new international law to establish the United Nations and create the Nuremberg and Tokyo war crimes tribunals. These reaffirmed the legal obligation of top government officials and their subordinates to respect international laws prohibiting war crimes, crimes against humanity, and crimes against the peace. Despite the flawed nature of the war-crimes judicial proceedings, insofar as they were victors' justice, they and the subsequent treaty prohibiting genocide did clarify and reinforce fundamental norms that were considered by governments around the world to be non-derogable. Even more important, they opened an unmistakable door, which had heretofore been invisible or closed, to the idea that *individuals* could be held accountable to *international* law, *even if they were prime ministers, presidents, or generals*.

The US Chief Counsel at Nuremberg, Robert Jackson, emphasized that the legal process of holding individual government officials morally and legally responsible for respecting laws prohibiting war crimes would be compelling *only* if the victorious countries would apply the same standard to themselves in the future.[15] As a sign of good faith present in the Nuremberg process, he promised that the United States would do so. The United States in recent decades has forgotten this US pledge; it has violated some of the same laws and refused to participate in a new court designed to hold officials accountable.

4.3 MISSING OPPORTUNITIES FOR A "NEW ERA"

When the Cold War ended in 1989, punctuated by the opening of the Berlin wall, many new opportunities arose for the United States that had not existed for a half century and, in fact, ever before. US officials faced a fundamental fork in their policy road. They could strengthen multilateral legal institutions and further demilitarize the global system—continuing the path chosen right after the world war, which then became the road less traveled during the tensest Cold War years. Or they could implement the policies and customs that they had come to know and prefer during the height of the Cold War, which asserted US military primacy, even though the original reasons that called the United States toward the primacy road no longer existed. There simply were no strategic rivals to United States' military power. US policymakers could have innovated new forms of global governance without serious risk. They chose not to take this path.

---

[15] Jackson, "Opening Statement."

US policy became less inclined to represent all people fairly in international institutions such as the World Bank. In addition, the permanent members of the UN Security Council refused to expand their circle beyond the allied victors in World War II, long after worldwide representation should have become more equitable. Moreover, rather than inviting Russia to join NATO or transforming NATO from a collective defense organization of over-against-ness into a regionally inclusive collective security organization (that would include Russia and all of eastern Europe), NATO still functioned in its anti-Moscow tradition and began to expand eastward to include members of the former Warsaw Pact in ways that Moscow found threatening. This contributed to Russian decisions that resulted eventually in Moscow's militarily aggressive, illegal conduct in Crimea and Ukraine.[16]

Because this inertia-induced policy orientation illustrates the kind of missteps that US policymakers were taking almost everywhere, it bears further discussion. The highly revered diplomat, George Kennan, who conceived and authored the US containment strategy for the Soviet Union, always felt that others gave an excessively militaristic emphasis to containment. He thought it should have emphasized political and diplomatic containment more than an arms race. He later believed that expanding NATO "to bring it to the borders of Russia was a terrible mistake."[17] He wrote in a *New York Times* article that "expanding NATO would be the most fateful error of American policy in the entire post-cold war era." "Such a decision," he warned, "may be expected to inflame the nationalistic, anti-Western and militaristic tendencies in Russian opinion; to have an adverse effect on the development of Russian democracy; to restore the atmosphere of the Cold War to East-West relations; and to impel Russian policy in directions decidedly not to our liking."[18] His warnings were ignored by the US national security policymaking community.

Even though his dire predictions about negative consequences in Russia from US alliance expansion have come true, there is no discernible evidence that US policymakers have learned anything from this experience, even though it has severely damaged US and European interests. From Kennan's perspective, the United States contributed to the demise of democracy in Russia just as it was beginning to take root. Kennan's view has been shared by enough other prominent members of the diplomatic community to confirm that it contained some wisdom, even though a sufficient number of policymakers and members of Congress did not agree to change US policy. Eighteen former high-level officials signed a public letter opposing NATO eastward expansion and warned that "this policy risks . . . significantly exacerbating the instability that now exists in the zone that lies between Germany and Russia, and convincing most Russians that the United States and the West are attempting to isolate, encircle, and

---

[16] See John J. Mearsheimer, "Why the Ukraine Crisis Is the West's Fault," *Foreign Affairs* 93, no. 5 (2014), https://www.foreignaffairs.com/articles/russia-fsu/2014-08-18/why-ukraine-crisis-west-s-fault.

[17] Quoted by Tim Weiner and Barbara Crossette, "George F. Kennan Dies at 101; Leading Strategist of Cold War," *New York Times*, March 18, 2005.

[18] Quoted by Weiner and Crossette, "Kennan Dies."

subordinate them, rather than integrating them into a new European system of collective security."[19] The signatories included Paul H. Nitze, former secretary of the navy and deputy secretary of defense; Jack F. Matlock Jr., former US ambassador to the USSR; and John A. Armitage, former deputy assistant secretary of state for European affairs.[20] They also favored a more inclusive US policy orientation that would have given Russia membership in a new international Committee on European Security and called for joint NATO-Russian security assurances for the belt of states from the Baltic to Albania, rather than incorporating them into NATO. The US habit of dissociative strategic thinking, stereotyping of adversaries, and the over-against-ness built into alliance structures contrasted sharply with an associative strategy[21] that could have included Russia structurally in a collective security system embracing Europe and part of Asia. This dissociative orientation dominated most US policy decisions from the time of Reagan forward, repeatedly rejecting opportunities for more inclusive, institutionalized peacebuilding that would have been possible after the end of the Cold War.

One notable exception, the successful use of the Security Council to reverse Iraq's invasion and annexation of Kuwait in 1990, suggests what might have developed at the UN as most of the world cooperated to reverse an act of military aggression. But the intellectual inertia of US national security policymakers inhibited their use of the rare diplomatic opportunity of having no serious strategic rivals or security threats in order to reform international institutions and establish global governance that might have made the international system a bit safer and fairer. Many members of Congress not only hesitated but also fiercely back-tracked, lacking willingness to attempt to increase the governability of the international system.

---

[19] Richard T. Davies, "Should NATO Grow? A Dissent, *New York Review of Books*, September 21, 1995, https://www.nybooks.com/articles/1995/09/21/should-nato-growa-dissent/.

[20] The complete list of signatories included John A. Armitage, Deputy Assistant Secretary of State for European Affairs, Department of State, 1973–1978; Robert R. Bowie, Counselor, Department of State, 1966–1968; William I. Cargo, Ambassador to Nepal, 1973–1976; William A. Crawford, Ambassador to Romania, 1961–1965; Richard T. Davies, Ambassador to Poland, 1973–1978; Martin J. Hillenbrand, Ambassador to the Federal Republic of Germany, 1972–1976; U. Alexis Johnson, Deputy Under Secretary of State for Political Affairs, 1961–1964 and 1965–1966, Ambassador to Japan, 1966–1969; James F. Leonard Jr., Deputy Permanent Representative to the United Nations, 1977–1979; Jack F. Matlock Jr., Ambassador to the USSR, 1987–1991; Paul H. Nitze, Secretary of the Navy, 1963–1967; Deputy Secretary of Defense, 1967–1969; Special Advisor to the President and the Secretary of State on Arms Control Matters, 1985–1989; Herbert S. Okun, Deputy Permanent Representative to the United Nations, 1985–1989; James K. Penfield, Ambassador to Iceland, 1961–1967; Jack R. Perry, Ambassador to Bulgaria, 1979–1981; John D. Scanlan, Deputy Assistant Secretary of State for European Affairs, 1981–1982; William E. Schaufele Jr., Ambassador to Poland, 1978–1980; Galen L. Stone, Ambassador to Cyprus, 1978–1981; Emory C. Swank, Deputy Assistant Secretary of State for European Affairs, 1969–1970, Ambassador to Cambodia, 1970–1973; Philip H. Trezise, Assistant Secretary of State for Economic Affairs, 1969–1971.

[21] To oversimply only slightly, a "dissociative strategy" tries to resolve conflicts by separating one group or groups of people and their interests from other groups with whom they are in conflict. In contrast, an "associative strategy" encourages groups in conflict to arrange ways, often involving legal processes, to transform their conflicts into forms of cooperation or at least stable tolerance of differing as well as common group interests.

In reflecting on the portentous Security Council actions that liberated Kuwait in 1991, Republican President George H. W. Bush, a seasoned former CIA director and Cold War realist, explained to a joint session of Congress: "Out of these troubled times . . . a new world order can emerge." This "new era" could be "freer from the threat of terror, stronger in the pursuit of justice, and more secure in the quest for peace." It could be "an era in which the nations of the world, East and West, North and South, can prosper and live in harmony." "Today," he said, "that new world is struggling to be born, a world quite different from the one we've known. *A world where the rule of law supplants the rule of the jungle.* A world in which nations recognize the shared responsibility for freedom and justice."[22]

However, rather than trying to usher in this new world, most US political leaders and members of Congress expressed narrow nationalism and opposed efforts to reform the international system to enable it to address conflicts from Rawandan-like genocides to the threat of nuclear weapons to keeping pace with changing needs for representation in international institutions and strengthening international law.

The narrower nationalism of the George W. Bush and Trump administrations led them not simply to dismiss international law but to be willing to unravel and violate it.[23] This cavalier attitude toward international law actually *weakened* it and *shrank* sovereignty, in the sense of pulling it back from incorporating respect for others and from making "their" sovereignty sensitive to "ours." This common attitude ignores that sovereignty has *two* dimensions. It both grants and limits power: it gives my national government supreme power and authority within its territory; it also limits the sovereignty of another national government to assert power beyond its territory, especially in my territory. By habit we emphasize our own government's power at home. Now we need to give more attention to employing US external sovereignty to limit other governments' sovereign powers beyond their territories. For example, no government's sovereignty should entitle it to let radioactive fallout drift across its borders into neighboring countries.

---

[22] George H. W. Bush, "Address Before a Joint Session of Congress on the Persian Gulf Crisis and the Federal Budget Deficit," Washington, DC, September 11, 1990, George Bush Presidential Library and Museum. Italics added. Quoted also in Richard Haass, *A World in Disarray: American Foreign Policy and the Crisis of the Old Order* (New York: Penguin Press, 2017), 4.

[23] The extensive public statements of leaders and White House legal memoranda justifying torture are examples. See Jane Mayer, "Outsourcing Torture: The Secret History of America's 'Extraordinary Rendition' Program," *New Yorker*, February 14, 2005; Bob Herbert, "Much of What Has Happened to the Military on Donald Rumsfeld's Watch Has Been Catastrophic," *New York Times*, May 23, 2005; Dana Priest and Barton Gellman, "U.S. Decries Abuse but Defends Interrogations," *Washington Post*, December 26, 2002, A 01; Joby Warrick, "CIA Tactics Endorsed in Secret Memos," *Washington Post*, October 15, 2008, A 01; Mark Tran, "FBI Files Detail Guantánamo Torture Tactic," *Guardian*, January 3, 2007; Human Rights Watch, "U.S.: Vice President Endorses Torture," press release, October 26, 2006; Human Rights Watch, "Descriptions of Techniques Allegedly Authorized by the CIA," press release, November 2005; CNN, "Previously Secret Torture Memo Released," July 24, 2008; Associated Press, "Pentagon Official Says 9/11 Suspect Was Tortured," January 14, 2009; CNN, "Senate Report: Rice, Cheney OK'd CIA Use Of Waterboarding," April 23, 2009; "New CIA Docs Detail Brutal 'Extraordinary Rendition' Process," *Huffington Post*, August 28, 2009.

US policymakers have seemed unconcerned about setting bad examples for others in violating laws prohibiting torture and the threat or use of military force for purposes other than self-defense; in withdrawing from a nuclear agreement with Iran with which it was complying; and in undermining the International Criminal Court. A majority of senators continued their indifference to honoring the Geneva Conventions when they approved Gina Haspel as director of the CIA, despite "her refusal to acknowledge torture's immorality," as Senator John McCain put it in explaining his vote against her confirmation.[24]

Although the Obama administration did provide opportunities for the United States to strengthen international institutions, these did not find sufficient support in the United States Congress to enable them to succeed. Republican members fiercely opposed President Obama's modest multilateralism and voiced withering criticism of him for not employing US military power more forcefully. Once Republicans took over the White House and both Houses of Congress in 2017, new US policies took any remaining wind out of tattered internationalist sails. US policy became a deliberate expression of exclusionary nationalism, sharply reducing the financial lifeblood that Washington had been providing in paying dues to international institutions and reversing the policies that haltingly had begun to lay some foundations for a world increasingly governed by international law and institutions.

As the Trump administration took over in 2017, narrowly nationalistic attitudes that had been previewed among conservatives in George W. Bush's first administration were revived: his appointees, illustrated by John Bolton and Robert C. O'Brien as national security advisers, did not appreciate international law or institutions.[25] Voices from the White House and the Republican-controlled Congress articulated a form of nationalism much narrower than the voices of those, like George Marshall, who had forged new institutional architecture to strengthen international economic cooperation as a bulwark against future war.

The Trump administration's surface attitudes revealed deeper problems of misaligning US power to achieve security. US officials' pejorative speech about people of other nations interfered with building cooperative attitudes. A low point may have been President Trump's complaint that some people entering the United States were coming from "shithole countries."[26] He characterized African Americans as "thugs" and

---

[24] Roger Cohen, "The Moral Rot Threatening America," *New York Times*, May 19, 2018, A 21.

[25] This was most directly expressed by John Bolton, who said the US goal should be to squeeze the ICC so hard that it would wither and die. John Bolton, "No, No, No to the International Criminal Court," *Human Events*, August 21, 1998, 8; Owen Bowcott, Oliver Holmes, and Erin Durkin, "John Bolton Threatens War Crimes Court with Sanctions in Virulent Attack," *The Guardian*, September 10, 2018, https://www.the-guardian.com/us-news/2018/sep/10/john-bolton-castigate-icc-washington-speech.

    In 2019, Bolton summed up the US attitude: "We will not cooperate with the ICC. We will provide no assistance to the ICC. We will not join the ICC. We will let the ICC die on its own. After all, for all intents and purposes, the ICC is already dead to us." Rick Noack, "Why Does the Trump Administration Hate the International Criminal Court So Much?" *Washington Post*, April 5, 2019, https://www.washingtonpost.com/world/2019/04/05/why-does-trump-administration-hate-international-criminal-court-so-much/.

[26] "Why are we having all these people from shithole countries come here?" President Trump once asked his advisers. Josh Dawsey, "Trump Derides Protections for Immigrants from 'Shithole' Countries,"

undocumented Mexicans as "rapists."[27] Even when rhetoric has been less inflammatory, US officials at times have used dishonest assertions and negative innuendoes to accuse other countries, some of whom are US allies, of being foolish or incompetent, immoral, or ignorant freeloaders on US generosity. Because leaders' use of bigoted language influences public attitudes on both sides of national boundaries, such language misaligns nationalism's potential for extending solidarity rights.[28] In contrast, to emphasize how universal values of human dignity entail some "sovereign obligation" to all other sovereign nations,[29] as Richard Haass points out, is a healthier expression of US nationalism.

When nationalism exalts one group above others, and sometimes above all others, it tempts a great power to forget internationalism and to take advantage of weaker nationalities while feeling few qualms of conscience about reaping the profits and political benefits of denying equal rights to others. In Richard Falk's view, after the terrorist attack on the World Trade Center and Pentagon, many US officials and citizens "reverted to a tribalist sense of the good citizen as . . . mindless supporter of national truth." This "allowed our elected leaders to enact their program of continuous warfare at great cost to ourselves" and "damage to the authority of international law and the United Nations." In addition, "by diverting our attention from the ticking bombs of climate change and energy scarcities, we are irresponsibly putting our own future and that of all humanity under a darkening cloud of risk and an almost preordained and heightened prospect of collective calamity."[30]

President Trump laid out the US approach in his first speech to the United Nations General Assembly in September of 2017, repeatedly emphasizing that national sovereignty should be the guiding principle for every country's conduct. For him, that meant the United States would always put its interest first and above everyone else's. His was

---

Washington Post, January 12, 2018, https://www.washingtonpost.com/politics/trump-attacks-protections-for-immigrants-from-shithole-countries-in-oval-office-meeting/2018/01/11/bfc0725c-f711-11e7-91af-31ac729add94_story.html?utm_term=.e1af8d8520bb. For additional reports of President Trump's language: https://www.cnn.com/2018/01/11/politics/immigrants-shithole-countries-trump/index.html.

[27] Reported in Brian F. Schaffner, "Follow the Racist? The Consequences of Trump's Expressions of Prejudice for Mass Rhetoric," Tufts University Report, https://tufts.app.box.com/s/zhpop8u1sjw6g7y4zx81074ugl9ord1i.

[28] "Elites can influence what people think and how they think about it. . . . Trump's prejudiced rhetoric causes people to express more prejudice themselves. . . . People's commitment to anti-prejudice norms is undermined even when exposed to prejudiced rhetoric attributed to unnamed politicians. These findings are consequential; if politicians increasingly feel at liberty to express explicit prejudice, then the mass public is likely to take cues from such behavior, leading them to express more prejudice themselves." Brian Schaffner, *The Acceptance and Expression of Prejudice During the Trump Era* (Cambridge: Cambridge University Press, 2020), https://doi.org/10.1017/9781108924153.

[29] Richard Haass discusses state obligation to other sovereign states in *Disarray*. A parallel sense of obligation can be employed with an emphasis on individual moral obligation to all, undergirding a degree of cosmopolitanism.

[30] Richard Falk, *On Humane Governance: Toward a New Global Politics* (Cambridge: Polity Press, 1955), 202–203.

a selfish national sovereignty. He shrank sovereignty's possible acknowledgement of the reciprocal rights of others or of mutually limiting conditions on sovereignty. He voiced nary a word about international responsibility for human rights or the rule of law. In this presentation, which some observers characterized as a "defiant speech, peppered with threats and denunciations,"[31] he warned that the United States would act aggressively, unilaterally if necessary, against North Korea, Iran, and Venezuela. If the United States were forced to defend itself "we will have no choice but to totally destroy North Korea."[32]

President Trump employed sovereignty in ways that dictatorial governments have done historically at the United Nations to deflect international criticism from their acts of oppression or aggression, rather than as a superpower that had established global institutions over the past 70 years to enshrine its interests and induce other countries to cooperate on interests that might be shared. Endorsing what could appear to be mutually exclusionary nationalisms, the president promised, "I will always put America first, just like you, as the leaders of your countries, will always and *should always* put your countries first."[33] He offered no thoughts, other than complete destruction, about how he would respond to other governments when they put their interests first in ways that he opposed. He ignored that other sovereign governments might believe they were serving their own countries first when they sought nuclear weapons or trade arrangements that Donald Trump deplored. US officials overlooked that by extolling a selfish sovereignty as the primary virtue in international relations, there could be no basis for criticizing North Korea's obtaining nuclear weapons or violating human rights. In Pyongyang's view, it might simply be exercising its national sovereignty to deter attacks by others.

This selfish version of sovereignty, widely applauded by congressional Republicans,[34] departs from a realistic understanding of US security interests and more recent international acceptance of "conditional sovereignty,"[35] which is beginning to affirm that sovereign governments are not entitled to immunity from outside intervention if they do not protect their own people from gross violations of human

---

[31] Mark Landler, "President Reshapes Vision for US Role with Emphasis on One Word: Sovereignty," *New York Times*, September 20, 2017, A1.

[32] Landler, "President Reshapes Vision," A-9.

[33] Landler, "President Reshapes Vision," A1. Italics added. John Halpin, "Why We Need Inclusive Nationalism," *Democracy: A Journal of Ideas*, July 29, 2020, https://democracyjournal.org/arguments/why-we-need-inclusive-nationalism/.

[34] Peter Baker and Rick Gladstone, "Heralding 'America First' in Combative Speech, Trump Airs List of Threats," *New York Times*, September 20, 2017, 9; Landler, "President Reshapes Vision," A-1.

[35] UN Secretary-General Kofi Annan emphasized a "developing international norm . . . that massive and systematic violations of human rights wherever they may take place . . . should not be allowed to stand." Although this evolving doctrine risks allowing pernicious interventions, its emphasis on sovereign obligation to respect human rights is an important recognition that governments do not have an absolute sovereign shield or legal defense behind which they can commit crimes against humanity with impunity. See UN Secretary-General Kofi Annan, Secretary-General Statements and Messages, "Secretary-General Presents His Annual Report to General Assembly," SG/SM/7136, GA/9596, September 20, 1999, https://www.un.org/press/en/1999/19990920.sgsm7136.html.

rights.[36] "As long as I hold this office, I will defend America's interest above all else," President Trump explained, which meant, among other goals, that the United States should not pay "unfair" financial burdens like the duly apportioned US obligation for its portion (22 percent) of the UN budget, which came to just over \$1 billion a year.

The Trump administration's policies merely punctuated the US departure from an earlier security policy consensus supporting multilateralism. Although President Trump presented a more constricted vision of world order than any US president in over a century, policies of earlier administrations and congressional actions already had eroded prospects for enhancing international law and institutions. In addition to dismissing the views of the UN Security Council and the restraint of international law in the attack on Iraq, George W. Bush had labeled Iran, North Korea, and Iraq an "axis of evil." Many people nodded in agreement, even though this way of "putting the United States first" probably stimulated desires for obtaining weapons of mass destruction in those countries. When in his state of the Union speech to both houses of Congress, President Bush declared that the United States "will never seek a permission slip"[37] before launching an attack to defend US security, members of both parties immediately sprang to their feet in an enthusiastic standing ovation, even though a thoughtful legislator would know that the United States wanted Iraq and North Korea and Iran to ask for an international permission slip before *they* obtained weapons-grade fissile material or tested such weapons. President Trump's emphasizing military means was simply a jingoistic expression of double standards that had been expressed previously by conservative presidents and legislators. For several decades the Senate had blocked development of international law and refused to ratify treaties in the US interest, in contrast to an earlier Senate's approval of the UN Charter and other international institutions, substantial foreign assistance after World War II, and constructive use of sovereignty's elasticity.

Stephen Walt, a leading political realist who may not be in agreement with all the empirical realist proposals described here, provides a persuasive criticism of several decades of US foreign policy: "Instead of a series of clear and obvious successes, the years after the Cold War were filled with visible failures and devoid of major accomplishments."[38] Often the failures were "missed opportunities, such as the bipartisan failure to capitalize on the Oslo Accords and achieve a lasting solution to the Israeli-Palestinian conflict. Other debacles—such as the Iraq and Afghan wars—were costly, self-inflicted wounds. In a few cases, what were advertised as farsighted and constructive US initiatives—such as the decision to expand NATO or the policy of 'dual

---

[36] "After centuries of more or less passive and mindless acceptance of the proposition that state sovereignty was a license to kill and repress, it is now clear that sovereigns have the duty to govern responsibly." Indeed, "the reconceptualization of state sovereignty . . . is seen as the duty to protect human rights and respect human security when the politics are right." Weiss, Forsythe, Coate, and Pease, *The United Nations and Changing World Politics*, 123.

[37] George W. Bush, "Address Before a Joint Session of the Congress on the State of the Union," January 20, 2004, http://www.presidency.ucsb.edu/ws/?pid=29646.

[38] Walt, *The Hell of Good Intentions*, 7.

containment' in the Persian Gulf—ended up sowing the seeds of future troubles." He accurately concludes: "None of these decisions made Americans more secure or prosperous."[39]

Walt's analyses show that US policy failures occurred because US "leaders pursued a series of unwise and unrealistic objectives and refused to learn from their mistakes. In particular, the deeper cause of America's recurring policy failures was the combination of overwhelming US primacy, a misguided grand strategy, and an increasingly dysfunctional foreign policy community."[40] An empirical realist might say that US military *over*-preparedness produced a "primacy" which in turn caused errors of hubris. The United States' "misguided grand strategy," which was not based on a realistic grasp of the limits of military power and of the possibilities of non-military means of influence, kept policy in a familiar yet increasingly ineffective rut. Meanwhile, the "dysfunctional foreign policy community" kept repeating time-honored policies even though they had turned into failures. Still, this community would not allow alternative views to penetrate the policymaking community. Barry Posen, another political realist, noted that the inertia in the US policymaking community and the continued pursuit of familiar US policy priorities "will likely prove not merely costly and counterproductive, as it has been in the recent past, but disastrous."[41]

Although US policymakers were, in the eyes of these political realist critics, pursuing "liberal hegemony," these US officials shared political realist emphases on maximizing military power and downplaying multilateralism. They considered themselves in full harmony with political realism, despite their public rhetoric justifying their military dominance by calling for spreading democratic values through military means. These policies also had been supported by majorities in Congress for several decades. They replaced the liberal internationalism of earlier years, which had not allowed military primacy to overshadow multilateral priorities. By 2020, the possibility of re-shaping national security policy to establish stronger multilateral institutions was low and the opportunities of the 2010s were unlikely to be repeated. Whereas early liberal internationalism had been a largely bi-partisan policy success in dealing with global problems, narrower nationalism began spewing out a hostile poisoning of the international atmosphere. By 2020, it had brought to an end any possibility that liberal internationalism might remodel itself enough to succeed in the next chapter of history. US leadership stepped back at precisely the moment that it needed to step forward with new creativity to succeed in building a safer world.[42] Donald Trump was more a symptom than a cause[43] of a long-standing problem of less benevolent US nationalism and adversarial stereotyping even though the Cold War was over. Indeed, US diplomatic

---

[39] Walt, *The Hell of Good Intentions*, 7.

[40] Walt, *The Hell of Good Intentions*, 13.

[41] Posen, *Restraint*, 165–166.

[42] Nye, "Will the Liberal Order Survive?"

[43] President Trump "is a symptom of powerful socioeconomic forces unleashed by modernity." Howell and Moe, *Crisis of Democracy*, 1.

and civic educational failures were far advanced by the time he became popular. They helped enable his success. George H. W. Bush could see a new horizon, but most in the national security community chose not to explore the road toward that soon-forgotten horizon.

To conjecture a bit about the road not taken, imagine at what a better place the world might be today if the United States had led the world's democracies and as many other countries as would come along to implement the concrete recommendations of the Brandt Commission on International Development (1980),[44] the Brundtland Commission on Environment and Development (1987),[45] and the Commission on Global Governance (1995)[46] for expanding the rule of law. These were reasonable sets of suggestions by study commissions made up of eminent statespersons and experts from around the world and endorsed by most enlightened national governments. If implemented, they would have changed the modern world with vastly enhanced economic equity and reasonable prospects for an internationally enforced peace and sustainable environmental well-being.

It would not have been unrealistic to expect that by 2030 the world would have a set of legally binding carbon emission guidelines including most countries of the world that would be monitored and enforced through legal and economic means. Nuclear weapons might have been reduced to such low levels that all nuclear powers and would-be nuclear powers would have a common interest in enforcing a ban on the further spread of weapons to any other country as the arsenals of nuclear-weapons countries were scheduled for eventual elimination or were placed under internationally verified control. Any head of government indicted by the International Criminal Court could be obligated to show up for a trial or face worldwide economic sanctions until doing so. The UN Security Council could have gained new legitimacy and authority because it would have been reformed by making it proportionally representative of the world's people rather than a throwback to the victorious alliance in World War II. Gross world poverty could have been eliminated; free, good quality elementary education could be available for every girl and boy in the world.

Many of the proposed policies, laws, and institutions could have been initiated without Russian or Chinese participation during their infancy, but very few could be established in the face of US opposition. The World Trade Organization, for example, grew strong without Russia and China, even though they eventually became eager to join. Russia underwent 18 years of negotiations before it was accepted as a member. Because the United States has moved away from the internationalism of its own earlier, more successful diplomacy, now the like-minded democracies in the rest of the world need to

---

[44] Independent Commission on International Development Issues (also known as the Brandt Commission), *North-South, a Programme for Survival: Report of the Independent Commission on International Development Issues* (Cambridge, MA: MIT Press, 1980).

[45] World Commission on Environment and Development (also known as the Brundtland Commission), *From One Earth to One World: An Overview* (New York: Oxford University Press, 1987).

[46] Commission on Global Governance, *Our Global Neighbourhood*.

take initiatives, such as recommended by the Commission on Global Governance, even if the initiatives must be, at first, without Washington, Beijing, and Moscow.

It is also at least possible that Russia, soon after Gorbachev ended the Cold War, and China, in the 2000s, might have evolved in a more multilaterally sensitive direction if the international community, led by the United States, had been more welcoming. Expanding NATO to the east, for example, instead of integrating Russia into a larger security framework was particularly unwise. Because of these attitudes, nationalism in its narrower form has come to dominate policy. A few initiatives, such as the world's first International Criminal Court, did succeed even without US, Russian, and Chinese support, but it would be far more successful with it.

In sum, the narrowing of US nationalism over the past half century has weakened international law and institutions, shrunk US sovereignty's potential influence, expressed less magnanimity toward the newly independent countries than toward Europeans after World War II, and led the United States away from giving constructive attention to the changing realities in international relations noted in Chapter 1. As a result, this shift has undermined the security of US citizens and diminished the legality and morality of its conduct.

4.4 IGNORING DEFICIENCIES OF THE NATION-STATE

No officials with much political power in Washington are working to change the international system, even though that is the foremost need for improving US and human security today. Yet sticking with familiar national policies will produce less security in the future than they provided in the past.[47] This pessimistic conclusion seemed confirmed by a series of events: attacks by 19 terrorists on 9/11; the poor security results from decades-long wars in Afghanistan and Iraq; unconscionable killing and inhumanity in Syria; the North Korean nuclear-missile standoff and other non-proliferation failures; violence and unrest in the Middle East; unmanageable and sometimes unknown cyberattacks; failures to manage the global economy effectively and fairly; the demise of a healthy environment; and the rampage of a pandemic. Without deliberate redesign of institutions over the long run, the existing security architecture will produce less and less security as time goes by. Astrophysicist Martin Rees has concluded that "the odds are no better than fifty-fifty that our present civilization on Earth will survive to the end of the present century without a serious setback."[48] Further failure to

---

[47] This is confirmed by the National Intelligence Council research published in 2021 noting that "The international system—including the organizations, alliances, rules, and norms—is poorly set up to address the compounding global challenges" facing all nations. "The scale of transnational challenges, and the emerging . . . fragmentation, are exceeding the capacity of existing systems and structures." National Intelligence Council, *Global Trends 2040*, 2–5. Held concludes that "the structural limits of the present global political arrangements . . . can be summed up as 'realism is dead' or, to put it more moderately, *raison d-etat* must know its place." Held, "Reframing Global Governance," 304.

[48] Martin Rees, *Our Final Century* (London: Arrow Books, 2003), 8.

change the system's architecture is like living apathetically in a high-rise apartment built long before there was any building code mandating structural strength in a geological zone where major earthquakes regularly occur, with the odds increasing every year that this building (our international house of cards) will collapse.

The militarized balance-of-power system's declining capacity to protect has become a direct, daily impediment to sustainable peace.[49] US citizens face not merely a poorly functioning international system; they (and others) are staring, like startled deer looking at headlights, into system breakdown. The system's most serious failure is its inability to provide genuine security for anybody, even the most powerful, or an effective antidote to violence for everybody. As the utility of military power for achieving desired political goals has declined, the utility of the international system that relies on military power has also declined. The security problem for a country or for humanity is not that one or two superpowers have been too weak militarily; it is that their reliance on the military instrument cannot deliver security and betrays a simplistic grasp of the complexities of effective power. Changes in international relations have exacerbated the inadequacies of the international system because the forces of disruption are growing among more diverse actors and in issue areas where the militarized balance-of-power system and states acting separately cannot function well or manage rising crises.

Ominously, most national security planners in the world's major powers share key assumptions and beliefs about the interstate system that are informed by political realism, which is an unnecessarily and unwisely limited way of understanding power and change. In the United States and Europe, many shared beliefs are still based on thinking of the Italian political adviser, Niccolò Machiavelli[50] (d. 1527), the writings of English philosopher Thomas Hobbes[51] (d. 1679), the practice of political leaders like Otto von Bismarck, and more recently the work of influential theorists E. H. Carr, John Herz, George Kennan, Hans Morgenthau, Henry Kissinger, Kenneth Waltz, John Mearsheimer, and others. Other cultural regions refer to their own exponents with similar views.[52] The point is not to dismiss the benefits of these earlier philosophers, political leaders, or more recent theorists, but to update any wisdom in their contributions by more carefully applying it to the new conditions that exist.

Most national security managers in the great powers hold similar assumptions and practice some version of political realism,[53] whether capitalist or communist, democrat

---

[49] This international system was born from the ruins of the Thirty Years' War in Europe, which ended with the peace of Westphalia in 1648.

[50] Niccolò Machiavelli, *The Prince*, Project Gutenberg, 2005, http://www.gutenberg.org/files/57037/57037-h/57037-h.htm.

[51] Nancy Stanlick, Daniel P. Collette, and Thomas Hobbes, *The Essential Leviathan: A Modernized Edition* (Cambridge, MA: Hackett, 2016).

[52] This thinking arises early in history and from culturally diverse sources, including the Greek philosopher Thucydides and the Chinese philosopher Sun-Tzu. Kennan in his later years embraced more cooperative approaches and became skeptical of military solutions.

[53] As Falk acknowledges: "Almost all governments continue to be led by political realists." Falk, *Power Shift*, 241.

or authoritarian, and North or South, which is why those who hold an empirically informed version of realism highlighting a need for system change have a difficult time making progress. Because policymakers see relations between states occurring in an anarchical international system in which states seek to maximize their military power as the best strategy for achieving their security,[54] impartial international law, representative international institutions, international morality, and human rights do not play significant roles. Perhaps most problematic of all, because political realists doubt that the existing international system can change, they do not try to change it. They actively resist and ridicule the idea of system change.[55] Yet system change is in fact possible, as one is reminded by several quite different international systems that have existed on the European continent: the ancient Roman Empire, the Holy Roman Empire with its hundreds of political entities, and the rise of the nation-state system following the Peace of Westphalia in 1648.

Although the existing international system had its modern construction less than four centuries ago, many policymakers and political realists treat the system as given and, in many ways, rooted in human nature. They doubt that qualifications to it are possible, even though sovereignty is being modified continuously, if often imperceptibly, by technological and ideational change.[56] Cyberattacks on the US Department of Defense and nuclear weapons laboratories, which may go on for months before any US officials know about them, should end arguments about sovereignty's change. Yet given the continued assumption that the system is here to stay, it is easy for a society to become trapped by unimaginative beliefs of leaders about feasibility that confine the future to little more than "an incremental continuation of the past," except for the possibility that the number of state actors might change as a result of war. Such "confinement of the political imagination coupled with a suppression of the moral imagination disables citizens and leaders alike from thinking clearly and benevolently about how to solve existing problems, whose solution requires non-incremental policy responses."[57] To dismiss structural changes as infeasible restricts policy initiatives to reactions to immediate crises, which always means that decision-making occurs too late to plan for averting larger, long-term catastrophes.

Historically, revolutions in ideas about what constituted legitimate sovereign authority "profoundly altered the 'constitution' that establishes basic authority in the international system."[58] Changes in ideas, as well as in material power, are why the

---

[54] This system became well established after the Peace of Westphalia in 1648.

[55] As Deudney summarizes, political "realists advise against, seek to prevent, and do not expect the establishment of authoritative supranational government." Daniel Deudney, "Regrounding Realism: Anarchy, Security, and Changing Material Contexts," *Security Studies* 10, no. 1 (2000), 4.

[56] Consider how cyber threats penetrate sovereignty, including top secret government departments. Cyber attacks destroy the impermeability of national boundaries and undermine the assumption of political realists that the state is analogous to a billiard ball. For how ideas shape sovereignty, see Philpott, *Revolutions in Sovereignty*.

[57] Richard Falk, "Horizons of Global Governance," in *Critical Perspectives on the Crisis of Global Governance: Reimagining the Future*, ed. Stephen Gill (New York: Palgrave Macmillan, 2016), 25–26.

[58] Philpott, *Revolutions in Sovereignty*, "Abstract," https://press.princeton.edu/books/paperback/9780691057477/revolutions-in-sovereignty.

Westphalian state system came into being. Ideas, as well as military and economic power, can shape today's international system and conduct within it. Abram and Antonia Chayes describe a new reality: "No single country—or small group of countries—no matter how powerful, can consistently achieve its objectives through unilateral action or ad hoc coalition. It is this condition that we call the new sovereignty."[59]

Nonetheless, for a critic in the national security policy community to question fundamental beliefs of political realists is to lose credibility in professional conversations and decision-making circles. Because nothing seems more precious in this community than credibility, policymakers shun new thinking if others view it as "incredible." As a result, almost all great power national security planners follow the familiar motto: If you want peace, prepare for war. They do not imagine how to institutionalize peace and security.

Somewhat surprisingly, many international relations scholars and national security policymakers follow widely accepted diplomatic strategies even though these ignore one of the hallmarks of political realism in an earlier age, when it first earned its strong reputation: the importance of considering how changing material realities, such as radically more dangerous technologies of destruction, influence whether it makes good sense to allow a continuation of the anarchy of the existing international system.[60] For example, although national security planners do look at ways that nuclear weapons influence the configuration of power and interstate interactions, they do not examine how those weapons call into question whether the international system itself can any longer provide security—which is the state's primary external purpose and reason for being. To state this more precisely, prevailing thinking, such as expressed in the work of political realists, has not taken a hard look at how nuclear weapons make the international system so dangerous that states within that system cannot provide lasting security for their people.

On the other hand, a largely ignored group of scholars have examined the meaning of nuclear weapons for the international system in which much of humanity has lived from 1648 to the present. They have concluded, as did Einstein and others in 1945, that the vast increases in destructive capacity make the anarchic international system positively dangerous. It allows nationally controlled nuclear arsenals which harbor unacceptable risks of nuclear destruction. Morgenthau, the most influential founder of political realism in the United States and the scholar whose writings were most used to teach generations of students in international relations, and other eminent realists like Herz, had earned high reputations as leading international relations scholars in their day. Surprisingly, key parts of their thinking have been totally ignored by today's political realists who have come to dominate the field of international relations and national security decision-making in the United States. The loss of empiricism in the thinking of policymakers became evident when they ignored insights of Herz,

---

[59] Abram Chayes and Antonia Handler Chayes, *The New Sovereignty: Compliance with International Regulatory Agreements* (Cambridge, MA: Harvard University Press, 1995), 123.

[60] For a brilliant analysis of this deficit in political realism, see Deudney, "Regrounding Realism," 1–42.

Morgenthau, Reinhold Niebuhr, Einstein, and others that an anarchic international system could no longer provide sustainable national security.[61] This more "realistic realism," was overwhelmed by advocates of more military power.[62]

The advent of competing, proliferating nuclear-weapons arsenals led Morgenthau to emphasize that all security actors were part of one world and that none could protect itself even though it could devastate its opponent. Morgenthau saw that "nuclear weapons had rendered the nation-state *militarily* obsolete."[63] He wrote: "The feasibility of all-out atomic war has completely destroyed this protection function of the nation state. No nation state is capable of protecting its citizens and its civilization against all-out attack."[64] He "emphasized the military obsolescence of the nation-state and the need for a world-state."[65] As Daniel Deudney has pointedly noted, "Morgenthau's nuclear one-worldism has been largely abandoned by his many followers." Because Morgenthau logically concluded that peace could not be maintained without some form of world organization, he explicitly valued world federation, indicating that "only a world state with a monopoly on violence could solve the problem of insecurity created by nuclear weapons."[66]

Why did the powerful intellects and towering reputations of Morgenthau and Herz fail to persuade others? They, along with the renowned realist Reinhold Niebuhr, concluded that nation-state architecture, as it stood, could not guarantee peace even though a peace guarantee was needed to avoid the possibility of destroying the very national societies that sovereignty and national security strategies were intended to protect.[67] Intellectual habits and political interests apparently blotted out unpleasant empirical realities and logic for most policymakers. This denial of reality became easier to overlook as time passed without nuclear war,[68] even though the threat had not diminished.

---

[61] Campbell Craig, "The Resurgent Idea of World Government," *Ethics and International Affairs* 22, no. 2 (Summer 2008): 134–136. x

[62] This reaction is similar to policymakers' reaction to a call for nuclear disarmament by former policymakers with superb political realist reputations—a call that was widely noted but then entirely ignored by the policy community within which these experts earned their reputations. George P. Shultz, William J. Perry, Henry A. Kissinger, and Sam Nunn, "A World Free of Nuclear Weapons," *Wall Street Journal*, January 4, 2007.

[63] Deudney "Regrounding Realism," 20. Emphasis in original.

[64] Hans Morgenthau, *The Purpose of American Politics* (New York: Knopf, 1960), 170.

[65] Deudney, "Regrounding Realism," 20. For an analysis of Morgenthau's nuclear one-worldism, see James P. Speer, "Hans Morgenthau and the World State," *World Politics* 20, no. 2 (January 1968): 206–227; see also Richard Rosecrance, "The One World of Hans Morgenthau," *Social Research* 48, no. 4 (Winter 1981): 749–765.

[66] Deudney, "Regrounding Realism," 20.

[67] These three influential realists "had concluded by 1960 that a 'world state' was logically necessary in light of the nuclear threat." Weiss, *Global Governance: Why?*, 183.

[68] As Falk correctly observes, "Some feel reassured that there has been no use of a nuclear weapon since 1945, but a more careful scrutiny of this period would suggest that the world escaped nuclear war on several occasions by the narrowest of margins. Recent research suggests that even a limited regional nuclear war would likely induce a global famine of ten years' duration that would cause an almost total collapse of organized life on the planet." Falk, *Power Shift*, 257.

Most political realists were not willing to follow Morgenthau's logic to the point of believing that strong international institutions were necessary, perhaps because they downplayed the instability and interdependency of nuclear powers' violent capabilities.[69] In addition, Morgenthau seemed hesitant to believe that what was necessary in governance was possible or might become possible in the foreseeable future. He wrote that "in no period of modern history was civilization more in need of permanent peace and, hence, of a world state, and . . . in no period of modern history were the moral, social, and political conditions of the world less favorable for the establishment of a world state."[70] Although thoroughgoing world community admittedly remains a distant goal, some prospects for establishing more effective global governance have become possible by 2020. They can be advanced by Morgenthau's and empirical realists' recognition that

(1) even the most powerful superpower is incapable of preventing the annihilation of its citizenry in nuclear war or of preventing nuclear winter, even though it has the power needed to destroy its adversary;

(2) the preceding reality has brought the demise of the most basic justification for national sovereignty, which is protection of its people;

(3) the meaninglessness of "victory" after nuclear war "made the defence of the national interest in an anarchic world based on the possibility of nuclear war problematic";[71] and

(4) nuclear weapons themselves might help to unite international initiatives because of a common fear among nations of nuclear destruction.[72]

Although Morgenthau, Herz, Niebuhr, and Einstein accurately foresaw the limits of the interstate system for managing nuclear threats, few political realists have given attention to working for even limited structural change.[73] If more had followed Morgenthau's logic, international relations would doubtless be in a more governable state today.[74]

---

[69] Daniel Deudney, "Left Behind: Neorealism's Truncated Contextual Materialism and Republicanism," *International Relations* 23, no. 3 (2009): 341–371.

[70] Hans Morgenthau, *Politics Among Nations* (New York: Knopf, 1967), 402, 502.

[71] Nicolas Guilhot, "Politics Between and Beyond Nations: Hans J. Morgenthau's Politics among Nations," in *Classics of International Relations: Essays in Criticism and Appreciation*, ed. Henrik Bliddal, Casper Sylvest, and Peter Wilson (New York: Routledge, 2013), 76. This point is also discussed in Hans J. Morgenthau, "What the Big Two Can, and Can't Negotiate," *New York Times*, September 20, 1959, https://www.nytimes.com/1959/09/20/archives/what-the-big-two-can-and-cant-negotiate-the-cold-war-is-an.html?searchResultPosition=2; and Campbell Craig, *Glimmer of a New Leviathan* (New York: Columbia University Press, 2003), 107–116.

[72] Morgenthau, "What the Big Two."

[73] One of the few calling for a stronger international system is Michael Walzer: "We need . . . a campaign for a strong international system, organized and designed to defeat aggression, to stop massacres and ethnic cleansing, to control weapons of mass destruction, and to guarantee the physical security of all the world's peoples." Michael Walzer, *Arguing About War* (New Haven, CT: Yale University Press, 2004), 155.

[74] One could make similar arguments about the futility of states acting on their own to address other global threats, such as environmental ruin and international terrorism.

4.5 RECOGNIZING THE DESIRABILITY AND IMPOSSIBILITY
OF WORLD GOVERNMENT

Because Morgenthau, along with Herz and Niebuhr, doubted that an effective world federal state could be created in the foreseeable future because of insufficient political community to sustain such an organization, he hoped to move closer to a sense of world community if national policymakers could "resolve or ameliorate world tensions through . . . wise diplomacy."[75] When asked what conditions would be sufficient for world society to sustain a world federation, Morgenthau answered that "the creation of an international community presupposes at least the mitigation and minimization of international conflicts so that the interests uniting members of different nations may outweigh the interests separating them."[76] He believed that both "the state-system and modes of consciousness it has generated need to be radically changed for security reasons."[77] If true, it may be time to give more emphasis to building international institutional structures and law as a way of helping to build new consciousness. Indeed, the father of neo-realism, Kenneth Waltz, believed that "men [and women] need the security of law before improvement in their moral lives is possible."[78] Securing the law and improving moral lives probably need to progress hand in hand.

In one of his last writings, Morgenthau warned, "Instead of trying in vain to assimilate nuclear power to the purposes and instrumentalities of the nation-state," citizens and national governments instead should "adapt these purposes and instrumentalities to the potentialities of nuclear power."[79] Morgenthau recognized that this goal "requires a radical transformation—psychologically painful and politically risky—of traditional moral values, modes of thought, and habits of action." Yet without such changes "there will be no escape from the paradoxes of nuclear strategy and the dangers attending them."[80] He wrote that "the question to which we now must direct our attention concerns the manner in which a world state can be created."[81] He insisted that "the difficulties standing in the way of the building of supranational political

---

[75] Speer, "Hans Morgenthau," 207.

[76] Morgenthau concluded: "It is only when nations have surrendered to a higher authority the means of destruction which modern technology has put in their hands—when they have given up their sovereignty—that international peace can be made as secure as domestic peace." Hans Morgenthau, *Politics Among Nations: The Struggle for Power and Peace* (New York: Knopf, 1967), 502, 534.

[77] Deudney, "Regrounding Realism," 20.

[78] Kenneth Waltz, *Man, the State and War* (New York: Columbia University Press, 1959), 163.

[79] Hans J. Morgenthau, "The Four Paradoxes of Nuclear Strategy," *American Political Science Review* 68, no. 1 (March 1964): 35; quoted also by Deudney, "Regrounding Realism," 20.

[80] Morgenthau, "Four Paradoxes," 35. Speer reports that "(1) the most significant function of the world state would be the control of the weapons of mass destruction, thus implying a federal arrangement in which the world government would have severely limited authority, and that (2) the sense of self-preservation may serve to activate the latent sense of a common humanity to the extent that a world community of a sort adequate to support a limited world government may be said to exist, without prejudice to the leaving of the more organic factors of community in national hands." Speer, "Hans Morgenthau," 219.

[81] Morgenthau, *Politics Among Nations*, 477.

institutions, such as the lack of a well-developed world community, are no longer to be emphasized, but rather the urgency of building those institutions."[82]

4.6 CONSIDERING A NEW SYSTEM

What I will call the "empirical realist conclusion"—that a new international system is necessary and that the only reason not to create it immediately after 1945 was that insufficient community existed to do so—is an enormously important conclusion. If more opportunities to build community exist today than when Morgenthau and Herz wrote in the 1950s and 1960s, as they certainly do, then we should, according to empirical realism, be cautiously attempting to construct worldwide institutional constraints on nuclear weapons instead of threatening to rain down fire and fury on those weaker societies who have an appetite to become more equal to the great powers in weaponry.

Today it is possible to find ways to overcome an anarchic international system that were not in view when they wrote. Since then, the material dangers have increased, in part due to the increased speed and scope of violent destructive capabilities, in part due to the broader scope of vulnerabilities, such as cyber-insecurity, and the danger that now includes threatened death to parts of the biosphere from nuclear war or global warming, in part to the larger number of nuclear-weapons states and non-state actors, and in part to more honest recognition that irrational human beings, acting impulsively, will have their finger on a nuclear trigger somewhere in the world.

There are four reasons that US citizens can be more optimistic about prospects today than when Herz and Morgenthau wrote. First, more international institutional capacity and experience exist today for making cooperative decisions on political and economic matters. Second, more economic, environmental, and political incentives exist for developing cooperative, enforceable community relationships. Adding to the war-prevention benefits of international system change today is the recognition of drastic threats posed by global warming, plus knowledge of the catastrophic harm that would occur from nuclear war and a possible nuclear winter. These dangers and the possibilities that a global rule of law might grow could demonstrate that, in Morgenthau's words, "the interests uniting . . . nations may outweigh the interests separating them."[83]

Third, Morgenthau and Herz may have overstated the assumption that governments must wait for more political community to develop before starting to build stronger international institutions. Such an assumption can result from a linear concept of change, as if one cannot build some foundation for new architecture before all the materials are available for the final, completed structure. A more dynamic

---

[82] Morgenthau, *Purpose of American Politics*, 308–310. Also quoted by Speer, "Hans Morgenthau," 221. On Morgenthau's belief that a world government was needed, see also Rosecrance, "The One World of Hans Morgenthau," 749–765.

[83] Morgenthau, *Politics Among Nations*, 502.

understanding recognizes that strengthening existing international institutions could help to generate stronger community and build some trust among societies. Stronger community, in turn, could enable even stronger institutions. The two—institutions and community—may grow in mutually beneficial ways, each reciprocally aiding constructive growth in the other.

Fourth, to control the nuclear genie may not require as onerous a task, as extensive a world federation, or as formidable an overarching structure as people may have assumed. Some vertical dispersal of sovereignty can occur without causing major counter-reactions, and some planetary federal processes may share sovereignty vertically as well as horizontally in ways that increase global democracy while honoring a continuation of much domestic sovereignty in harmony with the principle of subsidiarity.

In any case, it is sensible at this time in history to focus more on the desired international architecture and how to build it, including growing the community needed to sustain the structure. As Morgenthau had earlier warned, if people's focus did not shift to how to create the necessary world organization, then, tragically, "the purpose of America [to spread equality in freedom] may well turn out to be an exercise in futility, like designing a house for the top of a volcano that, barring a miracle, cannot fail to erupt."[84] As a result, Morgenthau called on Americans "to take the lead in establishing a world government, using propaganda and foreign aid to that end in order that the volcano may be defused." Morgenthau, in effect, "equates the American national interest not with power but with a governed world in which 'equality in freedom' may flourish."[85] He recognized that American national purpose does not consist primarily of maintaining its military power position. It lies in constructing a governable world sympathetic to freedom and equality.

Of course, building world community institutions remains a daunting task, but no longer is it necessary to doubt the possibility of doing so. As Deudney has wisely noted, the "tragic impasse" resulting from insufficient world community to sustain building world federation "stems from the disjunction between inherited political arrangements and emergent material realities, rather than from timeless flaws in human nature."[86]

Some common theoretical ground exists between empirical realism and world federalism[87] on the point that nuclear weapons require a security system commensurate with the scale of the security threat they impose—which is global. The gap that existed between Herz's and Morgenthau's skepticism about what could done, on the one hand,

---

[84] Morgenthau, *The Purpose of American Politics*, 308–310.

[85] Speer, "Hans Morgenthau," 221.

[86] Deudney, "Regrounding Realism," 21. Deudney notes that Morgenthau's reasoning differs from Niebuhr's "claim that human frailties precluded a world state." See Reinhold Niebuhr, "The Illusion of World Government," *Foreign Affairs* 27, no. 2 (April 1948): 379–388.

[87] Cord Meyer Jr., *Peace or Anarchy* (New York: Atlantic, 1947); A. C. Ewing, *The Individual, the State and World Government* (New York: Macmillan, 1947).

and people's belief that unleashing the nuclear genie required steps toward world federal government, on the other, was one of timing, not direction. Herz and Morgenthau were consistent in applying Hobbesian logic to the empirical realities of the nuclear era in recognizing that "nuclear weapons had created a state-of-nature situation of mutual vulnerability that necessitated a sovereign consolidation of authority" for governing international relations.[88] This is analogous to the need to create a state leviathan for national government to ensure that domestic life would not be, in Hobbes's celebrated words, "solitary, poor, nasty, brutish, and short."[89]

Indeed, one can argue that a new global democratic leviathan is needed. The order-keeping function of a national leviathan, which Hobbes foresaw and described, is now also needed to govern global interactions and maintain order, yet without imposing oppressive measures on any society while reducing the risk of nuclear war and other means of annihilation, environmental destruction, and pandemic infections. Humanity knows how to keep order without oppressing people. This happens every day in numerous societies. The key is democratic representation with all-inclusive participation and accountability of governing bodies to those who legitimate them. A second key is having a monopoly on the legitimate use of physical force, from global to local domains. If that monopoly is established in legitimate ways, it can keep order without oppressing or ever intending to kill.[90]

Human history reveals that an increase in the size of human groups and their cooperative enterprises has progressed throughout history because "evolution had a tendency to create forms of life featuring greater and greater complexity."[91] Some observers believe that the "evolution of technology, and of culture more broadly, was very likely to enrich and expand the social structure . . . , carrying social organization to planetary breadth." Without believing that anything in political history is determined, it may be possible that "the current age . . . is the natural outgrowth of several billion years of unfolding non-zero-sum logic."[92] Of course this provocative statement tells us nothing about how the next chapter of history will unfold. It does suggest that humans have the capacity to develop more inclusive and more complex organizations when some or many interests of separate individuals and groups overlap and when enlargement of group boundaries may mutually serve separate groups simultaneously. All humans now hold some interests in common.

---

[88] Deudney, "Regrounding Realism," 21.

[89] Thomas Hobbes, *Hobbes' Leviathan* (Oxford: Clarendon, 1958), xiii, 9.

[90] The purpose of law enforcement can be to protect people, to apprehend those accused of law violations, and to bring them before a court or truth commission for examination of their misdeeds, not to kill them in the street. Such a benign yet effective leviathan might function with a minimum of violence.

[91] "Both organic and human history involve the playing of ever-more-numerous, ever-larger, and ever-more-elaborate non-zero-sum games." Wright, *Nonzero*, 4–6.

[92] Wright, *Nonzero*, 5, 7.

4.7 HANGING ONTO DIPLOMATIC HABITS

Because the United States, like other great powers, seems frozen in policies that worked once but are not working now, it is instructive to look more closely at the policy habits that make it difficult to relinquish policies that have lost their value. US national security managers no doubt normally implement their preferred policies in good faith, even though they ignore some social science research that suggests a different path could be more productive. They dismiss alternatives to their policy preferences from those who do not share their diplomatic habits and their fears that it would be dangerous to re-think grand strategy in order to try to reduce international anarchy.

Yet to practice old diplomatic habits amid new realities yields many diplomatic and military setbacks. The interdependence of states and the permeability of every state's borders have increased so much that national security and economic well-being cannot be achieved by a single country for itself, even it if devotes much time, effort, and money to secure itself. This reality—the insufficiency and inadequacy of self-help—is seldom mentioned in public debate by US national security planners, but the often disappointing consequences of self-help alone are a major reason, often unrecognized, that many citizens in the United States and Europe have not been feeling good about the paths their own societies have been taking in recent years. Some have turned to populist, right-wing ideologies, which is understandable as an effort to become more secure, but this will eventually prove to be an unhelpful response to the pain they genuinely feel. For the same reason, members of Congress have been frustrated in their efforts because national legislators cannot get traction for measures that will actually solve problems, so they engage in tribal denunciations of "the other," including those of an opposing party whom in earlier times they would have regarded as the "loyal opposition." As things stand, many people acknowledge that Congress is "broken," but they do not understand what to do about it because they are not looking at the systemic flaws that inhibit new thinking and acting.

National security planners and their supporters mean well, yet they do not feel comfortable directly addressing new realities and taking reasonable risks to reform the international system. More independent observers, including some former US officials, would agree with the UN High-Level Panel on security challenges: "No State, no matter how powerful, can by its own efforts alone make itself invulnerable to today's threats. Every State requires the cooperation of other States to make itself secure. It is in every State's interest, accordingly, to cooperate with other States to address their most pressing threats, because doing so will maximize the chances of reciprocal cooperation to address its own threat priorities."[93] Yet within the self-validating

---

[93] United Nations High-Level Panel on Threats, Challenges, and Change, *A More Secure World: Our Shared Responsibility: Report of the High-Level Panel on Threats, Challenges, and Change* (New York: United Nations, 2004), 21, para 24, A/59/565. This panel included Anand Panyarachun, former prime minister of Thailand, Robert Badinter (France), João Baena Soares (Brazil), Gro Harlem Brundtland (Norway), Mary Chinery Hesse (Ghana), Gareth Evans (Australia), David Hannay (United Kingdom), Enrique Iglesias (Uruguay), Amre Moussa (Egypt), Satish Nambiar (India), Sadako Ogata (Japan), Yevgeny

community of intellectuals and national-security elites, US policymakers are able to justify continuing outmoded policies and the existing international system by recalling time-honored fears and insecurities flowing from the international anarchy of the current system, going back to the disastrous appeasement policies used unsuccessfully against Hitler.

Continuing past practices keeps the international system an expensive and divisive military competition, frequently threatening for most states.[94] The most powerful individual states in the system exercise more power than the center of the system itself, and they generally discourage changes in the system because they like their power advantages. Indeed, the international system of 193 states lacks a unitary center, although international institutions like the United Nations, the World Bank, the World Trade Organization, and a number of courts[95] constitute parts of the international system, along with customary patterns of economic and social interactions as well as a number of regional organizations like the European Union and African Union. Because nationalism and nation-states emphasize the good of one part of the human species rather than the good of the whole, nationalism, unless quite open-handed, interferes with efforts to find common solutions to global problems, such as environmental destruction.

4.7.1 Populism Impedes Constructive Change

A particularly serious problem has arisen in the United States because some strongly nationalistic citizens, disgruntled with the US governing elite, support strongman leadership to rid themselves of ineffective government by a political class who for too long have ignored many citizens' interests, or at least are perceived to have ignored them. US citizens' growing support for populism fits a classical populist pattern that is not limited to the United States or to this period of history. An accurate grasp of the populist threat to democracy and cosmopolitanism recognizes that "Trump himself is not the main reason America faces such troubled times. He is a symptom of powerful socioeconomic forces unleashed by modernity." These forces were at work but not widely understood before Trump became president and continue to be threatening after his departure, even if a Biden administration is able for a time to restore a sense of near normalcy.[96]

Primakov (Russian Federation), Qian Qiqian (China), Salim (United Republic of Tanzania), Nafis Sadik (Pakistan) and Brent Scowcroft (United States).   ı

[94] Wendt points out that "competitive security systems are sustained by practices that create insecurity and distrust. In this case, transformative practices should attempt to teach other states that one's own state can be trusted and should not be viewed as a threat to their security. The fastest way to do this is to make unilateral initiatives and self-binding commitments of sufficient significance that another state is faced with 'an offer it cannot refuse.'" Alexander Wendt, "Anarchy Is What States Make of It: The Social Construction of Power Politics," *International Organization* 46, no. 2 (Spring 1992), 421.

[95] See Alter, *New Terrain*.

[96] Howell and Moe, *Crisis of Democracy*, 2.

For the past half century, the modern world has been disrupted by forces of globalization, technological change, demographic changes and migratory pressures, and shifting sources for economic growth. These changes caused many US citizens, especially working-class people without sustained financial strength, to feel left out and emotionally distressed by their economic plight and loss of realistic hopes for realizing their aspirations. Immigrants, racial justice, women's liberation, and most of all, ineffective US government responses led them to turn against Washington elites and the workings of democracy itself. The federal government did respond in part, but its response was weak and ineffective. As a result, "the problems have intensified, people have grown angry, and populist appeals have found a receptive audience."[97]

Several causes contributed to the ineffectiveness of the US government's responses as problems mounted: many legislators have not fully or accurately understood why they cannot govern more effectively; many have not been as dedicated to serving the broad human interests of the US population as to serving the special interests of those who paid for their campaigns; many have been conditioned to be so partisan that they would rather see the middle and lower classes of US citizens suffer than an African American president (or any president of an opposing party) succeed; money from very wealthy individuals and corporate giants corrupted elections, much of the mass media, and the between-elections governing process itself; and social media, exploited by unscrupulous US individuals, organizations, and foreign governments have, in practice, cast truthfulness to the winds. All of these are partial explanations, but two overshadow others: (1) the incapacity of the US government to govern effectively, in part because of its structural encouragement of power-holders and leaders to play to a narrow base rather than to serve the common good, and (2) no national government, even the US superpower, is large enough to solve the global problems that press down on citizens. US governing ineffectiveness has happened at a time when economic, political, environmental, human rights, military, and even medical problems have significant global causes and consequences. Today's political structures prevent even good, smart people from governing effectively. Today's structures actually provide incentives for good people to be less good, because they encourage them to be unjustifiably partisan, both within United States politics and within world politics.

As Howell and Moe have concluded in their study of the rise of populism, US government ineffectiveness is unavoidable in this rapidly moving interdependent age, because Congress is not structurally set up to solve pressing international problems in a collaborative spirit aimed at serving the broad national interest.[98] Most senators and representatives serve vested interests in their home districts or states and especially the corporations and donors that finance their re-election campaigns. They do not naturally support what serves the common good in the United States. Their re-election does not benefit from helping anyone in the opposing party to achieve

---

[97] Howell and Moe, *Crisis of Democracy*, 4.
[98] "Congress is simply not wired to solve national problems in the national interest." Howell and Moe, *Crisis of Democracy*, 5.

governing success. If senators and representatives have difficulty serving national interests rather than their own vested interests, they will be far less able to address the global, human interest.[99] Yet without doing so, the irritating social forces of globalization, which have been a main cause of populism, will grow.

Perhaps the most dangerous characteristic of populist movements is that their support for authoritarian or "strongman"[100] leaders uses the popular backing of democracy to destroy democracy. This ominous reality arose on January 6, 2020, when a mob aroused by the US president penetrated the US Capital to prevent Congress from certifying the results of a democratic election. If people become so fed up that they support someone they consider a political savior, the democratic act of people selecting their preferred leaders can undermine democratic values and even destroy a democracy. To differentiate the authoritarian populist from the more genuine advocate of popular policies in harmony with democracy requires answering two questions: First, does the one running for office claim to be the only one who can save the country? Or does he or she have a plan to solve problems and genuinely help the poor and the left behind? Second, does the candidate genuinely support human rights, human equality, and the rule of law or only voice demagogic support for these to gain power?

A populist leader's promise to return America to greatness is false in part because it assumes an idyllic past that never was good for those who suffered genocide or chronic violation of their rights. Moreover, the forces of globalization, technological innovation, and cultural diversity will not go away. Of course, because these forces will be with us, the populist threat also will not simply fade away. The ineffective governmental, economic, environmental, and human rights causes of populist discontent need to be dealt with through enhanced national and global governance. In either context, governance cannot succeed for long unless it is democratic.

Yet many US citizens who were considered mainstream in the past have become populist supporters because of their disgust with the ineffectiveness of the US government, fears about the rising influence of others as the white majority in the United States declines and disappears, and disappointment with not meeting their aspirations. As a result, Howell and Moe's study concludes that "the Republican Party is now the organized means by which populism in America finds expression and exercises power. Though its members like to think of themselves as protectors of freedom and the Constitution, the party has become a danger to our democratic system."[101] Of

---

[99] Thomas Mann and Norman Ornstein conclude that Congress often elevates "political expedience above the national interest and tribal hubris above cooperative problem solving." *It's Even Worse Than It Looks: How the American Constitutional System Collided with the New Politics of Extremism* (New York: Basic Books, 2016), 4.

[100] I use "strongman" in this context to refer to both men and women who lead or control political power by force of will and character, often by using executive power to put leadership in the hands of other family members or sycophantic loyalists, employing payoffs and pardons to silence opponents and reward friends, and using police and intimidating methods to dominate rather than by respecting human rights and the rule of law.

[101] Howell and Moe, *Crisis of Democracy*, 16, 81, 98. See also John Sides, Michael Tesler, and Lynn Vavreck, *Identity Crisis: The 2016 Presidential Campaign and the Battle for the Meaning of America* (Princeton,

course not all Republicans are populists, and the party could reform itself. Yet the party's timidity during four years of the Trump administration to call its members and supporters to oppose bigotry and uphold democratic customs, values, and impartial laws raises serious questions about why it has been accepting anti-democratic strongman leadership and has tolerated or supported chronic lying that undermines democratic processes.

Given the populist contestation of democratic values in many societies around the world, it is particularly vexing that the most powerful political structures, which remain states throughout most of the world, are not adequate for managing the pressing problems that are global in extent. The lack of symmetry between the interconnected global forces causing problems and the merely national structures vainly trying to shape solutions causes much frustration, gridlock, and angry polarization, both within countries and between countries. Many people feel left behind, and many are, while globalization proceeds and benefits the wealthy of the world. Those underrepresented in governing decisions lash out at globalization. This backlash may take the form of (1) electing an anti-establishment strongman to restore a romanticized image of national glory or (2) joining a violent network of rebels or religious extremists. In the United States, it might mean connecting with a movement to downplay equal rights for African Americans or women, blocking refugees and migrants who flee violence and oppression, opposing international trade or environmental agreements as the cause of job losses, or amassing more military power in a largely vain hope that military dominance will make one's country great.[102] At precisely the moment that more global governance is needed, populism rises against globalization. Yet to maintain the state system unchanged is likely to undermine government effectiveness and thereby strengthen populism.[103]

4.7.2 Narrow Nationalism Reinforces Systemic Dysfunction

Even without populism, an ingrown nationalism will maintain an unchanging international system. The dysfunctions of the international system, such as its resistance to closing loopholes in the constraints on violence, when combined with the dysfunctions of exclusionary nationalism, such as its tendency to ignore the fears of other nations even when those fears may deepen a desire for weapons of mass destruction, feed upon and amplify each other.[104] Existing forms of nationalism and the existing

---

NJ: Princeton University Press, 2017); Amanda Taub, "The Rise of American Authoritarianism," *Vox* (2016), https://www.vox.com/2016/3/1/11127424/trump-authoritarianism.

[102] This hope was present in both North Korea and the United States in 2017–18.

[103] Dissatisfaction with national governments' ineffectiveness is likely not only in the United States but also in many other countries because of the "growing mismatch between what publics need and expect and what governments can and will deliver." National Intelligence Council, *Global Trends 2040*, 8.

[104] Exclusionary nationalism is on the rise in many countries according to the National Intelligence Council, *Global Trends 2040*, 8–9, 12, 69, 75–76, 117.

international system perpetuate one other. They are likely to continue doing so until they are deliberately disengaged. For example, because Washington officials know that they do not plan to initiate an attack against North Korea, they find it hard to believe that the insecure North Korean dictator is seeking nuclear weapons to enable him to deter a US threat or attack. As a result, US officials may boast: my "nuclear button . . . is much bigger and more powerful" than Kim Jong Un's.[105] That attitude narrows and intensifies nationalism in both countries and makes the international system harder to change. In contrast, if governmental actions were informed by peacebuilding research, policymakers would recognize that they are impeding systemic changes that could verifiably limit some military power.

One particular problem with US nationalism is the extent to which exaltation of it is embedded in the common discourse describing the United States as a morally exceptional country. It is true, of course, that there is no other country quite like the United States. Yet commonly held beliefs about US exceptionalism include these: *The United States does not pursue selfish interests to the extent that other states do. It is not militaristic or aggressive. It has not committed genocide or deliberately tortured. It does not fight illegal or ethically dubious, unjust wars. It always sides with freedom against oppression and with international law enforcement of human rights against predatory forces.* Such beliefs are oversimplifications and, if tested empirically, many are simply untrue. The tendency of nationalists around the world to see themselves as morally better than in fact they are is easiest to see, of course, when observed in a national group other than one's own, as illustrated in imperial powers' dominance of others during colonialism, in the racial supremacy of apartheid, in many acts of ethnic cleansing and genocide, in the religious-racial-cultural prejudice of Nazism, or in other "me-first" nationalisms.[106]

If fear-generated expressions of exclusionary nationalism arise in the United States or if members of an out-group do not behave in the ways that US nationalists prefer, bullying nationalism can arise. It can be identified by stereotyping disliked people with frequent blaming, racial or religious slurs, and predatory impulses. It draws misguided satisfaction from attacking others, especially vulnerable or religiously and culturally different groups. Because narrow nationalists on any continent may willingly take unfair advantage of other groups, their policies can be cruel and predatory. Intimidation and torture may be justified even though such measures have been internationally outlawed. Such conduct usually arouses the most violent reactions from those that one negatively stereotypes.

US officials at times have encouraged narrow nationalism, even though it generates misunderstanding and US insecurity in the long-run, rather than nurturing healthy nationalism in support of human dignity that manifests security for all. To address

---

[105] President Trump made this claim. Peter Baker and Michael Tackett, "Trump Says His 'Nuclear Button' Is 'Much Bigger' Than North Korea's," *New York Times*, January 2, 2018, https://www.nytimes.com/2018/01/02/us/politics/trump-tweet-north-korea.html.

[106] "Me-first" forms of nationalism exalt and seek advantages for one's own group at the expense of other groups rather than respect reciprocal rights.

the new threats to US security more successfully, policymakers need to align nationalism's positive potential with the purpose of increasing peace and justice for all rather
than trying to advance US interests mainly through military primacy and national self-
help, often viewed with suspicion by adversaries. Exclusionary nationalist practices
will be less successful in the future because the human condition itself is cosmopoli-
tanizing. The evolving world "urgently demands a new standpoint, the cosmopolitan
outlook, from which we can grasp the social and political realities in which we live and
act."[107] To ignore this standpoint puts US power at cross purposes with US security. Of
course, cosmopolitanism alone is not the answer, because nurturing human rights and
democracy requires national and local bases as well as universal understanding and
vision. In any case, this much is clear: absolute national differentiations between "us"
and "them" and rigid separations of "national" from "international" no longer enable
empirically realistic or creative means for addressing the crises we face.

Although identities and perceived interests can be transformed, even in today's relatively anarchic system,[108] cultivating a more inclusive perspective requires sustained
leadership. A global perspective is unfamiliar to many and is feared by those with
narrower national conditioning. Some forms of nationalism resistant to change have
developed tap roots in psychological motivations that are shared among people who
validate each other's prejudices, fears, paranoia, or even developmentally unhealthy
family or social conditions.[109] Exclusionary identities may express attributes associated with authoritarian, narcissistic, or other personality disorders in individuals who
stereotype and blame others for most problems arising in their relationships, regardless of whether evidence supports their blaming and prejudice. When nationalism

---

[107] Beck, *Cosmopolitan Vision*, 2.

[108] "State identities and interests can be collectively transformed within an anarchic context by many
factors—individual, domestic, systemic, or transnational." Wendt, "Anarchy Is What States Make of
It," 425.

[109] Darcia Narvaez explains, "When a child does not receive appropriate care, the more primitive brain systems may dominate social relations, curtailing optimal moral growth. Stress reactivity will overwhelm
psychological and moral functioning." Chronic stress responses cause "usually protective mechanisms"
to "become harmful," transforming personalities into dysfunctionality or pathology.

   Overactive stress responses undermine physiological and mental health. "Stress can put us into a
different moral mindset—from brain-freeze paralysis to combativeness." "The stress response," which
is shaped by early caregiving, "impairs higher-order thought and compassion." The age 18 to 48 months
can be a critical time for childhood personality development.

   Maternal separation and parental neglect can cause programmed cell death in multiple areas of the
immature brain, leading to impaired social skills and self-destructive behavior. Biopsychosocial disorders, such as borderline personality disorder, impair neuroception and social capacities causing relationships to become "very difficult and the moral life tempestuous." Disorders caused by early stress
look much like moral character issues, although their origin is much different. It becomes hard for a
person to feel compassion or behave in a prosocial manner. Anti-social conduct can look like "deficient
moral character when really it is biological reactivity and the breakdown of coping ability from too
much stress." Darcia Narvaez, *Neurobiology and the Development of Human Morality: Evolution, Culture,
and Wisdom* (New York: Norton, 2014), 127, 14, 141–145. See also Erich Fromm, *Escape from Freedom*
(New York: Farrar & Rinehart, 1941); Alice Miller, "Poisonous Pedagogy," *For Your Own Good*, ed. Alice
Miller (New York: Farrar, Straus and Giroux, 1983) xiii–xvii; 3–17, 58–101; and Alice Miller, "The Political
Consequences of Child Abuse," *Journal of Psychohistory*, 26 (1998): 574–585.

relinquishes psychologically unhealthy attitudes toward outgroups, it can draw on its underutilized potential for expanding people's identities beyond caring only for their own group.

An example of the inability to relinquish a modest degree of national exaltation, which produces far-reaching political consequences, seems evident in the nationalist impediments to opening slightly the category of permanent membership in the UN Security Council. This category of membership was an effort, not fully successful as it turned out, at the end of World War II to break free of the straitjacket that national sovereignty had put on collaborative multilateral action since 1648, including during the life of the League of Nations. The fifteen-member Council is authorized to make legally binding decisions for the entire international community of 193 countries. This was a major innovation that bridled sovereignty a bit for all UN members *except* the five permanent members, each of whom can unilaterally stop any decision from being made. Their veto power was a necessary concession at San Francisco to ensure the participation of the United States, which had refused to join the League of Nations, and probably some of the other great powers who had won World War II. But those five countries' refusal over three-fourths of a century (since 1945) to revise, even slightly, either the application of the veto power of permanent members or the selection process for whom may become permanent members has blocked adjustments needed to increase Council legitimacy and make reasonable decisions responsive to ever-changing realities.

4.7.3 An Integrative Approach

National security managers in the United States and other great powers focus primarily on security for their own state. Yet as US officials continue to base US security policy primarily on this older "Westphalian ethic," they accept unnecessary risks of nuclear war-fighting and they unnecessarily validate existing inequalities and disparities between rich and poor.[110] This nation-state focus means policymakers' plans do not develop a global grand strategy for *world* peace, unless it would be a world peace dominated by the US government's military primacy, a condition not likely to be supported around the world, thereby undercutting its success.

To hope for security by operating with an older "national logic" is to practice an illusion in a new world where no state, not even the world's sole superpower, can secure itself by itself any longer. US security, broadly understood, can be sustained only with help from many other countries, and that requires embracing reasonable security for other countries, as *they* perceive it, not as US officials wishfully perceive it. To become more successful, US security policy will need to avoid generating fears and insecurities for others that could motivate them to increase insecurity toward the United States as a consequence of their effort to increase security for themselves.

---

[110] Richard Falk, "International Law and the Future," *Third World Quarterly* 27, no. 5 (2006): 734.

Conditioned by fears and old ways of thinking, many people do not see the potential opportunities that lie in more cooperative initiatives, such as strengthening international enforcement of law and encouraging more effective applications of nonviolent action to address oppression throughout the world. Although these could help to make the international system safer by reducing dependency on national military power, a too-narrow nationalism would perpetuate the existing anarchic international system at its base. International anarchy in turn encourages nationalism to remain narrow. The two become one self-fulfilling prophecy. As a result, the United States and other great powers follow a time-honored, yet inertia-bound, fear-driven strategy: They aim at security for one country, the only entity that they feel they can trust, which leads to *insecurity* and makes it difficult for them to address successfully the new realities in international relations that require cooperative, worldwide action and associative solutions rather than dissociative solutions that are more common conflict-mitigation practices for ruthlessly competing sovereignties.[111]

One of the main guidelines for successful peacebuilding, as Lederach and Appleby point out, is to take an "integrative" approach, linking "immediate need with the desired vision of change," responding to emerging conflicts and needs in ways that will reinforce mutual cooperation among all former adversaries and build laws, social structures, and political institutions "supportive of change processes" that can be supported by all.[112] This key to success in intra-state peacebuilding is equally important in international peacebuilding. The latter requires previously distrustful national societies to develop some trust in the transparent governing institutions and the legally spelled-out international enforcement treaties that would be set up to serve the security commons, but states are *not* required to trust the unknown intentions of the other governments in the system.[113]

An integrative approach also provides some help in addressing fears that understandably arise in most people about how decisions would be made in a global system, because every nationality, looked at by itself, is a *minority* in the entire global community. Just as a minority of citizens within a democratic national society cannot achieve or maintain full rights for themselves if they try to segregate themselves from others and focus only on the interests of their own minority, so a nation-state today cannot achieve full rights or security for itself in world society if it tries to separate itself from others and focus mainly on its own national interests. Any reformed international organization would need to give careful attention to ironclad protections to the rights of minorities. These should be upheld by all as a matter of *self*-interest for oneself as

---

[111] For discussion of these approaches, see Johan Galtung, "Twenty-Five Years of Peace Research: Ten Challenges and Some Responses," *Journal of Peace Research* 22 (1985): 141–158; Kenneth E. Boulding, "Twelve Friendly Quarrels with Johan Galtung," *Journal of Peace Research* 14, no. 1 (1977): 75–86. Wallensteen notes that "inter-state regional integration," an associative strategy, "serves to improve the quality of . . . internal war outcomes." Wallensteen, *Quality Peace*, 207.

[112] Lederach and Appleby, "Strategic Peacebuilding," 41.

[113] See suggestions for implementing common security in Independent Commission on Disarmament and Security Issues, *Common Security: A Programme for Disarmament* (London: Pan Books, 1982).

well as of *human* rights for others. However, most great powers are not connecting their own well-being to robust respect for minority rights. Instead, they are content to perpetuate the existing international system of segregated sovereignties, in effect treating only their own rights as very important, rather than considering favorably the need for recognizing the benefits of multilateral cooperation to uphold the rights of all, perhaps with some shared sovereignty to enforce respect for all people, regardless of nationality.

4.8 CONSIDERING A GLOBAL GRAND STRATEGY

To develop policies more attuned to current realities, four suggestions may be helpful. First, US policymakers and citizens need to relinquish the mistaken assumption that continuing familiar diplomatic habits and military policies, which brought Americans to sole superpower status, will give the United States and the world as good a future as it has a past. This is unlikely, because many security issues are beyond the reach of military primacy. Recognizing this opens the door to change. To illustrate the changing reality, economically, the United States produced 50 percent of global output at the end of World War II. Its share had fallen to 22.5 percent by 1985, 15.1 percent by 2018, and the IMF projects that it will fall to 13.7 percent by 2023.[114] Approximately three-fourths of world purchasing power and 95 percent of world consumers are outside US borders.[115] The decline in the US share of the world's productivity suggests that adjustments are required in how the United States approaches the world economy and intends to share the management of it. For the world economy to be managed successfully, more cooperation and less unilateralism will be needed. Leadership will necessarily be more collaborative and rule-based. It will require overcoming past US disdain for multilateral conversations and institutions.

Second, to increase security and overcome fear-driven threats toward other countries, policymakers and citizens should consider amending the widespread belief that today's militarily competitive balance-of-power system is unchanging. Many assume that this international system is a given.[116] To be sure, it is "given" to us by preceding

---

[114] Preble, "Adapting to American Decline," IV: 6; Kimberly Amadeo, "U.S. Manufacturing, Statistics, and Outlook," https://www.thebalance.com/u-s-manufacturing-what-it-is-statistics-and-outlook-3305575; Govind Bhutada, "The U.S. Share of the Global Economy Over Time," January 14, 2021, https://www.visualcapitalist.com/u-s-share-of-global-economy-over-time/. China has become the world's top manufacturing country in producing 20 percent of the world's goods. Darrell M. West and Christian Lansang, "Global Manufacturing Scorecard: How the US Compares to 18 Other Nations," July 10, 2018, https://www.brookings.edu/research/global-manufacturing-scorecard-how-the-us-compares-to-18-other-nations/.

[115] Office of the US Trade Representative, "Economy and Trade," https://ustr.gov/issue-areas/economy-trade.

[116] Many different relationships can exist between political authority and territory. "Sovereign states, or sovereign state systems, are not a natural form of authority or an inevitable equilibrium. . . . Sovereign state systems are only one of many schemes of international society." Philpott, *Revolutions in Sovereignty*, 253.

generations, but it is likely to change over time as a result of technological innovations and inadvertence if not by deliberate decisions. To be sure, the existence of the present international system shows that it is *allowed* by human nature, but that does not mean that alternative systems could not exist within the scope of what else human nature may allow. Divine right monarchies were once thought to be congruent with human nature until one day people quit asking "Who shall be the king?" and instead asked, "Do we need a king?"

Thoughtful social scientists have long known that policymakers "should not act as if today's international political order were immutable or preordained."[117] The international system is neither "natural" nor, in recent years, very helpful. To be sure, whenever state power begins to concentrate, countervailing power may arise to check it, but balancing processes do not need to remain primarily military in order to balance. Nonmilitary political power, legal power, and economic power—checks and balances—are all parts of the balancing processes. It is imaginable that the military component of the balancing process could be relegated to a proportionately smaller and smaller role if there were determined efforts to institutionalize checks and balances aimed at diminishing the role of military power in balancing processes.

A third positive step would be to begin to reverse the shift that has occurred in bureaucratic power in the US government away from diplomatic, peacebuilding hands to military hands. The problem is *not* that the latter are against peace, because they are generally *for* peace. The problem, as Republican President Eisenhower first warned, is the massive influence of the military-industrial complex on thought, beliefs, and bureaucratic power within the government, and its pervasive influence through the country and now even the world. It encourages reliance on the habit of military preparedness and the unquestioned acceptance of a militarized balance-of-power system. This unwarranted emphasis on the role of military influences often comes more from civilians than from career military people, perhaps because the latter may be more familiar with the costs of military action.

George W. Bush's presidency illustrates the bureaucratic steamroller impact of a more highly militarized form of foreign policy.[118] His administration gave the Department of State insufficient budget for its policies and programs, except for anti-terrorism. Secretary of State Madeline Albright later confirmed that the State Department "ceded a lot of authority to the Defense Department" after 2001. The Bush administration cut the State Department out of many decisions that normally would have belonged to the department. Secretary of State Colin Powell "learned of Bush's plan to withdraw from the Kyoto Protocol . . . only after it had been decided."[119] As the Department of State was defunded, spending skyrocketed at the Department of Defense. One result of too large a military-industrial complex and too small a US peacebuilding presence was the

---

[117] Dan Plesch and Thomas G. Weiss, "1945's Lesson: 'Good Enough' Global Governance Ain't Good Enough," *Global Governance*, 21 (2015), 203.

[118] Farrow, *War on Peace*, xxiii.

[119] Farrow, *War on Peace*, xxiv.

Iraq war. The decline of the Foreign Service continued through both the Obama and Trump administrations with the Department of State being underutilized, especially after 2016. Military officials have increasingly handled international negotiations to end fighting and arrange economic reconstruction—functions that earlier were handled by people trained in diplomacy and conflict resolution. As a result of such changes, "a different set of relationships have come to form the bedrock of American foreign policy. . . . Where civilians are not empowered to negotiate, military-to-military dealings . . . flourish."[120] As a result, the US military-industrial complex has spawned local, indigenous "military-industrial complexes," or their functional equivalent, in Vietnam, Iraq, and other countries. The bureaucratic power and budgetary clout of military institutions can unintentionally pull overseas policies away from preparing as robustly for a non-military path in the future as for a military path.

Many members of Congress also encourage less funding for diplomatic priorities and more for the military-industrial complex. The decline of internationalism in Congress was underscored when Jesse Helms become chairman of the Senate Committee on Foreign Relations in 1994,[121] a sharp contrast to the role played by Congress during the years when the committee was chaired by J. William Fulbright, who warned about "the arrogance of power" in trying to call policymakers to account as they escalated the war in Vietnam.[122]

In addition to many legislators' sharing political realists' desire for US military primacy, they also smile on the ability of the Departments of Defense and Energy to employ large numbers of people, with constituents employed in every congressional district in the country. In addition, members of Congress and advocates of military preparedness usually believe that military spending is a great creator of jobs and a boon to the economy. Yet an equal amount of spending in non-military categories usually would create more jobs than military spending. The problem is that non-military spending simply does not obtain the congressional votes as easily as military spending. Expenditures on solar energy, for example, employ 21 percent more people than equivalent spending in the military.[123]

Not one of the destabilizing new realities mentioned in Chapter 1 can be addressed by high levels of military preparedness in the old balance-of-power system. If the United States and other great powers continue to follow traditional priorities over the next two decades, for example, they will put low-lying homes and croplands for tens of millions of people under water—hardly a security gain. Spending trillions on more military power will only add to environmental disaster, because the Pentagon and its counterparts in other countries are among the largest polluters in the world.

---

[120] Farrow, *War on Peace*, xxi, xxx.

[121] Farrow, *War on Peace*, xxii.

[122] J. F. Fulbright, *The Arrogance of Power* (New York: Random House, 1966).

[123] See Heidi Garrett-Peltier, "Study Says Domestic, Not Military Spending, Fuels Job Growth," Costs of War Project, Watson Institute for International and Public Affairs, Brown University, https://www.brown.edu/news/2017-05-25/jobscow.

Military purchases also take money away from serving human needs and the spread of clean energy which, if funded, would help reduce global warming and political polarization that simply must be decreased if one is serious about curtailing terrorism and unwanted migration. So US military spending and the military-industrial complex's pervasive presence need to be reduced and the US peacebuilding agenda and assets greatly expanded in order to increase security for people in the United States and everywhere else.

Fourth, future policy could also benefit from taking into consideration the role that fear plays in international relations and from striving not to generate fear. As James Speer has noted, the primary psychological reaction to international anarchy "is not the lust for power but simply fear. In such a milieu the . . . Hobbesian passion is fear, and the power thrust ought properly to be seen as a secondary phenomenon, that is, as a reaction to fear." A national government can never be sure of what a rival's intentions may be (as long as states retain this international system). A fear reaction may be "especially true when the anarchic environment is marked by a [nuclear] technology that has first drawn all peoples into close proximity and then threatened them with imminent and total mutual destruction. In such an ecology, fear becomes paranoiac."[124] Add to this fear the possibilities of irreversible scarcities of fresh water and global warming and of cyber vulnerabilities. Fears are understandable, and fears are devastatingly consequential for thinking and acting, but policymakers have not brought them thoughtfully into strategic thinking about the need for global institution-building to address the reasons that fears arise. International institutions can reduce fears if they increase transparency, communication, monitoring, and enforcement.

Policymakers' focus on *national* security becomes self-defeating because a singular national focus generates fears for others. It motivates high US military preparedness. This in turn stimulates new fears in the minds of adversaries, who then strengthen themselves in ways that produce new worries for the United States—the well-known security dilemma. Speer observes, "Fear tends to drive out reason. Hence, if the fear be great, as under the nuclear terror, a rational diplomacy will have but intermittent opportunities at best, and its accomplishments will tend to dissipate in the next crisis when fear again reaches a climax."[125] Yet if diplomacy has only scant and intermittent opportunity to overcome fear, then it has little opportunity to be truly effective because it needs to attempt to change the international ethos and create an effective world organization with sustained, dependable security measures that may reduce fears, moving toward international limits on the means of destruction. Speer questions Morgenthau's reliance on the slender reed of diplomacy to move toward a world system, rather than upon global governance, "to create the order out of which a sense of community can grow."[126] He suggests that a "better thesis would appear to be that, whether men [and women] and states are seen as power-lusting or as fearful, they are

[124] Speer, "Hans Morgenthau," 223.
[125] Speer, "Hans Morgenthau," 224.
[126] Speer, "Hans Morgenthau," 227.

to be tamed or reassured only by government." Speer argues that "only within a governed ecology can the . . . empathetic community grow and prosper." In other words, some form of international organization "is the *beginning* of community in its fuller sense, rather than its culmination."[127] In the contemporary context, one might argue that gradual strengthening of international laws and institutions could establish relationships that will in turn nurture enough community gradually to reduce anarchy and enable a safe international public limit on weapons of mass destruction.

In the pre-nuclear age, international anarchy was acceptable because it did not threaten a state's security. But with the coming of nuclear weapons and supersonic delivery systems, acute cyber vulnerabilities, and environmental destruction, anarchy plus continued belief in 19th-century national identities have become problematic, because they block dependable peace.[128] All nations have become vulnerable to destruction. Nuclear weapons changed anarchy's relationship to security because security invulnerability became impossible. Vulnerability became inevitable unless a world organization could reduce anarchy.

This reality has not been addressed by US grand strategy. In examining debates over grand strategy,[129] one finds national security policymakers discussing extensively how to maximize US military power and security, but one looks in vain for discourse about how to establish a sustainable world of peace and justice for all people or how to overcome the fears that exacerbate the nuclear danger. Neither the carefully crafted arguments for "deep engagement"[130] for the United States nor those for "retrenchment"[131] come to grips with the need to initiate a global peace strategy, without which national security can never again be sustained. In their excellent comparison of "competing

---

[127] Speer, "Hans Morgenthau," 227. Italics added.

[128] Deudney notes that "the relationship between anarchy and security is that it depends on levels of vulnerability rooted in the material context." Great insecurity, such as in the nuclear age, might lead to a rejection of anarchy. "Regrounding Realism," 24.

[129] Posen and Ross, "Competing Visions," 5–53; Rodger A. Payne, "Cooperative Security: Grand Strategy Meets Critical Theory?" *Millennium: Journal of International Studies* 40, no. 3 (June 2012): 604–624; Stephen G. Brooks, G. John Ikenberry, and William C. Wohlforth, "Don't Come Home, America: The Case against Retrenchment," *International Security* 37, no. 3 (Winter 2012/13): 7–51.

[130] See Brooks, Ikenberry, and Wohlforth, "Don't Come Home," 7. They argue, "A grand strategy of actively managing global security and promoting the liberal economic order has served the United States exceptionally well for the past six decades, and there is no reason to give it up now." See also, Ikenberry, *Liberal Leviathan*; Robert J. Lieber, *Power and Willpower in the American Future: Why the United States Is Not Destined to Decline* (New York: Cambridge University Press, 2012).

[131] Barry R. Posen, "The Case for Restraint," *American Interest* 3, no. 1 (November/December 2007): 7–17; Barry R. Posen, "A Grand Strategy of Restraint," in *Finding Our Way: Debating American Strategy*, ed. Michele A. Flournoy and Shawn Brimley (Washington, DC: Center for a New American Security, 2008), 81–102; John J. Mearsheimer, "Imperial by Design," *National Interest*, no. 111 (January/February 2011): 16–34; Paul K. MacDonald and Joseph M. Parent, "Graceful Decline? The Surprising Success of Great Power Retrenchment," *International Security*, 35, no. 4 (Spring 2011): 7–44; Christopher Layne, *The Peace of Illusions: American Grand Strategy from 1940 to the Present* (Ithaca, NY: Cornell University Press, 2006); Robert A. Pape, "It's the Occupation, Stupid," *Foreign Policy*, October 18, 2010, http://www.foreignpolicy.com/articles/2010.10/18/it_s_the_occupation-stupid; Robert A. Pape and James K. Feldman, *Cutting the Fuse: The Explosion of Global Suicide Terrorism and How to Stop It* (Chicago: University of Chicago Press, 2010).

visions" for a desirable grand strategy, Barry Posen and Andrew Ross make clear, although without emphasizing the importance of this finding, that the major purposes of *all* grand strategies under consideration—neo-isolationism, selective engagement, cooperative security, and primacy—range only from a "narrow commitment to the basic safety of the United States to an ambitious effort to secure permanent US global preeminence."[132] Among the major powers and even in debates within the United Nations Security Council, there is no grand strategy under consideration to establish an international system capable of reducing anarchy and building a just, sustainable peace for all the world's people.

Yet without such a strategy, every nation's security is in danger. Posen and Ross acknowledge that attempting to pursue US security with even the most plentiful military power in a grand strategy of primacy "is probably unsustainable and self-defeating."[133] The most telling criticism of grand strategies currently under debate is that the institutionalization of peace processes and the transformation of malleable elements of the existing balance-of-power system sufficient to make peace sustainable, along with generating the necessary political support, are not being studied.

On the one hand, exponents of US retrenchment claim that the current US grand strategy, especially the involvement in the Middle East and southwest Asia, is not serving the national interests of the United States. These exponents are probably correct that the outflow of money, time, and effort for US far-flung military deployments does not produce benefits commensurate to the expenditure. Indeed, these priorities seem to be counter-productive in terms of what the deployments accomplish. They may even encourage more hostility toward the United States—*unless*, one might add, these efforts would be modulated by and tightly connected to institutionalizing global peace for all in the long run.

On the other hand, the exponents of liberal internationalism and deep engagement are probably correct that retrenchment, in itself, will not encourage, let alone enable, the forms of help and cooperation with other nations that are needed for US security in the future—*unless* a US military pullback would be connected closely with the institutionalization of a peace plan, rooted in multilateral norms and institutions, that will not only take the place of a US forward-based military presence but also move far beyond it, both in diminishing the role of military power (i.e., nuclear free zones) and in increasing the role of international law and institutions in modest vertical dispersal and melding of sovereignties.

All four of the prevailing schools of US strategic thought—neo-isolationism, selective engagement, cooperative security, and primacy—could become stronger and wiser if they would connect their criticisms of the other schools by addressing the need for a plan from their own perspective for sustainable peace in a more stable, fair, and reliably structured international system. As presently constituted, all, with the

---

[132] Posen and Ross, "Competing Visions," 5.
[133] Posen and Ross, "Competing Visions," 41.

partial exception of cooperative security, are an invitation to more interstate struggle and military competition. Since conflicts and struggles will never go away, the key to a desirable security arrangement is to direct as much struggle as possible into expanded and more predictable legal and political processes, away from military contestation.

Does humanity have a choice, national security managers might ask, between accepting war and terror as a recurring reality in life and building dependable peace and justice? Although the architecture of the presently militarized balance-of-power system may appear to prevent the human species from governing itself in ways that will enable it to survive with dignity intact, the question remains: Why can humans not devise a better system, one that would enable enough cooperative behavior to improve their mutual security? Certainly the human capacity to govern millions of diverse people within large and culturally diverse political units, such as are now governed in India or the United States, suggests that it might be possible, with some vertical dispersal of sovereignty, to balance centralization and decentralization, majority decision-making and minority rights sufficiently to improve the architecture of the international system to enhance security for all people.

For this to happen, however, strategic thinking would need to shift from a focus on security for one country to shaping a *global* system capable of delivering sustainable *human* (rather than narrowly *national*) security. Grand strategy, which Barry Posen characterizes as a state's "theory about how to produce security for itself,"[134] could shift focus from a nation-state perspective to a human-species perspective that aims to secure all people. If wisely designed and implemented, an empirically based global grand strategy, elaborated in the next chapter, could empower people and emancipate them, creating opportunities to choose between accepting war and terrorism—more of what we have—or building sustainable peace with more justice and environmental health.

---

[134] Posen, *Restraint*, 1.

5

Developing a Security-Enhancing Strategy

EVEN THOUGH INTERNATIONAL peacebuilding is complex and research offers few clear-cut guarantees, a synthesis of diverse research findings from studies of war and peace over several decades suggests six correlates of sustainable peace and security. Peace reigns when these conditions are present: (1) Nations' specific security fears are being addressed. (2) People are able to meet their basic needs. (3) Nations enjoy reciprocal rights and duties in their interactions. (4) Nations are treated equitably in their relationships. (5) Nations' and people's lives are predictable, insofar as possible, and their human rights are assured because they live in an international system governed by the rule of impartial law. (6) Nations and people participate in the decisions that affect their lives through fair representation in democratic global governing processes.

Research has uncovered no reason that these conditions cannot be met in a future international system, and much evidence indicates that they could be implemented—not perfectly, but substantially enough to be workable. That these conditions are conducive to peace is substantiated by our synthesis of research and by much more research from more disciplines than one book can compile.[1] These correlates of peace are stated in Table 5.1 near the end of this chapter in a form that enables them to be used as guidelines to shape a global grand strategy for peace and human security. These six conditions treated as independent variables should not be expected singularly to produce the desired results, but together they are highly likely to do so.

---

[1] Much of this research is cited in the notes in the Introduction, but it is not limited to that chapter alone. Somewhat different recent syntheses have been done by Wallensteen, *Quality Peace*, and Cortright, Seyle, and Wall, *Governance for Peace*.

These correlational guidelines can shape a strategy to address all security needs and provide dependable peace. Of course, there is not agreement among experts on exactly how to employ these six influential factors. Yet ample research shows that negating their substantive content contributes to polarization and violence and that implementing them contributes to peace. In addition, much evidence from historical experience and wisdom and philosophical traditions reinforces them, which should raise them to a high level of importance for decision-making. These guidelines do not end debate over how to proceed, but they do suggest a promising direction to follow and good reasons to do so. If citizens and policymakers seek a new grand strategy based on these contributors to the common good, rather than continue a strategy serving mainly only one national part of it, then the prospects for building a reformed world order with sustainable peace and increased justice will be greatly enhanced.[2]

5.1 REDUCING FEARS

First of all, it is necessary to strengthen both the attitudinal and structural foundations on which peace and security can be constructed. Although this point seems obvious, in practice most governments, in focusing on national military security, have not genuinely attempted to lay the foundations for sustainable peace. As indicated previously, the prevailing guideline in policy planning is still the ages-old maxim: If you want peace, prepare for war.[3] Yet preparing for war is not equivalent to preparing to maintain peace. Nonetheless, most powerful governments assume that if they are prepared to fight the next war, it will not occur, because no one will attack. If no one attacks, the thinking goes, peace will be the default result. That simple-minded strategy may have given the impression of succeeding in the short run, but sustainable peace is not simply a default setting that manifests itself as a result of avoiding war by maintaining high military preparedness. To be dependable and sustainable, peace must be routinized and institutionalized while war is rendered both less necessary and less possible.

The human species seems reluctant to embrace this fundamental truth, clearly articulated by Immanuel Kant in 1795: "The state of peace among men [and women] living side by side is not the natural state; the natural state is one of war . . . , at least an unceasing threat of war. A state of peace, therefore, must be *established*, for in order to be secured against hostility it is not sufficient that hostilities simply be not committed."[4] For more than two centuries, national security planners have largely ignored this insight and not worked at establishing the conditions necessary to sustain peace.

---

[2] An earlier version of some ideas in this chapter first appeared in Robert C. Johansen, "Developing a Grand Strategy for Peace and Human Security: Guidelines from Research, Theory, and Experience," *Global Governance* 23, no. 4 (2017): 525–536.

[3] See, for example, United States Joint Forces Command, *Joint Operating Environment 2010: US National Security Posture Statement*, 62, http://www.fas.org/man/eprint/joe2010.pdf.

[4] Italics in original. Immanuel Kant, *Perpetual Peace* in *Immanuel Kant: On History*, ed. Lewis White Beck (Indianapolis, IN: Bobbs-Merrill, 1963), originally published in 1795.

A domestic analogy clarifies the wisdom in Kant's point. Within a society, a peaceful social fabric is not woven by merely preventing riots and violent clashes among differing races or other contending groups, important though that is. Additional initiatives are needed to transform institutionalized racial, ethnic, religious, economic, or other forms of conflict and insecurity-inducing relationships in order to provide reliable rules, institutions, and opportunities for competing groups, meanwhile encouraging healthy cross-cutting social cleavages among different groups on diverse issues.[5] Such interactions, occurring while maintaining peace through legal processes, can gradually build mutual respect and trust, transform an imagined community[6] into a genuine community, and nurture more inclusive identities that discourage violence even in moments of crisis. Analogous initiatives are needed internationally to reduce inequities and strengthen representative international institutions in order to increase all societies' stake in a peaceful and secure world order that enhances, in Morgenthau's words, human "equality in freedom."[7]

Focusing on a high level of military preparedness while underemphasizing the institutionalization of peace throws life out of balance. It often causes new insecurities to arise among international adversaries because a government with superb military preparedness may unintentionally generate an arms rivalry with other governments that may feel threatened by its preparedness. Empirical studies show that "arms races of military build-ups do in fact, by their mere presence, make it more likely that a serious dispute will escalate to war."[8] In addition, it may be tempting to initiate an unnecessary war if a country's military assets enable it to make and win war with impunity. High military preparedness encouraged the US decision to attack Iraq in 2003, for example, but the anticipated easy victory for peace eluded Washington officials because, in mistakenly assuming that peace is simply a default setting after war, they did not plan for constructing real peace in Iraq. Violent insecurities have plagued Iraqi society ever since the US invasion. These have spread additional violence far beyond Iraqi borders, fertilizing nearby fields for the growth of Al-Qaeda and the Islamic State to take root. The lack of a serious plan for building peace globally is as true and fraught with danger today as it was for building peace in Iraq in 2003.

Research confirms that policymakers and citizens should stop expecting a dependable peace to be a side benefit or default consequence of preparations for war or even the termination of a war.[9] Yet that continues to be the prevailing approach of major powers around the world, commanding enormous resources. Although preparing for war to bring peace may give policymakers a sense of security when operating with a

---

[5] See Ashutosh Varshney's brilliant study of violence and peace within a country: *Ethnic Conflict and Civic Life: Hindus and Muslims in India* (New Haven, CT: Yale University Press, 2003).

[6] Benedict R. Anderson, *Imagined Communities* (London: Verso, 2016).

[7] Morgenthau, *Purpose of American Politics*, 309.

[8] Vasquez, "Steps to War," 137.

[9] Note the deliberate, elaborate efforts after World War II to build a peaceful European community, contrasted to efforts following World War I to achieve peace within Europe through renewed preparations for war with high levels of military preparedness.

short-range view and a national viewpoint, from a global perspective in an increasingly interdependent world, it provides no structure for sustainable peace.

However, if anyone attempts to change strategies to embrace the goal of preparing for peace, another problem arises: One's credibility is questioned by national security planners. Why is groundwork for peace needed, security specialists will ask, when violence threatens around the world? Military analyses on the future of US security frequently emphasize that we live in a time of endless violence. As far as military officials can see into the future, US forces "will be continually engaged."[10] As a *Washington Post* article on one of these reports explained, "[Because] America's wars are unending . . . any talk of peace is quixotic or naïve." Well before Donald Trump moved into the White House, "peace . . . has become something of a dirty word in Washington foreign-policy circles."[11]

The widespread belief that peace is quixotic and naïve shapes national conduct.[12] For example, when the Republican-led US House of Representatives passed its preferred national budget several years ago, one of its goals was to cut funding for the US Institute of Peace to zero. Yet this publicly supported agency has been one of the most interested in research on making peace sustainable. At the time of the House vote, Richard Solomon, the Institute's president, lamented: "Peace doesn't reflect the world we are dealing with."[13] Diplomatically, when a military power suffers attacks by violent extremists, the prevailing approach calls for responding with military power even though abundant evidence (for example, from experience with terrorism in Israel, Algeria, Vietnam, Afghanistan, and Iraq) demonstrates that this frequently stimulates more violent extremism.

If peace is not prominent in the mental picture that shapes the mindset of esteemed political elites, it is important to bring to our conscious attention that the era of recurring or "unending" wars arose in part because the preparations-for-war approach simply has not worked. It has not built a foundation for peace that could enable it to occur. The prevailing US approach has not included a plan to institutionalize peace, which might enable it to happen.

To develop an effective peacebuilding plan, the place to begin is by listening carefully to people's existential fears about insecurity, because "at the root of all war is fear."[14] Fears drive arms races and underpin many threats. Indeed, the quality of peace that can be created is determined by "the nature and quality of relationships developed

---

[10] United States Joint Forces Command, *Joint Operating Environment*, 4.

[11] Gregg Jaffe, "A Decade After the 9/11 Attacks, Americans Live in an Era of Endless War," *Washington Post*, September 4, 2011, http://www.washingtonpost.com/world/national-security/a-decade-after-the-911-attacks-americans-live-in-an-era-of-endless-war/2011/09/01/gIQARUXD2J_story.html.

[12] Many studies indicate that false understandings often shape conduct. See, for example, Daniel L. Schacter, *The Seven Sins of Memory: How the Mind Forgets and Remembers* (New York: Houghton Mifflin, 2001); Rose Eveleth, *How Fake Images Change Our Memories and Behavior*, http://www.bbc.com/future/story/20121213-fake-pictures-make-real-memories.

[13] Jaffe, "Endless War," 4.

[14] Thomas Merton, *New Seeds of Contemplation* (New York: New Directions, 1961), 112; Jim Forest, *The Root of War Is Fear: Thomas Merton's Advice to Peacemakers* (Maryknoll, NY: Orbis, 2016).

with those most feared."[15] Research confirms that one can bring peace realistically into people's picture of the world and can gain credibility while endeavoring to build peace *only* if one simultaneously addresses people's existential security fears.[16] It is not built by manipulating people or "by forcing one or the other's hand."[17]

Of course, it is not enough to deal with the security fears felt by people in one's own country alone; the security fears of people in *all* relevant countries must be addressed[18] with genuine understanding if one wants to transcend self-defeating insecurity syndromes. Peacebuilding is a task for those strongly committed to building a better world because aiming for such a world brings constructive engagement with "those people and things we least understand and most fear." It is an "inevitably perilous but absolutely necessary journey"[19] that leads eventually to building genuine community with many with whom we disagree, enabled in part because as parts of the same species we also share a common fate that can bind us together.

Unaddressed fears close people's minds to useful peacebuilding knowledge and undermine political support for its utilization.[20] Fears freeze perspectives and lead at times to panic-driven activity. If one does not develop sensitivity to others' fears, one cannot gain their support, which one needs to build sustainable peace. UN Secretary-General Dag Hammarskjöld believed that "you can only hope to find a lasting solution to a conflict if you have learned to see the other objectively, but, at the same time, to *experience* his [or her] difficulties subjectively."[21] Doing this requires an approach that takes all security threats seriously as the only way to overcome the classic security dilemma of unintentionally increasing the threat felt by one's adversary while trying to increase military security for oneself.

So the first guideline is to develop a credible *plan for peace-maintenance*[22] in which the primary goal is to address all nations' security fears,[23] even the fears of one's adversaries, by growing the attitudes, values, policies, laws, and institutions that mitigate

---

[15] Lederach, *Moral Imagination*, 63.

[16] Commission on Global Governance, *Our Global Neighbourhood*, 78–134.

[17] Lederach, *Moral Imagination*, 85.

[18] The United States failed to do this in calling for a centralized government in Kabul in the first years of its long war there, even though Afghanis were a diverse set of clans or tribes who may not have wanted a unified central government. For many people there, the United States was taking sides in a civil war. Taking sides gives some people a feeling that US forces are an occupying army, triggering suicide bombing attacks, and other violence that has made this the longest war in US history.

[19] Lederach, *Moral Imagination*, 173.

[20] Both peacemaking and peacebuilding have been moderately successful in strategic peacebuilding. See Human Security Report Project, *Causes of Peace*, 78; Philpott and Powers, eds., *Strategies of Peace*; Crocker, Hampson, and Aall, *Leashing the Dogs of War*; Weiss, Forsythe, Coate, and Pease, *The United Nations and Changing World Politics*; Doyle and Sambanis, *Making War and Building Peace*.

[21] Dag Hammarskjöld, *Markings* (London: Faber & Faber, 1965), quoted by Henning Melber, https://www.daghammarskjold.se/2341-2/. Italics added.

[22] "The result [of strategic thinking] is a plan, informed by the past, linked to the present, for achieving some future goal." Gaddis, *Grand Strategy*, 24.

[23] Marlies Glasius and Mary Kaldor note that to address "the real security needs of people in situations of severe insecurity [in other countries] . . . will . . . make the world safer for Europeans." Glasius and Kaldor, "A Human Security Vision," 4.

fears and contribute to everyone's security. Investments in peacebuilding to address fears do pay off.[24] As indicated above, these are not simply byproducts of preparations for war, nor is peace a default condition that prevails in the absence of armed conflict. To become dependable, a peaceful system must be imagined, built, institutionalized, and maintained, the topics that are addressed in the five remaining correlates.

5.2. EMPHASIZING HUMAN SECURITY

Foremost among the values of human dignity is the right to life—a life of dignity for every person on Earth. The second correlate of peace underscores that value by focusing on the security that human beings feel when they are able to meet all their basic needs. Emphasizing human security contrasts quite sharply in two ways from emphasizing national security. First, the subject of attention shifts to all human beings from just one national group of people. Second, the human needs of people are the focus rather than the power needs of the state. The latter, of course, is the primary concern of national security policymakers.

A comprehensive understanding of "human needs" can include everything that is required for physical and psychological health as well as the right to peace, freedom from being arbitrarily killed, and the presence of opportunities to realize one's human potential. This collection of human needs can also be expressed in the terms "human security." Both concepts have been widely used in the United Nations Development Program Reports. Many analysts now prefer to use "human security" rather than "human needs" to convey the urgency associated with inability to meet needs and also because of the parallels and contrasts that human security provides with national security. Human security may more clearly communicate the importance of addressing fear as well as want. To clarify and keep "correlate" analytically separate from "effect" in this book, the emphasis here will be that meeting basic human security needs in national contexts will contribute to achieving peace and security for the species in planetary context.

5.2.1 Defining Human Security

The UN General Assembly declared in 2012 that "human security" is an approach to assist in identifying and addressing "challenges to the survival, livelihood, and dignity" of peoples.[25] Commitment to this correlate means that any deliberate taking of innocent life, whether by states or non-state actors, is unacceptable. Because all

---

[24] For example, research shows that a robust international peacekeeping presence in conflict-ridden areas reduces violence and war. Håvard Hegre, Lisa Hultman, and Håvard Mokleiv Nygård, "Evaluating the Conflict-Reducing Effect of UN Peacekeeping Operations," *Journal of Politics* 81, no. 1 (2019): 215–232, doi:10.1086/700203, https://search.datacite.org/works/10.1086/700203.

[25] United Nations, General Assembly, Res 66/290. United Nations Trust Fund for Human Security, https://www.un.org/humansecurity/what-is-human-security/.

governments and individuals are called by the Universal Declaration of Human Rights to act toward all human beings in a spirit of brotherhood and sisterhood, all people should do what they can to get not only their own government but all governments to enable lives of dignity for all.[26] To replace a national security emphasis with a human security perspective focuses the new strategy solidly on the most fundamental unit of concern: human beings, their security, and their core rights, which include meeting their basic needs.[27] Former UN Secretary-General Kofi Annan recognized that the UN Charter's guarantee of sovereign independence for states should not obscure the organization's primary concern: "As long as I am Secretary-General," Annan said, the United Nations "will always place *human beings* at the center of everything we do." To be sure, "fundamental sovereignty, territorial integrity, and political independence of states" are cornerstones of the existing international system, but Annan warned that sovereignty must not provide "excuses for the inexcusable."[28] The most sensible and fitting language that captures what ought to be emphasized in a genuine quest for world peace and security is "human security,"[29] not merely state security or national security. As the UN's High-Level Panel on Threats, Challenges, and Change put it, "What we seek to protect reflects what we value." States are protected "not because they are intrinsically good but because they are necessary to achieve the dignity,

---

[26] Perry, *Global Political Morality*, 27.

[27] Human Security Report Project, *Causes of Peace; Human Security Report 2013: The Decline in Global Violence: Evidence, Explanation, and Contestation* (Vancouver, BC: Human Security Press, 2014); Shaun Breslin and George Christou, "Has the Human Security Agenda Come of Age? Definitions, Discourses and Debates," *Contemporary Politics* 21, no. 1 (2015): 1–10; Fen Osler Hampson and Mark Raymond, "Human Security as a Global Public Good," in *International Organization and Global Governance*, ed. Thomas G. Weiss and Rorden Wilkinson (New York: Routledge, 2013), 524–534; Nik Hynek, *Human Security as Statecraft: Structural Conditions, Articulations and Unintended Consequences* (New York: Routledge, 2012); Michael D. Intriligator, "Global Security and Human Security," *International Journal of Development and Conflict*, 1 (2011): 1–10; Mary Kaldor and Shannon D. Beebe, *The Ultimate Weapon Is No Weapon: Human Security and the New Rules of War and Peace* (New York: Public Affairs, 2010); S. N. MacFarlane and Yuen Foong Khong, *Human Security and the UN: A Critical History* (Bloomington: Indiana University Press, 2006); Wallensteen et al., "Violence, Wars, Peace," 411–456; Weiss and Thakur, *Global Governance and the UN*; Donna J. Winslow, "Human Security," in *The Role of the United Nations in Peace and Security, Global Development, and World Governance: An Assessment of the Evidence*, ed. Michaela Hordijk, Maartje van Eerd, and Kau Hofman (Lewiston, NY: Edwin Mellen Press, 2007), 103–124. On rights, see Pogge, *Politics as Usual*, 8, 28–29, 52. Nussbaum argues "that the same considerations that support political liberalism for Western societies also support it for other world societies, both internally, and in the construction of the international society of which Grotius spoke." Nussbaum, *Cosmopolitan Tradition*, 217.

Seventy-four percent of Europeans think that "the EU should guarantee human rights around the world, even if this is contrary to the wishes of some other countries." European Commission, "A Human Security Doctrine for Europe" 3, no. 6 (2004): 3.6, as cited by Glasius and Kaldor, "A Human Security Vision," 17.

[28] Italics supplied. Quoted by Judith Miller, "Sovereignty Isn't So Sacred Anymore," *New York Times*, April 18, 1999, IV, 4.

[29] See Fen O. Hampson and Christopher K. Penny, "Human Security," in *The Oxford Handbook on the United Nations*, ed. Sam Daws and Thomas G. Weiss, http://www.oxfordhandbooks.com.proxy.library. nd.edu/view/10.1093/oxfordhb/9780199560103.001.0001/oxfordhb-9780199560103-e-031?rskey=BGlQXH&result=1.

justice, worth and safety of their citizens."[30] Human security is founded on "the inherent dignity . . . of all members of the human family."[31] From this foundation, "the equal and inalienable rights of all members of the human family . . . derive."[32]

Human security begins with no direct physical harm, violence, or war to threaten anyone's life.[33] In addition, human security "embraces far more than the absence of violent conflict. It encompasses human rights, good governance, access to education and health care and ensuring that each individual has opportunities and choices to fulfill his or her own potential."[34] Simply stated, "From the perspective of human security, death, whether it be from violence or disease, is equally to be feared."[35] In the words of the International Commission on Intervention and State Sovereignty, it "means the security of people—their physical safety, their economic and social well-being, respect for their dignity and worth as human beings, and the protection of their human rights and fundamental freedoms."[36] It includes both preventing violent conflict and reducing poverty. Annan explained, "Freedom from want, freedom from fear and the freedom of future generations to inherit a healthy natural environment—these are the interrelated building blocks of human—and therefore national—security."[37] Human security breathes new life into the meaning of human solidarity and imposes helpful conditionality on the meaning of state sovereignty.

In addition to meeting human needs, human security strives to implement other fundamental human rights, including the right to peace and economic, social, and cultural rights.[38] It derives its nature from the international bill of human rights,

---

[30] United Nations High-Level Panel on Threats, Challenges, and Change, *A More Secure World: Our Shared Responsibility: Report of the High-Level Panel on Threats, Challenges, and Change* (New York: United Nations, 2004), 22, para. 30.

[31] Preamble, Universal Declaration of Human Rights; Michael J. Perry, *A Global Political Morality: Human Rights, Democracy, and Constitutionalism* (Cambridge: Cambridge University Press, 2017), 25.

[32] Both Covenants make this declaration. See Perry, *Global Political Morality*, 27–28. The UN General Assembly Resolution, "Setting International Standards in the Field of Human Rights," declares the "inherent dignity and worth of the human person." A/RES/41/120.

[33] For different conceptions of human security, see Hampson and Raymond, "Human Security as a Global Public Good," 525–526.

[34] United Nations Secretary-General Kofi Annan, "Secretary-General Salutes International Workshop of Human Security in Mongolia," Press Release SG/SM/7382 (May 8, 2000): 103, https://www.un.org/press/en/2000/20000508.sgsm7382.doc.html; quoted also by Donna J. Winslow, "Human Security," in *The Role of the United Nations in Peace and Security, Global Development, and World Governance: An Assessment of the Evidence*, ed. Michaela Hordijk, Maartje Van Eerd, and Kaj Hofman (Lewiston, NY: Edwin Mellen Press, 2007), 103. The concept of human security from its beginning included freedom from fear and freedom from want. Winslow, "Human Security," 106.

[35] Anne-Marie Slaughter, "Security, Solidarity, and Sovereignty: The Grand Themes of UN Reform," *American Journal of International Law* 99, no. 3 (2005): 619.

[36] See International Commission on Intervention and State Sovereignty, Gareth Evans and Mohamed Sahnoun, co-chairs, *The Responsibility to Protect: Report of the International Commission on Intervention and State Sovereignty* (Ottawa, Canada: International Development Research Centre, 2001), 15.

[37] Annan, "Secretary-General Salutes International Workshop of Human Security in Mongolia."

[38] A broad endorsement for implementing a concept of human security based on human solidarity is contained in United Nations Development Programme, "A World Social Charter," *Human Development Report 1994* (New York: Oxford University Press, 1994), 6.

particularly the Universal Declaration of Human Rights and the two main treaties spelling out international human rights.

This human needs-human security approach also embraces duties. All actors, from individuals to governments, have at least a negative duty not to violate others' rights, and ideally a positive duty to help implement everyone's basic rights. The international community expressed states' obligations by adopting a "world social charter" in which nations pledged "to build a new global civil society, based on the principles of equality of opportunity, rule of law, global democratic governance and a new partnership among all nations and all people."[39] When states sign the UN Charter to become members of the UN, they "accept a responsibility both to protect their own citizens and to meet their international obligations to their fellow nations. Failure to fulfill these responsibilities can legitimately subject them to sanction." In effect, human security means that "membership in the United Nations is no longer a validation of sovereign status and a shield against unwanted meddling in a state's domestic jurisdiction. It is rather the right and capacity to participate in the United Nations itself, working in concert with other nations to sit in judgment of and take action against threats to human security whenever and wherever they arise."[40]

Implementing human rights generally contributes to human security not only because rights protect people from mistreatment, but also because they bring practical social benefits for human security. For example, increasing women's participation in political and economic institutions generally and in ceasefire negotiations specifically increases the prospects for peace, economic development, social justice, and sustainable democracy. Simply respecting equality for women reduces the likelihood of violence both within societies and between them. Women's inclusion in power structures helps to prevent violent conflict, create peace, moderate extremism, sustain peace after violent conflicts end,[41] and increase the prospects for democracy, social justice, and economic development to meet human needs.[42]

Higher percentages of women in parliaments correlate with reduced risks of civil war.[43] To allow the currently diminished roles for women in many countries to continue increases the likelihood of child abuse and neglect as well as of violence and war. Research on 58 violent conflicts within states between 1980 and 2003 found that when there were no women in the legislature, the risk that violence will recur increases over

---

Care needs to be exercised to ensure that human security initiatives are not too narrowly defined and do not instrumentalize human rights or give the impression that human security goals may limit or diminish the importance of basic rights, including the right to be free of torture and arbitrary death.

[39] United Nations Development Programme, *Human Development Report 1994*, 6.

[40] Slaughter, "Security, Solidarity, Sovereignty," 619–620.

[41] Valerie Hudson, Bonnie Ballif-Spanvill, Mary Caprioli, and Chad F. Emmett, *Sex and World Peace* (New York: Columbia University Press, 2012); Mary Caprioli, "Gendered Conflict," *Journal of Peace Research* 37, no. 1 (2000): 53–68; Mary Caprioli and Mark Boyer, "Gender, Violence, and International Crisis," *Journal of Conflict Resolution* 45 (August 2001): 503–518; Patrick M. Regan and Aida Paskeviciute, "Women's Access to Politics and Peaceful States," *Journal of Peace Research* 40, no. 3 (2003): 287–302.

[42] Cortright, Seyle, and Wall, *Governance for Peace*, 19.

[43] Erik Melander, "Gender Equality and Intrastate Armed Conflict," *International Studies Quarterly* 49, no. 4 (2005): 695–714.

time, but when women constitute as much as 35 percent of the legislature, the risk of relapsing into violence "is near zero."[44]

Although the causal links are not easy to specify given the complexity of social influences on violence and extremism, multiple studies show that gender inequality is associated with violent conflict both within states and between states. Where women are "empowered in multiple spheres of life, countries are less likely to go to war with their neighbors, to be in bad standing with the international community, or to be rife with crime and violence within their society."[45] Also, when women participate in and influence decisions about war and peace and when they play a leading role in addressing extremism, their "inclusion helps prevent [violent] conflict, create peace, and sustain security after war ends."[46] Indeed, some studies report that "gender equality is a better indicator of a state's peacefulness than other factors like democracy, religion, or GDP."[47] In all these cases, advancing human rights also aids prudential politics and peacebuilding.

Including women in negotiating processes generally increases the likelihood of peace, justice, and human security, yet only 2 percent of mediators and 9 percent of negotiators in 31 peace processes between 1992 and 2011 have been women.[48] Because women's identities also tend on average to be more inclusive than men's,[49] they are statistically more likely to be good peacebuilders and to contribute to a culture of peace.[50] Raising women's inclusion generally will almost certainly increase peace and justice, suggesting an enormous potential increase in human security is possible and within reach.[51]

---

[44] See Jacqueline H. R. Demeritt and Angela D. Nichols, "Female Participation and Civil War Relapse," *Civil Wars* 16, no. 3 (2014): 362.

[45] Marie O'Reilly, "Why Women? Inclusive Security and Peaceful Societies," *Inclusive Security*, October 2015 Report, 4, https://www.inclusivesecurity.org/wp-content/uploads/2017/06/Why-Women-Report-2017.pdf.

[46] O'Reilly, "Why Women?" 3–5; Hudson, Ballif-Spanvill, Caprioli, and Emmett, *Sex and World Peace*.

[47] "War-ravaged Syria, for example, has the third-most discriminatory social institutions of 108 countries surveyed." O'Reilly, "Why Women?" 4.

[48] United Nations Office for the Coordination of Humanitarian Affairs, OCHA Services, "Women's Participation in Peace Negotiations: Connections between Presence and Influence" (October 2012): 3 https://reliefweb.int/report/world/women%E2%80%99s-participation-peace-negotiations-connections-between-presence-and-influence; O'Reilly, "Why Women?" 3.

[49] See, for example, O'Reilly, "Why Women?" 4–11; Frances Stewart, *Horizontal Inequalities as a Cause of Conflict: Understanding Group Violence in Multiethnic Societies* (New York: Palgrave Macmillan, 2008); Daron Acemoglu and James Robinson, *Why Nations Fail: The Origins of Power, Prosperity and Poverty* (New York: Crown, 2012).

[50] Desiree Nilsson, "Anchoring the Peace: Civil Society Actors in Peace Accords and Durable Peace," *International Interactions* (2009) 38, no. 2, 243–266; Sanam Naraghi-Anderlkini, "21st Century Diplomacy: From Power Sharing to Responsibility Sharing," International Civil Society Action Network, *The Better Peace Tool* (2015): 3–28; Thania Paffenholz, ed., *Civil Society and Peacebuilding: A Critical Assessment* (Boulder, CO: Lynne Rienner, 2010); Hudson, Ballif-Spanvill, Caprioli, and Emmett, *Sex and World Peace*.

[51] On the inclusion of women, see Commission on Global Security, Justice and Governance, *Confronting the Crisis of Global Governance: Report of the Commission on Global Security, Justice and Governance* (The Hague: Hague Institute for Global Justice and Stimson Center, 2015), xvii, 24, 32; Commission on Global Governance, *Our Global Neighborhood*, 17, 22, 36, 143, 284–285, 346.

Because human security embodies the principle that every human life is of equal moral worth, a grand strategy that aims straightforwardly to achieve human security will integrate concern for core rights in all situations.[52] Although human rights discourse may vary from culture to culture, human rights are the foundation of all law, politics, government, and sovereignty itself—*if* these possess international legitimacy. Taking human dignity seriously sometimes requires citizens to go around and beyond their governments, not always through them. The concept of human security can enjoy high ethical, philosophical, and political standing because it calls forth people's compassionate recognition that other people, no matter how different, are part of a common humanity.

5.2.2 Harmonizing Human Security and National Security

The concept of human security includes many traditional national security goals, such as peace and economic well-being. These might be achieved more reliably if they were recognized as common security goals that apply to all nations. However, supporters of the militarized balance-of-power system and traditional national security policies are less comfortable with the human security emphasis than with the familiar national security paradigm that highlights group behavior motivated by narrow self-interest and often by international aggression, as of course it *may* be. Yet human behavior is not in fact limited to such motivation, as social science research increasingly demonstrates. For example, an international group of social scientists specifically asked to examine the origins of human aggression reported that "just as 'wars begin in the minds of men,' peace also begins in our minds. The same species who invented war is capable of inventing peace." In their concluding statement, which was adopted by UNESCO's General Conference, they said, "It is scientifically incorrect to say that war or any other violent behaviour is genetically programmed into our human nature."[53]

Cooperative international behavior does occasionally cross boundaries of primary national identity,[54] especially when potential mutual benefits seem clear. Possibilities for such behavior are deeply ingrained in human beings because of evolutionary history,[55] which contains as many non-zero-sum (cooperative) as zero-sum (competitive) activities. The scale and intertwining density of cooperative interactions between

---

[52] Christin Chinkin, "International Law Framework with Respect to International Peace and Security," in *A Human Security Doctrine for Europe: Project, Principles, Practicalities*, ed. Marlies Glasius and Mary Kaldor (London: Routledge, 2006), 175.

[53] UNESCO General Conference, November 16, 1989, "Culture of Peace Programme," http://www.unesco.org/cpp/uk/declarations/seville.pdf, 3; Alfie Kohn, "Are Humans Innately Aggressive?," *Psychology Today* (June) 1988, http://www.alfiekohn.org/article/humans-innately-aggressive/; Fromm, *The Sane Society*; Ralph White, *Fearful Warriors: A Psychological Profile of US-Soviet Relations* (New York: Free Press, 1984); Erik H. Erikson, *Gandhi's Truth* (New York: Norton, 1969).

[54] See Monroe, *Heart of Altruism*; Boulding, *Three Faces of Power*.

[55] Samuel Bowles and Herbert Gintis, *A Cooperative Species: Human Reciprocity and Its Evolution* (Princeton, NJ: Princeton University Press, 2011), 13; Christakis, *Blueprint: Evolutionary Origins*, 272–308.

previously separate groups has grown throughout human biological and cultural history.[56] Natural selection processes have built into human genes an ability to organize reciprocal benefits across identity boundaries as well as to enlarge identities.[57] Of course this evidence does not mean that international cooperation is inevitable, but it does suggest that new forms of boundary-crossing cooperation are possible and have happened many times in history. There also is evidence that these possibilities are found in all cultures.[58]

Prudence should caution strategic thinkers against focusing only or even primarily on zero-sum forms of competition, although that clearly is part of international relations. The human security paradigm takes seriously (1) that humans can be motivated for positive ends toward others either for self-interested reasons or a combination of self-interested and altruistic reasons, and (2) that there is a stronger argument than is usually acknowledged among policymakers in the great powers that a different system of international relations could take root and embody a less violent character than the system that we have lived within since the rise of the modern nation-state system.[59] It might be possible, in this era of new communication and interdependence, for human identities to include respect for all people and for social and political organizations to become more democratic and global in scope.[60]

Peacebuilding usually benefits when identity changes occur moving from narrow nationalism to slightly more cosmopolitan nationalism. This may happen when a person feels called to change by friends or authority figures whom one respects, because they can encourage awareness that inclusive identity and mutual respect are attributes of exemplary human conduct. Change also is encouraged when a person begins to change the relative weight he or she gives to various criteria of what constitutes fulfillment of who one "really is."[61] Both conditions would be present, for example, if one's friends would advocate equal opportunity for all women as a human right, and one would begin to value upholding human rights as a duty.

Because individuals possess multiple identities and multiple standards for their identities, possibilities for identity change are always present, although complicated. First, increased recognition by people that they are operating in a new security environment facilitates identity change. Second, recognizing differences between national security and human security also spurs change. Inner resistance to more inclusive identity can be eased by understanding that long-range national security often is better sustained by upholding human security. Third, identity change can be stimulated by growing awareness that one's identity standard (e.g., being a law-abiding world

---

[56] Wright, *Nonzero*, 251–336.

[57] See Wright, *Nonzero*; and Robert Wright, *The Moral Animal: Evolutionary Psychology and Everyday Life* (New York: Pantheon Books, 1994).

[58] Christakis, *Blueprint: Evolutionary Origins*, 410–419; Wright, *Nonzero*, 23.

[59] Bowles and Gintis, "A Cooperative Species," 13.

[60] Christakis, *Blueprint: Evolutionary Origins*.

[61] Julie Putnam Hart and Anjel N. Stough-Hunter, *Pathways to Pacifism and Antiwar Activism among US Veterans* (New York: Lexington Books, 2017), 17.

citizen) is not being met in one's actual behavior as it has been channeled by one's own government (e.g., not respecting the Charter prohibition of aggressive use of force). Fourth, identity change is more likely when a person feels a psychological need to affirm others' identities in order to remain a member in good standing within a larger group.[62] For example, identifying with others in a compassionate religious tradition should encourage kind treatment for all others, even when they are of a different race, religion, or nationality.

The process in which a person's identity may expand to include all people can occur because people naturally seek verification that their identity conduct harmonizes with their identity standards based on valuing human dignity.[63] If there is dissonance between one's standards and one's behavior, change eventually brings consistency between them. More inclusive behaviors and identity standards may grow mutually.[64]

The aforementioned understandings of human nature are not necessary to demonstrate that a human-centered concept of security makes good sense, but they add strength to its prospects. This evidence and examples of system change throughout history might ease some people's hesitations about seriously considering a human security framework. Exploring the evidence might provide a basis for exponents of human security and national security to find more common ground.

The remarkable changes in long-standing hostile German and French identities and separate military interests illustrate how quickly these identities and national interests can change. They were transformed into common security interests in less than two decades between the onset of World War II and the start of the European Coal and Steel Community. War might have made each nation more resistant to identity change, as had happened following previous wars, but even the extremely bitter, violent World War II conflict did not prevent major, rapid identity changes.

In more recent years while calling for a common European foreign policy, some experts have emphasized the appeal of the human security paradigm: "It posits that human beings have a right to live with dignity and security, and a concomitant obligation to help each other when that security is threatened." It "does not accept that human lives become cheap in desperate situations. There is nothing distinctively European about such moral norms. On the contrary, they are by their nature universal."[65]

---

[62] For analysis of identity change, see Peter J. Burke and Jan E. Stets, *Identity Theory* (New York: Oxford University Press, 2009), 175–196; Hart and Stouch-Hunter, *Pathways*, 8–9.

[63] On the other hand, exclusionary identity-based loyalties may resist bringing one's identity into conformity with human dignity. Such identity-based beliefs often override truth-seeking because of a person's psychological need to belong to one's in-group, obtain status there, understand the world from that narrow perspective, and feel morally justified in one's attitudes. See National Intelligence Council, *Global Trends 2040*, 74–75. This is one reason that a large number of US citizens steadfastly believe information that is clearly untrue. When inaccuracies are pointed out to them, they tend to attack the truth-teller rather than change their beliefs.

[64] For discussion of identity verification processes and identity change, see Burke and Stets, *Identity Theory*, 175–196.

[65] Glasius and Kaldor, "A Human Security Vision," 8.

To give human security needs at least as much attention as national security goals could remind everyone that, despite one's differences with adversaries in other states, all sides in a conflict are human and all share some common security needs.[66] Because human security should be founded on "the primacy of individuals, not states," it encourages multilateral commitments to international law and international institutions, some at the global level, and "a bottom-up approach at the local level."[67]

In sum, human security provides a useful conceptual foundation for bringing people across the world together to work on common purposes such as to overcome poverty, authoritarianism, militarism, racism, sexism, corruption, and predatory elements of capitalism or state socialism while supporting movements for democracy, human rights, and a healthy environment. This collaborative potential is almost unlimited because the concept of human security encompasses all fundamental threats to people's security, seeking not only to achieve negative peace, understood as the absence of war and genocide, but also to establish positive peace, understood as reducing the structural violence of extreme poverty, oppression, and other injustices that significantly reduce life expectancy.[68]

Citizens and states are already obligated to uphold, or at least not to trample on, human security insofar as its goal is to honor people's human rights, including their basic needs. States simply need to fulfill more conscientiously what they have already agreed on. Every state that is a member of the United Nations has committed itself to "universal respect for, and observance of, human rights and fundamental freedoms for all without distinction as to race, sex, language, or religion."[69] States pledge themselves "to take joint and separate action . . . for the achievement" of all people's human rights.[70] States have reaffirmed this obligation in many times and places, including the Universal Declaration of Human Rights, the International Covenant on Civil and Political Rights, the International Covenant on Economic, Social and Cultural Rights, and the Vienna Declaration of 1993.[71] In exemplary initiatives, the European Union has

---

[66] In defining "human security," the *Human Security Report* notes, "At a minimum, human security means freedom from violence and from the fear of violence," http://www.hsrgroup.org/press-room/human-security-backgrounder.aspx.

   The United Nations Development Project, which brought early attention to this concept, defined "human security" to mean "freedom from fear and freedom from want." United Nations Development Programme 1994, *Human Development Report*, 24.

[67] Glasius and Kaldor, "A Human Security Vision," 17.

[68] Some analysts criticize human security as being "so vague that it verges on meaninglessness." Roland Paris, "Human Security: Paradigm Shift or Hot Air?" *International Security* 26 (2001): 102.

   The main problem for critics of human security often seems to be that it is not state centric and is far more comprehensive than traditional concepts of national security. There is no necessary reason that human security cannot be as clear as national security. It simply shifts focus (1) from the national state to taking all human beings as important reference points for the object of security policies and (2) from threats to a state's power to threats to the most fundamental qualities of life for individuals. These factors are noted in United Nations Development Programme, *Human Development Report 1994*, 23.

[69] UN Charter, Article 55.

[70] UN Charter, Article 56.

[71] These were also affirmed by the European Union. See Glasius and Kaldor, "A Human Security Vision," 9.

also declared its intention to relate to other states by contributing to "peace, security, the sustainable development of the earth, solidarity and mutual respect among peoples, free and fair trade, eradication of poverty and protection of human rights . . . as well as to strict observance and development of international law, including respect for the principles of the United Nations Charter."[72]

Support for human security can benefit from the growing acceptance of international human rights standards as relevant for evaluating government conduct. This is reflected in recent agreement that sovereignty is "conditional" rather than absolute, and the recognition that the international community has a "responsibility to protect"[73] citizens victimized by their own government if it threatens or commits gross violations of human rights. The recognition that sovereignty's legitimacy depends on respect for basic human rights is a strong normative step forward. But to allow one or more other countries to intervene militarily in a delinquent country for largely self-interested reasons, misleadingly cloaked in human rights rhetoric, is not.

To the extent that the responsibility to protect can avoid unwarranted justifications for military intervention in another society, it illustrates how to build the normative groundwork for peace that a human security emphasis should pursue. Quite different examples of innovative institutional structures that can help to advance human security, despite their current limitations and difficulties, include the European Union, the International Atomic Energy Agency, conflict-adjudicating aspects of the World Trade Organization, and the International Criminal Court.

To ensure that the responsibility of the international community to protect actually serves a global strategy for human security, it needs strict guidelines for governing any intervention. Without those, strong states that are well represented in the Security Council could intervene in weaker states that are treated almost as de facto trusteeship territories in an international system "bifurcated" between weak and strong.[74] Intervention should protect people, not wage major combat. Those to be protected need to participate in decisions regarding their political fate during and after the time they are protected, receiving robust attention to their human rights rather than being treated as wards of external charity. They should not simply be turned over to the same power structures, without genuine international guarantees, that violated their rights in the first place. Nor should they simply be assigned to the care of humanitarian organizations if these ignore people's agency.

Moreover, constant attention is required to ensure that powerful states do not escape scrutiny from the international community if they engage in violent

---

[72] Treaty on European Union, Article 3 (5), https://eur-lex.europa.eu/legal-content/EN/TXT/HTML/?uri=CELEX:12008M003&from=EN.

[73] The UN High-Level Panel endorsed the "responsibility to protect" and confirmed that the international community carries a duty to intervene in states that cannot or will not protect the most basic rights of their people to be free of "genocide and other large-scale killing, ethnic cleansing or serious violations of international humanitarian law." *A More Secure World*, 57, para 203.

[74] On these points, see the provocative analysis by Mahmood Mamdani, "Responsibility to Protect or Right to Punish?" *Journal of Intervention and Statebuilding* 4, no. 1 (2010): 53–67.

"counterinsurgency operations" against their own people. The goal should be to develop as wide an agreement as possible on the legal justification for intervention and how it should be conducted[75] to protect human security.

The main goal of human security is to increase the security of every human being on the planet by bringing national security policies into harmony with meeting human security needs in order to enhance everyone's overall security and peace. Perhaps the best way to engage everyone on Earth in pursuing common security is to root initiatives in the right of every person to human security and a life of dignity. On the foundation of nurturing human life through reducing direct and structural violence, new security initiatives also can encourage more inclusive identities and deepen a sense of human solidarity based on the belief that people have equal moral worth.[76] This approach underscores the inseparable interconnections between legitimate national security goals and human security.[77]

The concept of human security has been criticized by some for being vaguely idealistic or foolishly unrealistic in downplaying national security. Yet if governments try to emphasize national security alone or at heavy cost to human security, their policies would be unlikely to succeed in areas that require cooperative action or a worldwide response, such as a need for shared intelligence to avert terrorist acts or for global efforts to constrain nuclear weapons. If some national security policies were to recede as the human security emphasis were foregrounded, exactly what would be left behind would be determined by negotiations among all national governments, of course, and no doubt would be implemented gradually over sufficient time for all to feel secure. It would be sensible to include constraints such as these: no government would be allowed to commit genocide or ethnic cleansing; no state or non-state actor could violate the law of civilian immunity; no state would be allowed to engage in the threat or unilateral use of military force;[78] no state could maintain a first-use nuclear weapons policy; and no one could develop new nuclear weapons or perhaps any weapons of mass destruction. Eventually, perhaps no independent national nuclear weapons forces might be allowed. Of course, the human security emphasis also stands against illegitimate national security actions at the present moment, such as bombing civilians or using rape as instruments of national policy. Some elements of current national security policies probably would be constrained because they threaten human security. At the same time, the elements of national security policy that serve the security of all people would be folded into the human security emphasis. All people would be

---

[75] See Ikenberry, *A World Safe for Democracy*, 297–298.

[76] Nations might "view their separate identities not as a cause for war, but as unique contributions to the celebration of a common humanity." See Henri J. Nouwen, *Lifesigns: Intimacy, Fecundity, and Ecstasy in Christian Perspective* (St. Anthony Messenger Press, 2007), 117.

[77] Annan, "Secretary-General Salutes International Workshop of Human Security in Mongolia," 103. See also Jan Van Dijk, "Human Security: A New Agenda for Integrated, Global Action, International Conference on Space and Water: Towards Sustainable Development and Human Security," Santiago, Chile, April 1, 2004, hhttp://www.unodc.org/speech_2004-04-01_1.html.

[78] This would be an enforceable and strengthened version of Article 2 (4) of the UN Charter.

guaranteed the right to be secure in their own national culture while practicing their own preferred way of life.

In brief, enlightened forms of national security and human security do not contradict each other. Pursuing human security does not negate upholding national security or security for everyone in one's nation. Human security includes familiar values of territorial integrity and economic prosperity. Indeed, a "holistic view of security," as advanced by the UN High-Level Panel, "understands state security and human security to be fundamentally intertwined."[79]

Other critics of the human security concept have feared that it might be a neo-imperial initiative, whether conscious or unconscious, to bring the world into a Western cultural orbit, because the concept has seldom called into question the existing international system and state-centered solutions while perhaps drawing too much on Western language for defining its goals. Yet the concept can be shaped multiculturally and address the preceding criticisms while taking a critical approach to examining unfair international structures, not merely policies, that contribute to wars, inequities, and violations of human rights.

5.2.3 Securing People Liberates Them

Implementing human security can liberate people everywhere because it invites the empowerment of all while protecting the rights of all from encroachment by others. Human security is not simply "delivered" by some advantaged people for hapless other people who need help to be secure. It empowers all people to share in meeting security needs for one's own group and for others as well. It also enables holding all accountable. By including all people, this approach reduces conditions that give rise to extremism and terrorism.

Helping people feel secure also invites them to support wider collective action. The dispossessed and underrepresented of the world could be encouraged to support a global peace strategy, thereby enlarging the coalition of those with a direct stake in securing further freedom and security for all. Those now dismissive of institutionalizing peace might be more likely to become interested in supporting a world peacebuilding strategy if it fairly benefited all people. Such a strategy lays the foundation for worldwide political support and transnational coalitions moving beyond fear.

A plan to implement the strategy proposed here could empower human beings and emancipate them from many genuine fears. Policy planning in low-income countries might move beyond the question "How can we survive?" to consider the likelihood that national survival would be most assured if policymakers would become seriously concerned with meeting the human needs and security of all those suffering in their country or elsewhere. Well-off countries might be willing to provide no more and no less than their fair share of resources toward human security because it would serve

---

[79] Slaughter, "Security, Solidarity, Sovereignty," 621.

their own security. A policy that elevates being human to the level of one's own nation can liberate people from self-defeating virulent nationalism and increase respect for one's common humanity. This is the path toward spreading the more precious value, "equality in freedom," which is being undermined now by national priorities that detract from helping to achieve the global human interest.[80]

Human security could be a useful driver of policy planning for several reasons:

1. Human beings should be the beneficiaries of all security policies (and of sovereignty itself). Focusing on people within a country encourages security policy to address what people need to be secure rather than to secure mainly what ruling elites want.
2. The concept of human security provides a prudential framework for connecting practical security goals with an identity that includes all people, opening minds to thinking about all people, not merely the people of one's own nation.
3. To focus on helping people to meet their basic needs encourages thinking more imaginatively about building a world society that enables human flourishing while transcending respectfully the boundaries between nations, religions, genders, and South and North. This advances both prudential and normative values in security planning.

To serve human security needs can work well both in theory and practice; it can become an exemplary guide for policymaking. It is buttressed by principles that governments have already inscribed in international laws supporting human dignity. Politically, these laws are secular and enshrined in international treaties and diplomatic practice; scientifically, they are undergirded in research on conflict and human health;[81] and interpersonally, they express revered moral principles rooted in the world's major religious and wisdom traditions.[82] Standards for assessing progressive realization of human security could be rooted in the concept of "quality peace," which seeks to assess societies' ability to meet not only standards of security and predictability but also of human dignity.[83]

---

[80] Robert C. Johansen, *The National Interest and the Human Interest* (Princeton, NJ: Princeton University Press, 1980), 22–23, 391–393.

[81] See, for example, the Seville Statement, UNESCO General Conference, Culture of Peace Programme (November 16, 1989), 3, http://www.unesco.org/cpp/uk/declarations/seville.pdf; Kohn, "Innately Aggressive?"; Fromm, *Sane Society*; White, *Fearful Warriors*; Erikson, *Gandhi's Truth*.

   Coleman also notes that the myth that humans are innately aggressive "has been roundly refuted by archaeological evidence finding that war is a relatively new invention and humans lived in peace for millions of years prior to the onset of the scourge of war." Peter Coleman, "Half the Peace: The Fear Challenge and the Case for Promoting Peace," *Courier*, Summer 2018, note 1, 10.

[82] See Brian D. Lepard, *Rethinking Humanitarian Intervention: A Fresh Legal Approach Based on Fundamental Ethical Principles in International Law and World Religions* (University Park: Pennsylvania State University Press, 2002).

[83] See Wallensteen, *Quality Peace*, 3.

5.3 RESPECTING RECIPROCITY

Third, one of the most currently influential guidelines for successful peacebuilding is to uphold the principle of positive reciprocity in human conduct, both in the practice of international relations among countries and in intergroup relations within countries. Reciprocity simply means that people of one country or group do not claim any right for themselves that they do not grant to others, and they do not seek to impose a duty on others that they do not accept for themselves. Reciprocal rights are understood and valued by people in nearly all cultures on Earth.[84]

Reciprocity "seems to be the most effective strategy for maintaining cooperation among egoists."[85] It is the traditional means of enforcing all international law[86] and remains the "condition theoretically attached to every legal norm" in international relations.[87] Throughout the Cold War, presidents and other leaders of both the Republican and Democratic parties invoked the principle of reciprocity frequently in discussing trade relations generally and arms control negotiations between the United States and the Soviet Union at a time when no other basis for agreement seemed possible. In contrast, absent reciprocity, prosocial behavior unravels, and short-term, proself behavior grows.[88]

For hundreds of years, reciprocal rights have been enshrined in the idea of sovereign equality, fair treatment, numerous treaties, and general international law.[89] A national government almost always insists that it enjoy reciprocal rights for itself. The test of sincerity in honoring the principle arises when thinking about granting reciprocal rights to others,[90] rights that are commensurate to what one insists on for oneself and when accepting duties and obligations for oneself that one expects of others. The United States is happy to enforce obligations to obey laws prohibiting war crimes and crimes against humanity on officials in the former Yugoslav republics, Rwanda, Uganda, Sudan, and Kenya through ad hoc courts or the permanent International Criminal Court. But US officials do not recognize the reciprocal duty for themselves to

---

[84] See Ernst Fehr and Simon Gächter, "Fairness and Retaliation: The Economics of Reciprocity," *Journal of Economic Perspectives* 14, no. 3 (Summer 2000): 159–181; Matt Ridley, *The Origins of Virtue* (London: Penguin 1998); Allison Dundes Renteln, *International Human Rights: Universalism Versus Relativism* (Newbury Park, CA: Sage, 1990).

[85] Robert O. Keohane, *After Hegemony: Cooperation and Discord in the World Political Economy* (Princeton, NJ: Princeton University Press, 2005), 214.

[86] John H. Barton and Barry E. Carter, "International Law and Institutions for a New Age," *Georgetown Law Journal* 81, no. 3 (1993): 535, 540; Robert O. Keohane, "Reciprocity in International Relations," *International Organization* 40, no. 1 (1986): 1–27.

[87] Elizabeth Zoller, *Peacetime Unilateral Remedies* (Dobbs Ferry, NY: Transnational, 1984), 15, as cited in Keohane, "Reciprocity in International Relations," 1.

[88] Joshua D. Kertzer and Brian C. Rathbun, "Fair Is Fair: Social Preferences and Reciprocity in International Politics," *World Politics* 67, no. 4 (2015): 613, 617.

[89] Barton and Carter, "International Law," 535.

[90] For culturally universal support of the principle of reciprocity, see Allison Renteln, *International Human Rights: Universalism Versus Relativism* (Newbury Park, CA: Sage, 1990).

join the ICC or to accept international scrutiny of any alleged US misconduct regarding the very same laws.

The constancy, persistence, and universality of reciprocal behavior evoke evolutionary roots.[91] Many cultural anthropologists believe that the very nature of human evolution was shaped by early human discovery of the benefits of positive reciprocal action. Human groups survived because they learned to share goods and services and honored a network of obligation. Through the custom or rule of reciprocity, dependable systems of trade and mutual aid made possible clear benefits for societies utilizing reciprocal inter-group relations. These benefits encouraged the persistent custom among societies and the internalization of reciprocity within human personalities. This has shaped contemporary customs and evaluations of what constitutes good behavior, even in relatively anarchic international relations.[92]

In this discussion, I frequently shorten "positive reciprocity" to simply "reciprocity" to refer to reciprocal behavior expressing what different groups mutually recognize as good conduct. Ernst Fehr and Simon Gächter, among others, distinguish "positive reciprocity" from "negative reciprocity," which expresses retaliation by a group that previously has suffered harmful conduct inflicted by another group. Negative reciprocity takes an eye in retaliation for an eye that was taken.

Reciprocity's utility arises from its capacity to provide a principled basis for cooperation to emerge even in a system of anarchy. It provides a widely understood standard for behavior and deters non-performance or violation of agreements. Once it succeeds in encouraging cooperation in a specific area, such as an equal trading relationship, it may also encourage the growth of a broader "diffuse reciprocity" that could apply more generally and encourage the growth of trust.[93] Research and experience also show that positive reciprocity correlates with peacebuilding and sustainable peace: "A reciprocating strategy provides the best overall outcome while avoiding war . . ." reports John Vasquez, whereas "a bullying strategy is usually associated with disputes escalating to war.[94]

Although the principle of reciprocity already is a central feature of international law, social science research on human motivations for reciprocity sheds further light on whether to strive for operationalizing a more strictly principled system of reciprocal international relations. Research indicates that policymakers who honor positive reciprocity often do so because they have a social preference to treat others fairly. They may be partly motivated by altruism and willingness to sacrifice for the good of others beyond conditions attributable simply to self-interest,[95] but altruism need

---

[91] Bowles and Gintis, "A Cooperative Species"; Rajiv Sethi, and Eswaran Somanathan, "Understanding Reciprocity," *Journal of Economic Behavior & Organization* 50, no. 1 (2003): 1–27.

[92] Fehr and Gächter, "Economics of Reciprocity;" Richard Leakey and Roger Lewin, *People of the Lake: Man, His Origins, Nature and Future* (Cork, Ireland: Collins Press, 1979); Ridley, *Origins of Virtue;* Gintis and Bowles, "A Cooperative Species."

[93] Keohane, "Reciprocity in International Relations," 1–28.

[94] Vasquez, "Steps to War," 139.

[95] Bowles and Gintis, "A Cooperative Species," 209.

not be present for reciprocity to thrive. A social preference among many people for reciprocity, fairness, equity, and equality can all be important motivators for prosocial behavior even when altruism is not present.[96] People frequently expect that they will be treated fairly by another group if they treat it fairly. They feel cheated by any who do not respect reciprocal action or who take advantage of others by being a free rider when reciprocity has been expressed by others. This is one reason that reciprocity naturally arouses an obligation to comply and to punish free riders,[97] even in international relationships devoid of other governing principles or institutions. As a consequence of this obligation and a willingness to impose legal or economic penalties on those who do not respect reciprocity, a high level of cooperation can be achieved for the exercise of power that can encourage collective, cooperative actions and help to enforce international norms.[98]

To concretize this principle in a vital area where acceptable conduct is highly contested, it is instructive to consider how implementing reciprocity could help to halt the proliferation of nuclear weapons. At first glance, many people see the proliferation problem as arising from the provocative conduct of North Korea or Iran, which are frequently denigrated by being called rogue regimes. This seems to make sense, to a degree, but a deeper understanding of the proliferation problem is that there are eight other countries who already have many nuclear weapons, who keep saying that *their* nuclear weapons are necessary for *their* security, and that they intend to keep *their* weapons. This message whets the appetite of additional countries to obtain them, particularly those that may fear attack. Not following the reciprocal principle proposed here, the US president probably deepened the fears of Iraqi, Iranian, and North Korean officials by calling them an "axis of evil,"[99] and then he attacked one of these countries, Iraq, without justifiable cause of self-defense or UN authorization, thereby unintentionally teaching the lesson to others that those who want to protect themselves against attack may want to obtain nuclear weapons.

The existing nuclear weapons countries understandably have asked North Korea not to develop any more nuclear weapons and Iran (1) to place all of its nuclear installations under strict inspection by the International Atomic Energy Agency, (2) to refrain from developing any weapons-grade enrichment capabilities, and (3) to refrain from developing or possessing any weapons grade nuclear materials or nuclear weapons. Yet the existing nuclear powers have not implemented *any* of those measures themselves, and they have no plans to do so. In addition, the US Senate has repeatedly refused to ratify the Comprehensive Nuclear Test-Ban Treaty,[100] which calls for a comprehensive

---

[96] Kertzer and Rathbun, "Fair Is Fair," 617.

[97] "People also enjoy punishing those who exploit the cooperation of others, or feel morally obligated to do so. Free-riders frequently feel guilty, and if they are sanctioned by others, they may feel ashamed." Bowles and Gintis, "A Cooperative Species," 14.

[98] Fehr and Gächter, "Economics of Reciprocity," 160.

[99] George W. Bush, "State of the Union," January 29, 2002, https://georgewbush-whitehouse.archives. gov/news/releases/2002/01/20020129-11.html.

[100] Adopted by the United Nations General Assembly on September 10, 1996, but never entered into force because of non-ratification.

ban on all further testing. For the United States to ratify this treaty would simply reciprocate what US officials are asking of others. The treaty was agreed to by 166 other countries, still awaiting US ratification a quarter of a century later, with no likelihood in sight.

To advance reciprocal rights and obligations, nuclear weapons countries should also approve a treaty ban on the further production of all highly enriched fissile materials as they seek to halt production by those whose proliferation they oppose and fear.[101] Until the nuclear weapons countries take strides toward reciprocity, they will be unlikely to establish an effective long-term non-proliferation policy, regardless of how much pressure they apply to Iran or North Korea, and even though a delay in Iranian development had been negotiated for the short run.[102]

As suggested previously, a deeper understanding of proliferation problems arises from simple recognition that the international system, in its present form, does not provide reliable means (1) to know exactly what other states are doing with their nuclear technology, thereby making it potentially more fearful, or (2) to enforce rules for reciprocal constraint of nuclear capabilities. Yet until governments change the international system enough to provide the means to address these fears, truly effective non-proliferation will be unlikely.

The United States and its allies would probably be safer today if years ago they had created treaty law to prohibit all further testing and manufacture or stockpiling of nuclear materials by all nuclear-weapons countries, and subsequently negotiated the gradual elimination of nuclear weapons, including robust verification of all constraints by the IAEA. Then they would have been in a strong, reciprocal position to stop proliferation by others. By not taking this path, the United States found itself being unable to stop North Korean proliferation without risking catastrophic war and possibly further militarization and proliferation by its allies, South Korea and Japan. By 2017, polls showed 60 percent of South Koreans favored building their own nuclear weapons; nearly 70 percent wanted the United States to reintroduce tactical nuclear weapons in South Korea for battlefield use. South Korea had stockpiled enough spent fuel to fabricate more than 4,300 bombs if it decided to do so.[103] Of course, those developments occurred against a backdrop of US rejection of reciprocity and Donald Trump's

---

[101] Several US administrations have favored a Fissile-Material Cutoff Treaty to prohibit the further production of weapons-grade nuclear materials. Although President Clinton advocated such a treaty, the Bush administration announced in 2004 that it opposed the inclusion of a verification mechanism in a proposed treaty because it could not be effectively verified. See also UN High-Level Panel, *A More Secure World*, 44, para 138.

[102] The agreement of June 2015 illustrates both short-term success in slowing Iranian technological advances and the continuation of long-term intentions, by both Iran and the nuclear weapons countries, toward efforts to limit production of nuclear weapons.

[103] David E. Sanger, Choe Sang-Hun, and Motoko Rich, "Allies Weighing Nuclear Options as Threat Looms," *New York Times*, October 29, 2017.

speaking favorably about the possibility that South Korea and Japan might obtain their own nuclear weapons.[104]

In a further demonstration of how the United States did not respect reciprocity, Secretary of Defense James Mattis criticized North Korea for the "threat that it poses to its neighbors and the world through its illegal and unnecessary missile and nuclear weapons program," while he also laid plans to develop extensive new US nuclear weapons, which he considered fully legal and necessary. Although claiming that the United States needed to update its nuclear weapons, the United States "does not accept a nuclear North Korea" or the updating of its weapons. To develop nuclear weapons that would amount to only a tiny fraction of the US arsenal, North Korea was engaging in "outlaw behavior, threatening behavior."[105] The legal basis for Secretary Mattis's argument no doubt lies in UN Security Council resolutions requesting North Korea to stop testing. Yet a long-standing US treaty obligation to move toward nuclear disarmament is ignored.

To be sure, the North Korean development of nuclear weapons and missile technology is destabilizing and threatening. From a US point of view, this development is simply unnecessary. But a plausible case can be made that the North Korean government wanted nuclear weapons to serve as a deterrent,[106] the same argument the United States has used to justify its nuclear weapons. When one recalls President Bush's portrayal of North Korea as part of an axis of evil, along with Iraq, a country he soon attacked, and President Trump's extolling the virtue of self-centered national sovereignty for the United States and other governments, there was little persuasiveness in the US argument against North Korean military policies, in part because it did not value reciprocity.

Moreover, before President Trump reported that he "fell in love" with Kim Jung-un,[107] he more than once threatened North Korea militarily, thereby implicitly giving a reason to North Korea to want a nuclear deterrent. He belittled the North Korean leadership and at one point said in all seriousness that North Korea's leaders "won't be around much longer."[108] North Korea called his threats a declaration of war by the United States. Without endorsing any of North Korea's foreign or domestic policies, an objective observer can see that North Korean-US relations have been characterized more by applying double standards, one for "us" and another for "them," than

---

[104] This specific statement was made during his election campaign. Sanger, San-Hun, and Rich, "Allies Weighing."

[105] Helene Cooper, "Mattis Says North Korea Accelerating War Threats," *New York Times*, October 29, 2017.

[106] North Korean officials have frequently mentioned what happed to Gadaffi only a few years after he gave up Libya's nascent nuclear program. Malfrid Braut-Hegghammer, "Why North Korea Succeeded at Getting Nuclear Weapons—When Iraq and Libya Failed," *Washington Post*, January 2, 2018; Malfrid Braut-Hegghammer, "Revisiting Osirak: Preventive Attacks and Nuclear Proliferation Risks," *International Security* 36, no. 1 (2011): 101; Malfrid Braut-Hegghammer, *Unclear Physics: Why Iraq and Libya Failed to Build Nuclear Weapons* (Ithaca, NY: Cornell University Press, 2016).

[107] Associated Press, "Trump on Kim Jong-un: 'We Fell in Love,'" *New York Times*, September 30, 2018.

[108] Associated Press, "Trump on Kim Jong-un."

by a reciprocal sensitivity to what each wants for itself as a guide for what it is able to understand about the other's needs and motivations.

US policymakers, citizens, and most news analysts conveniently forgot that "it was the United States, in 1958, that broke the provisions of the 1953 Korean Armistice Agreement [with North Korea,] when the Eisenhower administration sent the first atomic weapons into South Korea."[109] The armistice agreement, which had ended three years of bloody fighting, specified that no new weapons or ammunition was allowed to be introduced anywhere in the Peninsula by the United States or by North Korean or Chinese forces. International monitoring teams from neutral nations were established to inspect arms coming into North or South Korea. The United States violated this agreement during and following the Eisenhower presidency. By the mid-1960s, the United States had deployed more than 900 nuclear bombs and artillery shells, missiles, and nuclear land mines in South Korea.[110] The illegal US deployment of nuclear weapons just across the armistice lines no doubt spurred the North Korean nuclear program and justified it in North Korean eyes. Even without an international agreement, US respect for reciprocity would have meant that the United States would not have deployed nuclear weapons in or near the Korean peninsula to encourage North Korea not to develop or deploy similar weapons.

US citizens favoring reciprocity have wanted the United States to honor international duties that the United States expects of other states, such as ratifying the Comprehensive Test Ban Treaty or strictly obeying the Non-Proliferation Treaty's call to negotiate nuclear arms reduction, to say nothing of honoring the Charter prohibition of unauthorized threat or use of force when not in self-defense. They believe that whenever the United States declines to modernize and produce new nuclear weapons, it adds strength to the argument that non-nuclear weapons states should remain nonnuclear. Similarly, whenever the United States reciprocates the right of other states not to be threatened or attacked, it helps to weave the customary legal fabric that serves US citizens well in the long run.[111]

5.4 IMPLEMENTING EQUITY

Advancing equity and human equality is the fourth correlate for building peace in a violent world. Peace requires constructing more equitable relationships among diverse societies as well as among diverse groups within each society. Relationships should be fair, mutually beneficial, and to the extent possible, mutually satisfactory, with people being treated equally before the law. No group can get all of what it wants, but every

---

[109] Walter Pincus, "The Dirty Secret of American Nuclear Arms in Korea," *New York Times*, March 19, 2018, https://www.nytimes.com/2018/03/19/opinion/korea-nuclear-arms-america.html.

[110] Pincus, "Dirty Secret."

[111] Although peacebuilding within states is not a primary focus here, measures for transitional justice within states also benefit from sensitivity to the principle of reciprocity, so cultivating this norm for behavior is mutually reinforcing in all political life.

group must have assurance of processes in which it will not be discriminated against and can obtain a fair share of everything to which it is entitled.

This correlate of peace is underscored in the first article of the Universal Declaration of Human Rights: "All human beings are born free and equal in dignity and rights."[112] The International Human Rights Covenants recognize that human rights are equal and inalienable and "derive from the inherent dignity of the human person."[113] The principle of equality and non-discrimination is the most fundamental element of international human rights law. It establishes the equal moral worth of every person at birth,[114] an entitlement that does not need to be earned. All people should be treated equally before the law "without distinction of any kind, such as race, color, sex, language, religion, political or other opinion, national or social origin, property, birth or other status." In addition, "no distinction shall be made on the basis of the political, jurisdictional or international status of the country or territory to which a person belongs."[115] The "principle of equality and non-discrimination guarantees that those in equal circumstances are dealt with equally in law and practice."[116]

Although human rights are often considered a product of Western liberal thought, this is not an accurate account of the origins of rights as fundamental as equity.[117] Human rights expert Paul Lauren notes that the most fundamental rights are not simply enshrined in recent documents, like the Universal Declaration, a cornerstone of the "global constitution." Fundamental rights also draw support from most major religious traditions and many philosophical traditions. Indeed, the call to express kindness and respect for the equal dignity of others, even strangers, originates in ancient scriptures of Hinduism, Buddhism, Judaism, Christianity, and Islam.[118] On the matter of equality, for example, Islam teaches "that there should exist absolute equality among races and

---

[112] Universal Declaration of Human Rights, Article 1.

[113] Jack Donnelly, *International Human Rights* (Boulder, CO: Westview, 2013), 22–23.

[114] See Perry, *Global Political Morality*, 43–62. Governments have said "all persons are equal before the law and are entitled without any discrimination to the equal protection of the law." International Covenant on Civil and Political Rights (ICCPR), Article 26. The African Charter on Human and People's Rights says that "every individual shall be equal before the law" and "entitled to equal protection of the law." Article 3 (1) and (2). The South African Constitution says, "Everyone is equal before the law and has the right to equal protection and benefit of the law" (Article 9). The US Constitution declares "the equal protection of the laws" in the Fourteenth Amendment.

[115] Universal Declaration of Human Rights, Article 2.

[116] See Icelandic Human Rights Centre, "The Right to Equality and Nondiscrimination," http://www.humanrights.is/en/human-rights-education-project/human-rights-concepts-ideas-and-fora/substantive-human-rights/the-right-to-equality-and-non-discrimination.
"Everyone has the right to freedom of opinion and expression; this right includes freedom to hold opinions without interference and to seek, receive and impart information and ideas through any media regardless of frontiers." UDHR, Article 19. In addition, "Everyone has the right to freedom of peaceful assembly and association." Article 20 (1). The International Covenant on Civil and Political Rights amplifies the right described in the UDHR, especially in Articles 19, 21, and 22.

[117] Mary Ann Glendon, *A World Made New: Eleanor Roosevelt and the Universal Declaration of Human Rights* (New York: Random House, 2001).

[118] Paul Lauren, *The Evolution of International Human Rights: Visions Seen* (Philadelphia: University of Pennsylvania Press, 2011), 5–10.

that religious toleration should be guaranteed."[119] Muhammed declared that "Jews [and later Christians] who attach themselves to our commonwealth shall be protected from all insults and vexations; they shall have an equal right with our own people . . . and shall practice their religion as freely as the Muslims."[120] Huston Smith characterized this declaration of equal right "the first charter of freedom of conscience in human history."[121]

Widespread belief in the inviolability of human equality makes violations of it a frequent cause of unrest and even violent conflict. Wherever violence erupts, more inequality usually attends. Respect for or denial of equality and non-discrimination affects all aspects of life within a state and in relations among them. Implementing more equality and equity within a rule-of-law society, both domestically and internationally, builds peace and human security in the long run.[122] Moreover, many indicators of equitable economic development, high levels of trade among states, participation in international organizations, and democratic governance lower the risk of armed conflict and in the long run correlate with peace.[123]

The concept of equity grows from belief in the virtue of equality. Whereas equality calls for people to be treated the same, equity calls for people to be treated fairly. Equity builds on equality yet moves beyond it because fair treatment is not synonymous with mathematical equality. Immediately after the Universal Declaration declares that "all human beings are born free and equal in dignity and rights," it affirms the equitable virtue that all human beings "should act towards one another in a spirit of brotherhood [and sisterhood]."[124] The first affirmation emphasizes equality while the second calls for equity (fair treatment) and even more: compassion for others. In a familial ethic, all are welcome at the table. Each contributes what he or she can and receives what he or she needs, or as much of it as the family can provide.

Equality of opportunity and equity (fairness) of outcomes are fundamental measures in human security. A commitment to equity as a correlate of peace means that the international community would strive to ensure that the central human capabilities of every person, as outlined by the UN Human Development Program and detailed in the earlier discussion of Nussbaum, would be pursued to enable development of each person's potential.

---

[119] Lauren, *International Human Rights*, 8.

[120] Huston Smith, *The Religions of Man* (New York: Harper & Row, 1958), 249; Lauren, *International Human Rights*, 8. See also Ann Elizabeth Mayer, *Islam and Human Rights* (San Francisco: Westview/HarperCollins, 1998); Riffat Hassan, "On Human Rights and the Qur'anic Perspective," in *Human Rights in Religious Traditions*, ed. Arlene Swidler (New York: Pilgrim Press, 1982), 51–65; Mahmood Monshipouri, "Islamic Thinking and the Internationalization of Human Rights," *Muslim World* (July–October, 1994), 217–239.

[121] Smith, *Religions of Man*, 249.

[122] "If inequality causes violence, it can reasonably be expected that decreasing inequality will lead to pacification." See Wallensteen et al., "Violence, Wars, Peace," 444.

[123] See Russett and Oneal, *Triangulating Peace*, 271–305; Cortright, Seyle, and Wall, *Governance for Peace*, 180.

[124] Article 1, Universal Declaration of Human Rights.

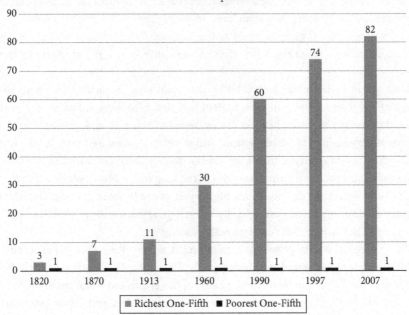

Income Ratios Comparing Richest One-Fifth to Poorest One-Fifth
of World Population

FIGURE 5.1 Income Ratios Comparing Richest One-Fifth to Poorest One-Fifth of World
Population

Sources: United Nations Development Programme, *Human Development Report 1992: Global Dimensions of
Human Development*; *Human Development Report 1999: Globalization with a Human Face*; *Human Development
Report 2018: Statistical Update: Human Development Indices and Indicators.*

5.4.1 One System, Two Worlds

To grasp a measurable element of equality and equity, it is helpful to compare the income
of the richest 20 percent of the world's population to the poorest 20 percent over the past
two centuries. This is shown in Figure 5.1. In 1820, the richest one-fifth of people on average made only three times as much as people in the bottom one-fifth. The income advantage of the well-off had more than doubled to 7 to 1 by 1870. It had increased to 11 to 1 in
1913, 30 to 1 in 1960, 60 to 1 in 1990, 74 to 1 in 1997, and 82 to 1 in 2007. One UN estimate
even indicated that the income of the richest one-fifth of the world's people had risen to
150 times more than the poorest one-fifth.[125]

---

[125] UN Development Programme, *Human Development Report 1992, Global Dimensions of Human Development*
(New York: Oxford University Press, 1992), 1, 34, 96; United Nations Development Programme,
Human Development Report 1999, Globalization with a Human Face, 2–3, 11, 38, http://www.hdr.undp.
org/en/content/human-development-report-1999; United Nations Development Programme, *Human
Development Report 2018, Statistical Update: Human Development Indices and Indicators*, 4, 33, 106–107,
http://hdr.undp.org/en/content/human-development-indices-indicators-2018.

Wealth is even more unequal than income. The wealthiest 10 percent of the world's people control 86 percent of the world's wealth,[126] while the poorest half of the world's people own less than 1 percent of the wealth.[127] The wealthiest tenth of the world's people are 400 times richer, on average, than are the bottom 50 percent. The top 1 percent are about 2,000 times richer than the poorer half.[128] Income inequality characterizes US society also: the wealthiest one-fifth receive more after-tax income than the bottom 80 percent of citizens combined. The top 0.1 percent receive in a *day and a half* what the bottom 90 percent earn in a *year*.[129]

There is no justification for such extreme inequality. Because there is only one international economic system, all people throughout the world participate in this systemic inequality.[130] These wealth and income ratios show that the international and domestic economic systems have been increasing inequality for two centuries, despite some recent improvement in the absolute number of people not living in abject poverty. The wealthy societies perpetuate this inequitable system, whether deliberately or not.[131] In practice over the past two centuries, the international economic system has failed to deliver the central moral claim of democratic capitalism, "that it provides the optimum political and economic conditions for all human beings to actualize their potential."[132] This international system has produced, maintained, and increased gross inequality and inequity.[133]

Imagine how a family might feel if, despite each person's best efforts, they struggled in the group at the bottom—not only for the current year, but for a decade or for generations. Inequalities of wealth produce inequalities of power, opportunity, physical and mental health, education, and life expectancy. The poor are more often subjected to violence, domestic or foreign, and environmental disruption. In addition, the poor see wealthy countries making huge payments for purchasing natural resources to *any* political leader, no matter how corrupt, who is able to control territory where valuable exports originate. In doing this, wealthy countries enable violent despots, the poor's oppressors, to stay in power. Often the authoritarian governments buy weapons from

---

[126] Credit Suisse Research Institute, *Global Wealth Report 2013*, 10, https://web.archive.org/web/20150214155424/https:/publications.credit-suisse.com/tasks/render/file/?fileID=BCDB1364-A105-0560-1332EC9100FF5C83.

[127] Elizabeth Anderson, "Economic Inequality and Human Development," *UN Development Report 2019*, 89, http://hdr.undp.org/sites/default/files/hdr2019.pdf.

[128] James B. Davies, Susanna Sandstrom, Anthony Shorrocks, and Edward N. Wolff, *The World Distribution of Household Wealth* (Santa Cruz, NM: Center for Global, International, and Regional Studies, University of California, 2007), https://escholarship.org/uc/item/3jvo48hx.

[129] Joseph E. Stiglitz, *The Price of Inequality: How Today's Divided Society Endangers Our Future* (New York: W.W. Norton, 2012), 4. Compensation for CEOs in the United States jumped by an unbelievable 725 percent between 1978 and 2011. This rise was 127 times faster than that of the average worker and an average income of $10 million a year was 209 times higher than that of the average worker.

[130] As indicated by the Commission on Global Governance, "In the field of finance, national frontiers have little meaning; 'the end of geography' is approaching." *Our Global Neighbourhood*, 137.

[131] Pogge, *Politics as Usual*, 1–56.

[132] Gill, "Historical Crossroads," 182.

[133] Thomas Piketty, *Capital in the Twenty-First Century* (Cambridge, MA: Harvard University Press, 2014).

the same industrialized countries to whom they sell their oil or other raw materials. There is a mutually self-serving relationship in which an authoritarian government exports to the wealthy what they want to buy and the wealthy sell to autocratic elites the instruments of oppression through which they remain in power by oppressing everyone else. The well-off countries and the oppressors in the poor countries together perpetuate the international system that enables the symbiotic, inequitable relationships to continue.

For US citizens favoring equity, raising US sensitivity to these two unequal worlds is made difficult because the United States has allowed inequality to spike at home in recent decades. Chief executive officers in major corporations now are paid 278 times the income of the average US worker. Their wealth increased by 1,008 percent between 1978 and 2018, while typical worker pay rose only 12 percent.[134] In 1965, the compensation ratio of chief executives to workers was 20 to 1. By the end of the Reagan administration it had risen to 58 to 1. It is 320 to 1 today.[135]

The existing global economic system imposes poverty on nearly half of the world's people, enabling the richest 26 people in the world to possess as much wealth as the total wealth of the poorest 3.89 billion people.[136] On average 50,000 people, 30,000 of them children, die preventable deaths every *day*, many from causes such as hunger and bad drinking water. This system kills roughly 18 million people each year.[137] A world expert on poverty, Thomas Pogge, has concluded that "an appeal to permissible [national] partiality cannot justify the imposition, by the most powerful governments on the rest of the world, of an unjust global institutional order under which a majority of humankind is foreseeably and unavoidably deprived of anything resembling a fair start in life."[138] The policies of the globally rich and powerful that in practice perpetuate poverty are simply, "crimes against humanity."[139] In Pogge's view, the industrialized countries "are participants in the largest human-rights violation in human history."[140]

---

[134] In 2018, CEOs in the country's top 350 businesses were paid $17.2 million on average. Employees working in those industries—ranging from retail to technology and manufacturing—typically earned $64,500. Andrew Keshner, "CEOs Are Paid 278 Times More Than the Average US Worker," *Market Watch*, August 31, 2019, https://www.marketwatch.com/story/ceos-are-paid-278-times-more-than-the-average-us-worker-2019-08-15.

[135] Economic Policy Institute, Lawrence Mishel and Jori Kandra, *CEO Compensation Surged 14% in 2019 to $21.3 Million: CEOs Now Earn 320 Times as Much as a Typical Worker*, Economic Policy Institute, 2020, https://www.epi.org/publication/ceo-compensation-surged-14-in-2019-to-21-3-million-ceos-now-earn-320-times-as-much-as-a-typical-worker/#:~:text=Using%20the%20realized%20compensation%20measure%2C%20the%20CEO%2Dto%2Dworker,1970s%2C%201980s%2C%20or%201990s.

[136] Marc Benioff, "We Need a New Capitalism," *New York Times*, October 14, 2019.

[137] Pogge, *Politics as Usual*, 11, 31.

[138] Pogge, *Politics as Usual*, 24, 26–56.

[139] Pogge, *Politics as Usual*, 2.

[140] Pogge, *World Poverty*, 264.

5.4.2 *Economic Nationalism or Multilateralism?*

The nearly unbelievable acquiescence of the rich in perpetuating poverty for the poor may sound overstated. Yet the ways in which bureaucratic systems, whether privately owned or governmental, go after profits at the expense of people's health and safety do illustrate breathtaking selfishness when seen in a global context. Because corporations may legitimately, yet ruthlessly, seek and acquire great wealth and power, a large corporation may behave in ways that, if evaluated as a human being, "it would be [considered] a sociopath."[141] For example, UN and world health officials were stunned when the United States opposed a UN resolution that called on governments to encourage mothers to breastfeed their babies and to discourage misleading corporate marketing of substitutes for breast milk.[142] The UN resolution, which was expected to pass easily with nearly all governments supporting it, was based on decades of medical research around the world demonstrating that babies are healthiest when breastfed by their mothers because this practice provides the best nutrition, including natural "antibodies that protect newborns against infectious disease."[143] Because artificial infant formulas lack these nutrients and often are prepared with unsafe water, babies are more likely to become sick or die. A 2016 study concluded that breastfeeding would save 800,000 infant lives every year and save $300 billion in reduced healthcare costs and improved economic outcomes for those raised with breast milk.[144]

Not only did US officials oppose this resolution protecting babies, they threatened retaliatory action against the Ecuadorean government because it planned to introduce the resolution. They told Ecuadoreans that if they refused to drop the resolution, Washington would "unleash punishing trade measures and withdraw crucial military aid." Needing US assistance, the Ecuadorean government immediately acquiesced. At least a dozen other countries in Africa and Latin America, adversely affected by misleading marketing of artificial milk, also backed away from the resolution, "citing fears of retaliation" by the United States.[145] Patti Randall, the policy director of Baby Milk Action and a participant in the World Health Organization's meetings since the late 1980s, reported: "What happened was tantamount to blackmail, with the US holding the world hostage and trying to overturn nearly 40 years of consensus on the best way to protect infant and young child health."[146] In protecting corporate interests by threatening to cancel military aid to countries that wanted to protect their children,

---

[141] Tim Wu, quoted by Sally Lee, "Losing at Monopoly," *Columbia Magazine*, Spring 2019, 40.

[142] Andrew Jacobs, "US Delegation Disrupts Accord on Breast Milk," *New York Times*, July 9, 2018, A1.

[143] Jacobs, "US Delegation Disrupts Accord," A1.

[144] Jacobs, "US Delegation Disrupts Accord," A7.

[145] Jacobs, "US Delegation Disrupts Accord," A1.

[146] Jacobs, "US Delegation Disrupts Accord," A7. The American Academy of Pediatrics disagreed with the Trump administration's position on breastfeeding and human milk, as did the American College of Obstetricians and Gynecologists. See Roni Caryn Rabin, "Trump Stance on Breast-Feeding and Formula Criticized by Medical Experts," *New York Times*, July 9, 2018, https://www.nytimes.com/2018/07/09/well/breastfeeding-trump-resolution.html?action=click&module=RelatedCoverage&pgtype=Article&region=Footer.

US officials cast doubt on whether US security policies toward poor countries were designed primarily to serve security or instead profits for corporate friends who would fund their US re-election campaigns. When Russian officials decided to introduce the infant-formula resolution that US officials had bullied Ecuadorians into dropping, US officials then threatened to cut US contributions to the World Health Organization (WHO) as a more global form of retaliation.

US officials seemed to prioritize profit over human health in other contexts by opposing language in trade negotiations that would discourage consumption of soda and require warning labels on junk food and sugary beverages made by US multinational corporations. To support profits by the pharmaceutical industry, Washington also thwarted a World Health Organization initiative to enable poor people to obtain access to medicines. Some experienced health advocates feared that US officials would do lasting damage to international health institutions because of their hostile attitudes toward public health efforts. "If you can't agree on health multilateralism, what kind of multilateralism can you agree on?" asked Ilona Kickbusch, director of the Global Health Centre at the Graduate Institute of International and Development Studies in Geneva.[147]

Widespread support among capitalist elites for what has been called neoliberalism or the "Washington Consensus"[148] needs to be revisited and replaced with a perspective that supports substantial freedom for markets while at the same time insisting that markets operate within an economic framework that protects the vulnerable from disease, predation, joblessness, and extreme poverty.[149] Not only should poverty be abolished; extreme wealth should also be questioned because of its connection with inequitable power and control by the wealthy.[150] Nobel Prize winner and World Bank economist Joseph Stiglitz, among others, has noted that commonly believed flaws in the neoliberal perspective include "the fundamentalist notion that markets are self-correcting, allocate resources efficiently, and serve the public interest well." Sitglitz

---

[147] Jacobs, "US Delegation Disrupts Accord," A7.

[148] The Washington Consensus or neoliberalism refers to a set of free-market economic policies supported by prominent financial institutions in Washington, including the International Monetary Fund, the World Bank, and the US Treasury. These have advanced economic prescriptions in developing countries calling for macro-economic stabilization, economic openings for both trade and investment, and the expansion of market forces within domestic economies.

The Washington consensus favors free trade, floating exchange rates, largely unregulated markets, and low government borrowing. The terms sometimes are used to refer simply to a general orientation in favor of a strongly market-based approach that critics describe as market fundamentalism or neoliberalism. They argue that an excessive strengthening of domestic market forces has come at the expense of key functions of the state in establishing a social net for vulnerable people. Other critics point out that the Washington Consensus has omitted the importance of domestic institution-building and policies designed to improve opportunities for the weakest in society. For analysis, see Janine Brodie, "Income Inequality and the Future of Global Governance," in Critical Perspectives on the Crisis of Global Governance: Reimagining the Future, ed. Stephen Gill (New York: Palgrave Macmillan, 2016), 45–88.

[149] See John Ruggie, "Taking Embedded Liberalism Global: The Corporate Connection," in Taming Globalization, ed. David Held and Mathias Koenig-Archibugi (Cambridge: Polity, 2003), 93–129.

[150] Anderson, "Economic Inequality," 89.

warns, "It was this market fundamentalism that underlay Thatcherism, Reaganomics, and the so-called 'Washington Consensus' in favor of privatization, liberalization, and independent central banks focusing single-mindedly on inflation." Rather than aiming to serve human or environmental needs, "neo-liberal market fundamentalism was always a political doctrine serving certain interests. It was never supported by economic theory. Nor, it should now be clear, is it supported by historical experience."[151]

Amartya Sen points out that implementation of distributive justice, informed by the UNDP's capabilities approach, is also hampered by "national particularism" in which policymakers motivated by exclusionary nationalism define equality and justice in a strictly nationalist context that ignores worldwide implications. In contrast, to implement equity conducive to human security will require "interpersonal sympathies and solidarities across borders." Fairness can and should be envisaged in global yet interpersonal, ethical terms.[152] Many independent international economists agree with Sen that "equity problems have to be addressed, especially in dealing with serious deprivations."[153]

5.4.3 *Denying Equity Generates Conflict*

In addition to violating human rights, gross economic inequities increase tensions among social groups within countries and between them. Empirical studies show that poverty brings higher risks of war whereas more equitable economic conditions increase the chances of maintaining peace.[154] Disrespect for the poor also increases polarization. Desperately poor people may be driven to civil unrest within their society, especially when they are treated unfairly. Violence may be used by those trying to quell protests and those trying to mount them.[155] The negative consequences of poverty are magnified further because people born into a culture of poverty are deprived of equitable opportunities to escape it, often including equal access to education and ability to use judicial processes.[156] Of course, slum dwellings impede and deny human potential. Poor living conditions create refugees by the thousands and millions. Distributive inequality also undermines trust among citizens and promotes conflict. It depresses the vitality of civil society.

---

[151] Joseph Stiglitz, "The End of Neo-liberalism?" *Project Syndicate*, July 7, 2008, https://www.project-syndicate.org/commentary/the-end-of-neo-liberalism?barrier=accesspaylog.

[152] Amartya Sen, "Global Justice and Beyond," in *Global Public Goods*, ed. Inge Kaul, Isabelle Grunbert, and Marc A. Stern (New York: United Nations Development Program, 1999), 120.

[153] Amartya Sen, *Development as Freedom* (New York: Alfred Knopf, 2000), 119.

[154] Human Security Report Project, *The Causes of Peace*, 38, 52.

[155] The IMF has expressed concern that the growth of inequality contributes to civil wars. Ambrose Evans Pritchard, "IMF Raises Spectre of Civil Wars as Global Inequalities Worsen," *The Telegraph*, February 1, 2011, http://www.telegraph.co.uk/finance/globalbusiness/8296987/IMF-raises-spectre-of-civil-wars-as-global-inequalities-worsen.html.

[156] Anderson, "Economic Inequality," 89.

Societies stunted by economic strife undermine democracy by sometimes "enabling the rich to capture the state and thereby appropriate a disproportionate share of public goods, shift tax burdens in a regressive direction, enforce fiscal austerity and avoid accountability for predatory and criminal behaviour."[157] Grossly inequitable conditions often empower authoritarian rulers. It should not be a surprise that Freedom House has indicated that 22 of 41 democracies have become less free in the last five years as inequality and populism have increased.[158] Both within countries and between them, armed struggles arise for control of economic resources such as oil, valuable minerals, water, and agricultural land.

Whether intentionally or inadvertently, US policies have for decades helped to perpetuate gross inequities that make it impossible to strengthen an international society and build world community capable of scaling back international anarchy as well as poverty. Because economic and power inequities are mutually reinforcing, they exacerbate international conflict and increase international injustice. They make international society almost ungovernable. Democratic deficits in international institutions, as well as in national societies, result from wealth inequities as well as contribute to it. Because inequities increase social tensions and risks of violent conflict, pursuing equity and democratization in international institutions would contribute to security and peace.[159]

Desperate economic conditions, often found in countries that have not received an equitable share of capital for human development, motivate people to take extreme risks to migrate to societies with abundant capital. Because the United States and other capital exporting countries historically refused to move enough capital into poor societies to support human development, universal education, and human rights, some dispossessed people, being denied equitable opportunities at home, began trying to move to countries where capital existed in excess, even though migrants often moved against the wishes of people in those wealthier societies. In many well-off countries, migratory pressures have stirred fears and hatred of refugees and immigrants, often exacerbating conflicts and polarization at home while stimulating more narrow nationalism and populism.

Inequity may even impede environmental protection because the rich often feel the poor expect to be free riders in not paying an equal share of the burden of environmental health, while the poor point out that the rich developed their wealth by polluting with abandon. In addition, a more equitable distribution of wealth globally would provide a better context for sorting out ways to constrain consumption for the sake of environmental protection.[160] In contrast, the principle of equity could help allocate

---

[157] Anderson, "Economic Inequality," 89.

[158] Freedom House, "Freedom in the World: Report 2019," https://freedomhouse.org/report/freedom-world; https://freedomhouse.org/countries/freedom-world/scores.

[159] Commission on Global Governance, *Our Global Neighbourhood*.

[160] As Ernst F. Schumacher has reminded us, "Infinite growth of material consumption within a finite world is an impossibility." Quoted by Schwartzberg, *Transforming*, 272.

responsibility for those who may cause or resolve problems in the global commons. The most effective human development occurs when linked via multilateral decision-making aiming at environmental sustainability and based on the commitment of the world's countries "to build a humane, equitable and caring global society cognizant of the need for human dignity for all."[161]

5.4.4 *Increasing Equity Builds Community*

The international economic system needs to change because its inequity, its waste, and its inhumanity are not morally desirable or politically prudent for achieving sustainable peace. It is unrealistic to expect sustainable peace or an end to political extremism amid extreme inequity, regardless of how much military preparedness the well-off may amass.[162] In contrast, new efforts to listen to and represent the dissatisfied of the world in the international system would signal willingness to give up old habits of maintaining inequity and to address new realities fairly. Ample evidence shows that eliminating poverty and inequity generally benefits peace at home and abroad. Within countries, more equitable economic development aids initiatives for conflict prevention.[163] Internationally, equitable trade and foreign investment practices reduce the risk of violent conflict.[164]

Most governments have already acknowledged in the International Covenant on Economic, Social, and Cultural Rights that "everyone has the right to a standard of living adequate for the health and well-being of himself and of his family, including food, clothing, housing and medical care and necessary social services, and the right to security in the event of unemployment, sickness, disability, widowhood, old age, or other lack of livelihood in circumstances beyond his control."[165] Moreover, "children, whether born in or out of wedlock, shall enjoy the same social protection."[166] National

---

[161] Statement adopted at the World Summit on Sustainable Development, "Annex 1: Johannesburg Declaration on Sustainable Development," *International Environmental Agreements: Politics, Law and Economics* (Amsterdam: Kluwer Academic, 2002): 403–406.

[162] The National Intelligence Council points out that rising or persistent inequality threatens people's faith in government, undermines trust in one another, and encourages polarization and conflict. *Global Trends 2040*, 78–80. See also Patricia Justino, "Poverty and Violent Conflict: A Micro-Level Perspective on the Causes and Duration of Warfare," *Journal of Peace Research* 46, no. 3 (2009): 315–333; Lopez-Claros, Dahl, and Groff, *Global Governance*, 312–313; Frances Stewart, "Root Causes of Violent Conflict in Developing Countries," *British Medical Journal* 324, no. 7333 (February 9, 2002): 342–345. Perhaps "we cannot have peace if we are only concerned with peace," because "war is not an accident. It is the logical outcome of a certain way of life." A. J. Muste, quoted by Nat Hentoff, "Introduction," in *The Essays of A. J. Muste*, ed. Nat Hentoff (New York: Bobbs-Merrill, 1967), xvii.

Muste felt strongly that "in a world built on violence, one must be a revolutionary before one can be a pacifist." "A. J. Muste," https://en.wikiquote.org/wiki/A._J._Muste.

[163] Human Security Report Project, *Causes of Peace*, 60.

[164] Human Security Report Project, *Causes of Peace*, 29. Russett and Oneal, *Triangulating Peace*, 271–305.

[165] Governments also emphasized "the fundamental right of everyone to be free from hunger." International Covenant on Economic, Social, and Cultural Rights, Articles 9, 11. See also Articles 12 and 13 and UDHR, Articles 22, 25, and 26.

[166] International Covenant on Economic, Social, and Cultural Rights, Article 25 (2).

governments have also said that all people have a *duty* to stop perpetuating any system that deprives anyone, including the underrepresented and the poor, of access to their rights, including the economic right to meet basic needs. If the international community would begin to take equity seriously, it would doubtless produce a major improvement in the state of world community, thereby making solutions to many other problems far easier.

The international community has opportunities to transform the international economic system in ways that could increase equality of opportunity and also reduce incentives for polarization, terrorism, and war.[167] To relieve unjust inequities, it could require a small percentage of the income earned by poor countries from the export of their natural resources to be put into an internationally shielded development fund to be used for the benefit of the citizens of the countries from which the exports come.[168] Or, if the wealthiest one-tenth of the world's population would contribute only 1 percent of their annual income for intelligent programs designed to meet human needs, all people on Earth could be raised out of poverty.[169] If the richest one-tenth of the world's people would take this "one percent step" to abolish poverty, the quality of their lives would not be diminished in any significant way, yet the lives of those rising out of poverty would be immensely improved, as would the lives of compatriots no longer facing massive poverty as a subculture in their societies. Despite this fact, the well-off maintain an international system that refuses to enable such an easy yet major advance in equity to occur. In a typical year in the past decade, the 100 richest people in the world added $240 billion to their wealth, which would be more than the $175 billion needed per year for 20 years to end extreme poverty.[170] A grand strategy aiming for equity could abolish poverty in a relatively short time.

It would also be possible to develop an alternative source of international revenue that could help abolish poverty, increase equity, and enforce world law. This might come from a tiny international levy on all international currency exchanges. Because of the massive amounts of currency changed on international markets each day,[171] a small fee of less than half of 1 percent could generate a billion or more dollars each *day*. This idea was originally proposed in 1972 by Nobel prize–winning US economist James Tobin with the intention of discouraging short-term currency speculation.[172]

Three additional arguments show why including equity in a strategy for human security could be realistic. First, much of the recent growth of income inequality around

---

[167] See Paul Collier, *The Bottom Billion* (Oxford: Oxford University Press, 2007).

[168] See Pogge's proposal for a Global Resources Fund, which asks for 0.67 percent of natural resource usage to be used to end hunger and other severe deprivations of the poor. *World Poverty*, 210–214.

[169] Thomas W. Pogge, "Human Rights and Human Responsibilities," in *Global Responsibilities: Who Must Deliver on Human Rights*, ed. Andrew Kuper (New York: Routledge, 2005), 4.

[170] This is the estimate provided by Jeffrey Sachs and reported by Lea Gorius, "How Much Does It Cost to End Poverty?" The Borgen Project, https://borgenproject.org/how-much-does-it-cost-to-end-poverty/#:~:text=So%2C%20how%20much%20does%20it,per%20year%20for%2020%20years.

[171] Foreign exchange averaged $5 trillion a day in 2016.

[172] Heikki Patomäki, *Democratizing Globalization: The Leverage of the Tobin Tax* (New York: Zed Books/Palgrave, 2001).

the world has arisen from deliberate policies implemented during and since the Reagan administration, not simply from globalization and technological change.[173] Changing those policies could help reduce inequalities. Second, extreme inequality harms everyone in national and global societies because it depresses demand and increases political polarization and instabilities arising from social liabilities, resentments, fears, and unnecessary conflicts, so greater equity should be politically and economically attractive. Third, most national economies and the international economy will not become healthy until governments and social movements bridle markets enough to ensure a more equitable distribution of income, wealth, and politico-economic decision-making power.[174]

With help from strong public pressure, the United States and other well-off countries might be induced to support enough equity to enable half of the world's people to rise from perpetual poverty. Without such change, the world will be plagued with unrepresentative international institutions. International economic and political strains will increase because of wasteful consumption by the wealthy, lingering neo-imperial ambitions,[175] and deprivation of the poor. Environmental deterioration will be more difficult to address. Migration pressures will mount. As US fears of communism at the end of the Cold War gave way to national economic selfishness and fears of terrorism, migration, Islamic societies, and other perceived threats, US magnanimity and support for limited equity declined, but it could be revived. New commitment to equity could include not only consideration of measures to end chronic poverty but also such attractive goals as to relieve suffering of refugees and displaced persons, ensure free primary and secondary education for all children, place some kind of levy on carbon production and currency exchanges, curtail the flow of capital to tax havens,[176] and

---

[173] Brodie, "Income Inequality," 67.

[174] A number of respected economists and detailed studies support these conclusions and generally repudiate the neoliberal economic and political policies that have brought enormous economic inequalities and inequities. See Brodie, "Income Inequality," 66–67; Paul R. Krugman, *Arguing with Zombies: Economics, Politics, and the Fight for a Better Future* (New York: W.W. Norton, 2020); Paul R. Krugman, *End This Depression Now!* (New York: W. W. Norton, 2013); OECD, *Divided We Stand: Why Inequality Keeps Rising* (Paris: OECD Publishing, 2011); OECD, *In It Together: Why Less Inequality Benefits All* (Paris: OECD Publishing, 2015); Oxfam Media Briefing, "The Cost of Inequality" (January 18,2013), https://oxfamilibrary.openrepository.com/bitstream/handle/10546/266321/mb-cost-of-inequality-180113-en.pdf;jsessionid=7F31C9518AF10A15A3E636EE726C666F?sequence=1; Robert B. Reich, *Beyond Outrage: What Has Gone Wrong with Our Economy and Our Democracy, and How to Fix It* (New York: Vintage Books, 2012); Jeffrey Sachs, *The Price of Civilization: Economics and Ethics After the Fall* (London: Vintage, 2012); Joseph E. Stiglitz, "The End of Neo-Liberalism?" *Project Syndicate* (July 7, 2008), https://www.project-syndicate.org/commentary/the-end-of-neo-liberalism?barrier=accesspaylog; Stiglitz, *Price of Inequality*.

[175] Ikenberry, "America's Imperial Ambition," 44.

[176] The absence of global governance over corporations that keep their capital in tax havens allows structural reinforcement of global inequities and the failure of corporations to pay their fair share of the costs of running modern urban societies from which they earn unreasonable profits. See Gill, "Historical Crossroads," 189–190.

require that global supply chains operate with the principles in mind of protecting health and respecting fair labor practices.[177]

5.5 STRENGTHENING LEGAL MUSCLES

To strengthen the rule of law in world affairs is the fifth guideline in a global strategy for ending today's prolonged violent conflicts and preventing new ones. The "democratic rule of law"[178] is the most effective instrument human beings have yet created for managing conflicts between large groups of people who may strongly disagree. Secretary-General Kofi Annan provided a useful description for this correlate of peace when he said the rule of law is "governance in which all persons, institutions and entities, public and private, including the state itself, are accountable to laws that are publicly promulgated, equally enforced and independently adjudicated, and which are consistent with international human rights norms and standards." It requires "measures to ensure adherence to the principles of supremacy of law, equality before the law, accountability to the law, fairness in the application of the law, separation of powers, participation in decision-making, legal certainty, avoidance of arbitrariness and procedural and legal transparency."[179]

Evenhanded law is useful for maximizing justice and minimizing violence while managing conflict, both within societies and between them. It also enables increasing the equity of democratic representation in international decision-making. Although international law is sometimes overridden by a country asserting its material power in violation of law, international law often does influence national conduct. Despite widespread skepticism about the utility of international law for enforcing peace, as Louis Henkin famously said, "Almost all nations observe almost all principles of international law and almost all of their obligations almost all the time."[180] Although enforcement mechanisms for international law are commonly weak, some kind of

---

[177] See Brodie, "Income Inequality," 45–88.

[178] The "democratic rule of law" occurs where fair, representative processes undergird the legislating of laws and writing of treaties, both of which are impartially interpreted and enforced within the context of respect for human rights, including minority rights, and equal protection of all under the law. In international society the element of "democracy" is seriously limited by the existence of authoritarian domestic political systems. Nonetheless, such societies need a place at the diplomatic table because of wide recognition that even flawed processes for selecting representatives from a country are often preferable to no representation at all. International institutions should be structured as democratically as possible.

[179] UN Secretary-General Kofi Annan, *The Rule of Law and Transitional Justice in Conflict and Post-Conflict Societies: Report of the Secretary-General* (New York: United Nations, 2004), 4; https://www.un.org/ruleoflaw/blog/document/the-rule-of-law-and-transitional-justice-in-conflict-and-post-conflict-societies-report-of-the-secretary-general/; https://www.un.org/ruleoflaw/files/2004%20report.pdf.

On corporate capitalism as instruments of governance, see A. Claire Cutler, "New Constitutionalism, Democracy and the Future of Global Governance," in *Critical Perspectives on the Crisis of Global Governance: Reimagining the Future*, ed. Stephen Gill (New York: Palgrave Macmillan, 2016), 89–109.

[180] Louis Henkin, *How Nations Behave* (New York: Columbia University, 1979), 47.

sanction exists for all international laws, although with widely varying consequences. States frequently obey international law because it helps them achieve their goals and makes international relations more predictable, not because they fear a sanction for violating law. One country's compliance encourages reciprocal compliance by others. Non-compliance undermines others' trust in a particular norm and in other states' conduct. Non-compliance often leads to reprisals.

Much can be done to strengthen international law without undergoing dangerous risks, even from a political realist perspective, if there is interest in doing so and willingness to experiment. One of the most doable, safest measures for strengthening international law is for the United States (and other states) simply to be more faithful in complying with existing laws,[181] thereby strengthening customary law. In addition, to rely on judicial processes for resolving disputes and to develop more incentives for states' compliance with law, backed by coercive enforcement mechanisms when needed, would be useful.

The Ottawa treaty banning anti-personnel land mines even illustrates how legalization processes may at times "legislate" new norms. This treaty "would appear to be a case where norms shaped practice, rather than one where prevailing practice became codified into law."[182] Instructively, this process did not follow the political realist expectation that international law is nothing more than the product of dominant nations' preferences. Non-governmental organizations and small and medium-sized states pressed for this treaty to constrain violence by great powers that often has maimed or killed civilians, especially children.

Another impetus for expanding law is that commerce flourishes with predictability and reciprocity that only law can provide, both internationally as well as domestically. As interdependence grows and the ease of moving corporate economic operations offshore and around the world increases, national governments will find it harder and harder to enforce domestic laws for worker safety and fair play, environmental standards, a level economic playing field, and taxes unless they coordinate domestic law enforcement with offshore financial "sanctuaries" and economic activity in other countries. National governments may want to coordinate lawmaking among countries in North America and the EU, for example, to regulate companies with the sweep of Google, Facebook, Microsoft, and Amazon.

Unless international law is strengthened and relied upon, it is difficult to see how the values of human dignity can be widely implemented or even how the human species will be able to survive with dignity and a reasonable degree of civilization in the future. It is foolish to discard the possibilities presented by imaginative use of law,

---

[181] In the words of historian Stephen Wertheim, "After decades of unilateral actions, crowned by the aggressive invasion of Iraq, it is US military power that threatens international law and order. Rules should strengthen through cooperation, not wither through imposition." Stephen Wertheim, "The Only Way to End 'Endless War,'" *New York Times*, September 14, 2019.

[182] Matthew Evangelista, Henry Shue, and Tami Davis Biddle, *The American Way of Bombing: Changing Ethical and Legal Norms, from Flying Fortresses to Drones* (Ithaca, NY: Cornell University Press, 2014), 13. The United States was a major world producer of land mines prior to the treaty banning them.

especially when the growth of international law over the past century now presents us with "the opportunity to extend the rule of law over international human affairs for the first time in human history."[183] Some will argue that "without a trusted system of laws, no sustainable [global] community can be brought into being, and hence no genuine bonds of [global] citizenship can be established."[184] Although some people with inclusive identities or universal religious or philosophical commitments do harbor feelings of global citizenship even before a trusted system of laws is well established, the central role of international law in constructing global community seems beyond doubt.

The international actors and relationships "that provided the basis for governance for nearly 400 years are changing." International law is becoming "a dense system of legal interactions with connections to national and subnational institutions, international organizations, and a host of private actors."[185] Even in the absence of deliberate intentions to enhance international legislative functions, some norm-making occurs through statements of principle from non-governmental organizations, texts prepared by expert groups, and self-regulating codes of conduct for networks of professionals and multinational corporations.[186] "A growing body of empirical work shows that such informal mechanisms do influence state behavior."[187] Because of incentives for predictable international behavior, some "compliance can be achieved regardless of whether the norm is hard or soft[188] as long as there is a culture that encourages adherence to the norm."[189]

5.5.1 Providing an Antidote to Violence

Developing impartial, rights-sensitive international law is the only effective means available for increasing and sustaining peace, economic justice, human rights, and environmental health in the long run. Because "good law"[190] helps make human conduct more predictable and trustworthy, it enables governments to maximize human freedom and justice while minimizing violence in their transactions. Because war "can be regarded as a way of making political decisions under conditions of anarchy, the creation of a system of rules by which to make political decisions can serve as the

---

[183] Thomas J. Schoenbaum, *International Relations: The Path Not Taken: Using International Law to Promote World Peace and Security* (New York: Cambridge University Press, 2006), 304.

[184] Falk, *Power Shift*, 243.

[185] Ku, "Evolution of International Law," 40.

[186] For example, the MacBride and Sullivan Principles establish a corporate code of conduct regarding human rights and labor standards.

[187] Ku, "Evolution of International Law," 41.

[188] Soft law refers to agreements, principles, and declarations that are not legally binding.

[189] Ku, "Evolution of International Law," 41.

[190] In this analysis, "good law" refers to laws that uphold human dignity. Boaventura de Sousa Santos captures part of its spirit in "international law from below." *Toward a New Legal Common Sense: Law, Globalization, and Emancipation* (London: Butterworths, 2002).

functional equivalent of war."[191] Making treaty law is a primary way to "legislate" rules of understanding and reciprocity among countries to bridle unruly states in a system of relative anarchy. Substantial evidence indicates that where major powers make serious efforts to develop a set of rules to guide their relationships, they are unlikely to fight major wars.[192] Indeed, "the purpose of law is peace."[193] Even without relinquishing their hold on military force, sovereign states "can come to see themselves in a constitutionalized world society as peaceful members of the international community and at the same time as capable players in international organizations."[194]

Arms control treaties provide another example of how to use legal constraints on the procurement of destabilizing armaments to create weapons controls or weapons-free zones and increase the likelihood of peace while expanding the rule of law generally. Historical experience demonstrates that arms control contributes to peace when it constrains arms races and discourages accumulation of destructive power, in part because the militarily most powerful states are the most war-prone.[195] If not constrained, new military technologies usually are destabilizing because they increase some or all countries' vulnerability, as illustrated by nuclear weapons proliferation, cyberwarfare, under-the-radar drone attack weapons, and the potential threat of space-based attack weapons.

Consider what the utility of treaty law might have been if it had been used, for example, to constrain China's production of thousands of drones and its willingness to sell the Chinese imitation of the US-developed Predator, for only $1 million each, often to destabilizing buyers. The Pentagon's Defense Science Board described China's intense pursuit of attack drones as simply "alarming."[196] Of course, the drone appetite internationally has been whetted, not constrained, by the pace-setting United States, which has been the first country to make widespread use of attack drones. International legal restraints also would have been useful to constrain US allies from undermining US security: in the 1990s, Israel sold 100 Harpy armed drones to the Chinese government, facilitating their early development program.

---

[191] Vasquez, "Steps to War," 144; Quincy Wright, *The Role of International Law in the Elimination of War* (New York: Oceana Publications, 1961).

[192] See Peter Wallensteen, "Universalism vs. Particularism: On the Limits of Major Power Order," *Journal of Peace Research* 21, no. 3 (1984): 243–257.
    Major wars did not occur in the 19th century in part because norms and rules were more widely accepted as constraints than in the 20th century. See Vasquez, "Steps to War," 130, 143.

[193] Mary Ellen O'Connell, "Belief in the Authority of International Law for Peace: A Reflection on Pacem in Terris," in *Peace Through Law: Reflections on Pacem in Terris from Philosophy, Law, Theology, and Political Science*, ed. Heinz-Gerhard Justenhoven and Mary Ellen O'Connell (Baden-Baden, Germany: Nomos, 2016), 45. See also Richard Falk's confirmation of the utility of "a law-oriented approach that is increasingly committed to cosmopolitan values and procedures and to an ethos of *global* democracy." Italics in original. Falk, "International Law and the Future," 728; Anthony Appiah, *Cosmopolitan Ethics in a World of Strangers* (New York: Norton, 2006); and Held and Koenig-Archibugi, *Taming Globalization*.

[194] Habermas, "Political Constitution," 273.

[195] Human Security Report Project, *Causes of Peace*.

[196] Edward Wong, "Hacking US Secrets, China Pushes for Drones," *New York Times* September 21, 2013, A 3.

Good law, unlike mere political interactions, offers precision and mutual obligation in written texts to narrow gaps between loose rhetoric and punitive actions by specifying what conduct or behavior is consistent with a professed value. It aids enforcement. Good law discourages irresponsible rhetoric and action in times of crisis. If officials truly respect their own government's rhetorical support for peace, they should be less willing to threaten war in violation of UN Charter law against it.[197]

Among other benefits, better use of international law can enable separate, power-seeking sovereignties to overcome chronic impediments to developing mutually peaceful policies and more trustworthy cooperative international relations generally. Law can help close the destabilizing gap between nice-sounding rhetoric and not-so-nice actions, between claims that officials often make about who will benefit from a particular policy and those who really will benefit or suffer from it. Law can expose or adjust the gap characterized by double standards such as, "Our country may develop nuclear weapons but yours may not."

Good international law can strengthen peacebuilding processes because it provides a precise and principled means for doing systematic value clarification and careful assessment of how official rhetoric compares to the value consequences of government actions. Because the powerful frequently succumb to the temptation to deliberately claim or unconsciously believe that they serve others' interests or the general interest when in fact they primarily serve their own narrower interests, peacebuilders and private citizens need always to ask "Who benefits?" and "Who pays?" for any particular decision. If value clarification proceeds systematically with legal norms as standards for resolving conflicts, it is an effective way that individuals and groups may unmask gross violations of human rights and speak truth to power without inciting violence.[198]

Negotiated legal settlements to end violent conflicts enable equitable representation of multiple stakeholders, which more often results in lasting peace and democracy after the conflicts end than do military victories.[199] Many studies show the desirability of compromise agreements that respect the dignity and rights of all parties, qualities enabled by the rule of law. Benefits accrue to the people associated with all the warring parties, to the nature of their future governments, and to international society. The risk of renewed violence in war-torn societies declines by 50 percent when civil society and women are included in negotiations, which legal processes enable.[200]

---

[197] They would honor Articles 2 (4) and 51 of the Charter.

[198] For examples, see Johansen, *The National Interest and the Human Interest*, chapter 1; Milton Rokeach, *Understanding Human Values: Individual and Societal* (New York: Free Press, 1979); Milton Rokeach, "Inducing Change and Stability in Belief Systems and Personality Structures," *Journal of Social Issues* 41, no. 1 (1985): 153–171.

[199] Wallensteen, *Quality Peace*, especially 205–210.

[200] Desirée Nilsson, "Anchoring the Peace: Civil Society Actors in Peace Accords and Durable Peace," *International Interactions* 38, no. 2 (April 1, 2012): 243–266, http://www.tandfonline.com/doi/abs/10.1080/03050629.2012.659139.

To make the rule of law more reliable and effective internationally, as the functional substitute for war, would enable countries gradually to rely less on military instruments[201] and more on law and international institutions to protect all parties' legitimate interests and to enforce norms of reciprocity, equity, and peace. Empirical studies indicate that temptations to use military force are stronger in countries with larger size and power, resulting in a greater risk of war. On the other hand, evidence shows that international laws and institutions designed to constrain temptations to use force actually do so in some cases.[202]

Perhaps the foremost scientifically documented benefit of spreading rule-of-law institutions with democratic values domestically and internationally is that the incidence of war is almost certain to go down as these institutions spread. Although democracies are not inherently more peaceful than authoritarian societies, mature democracies generally do not engage in overt warfare against each other.[203] If the number of democracies in the international system increases, the number of war-prone dyads decreases.[204]

Finally, law provides an antidote to violence by empowering peace-minded governments and citizens everywhere to clarify and, when necessary, to enforce their desire to uphold norms restricting violence, including the existing laws against military aggression and for protecting civilian immunity. Law provides a handle to grasp in developing new legal standards to constrain dangerous technologies, violence, and weapons of mass destruction. It enables citizens to discourage their own government, as well as others, from making violent threats against others,[205] to participate watchfully in the work of the International Court of Justice, and to press US officials and members of Congress to support joining the International Criminal Court as ways of moving disputes from battlefields to courtrooms.[206] Additionally, the UN Security Council should much more frequently "use the authority it has under the Rome Statute to refer cases of suspected war crimes and crimes against humanity to the International Criminal Court."[207]

---

[201] Some reductions in the number of violent conflicts can be attributed to the increase in the number of democracies, an increase in the acceptance of human rights, and the decline in government discrimination against minorities. See Human Security Report Project, *Causes of Peace*.

[202] Human Security Report Project, *Causes of Peace*.

[203] See, for example, Russett, *Grasping the Democratic Peace*; Bruce Russett, Christopher Layne, D. E. Spiro, Michael Doyle, "The Democratic Peace: And Yet It Moves," *International Security* 19, no. 4 (October 1995): 164–175.

[204] "The risk of [violent] conflict declines as the proportion of democracies in the international system increases." Russett and Oneal, *Triangulating Peace*, 275.

[205] Article 2 (4) of the UN Charter prohibits "the threat or use of force."

[206] For good suggestions about providing appropriate education for senators and representatives, see Lorelei Kelly and Elizabeth Turpen, *Educating Congress on Peace and Security* (Washington, DC: Henry Stimson Center, 2004), https://www.stimson.org/wp-content/files/file-attachments/Policy%20 Matters%20FINAL.pdf.

[207] UN High-Level Panel, *A More Secure World*, 35, para 90.

Aligning US power to strengthen impartial international law and increase states' compliance with it would benefit US interests in the long run because the practice of international law can indeed become a functional replacement for war.[208]

5.5.2 Supporting Justice and Law Enforcement

One way in which law dampens violence is to make it possible to design a fair, systematic way of representing all people or groups in decision-making, thereby enabling legal processes to lower pressures for and replace violent conflicts. The absence of fair representation in decision-making often encourages violence, especially when there are sharp differences between those who have power to make policy and those who are affected by it. Seldom in international relations do all of those who are affected by a decision have a fair measure of power to decide it. In this democratic deficit, government officials of one country in practice say: "Our country has the right to make this decision, and yours does not, even though the decision may affect your country." Good lawmaking processes potentially can bring everyone affected by a political decision into a fair decision-making process. If, for example, everyone on Earth is affected by the atmospheric testing or use of nuclear weapons—and all are—then all should have a say in whether and how these might or might not occur.

In the long run, the sovereign equality of states, established at Westphalia, needs to be transformed by giving new representational weight to human equality. The Security Council, for example, cannot acquire the legitimacy or power it needs to do its peacemaking job effectively and with a minimum of violence if the people in the world's largest democracy (India) have no permanent seat there while people in two far less populous states (United Kingdom, France), who represent the same continent (Europe), do. Law enables and encourages reasonable balancing of representation for decision-making.

Good international law also can maximize freedom, justice, and nonviolent political instruments by clarifying and channeling acceptable conduct, such as respect for rules governing warfare, including non-aggression and civilian immunity from attack, and establishing legal means for enforcing law on heads of governments and military organizations. One essential requirement for law to move toward being a functional replacement of war is to be able to conduct coercive enforcement of laws when coercion is needed, even while seeking to conduct law enforcement with as little war-fighting as possible.

If future international law can be strengthened by increasing incentives to induce officials' compliance and by establishing fairer representation of underrepresented peoples in international lawmaking processes, it could play a more successful role in reducing felt needs for using violence and in building support for transnational

---

[208] See Louis Henkin, *How Nations Behave: Law and Foreign Policy* (New York: Columbia University Press, 1979); O'Connell, *Power and Purpose*, 105–149.

political change. Many people who already feel the weight of a global system on their shoulders experience "a lack of substantive representation in the programs and actions that have a dramatic influence on their lives." Indeed, "local perspectives are usually diluted at best or absent at worst from the global governors whose focus invariably is the macro [level]."[209] The promise of more adequate representation and feedback loops would encourage many young people to look forward to more responsive systems of governance, starting locally while also connecting internationally.

The security benefits from stronger international law also can be increased by educating people to exploit the utility of nonviolent action for ousting tyrants, preventing war, upholding human rights, and promoting democratic social change.[210] Civilian resistance in the form of nonviolent direct action, which requires planning and training but no weapons or huge, military-like budgets, can do much more to protect human security and enable civilians to influence political decision-making than is commonly recognized or utilized. Erica Chenoweth's and Maria Stephan's research[211] shows that nonviolent means for overcoming an authoritarian government or resisting a foreign occupation, although no panacea, are far more likely than violent means to succeed and far more likely to lead to democratic government after an anti-government campaign, even against highly authoritarian governments.

Strengthening the rule of law is a daunting task that requires being both principled and firm. If one is not principled, then it is difficult to be firm with others because unprincipled, double standards will continue to rule the day in international relations, obstructing universal commitments and impartial enforcement. At the same time, one must be firm to enhance the law because enforcing the law sometimes requires coercion to stop deviant behavior. The kind of coercion that seems most desirable, and which might be feasible in a growing number of situations with gross violations of human rights, could take the form of economic pressures and perhaps smart sanctions backed by cosmopolitan law enforcement,[212] rather than relying on traditional military combat. This would enable diplomacy to aim at moving gradually toward international equivalents of judicial and police enforcement familiar in well-functioning domestic legal systems.[213]

---

[209] Thomas Weiss and Rorden Wilkinson, "The Globally Governed—Everyday Global Governance," *Global Governance* 24, no. 2 (2018): 206.

[210] Erica Chenoweth and Maria Stephan, "Why Civil Resistance Works," *International Security* 33, no. 1 (2008): 7–44; Erica Chenoweth and Maria Stephan, "Drop Your Weapons: When and Why Civil Resistance Works," *Foreign Affairs* 93, no. 4 (July/August 2014): 94–106; Chenoweth and Stephan, *Why Civil Resistance Works*. See also Mel Duncan, "Greater Than the Tread of Mighty Armies: Unarmed Civilian Protection Gaining Momentum Worldwide," *Courier*, 91 (Fall 2017): 3–7.

   More than 39 civil society organizations are working nonviolently to protect civilians in 21 countries, including Myanmar, Iraq, South Sudan, and the United States.

[211] See Chenoweth and Stephan, *Why Civil Resistance Works*, 3–29.

[212] For discussion of cosmopolitan law enforcement, see Kaldor, *New and Old Wars*.

[213] Throughout this analysis, I use "police" and "policing" to refer to life-preserving, violence-reducing police enforcement led by civilians informed by respect for human rights and community-based decision-making. See Ferreira Bertus, *The Use and Effectiveness of Community Policing in a Democracy*

Insofar as possible, efforts to ensure lawful conduct could be "based on law enforcement rather than war-fighting, premised on the equal value of all human lives instead of privileging one side, aimed at protecting people and arresting individual criminals rather than defeating an enemy, and situated within a framework of international law." Marlies Glasius and Mary Kaldor conclude that "such an approach is the only realistic version of a European security policy."[214] One might add that it also could begin to be a realistic global security policy in some cases, gradually opening the door to more applications if confidence in such an approach increased.

To set a good example of being principled and firm in strengthening the rule of law, the United States, as well as Russia, China, and India, should reconsider their dismissive attitude toward the International Criminal Court. Although the United States has asked this court to prosecute others, US officials have refused to accept the court themselves. This hypocritical double standard undermines lawmaking processes, discourages lawful conduct by other actors, and diminishes the effectiveness of the court.

Although custom may be a disappointingly slow way to create law, it also is an encouragingly accessible way for governments to create law in the absence of a global legislature, and its growth could be speeded given the will to do so. Every country's day-to-day actions contribute to custom, so technically no government and no people are totally excluded from this kind of "legislative" process if they respect and insist that others respect the rule of law.

Constructing the necessary new legal architecture requires the United States and other societies to take immediate steps—small and safe yet significant—to strengthen the rule of law throughout all of international relations. Because preventing war requires creating a political system capable of making and enforcing rules to accommodate differences and not allow separate decisions to employ large-scale violence, sustainable peace depends on institutionalizing procedures to resolve competing political demands.[215] There are no persuasive arguments against moving in this direction. The most common excuse is that more effective law restricts a superpower's freedom of action. But that is misleading if the law embodies positive values, because the law increases freedom and effectiveness in doing what is desirable when others' conduct follows constructive rules. Good law may restrict one's freedom to do bad things, and one cannot escape the possibility that this kind of constraint is behind some objections to strengthening international law. Yet if it also prevents others from doing unwanted things, it may be a good bargain.

(Washington, D.C.: National Institute of Justice, 1996); and Gerald W. Schlabach, ed., *Just Policing, Not War: An Alternative Response to World Violence* (Collegeville, MN: Liturgical Press, 2007), 3–19, 93–106.

[214] Glasius and Kaldor, "A Human Security Vision," 17.

[215] Vasquez comes to a similar conclusion: "If we assume that war avoidance . . . involves the creation of a political system . . . capable of making decisions, then how long the peaces . . . will last depends upon their success in creating an order that institutionalizes procedures for the resolution of political demands." Vasquez, "Steps to War," 144.

5.5.3 *Demanding Public International Law*

Establishing a more effective rule of law in world affairs would be possible *if* enough people would insist on it. More might be inclined to do that if it became clearer that the most promising way to stop mutually reinforcing, compounding tragedies of the commons from arising in today's nationally divided, segregated international system is to modernize the international legal architecture to make decision-making fairer and to extend freedom and the rule of law beyond national borders to effectuate more security and human rights around the world.[216] If international law would be constructed *strategically*, it could begin to set limits on other countries' war-making and environmentally destructive capabilities. However, such limits will be accepted by other states only in return for reciprocal constraints on one's own national conduct and for democratizing international decision-making. To give up some discretion for one's own nation may be wise if in return one obtains more predictability, cooperation, and legal compliance from others.[217] Yet some policymakers, especially in the more powerful states, are not sure they want stronger international law. The benefits of law appear to be less obvious to the powerful than to the weak, because the former hope to get most of what they want by imposing their will on others without any legal constraints on their own conduct. Yet empirical realists recognize that "the institutionalization of measures for the nonviolent settlement of international conflicts . . . [is] the central problem of international politics and international law."[218]

If the law is impartial, the growth of international law governing international conduct could be seen by US and other national officials as a desirable trade-off rather than a reluctant concession to new realities, especially if one considers all the consequences of a largely lawless world compared to one where the war-making, human rights-denying, or environment-destroying functions of sovereignty have been mutually, reliably limited. Even more important philosophically, the international law that limits and frees states can, with the help of a more cosmopolitan nationalism in the future, become cosmopolitan law that governs and liberates individuals. In the new architecture proposed here, individuals benefit not only from being subjects of a demilitarized national order, but also by becoming significant subjects as citizens whose dignity is upheld in a legally constituted global society.

The best evidence for how legalization processes may proceed, even without an overall, explicitly agreed-on strategy to do so, is contained in Karen Alter's *The New Terrain of International Law*. This careful analysis shows how international law can exert sustained influence on national decisions, thereby establishing new transnational

---

[216] The opportunities for doing this present themselves in increased interdependencies among nations as boundaries become more permeable.

[217] G. John Ikenberry, *Liberal Order and Imperial Ambition* (Cambridge: Polity Press, 2006), 122; Cortright, Seyle, and Wall, *Governance for Peace*, 230.

[218] Werner Levi, *Law and Politics in the International Society* (Beverly Hills, CA: Sage, 1976), 154, cited by David P. Forsythe, "United Nations Peacemaking," *Proceedings of the Academy of Political Science* 32, no. 4 (1977): 206.

political processes and coalitions of actors that both generate new laws to guide conduct and new political allies to carry influences further down the road of legalization and compliance. Her view is reinforced by Anne-Marie Slaughter's somewhat surprising observation that international networks of government officials, either appointed or elected, "can perform many of the functions of a world government—legislation, administration and adjudication—without the form."[219] Increasingly "disaggregated states" face "the rising need for and capacity of different domestic government institutions to engage in activities beyond their borders, often with their foreign counterparts. It is regulators pursuing the subjects of their regulations across borders; judges negotiating mini-treaties with their brethren to resolve complex transnational cases; and legislators consulting on the best ways to frame and pass legislation affecting human rights or the environment."[220]

However, as promising as Alter's and Slaughter's findings are, the growth of lawmaking processes appears insufficient and too slow for dealing with tough political and geostrategic issues. Although these findings enable us to imagine the gradual growth of lawmaking and judicialization of more international conduct and to catch a glimpse of the future, more direct efforts to expand democratic representation at the global level and to orchestrate new political institutions are necessary to increase human security sufficiently. In addition, effective new institutional architecture would be an impossible dream without substantial stabilization of political relationships among major actors in today's world, requiring gradual reform of the existing militarized balance-of-power system. Fortunately, peace and security research and lived international experience since World War II provide promising guidelines for how to move safely from the existing world to a transformed international system, with the aid of new realities that Alter, Slaughter, and others have brought to our attention.

To expand the willingness of citizens to support the growth of international law means recognizing that any stable relationship between large groups usually includes some limits on what all parties can do, even while opening new vistas of mutually beneficial cooperation. Growing interdependence has made cooperative relationships both more necessary and more fruitful than earlier in history. Many people oppose strengthening international law because they fear it would reduce US sovereignty. Yet if the United States favors the norms contained in a particular treaty, then all states that ratify it undertake some obligation to conduct themselves in ways that are preferred by the United States. US ratification of a desirable multilateral treaty can be viewed as extending US sovereignty's values around the world and increasing the obligation of other states to comply with the code of conduct that the United States prefers. Even though it reciprocally obligates the United States to honor the same norms and consolidate them into law, it might be a good bargain, a good way to use US sovereignty.

---

[219] Anne-Marie Slaughter, *A New World Order* (Princeton, NJ: Princeton University Press, 2004), 4.
[220] Slaughter, *New World Order*, 5, 12.

Conservatives with a profound understanding of treaty law could favor ratifying many treaties, not because they arguably place *limits* on US sovereignty but because they *expand* the influence of US values and uphold preferred norms of human dignity around the world. These often rein in government abuses and constrain governmental conduct, another conservative value. Smart limits on every national government's sovereignty expand human freedom and enable its exercise without fear of violence. Closing the door on abuses of sovereignty opens the door for human liberation. This process can proceed by the intermingling of healthy forms of nationalism and cosmopolitanism. International law, familiar as a law for states, can be transformed into cosmopolitan law as a law for individuals. Personal liberty can actually increase for individuals when they are not limited merely to being objects of international law but also attain status as subjects under cosmopolitan law[221] that may restrict violence against people and advance environmental health and human rights.

US policies have been especially short-sighted when one recognizes that we live in an era of relative US decline in international influence. With the passing of time, US ability to exert dominant influence on international norms may decline further. It is instructive to imagine what the world would be like today if the United States years ago had implemented many of the legal norms contained in treaties awaiting US ratification and that many other states did support (see Table 2.1). If the public had understood the enormous difference that US ratification and vigorous compliance would have had in advancing the rule of law, many more would probably have pressed for ratification. With US ratification, other countries that have not ratified many of the treaties would have felt increased pressure to do so. Indeed, ratification of important treaties could be made a condition of offering a state other benefits in the international system. Countries that have ratified some of the treaties but not fully implemented their provisions would be much more likely to take implementation seriously if the United States also were doing so. Additional international incentives could be offered for faithful compliance after ratification. In addition, had these treaties become fully and widely binding after their negotiation, many new initiatives, not even mentioned here, could have been given prominent space on the drawing boards of new global architecture for human security and prosperity.

Despite the absence of robust US support for lawmaking processes since the Reagan administration, some global dialogue around substantive international law has occurred, including more input from small and medium powers. This has helped to make universalism more "truly universal, not simply the universalism of major powers."[222] It has expanded the law's capacity to encourage compliance[223] and "to blend the

---

[221] See Habermas, "Political Constitution," 268.

[222] Wallensteen, "Universalism vs. Particularism," 257.

[223] Ian Johnstone notes that "the creation, interpretation, and implementation of law generate a predisposition towards compliance not shared by everyone, but sufficiently widespread to influence the climate of opinion." Johnstone, "The Power of Interpretative Communities," in *Power in Global Governance*, ed. Michael Barnett and Raymond Duvall (Cambridge: Cambridge University Press, 2005), 189.

wisdom of multiple cultures."[224] As World Court Judge Christopher Weeramantry of Sri Lanka, has noted, although international law "was cast largely in a Graeco-Judaeo-Christian mould," more recently "it has moved towards greater universalization. Many more universal perspectives drawn from all the world's cultural traditions can and must be fed into it as it develops to suit the needs of the 21st century."[225] International law "cannot afford to remain set in a narrowly monocultural mould" if it is realistically "to address problems which are truly global, multi-cultural and multi-traditional, which cry out for a universal solution." He expects that the future success of good international law "will depend heavily on the extent to which it can be further universalized by harnessing the strength available in the world's rich inheritance of cultural and ideological traditions." In his view, it is through international legal processes that "diverse cultures can reach consensus about the moral norms that we should commonly live by. People everywhere believe in law, believe in this alternative to force, as they believe in higher things."[226]

Mary Ellen O'Connell notes that international law expresses "the international community's shared goals . . . [of] peace, respect for human rights, prosperity, and the protection of the natural environment." Developing a better understanding of the power and potential of international law and promoting more widespread acceptance of it "should enhance its authority and, thereby, its power to achieve . . . [the preceding] goals on behalf of us all."[227] In sum, expanding the rule of law constitutes a strong correlate of peace and an essential part of a global strategy for human security.

5.6 GROWING GLOBAL GOVERNANCE

The analysis so far points toward two conclusions: (1) There cannot be lasting peace or sustainable security without increased global governance to help manage state behavior; and (2) to make global governance desirable and feasible, increased democratization of international institutions must occur. Therefore, to grow sufficient democratic global governance to ensure human security is the sixth correlate of peace and guideline for grand strategy.[228]

---

[224] O'Connell, *Power and Purpose*, 141.

[225] Christopher G. Weeramantry, *Universalising International Law* (Leiden, Belgium: Martinus Nijhoff, 2004), 2–3, as cited by O'Connell, *Power and Purpose*, 141.

[226] Weeramantry, *Universalising International Law*, 2–3, as cited by O'Connell, *Power and Purpose*, 370.

[227] O'Connell, *Power and Purpose*, 370.

[228] See Jan Tinbergen, "Global Governance for the 21st Century," in United Nations Human Development Programme, *Human Development Report 1994*, 98; Russett and Oneal, *Triangulating Peace*, 271–305.

    Numerous studies show that focusing on "quality governance and capable institutions offers the best prescription for . . . reducing the risk of armed violence." Cortright, Seyle, and Wall, *Governance for Peace*, 14–15, 227–250.

    A well-known earlier proposal for substantial military reductions combined with limited world federal government to enforce law is Grenville Clark and Louis Sohn, *World Peace Through World Law* (Cambridge, MA: Harvard University Press, 1958, and revised in 1960, 1966, and 1973). The Report of the High-Level Panel of Eminent Persons on the Post-2015 Development Agenda concluded that

Sustainable peace and security require a global extension of democratic values and institutions[229] to enable incorporating just enough additional global governance[230] to ensure that every state respects necessary rules, such as to constrain the use of weapons of mass destruction, limit greenhouse gases, or prevent genocide and crimes against humanity. The required growth in governing ability could occur either by encouraging democratization and strengthening of existing United Nations agencies or by establishing a new global democratic institution. In either case, the necessary features are (1) that all people on Earth should be fairly represented, (2) that the global agency should be authorized to make some security rules for the common good and legally binding on all, and (3) that it should be able impartially to monitor and enforce these rules without exception.

Because national sovereignty rather than democracy has been a guiding principle in most existing UN agencies, many are characterized by insufficiently diverse participation, weak accountability and legitimacy, and a tendency to serve the interests of a small number of large states. In making reforms, both the *global* and the *democratic* dimensions of new governance are essential. More *global* governance is needed to make, interpret, and enforce the laws of peace and environmental protection worldwide, for example, including constraints on the development, possession, and use of weapons of mass destruction, and limits on greenhouse gas emissions. Such governance could make globally coordinated, legally binding initiatives possible, with incentives and enforcement rules for all countries in order to sustain peace and implement a liberating rule of law to make international relations predictable and human dignity viable.

The *democratic* dimension is needed to make any necessary global expansion of governing authority desirable and politically feasible.[231] Most people would not want more powerful global institutions unless they were based on democratic values and enabled all people to be fairly represented in them. Of course, societies that lack fully functioning national democratic processes at home need to be included in global governance, as they are now in the United Nations. Yet to diversify and democratize representation from these and indeed every national society, reformed global institutions might encourage civil society organizations to participate or perhaps some representatives to

---

reducing the risk of armed conflict requires equitable economic development and "building effective and accountable institutions" of governance. United Nations, *A New Global Partnership: Eradicate Poverty and Transform Economies through Sustainable Development* (New York: United Nations, 2013), 9.

This conclusion applies to peacebuilding in both domestic and international contexts, as does Barbara Walter's finding that armed conflict is a clear sign that government is unresponsive to human needs and aspirations, unreliable, and weak. Barbara F. Walter, "Conflict Relapse and the Sustainability of Post-conflict Peace," *World Development Report* 2011 Background Paper (Washington, DC: World Bank, September 2010), 7–19.

[229] Russett, *Grasping the Democratic Peace*; Russett and Oneal, *Triangulating Peace*.

[230] Weiss, *Global Governance: Why?*

[231] More international attention should be given to sustaining healthy democracy where it exists and to its spread where it is not present. "As at the national level, so in the global neighborhood: the democratic principle must be ascendant." Commission on Global Governance, *Our Global Neighbourhood*, 65–67.

be directly elected to participate in a global institution, in addition to more traditional representation from national governing officials. A global democratic framework of course could not be fully realized immediately, nor would it need to be, as long as a few civilization-protecting rules were being followed by all countries in the meantime, facilitated by modest reforms in existing UN institutions.

5.6.1 Honoring the Right to Democracy

Democratic political processes are a human right.[232] Indeed, they are the political foundation for both human freedom and human security, one reason that starvation and violence are both less likely in democratic than in authoritarian societies. Following the moral imperative of treating others as we want them to treat us requires a commitment to democracy because the opinions, values, and interests of others, as well as of oneself, need to be taken into account in decision-making in a fair and systematic way. This right to democratic government has been internationally recognized for three-fourths of a century in the Universal Declaration of Human Rights: "Everyone has the right to take part in the government of his country, directly or through freely chosen representatives." Moreover, "The will of the people shall be the basis of the authority of government; this will shall be expressed in periodic and genuine elections."[233]

Democratic human rights obviously apply locally and nationally as well as globally, but they cannot be easily or quickly achieved in undemocratic or authoritarian states even though at the same time some democratic values can be implanted in international institutions—for example, by employing globally fair representation. Democratic values can be encouraged everywhere, as are human rights, through nonviolent means. Although the primary focus of the democracy discussion here is on overcoming democratic deficits in international settings, support for democracy at all levels of governance is part of this correlate of peace.

When questions arise about how to respond to undemocratic national governments throughout the world, the United States does not need to express support for democratization in authoritarian countries by encouraging violent revolution there or attacking an authoritarian government as it did Iraq. US policies might be more successful by adopting a long-term strategy that encourages authoritarian states to respect international human rights and to introduce liberal reforms gradually. This approach would probably increase the likelihood that democratization would succeed when it finally does occur.

Employing a long-range, nonviolent democratic framework is likely to be most effective, both in the international and national arenas, when constructed on principles that explicitly recognize the equal moral worth and dignity of all people, the

---

[232] UDHR, Articles 20, 21, 28.

[233] UDHR, Article 21, paragraphs 1 and 3. The International Covenant on Civil and Political Rights, to which the United States is a party, uses nearly identical language in Article 25.

consent of the governed in decisions that affect their lives, the necessity for shared decision-making through fair voting procedures, the requirement that every official representative exercise some political responsibility and accountability in his or her role, the principle of subsidiarity in locating decision-making power, and, at the least, the avoidance of serious harm to any country's rights and the enablement of meeting everyone's basic needs as institutions evolve.[234]

Because democracy requires free and fair elections to choose people's representatives, it would be useful to develop a robust framework for monitoring or at least evaluating national elections to ensure their integrity. The United Nations or an independent agency, perhaps with the help of organizations like the Carter Center or Freedom House, could note the extent to which all adult citizens vote and whether there has been voter suppression, candidate intimidation, or dishonest tabulation of votes. If possible, high-quality elections should be acknowledged and corrupt or unfair electoral practices discouraged. The UN High-Level Panel also suggests developing means to protect democratically elected governments from "unconstitutional overthrow."[235]

A striking example of the need for democratization in the international community to overcome the poorly aligned relationship between state power and legitimate authority is found in the effort to free the UN Security Council from the stranglehold imposed on it by the five permanent members. These five took permanent seats at the UN's founding because they were victors in World War II. Except for the permanent five, all 193 UN member states must compete to be elected before they obtain one of the 10 non-permanent seats on the Council. Once an elected member obtains a seat, it has no veto. Because the veto enables any one of the permanent five to block single-handedly any Security Council decision, representation is unfair, first to obtain a seat and then to exercise equal power once in a seat. All countries of the world are legally required to do what the Security Council asks when only the five permanent members and four other states vote for an action. On the other hand, all countries may be deprived of the possible benefit of a council decision if only one of the permanent members disagrees. This inequitable power configuration prevents the world's only general purpose political institution from developing fair legal processes for governing internationally. How can the Security Council obtain the necessary legitimacy,[236] authority, and power required to take important decisions for the maintenance of peace, security, and the environment without becoming far more equitable in its representation and exercise of power? Even without totally removing the status of the original five permanent members, a way could be found to extend at least informal

---

[234] See Held and Koenig-Archibugi, *Taming Globalization*, 93–129.

[235] See suggestions from the UN High-Level Panel, *A More Secure World*, 35, para 94.

[236] For an excellent discussion of Security Council legitimacy, see Robert O. Keohane, "Global Governance and Legitimacy," *Review of International Political Economy: Legitimacy and Global Governance* 18, no. 1 (2011): 99–109.

"semi-permanent" status to obvious candidates, such as India, Japan, or Brazil, without taking the veto away from any original permanent member unwilling to qualify it more reasonably.

Growing democratic global governance is not a call for full-blown or unitary world government, because abundant evidence suggests that would be both unfeasible and unwise in the immediate future.[237] The strategy proposed here would entail limited global political integration and vertical dispersal of national sovereignty,[238] consistent with the principle of subsidiarity, with more effective and more democratic governance in all contexts where possible, from local to global, where some sovereignty would be shared gradually and held in common, presumably in some form of federal architecture. Jürgen Habermas, for one, notes that the ways that a liberal constitution "limits the power of the state without constituting it . . . provides a conceptual model for a constitutionalization of international law in the form of a politically constituted world society without a world government." Nation-states can "be restricted in their scope of action without being robbed of their status as subjects of a global legal order."[239] A state may accept and require of other states some legal constraints established through international treaties, imagined even as a world "constitution," without more|political community than international relations now embody. States "can remain subjects of a world constitution without a world government."[240]

Despite Britain's 2016 decision to leave the European Union, notably with the "help" of Russian manipulations of public opinion, the peaceful changes in Europe over 70 years following World War II offer a profound experiment relevant to making desirable changes in building a worldwide security community today. The centuries-long experience of wars between the Germans and French was replaced after 1945 with economic collaboration in the European Coal and Steel Community by using an "associative" strategy of integrative conflict transformation. This made war less likely and eventually led to some supranational governance in the European Union. Architects of the EU thought about sovereignty in a new way and thereby changed it.

In the old way of thinking, sovereignty signified "the complete autonomy of the state to act as it chooses, without legal limitation by any superior entity,"[241] in particular to

---

[237] See the discussion of the rejection of world government in Weiss, *Global Governance*, 8–26; Richard Falk, *On Humane Governance: Toward a New Global Politics* (Cambridge: Polity Press, 1995); Slaughter, *A New World Order*, 8. Slaughter also argues that world government may not be necessary because "a world order self-consciously created out of horizontal and vertical government networks could . . . create a genuine global rule of law without centralized global institutions and could engage, socialize, support, and constrain government officials of every type in every nation." Slaughter, *New World Order*, 4, 261. Two problems with this suggestion are: (1) the difficulty of making networks effective decision makers and, (2) if they could become effective, how could such networks be held accountable to global constituencies?

[238] See Pogge, *World Poverty*, 174–201; Thomas Pogge, "Cosmopolitanism and Sovereignty," *Ethics* 103:1 (1992) 48–95.

[239] Habermas, "Political Constitution," 269.

[240] Habermas, "Political Constitution," 269–270.

[241] Chayes and Chayes, *New Sovereignty*, 26.

make war on its neighbor with abandon. Sovereignty for a separate, unitary state was, in Slaughter's words, "the power to be left alone"[242] or to be left out of a neighbor's hostile decision. In the past, the state may have "realized and expressed its sovereignty through independent action to achieve its goals." But when states are no longer completely independent of one another, they cannot achieve their main goals of security and economic well-being for their citizens without the cooperation of other countries. The old concept of sovereignty, as Abram Chayes and Antonia Chayes concluded, "no longer has any real world meaning."[243] Now states express sovereignty "through participation in the various regimes that regulate and order the international system." For most countries, "sovereignty no longer consists in the freedom of states to act independently, in their perceived self-interest, but in membership in reasonably good standing in the regimes that make up the substance of international life." Indeed, "to be a player, the state must submit to the pressures that international regulations impose."[244] If they do not, as Robert Putnam has noted, "the sanction for violating [the norms of an international regime] is not penal, but exclusion from the network of solidarity and cooperation."[245]

Slaughter sums up the new sovereignty as "the capacity to participate in international institutions of all types—in collective efforts to steer the international system and address global and regional problems"[246] in collaboration with transnational networks encompassing all relevant parties—states, international organizations, and non-governmental organizations. Although to increase compliance with international norms by operating with this understanding of sovereignty and utilizing processes of legal justification and political persuasion "is less dramatic than using coercive sanctions . . . it is the way operational regimes in the real world go about it, for the most part."[247] Even if one debates how broadly this description applies to international relations today, it does explain an opening window for strengthening compliance with international law.

Drawing on a new understanding of sovereignty and developing associative strategies for war prevention could help replace recurring wars and structural violence in global affairs with dependable peace and greater justice, even acknowledging the large contextual differences between the European community and the world community, and despite the current divisions in the European community. The EU experience also highlights outcomes to avoid, such as allowing regional democratic deficits to linger

---

[242] Slaughter, *New World Order*, 267.

[243] Chayes and Chayes, *New Sovereignty*, 26–27; Stephen D. Krasner, "Contested Sovereignty: The Myth of Westphalia," unpublished manuscript, 1944, as reported in Chayes and Chayes, *New Sovereignty*, note 98, 312.

[244] Chayes and Chayes, *New Sovereignty*, 27.

[245] Robert D. Putnam, *Making Democracy Work: Civil Traditions in Modern Italy* (Princeton, NJ: Princeton University Press, 1993), 183.

[246] Slaughter, *New World Order*, 267.

[247] Chayes and Chayes, *New Sovereignty*, 28.

too long before addressing hard questions regarding the need for more inclusive representation.

In addition to making Europe peaceful after centuries of recurring wars, there is much empirical, logical, and normative support for using law with economic and political integration to substitute for war-fighting as a means of settling disputes in a variety of different regional contexts. Studies of recent armed conflicts indicate that active involvements by the United Nations and regional international organizations have helped to prevent violent conflicts, to end violent conflicts, and to sustain peace agreements once established.[248] The quality of internal peace following violent domestic conflicts improves in the presence of "inter-state regional integration."[249] These studies also confirm that democratic governance, equitable trade, and shared memberships in intergovernmental organizations together reduce risks of violent conflict.[250] Because democracies normally find a way to feed their people and do not engage in war with other mature democracies, they contribute directly to human rights and peace.[251]

Democratic values and institutions in a global context can rightfully be understood as constituting a system of peaceful conflict resolution, because they gradually can take over the decision-making and ordering role of war through less threatening and more reliable means.[252]

5.6.2 Recognizing Democracy's Extent

With societies as heavily interdependent as they are today, the human right to democracy cannot be fulfilled in a national context alone, because one country's decisions affect people in neighboring countries also. Without the latter's representation in the former's decisions, democracy is compromised and may be contradicted. Although this problem arises for citizens of all countries, including the United States, China, Russia, and India, it is especially glaring for citizens living in small powers who bear the burden of even heavier democratic deficits because they are usually ignored when the big powers make decisions. For years, decisions by the United States and other powerful actors have violated the fulfillment of the democratic principle for many people throughout the world who are affected by great power decisions but who exercise no influence over them.

After the dawn of the nuclear-cyber-environmentally threatened age, citizens of every nation need to have some dependable democracy in the global sphere, at the least to have their basic human rights respected where they have no reliable political

---

[248] Human Security Report Project, *Causes of Peace*, 20, 78.

[249] Wallensteen, *Quality Peace*, 207.

[250] Russett and Oneal, *Triangulating Peace*; Human Security Report Project, *Causes of Peace*.

[251] Although scholars vigorously disagree about the best explanation for why the theory of democratic peace is true, there is not much evidence casting doubt on the validity of the main hypothesis: mature democracies do not make overt war on other mature democracies. Russett, Layne, Spiro, and Doyle, "The Democratic Peace," 164–175.

[252] Wallensteen et al., "Violence, Wars, Peace, Security," 444.

influence over others' decisions. Progress in democratizing basic decisions internationally is necessary if we are not to lose democratic ground nationally. As interdependence advances it inevitably moves some control of decisions out of exclusively national hands, a reason that democratization is an essential ingredient in the proposed plan for human security. If global governance is to reduce all nations' security fears, then all need to be fairly represented in its lawmaking institutions. Fair representation may also have important community-building consequences because working collaboratively with others often reduces hostilities toward them.[253]

Moreover, a pragmatic benefit arises with the understanding that mobilizing the necessary grassroots political support for global reform in every country will not happen without genuine promise that each group of people will be fairly represented. The democratic principle simply cannot be fulfilled in this stage of history unless it is implemented, to a minimal degree, in a worldwide context. Thus, some *global* representative governance eventually is a necessity. Reforms should always include full representation of women and other groups who have been discriminated against in the past. Of course, careful listening to underrepresented voices can help to "democratize" processes and pave the way even before institutions are sufficiently reformed.

Under appropriate conditions, democracy and globalization can be mutually reinforcing, because in a world of much interdependence, no nation should be left out of any major decision, made anywhere on Earth, if that major decision significantly affects it. Some of the burden of carbon dioxide emissions or virus infections arises from people living outside one's own national boundaries, vivid reminders that "internal and external security are now inseparable."[254]

5.7 SIGNS OF HOPE

Hope for the future arises from (1) the potential in international lawmaking and democratizing processes currently under way and (2) the development of a grand strategic plan for human security based on the correlates of peace elicited from peace and security research. These are summarized in Table 5.1.

Implementing these correlates would encourage more representative international political processes, nurture more effective international institutions, and draw into being new transnational political coalitions that rise above traditional boundaries to bringing needed growth of more democratic global processes. Alter's research details how political coalitions are crisscrossing borders, often on a daily basis, in order to influence compliance with judicial decisions, especially affecting international commerce, by one of the world's 24 permanent international courts. These have rendered

---

[253] David Held, *Democracy and the Global Order* (Cambridge: Polity Press, 1995); Parker J. Palmer, *Healing the Heart of Democracy: The Courage to Create a Politics Worthy of the Human Spirit* (San Francisco: Jossey-Bass, 2011), 5.

[254] Glasius and Kaldor, "A Human Security Vision," 4.

TABLE 5.1

Correlates of Peace

1. Address all nations' security fears
2. Emphasize human security no less than national security
3. Establish positive reciprocity in all international relationships and institutions
4. Implement equity in economic, political, and environmental processes and decisions
5. Expand the rule of law in the international community
6. Build democratic global governance to enable formation and enforcement of laws
   essential for human security

more than 37,000 decisions, mostly since 1989.[255] More than 80 percent of these have some form of compulsory jurisdiction, and 84 percent authorize non-state actors—supranational commissions, prosecutors, or private actors—"to initiate litigation." These processes are bringing "a judicialization of international relations and diminishing [national] government control over how international legal agreements are understood domestically and internationally." These politico-judicial processes actually alter international politics in small ways because they almost automatically motivate government agencies, bureaucracies, and diverse non-governmental actors to build "compliance constituencies" that lubricate transactions and make them more predictable. International law "is the source of the international courts' power and it is what broadens and unites compliance constituencies." Governments' delegation of decision-making power and authority to international courts "is part of a forward-looking project of building respect for international law."[256]

Some international legal processes increasingly reflect "true worldwide participation"[257] that can be understood as "dialogue" among nationally diverse actors,[258] expressing global consensus about specific rules "as well as the purpose of the law and more general values and principles."[259] These governing processes can be employed more influentially than in the past because of the ease of communication. For the first time in world history, people can know "the international community's values" in real time and promptly debate the universality of human rights law.[260]

---

[255] Alter, *New Terrain*, 4.

[256] Alter, *New Terrain*, 5, 26.

[257] O'Connell, *Power and Purpose*, 141. O'Connell notes that An-Na'im, Weeranmantry, and Diane Otto find dialogue over norms encouraging universal consensus.

[258] Diane Otto cautions against assuming that universal values will coincide with Western values even while acknowledging that a new universality is a possible outgrowth of genuine dialogue. Diane Otto, "Rethinking the 'Universality' of Human Rights Law," 29 *Columbia Human Rights Law Review* 1, no. 5 (1997): 1–7.

[259] O'Connell, *Power and Purpose*, 141.

[260] Otto suggests "the potential for rethinking universality, rather than dispensing with it." She argues "that universality still has a place in a transformative paradigm [for major international change], provided people re-understand universality as continuing dialogue and struggle rather than as a civilizing

Sufficient growth in legal enforcement processes has occurred globally and regionally in Europe to demonstrate some possibilities for taking steps to strengthen global governance by enlivening existing institutions in ways that would threaten no one today and that could enable more effective enforcement and peacebuilding measures tomorrow. Necessary legal restrictions and political compromises could increasingly be enforced by an evolving combination of local, regional, and worldwide incentives, processes, and institutions.

Of course, wisdom calls for fair representation of people at all levels of society, insofar as possible, and for transparency[261] to maintain the political support necessary for successfully establishing necessary representational and enforcement processes. Had the European Union and the United Kingdom been more astute and politically capable on these matters, for example, the United Kingdom would have been less likely to have 52 percent of its voters favoring withdrawal in 2016. Indeed, even before Britain exited the EU four years later, polls showed that 57 percent of UK citizens favored *staying in* the EU.[262] In acknowledging that "liberal democratic theory does not match well with the actual practices of global governance," Keohane notes that "there is no coherent global public engaged in discussions over issues, little shared sense of fate, and no common political culture of democracy." This easily could change, given modern communication technology. He notes that "the standards we use for assessing the legitimacy of global governance practices should be derived from democratic theory," but "the threshold of acceptability that is appropriate . . . should be lower than it would be in a well-ordered domestic society."[263] Approaching global governance with an eye to the possibility of its continual improvement makes good sense. With too high a threshold, "no feasible institutions would be legitimate. Since no global institutions would meet a high threshold of liberal democracy, the concept of legitimacy would provide us with little leverage for distinguishing among governance institutions."[264]

To adopt the proposed strategy for human security need not be viewed as a sad concession necessary for managing a world of new threats. Limited yet expanded democratic global governance could bring a sense of liberation and well-being. Done thoughtfully, it would free people from their deepest fears of destruction or environmental devastation. It would secure human needs for more people than ever before in

---

mission of Europe. Such transformative dialogue involves creating a politics out of multiple differences and incommensurabilities in place of the modern dualities of sameness and difference."

At the center of a transformative project of universality "is the articulation of ethical principles which address disparities in power, insist on the unlearning of privileged epistemologies, and promote the indivisibility of the material aspects of human dignity. Furthermore, universality in a transformative sense is informed by the productive tensions and intersection between local and global knowledges, and the interests of the individual and her or his community." Otto, "Rethinking the 'Universality,'" 45–46.

[261] Transparency contributes to agreements being upheld over time. Wallensteen, *Quality Peace*, 207.
[262] PBS News Hour, December 7, 2020, https://www.pbs.org/newshour/show/december-7-2020-pbs-newshour-full-episode.
[263] For an excellent discussion of realistic qualities of legitimacy for institutions in global governance, see Keohane, "Global Governance and Legitimacy," 99–100.
[264] Keohane, "Global Governance and Legitimacy," 100.

history. A shift in the direction of globalization, away from past inequitable or beggar-thy-neighbor economic and security doctrines toward social democratic globalization, would replace hegemonic military doctrines with international laws to constrain weapons of mass destruction, advance economic human rights, enable collective action to curtail terrorist acts and to protect the environment, and guarantee basic education[265] and improved public hygiene for all in a new covenant to serve the global family.[266]

One gains perspective on the current task by noting the war-fighting realities four centuries ago that confronted Hugo Grotius, the gifted Dutch diplomat, jurist, and scholar as he wrote his masterpiece, *De Jure Belli ac Pacis (On the Law of War and Peace)*, first published in 1625. He wrote as devastating religious wars raged in Europe, before the origin of modern sovereignty in the Peace of Westphalia. He created what is widely considered to be one of the greatest contributions in history to the development of international law.[267] It is no accident that he endowed international law "with unprecedented dignity and authority by making it part not only of a general system of jurisprudence but also of a universal moral code."[268] He chose not to create an international law based only on Christian beliefs, because he understood that international law needed a more universal or "natural" basis to enable it to appeal to people regardless of faith. He also could not base an adequate law on the foundation of rulers' agreements alone, since their agreements were too timid and self-interested. His work may appear

---

[265] Research studies show that better educated publics are associated with lower risks of violent conflict. Cortright, Seyle, and Wall, *Governance for Peace*, 18

[266] On a "new global covenant," see Held, "Reframing Global Governance," 303.

Peter Coleman emphasizes the need to track, measure, and promote the factors that foster peacefulness in societies even though "it is easier to see acts of violence and war than states of positive peace." Nonetheless, research shows that sustainable peace results from "an overarching identity that unites groups across their differences; interconnections among subgroups through trade, intermarriage, sports teams, or associations; cooperative forms of interdependence due to mutual ecological or economic dependencies or common security interests; socialization of non-warring values and taboos against violence in homes, schools, and communities; symbolism and ceremonies that reinforce and celebrate peace; and the physical safety of women."

In the international sphere he reports that additional research shows "norms against conquest and violent succession, and supporting peaceful decolonization, combined with an increase in the availability and use of conflict-management processes like mediation, are associated with . . . positive peace." Peter Coleman, "Half the Peace: The Fear Challenge and the Case for Promoting Peace," *Courier* (Summer 2018): 8–10. The factors contributing to domestic peace also promote international peace.

[267] This section draws on O'Connell, *Power and Purpose*, 48–55. Grotius argued in *On the Law of War and Peace* that there was a law that applied to all rulers and societies, regardless of location, and that set limits on their behavior in peace and in war. On these points, Grotius wrote with an overview unusual for his time. He said he was "fully convinced . . . that there is a common law among nations, which is valid alike for war and in war. . . . Throughout the Christian world I observed a lack of restraint in relation to war, such as even barbarous nations should be ashamed of." *Prolegomena*, 28, https://www.britannica.com/biography/Hugo-Grotius.

[268] Hersh Lauterpacht, "The Grotian Tradition in International Law," *British Yearbook of International Law* 23, no. 183 (1946), as cited by O'Connell, *Power and Purpose*, 54. This intellectual orientation is similar to John Gaddis's insight that Abraham Lincoln's strategic thinking "had shown the practicality, in politics, of a moral standard. I mean by this an external frame of reference that *shapes* interests and actions, not—like [his opponent, Senator Stephen] Douglas's—an internal one that only *reflects* them." Italics in original. Gaddis, *Grand Strategy*, 232.

to be "more a system of ethics applied to states than a system of law."[269] Of course, that is precisely what is needed today to motivate and constrain states that are too timid and self-interested to act internationally, even for their own good, as was true in the time of Grotius, before the rise of democratic government and the contemporary system of independent sovereign states.

Grotius encouraged the development of international law to be "binding on sovereigns even without their consent."[270] Today's expression of this concept would be to use the ICC to enforce international law on individual alleged violators who are government officials. The laws to be enforced would be *jus cogens*, the legal principles in international law from which derogation is never permitted by any actor under any circumstance. These include norms against piracy, slavery, genocide, extra judicial killing, racism and apartheid, and wars of aggression. These are the kinds of norms which, in Grotius's view, "could only come from an extra consensual source as they cannot be changed through the positive law methods of treaty and custom."[271] Although people continue to disagree about the *origin* of such basic norms in the international community, there is much agreement about the *content* of the most fundamental norms. When these norms are buttressed by prudential arguments that increased compliance with them will serve self-interest in an interdependent world, they provide a solid foundation for imagining how to change the international system and for designing new peacebuilding architecture, the two topics to which we turn in the next two chapters.

---

[269] Lauterpacht, "The Grotian Tradition," 183, as cited by O'Connell, *Power and Purpose,* 54.
[270] O'Connell, *Power and Purpose,* 54.
[271] O'Connell, *Power and Purpose,* 54–55.

6

Fostering System Change

PRECEDING CHAPTERS HAVE identified ways that US grand strategy has not aligned policy means—nationalist values, military power, and an anarchic balance-of-power system—with desirable policy ends of sustainable peace and human security. If one examines all contemporary security problems, ranging from terrorism and the spread of weapons of mass destruction to the weaponization of space, and from life-threatening poverty and gross violations of human rights to environmental destruction, one discerns that each of these challenges can be more effectively addressed if it is viewed as a problem of global *governance* rather than as a problem to be solved by deploying national *military power*—regardless of the amount deployed. A few necessary security functions can be carried out only if they are addressed as matters of participatory governance that includes everyone on Earth. To be sure, military means should not be dismissed as without consequence: they can buy time, but their recurring use is likely to increase danger because it raises the risks of proliferation, terrorism, and destructive conflicts in the future. What humanity needs are internationally agreed-on and enforceable rules that specify appropriate conduct and enable reliable enforcement—in short, more effective governance.

New global architecture not to replace states but to supplement and moderate them is needed in order to address effectively those security issues that encompass the entire Earth and are more extensive than for any single state.[1] To solve global problems,

---

[1] See Cortright, Seyle, and Wall, *Governance for Peace*.

global security should become a *national* priority. An approach that is both prudent and morally desirable would harmonize what is best for one's own nationals with what is best for the human species. Departing from the familiar old adage, the new guideline should be this: If we want peace, let us prepare to institutionalize peace globally.

New forms of governance are possible whenever the voluntary submission of individual states to a world authority can produce benefits that exceed what it exacts in costs by solving problems that require higher-level cooperation. The goal is to enable and require politics in the future to respond to demands for order, peace, social justice, and environmental health from the local to the global domains, institutionalizing pragmatic elements of cosmopolitan democracy where possible. The future can be built on global governance processes sufficient to address issues effectively while retaining checks and balances against excessive concentration of power. New institutions should increase national officials' accountability to global security responsibilities.

A more cosmopolitan sense of citizenship need not exclude territorially based nationalism with which we are familiar, although human identity would be extended beyond that. Instead of being based on territoriality, citizenship could also build on the value of human dignity and the correlates of peace and human security, applied in a rich diversity of cultural settings. The new architecture would help bring forth a politico-cultural context for all persons to enjoy equal human worth, freedom, and opportunity. "Only a democratic citizenship that does not close itself off in a particularistic fashion can pave the way for a *world citizenship*, which is already taking shape today in worldwide political communications."[2] Gradual transformation of existing identities rather than a violent re-definition of identities should be possible because "state citizenship and world citizenship form a continuum whose contours . . . are already becoming visible."[3]

Harmonization of diverse nations' interests, rather than exaltation of one's own, will become more obviously necessary because one country's pursuit of a singular set of interests fails to take seriously the asymmetry between the global scope of pressing problems and the national scope of officials' vision in attempting to solve the problems. Issues like climate change, cyberattacks, or the spread of nuclear weapons have global consequences; when solutions are sought from the vantage point of national perspectives and answer only to particular national constituencies, they cannot succeed. The cosmopolitanization of functional reality is more advanced than the cosmopolitanization of people's subjective identities and institutions, suggesting a need to limit the most dangerous aspects of national independence now, insofar as possible, allowing time for attitudes to catch up.

---

[2] Jürgen Habermas, *Between Facts and Norms: Contribution to a Discourse Theory of Law and Democracy*, trans. W. Rehg (Cambridge: Polity, 1996), 514. Italics in original. See also Held, *Cosmopolitanism: Ideals and Realities*.

[3] Habermas, *Between Facts and Norms*, 515.

6.1 TRANSCENDING HYPER-INDEPENDENCE

Destabilizing changes in the nature of international relations, growing populist unrest with rising globalization, and inadequate governing capacities in the existing international system alert us to the need for more effective governance throughout the world. Such governance could help free us from death-dealing insecurities about the dangerous degree of independence exercised by other states, which we might call their "hyper-independence," whereby a national government (or other international actor) may claim that its right to independence gives it an unlimited right to develop and recklessly deploy nuclear weapons, or to allow people to plan terrorist actions from within their country, or to permit corporations to dump huge amounts of CO_2 annually into the atmosphere, or perhaps to experiment with biological weapons without following international safety standards.

Despite the obvious need for more effective global governance to constrain hyper-independence, no consensus among citizens or national governments exists about how to establish it. In fact, there is disagreement about the advantages and disadvantages of today's capitalism, nationalism, globalization, international organizations, and the militarized balance-of-power system. Many people resist more effective global governance out of fear that constraints on hyper-independence of some sovereignties or capitalist actors would eventually destroy both, end their own national traditions, and undermine their personal wealth and other benefits.

Jean Jacques Rousseau, writing almost three centuries ago, can help us understand and, perhaps, address these fears. He told what has become a celebrated story that remains instructive for understanding human beings' need for, yet resistance to, establishing more effective governance to enable them to survive. He asked his readers to imagine five hungry men living in a state of nature who commit themselves to hunt together in order to catch a stag. If they succeed, each will have enough food for himself and his family. They embark on a hunt. As they encircle a stag, one hunter sees a hare that he can catch by himself. It will satisfy his needs alone. He hesitates, because he knows that if he pursues the hare, the stag might get away. After reflection, he goes after the hare, because he fears that if he does not, someone else in the hunting party might see the hare, chase it, and leave *him* with nothing. So he catches the rabbit; the stag gets away.[4]

Rousseau's parable teaches the lesson that, in the words of the eminent political realist, Kenneth Waltz, "even where all [parties] agree on the goal and have an equal interest in [the success of] the project, one cannot rely on others."[5] This central belief of political realists undergirds the militarized balance-of-power system. It makes good sense in a limited context, but not if people exercise imagination and take action. If the five hunters would have established a modest contract or governing arrangement

---

[4] Jean Jacques Rousseau, *A Discourse on the Origin of Inequality* (New York: Penguin, 1984), 111.
[5] Waltz, *Man, the State and War*, 168.

among themselves, they could have transformed their conduct enough that they *could* rely on others. With such an arrangement, cooperation to meet everyone's needs could have been assured. If the hunters had made a binding agreement that anyone who leaves his assigned post in a stag hunt, in order to catch a hare instead, would be required to share the rabbit equally with the rest, then the stag hunt would have continued and the common good could have been served. Governance matters.

It can improve human conduct. System change in the form of more inclusive governance can replace former adversaries' inclination to fight each other with more reliable relationships. One might think of an agreement among the hunters as a cooperative security arrangement that could have been constructed without jeopardizing other valued dimensions of their lives. Such an arrangement could have become reliable because it could be enforced without violating anyone's rights, by providing genuine security benefits or incentives for cooperation and effective sanctions for non-compliance. An analogous change in today's "state-of-nature" international system could occur without jeopardizing most benefits of healthy national identities. Indeed, most national traditions could more fully and safely blossom when less burdened by fears of others' hyper-independence.

Note that more armament, or "military preparedness," would not have helped the hunting party. A club or even a firearm, in the absence of any compact, would not have changed the underlying dynamic. Indeed, if all hunters had a gun, they might have bagged the stag faster, but if they encircled it from a distance to get close enough to shoot accurately, they also might accidentally have shot one another. Although more armed preparedness in itself would not have helped the hunters much, an enforceable agreement could have made a profound difference.

Two sharply differing lessons may be drawn from Rousseau's parable if one looks deeply enough to understand that changing human relationships may be possible, even without changing human nature. This distinction is crucial because political realists correctly assume that human nature is unchanging; but they ignore some possibilities that human interactions can be changed nonetheless. In the first lesson, political realists conclude that even rational conduct will not lead to reliable cooperation among actors in a state of anarchy. It was rational for one hunter to catch the rabbit. In the second lesson, empirical realists might conclude that where all parties agree on the goal and share an interest in binding others to rules agreed on for success, one can change the relationships enough to produce reliable cooperation and more benefits for each hunter overall. Human conduct, aided by new governance, may change, even though human nature remains the same. The architecture needed to change human relationships would enable insecurity to be overcome by making human interactions more dependable. All five and their families could have had a large meal.

If the "anarchy" expressed in the system of governance that prevailed in the failed stag hunt could be transformed into reliable cooperation or simply rule-governed rivalry, the hunters would have been likely to succeed. The groundbreaking theorist of international relations, Alexander Wendt, made a similar point when he said that "self-help and power politics do not follow either logically or causally from anarchy." He points out, "State *cognition* depends on states' systemic *culture*."[6] Officials' ideas about the capabilities of the international system are given content and meaning "by the ideas which they share with other states." As a result, "the more deeply that states have internalized the culture of the states system the more difficult it will be to change."[7] True enough, most officials in the great powers do not imagine that a less dangerous or less anarchic system of relationships is possible.

This is why asking diplomats and national security managers to change the international system usually has been a lost cause. Unless some catastrophic event, such as a major war, climate disruption, or a severe pandemic, forces them to think differently, they have so deeply internalized the culture of the states system that they are almost incapable of changing it. Wendt notes that human beings create social ideas that they reify as time passes. Then they forget or downplay that they constructed both the ideas and the related institutions. If they remembered and understood, they could change them, but almost no policy planners think about changing the international system.

If we do not look in the right places for different ways of thinking and acting, we seldom see them. Political scientists, policy planners, and CIA officials did not anticipate the end of the Soviet Union and the Cold War even a short time before both happened.[8] Given Wendt's understanding that ideas and culture constitute the international system, he explains why the actions of Mikhail Gorbachev, general secretary of the Communist Party and president of the Soviet Union, were so surprising: "Gorbachev's New Thinking was a deep, conceptual reassessment of what the US-Soviet relationship '*was*.'"[9] Gorbachev did "constitutive theorizing." As a result, Russian officials "were able to end, unilaterally and almost overnight, a conflict that seemed like it had become set in stone." In analyzing Gorbachev's abrupt break with the past in his new policies of glasnost (openness) and perestroika (restructuring), Wendt points out: "It may be that objective conditions were such that the Soviets 'had' to change their ideas about the Cold War, but that does not change the fact that in an important sense those ideas *were* the Cold War, and as such changing them by definition changed the reality."[10] To be sure, Soviet officials faced daunting challenges in keeping up with US weapons technology, but it remains nonetheless true that changing their *ideas* about the US-Soviet relationship in fact *changed* it and with it part of the structure of international relations.

---

[6] Wendt, *Social Theory*, 372.

[7] Wendt advises: "In analyzing what states think, it makes sense to start with the culture of the international system and work top-down, rather than start with unit-level perceptions and work bottom-up.... [International relations] scholars should think more like structural anthropologists than economists or psychologists." Wendt, *Social Theory*, 372.

[8] Scholars in the discipline of international relations, dominated by political realism, also did not expect the dismantling of apartheid without a bloodbath, the attacks of 9/11, and the rise of the Arab Spring.

[9] Wendt, *Social Theory*, 375. Italics added.

[10] Wendt, *Social Theory*, 375.

With more openness, structural imagination, and "constitutive thinking" about system change, US policymakers could have launched world politics on a much different vector. They probably could have begun building a system of dependable peace and security and environmental health, but they lacked creativity and did not feel enough grassroots support, let alone pressure, to change their thinking. Change did not happen. That does not mean that it *could not* have happened, but that conclusion is what most political realists have claimed. They still believe that the international system remained the same because one state could not rely on another, even though the formula for enhancing reliability might have changed. Gorbachev's constitutive-thinking was either never understood or quite quickly forgotten by *both* US and Russian officials, even though—no one can dispute—it did happen. The hold on the human mind of traditional thinking about the international system is so strong that the constitutive-thinking breakthrough was not built upon even in the policymaking community in Russia where it first transformed the Soviet-US relationship.

For those who aspire to base domestic and global societies on the values of human dignity, these insights can hardly be overemphasized. Constitutive theorizing "enhances our collective capacity for critical self-reflection or 'reflexivity.'" This "gives us perspective on our social environment and helps us to overcome any false sense of determinism. It also opens up the possibility of thinking self-consciously about what direction to go in."[11] Although political realists take states for granted, states did not always exist.[12] The international system is at its foundation a set of ideas about political organization. Because those ideas and this organization may change, a primary goal for strategic thinkers should be security for humanity rather than security for a single nation-state. A relatively small number of national officials, especially found among non-great powers, do see themselves as part of a society of states. They do think about what is required to keep international public order. They embody what Wendt describes as an "emerging collective self-consciousness that is expressed in the 'public sphere' of international society, an emerging space where states appeal to public reason to hold each other accountable and manage their joint affairs."[13]

Moreover, "the emergence of an international public sphere signals the emergence of a joint awareness, however embryonic at this stage, of how . . . [state officials'] ideas and behavior make the logic of anarchy a self-fulfilling prophecy." If awareness grows of how policymakers' ideas and the culture of the state system constitute the system and cause self-defeating consequences, such awareness could nurture "a potential for self-intervention designed to change the logic and bring international society under a measure of rational control. In individuals we might call this 'therapy' or 'character planning'; in social systems like international society it would be called 'constitutional design,' 'engineering,' or 'steering.'" Policymakers and concerned citizens can contribute much more to solving international problems if they would approach them from

---

[11] Wendt, *Social Theory*, 375.

[12] See Wright, *Nonzero*, 179

[13] Wendt, *Social Theory*, 376.

a "design orientation toward international life." Although intentional re-design of the international system would no doubt produce some unintended consequences, "at least in a reflexive system there is a possibility of design and collective rationality that does not exist in a reified system."[14]

Political realism is based on the idea that "the culture of international life does not depend on what states do." In this mistaken view, international relations scholars assume that the culture is "given." They "reify it" and simply "focus on helping states do the best they can within it." When they do that, "the kind of knowledge produced by this [political realist] theory is useful for solving problems within the existing system, but not for changing the system itself. The result is that problem-solving theory has the practical effect of helping to reproduce the status quo, and in this way [political] Realism, despite its claim of objectivity, becomes a normative as well as a scientific theory."[15]

In contrast, the concerned citizens and policymakers embracing empirical realism would understand that the norms and culture of international life are shaped by what states do. These are not given. By focusing on how states create international norms and international culture by their own conduct, empirical realists explore the goal of transforming the international system. This approach opens the mind to thinking that there is a change-inducing role for the individual as well as for the state. For the individual, a high calling could be to imagine a politics without intended killing and an international society governed by security-enhancing international law and human rights. The thinking of both the traditional realist and the new empirical realist can contribute to shaping international relations, although with quite different outcomes: the former to maintaining the existing system with its insecurities of hyper-independence, and the latter to changing it. Even if they both use some scientific methods, their perspectives lead to different normative ends.

6.2 ENLARGING THE SECURITY COMMUNITY

Understanding Rousseau's parable, in which insecurity is accepted by independent actors who continue living in an anarchic system, can lead concerned citizens and policymakers to explore how to transform the "hunting dynamic" of the international system to make conduct more reliable. Examining an analogy between the insecurities of medieval Europeans and the insecurities of those living in the contemporary international system can expand our understanding of how to build the necessary architecture to increase human security today.

The feudal security system was based on well-fortified castles—until a new technology of gunpowder-firing cannons was invented. Then the range and destructiveness of new weapons transformed the very constitution of that security system. Impenetrable

---

[14] Wendt, *Social Theory*, 376.
[15] Wendt, *Social Theory*, 376.

castles were transformed almost overnight from secure fortresses into little more than tourist attractions. Because new technologies of destruction caused the castle system to lose its ability to provide security, small feudal manors amalgamated into larger kingdoms with monarchs and eventually into nation-states. To be defensible with the new technologies, security units needed to become territorially larger. Forward-looking leaders pressed for changing their existing system to increase security and to expand space for safe commerce. Making feudal governance more inclusive produced peace within larger political units.

Of course, many people resisted relinquishing the familiar security system in which they enjoyed power and wealth. After a system had been in operation for roughly 600 years, wasn't it "given"? Eventually feudalists were forced to change their minds or they were overwhelmed by the forces for national unification. The larger territorial units usually included more diverse people within each state security community (which did cause some conflicts within the states).[16] In any case, the new security unit in Europe expanded from the feudal kingdom to the nation-state. The security unit then expanded again, this time beyond the nation-state, because the French and German nation-states faced recurring wars in the European balance-of-power system. Globally, many states are defenseless before myriad security threats, unless and until a worldwide system can provide enough global governance to enforce rules capable of making peace as dependable throughout the world as it is now within stable national societies. Weapons of mass destruction and non-military security threats together are destroying the separateness of nation-states today as surely as gunpowder and cannon destroyed the utility of the castle in separate feudal kingdoms. To protect human life and increase security for reformed states, the security unit eventually will need to become commensurate with the destructive extent of modern weaponry, which is global.[17]

Even though today's nation-state is analogous to yesterday's feudal kingdom, many of those who enjoy power and wealth within today's system do not want to acknowledge the empirical truth about the nation-state's limitations. Nonetheless, the rise of interdependence and the advance of technologies of destruction have brought humanity to a point in history when it is no longer possible for countries to be secure if they rely primarily on self-help. The days of national territorial invulnerability and relatively impermeable national borders, essential for success in past security policies, are drawing to a close. Human societies need to re-size their security community to fit global weaponry.[18] No one can rationally deny weapons' global reach, yet many seem to deny it in practice. As reported throughout this analysis, the threats posed

---

[16] The European Union is a more recent example of a somewhat analogous, albeit a less far-reaching, transformation.

[17] "What basic historical forces are doing is driving the system toward a new equilibrium, in which social structures will be compatible with technology." Wright, *Nonzero*, 204–205.

[18] See Deudney, "Regrounding Realism," 1–45, 18–20; Wendt, "Why a World State Is Inevitable," 491–542.
  "Governance has always tended to expand to the geographic scope necessary to solve emerging non-zero-sum problems that markets and moral codes can't alone solve." Wright, *Nonzero*, 211.

by environmental destruction and by nuclear, biological, and chemical weapons; the weaponization of space; a global pandemic requiring a global vaccination plan; and the availability of destructive capabilities to any determined, anti-social state and even to non-state actors—all these press humanity toward some form of federated global security system analogous to how technological change expanded the security unit beyond the feudal kingdom. The needed new architecture would bring everyone within the same security tent, or more accurately, acknowledge the extent to which everyone is already there, even though not acting on this reality.[19]

A synthesis of historical experience and peace and security research demonstrates that the "permissive cause" of recurring wars, terrorism, chronic poverty, and environmental degradation is the existing international system.[20] In his pathbreaking synthesis of security research, John Vasquez concludes that when states "have taken a more Grotian approach [respecting and enforcing positive normative constraints], they have succeeded in avoiding war among themselves."[21] International law and enforcement probably could replace many functions now played by war. Today's national security managers in the great powers may be analogous to Rousseau's hunters in a state of nature insofar as the international system allows sovereign states to take the "hare option," rather than design a more cooperative hunt that would serve the common security interests of everyone. Nuclear-weapons states keep their "catch" of nuclear weapons for themselves while refusing to honor their obligations under Article VI of the Nuclear Non-Proliferation Treaty to pursue nuclear disarmament together, which if achieved, would produce at least one common security benefit of catching the security stag for everybody.[22] To replace hyper-independent-actor relations with collaborative-actor relations could enable successful, recurring security hunts that steadily replace the role of dangerous independent military actions with enforceable international law constraining armaments just as it could constrain overgrazing in the medieval commons.

A successful hunt, if guaranteed by a global compact for implementing and enforcing collaboration, could produce common security. Continuing to fall back on extreme self-help security mechanisms is like going after the hare for oneself. The hare satisfies one's security appetite today, but it leaves people's future appetite for security unsatisfied. Catching the security hare produces a frightening future because it encourages other hunters to be more selfish since they have been left alone in a world of security

---

[19] The spread of COVID 19 has confirmed this.

[20] Waltz, *Man, the State, and War*, 232–238.

[21] Vasquez, "Steps to War," 145.

[22] To be sure, nuclear weapons countries may claim that their rabbit-catching yields a generalizable benefit for all if it deters nuclear war by other nuclear powers. However, those states aspiring to own nuclear weapons usually fear at least some of the countries with nuclear capabilities and resent their own inferior power status that they suffer because they do not possess nuclear weapons. Therefore, even an assumed generalizable benefit may not be influential in stopping the spread of nuclear weapons to additional governments, some of whom do not feel protected by a generalized benefit that is claimed by those choosing the hare option.

scarcity. Because the permissiveness of the existing international system for negative forms of independence threatens every person and every country on Earth, every society could benefit from establishing an all-inclusive compact that makes other states' conduct less "hyper" and more dependable.

Although the permissiveness of the international system threatens people because its anarchy occasionally allows horrendous violence, at the same time it attracts people because it conjures up past national glories and requires few constraints on "me and mine" within one's own state. Empirical study suggests that the threats of disaster, which could include very long-lasting radioactivity, should be given no less attention than the attractions of military victory, which often do not last long. Yet the permissiveness of the international system seduces, because it promises, falsely, that we can have most of what we want without international constraints. Believing this gives in to short-term emotion and illusion rather than being guided by reason and empirical understanding. That may explain why today's "management" of the environmental and security commons is a tragedy, why the common interest in hunting for security is cast aside by the independent sovereign hunter prioritizing his own appetite, and why the richest people on Earth refuse to contribute even 1 percent of their annual incomes to abolish poverty and advance equity.

To be clear about the preferred path, citizens should recognize what current national security planners seldom acknowledge: To continue relying on today's militarized balance-of-power system is no longer an effective policy for addressing future questions of life and death. In addition to being a permissive cause of war and other threats to human security,[23] the balance-of-power system itself will not overcome the low utility of military power for achieving desired outcomes.[24] It will be unable to "balance" safely against new technologies that pose instantaneous, catastrophic destruction. By itself, the fragmented international system has no effective way to stop terrorists and non-state actors. It is failing to address non-military threats like environmental destruction and non-territorial threats like weaponization of space. Given the complex nature of new security problems, genuine security simply requires more worldwide governing functions than a militarized balance-of-power system can provide.[25]

6.3 DELIVERING MORE THAN NATIONAL GOVERNMENTS

Research and historical experience with international institution-building since World War II, as well as the feudal security analogy and Rousseau's parable, suggest a way out

---

[23] Vasquez, "The Steps to War," 142; 133, note 76.

[24] The National Intelligence Council points out that military power "will be insufficient for securing and maintaining favorable outcomes" in U.S. foreign policy. National Intelligence Council, *Global Trends 2040: A More Contested World*, March 2021, https://www.dni.gov/index.php/global-trends-home, 92.

[25] "The management of world order can no longer be reliably entrusted to the decentralized workings of a system of sovereign states, a system that operates according to statist geopolitics." Falk, "International Law and the Future," 727.

of our security dead end. In the simplest terms, we could have world peace with much more justice and environmental balance if we would construct the architecture needed for managing conflict, upholding human rights, and strengthening the rule of law. With this knowledge, we can imagine a system that is global, human-centered, and capable of delivering more than national governments alone can do.

Design for peace and security is more a matter of political, economic, environmental, and security cooperation, to ensure that differences are addressed and conduct is made predictable and beneficial (non-zero-sum), than of military balancing. Empirical realists observe that the existing balance of military power actually encourages violence and extremism internationally and domestically because this system induces adversarial relations and exclusionary identities; it perpetuates political inequity and global poverty; it fails to address unemployment worldwide; it causes unfair exclusion of millions of people from participating in decisions that affect their lives; it works against effective environmental protections; it inhibits international law enforcement and worldwide intelligence gathering on terrorism; and it generally impedes finding *global* solutions to global problems. Similarly, global institutions are needed because the sources of economic instability also are "increasingly located on international and global scales and thus outside the jurisdictional reach of national governments."[26]

An international system dating from the 17th century and operating with military enforcement strategies and security thinking from the 19th and 20th centuries is insufficient for 21st-century security needs. The rationale for the necessary new architecture to liberate humanity from perpetual denial of the right to live in health, dignity, and peace lies in Article 28 of the Universal Declaration of Human Rights: "Everyone is entitled to a social and international order in which the rights and freedoms set forth in this Declaration can be fully realized."[27] Yet because many people's identities are primarily national, not universal, they and the governments they support have been generally incapable of delivering truly effective solutions, which would include a changed international order. Although nationalism and the nation-state are resilient, they cannot by themselves solve pressing problems nor provide legitimacy for global decision making. Each national government is somewhat suspect in the eyes of other nations. Chronic suspicion causes unwise decision making, yet the existing balance-of-power system has no effective way of reducing suspicion, thereby discouraging plans for institutional change. Although the existing system does help keep states independent from one another, its failure to establish centrally coordinated decision making, to reduce uncertainty about other states' motives and to represent all societies equitably in international decision making are impediments to future security.

Astute observers saw these dangers coming long ago. In the 17th century, Thomas Hobbes, well known for his endorsement of a strong state to maintain *domestic* social order, also acknowledged that a lawful *interstate* order could be possible and

---

[26] Brodie, "Income Inequality," 49.
[27] Article 28.

desirable.[28] In the 18th century Immanuel Kant described three conditions necessary for perpetual peace: "a republican constitution [within states] that guarantees freedom and equality of citizens through the rule of law and representative institutions," a federation of states to facilitate relations among them, and "observance of [a] cosmopolitan right of universal hospitality."[29] Today, Habermas sees Kant's federalism as "a transitional stage *en route* to a world republic."[30] To secure peace, Einstein concluded, "a world government must be created which is able to solve conflicts between nations by judicial decision. This government must be based on a clear-cut constitution which is approved by the governments and nations and which gives it the sole disposition of offensive weapons."[31] Falk believes that "humane governance can be achieved without world government, and that this is both the more likely and more desirable course of action."[32] This would entail enhancing international law and institutions through "transnational democratic initiatives" in which civil society organizations and progressive states would work with a reformed United Nations system to challenge statist and market forces obstructing solutions to contemporary problems.

Classical realists like Niebuhr, Carr, Morgenthau, and Herz, also seemed more aware and willing than current US officials to examine structural issues and to acknowledge the need for building global institutions to limit the risks of nuclear destruction. They saw that unavoidable interdependence in violence potential and economic matters necessitated more world organization. They simply were doubtful about whether it was possible to build the community necessary to operate effective global institutions. Yet as the initial shock of nuclear weapons receded, most US policymakers and political realists have denied the utility of global institution-building.[33] There is a significant difference between (1) classical realists' acknowledgment that a desirable end-goal included "global political change toward a world government in the form of a global federal system" as soon as it became feasible,[34] and (2) contemporary political realists' rejection of any desirable end-goal other than maintenance of the militarized balance-of-power system.[35] The latter's dominance of decision making and the training of scholars and diplomats has discouraged study of system change that might have addressed the present quandary.

---

[28] Catherine Lu, "World Government," *The Stanford Encyclopedia of Philosophy* (2016), ed. Edward N. Zalta, https://plato.stanford.edu/entries/world-government/.

[29] Lu, "World Government," 5.

[30] Habermas, "Political Constitution," 268.

[31] Albert Einstein, "Towards a World Government," in *Out of My Later Years: The Scientist, Philosopher and Man Portrayed Through His Own Words* (New York: Wings Books 1956), 138.

[32] Falk, *On Humane Governance*, 8.

[33] See, for example, Mearsheimer, "False Promise," 5–49. Scheuerman notes that "classical realists" of the 1960s and 1970s saw more utility in global institutional reform than contemporary realists. See William Scheuerman, *The Realist Case for Global Reform* (Cambridge: Polity Press, 2011), 73.

[34] Scheuerman, *The Realist Case*, 73.

[35] See Lu, "World Government."

6.4 DISCIPLINING SOVEREIGNTY

Sovereignty's inadequacies could become a driver toward global governance if the self-destructive consequences of national sovereignties become empirically acknowledged and widely understood. The ever-growing harmfulness of advancing military technology probably will render a state's seeking recognition and power through violent means increasingly intolerable to most other states. That feeling was expressed a half-century ago by historian Arnold Toynbee when he called attention to "the moral consequences of the factual interdependence to which the world has come." In his view, states "no longer have the moral right to exercise 'sovereignty' or 'independence' which is now no more than a legal right to act without regard to the harm which is done to others."[36] In any case, growing dangers may erode states' satisfaction with the benefits of self-help for themselves when it is also allowed for others, perhaps enabling them to develop what Wendt has called "supranational We-feeling."[37] This appears to be what is needed to overcome current resistance to reasonable global governance, yet at present this does not seem likely without enormous grassroots pressure.

Scholars taking a long view believe that some kind of a world security organization may be nearly inevitable, if the species is able to survive, but they do not agree on whether it will come in time to avert major catastrophe. Pessimists expect that military-industrial vested interests and exclusionary nationalisms will perpetuate hyper-independent, globally irresponsible sovereignties until Armageddon. In a more hopeful view, separate states' increasing awareness of their "violence interdependency" may drive them to seek a unified security system to govern modern weaponry and other threats to survival.

In response to the instabilities of national and other sub-global systems, Wendt expects that the current anarchic international system of states gradually will become a society of states, then a world society, and eventually an integrated world system of governance. Because the interstate system "generates a tendency for military technology and war to become increasingly destructive,"[38] competition among states could lead to "collective identity formation" essential for more global governance.[39] Indeed, the need for "a global monopoly on the legitimate use of organized violence" will make "a world state . . . inevitable,"[40] predicts Wendt, unless the species destroys much of itself and its civilization first. The passage from zero-sum to more non-zero-sum security relationships seems likely to bring increased risks the longer it is postponed.

Wendt's argument that a "world state is inevitable" need not be taken as a prediction of what will happen, because it is possible that a nuclear war could occur at almost

---

[36] Reported in William McNeill, *Arnold J. Toynbee: A Life* (Oxford: Oxford University Press, 1989), 184.

[37] Wendt, "Why a World State Is Inevitable," 517.

[38] Wendt, "Why a World State Is Inevitable," 491

[39] Wendt, "Why a World State Is Inevitable," 493.

[40] Wendt, "Why a World State Is Inevitable," 491. He uses the terms "world state" to mean an integrated world system with authority to control the legitimate use of organized violence, not a singular hierarchical system with powers over other domains of life, many of which would remain with states.

any time in the existing international system and bring such widespread destruction that insufficient human civilization and organizational capacity would remain to establish a world state. However, Wendt's analysis remains a useful statement of logic about what may be necessary to avoid cataclysmic destruction because of great powers' military interdependency and mutual vulnerability.

For movement toward global governance to succeed at reasonable cost, global institutions would need to embrace healthy nationalisms, not suppress them.[41] A successful global system seems likely to be a federal arrangement following the principle of subsidiarity, allowing much national and local autonomy and perhaps even more national cultural diversity than exists now, even though hyper-independent war-making functions of today's great-power sovereignties would be bridled.

Historically, political authority has moved toward larger and larger units, not uniformly or without temporary reversals, but relentlessly. Robert Carneiro estimates that in 1000 BCE there were roughly 600,000 independent political communities on Earth.[42] These have been amalgamated until today there are approximately 200 independent states.[43] Because of the negative consequences of separate conflicting sovereignties, such as symbolized in the stag hunt and witnessed historically in feudalism, they repeatedly have given birth to opportunities to centralize.[44] The 97.7 percent decline in the number of independent security units over the past 3,000 years is not likely to be reversed, so wisdom suggests that it is time to make plans for future political and economic integration that will serve human dignity rather than some hegemon's global tyranny.

Regardless of whether the pessimistic or the hopeful scenario seems more likely, it is useful to imagine how movement toward a desirable global authority might occur, with the understanding that one's efforts to orchestrate a worldwide system to serve human dignity can always be encouraged even if it cannot be assured. Just as individuals have found it functionally useful, as Hobbes anticipated four centuries ago, to come together in many *nationally* governed states, each with a monopoly on the legitimate use of violence, so too might citizens lean toward a *globally* governed system to establish a newly inclusive monopoly on the legitimate use of violence.[45] A "universal security community" could emerge in which states expect one another to resolve conflicts peacefully rather than through military combat.[46] If attempts to violate this expectation would occur, a universal security system could ensure the protection of

---

[41] Wendt, "Why a World State Is Inevitable," 527.

[42] Robert Carneiro, "Political Expansion as an Expression of the Principle of Competitive Exclusion," in *Origins of the State*, ed. Ronald Cohen and Elman Service (Philadelphia: Institute for the Study of Human Issues), 205–223.

[43] Cited by Wendt, "Why a World State Is Inevitable," 503.

[44] Recent historical examples include establishing the Concert of Europe in 1815 after the Napoleonic wars, the League of Nations after the trauma of World War I, and the United Nations after World War II.

[45] Wendt, "Why a World State Is Inevitable," 508.

[46] Karl W. Deutsch anticipated this in his research on pluralistic and amalgamated security communities. *Political Community and the North American Area: International Organization in the Light of Historical Experience* (Princeton, NJ: Princeton University Press, 1968).

each member with the help of a supranational authority empowered to make binding decisions about the collective use of force and to enforce them.[47]

Enjoying the benefits of their exalted status in the current system, the great powers may be most resistant to the formation of global governance. However, with the diffusion of greater violence potential to smaller powers, such as Pakistan, Israel, North Korea, and Iran, "the ability of Great Powers to insulate themselves from global demands [of other states] for recognition will erode, making it more and more difficult to sustain a system in which their power and privileges are not tied to an enforceable rule of law."[48] Although the United States and other great powers have expressed frustration with the dilemma they face with North Korean and Iranian demands for status and recognition, they have not been able to turn back the clock. To achieve stability, a world system is needed in which states will have lost their negative freedom to engage in aggressive war but will have gained positive freedom of being recognized as a full member of the community without needing to risk war to gain attention.[49]

The flowering of effective global governance will doubtless take time, but perhaps it is not as far off as has been assumed by those who believe that an integrated world community is a *prerequisite* for stronger international institutions. Strengthened community and strengthened institutions may develop concomitantly. Indeed, some instructive institutions are already in our midst, as the experience of the European Union and the "new terrain of international law" detailed by Alter demonstrate. Substantial evidence shows that at least some of what is needed immediately to address the most serious security dangers is possible now. Immediate changes could reduce the gravest risks of war and environmental destruction while opening doors to further advances thereafter. If current experiences with the development of international organizations would lead to spreading webs of interactions encompassing the globe, the world would be moving toward effective global governance. Although there is nothing inevitable about future governance, it seems likely that the pressures and opportunities for world public authority will grow and draw a positive response at least from those citizens seeking to uphold human dignity rather than act out ideologies of exclusive nationalism, hyper-independence, unregulated capitalism, or proselytizing religion.

A centrally focused vertical dispersal of the most dangerous aspects of national sovereignty could employ part of every country's sovereignty more wisely but without eliminating it. Such a dispersal would enable all "legitimate independences" to thrive by bridling "hyper-independences." This is similar to what previously warring states in Europe did in creating the EU to end Franco-German wars. In the words of German foreign minister Joschka Fischer, "European integration was the response to centuries of a precarious balance of powers on this continent which again and again resulted in terrible hegemonic wars culminating in the two World Wars between 1914 and 1945."

---

[47] Wendt, "Why a World State Is Inevitable," 505.
[48] Wendt, "Why a World State Is Inevitable," 524.
[49] See Wendt, "Why a World State Is Inevitable," 525.

European international system change in the form of more inclusive governance replaced war. As Fischer unambiguously confirmed: "The core concept of Europe after 1945 was and still is a rejection of the European balance-of-power principle and the hegemonic ambitions of individual states that emerged after the Peace of Westphalia in 1648, a rejection that took the form of a closer meshing of vital interests and the transfer of nation-state sovereign rights to supranational European institutions."[50] This description by the German foreign minister succinctly expresses the central argument for a global strategy for human security proposed here: more inclusive, limited governance can replace war.

Vertical dispersal of some sovereignty could move the extreme war-making function of sovereignty to a centrally coordinated global level,[51] thereby constraining weapons of mass destruction and unilateral threats to inflict violence on others. By facilitating a global monopoly on the means of extreme violence, peace could be better maintained. Yet, channeling the most dangerous war-making function of sovereignty to the center of a global system would not eliminate the effective functioning of other aspects of sovereignty at national and subnational levels. In addition, once the extreme war-making function of national sovereignty is bridled, other dimensions of national sovereignty may more safely flourish. Additional resources would be available for meeting human needs, thereby generating political support for these war-dampening initiatives. Human freedom for all could grow without endangering anyone with military aggression. Indeed, by taking weapons of mass destruction and possibly major war off the agenda, a global federal authority, perhaps in the form of a revised UN Security Council, could create new capacities for legally binding collective action to meet developmental, environmental, and all other human security needs in ways that national governments could never achieve in the present international system. This kind of world order design holds exciting promise for all.

6.5 ENLIVENING PEACE

Many citizens do not know the seriousness with which some US officials began advancing the idea of constructing a more reliable global security system even before World War II ended.[52] After Roosevelt's death in 1945, these conversations continued at the San Francisco conference to construct the United Nations, but the architecture eventually agreed on fell short of the changes needed. After two world wars had brought, as the UN Charter described, "untold sorrow to mankind,"[53] sacrificed 100 million people,

---

[50] Joschka Fischer, "From Confederacy to Federation—Thoughts on the Finality of European Integration," speech at Humboldt University, May 12, 2000, https://ec.europa.eu/dorie/fileDownload.do?docId=192 161&cardId=192161.

[51] As Wendt puts it, "Loss of some agency at the micro-level may create agency at the macro-level." Wendt, "Why a World State Is Inevitable," 502.

[52] A good summary of this is in Weiss, *Global Governance*, 21–26.

[53] United Nations Charter, Preamble.

and grievously damaged the ways of life for hundreds of millions more, the victorious countries had come together at San Francisco to create a replacement for the League of Nations, with their purpose being "to save succeeding generations from the scourge of war."[54] That goal, written in the first sentence of the Charter, suggests that peace is both desirable and possible. Yet the familiar great power habit of clinging to their separate national military organizations rather than putting war-making more fully under international control resurfaced as soon as the war-time pressures for multilateral cooperation diminished. Retaining the war-making function of sovereignty in their own national capitals caused the conference to fall short of endorsing a plan that, as some proposed, sought to strengthen more direct international enforcement through world law.[55] Far-reaching steps aimed at establishing international control over arms production and deployment were advanced by the United States and Soviet Union in the 1950s and early 1960s, but these never bore fruit.

Although the world's governments have repeatedly emphasized people's right to peace, they have never sought to mobilize people around this right, perhaps because of their own ambivalence toward it. Some governments question whether peace should be called a "human right," but that question is raised on somewhat technical grounds because the desirability of peace for all people and their entitlement to it seem beyond question. Enlivening people's right to peace could enable them to feel and touch something that directly affects many of their lives.[56] Some *feeling* is necessary for people to become engaged in actively supporting a global strategy for human security. Publicizing this right can draw upon the 1948 UN declaration that "everyone has the right to life, liberty, and security."[57] Three decades later the General Assembly declared: "Every nation and every human being regardless of race, conscience, language or sex, has the inherent right to live in peace."[58] The world's governments in 2018 solemnly proclaimed "a sacred right to peace" which stands as "a fundamental obligation of each state."[59]

The heart of the UN Charter insists that "All members shall refrain in their international relations from the threat or use of force."[60] In addition, the Charter urges the institutionalization of peace. Every country is obligated to ensure that its policies are "directed towards the elimination of the threat of war."[61] All UN members shall find

---

[54] United Nations Charter, Preamble.

[55] The great powers could have retained much of their sovereignty and power while still creating a new system that strengthened multilateral means of enforcement while constraining the war-making function of their rivals as much as it would have constrained their own. Clark and Sohn described one approach in their discussion of world federation, *World Peace Through World Law*.

[56] Lederach discusses the importance of enabling people to feel the meaning of political projects in *Moral Imagination*, 56–57.

[57] Article 3, Universal Declaration of Human Rights.

[58] UN Documents, Resolution 33/73. "Reaffirming the Right of Individuals, States and All Mankind to Life in Peace," http://www.un-documents.net/a33r73.htm.

[59] UN General Assembly Resolution 39/11, "Declaration on the Right of Peoples to Peace," https://www.ohchr.org/EN/ProfessionalInterest/Pages/RightOfPeoplesToPeace.aspx.

[60] UN Charter, Article 2 (4).

[61] UN General Assembly Resolution 39/11.

ways to "settle their international disputes by peaceful means in such a manner that international peace and security, and justice, are not endangered."[62] States are required to resolve disputes through negotiations or judicial processes, never to claim or justify territorial changes as a result of war, and to eliminate causes of violent conflict, including to refrain from arms races.

Citizens might insist that their governments take these obligations seriously and ask other governments to do so, in part because "peace is a vital requirement for the promotion and protection of all human rights for all."[63] To chart a preferred course in international relations, UN members should take seriously that "the education of humanity for justice, liberty and peace are indispensable to the dignity of human beings and constitute a *duty* that all nations must fulfil in a spirit of mutual assistance and concern."[64] The international community should incentivize states' obligation to "respect, implement and promote" key principles grounded in the values of human dignity, including freedom from fear and want.[65] The UN called on all of the following to take personal responsibility for building a culture of peace: parents, students, teachers, politicians, journalists, religious leaders and groups, academics and other intellectuals, artists, entertainers, scientists, health and humanitarian workers, social workers, business leaders and managers, as well as civil society organizations.[66]

Many are understandably skeptical of high-minded UN declarations that do little to change political realities. Yet these statements demonstrate widespread support for peace and for the belief that all should be working to realize it. What have been missing are practical ideas to institutionalize peace and the will to implement agreed-on values, the subjects of this book. For concerned citizens in the United States and other countries to ignore any longer the need to build a movement to implement the correlates of peace would be counter-productive because that takes away "the most powerful weapon against the forces of inhumanity—respect for freedom, democracy, human rights, and the rule of law."[67] How might concerned citizens and policymakers move toward practical policies capable of contributing to genuine security while nurturing the values of human dignity to broaden political support? The suggestions in the next chapter point toward that goal.

---

[62] UN Charter, Article 2 (3).

[63] See Official Records of the General Assembly, 67th Session, Supplement no. 53 and corrigendum (A/67/53 and Corr. 1), chapter IV, https://documents-dds-ny.un.org/doc/UNDOC/GEN/G12/173/25/PDF/G1217325.pdf?OpenElement.

[64] UN General Assembly Resolution 39/11, Declaration of the Right of Peoples to Peace, L. 29, p. 5. Emphasis added.

[65] Resolution A/71/189.

[66] Resolution A/71/189.

[67] Schoenbaum, *International Relations*, 305.

7

Designing Life-Enhancing Architecture

NEW INSTITUTIONAL ARCHITECTURE to realign US power and purposes to meet human security needs can be built now without carrying unacceptable risks while also opening doors for deeper structural change down the road. In many cases, promising initiatives can be grafted onto existing institutions and processes. This is a good formula for advancing system change. To illustrate how this may be done, a half dozen quite different initiatives are discussed here, each a vital area in the proposed grand strategy for human security: invigorating international lawmaking, expanding global monitoring, establishing multinational police enforcement, advancing global legislative conversations, achieving economic well-being for the poor, and improving environmental health.

7.1 STRENGTHENING INTERNATIONAL LAW

Strengthening laws to encourage desirable conduct is perhaps the most important and powerful action that the United States can take to stop violence and foster human freedom.[1] There are many ways to go about that. Many world-minded people have long favored making the United Nations a more effective organization in which national governments would relinquish their right to wage war in return for reciprocal

---

[1] This has been well documented in both domestic and international legal contexts. For example, see Schoenbaum, *International Relations*; O'Connell, *Power and Purpose*; Wright, *The Role of International Law*; Lu, "World Government."

relinquishments by others. States would submit disputes to authoritative international judicial and enforcement institutions. As Grenville Clark and Louis Sohn wrote in what became a well-known book published in 1958, world peace could only be achieved through the strengthening of world law.[2] They proposed a revised UN Charter in which votes in the General Assembly would be based on the populations of member nations; the UN Security Council would be replaced with an Executive Council that included China, India, the Soviet Union, and the United States as permanent members but with no veto power; and a world police force would be created and eventually become the only military force permitted in the world. Interest in these proposals declined as the rivalry with the Soviet Union increased during the Cold War. They seemed to require more trust than existed at the time and probably understated the political struggle that would accompany such major changes. Nonetheless, it is instructive to examine more modest law-strengthening measures that could be added to existing processes and institutions, including one striking initiative by President Kennedy and Adlai Stevenson to create "a world without war."[3]

The prudential promise of strengthening law to reduce violence has been underscored by many scholars and practitioners both before and after the Clark-Sohn proposals.[4] The Commission on Global Governance, a blue-ribbon international panel meeting a quarter-century ago, concluded that the world community of the future should be "characterized by law, not by lawlessness; by rules that all must respect; by the reality that all, including the weakest, are equal under the law and that none, including the most powerful, is above the law."[5] This goal is both ethically desirable and politically possible. It simply requires "a will to lead by those who can, and a willingness by the rest to join and help in the common effort."[6] Another recent formulation comes from Glasius and Kaldor's depiction of a preferred European security strategy, which could be sensible for the entire world as well: "Security policy . . . should be rooted firmly in a multilateralist commitment to international law. . . [and] it should be based on methods or guidelines appropriate to a human security approach."[7] Political leaders, the military, police, and civilians could attempt to work together to enforce desirable law.

Wendt has argued that US grand strategy should adjust to where history may be headed: "If [political] Realists are right that anarchy is programmed for war, then it makes sense to define one's sovereignty and interests in egoistic terms and act on

---

[2] Clark and Sohn, *World Peace Through World Law*.

[3] This initiative followed earlier systemic initiatives in the Baruch Plan, Acheson-Lilienthal proposals, and McCloy-Zorin guidelines, all designed to take multilateral control of nuclear weapons and the capability to build them. See Adlai E. Stevenson, "Working Toward a World Without War," *Disarmament: The New US Initiative* (Washington, DC: US Arms Control and Disarmament Agency, 1962), 13–28.

[4] See, for example, Clark and Sohn, *World Peace Through World Law*; Weiss, *Global Governance: Why?*; Wendt, "Why a World State Is Inevitable"; Schoenbaum, *International Relations*; O'Connell, *Power and Purpose*.

[5] Commission on Global Governance, *Our Global Neighbourhood*, 332.

[6] Commission on Global Governance, *Our Global Neighbourhood*, 332.

[7] Glasius and Kaldor, "A Human Security Vision," 10–11.

that basis. International law is irrelevant or an impediment to the national interest, and one should pursue a unilateralist policy whenever possible."[8] On the other hand, if more global governance might be needed and actually comes into being, then a different grand strategy makes sense. Rather than a vain attempt to rely on militarized self-help for security in the long run, Wendt says the United States should immediately try to shape, strengthen, and participate in the emerging global constitution to enable it to save the security commons before further tragedy in the commons occurs (e.g., proliferating weapons). That would mean acceptance of international law and supportive participation in multilateral institutions.

Great powers typically have little enthusiasm for expanding the rule of law to reduce the role of military power because, being great powers, they prefer relying on military self-help to manage international relations rather than on legal processes that are less subject to their own control. Until this tendency is recognized and addressed by citizen education and political action, the militarily powerful states, including the United States, are likely to impede legal processes from supplanting military processes. As previously indicated, US policymakers and conservatives in Congress have blocked progress on many lawmaking initiatives since the Reagan administration. The George W. Bush administration, for example, in addition to launching aggressive war and justifying torture, first elevated John Bolton, the arch critic of international law and institutions, into the post of US ambassador to the United Nations where he undermined UN agencies, from Security Council proceedings against war crimes, to General Assembly budget allocations, to law enforcement by the International Criminal Court.

Two foundation stones can strengthen the role and the rule of law internationally. First, the United States needs scrupulously to honor existing international laws that constrain war-fighting and to take new legal initiatives to prevent war and to render it less destructive, if it occurs. In addition, the conflict-resolving capacities of the law should be more widely utilized by the United States and others. The United Nations Charter is a treaty that all countries who are members have ratified and is, according to the US Constitution, part of the supreme law of the land. Its explicit prohibition of war, save two limited exceptions,[9] should be carefully honored by all leaders, citizens, and governments. Preventive wars, such as the US invasion of Iraq in 2003 are generally illegal[10] as well as unjust and immoral. Violating these norms governing the use of force usually subverts United States' basic interests, even when it may seem that it does not, because US violations open the door more widely for others to violate norms also. Because the United States is a major influence in international relations, for it explicitly to comply with specific laws strengthens the law. US compliance with

---

[8] Wendt, "Why a World State Is Inevitable," 529–530.

[9] The exceptions are (1) when the Security Council authorizes the use of force for the maintenance of peace and security, and (2) if a country has been attacked, it is authorized to use military force in self-defense until the Security Council has had time to come to its defense.

[10] Referring to the US-British attack on Iraq, UN Secretary-General Kofi Annan said that "From our point of view and the UN charter point of view, it was illegal." Quoted by Colum Lynch, "U.S. Allies Dispute Annan on Iraq War," *Washington Post*, September 17, 2004, A 18.

violence-constraining laws, explicitly stated, should be the first element in new legal architecture.

Second, although the world could use a global legislative institution to formulate needed laws that would be binding on all actors in order to assure human survival, until the Security Council takes such a responsibility seriously or another more representative institution is created, the United States and other governments can still nurture the growth of law in the existing relatively anarchic framework in order to pave the way for future innovations. Concerned policymakers and citizens can address the present state of institutional legislative weakness by elaborating and formally consolidating standards for state conduct through the UN's International Law Commission (ILC).[11] UN member states established the ILC to undertake the mandate in the UN Charter to "initiate studies and make recommendations for the purpose of . . . encouraging the progressive development of international law and its codification."[12] More than two decades ago, the Commission on Global Governance suggested that the ILC be revamped so it could effectively co-ordinate making international law. If activists and progressive governments would press toward this goal, they could "give international lawmaking the prominence it requires"[13] even before a global legislative function is more formally established.

Although at first new standards arising from ILC codification might technically be non-binding, they could have substantial influence on national behavior. The ILC has been quite successful in winning compliance for much of its work. As its standards are followed by more and more countries, the standards assume added gravitas. Because custom is a source of international law and large incentives could be provided to foot-draggers when political will is present in a good number of lawmaking countries, it would be possible to establish many desirable customs that could be codified as legalization progresses. This process could gradually harden soft law into strictly enforced hard law.

Although great powers may be slow to endorse lawmaking if it encroaches on their freedom to act unilaterally, democratic governments generally do favor strengthening international law and the role of the ILC. If the Biden administration chooses to emphasize its role as a leader of democracies interested in multilateral institution-building, then the prospects for enhancing the rule of law will greatly improve. Indeed, a major, constructive strategic role awaits the United States in democratic internationalism[14] if US officials would decide to breathe life into a new coalition of democracies for lawmaking. Regardless of the role played by the United States or any particular democracy, it would be useful for all the world's democracies to strengthen and possibly

---

[11] See United Nations, Office of Legal Affairs, "International Law Commission," http://legal.un.org/ilc/.

[12] UN Charter, Article 13 (1) (*a*).

[13] Commission on Global Governance, *Our Global Neighbourhood*, 331.

[14] In this regard, much can be learned from Deudney and Ikenberry's earlier articulation of "democratic internationalism" as a possible US strategy, although that formulation does not appear to emphasize the need for a global strategy for system change and citizen pressure as much as this analysis. Deudney and Ikenberry, "Democratic Internationalism."

to institutionalize their own collaboration to enable like-minded governments to build more effective international laws and institutions. Illiberal states might certainly join such initiatives, but the foot-dragging states, regardless of ideology, should not determine the future lawmaking agenda.

In addition to more strict compliance with existing legal constraints on the uses of force, to elevating the role of the International Law Commission, and to sharing multilateral leadership within a strengthened political coalition of democracies for lawmaking, the United States could also benefit from considering the specific role of law in these four illustrative areas: to constrain destructive technologies, to protect civilians, to enforce law on governmental officials as individuals, and to curtail terrorism.

7.1.1 Constraining Destructive Technologies

One of the most pressing needs for enhancing human security is gradually to increase public controls over extremely dangerous means, particularly to prevent the manufacture, deployment, or use of nuclear, chemical, and biological weapons of mass destruction; to prohibit deploying attack weapons in space; and to strengthen the international community's ability to monitor and enforce agreed constraints on weapons. Yet the main impediment to arms control for limiting these dangers seems to be inertia—inclination to follow past patterns and fear of change. As a result, we discuss here some viable opportunities to relinquish this patterned thought and behavior.

The need to employ new forms of global governance to manage weapons of mass destruction has been strongly recommended in the widely noticed but immediately ignored proposal by former secretary of state and national security adviser Henry Kissinger, former secretary of state George Schultz, former secretary of defense William Perry, and former chairman of the Senate Committee on Armed Services Sam Nunn to establish international rules and enforcement to achieve "a world free of nuclear weapons" and "ultimately ending them as a threat to the world."[15] Henry Kissinger has been held in especially high esteem as a leading theoretician and policymaker on nuclear deterrence, and the other three former officials also possess impressive credentials endorsing US nuclear policy across the boards during their earlier professional careers. Significantly, "a world free of nuclear weapons . . . has been endorsed by no less than two-thirds of all living former secretaries of state, former secretaries of defense, and former national security advisers."[16] Yet the Kissinger-Schultz-Perry-Nunn proposal for decreasing reliance on nuclear weapons was not taken seriously by the national security policymakers occupying the offices that the four formerly held. Significantly, the four did not publicly advocate these policies while in office, and they were not particularly influential after they were out of office, underscoring the need

---

[15] Shultz, Perry, Kissinger, and Nunn, "A World Free of Nuclear Weapons."

[16] Ivo Daalder and Jan Lodal, "The Logic of Zero: Toward a World without Nuclear Weapons," *Foreign Affairs* 87, no. 6 (2008): 81.

for strong citizens' pressure to take desirable steps toward constraining weapons of mass destruction through law enforcement.

This notable difference between their earlier positions and their later positions suggests an important political reality. It is unlikely that, in the absence of enormous public pressure, US policymakers will implement wise, boundary-transcending, system-changing policies while in office. It is also unlikely that the same people, after leaving office and advocating wiser policies, will exercise much influence. Former secretary of defense Robert McNamara is another powerful former official whose revisions of his Vietnamese and nuclear policy positions after leaving office confirm the rule of narrow nationalism while in power and the lack of influence while speaking for more inclusive policies after departing from office.

In any case, the proposal to move away from reliance on nuclear weapons and eventually to eliminate them should be vigorously pursued in the new architecture. Highly respected independent experts,[17] President Obama,[18] and many civil society groups[19] have supported the idea. But rather than pursue new opportunities to reduce nuclear arms, US officials and the other nuclear-weapons countries continue to satisfy their own separate nuclear appetites, while trying to prevent others from satisfying theirs. The point is not to suggest that nuclear-armed officials are malicious or even that their conduct is not rational under limited circumstances, as it was for the single hunter in Rousseau's parable. The point is that today's international system, if left as it is, encourages pursuing security separately; this undermines collaboration for the common good, even though the international system *could be changed* to implement the good of all. As long as the overly permissive international system remains structurally unchanged, it will be unable to prevent hyper-independent states from using nuclear weapons in a crisis or additional states from seeking a nuclear capability.

More grassroots pressures are needed to change policies. Those designing new global security plans should be encouraged to recognize that ultimately there will be no security apart from common security—security sustained by limited yet dependable rules enforced by global authority on behalf of all for the benefit of all.[20] Yet like dinosaurs lounging on their path to extinction, many humans have been lulled into complacency. They may ask: What is there to fear? Nuclear weapons have been around since 1945 and used only twice at Hiroshima and Nagasaki. Yet, the longer the weapons are available, the more numerous are the opportunities and temptations to use them.

---

[17] Shultz, Perry, Kissinger, and Nunn, "A World Free of Nuclear Weapons."

[18] Jeffrey Lewis, "Obama's Dream of a Nuclear-Free World Is Becoming a Nightmare," *Foreign Policy*, March 29, 2017, https://foreignpolicy.com/2017/03/29/obamas-dream-of-a-nuclear-free-world-is-becoming-a-nightmare/.

[19] One such group is the US Conference of Catholic Bishops, "U.S. and European Catholic Bishops Call for Strategy to Eliminate Nuclear Weapons Globally," July 6, 2017, http://www.usccb.org/news/2017/17-121.cfm.

[20] Glasius and Kaldor conclude that "Europeans cannot be secure while others in the world live in severe insecurity. National borders are no longer the dividing lines between security and insecurity: insecurity gets exported." "A Human Security Vision," 10.

The longer they are deployed, the greater the risk that someone with psychological problems may use the power to launch nuclear weapons for psychologically motivated reasons that do not serve the security of an entire society or the world. As the Canberra Commission on the Elimination of Nuclear Weapons pointed out, it is simply incredulous that nuclear weapons can be deployed indefinitely but not be used either intentionally or inadvertently. Nuclear deterrence simply "can't last out the necessary timespan, which is roughly between now and the death of the sun."[21]

Many will argue that it made sense to risk annihilation in order to preserve freedom against the aggressions of Hitler and Stalin. At first these horrible weapons were seen as something that only the likes of Hitler and Stalin would want to acquire. Yet what happened after those threats disappeared? Now nuclearism, characterized by faith in nuclear weapons and preparations for total war, including elements of authoritarianism to manage them, is justified by the democracies of the West. Many earlier opponents of total war have become defenders of US, British, and French preparations to fight such war. In 2020, the United States leads the world in upgrading its nuclear weapons even though upgrades are not needed, as Kissinger and colleagues pointed out. The United States now justifies for itself what formerly was justified only as a necessity to oppose totalitarianism, as if this nuclear potion has become part of the American way of life and of killing in war.

Authoritarian governments seem to like nuclear weapons because they offer a false promise of giving those who possess them absolute control over opponents at home and abroad. They offer final, total destruction of enemies. They are great for making threats and feeling powerful. They are prepared with top secret targeting and top secret ways, means, and agents for firing. They are built in secret laboratories and manufacturing sites, with occasional understatements of their full costs and denials of how many have died or been irradiated in the process of development or use. They are designed to be fired quickly, not after open, participatory deliberations. Nuclear weapons almost seem to require quasi-authoritarian means for handling them.

Perhaps the most sobering prospect is that, if a nuclear war were to occur, nuclear winter might settle over the planet, threatening the entire species and of course non-human species also. Radiation would be horrible for most who remained alive. Historically, the fear that has often motivated people to fight has been that another country threatened their way of life. A national tradition might die if no one defended it. However, in nuclear war, humanity might die. Any people living during an approaching doomsday might face, too late, the death not simply of a national society, but the death of birth. It is the murder of the future for which every citizen of every nuclear-armed

---

[21] Australian Department of Foreign Affairs and Trade, Canberra Commission on the Elimination of Nuclear Weapons, *Report of the Canberra Commission on the Elimination of Nuclear Weapons* (Canberra: Department of Foreign Affairs and Trade, 1996), 18–22; Weiss and Thakur, *Global Governance and the UN*, 101–102; Martin Amis, *Einstein's Monsters* (London: Jonathan Cape, 1987), 16–17; Craig, "The Resurgent Idea," 136.

country must share some responsibility.[22] Is it rational to risk the death of birth in order to counter a threat to a nation? If not, then to allow the nuclear menace to continue year after year seems irresponsible.

For citizens to object strongly to the existing system's propensity for destruction would be a step toward responsibility and refusal to be accomplices to possible future atrocity and the worst killings ever conducted by any human beings. It is also a step away from being in a state of denial about the likelihood that nuclear weapons and the traditional state system can co-exist indefinitely. It is a step away from what might be called a "US extremism of the center" in which a widely shared centrist view accepts nuclearism and the possibility of committing suicide to defend one's nation. To reject nuclearism, rather than to continue the present order because it is familiar would be difficult, but it is not impossible.

At the United Nations in 2017, 122 countries voted for the Treaty on the Prohibition of Nuclear Weapons,[23] the first legally binding agreement to prohibit nuclear weapons, with a goal of their elimination. The treaty prohibits the development, testing, production, possession, stockpiling, stationing, transfer, use, and threat of use of nuclear weapons. The treaty takes a clear stance in favor of achieving and maintaining a nuclear-weapon-free world. To be sure, further negotiations will be required to specify the legal and technical measures required to put such a sweeping prohibition into practice. The treaty's proponents hope that the treaty will help to stigmatize nuclear weapons and catalyze a global movement for banning them. It will be difficult to implement effectively without US support, but the United States and other states possessing nuclear weapons are opposed. Sustained citizen support for this treaty can help to strengthen norms to delegitimize nuclear weapons.

In addition to employing international laws to limit nuclear weapons, public support is needed for broad arms control measures to prohibit deployment of new military technologies to avert the destabilization of political relationships that has occurred throughout history with manufacture of the cross-bow, gunpowder and cannon, machine guns, submarines, poison gas, aerial bombing, aircraft carriers, guided missiles, cruise missiles, and cyber warfare. Whoever first develops a new military technology is usually tempted to deploy it immediately because it gives its developers an advantage. But the advantage is usually short-lived, as competitors learn the technology and turn it against its inventor. Although this lesson has been obvious for centuries, governments repeat their mistake over and over. Atomic and hydrogen bombs, missile delivery systems, multiple independently-targetable-reentry vehicles, shoulder-held heat-seeking missiles, and drones all illustrate the self-defeating nature of recent arms deployments intended to give one side a decisive advantage, but causing losses in security over the long run.

---

[22] I am indebted to Daniel Deudney for this formulation. International Studies Association roundtable, "Assessing Jonathan Schell's Nuclear Legacy: Theoretical Innovations and Political Impacts," San Francisco, April 4, 2018.

[23] United Nations, https://www.un.org/disarmament/tpnw/.

In opposition to strengthening legal constraints on new weapons, the Obama and subsequently the Trump administrations' enthusiasm for drones led them to establish a precedent for the right to attack anyone they decided to target, without any authorization or justification outside of themselves. Instead, at the least, the United States should have established a rule that attacks would not be allowed against people in countries with which the US was at peace. It would have been helpful for US policymakers to have seen the wisdom in denying adversaries the "right" to attack anyone of *their* own choosing at any time, especially if potential targets lived in a country with which they were at peace. To help build new architecture for human security, US citizens should insist that their government return to traditional restrictions on when attack weapons may be used to kill others.[24]

In addition, to enhance sustainable peace, verifiable global rules and reliable enforcement measures are needed in all theaters of operations to ensure, for example, that no one will deploy attack weapons in space, no one will divert non-weapon nuclear materials to weapons purposes, no one will place weapons on a hair trigger, and no one will use military force, including attack drones, except within strict application of the Charter's limitations on the use of force. A strong initiative to limit conventional arms to defensive purposes and to reduce the trade in conventional arms further illustrate initiatives that would produce positive results. Although the difficulties of designing conventional arms so they do not pose an offensive threat to other countries are too complex to present here, simply establishing a clear intention to differentiate offensive and defensive functions would be a major step forward. Weapons' manufacturers strongly oppose this differentiation, in part because of fear that their sales and profits would diminish if procurement purchases emphasized defensive purposes.

The United States has weakened standards for limiting arms exports with the goal of increasing corporate profits,[25] but the US Arms Control Association reports that this claim is misleading.[26] These US policies are dangerous because increased arms sales are likely to lead to more violent conflicts, increase their destructiveness, and make existing conflicts more difficult to end. They raise the likelihood that some of these weapons will be sold to dictatorial governments using them to oppress their own people. The policies also increase the risk that dangerous arms will get into the hands of terrorists. Moreover, assault rifles and their ammunition, which make up a significant part of the small arms trade, are "weapons of choice" of drug trafficking organizations in Latin American countries. Even though arms sales may undermine security and increase oppression elsewhere in the world, the United States sells more conventional weapons

---

[24] David Cortright, Rachel Fairhurst, and Kristen Wall, *Drones and the Future of Armed Conflict: Ethical, Legal, and Strategic Implications* (Chicago: University of Chicago Press, 2014).

[25] Senator Ben Cardin of Maryland has reported that pro-gun lobbyists significantly influenced the administration to make the changes. Arms Control Association, Jeff Abramson, *Issue Briefs* 10, no. 6 (June 7, 2018), https://www.armscontrol.org/taxonomy/term/31.

[26] Arms Control Association, Jeff Abramson, *Issue Briefs*, 10.

in the international arms market than any other country.[27] Another modest yet desirable standard, which was strengthened in the Clinton administration, required that a purchaser's past record on human rights be considered before deciding to make a sale. The Trump administration removed that requirement.[28] As US manufacturers sell more weapons to countries with poor human rights records, international standards for responsible weapons sales become more difficult to uphold.

Restricting new destructive technologies is difficult because the manufacturing countries are eager to see how effective their new manufactures might be. They pursue the hare security option, allowing the collective benefit of catching the security stag to get away. An example of this arises from the possibilities of combining drone targeting technology with killer robots and lethal "autonomous" weapons systems. These rely on artificial intelligence and information technology to enable computers to use face recognition to make decisions about whom to kill. More than two dozen countries, including Algeria, Austria, Bolivia, Brazil, Chile, China, Colombia, Costa Rica, Cuba, Ecuador, Egypt, Ghana, Holy See, Iraq, Mexico, Nicaragua, Pakistan, State of Palestine, Uganda, and Zimbabwe, have urged a ban on such weapons before they become operational.[29] But the United States, the United Kingdom, Israel, and Russia have opposed any legally binding ban.[30] They believe they might benefit financially or strategically from such destructive technology, so they give little consideration to the benefit of halting development and preventing all states from obtaining it.

7.1.2 *Protecting Civilians*

A second area of lawmaking draws on the many legal codes and religious traditions throughout the world forbidding the deliberate killing of people who are not members of any armed forces, in support of the principle that it is wrong to kill civilians intentionally, even in war.[31] This principle of civilian immunity from attack, which means that non-combatants may not be deliberately targeted or killed by anyone for

---

[27] Alexandra Kuimova, Aude Fleurant, Nan Tian, et al., *Trends in International Arms Transfers*, 2017, https://www.sipri.org/sites/default/files/2018-03/fssipri_at2017_0.pdf; Security Assistance Monitor, *Arms Sales Dashboard*, https://securityassistance.org/contentnn/arms-sales-dashboard; A. Trevor Thrall and Caroline Dorminey, "Risky Business: The Role of Arms Sales in US Foreign Policy," *Policy Analysis*, CATO Institute (March 13, 2018), 1.

[28] Security Assistance Monitor, "Arms Sales Dashboard"; Thrall and Dorminey, "Risky Business," 1.

[29] Adam Satariano, "Will There Be a Ban on Killer Robots?" *New York Times*, October 19, 2018, https://www.nytimes.com/2018/10/19/technology/artificial-intelligence-weapons.html?searchResultPosition=2.

[30] Matthieu Ortiz, "Issue Briefs: Killer Robots," *Arms Control Association, Issue Briefs* 10, no. 6, June 7, 2018, https://www.armscontrol.org/taxonomy/term/31.

[31] For example, the Quran declares, "whoever kills one innocent human being, it is as if he has killed all of humankind (5:32)." A. Rashied Omar, *Islam Beyond Violent Extremism* (Cape Town, South Africa: Claremont Main Road Mosque, 2017), 55–63. See also Alex Bellamy, *Massacres and Morality: Mass Atrocities in an Age of Civilian Immunity* (Oxford: Oxford University Press, 2012), 1.

any reason, in wartime or peacetime, has been enshrined in international law. People widely agree that this prohibition is a fundamental moral and legal obligation.

Yet despite this generally endorsed principle, the deliberate killing of civilians repeatedly occurs, undermining one of the most important elements in the rule of law. The killers frequently have avoided much criticism or accountability. Often their political supporters have praised their actions. Willingness to violate this norm is shaped by many factors, two of which are whether other governments respect civilian immunity in their own conduct and how the international community responds to violations.

Because of civilian immunity's importance for honoring human dignity and the rule of law, stopping violations of it is one of the most important places in which to work for positive change. Most independent experts agree that "the battle for civilian immunity is perpetual and should be waged everywhere that the norm is challenged. There is simply no room for complacency."[32]

The international community has woven a web of laws and institutions to protect victims and hold perpetrators accountable, from the universally ratified Geneva Conventions to the principled actions of the International Committee of the Red Cross. Civil society organizations have sought to strengthen civilian protections by (1) developing international human rights and humanitarian law "to outlaw arbitrary killing in almost all of its forms"; (2) establishing and employing the International Criminal Court to provide international jurisdiction for prosecuting individuals accused of deliberate killing of civilians; (3) expanding international humanitarian assistance to victims; (4) educating people about and drawing on UN Security Council resolutions specifying that states must respect international humanitarian law; (5) shaping UN peace operations to protect civilians and nurturing an enforcement culture that does so; (6) taking regional initiatives to discourage harming of civilians; and (7) supporting states that emphasize sovereignty's conditionality and accept an international responsibility to protect victims whose national government is unable or unwilling to protect its own citizens from gross violation of human rights.[33]

Looking more closely at practices that strengthen or weaken civilian protections increases understanding of how citizens may help to bolster international law in the service of human security more generally.[34] Although the concept of legitimacy does not strictly determine states' conduct, it does influence what they are willing to do or try to get away with. State behavior is commonly believed to be legitimate if it

---

[32] Bellamy, *Massacres*, 14. See also Matthew Evangelista, *Law, Ethics, and the War on Terror* (Cambridge, UK: Polity Press, 2008).

[33] The United Nations affirmed the international community's responsibility to protect victims of their own government's misconduct first in 2005 (A/RES/60/1), and again in 2006, and 2009, in Resolutions 1674 and 1894. The Responsibility to Protect has been repeatedly affirmed in more than 80 resolutions. See *"UN Security Council Resolutions Referencing R2P: Global Centre for the Responsibility to Protect"* www. globalr2p.org.

[34] See Bellamy, *Massacres*, especially chapter 10. For an effort to identify causal links in mass murder, see Jonathan Leader Maynard, "Rethinking the Role of Ideology in Mass Atrocities," *Terrorism and Political Violence* 26, no. 5 (2014): 821–841 at 828.

corresponds with widely accepted standards expressed in the norms of international society. Because norms are shaped by what influential states do, their respect for positive norms is necessary to reduce arbitrary killings. In contrast, casual willingness by leading states to violate norms when it serves their interests to do so is harmful to the normative structure from which most states benefit overall.

In the second half of the 20th century and especially after the end of the Cold War, the growing influence of human rights and other civil society organizations helped progressive states in the international community strengthen a body of international law that informed states how they may and may not treat their own and other countries' citizens. These laws demonstrated a trend that expanded "norms on behalf of individuals . . . at the expense of state sovereignty."[35] Because behaviors are judged to be legitimate when they enjoy the support and voluntary compliance of others, following these reduces anticipated transaction costs. In contrast, "things thought to be illegitimate are likely to be criticized, resisted, and punished, increasing anticipated transaction costs for governments contemplating lawless actions."[36] For example, an indictment by the ICC after extensive Security Council and court prosecutorial investigations, may exact extensive diplomatic costs for an accused leader, e.g., Sudanese president Omar Hassan Ahmad al-Bashir, even though he continues to exercise power and evades arrest and trial. These are not always decisive, of course, but their influence may deter some future misconduct.

Historical studies of massacres show that the rise of public interest in human rights gradually reduced the level of deliberate civilian killing that could be justified by governments to the point that it offered little prospect of being accepted as legitimate.[37] Repeated statements over many years that civilians should never be targeted, coming from both liberal states and civil society (e.g., religious groups, Human Rights Watch, Amnesty International, and the Red Cross and Red Crescent societies), made it difficult for governments to justify mass murder by claiming "necessity" in battle or the professed desirability of selective extermination of disliked people. But there is no historical inevitability to this progress. Groups like Al-Qaeda and ISIS seem to have revived extermination of hated people as a justification.

Some contexts enable perpetrators of mass killings to avoid criticism from or punishment by the international community. During the cultural revolution in China, for example, the Chinese government killed millions of civilians "without . . . offering a plausible justification to international society" because of its relative isolation and reliance on communist solidarity to avoid censure. Similarly, Cambodia under the Khmer Rouge killed millions. While the number of deaths in the United States war in Indochina was smaller than these two examples, the United States also "complied with civilian immunity only when it believed that violations would be widely reported. Where it believed that violations would not be reported, as in Laos and Cambodia, US

---

[35] Evangelista, *Law*, 3, 7, 11.
[36] Bellamy, *Massacres*, 382.
[37] Bellamy, *Massacres*, 383; Evangelista, *Law*, 1–22.

strategy paid much less respect to the norm."[38] More recently, anemic protests by the United States and other democracies in response to Syrian and Russian gross violations of civilian immunity have allowed further weakening of this norm.

Governments usually try to justify their actions by claiming they are consistent with agreed standards. Violators of the sanctity of civilian life often try to reject universal standards associated with inclusive human identity. Their ideologies appeal only to their in-group: "white Europeans in the case of colonialism, Aryans . . . in the case of Nazism, the working class in the case of Stalinism, poor peasants in the case of Maoism, Khmer peasants in the Khmer Rouge's case, and Muslim fundamentalists in the case of Al-Qaeda."[39] Because out-groups are hated, constraints on perpetrators are more effective if they come from domestic sources, but of course these are difficult to mobilize. Yet even here, clearly upheld international standards are an important help in the long run.[40]

For US citizens seeking to advance a moral security policy consistent with the values of human dignity, it is painful to consider findings that the US and British governments in World War II, "justified the intentional bombing of German and Japanese civilians by arguing that civilians were not the actual targets of attack, a position that both governments knew to be inaccurate." To avoid the need to justify atrocities, US and British officials "argued . . . that massacre reports were false, that the victims were not civilians, that civilians were not killed deliberately, and that undeniable massacres were committed by 'rogue elements' or uncontrollable militia."[41] The success of such rationalizations demonstrates the way the context and reporting shape what is considered legitimate. It also underscores the need for a vigilant global watchdog to uphold and keep visible a universal concept of civilian immunity. Here is a place where advanced technology, such as satellite and smart-phone photography providing evidence of atrocities, can encourage more principled conduct and contribute to common interests in worldwide civilian immunity.

It is difficult to use big military firepower, which often causes unintended civilian deaths, to uphold the norm of civilian immunity, as demonstrated by US policies in Vietnam, Iraq, and Afghanistan. Yet no country can be persuasive in claiming that every civilian life is precious and immune from attack if it kills many civilians itself. As General David H. Petraeus, US commander in Afghanistan, acknowledged: "Every Afghan civilian death diminishes our cause. . . . We know [that] the measure by which

---

[38] Bellamy, *Massacres*, 385.

[39] Bellamy, *Massacres*, 386–387.

[40] Bellamy notes that "domestic politics and the decline of the material power of its principal adherents did most to rid the world of its three bloodiest forms of selective extermination—colonialism, Nazism/fascism, and communism." *Massacres*, 387. See also Hunjoon Kim and Kathryn Sikkink, "Explaining the Deterrence Effect of Human Rights Prosecutions for Transitional Countries," *International Studies Quarterly* 54, no. 4 (2010): 939–963.

[41] Bellamy, *Massacres*, 388.

our mission will be judged is protecting the population from harm by *either* side."[42] The negative political fallout that accompanies killing civilians means that advantages in military firepower may not produce advantages in political outcomes or serve political goals effectively. Because of instant communication with social media, accidentally bombing civilians or using excessive violence cannot easily be swept under a rug of public ignorance. For this reason, prudence suggests that military means need to be carefully evaluated because some may not be as helpful as assumed in the past.

Because civilian immunity is frequently violated, for states to strictly follow the law is especially necessary to protect it from breakdown. Support for civilian immunity could become an important legal cornerstone for US relations with other governments, from close allies to adversaries like Syria and Iran. One of the best forms of resistance to those who justify mass murder is to refrain from killing civilians oneself.

One of the changes in international relations—the speed and accessibility of worldwide communication—decreases perpetrators' ability to violate the norm with impunity because information often will get out.[43] To increase compliance with the law for protection of civilian life, national governments and the UN could strengthen communication with endangered groups further, improve UN capacity to conduct rapid analysis to confirm or deny claims that civilian immunity is being violated, strengthen the UN Office of the Special Adviser for the Prevention of Genocide, and expand it to include mass atrocities that fall short of genocide.

One of the promising developments in recent decades that should be strengthened is the recognition that sovereignty is conditional. No government should enjoy the protection of being immune from international accountability or outside intervention (sovereign immunity) if it is unable or unwilling to protect its citizens from being harmed (civilian immunity). As discussed in Chapter 5, the Responsibility to Protect[44] places a duty on international society to take action to protect those threatened by gross violation of human rights. To implement that goal, the Global Centre for the Responsibility to Protect recommends early analyses of emerging threats of genocide and mass atrocity and better co-ordination of international responses.[45] Of course, as noted previously, this concept needs its own checks to prevent unwarranted military interventions from causing unjustifiable harms themselves.

---

[42] Italics added. Rod Nordland, "U.N. Reports Rising Afghan Casualties," *New York Times*, August 10, 2010.

[43] Bellamy, *Massacres*, 390–391.

[44] See Edward C. Luck, "The United Nations and the Responsibility to Protect," *Policy Analysis Brief* (Muscatine, IA: Stanley Foundation, August 2008), 5, https://www.stanleyfoundation.org/publications/pab/LuckPAB808.pdf; International Law Commission, "Draft Articles on the Responsibility of States for Internationally Wrongful Acts," http://untreaty.un.org/ilc/texts/instruments/english/commentaries/9_6_2001.pdf); Louise Arbour, "The Responsibility to Protect as a Duty of Care in International Law and Practice," *Review of International Studies* 34, no. 3 (2008): 445–458.

[45] The Global Centre for the Responsibility to Protect, "Fulfilling the Responsibility to Protect: Strengthening Our Capacities to Prevent and Halt Mass Atrocities," September 24, 2010, https://reliefweb.int/report/rwanda/fulfilling-responsibility-protect-strengthening-our-capacities-prevent-and-halt-mass.

Widespread education of citizens in the United States and other countries is needed to increase understanding that civilian immunity requires every person on Earth not to target civilians or allow others to target civilians even if senior military or civilian officials may believe that killing civilians would help their cause by enabling "necessary" bombardments or by removing a hated population from coveted territory in what has euphemistically been called "ethnic cleansing." Educating civilians and soldiers is necessary, in part, because of difficulties enforcing this norm. When a national government engages in aerial bombing, some "collateral damage" of civilian killing is allowed, yet it is often difficult to know the difference between targeting civilians, which is illegal, and targeting nearby military targets, which is legal, even though some civilians die in the attack. In addition, when a non-state actor conducts a suicide bombing, the perpetrators may claim that an entire enemy population has mobilized against them, leaving no one, except perhaps babies, as non-combatants. In any case, these difficulties underscore the importance of principled efforts to uphold civilian immunity.

7.1.3 Enforcing Law on the Powerful

A third important area for strengthening international law is to expand possibilities for enforcing international law on *individuals* rather than on an entire society or a state, because the latter are difficult agencies to constrain. The lynchpin in employing law to diminish war is to hold officials as individuals accountable for any violations of the most basic, widely agreed upon international laws that prohibit crimes against the peace (e.g., wars of aggression), crimes against humanity (e.g., rape or mass killings of civilians), and war crimes (mistreatment of civilians or soldiers during war). Establishing individual responsibility for honoring the law both increases compliance and possibilities for enforcing the law. Although enforcing law on individual public officials is not easy, the potential payoff can be large, because as law can be enforced more effectively on individual officials, the felt need for war against an entire society diminishes.

At the conclusion of World War II, the Nuremberg war crimes tribunal clearly established that individuals exercising official roles are responsible for what they and their state do. Their personal responsibility cannot be waived by claiming that they are acting for the state and thus have no individual moral or legal responsibility for what they do or ask others to do. *Raison d'état* (reason of state) is never a legitimate defense argument for impunity when committing war crimes, crimes against humanity, or crimes against the peace.

This precedent should be upheld in every war throughout the world, taught to every new generation, and reinforced wherever possible. Nearly a half century passed after the Nuremberg and Tokyo war crimes tribunals before additional precedents occurred in the two ad hoc tribunals established for addressing crimes in the former Yugoslavia and Rwanda. Soon after these, a huge advance occurred in establishing the International Criminal Court—the first permanent international court in world history to hold individuals (rather than states) accountable. Although 123 countries have joined the court, the world's two largest democracies, the United States and India, as well as China and Russia have not.

Because the felt need for war would decline if it were possible to enforce law more frequently on heads of government to prohibit them from committing major crimes (such as the crimes for which German officials were held accountable following World War II), every opportunity should be pursued to make law enforcement on government officials successful. Yet although the International Criminal Court is able to hold individuals accountable for gross crimes committed in countries that ratified the statute, the United States, as noted previously, has opposed the court and actively undermined it by threatening other countries with loss of US assistance if they joined the court. US membership in the court would strengthen legal constraints on mass murders and would not undermine any part of the US judicial system or any US legal conduct. As international law expert Catherine Lu has concluded, "The ICC . . . may simultaneously limit *and enhance* states' rights and responsibilities. Global authority . . . need not undermine national authority structures."[46] Indeed, it would give a ratifying state an added right to expect others to conduct themselves lawfully. Moreover, it behooves the United States to keep its military conduct well within the law because this restraint increases the pressure on other national governments to comply with the same norms.

Because the United States found the court useful to refer cases to it from Sudan, Libya, and Kenya, the possibility of joining the court should be reconsidered. Unless the United States is likely to violate the prohibitions of major crimes, joining the court would strengthen US ability to hold other governments' officials accountable to norms of peace and human rights. Joining the ICC would also have a positive impact on the 123 other states that have become members and on the strength of the court's proceedings. US membership would harmonize US international law practices with legal practices of the United Kingdom, Germany, France, all other members of the European Union, Canada, Japan, Australia, South Korea, and others. Together they could encourage foot-dragging countries to join and other officials to honor the law prohibiting mass murder. US membership would not assure that Russia, China, and India would join, of course, but it would press them a bit more to join. Even countries staying outside the court probably would be slightly less likely to violate the relevant humanitarian and human rights laws.

As long as the United States stays outside the court, it cannot do much to get others to follow the law, to respect the court, or to help enforce the laws against the accused. On the other hand, if the United States vigorously bolstered international legal institutions against unconscionable atrocities, it could help move the world toward every country joining the court. Then, at last the world would have the opportunity to enforce the most basic international laws aimed at limiting violence and war by apprehending and putting on trial any individual leaders accused of violations.

---

[46] Lu, "World Government." Italics in original.

If the United States had strongly supported the court from the outset, the international community already would have gained much more valuable experience constructing reliable ways to hold individuals accountable to international law, to get indictees to show up for trial, and to replace lawless violence with the rule of law. To claim to support the rule of law while inconsistently applying the law to some others and refusing to honor the same law enforcement for oneself impedes the lawmaking process.

Of course, even without the United States ratifying the Rome Statute that established the court, other treaty laws governing war and human rights still obligate all states that have ratified them, including US officials. The genocide convention is an excellent example of the kind of lawmaking needed in the future, so it is instructive to learn from both the positive and negative aspects of US experience with this treaty, which was an international effort to ensure that the death and degradation of the holocaust would never again occur. On the positive side, the genocide treaty not only *prohibits committing* genocide, it also imposes a legally binding *duty to prevent* it and, if it occurs, to punish it.[47] Although desirable, the second obligation is not present in many other human rights treaties. This twofold obligation, to refrain from doing a misdeed and to commit oneself to preventing it everywhere else, should guide lawmaking in the future.

Also, on the positive side of US experience with this treaty, the United States eventually did ratify it, which is profoundly important. US ratification has given a solidity to the law that without its ratification would simply be lacking. However, on the negative side, US ratification was unconscionably delayed for 38 years by conservatives in the Senate. Such delays by the United States profoundly disrupt international lawmaking. A future "best practice" would be to ratify a treaty promptly after giving it due examination and discussion. This treaty, completed in 1948, defines genocide to include "acts committed with intent to destroy, in whole or in part, a national, ethnical, racial or religious group" by "(a) killing members of the group; (b) causing serious bodily or mental harm to members of the group; (c) deliberately inflicting on the group conditions of life calculated to bring about its physical destruction in whole or in part; (d) imposing measures intended to prevent births within the group; and (e) forcibly transferring children of the group to another group."[48] In addition to genocide itself, other illegal acts include "conspiracy to commit genocide; . . . public incitement to commit genocide; [any] attempt to commit genocide; [and] complicity in genocide."[49] Why

---

[47] Convention on the Prevention and Punishment of the Crime of Genocide, Article 1. It was adopted by the UN General Assembly, December 9, 1948, General Assembly Resolution 260. The Convention entered into force on January 12, 1951. https://www.un.org/en/genocideprevention/documents/atrocity-crimes/Doc.1_Convention%20on%20the%20Prevention%20and%20Punishment%20of%20the%20Crime%20of%20Genocide.pdf

[48] Convention on the Prevention and Punishment of Genocide, Article 2. https://www.un.org/en/genocideprevention/documents/atrocity-crimes/Doc.1_Convention%20on%20the%20Prevention%20and%20Punishment%20of%20the%20Crime%20of%20Genocide.pdf .

[49] Convention on the Prevention and Punishment of Genocide, Article 3.

should the United States have waited for 38 years to approve such treaty prohibitions, especially when there is no other global legislative process available for lawmaking? It is worth learning from this experience that, since the belated US ratification in 1986, no harms have come to US sovereignty as conservatives feared. Nonetheless, the United States continues to this day to oppose additional efforts to develop more effective laws for enforcing genocide prevention.

Another desirable lawmaking practice is for the United States to implement fully any treaty that it ratifies, because, as the Constitution specifies, it "shall be the supreme law of the land."[50] Yet recognizing this brings up another negative experience with this treaty, which the United States has not taken very seriously or done a good job of implementing, especially when it comes to the duty to prevent genocide elsewhere. When genocide began in Rwanda in 1994, State Department officials did not want to use the "g" word to describe events there, because of reluctance to heed the obligation to stop the violence if it were called "genocide." President Clinton in a 1998 visit to Rwanda delivered what later became known as the Clinton apology, in which he acknowledged US failure to respond to the Rwandan genocide. At the time, UN peacekeepers were present in Rwanda and almost certainly could have stopped it quickly if the Security Council had changed the peacekeepers' mandate to protecting people fleeing genocide. Instead, the United States and Belgium wanted UN forces not to get involved, even though they probably could have saved hundreds of thousands of human lives.

Another learning is that although the United States did not implement the Genocide Convention in Rwanda, it *could* have. It could have helped halt genocide without violating its national interests. But to do that, it would have needed to give a bit more weight to the *human* interest. The *national* interest, as interpreted by political realists, does not pay attention to much beyond the power-maximizing calculations associated with national interest. No US power was lost in ignoring genocide, some might argue. Yet in this case, the lawmaking process was well aligned with the human interest or, empirical realists would argue, the enlightened, long-range national interest. If the United States had exerted lawmaking leadership in implementing this treaty, and if it had not turned a nearly blind eye to genocide elsewhere, the world probably could have arrived at a better place by now, saved hundreds of thousands of lives in several countries, and made compliance with this particular international law more nearly universal.

It is fair to say that the United States has turned down many invitations by human rights groups and progressive states to advance international judicial enforcement, especially by the ICC, of the prohibitions of crimes against humanity, war crimes, and crimes against the peace.[51] If the United States would relinquish its past role of blocking lawmaking aimed at upholding the genocide ban and other human rights, even at times when no significant US interests would have been compromised by supporting

---

[50] Convention on the Prevention and Punishment of Genocide, Article VI, section 2.
[51] See Johansen, "International Criminal Court," 301–331.

lawmaking, it could, with like-minded governments, build robust legal measures to halt mass murder, encourage all other states to respect the law, and decrease the likelihood that many states or non-state actors would feel they might benefit by taking up armed conflict against civilians, regardless of their identities.

In a case notably different from and more challenging than Rwandan genocide, some conjecture about what might have occurred if the United States had tried a law-enforcement approach in Syria, rather than a war-fighting strategy, might be instructive. Can such a case offer insight into future lawmaking? The unrest began there in 2011 when nonviolent protestors against Syria's president Bashar al-Assad's government succeeded in mobilizing large numbers of people for political reform. Because they were violently attacked by Assad's security forces, some protestors decided to take up arms to protect themselves from his violence against peaceful protest. Later a full-scale civil war resulted, with more than 400,000 people killed, over half civilians,[52] vast areas of Syrian cities and countryside destroyed, more than 12 million refugees and displaced persons driven from their homes, and a half dozen regional and global powers, including Russia and the United States, drawn into the conflict.

The abject failure of all efforts by the United States and the world community to end senseless slaughter in Syria for more than nine years should motivate policymakers to try a different approach emphasizing some insights from this peacebuilding analysis. The arguments below are not a blueprint, but they do illustrate how human security thinking might actually result in more U.S. security. Such initiatives, even in the absence of full success, seem likely to produce a less disastrous outcome than what has transpired in Syria with a war-fighting strategy, and it would blaze a path that could hold more promise in future conflicts, including some lawmaking precedents. Such an alternative approach might consider the following suggestions.

First, choose principles to follow, not sides to oppose. Opposing a given leader ushers in problematic consequences because no political side is perfect, and the allies of the side that the United States might oppose, whether in that country or elsewhere, usually resent U.S. opposition. To be specific, the official US diplomatic slogan was for many years, "Assad must go." Probably this should have never been voiced, even though the value position behind it made sense. Assad was indeed a poor leader and probably guilty of many war crimes and crimes against humanity. Nonetheless, the anti-Assad slogan could have been replaced with a less contested and politicized principle, "the killing must stop."

This suggests the second guideline: Uphold a desirable principle such as the long-standing law of civilian immunity—the rule that no non-combatants should ever be targeted, even in war. That should have been and in the future should be the guiding

---

[52] Some estimates have been as high as 500,000. See Associated Press, "Timeline of the Syrian Conflict as It Enters Its 8th Year," March 15, 2018, https://apnews.com/792a0bd7dd6a4006a78287f170165408; Council on Foreign Relations, *Global Conflict Tracker*, https://www.cfr.org/global-conflict-tracker/conflict/civil-war-syria, accessed December 11, 2020; Statista, "The Syrian Civil War—Statistics & Facts," November 20, 2020, https://www.statista.com/topics/4216/the-syrian-civil-war/.

principle for policy. Then the United States, its allies, and the United Nations could clarify that the overriding goal of the international community is not to advance or undermine the political power of one side or another in Syria or anywhere. The effort to avoid taking sides among warring parties should not diminish the insistence on no killing of civilians by any and all sides. Instead of jockeying for power advantages among numerous imperfect Syrian factions at war, all external governments should insist on no killing of non-combatants and ensure that violence against civilians gets documented and prosecuted to the full extent of the law as soon as that becomes possible, whether the wrongdoers are one's friends or not.

Third, it is reasonable to acknowledge publicly that one's overall political goal, after stopping the killing, is to enable a fair and law-abiding leadership to govern Syria. As soon as possible, conversations might begin among all interested parties to discuss how to reconstruct life fairly in Syria. Instead of struggling to identify friends or enemies in the complicated conflict, simply make it clear that any person, friend or foe, who kills innocent civilians should be prosecuted according to existing laws and if convicted, should be barred from ever holding public office again.

Fourth, after clarifying the fundamental change in goals, the international community should create safe humanitarian corridors where all those people fleeing violence may live safely and securely until war ends. These could have been in northern Syria or beyond Syria but as near as possible while being far enough away from fighting to be secure. In early 2014, Senator Tim Kaine recommended that the United States sponsor a UN resolution to establish a humanitarian area in northern Syria to which any Syrians could go if they were fleeing violence, persecution, starvation, ISIS, the Taliban, Assad, or any other perpetrator. They could stay there in safety, protected by the international community until a political solution to the conflict could be negotiated.[53] If soldiers in the conflict become weary of fighting, they too could be allowed to move to a humanitarian corridor as long as they disarmed and would not return to battle. Of course, no arms could be allowed within humanitarian corridors. They must not become staging grounds for returning to combat.

Fifth, the international community should strictly monitor all Syrian borders and cut off the inflow of war material for all parties. If any Syrian factions were to be fearful of the consequences of stopping the importation of war material, they could consider leaving the country or demobilizing until normalcy returns. Empirical studies indicate that economic sanctions often help shorten wars,[54] but weak enforcement diminishes the effectiveness of sanctions,[55] underscoring the importance of the international community's buttressing its collective enforcement capabilities.

Without the inflow of new arms, ammunition, fuel, and spare parts, violence should decline. Cutting off war supplies to all parties would clarify that the international

---

[53] "Senator Tim Kaine Questions Legality of US Led Airstrikes," *All Things Considered with Michel Martin*, NPR, April 14, 2018.

[54] Human Security Report Project, *Causes of Peace*.

[55] Human Security Report Project, *Causes of Peace*.

community is insisting that the fighting stop. Of course, equal constraints on all actors do not produce equal consequences. A government that has better supplies would not be handicapped as much as a rebel group without an extensive weapons inventory. Still, if government officials used their "violence advantage" to harm civilians after rebels ran out of ammunition to protect themselves, they would undermine their own legitimacy and lose any claim to exercise a governing role in the future. Rebels who felt threatened by an arms embargo could move to humanitarian corridors if they demobilized. Any violations of civilian immunity while fighting diminishes would be closely monitored so as to hold perpetrators responsible for illegal acts.

Insofar as possible, the international community should have prevented exports from Syria from providing income to finance fighting. If oil exports were to be allowed at all by the international community, a substantial portion of income from those might be used to pay the costs of caring for people in the humanitarian corridors.

Sixth, after the fighting stops, all parties with stakes in the outcome, both inside and outside the country, should be included in the conversations about how to establish government to protect all people's rights in Syria. Those who may have disarmed, demobilized, and left the country would not have forfeited any of their claims. In some cases, they may be better able to advance their cause after having stopped their fighting rather than by continuing. In addition, until negotiations occur, no one can know the arrangements that will establish a fair and stable social order. Conversations about the future should be administered by the international community, based on fair representation for all interested parties, including those victimized during the conflict. No doubt some power-sharing among internal parties would be established and maintained with the help of external facilitators, monitors, and guarantors. During the years of transition, tranquility could be maintained by completely reconstituted civilian police drawn as much as possible from communities in which they worked, with help of international training and monitoring, collaborating as cooperatively as possible with local people from Syrian communities.

Seventh, insofar as possible, the costs of the international operations should be repaid by establishing a reasonable fee on the future extraction of natural resources within the country and on exports, so that repayment might occur over a sufficient number of years to recover the costs without strangling the renewing economy.

Eighth, any people whom the International Criminal Court indicted, based on evidence gathered before, during, and after the violent conflict, should be given a fair trial as soon as possible. If feasible and fair, the ICC should arrange for at least some trial venues to be in Syria or nearby. Because there is no statute of limitation for these crimes, the trials could occur at any time. Any persons who would shield from arrest someone who has been indicted could also be indicted, apprehended, and tried as an accomplice. Following a precedent used while negotiating the Dayton Accords for the former Yugoslavia, any person indicted by the ICC should not be allowed to participate in negotiations on the future of Syria, unless he or she has offered a credible agreement to face trial for alleged crimes. Agreeing to stand trial would entitle accused persons to participate in negotiations unless and until they were convicted. There is no capital punishment for those convicted by the ICC, so the accused could voluntarily accept trial without thinking that they might be condemning themselves to death.

Anyone convicted of serious crimes should be prohibited from ever holding political or military office again and from possessing or using weapons or engaging in violence against others at any time. Those convicted might engage in civilian public service if they chose to redeem themselves during the remainder of their lives.[56]

Such intrusive international intervention in Syrian national life would be justified because of strong evidence of recurring gross violations of fundamental human rights. The continuing slaughter and destruction, month after month, might legitimately employ the international community's "responsibility to protect." This widely endorsed development in the 1990s, which declared that sovereignty is not unconditional, specifies that a sovereign government loses its entitlement to govern without external intervention if it lacks the capacity or willingness to uphold core human rights. The international community would be exercising its responsibility to protect while emphasizing legal, economic, political, and humanitarian means.

Many countries, perhaps even most, could join in these proposed initiatives. Whether some national governments who supported Assad or ISIS would join the proposed effort is unclear, but the direction suggested here might seem acceptable even to them, compared to the slogan "Assad must go," indefinite bloodletting, and massive destruction. In supporting such initiatives, they would not be joining an international campaign to depose their ally. They could honestly say they are merely joining a campaign to stop killing that violates the principle of civilian immunity, a principle that people of all political systems and religious traditions have endorsed.

In any case, policies aimed at the ends proposed here, even if not fully successful, would not have been likely to have produced a *worse* outcome than has occurred from a strategy of choosing sides and war-fighting, which led the United States to depart from preferred principles and lose standing throughout the Middle East. The consequences of past policies prolonged war-fighting in Syria and caused truly incalculable, irreversible destruction of life, productivity, and culture in Syria. It also caused immigration pressures on Europe that led Britain to leave the European Union and the EU to face nearly insurmountable internal problems. Moreover, it stimulated the growth of racial and religious fears and cultural prejudice and the rise of lasting anti-democratic right-wing divisive influences in democracies in Europe, the United States, and elsewhere. Compared to the admittedly imperfect alternative that empirical realists might have suggested above, the actual outcomes have not been at all positive.[57]

If the conduct of a leader accused of mass murder could be investigated by the ICC and evidence were found to indict him, as in the case of Sudanese president Omar

---

[56] In the Colombian peace agreement, public service was offered to some belligerents in place of prison time.
[57] Even if the proposed approach would not have succeeded in achieving conflict transformation goals in the short run, it would have made a significant difference in furthering education of people and governments throughout the world that killing civilians is illegal and immoral and that ways and means of dampening violent conflict are available and can be used in the future.

Al-Bashir, the international community should insist that the indicted appear in court to face trial. At first glance, to replace the motto, "Assad must go," with insistence that "Assad must face the court" does not seem much different. But it is. As time passes and other governments repeatedly insist that he face trial, his situation begins to be viewed differently by people, perhaps even by some allies, compared to hearing the drumbeat of an adversary saying that he must abdicate. Asking the accused to face trial is not announcing preemptively and condescendingly that he must leave office. In asking him to face trial, one is repeatedly pointing at his conduct, not his person. Even if fighting continues in the short run, he may be less likely to engage in mass murder if there is any possibility that he ever might face trial for crimes for which there is no statute of limitations for anyone on Earth.

Asking a person to face trial communicates a different message than demanding that a person leave office because in the latter request an adversary has already judged him or her to be a totally unacceptable person. To ask a person to show up in court shifts the emphasis to enabling the accused to listen to his or her accusers and to artic-ulate a defense. It puts the spotlight on alleged misconduct and truth-telling. If one is too weak to show up for that, and many authoritarian leaders are, one's legitimacy is weakened in a way that demanding that a person leave office does not. That outcome may be the most that one can achieve without a trial, but even that is a normative gain for the international system. In any case, the emphasis on alleged misconduct does not immediately dismiss one's personhood, and it is the person's misdeeds that one cares about most in international relations.

To a small degree, the proposed legal emphasis might also call the bluff of the accused's allies who claim that the accused leader is a good head of government. If they are confident of innocence, they should not object to a fair trial. If they are not confi-dent, can they claim virtue in being the leader's uncritical ally? Of course, Russia and other Syrian allies may have been unlikely to agree with the preceding proposal, but it remains a serious aspirational standard that places negative weight on their rejection of the proposal. Some law-abiding states can and should seek to uphold it even if all states are not willing.

If the UN Security Council could not agree on a vote to authorize protecting civil-ians from being harmed by illegal government violence, then law-respecting UN mem-bers should coalesce to uphold principled conduct against killing unarmed protestors. Those countries in favor of multilateral law enforcement could resurrect the Acheson Plan or the Uniting for Peace Resolution which authorize General Assembly action when the Security Council is paralyzed by a veto.[58] Obtaining multilateral authoriza-tion is important to differentiate it from unilateral or national interventions.

---

[58] See United Nations General Assembly Resolution A/RES/377(V), November 3, 1950; Hans Kelsen, "Is the Acheson Plan Constitutional?" *The Western Political Quarterly* 3, no. 4 (1950): 512–527, doi:10.2307/442511; Rebecca Barber, "Uniting for Peace Not Aggression: Responding to Chemical Weapons in Syria Without Breaking the Law," *Journal of Conflict and Security Law* 24, no. 1 (2019): 71–110; Jean Krasno and Mitushi Das, "The Uniting for Peace Resolution and Other Ways of Circumventing the Authority of the Security Council," in *The UN Security Council and the Politics of International Authority*, ed. Bruce

Regardless of how one feels about the wisdom of the Syrian war-fighting, the United States and the international community need to give more attention to (1) constraining those indicted by the ICC but who have not faced trial and (2) incentivizing ways to bring the indicted into court. Incentives could be both positive and negative. Financial benefits could be given to the country of residence of an indicted person if it arrested the indicted and facilitated his or her being brought to trial. Monetary fines, travel restrictions, and smart economic sanctions could be imposed after an indictment until the accused appeared in court. Some such measures could be applied both to the accused and to any governments that may shield the accused from arrest and trial.

Although the ICC must reserve its limited time and personnel to the most influential of the accused, the international community also needs to devise ways and means of constraining, rewarding, or penalizing more ordinary accomplices of official misconduct until they face trial. The likelihood of being called to accountability could deter people in lower ranks of military operations from carrying out a leader's orders for genocide, ethnic cleansing, or other crimes. Trials for the accused should optimally be conducted in the country where the crimes were committed, perhaps with a hybrid tribunal including both international and national judges.

As trials become more familiar, the deterring impact of the law is likely to increase[59] because there is no statute of limitations for these crimes. A German court in 2021 convicted a former Syrian secret police officer of aiding and abetting crimes against humanity because nearly a decade earlier he had arrested and transported nonviolent protesters in Syria to an interrogation center known for torture. A Syrian lawyer, Anwar al-Bunni, said this conviction, sends "a message to all criminals . . . that the time of impunity is over."[60]

The preceding discussion includes only a few illustrations of many positive proposals that the international community might develop to work more intentionally on both good lawmaking and increasing compliance of leaders as individuals with existing international laws through more powerful, purposeful, yet primarily non-military means.

Cronin and Ian Hurd (London: Routledge, 2008), 173–195; Michael Ramsden, "'Uniting for Peace' and Humanitarian Intervention: The Authorizing Function of the U.N. General Assembly," *Washington International Law Journal* 25 (2016): 267–304; Dominik Zaum, "The Security Council, the General Assembly and War: The Uniting for Peace Resolution," in *The United Nations Security Council and War: The Evolution of Thought and Practice since 1945*, ed. Vaughan Lowe, Adam Roberts, Jennifer Welsh, and Dominik Zaum (Oxford: Oxford University Press, 2008), 154–174.

[59] Kim and Sikkink, "Explaining the Deterrence Effect," 939–963.
[60] Ben Hubbard, "German Court Convicts Former Syrian Official of Crimes Against Humanity," *New York Times*, February 24, 2021, https://www.nytimes.com/2021/02/24/world/middleeast/germany-court-syria-war-crimes.html.

7.1.4 Curtailing Terrorism

In a fourth area of lawmaking, a new strategic direction could curtail terrorist acts more effectively. Although many people believe that "killing bad guys" must surely be part of the strategy for defeating terrorism, empirical studies of 648 cases of terrorism show that increasing violence against insurgent groups does not work in the long term.[61] These studies indicate that military force is generally not effective against terrorists.[62] US officials will be unlikely to succeed in stopping future terrorist misdeeds by waging war in other people's countries or by launching drone attacks in countries with which the United States is at peace, because every US attack motivates additional people to hate the United States and to take the place of each terrorist killed.[63] Killing terrorists does not kill terrorism. Too often war on terrorism simply swells the sum of terror.

For that reason, to rely primarily on military means to counter terrorism will usually result in frustrated efforts not only because military combat seldom slows recruitment, but also because it cannot stop violent extremists from slipping through national territorial cracks. Terrorists build their strength through oppositional ideologies rather than through military might, and these ideologies flourish amid (1) US military presences in their regions of the world and (2) US alliances with oppressive national governments in those regions. US drone strikes and forward-based military forces both give life to extremist ideologies and create new terrorists to replace the old.[64]

Yet making war on terrorism seems an easy solution for US officials to embrace, perhaps too easy given all the arms US officials hold at the ready. That strategy does not encourage doing the hard work of looking closely at the underlying causes of extremism and of one's own connection, however remote, with its origins. As Robert Pape's research on terrorism shows, US forward-based military strategies have actually caused *losses* in US security. His findings confirm that nearly all suicide bombings against the United States in the Middle East and south Asia have had a similar purpose: to compel the withdrawal of external military forces from territory that the terrorists consider their homelands. US citizens may too easily forget that there were no suicide bombing campaigns in Iraq, Afghanistan, or Pakistan before US and other Western military forces moved into the Middle East and Central Asia. The Pakistani Taliban arose after the United States pressed the Pakistani army to invade the tribal regions of Northwest Pakistan to help with the US war in Afghanistan. There was no Al-Qaeda in Iraq before the US invasion in 2003 and overthrow of the Iraqi government.[65]

---

[61] Human Security Report, *Causes of Peace*.

[62] Seth G. Jones and Martin C. Libicki, *How Terrorist Groups End: Lessons for Countering al Qa'ida* (Santa Monica, CA: Rand Corporation, 2008), iii, rand.org/content/dam/rand/pubs/researchbriefs/2008/RAND_RB9351.pdf; Bradford Ian Stapleton, "The Problem with the Light Footprint: Shifting Tactics in Lieu of Strategy," *Policy Analysis* 792 (Washington, DC: Cato Institute, 2016).

[63] Schwartzberg, *Transforming*, 262.

[64] Feldman and Pape, *Cutting the Fuse*; Schwartzberg, *Transforming*, 262.

[65] Pape, *Dying to Win*.

If tit-for-tat violence inflicted by a government against opponents using terror tactics actually provided more security and peace, would not Israel be one of the most secure and peaceful places in the world? Understandable though the desire for revenge may be among some US citizens and members of Congress after suffering horrendous violence and even the glorification of killing by terrorists, military combat against an ism often is counter-productive. Despite all the understandable US reasons given for using violence against terrorism, that violence will be viewed as its own form of terrorism by those sympathetic to the goals of the people targeted, even if they disagree with terrorists' means. To do anything to generate this group's increased support for terrorists is self-defeating because those who sympathize with some of the terrorists' complaints, even while rejecting their means, are needed in the effort to constrain terrorists' acts. Without this group's voluntary cooperation, terrorism cannot be effectively monitored or discredited within its own culture.

Four guidelines are helpful in designing effective policies for reducing terrorist acts and, eventually, terrorism. First, public authorities should try to isolate acts of terror and separate unacceptable deeds, which must be opposed, from making public judgments about the doers' motivations and the people who may accept some of their goals but not their means. One reason that violence against "terrorism" generally misses the mark of diminishing terror is that almost any ism contains at least one or two rhetorical goals calling for justice or for a fairer economic deal, which many people find appealing even if they do not favor terrorist violence. There is no point pushing those two groups together, no reason for US war-fighting against many people in the Middle East or south Asia who do not engage in violent acts themselves, even though they endorse political goals or governments that differ from US preferences. The nuanced understanding needed here is that any person who is about to embark on terrorist acts must, insofar as possible, be denied weapons and explosives, restrained, discredited, disempowered, and, if unlawful deeds are done, held accountable. But this does not mean prolonged war-fighting against any ism. It is difficult to kill an ism with violent means when one is fighting in a different culture containing many people unsympathetic to US military goals. A more effective approach would adopt a gradualist, non-military strategy aiming to eradicate terrorism as a long-term goal, not on the battlefield, but through reducing the risk of terrorist attack through more cooperative intelligence, effective law enforcement, and, as indicated next, removal of many motivators for terrorist recruitment and incitement.

Second, it is useful to identify the underlying causes of terror and address those. That will be far more effective than military combat. Secretary-General Kofi Annan once commented, "People who are desperate and in despair become easy recruits for terrorist organisations."[66] Why are people desperate?[67] Most studies conclude that people become willing to commit terrorist acts when

---

[66] United Nations Secretary-General Kofi Annan, "Statement by UN Secretary-General Kofi Annan," September 19, 2001, www.un.org/News/Press/docs/2001/sgsm7964.doc.htm.

[67] For analysis of the complexities, see Martha Crenshaw and Gary LaFree, *Countering Terrorism* (Washington, D.C.: Bookings Institution Press, 2017).

(1) they believe that negotiations with their opponents over political differences are simply unavailable to them because opponents are immovable or will not talk seriously with them;

(2) they believe that nonviolent means are not available to address their grievances;

(3) they believe that further inaction by themselves will threaten their way of life forever and suffocate themselves and their families;

(4) they feel some divine sanction for their actions because of the extreme plight in which they find themselves; and

(5) they believe that those they oppose are supported by people who are culturally, economically, and religiously different from them and who think of themselves as superior to them.

Those opposed to terrorist acts can do something about some or all of these reasons, thereby reducing the number and intensity of desperate, despairing people. This strategy also means listening to grievances voiced by those who may support terrorists' political goals but not their terrorist acts, while trying to ensure that they do not evolve toward engaging in acts of terror themselves. Insofar as they have legitimate claims, these should be addressed effectively. Two effective antidotes are to work for good public education for all children and to ensure good employment opportunities for those who leave school.

Terrorists who are arrested should receive fair trials rather than summary execution in order to discredit their misdeeds rather than their personhood. Whereas violence against terrorism often spreads it, addressing its causes makes terrorist acts seem less "necessary" to those in a position culturally to enable or disable them. In addition to reducing the causes of people's willingness to commit violence, attention should be given to limiting the availability of means to inflict violence by developing international controls on arms, explosives, training, and communications.

Third, US officials and local authorities should address those who threaten or commit illegal acts through support for more effective enforcement of international and domestic laws,[68] especially those prohibiting violence against civilians. More effective enforcement of laws against terror would benefit a large majority of people in every country and hold wrongdoers accountable without attacking all of their political goals or cultural symbols. Legal processes are better than war at discrediting those advocating violence. Law also can help to restrain finances and preparations for terrorist acts.

Far more could be done to coordinate the combined intelligence and law enforcement capabilities of every state of the world, or at least of all those willing to cooperate, to address terrorist acts as criminal acts rather than as reason to do war-fighting, which often drives borderline allies into the shadows. Research shows that police forces are more effective in dampening terrorism than militaries.[69] Retraining and

---

[68] Schwartzberg, Transforming, 262–263.
[69] Jones and Libicki, How Terrorist Groups End, i–iii.

remodeling existing international police, intelligence, and judicial systems and creating more collaborative worldwide enforcement institutions, including among agencies in Europe and North America, could build cooperation that would produce long-term enforcement benefits in other areas as well. A focus on law enforcement also reminds governments that heavy-handed enforcement is generally less needed if social justice, good public education, and job opportunities are available in all societies.

Fourth, the United States and other governments should exercise increased care not to commit any violence themselves that might be perceived to be acts of terror initiated by a government, because such acts, even though conducted by a state, are quickly construed by adversaries to justify their terrorist attacks against those they oppose. If and when terrorist groups do stop their bloody work, it is usually because their leaders are brought into legitimate political processes or they fade away because of effective intelligence and police work that render their initiatives futile. Only about 7 percent of terrorist groups end as a result of military action against them.[70] The best antidotes to terror are effective police enforcement combined with programs to build a just society with opportunities for youth and insistence throughout the society that all human life be respected. If more opportunities become available for those who previously saw themselves as being cut out of reasonable prospects to build what they see as a more positive future, recruitment will decline. If parts of that image of the future seem to be misguided, such as denying women's basic rights, the international community should not enable those parts. On the contrary, including more well-trained women in police forces, for example, generally increases their effectiveness against domestic terrorism.[71]

International lawmaking also could benefit from focusing more heavily on countering terrorist supporters' use of modern technology to form networks across borders and their success in recruitment. The United States and the United Nations need to develop skills in working hand in hand across borders, with nearly every society, to obtain intelligence,[72] restrict instruments of violence, and conduct police enforcement of existing laws against terrorist acts. Worldwide collaboration also is needed to enhance unresponsive governments and to dry up the swamps of hatred, polarization, and lack of opportunity that give rise to terrorism. These are primarily functions to be addressed through global governing, not military power.

Research indicates that the most effective way to reduce terror in the long run is to address the human security needs of people living in severe insecurity. The UN General Assembly has noted that "the promotion and protection of human rights for all and the

---

[70] Of those integrated into political processes, 83 percent become legislators. Jones and Libicki, *How Terrorist Groups End*, iii.

[71] For example, women are more likely to report gender-based violence to women police officers. Policewomen are also more likely to de-escalate conflict than male colleagues. Jacqueline O'Neill and Jarad Ary, "Allies and Assets: Strengthening DDR and SSR Through Women's Inclusion," in *Monopoly of Force: The Nexus of DDR and SSR* (Washington, DC: National Defense University, 2010).

[72] The UN High-Level Panel concluded: "Cooperation in the sharing of intelligence by States is essential for stopping terrorism." *A More Secure World*, 21, para 25.

rule of law are essential to the fight against terrorism."[73] Moreover, "effective counter-terrorism measures and the protection of human rights are not conflicting goals, but are complementary and mutually reinforcing."[74] The UN High-Level Panel called for addressing the causes of terrorism, including "promoting social and political rights," encouraging "the rule of law and democratic reform; working to end occupations and address major political grievances; combating organized crime; reducing poverty and unemployment; and stopping State collapse."[75] To reduce terrorism, there is urgent need for a worldwide political program, which would draw on law and international police enforcement, with positive social goals that go beyond the national security of any single society, to reach out and nurture life for all people regardless of race, class, nationality, or religion—something to which like-minded people throughout the world can commit themselves while opposing terror and expressing solidarity with other well-intentioned people everywhere.[76]

7.2 EXPANDING GLOBAL MONITORING

Lawmaking without monitoring people's conduct is wasted motion of little consequence. But lawmaking coupled with accurate information about all countries' and people's conduct, especially when it poses threats of violence or violates the basic rights of others, can be supremely valuable new architecture for holding governments and non-state actors accountable to agreed-on norms. An opportunity to achieve this could be realized by creating a permanent international monitoring agency equipped with satellite and drone surveillance capabilities for multiple UN and other global governance applications.[77] Such an agency could, for example, strengthen existing and expanded monitoring functions for the International Atomic Energy Agency and implementation of the CTBT and thereby help to deter illegal weapons tests. It could supply photographic evidence to the International Criminal Court—whether investigating genocide, crimes against humanity, or war crimes, whether crimes are committed by governments or by those fighting against them. Such an agency is technologically possible, already previewed by private aerial and satellite surveillance and national systems of satellite and drone surveillance, and urgently needed to give global

---

[73] UN General Assembly, "Declaration on the Right to Peace," Resolution A/71/189, February 2, 2017.

[74] UN General Assembly, "Declaration on the Right to Peace," Resolution A/C.3/71/L.29, October 31, 2016 .

[75] The UN High-Level Panel, *A More Secure World*, 46, para 148; Glasius and Kaldor, "A Human Security Vision," 10.

[76] UN Secretary-General Kofi Annan recommended such a program following the UN High-Level Panel Report, *In Larger Freedom: Towards Development, Security and Human Rights for All*, Report of the Secretary-General, UN Doc. A/59/2005 & annex (2005), 58, para 6(h), http://www.un.org/largerfreedom/contents.htm.

[77] France first proposed an international satellite monitoring agency in 1978. United Nations Special Session of the General Assembly Devoted to Disarmament, "Study on the Implications of Establishing an International Satellite Monitoring Agency," UN Document no. A/AC 206/14 (New York: United Nations, 1981).

public authority the ability to know in real time what is happening that may require the international community's attention. It is possible that a global public monitoring agency could be financed in part by enabling private corporations or other agencies to access aerial photography useful in their activities in return for fees paid to the global agency.[78]

To combine expanded monitoring capability with new lawmaking to assist non-proliferation initiatives, the IAEA could be authorized to expand its oversight beyond non-weapons states to include all weapons states so that every major nuclear installation on Earth, without exception, would be monitored to ensure that all countries' nuclear facilities meet both safety and security standards. At present, the IAEA's 168 members mainly support work that the United States and other nuclear-weapons countries have specified to ensure that "horizontal"[79] weapons proliferation cannot proceed undetected and hopefully will not occur. It performs many vital functions to dampen negative forms of nuclear weapons competition.[80] But the agency does not inspect the facilities of the existing nuclear weapons countries and it does little to slow "vertical" proliferation of weapons by the nuclear weapons countries themselves. It would be useful to expand IAEA inspection to cover all nuclear-armed countries' nuclear installations as well as all nuclear reactors of states without nuclear weapons.

The move to monitor *all* countries could send a clear signal that the nuclear weapons countries have decided to get serious about non-proliferation and nuclear arms reduction. This added inspection would not threaten US or other countries' fundamental security. More comprehensive monitoring, such as proposed here, will be absolutely necessary someday for people to be secure. Why not begin it now and get immediate benefits in dampening the risks of further proliferation of both horizontal and vertical varieties?

Another example of how to turn arms control into system-changing legalization processes and institutions exists in the monitoring agency to watch over a comprehensive ban on nuclear testing. Somewhat surprisingly, this agency has been established while signatories wait for foot-dragging governments to ratify the Comprehensive Nuclear-Test-Ban Treaty, which would enable it to become fully operational. This is a treaty that most US presidents, excluding Donald Trump, have favored, but that conservatives in the US Senate have refused to ratify, preventing it from becoming legally binding. The Preparatory Commission for the Comprehensive Nuclear-Test-Ban Treaty Organization is based in Vienna, Austria, and reports its findings to the

[78] For suggestions on how to govern dangerous technologies, see Elizabeth Turpen, "Achieving Nonproliferation Goals: Moving From Denial to Technology Governance," June 10, 2009, Policy Analysis Brief for the Stanley Foundation (Washington, DC: Stimson Center, 2009), https://www.stimson.org/2009/achieving-nonproliferation-goals-moving-denial-technology-governance/.

[79] "Horizontal nuclear proliferation" is the spread of nuclear weapons to additional countries; "vertical proliferation" occurs when existing nuclear weapons countries develop new nuclear weapons. See section 4.3.

[80] Mark Hibbs, "Why Does the IAEA Do What It Does?" Carnegie Endowment for International Peace, https://carnegieendowment.org/2017/11/06/why-does-iaea-do-what-it-does-pub-74689.

Comprehensive Nuclear-Test-Ban Treaty Organization, established by the states that signed the treaty in 1996. Its main purpose is to establish a global verification institution to ensure that all nuclear tests are detected.

This international monitoring system will, when completed, consist of 337 facilities worldwide to watch the entire planet for signs of nuclear explosions. The system will include 50 primary and 120 auxiliary seismic monitoring stations; 11 hydro acoustic stations detecting acoustic waves in the oceans; 60 infrasound stations to detect very low-frequency sound waves in the atmosphere; 80 radionuclide stations using air samplers to detect radioactive particles released from atmospheric explosions and/or vented from underground or underwater explosions; and 6 radionuclide laboratories for analysis of samples from the radionuclide stations. More than 80 percent of these are already running.[81] This striking example demonstrates how easily major strides can be taken when the nuclear-weapons countries want them and how thoroughgoing and effective international governance can be even in the sunset years of international anarchy. Even though the treaty still lacks US ratification, establishing the monitoring capability puts all countries on notice that they will be unlikely to conduct tests clandestinely, a deterrent to making the attempt.

7.3 ESTABLISHING MULTINATIONAL POLICE ENFORCEMENT

No institutional innovation is likely to be more important for constraining violence than to establish a United Nations emergency police force or peace service from among individuals who might volunteer from any nation.[82] They could be carefully selected, highly trained, wisely commanded, and ready to deploy on a moment's notice to protect people threatened by mass murder.[83] This would meet the compelling need for the UN to have an international police mode of law enforcement. An emergency constabulary service could move quickly to stop ethnic cleansing, crimes against humanity, and

---

[81] Sonya Pillay, "Bringing the CTBT into Force: Looking Back at The 2011 Article XIV Conference," *VERTIC*, http://www.vertic.org/media/assets/Publications/VB16.pdf.

[82] An earlier version of ideas in this section appeared in Robert C. Johansen, "Proposal for a United Nations Emergency Peace Service," in *A United Nations Emergency Peace Service*, ed. Robert C. Johansen (New York: Global Action to Prevent War, Nuclear Age Peace Foundation, and World Federalist Movement, 2006), 21–41. See also Schwartzberg, *Transforming*, 225–271; Government of Canada, *Towards a Rapid Deployment Capability for the United Nations: Report by the Government of Canada* (1995), https://s3.amazonaws.com/piquant/Langille/Towards+a+Rapid+Reaction+Capability+for+the+Unite d+Nations.pdf; Brian Urquhart and Francois Heisbourg, "Prospects for a Rapid Response Capability," in *Peacemaking and Peacekeeping for the New Century*, ed. Olara Otunnu and Michael W. Doyle (Lanham, MD: Rowman & Littlefield, 1998), 189–199; William J. Durch, *Discussion of the Report of the Panel on UN Peace Operations: The Brahimi Report* (Washington, DC: Stimson Center, 2000). Weiss and Thakur also concluded that "some sort of an international ready-reaction capability will have to be established." Weiss and Thakur, *Global Governance and the UN*, 88.

[83] See Johansen, "Proposal for a United Nations Emergency Peace Service," 21–41; Schwartzberg, *Transforming*, 225–271; Government of Canada, *Towards a Rapid Deployment Capability for the United Nations*; Urquhart and Heisbourg, "Prospects for a Rapid Response Capability"; Durch, *Discussion of the Report of the Panel on UN Peace Operations*.

genocide; to protect civilians in humanitarian corridors when fleeing war or mass murder; and to prevent small-scale acts of aggression. Nearly all UN secretaries-general since the beginning of the UN have voiced the need to establish such a service.[84]

If such a service had been established at the origin of the United Nations, or at least at the end of the Cold War, it could have prevented some of the atrocities that have killed or wounded millions of civilians, forced tens of millions to become refugees or displaced persons, destroyed economies, and cost billions of dollars in needless destruction and required humanitarian assistance. Such a service could have prevented catastrophes such as happened in Rwanda in 1994. Most of that killing could have been prevented with a modest-sized UN peace service if only one had been ready to deploy quickly.[85] Many killings of innocent people in Cambodia, the former Yugoslavia, East Timor, Sierra Leone, the Democratic Republic of the Congo, Liberia, Syria, the Sudan, and elsewhere further illustrate what new UN architecture might address with an effective, mobile constabulary capacity.

Of course, such a service would not be a panacea for security problems in general. It would not be large enough for that, but it would be able to complement, not replace, other essential UN peacekeeping efforts. It could provide immediate protection in small crises and serve as an advance group to prepare the way for subsequent additional help, if needed, in larger conflicts. It also could help address extreme pandemic, environmental, and natural disasters in emergencies where other remedies are inadequate for averting major threats to human life.

The proposed UN emergency peace service should be permanent, made up of individually recruited volunteers and based at UN designated sites. It should include mobile field headquarters so it could move to quell an emergency within 24 hours after UN authorization. Because it would be staffed by individuals from around the world and not be made up of military units contributed by any single country's national military services, as are existing UN peacekeeping forces, it would not suffer the handicap of UN members' reluctance to deploy their own national units in dangerous contexts, a reluctance that enabled the Rwandan genocide.

Major independent studies have documented the need for more highly skilled personnel, sensitive to human rights, to be deployed during crises to prevent armed conflict, protect civilians, and enforce the law.[86] Because the proposed service could

---

[84] The need is so obvious that 69 percent of Europeans have said that a "rapid reaction force that can be sent quickly to trouble spots when an international crisis occurs" should be created by the EU in the absence of a UN force.

[85] Canadian Lieutenant-General Roméo Dallaire, serving as commander of UNAMIR, the United Nations peacekeeping force in Rwanda in 1993 and 1994, estimated that a UN force of approximately 5,000 to 10,000 could have stopped the spread of the genocide. See Scott. R. Feil, "Could 5,000 Peacekeepers Have Saved 500,000 Rwandans? Early Intervention Reconsidered," Institute for the Study of Diplomacy, *ISD Reports* (Walsh School of Foreign Service, Georgetown University) 3, no. 2 (April 1997).

[86] See, for example, Robert C. Johansen, "The Future of United Nations Peacekeeping and Enforcement: A Framework for Policymaking," *Global Governance* 2, no. 3 (September–December 1996): 299–333; Stephen P. Kinloch, "Utopian or Pragmatic? A UN Permanent Military Volunteer Force," *International Peacekeeping* 3 (Winter 1996); John G. Heidenrich, *How to Prevent Genocide: A Guide for Policymakers, Scholars and the*

integrate civilian, police, judicial, and military personnel prepared to conduct multiple functions in diverse UN operations, it would not suffer for lack of skills essential to peace operations or from confusion about the chain of command. By providing a wide range of functions, the UN emergency peace service could, for the first time in history, offer a rapid, comprehensive, internationally legitimate response to crisis. Its approximately 20,000 personnel would not fail in their mission due to lack of skills, equipment, experience in resolving conflicts, or gender, national, or religious imbalance. Of course, it would need to be carefully led and monitored to ensure that it did not succumb to enforcement malpractices and human rights violations that too easily have occurred among both UN and national police forces in many different contexts in the past.[87]

A UN police service could also help, from time to time, to re-educate and train domestic police inside countries that have been torn apart by civil war and require reconstituting their police from the ground up to ensure that they play a service rather than a predatory role in their communities. This in itself would contribute to improving human security.

One reason that such a force has never existed during the United Nations' 75-year history, despite the need for it from day one, is that the major powers have not wanted the United Nations to be capable of acting on its own, even though the five permanent members of the Security Council each possess a veto that could block action against their wishes. As a result of this configuration of state power and the resistance to developing a reliable UN enforcement mechanism, the initiative for breathing life into a UN emergency peace service needs to be taken by members of civil society, working with political allies in the UN and the most far-sighted governments.

The creation of a UN emergency peace service should produce enough true benefits to demonstrate to all societies that when it comes to stopping genocide and crimes against humanity, the human interest and national interests are congruent. The proposed UN service could, in limited ways, "teach" the international community how to curtail violence in divided societies, deflect venomous attacks between those of different identities and religious traditions, constrict a culture of impunity by law violators, encourage the concentration of scarce resources on meeting human needs rather than on destruction, and bring an energizing focus to the meaning of human security. It could produce benefits in lives saved, mothers and daughters protected against grievous violations, families still able to live at home, time and money never spent to kill and destroy, tolerance maintained, laws upheld, and communities at peace. By acting

---

Concerned Citizen (Westport, CT: Praeger, 2001); Challenges Project, *Challenges of Peace Operations: Into the 21st Century, Concluding Report* (Stockholm: Elanders Gotab, 2002); William J. Durch, Victoria K. Holt, Caroline R. Earle, and Moira K. Shanahan, *The Brahimi Report and the Future of UN Peace Operations* (Washington, DC: Henry L. Stimson Center Report, 2003); and Government of Canada, *Towards a Rapid Deployment Capability for the United Nations*.

[87] See United Nations Department of Peacekeeping Operations: Department of Field Support, *Guidelines: The Role of United Nations Police in Protection of Civilians: Ref. 2017.12* (New York: United Nations, 2017), 5, 20.

together to build this enforcement architecture, people could enliven that spark of human solidarity that lives, often hidden, within people everywhere on Earth.

After witnessing genocide, nearly everyone promises "Never again." But mass murder has happened again—and yet again. The time to stop it has come, at least in all those instances where the international community could have a reasonable probability of success. The proposed service could save lives and resources while also advancing the rule of law and more effective enforcement against heinous crimes. Although it would take money and leadership with integrity to establish it, it would be a cost-effective instrument for the international community. Finally, people could give real meaning to "never again."

7.4 BEGINNING GLOBAL LEGISLATIVE CONVERSATIONS

The world does not have an effective global legislative process, although some legislative functions occur in piecemeal fashion whenever nations gather to negotiate a treaty and bring it into force. In addition, the International Law Commission encourages the codification and progressive development of international law.[88] Its professional work often stimulates legalization processes. Because custom is also a source of international law, for the United States simply to engage in exemplary behavior by explicitly complying with specific laws gradually "legislates" strengthened rules for all actors in international relations. In addition, international law "can develop through networks and social movements rather than exclusively through institutions or governments."[89] Although social movements, like the outlawing of land-mines, come and go, their written normative legacies often stick around. Although these quasi-legislative methods are useful and need to be enhanced, they are too slow and cumbersome to produce the rules needed now for violence-prevention and environmental health. Additional legislative opportunities need to be designed and constructed.

One way to promote broader legislative conversations across borders than occur through diplomatic channels alone would be to construct a virtual World Democratic Parliamentary Assembly. This could be established almost immediately on the internet if members of the world's democratically elected parliaments would assert their desire to do so.[90] All of the world's democratically elected national legislators could be in frequent contact on line in order to share best practices (e.g., developing desirable national laws that are mutually reinforcing across borders) and to cooperate in addressing global problems by creating a virtual parliament in which they could discuss pressing issues and build transnational political coalitions of legislators. They might discuss, for example, a ban on weapons in space or a tax on carbon emissions

---

[88] UN Charter, Article 13 (1) a.

[89] Ku, "Evolution of International Law," 44.

[90] An earlier version of ideas in this section appeared in Robert C. Johansen, "The E-Parliament: Global Governance to Serve the Human Interest," *Widener Law Review* 13 (2007): 319–427.

or the creation of an intercontinental electrical grid to collect and sell solar-generated energy by moving it from countries with abundant sunshine to countries in short supply. If support from democratically elected legislators from many countries' legislatures could coalesce around some needed international legal innovations, this would greatly speed ILC or treaty-making processes.

To create such a virtual world parliament, all that would be required is to establish an authoritative certification process to identify those who presently are seated in democratically elected national parliaments or congresses throughout the world. They would be eligible to be seated in a virtual chamber to interact on issues of common interest. These legislators, whether members of parliaments or congresses (all referred to here as "MPs"), could pose formal questions to any or all of the world's democratically elected MPs, as well as to prime ministers and presidents, to assess support for an international law under consideration. It would be useful, for example, to know how many would favor legislation to limit their own country's greenhouse gas emissions to a globally equitable level that could prevent global warming from exceeding 2 degrees Celsius. The existence of such an assembly might also constitute an incentive for those in authoritarian societies to encourage democratization in their own country so they eventually could participate. A virtual democratic assembly also might encourage worldwide certification of electoral processes to confirm when legislators have been selected through honest democratic procedures.

At first this proposed collection of opinions from members of legislatures around the world would not produce any legally binding outcomes. However, they could have an influential, informal voice, given the ease of worldwide communication and the fact that they would, indeed, represent all people of the world who elect national legislators. In some instances, they might affirm or disconfirm a resolution being considered in the UN Security Council or General Assembly, thereby adding a direct people's voice to what foreign ministries have proposed. Of course, if a virtual assembly solidified its acceptance across the planet's continents, it eventually could be given authority to pass legally binding measures on behalf of the people who elected them to their national assemblies, perhaps in co-sponsorship with a democratized UN Security Council or General Assembly that still represented national governments exclusively.

Because globalization without democratization undermines human rights and also intensifies populist discontent, the search for ways to overcome the global democratic deficit raises interest in a second possibility: creating a Global People's Assembly. Rising interest in global affairs by civil society organizations and multinational corporations also underscores the need to create more space for conversation to work out differences and advance common interests. Richard Falk and Andrew Strauss make a compelling case for experimenting with a Global People's Assembly.[91] Whether at first popularly elected or selected indirectly, as occurred in the history of the European

---

[91] Richard Falk and Andrew Strauss, "Toward Global Parliament," *Foreign Affairs* 80, no. 1 (2001): 212–220; Richard Falk and Andrew Strauss, "On the Creation of a Global Peoples Assembly: Legitimacy and the Power of Popular Sovereignty," *Stanford Journal of International Law* 36, no. 2 (2000): 191–220.

Parliament, the costs of creating a virtual global forum have been brought within reach by online meeting technology. Because its members would interact directly as individuals, not as representatives of states, its mere existence might promote discussion and help resolve some conflicts. Although it would begin as a weak institution, it still might affirm some policy directions that would influence UN agencies. Over time, if an assembly "became the practical place for clashing interests to resolve differences, formal powers would likely follow."[92]

Because of the rising influence of opponents of globalization on both the right and the left, a global assembly might "serve as an attractive alternative to those people who, out of enlightened self-interest or even public spiritedness, wish to see the international system become more open and democratic."[93] A coalition of strong civil society organizations and forward-looking businesses could create it; because such an assembly would not represent states, it would not require state approval before being established. Of course, support from progressive states would be quite helpful in contributing to start-up costs and giving it initial gravitas.

Falk and Strauss also speculate that "tremendous transformative energy . . . could be unleashed when those people who have found their deep-seated aspirations for a better world so difficult to realize are presented with a viable vision of a [global people's assembly] . . . around which they can unite" and organize politically.[94] Regardless of whether that would happen, it might provide a concrete institutional example of the incipient practice of global democracy. No less important, either or both a Global People's Assembly or a World Democratic Parliamentarians' Assembly might provide an international body that could begin to build cohesiveness across borders to speak with authority and vision on global challenges.

7.5 ACHIEVING ECONOMIC WELL-BEING FOR THE POOR

In order for a grand strategy for peace and human security to be effective, the United States and the international community need to commit themselves to reducing global inequity, abolishing poverty and unemployment, and implementing all the economic dimensions of human rights. The world's governments have already recognized that "Everyone . . . has the right to social security and is entitled to realization . . . of the economic, social and cultural rights indispensable for his [or her] dignity and the free development of his [or her] personality."[95] Governments have also declared that "everyone has the right to work . . . and to protection against unemployment."[96]

---

[92] Falk and Strauss, "Toward Global Parliament," 218.
[93] Falk and Strauss, "Toward Global Parliament," 218.
[94] Falk and Strauss, "Global People's Assembly," 220.
[95] UDHR, Article 22. See also the International Covenant on Economic, Social, and Cultural Rights.
[96] UDHR, Article 23 (1).

However, the United States and many other governments have not taken seriously their own rhetoric and analysis of the consequences of unemployment and inequity. The existing "right to work" has not ended unemployment for millions of people. Yet chronic unemployment is not just a demoralizing denial of one's human rights, it also leads "to social unrest, political polarization, and growing tensions" in many countries.[97] In addition, some people hold jobs that do not offer sufficient income to enable survival with dignity. Yet governments have said that everyone is entitled to a job that provides "just . . . remuneration, ensuring for himself and his family an existence worthy of human dignity."[98]

When a society suffers, as many do, from youth unemployment as high as 20 to 50 percent, the prospects for establishing national societies capable of tranquility or a stable international community are sharply lowered. Far fewer people will develop positive feelings toward contributing to international stability or to respecting others' interests borne out of any sense of human solidarity. Indeed, massive unemployment leaves people, often both those with and those without jobs, feeling no sense of human solidarity. This is as understandable as it is unacceptable. To transform rhetorical aspirations to promote economic well-being for all into genuine reductions of inequalities within and among countries[99] suggests the new architecture needed in this area. Despite good rhetoric, the United States and many other governments have ignored economic human rights.[100] Yet with appropriate planning and resource allocation, the international community could deliver the right of all people on Earth to minimal social security and economic conditions sufficient for human dignity and the development of each person's potential.[101]

First, as the percentage of world population in agriculture declines, the right to employment[102] grows in importance because non-agricultural people have no place to turn for sustenance without gainful employment. Implementing people's right to earn income sufficient for a life of dignity should be taken more seriously by the global

---

[97] Muhammad Yunus, *A World of Three Zeros: The New Economics of Zero Poverty, Zero Unemployment, and Zero Net Carbon Emissions* (New York: Public Affairs, 2017), 92.

[98] Universal Declaration of Human Rights (UDHR), Article 23 (3). https://www.un.org/en/about-us/universal-declaration-of-human-rights.

[99] "Right to Peace," A/RES/71/189, L. 29, 4, https://documents-dds-ny.un.org/doc/UNDOC/GEN/N16/454/62/pdf/N1645462.pdf?OpenElement.

[100] An instructive exception might be the Mahatma Gandhi National Rural Employment Guarantee Act of 2006. It is an Indian social security measure that guarantees at least a partial right to work. It provides a minimum of 100 days of employment per year to every household in which an adult member volunteers to do unskilled work. The program was described by the government as "the largest and most ambitious social security and public works programme in the world." Government of India, Ministry of Rural Development 2012, *MGNREGA Sameeksha, An Anthology of Research Studies on the Mahatma Gandhi National Rural Employment Guarantee Act, 2005, 2006–2012 "Ministry of Rural Development"* (New Delhi: Orient BlackSwan), ix. The World Bank has characterized it as a "stellar example of rural development." See *Economic Times*, http://articles.economictimes.indiatimes.com/2013-10-10/news/42902947_1_world-bank-world-development-report-safety-net.

[101] All people have "the right to protection against unemployment." UDHR, Article 22.

[102] UDHR, Article 23 (1).

community[103] because without it people cannot live lives of stability, peace, and constructive engagement. Significantly, the happiest people on Earth live in societies with secure social nets that provide genuine opportunities to work and protect all citizens from severe deprivation and economic calamity.[104]

One of the first and most profoundly positive innovations that the international community could make would be to re-interpret the widely acclaimed "right to work" to mean that every adult, able-bodied person on Earth has the right to adequate employment or the opportunity to become an entrepreneur.[105] Global full employment could be brought within reach if national and international officials sought to embrace it. The goal would not be to "give" everyone a job or to require slave labor, but to ensure that every able-bodied person has the opportunity either to be employed or to initiate small-scale entrepreneurship.

Two promising tools might be used to help implement this kind of change in global governance: microfinance and social businesses. Mohammed Yunus, founder of the micro-credit movement and the Nobel Prize–winning Grameen bank, helped millions of illiterate, unemployed people rise out of poverty without government programs.[106] More recently, Yunus also has recommended providing modest self-sustaining help to enable unemployed people, regardless of social class or economic status, to become job *creators* rather than job seekers. Such programs enable the unemployed to develop social enterprises that meet real needs of poor people but that do not aim to generate profit for investors.[107] Enormous progress can be achieved in enabling productive work for unemployed people when policymakers stop waiting for profit-making corporations to decide to hire unemployed persons and instead "turn unemployed people into entrepreneurs"[108] who are able to employ themselves to meet human needs without being limited by a need to make profit for investors. Social businesses have succeeded

---

[103] UDHR, Article 23 (3). "Everyone has the right to a standard of living adequate for the health and well-being of himself and of his family, including food, clothing, housing and medical care and necessary social services, and the right to security." In addition, "everyone has the right to education." UNDHR, Articles 25 (1); 26 (1).

[104] The countries frequently at the top of the rankings include Denmark, Finland, Iceland, Netherlands, and Norway. *World Happiness Report 2019*, https://worldhappiness.report/ed/2019/; Maggie Astor, "Want to Be Happy? Try Moving to Finland," *New York Times*, March 14, 2018.

[105] Lopez-Claros, Dahl, and Groff, *Global Governance*, 8–10. Unemployment in Bosnia and Herzegovina, for example, was 40 percent in 2017. Yunus, *Three Zeros*, 133.

[106] Yunus has extensive experience in demonstrating what vast changes can be achieved by relying on human ingenuity and creative uses of severely limited capital. The success of the Grameen bank has demonstrated the power of making financial services available to poor women who were never taken seriously by profit-maximizing banks and national governments. The bank "is self-sustaining, runs with its own resources . . . is owned mostly by poor female borrowers," and established a 98 percent repayment record. Despite some criticisms, its four-decade history of success has provided millions with gainful employment and was recognized internationally with the Nobel Peace Prize in 2006. Yunus, *Three Zeros*, 217, 235.

[107] Yunus, *Three Zeros*, 3–66, 239–266.

[108] Yunus, *Three Zeros*, 91.

in scores of countries by empowering the poverty-stricken unemployed, in rich countries as well as poor.

These "social businesses," as distinguished from profit-maximizing businesses, may have almost unlimited purposes and possibilities to focus directly on solving problems. Yunus hopes that social enterprises could be an element "in the transition from our current greed-based civilization to a civilization based on the deeper human values of sharing and caring."[109] Regardless of whether that becomes true, with sufficient imagination, many economic or social problems can be turned into service enterprises that, although non-profit, are self-sustaining creators of jobs at the same time that they solve the problems.

Although microfinancing has provided liberating incomes for the poor, it has come under some criticism that can be drawn upon to improve its approach. On the positive side, microfinance "democratizes" capital by placing small loans in the hands of the very poor. They have no access to capital through traditional approaches to credit, from either the private sector or government banks. Microfinance invites the poor, especially women, into entrepreneurial roles that increase their dignity and income. This approach is often the only viable alternative to elites' predatory takeover of all political and economic institutions in a local community. It is a valuable "thorn in the side of predatory moneylenders," and provides "an opportunity for the landless poor to build assets."[110] However, critics say the Washington consensus for spreading capitalism worldwide and the Bangladeshi consensus for using microfinance to get capital into the hands of the poor have come together, producing mixed results because finance capital and development capital have "commodified development."[111] When this happens, it develops characteristics of subprime lending, including profiteering, predatory interests rates, and patriarchal disciplinary tactics. Moreover, the commodification of development programs has distracted from addressing the deeper causes of poverty. A premise of microfinance run by big banks or government programs "is that poverty is the lack of access to credit and capital. But poverty is in fact structural exclusion from power."[112] The best microfinance programs in the future can and should take on these issues.

A second focal point in the campaign to abolish poverty and reduce inequality for the United States and all well-off societies is to commit themselves strictly to meeting the familiar, yet chronically ignored, international standard of transferring 0.7 percent of GDP annually to international development assistance. This would put the world firmly on a path to abolish extreme poverty. States should also take initiatives in other areas, such as putting a small percentage of each payment for raw materials imported

[109] Yunus, *Three Zeros*, 142.

[110] Josh Leon, "Poverty Capitalism: Interview with Ananya Roy," *Foreign Policy in Focus* (2011), https://fpif.org/poverty_capitalism_interview_with_ananya_roy/.

[111] Ananya Roy, *Poverty Capital: Micro Finance and the Making of Development* (New York: Routledge, 2010), http://bvbr.bib-bvb.de:8991/F?func=service&doc_library=BVB01&local_base=BVB01&doc_number=0 18971867&sequence=000001&line_number=0001&func_code=DB_RECORDS&service_type=MEDIA.

[112] Leon, "Poverty Capitalism"; Roy, *Poverty Capital*.

from less developed countries in a publicly overseen fund to benefit the residents of the state from which the materials come.

A third step toward abolition of poverty would be for the United States and other affluent societies to use a combination of public education and legislation to encourage or possibly require all individuals within their own countries whose income places them in the top 10 percent of the world population to contribute 1 percent of their income annually to development overseen by an independent agency to ensure corruption-free administration. Without harming the wealthy, this "one-percent income redistribution" would vastly improve the standard of living for millions of people now dwelling in poverty. This measure could abolish poverty throughout the world in 20 years.

Fourth, some changes are needed in the governance of the World Bank, the IMF, the World Trade Organization, and perhaps other international institutions to provide fairer representation to all stakeholders. Reform considerations should include not only how to increase the power of underrepresented stakeholders, but also how to increase benefits from drawing on the expertise of relevant non-governmental organizations. Although the World Trade Organization (WTO) has effectively developed shared rules and institutions for resolving trade conflicts and constructively managing the global economy,[113] it also illustrates ways in which such management could be improved. Representation in decision-making needs to be broadened to reduce the extent to which trade negotiations are dominated by corporate interests and to increase the influence of labor, consumer, and environmental groups that have been shut out in the past.[114] In addition, the WTO has failed to give sufficient weight to labor and environmental standards that would raise wages and reduce pollution.

Ironically, a potentially better global trade organization was successfully negotiated by US officials in the aftermath of World War II when the need for cooperative trade rules was fresh in negotiators' minds. This experience illustrates another lawmaking opportunity that went unseized. Called the International Trade Organization, provisions focused on achieving full employment, fair competition, international labor standards, anti-monopoly provisions, rules to prevent cheating in currency exchanges, and additional rules to spread the benefits of trade equitably to more people. Successful negotiations for this organization, initiated in 1946 and completed in 1948, led 56 countries to sign the treaty. Later, conservative US senators serving their corporate benefactors surprised the world when they blocked US participation

---

[113] Significantly, Keohane points out that "in many countries, including the United States, the WTO enhances democracy, since its rules limit the ability of special interests to gain advantages at the expense of the public as a whole. Effective democratic governance requires devices to make it difficult for lobbyists seeking special advantage to siphon off economic rents; the WTO is one of the most effective such devices in existence, since its rules cannot be changed unilaterally by any single state. Hence it can properly be seen . . . as a democracy-enhancing institution." Keohane, "Global Governance and Legitimacy," 106–107; Robert O. Keohane, Stephen Macedo, and Andrew Moravcsik, "Democracy-Enhancing Multilateralism," *International Organization* 63, no. 1 (2009): 1–31.

[114] Aileen Kwa, *Power Politics in the WTO* (Bangkok: Focus on the Global South, 2003).

in the organization, which killed it. Yet internationally recognized trade expert Lori Wallach has argued that this "very different vision for a rules-based global trading system remains attainable, once we agree that the system is supposed to work for people around the world, not the world's largest corporations."[115] Such provisions, which could implement an increased emphasis on equity and human dignity, illustrate the direction to take reforms in international financial institutions.

Fifth, a more serious commitment to equity requires reviewing attitudes toward capitalism, at least in unbridled form, because without government intervention in the marketplace, wealth naturally flows toward higher and higher concentrations of capital in the hands of fewer and fewer people.[116] Economic inequities enable wealthy, controlling elites in the United States to keep themselves disproportionately in power through political contributions and lobbying. Corporations seeking primarily their own profit maximization may take advantage of workers, paying them less than the value of their labor when they can, and may take advantage of consumers who often are unable to influence prices or the quality of products marketed. Too often powerful corporations also buy self-serving political power through contributions to government officials who, in return for being financed heavily by corporate donors and wealthy individuals, gain re-election repeatedly and control legislation to make it favorable for keeping the ruling political and economic elites in power. As a result, many international problems remain unaddressed.[117] In the short run, legislators and the economic elite may benefit from not facing these.

The issue is not whether democratic government should intervene in the market place; it is already present there and being pressed by enormous corporate power intervening in governing processes. The key question is, What should be the nature of government involvement in economic policymaking in order to serve the common good? The current lack of market accountability should be corrected because it facilitates injustice and corrupts democracy, as well as renders unwise economic decisions in the long run, producing tragedies in the commons. Advertisers' influence in the media and the absence of transparency in and limitations on political contributions keeps the public poorly informed even about what serves their own interests, thereby producing a society that may appear democratic in form but is far from equitable and democratic in content.

What has been called the Washington Consensus—the preference of elites for allowing markets guided by profits to dominate decisions about what to produce and consume—has weakened the ability of humanity to govern its future by pulling political decision-making back from shaping development plans, meeting environmental

---

[115] See Lori Wallach, "The World Trade Organization Is Dying," *New York Times*, November 28, 2019, https://www.nytimes.com/2019/11/28/opinion/seattle-world-trade-organization.html?searchResultP osition=1.

[116] "Wealth concentration is an all-but-inevitable, nonstop process under the present economic system." Yunus, *Three Zeros*, 7. Thomas Piketty, *Capital in the Twenty-First Century* (Cambridge, MA: Harvard University Press, 2014).

[117] Howell and Moe, *Crisis of Democracy*, 153.

and human needs, and respecting equity and reciprocity at home and worldwide. This consensus has placed higher value on not constraining economic forces than on advancing social justice and environmental sustainability or on achieving economic effectiveness in reducing conflict and achieving economic justice.[118] An alternative perspective, perhaps as found in countries with strong social democratic traditions, shows that with nurturing human dignity as a clearly stated goal and economic experimentation as the preferred means, it is possible to be both friendly to legitimate business activity and oriented toward fulfillment of human potential.[119]

7.6 IMPROVING ENVIRONMENTAL HEALTH

Nurturing Earth's environmental health must become an urgent priority to turn our world away from the self-destructive, non-sustainable path it is on because of "its commitment to unlimited economic growth and the concomitant depletion of resources and degradation of the environment"[120] that are occurring. New global architecture can enable countries to work more closely together to develop and incentivize more stringent international legal standards to guide decisions toward implementing equitable guidelines for protecting planetary environmental health. One of the most pressing goals for the United States after re-joining the Paris climate agreement[121] should be to help save tens of millions of people from being driven from their homes and their livelihoods by rising sea levels, declining fresh water supplies, advancing desertification, and weather extremes affecting all regions of the world. To develop thoughtful internationally agreed-on guidelines and to make them legally binding on all, with the help of international financial assistance where needed, can slow environmental destruction and encourage conservation to enable human freedom and dignity to flourish throughout the world.

The following discussion emphasizes (1) public educational initiatives to build support for the changes required to address environmental destruction; (2) the need for an Environmental Security Council; (3) the necessity to formulate a comprehensive environmental treaty to establish basic guidelines for interactions; (4) the role that could be played by a UN Common Heritage Council; and (5) the potential benefits from building a green grid alliance.

First, US environmental groups and the Environmental Protection Agency can play a major constructive role by seizing the opportunity to promote change through extensive public education, demonstrating that environmental threats to human security are huge and need to be taken seriously. The prospects for constructive change are

---

[118] Held, "Reframing Global Governance," 297.
[119] See Held, "Reframing Global Governance," 302.
[120] Schwartzberg, *Transforming*, 292.
[121] United Nations Climate Change, *The Paris Agreement*, https://unfccc.int/process-and-meetings/the-paris-agreement/the-paris-agreement.

determined by what citizens and corporations understand and support, because the US government at best has been slow to lead. To enhance the prospects, massive educational efforts are necessary. To gain credibility all initiatives should be based firmly on scientific evidence that climate disruption is happening now. Globally, for example, "every one of the past 40 years has been warmer than the 20th-century average."[122] Wildfires and deforestation are increasing. Dangerously hot weather for humans, animals, sea life, and plants now occurs with ever more frequency. Scientists observe climate being disrupted, polar ice caps and permafrost melting, numerous species becoming extinct, topsoil eroding, deserts expanding, and fish harvests declining. Rising sea levels around the world threaten people's homes, fields, and towns. More rain falls during storms, increasing the risk of flooding, widespread erosion, and irretrievable losses of valuable topsoil. Enormous crises await the densely settled deltaic regions in Bangladesh and adjacent areas of India and the Hwang Ho and Yangtze deltas of China. These will generate refugee flows in the tens of millions and doubtless produce deep social unrest.[123] Diminishing glaciers in the Himalayan and Karakoram mountains are major sources of water for hundreds of millions of people in India, Pakistan, Bangladesh, Nepal, and China. Prolonged drought and severe water and food scarcity are almost certain to ensue in these regions, as will economic and political conflict.[124]

There is no longer doubt among informed and rational people that human conduct is overloading the atmosphere with carbon dioxide, causing increases in our planet's temperature. Even though US citizens are educated, wealthy in global context, and free to organize and speak for desirable change, they are living examples of how a massive tragedy of the commons, which also causes unconscionable human rights violations, can unfold in the midst of people with good intentions who are going about their daily tasks as usual, because they have unwisely trusted their government to take action when needed—but in vain. US citizens have known the truth (or easily could have) and presumably have wanted to save the Earth, but they have largely acquiesced with the US and other governments that, although they discussed saving the Earth in the decade of the 1980s, ultimately failed.[125] Part of the educational mission should be to document that it was unwise and perhaps catastrophic to wait for big governments to act.

Citizens have not pressed for change because they have been unsure of the economic consequences from new conservation initiatives, especially when they have been frequently misled by leaders who say that there is no environmental crisis and that environmental protection will be economically harmful. Many US political leaders

---

[122] Union of Concerned Scientists, https://www.ucsusa.org/global-warming#.WleVlq6nEdU.

[123] Schwartzberg, *Transforming*, 334.

[124] See Schwartzberg, *Transforming*, 333.

[125] For the startling historical record of this aborted effort, see Nathaniel Rich, "Losing Earth: The Decade We Almost Stopped Climate Change," *New York Times Magazine*, August 5, 2018, 7–70, https://www. nytimes.com/interactive/2018/08/01/magazine/climate-change-losing-earth.html?searchResultPosit ion=8.

reject reasonable proposals for environmental security because they fear that support-ing them will cause them to lose support from political or financial backers.[126] Some dismiss scientific evidence of global warming as "a hoax."[127] As a result, many US poli-cies have been increasing the tragedies in the commons, but good civic education can change that.

For decades, national and international laws have lagged far behind the negative consequences that human activities have been inflicting on the environment. The problem of legal lag became an even deeper problem in the United States with the rise of neo-conservatives' exclusionary nationalism and dismissiveness toward interna-tional laws and multilateral institutions pursuing environmental health. Despite legal lag, governments have developed some positive guidelines for environmental protec-tion, but they need more serious implementation. Because "all human beings have the fundamental right to an environment adequate for their health and well-being,"[128] states need to cooperate across borders where that is necessary to maintain ecosys-tems essential for the functioning of the biosphere. Similar cooperation is needed for maintaining biological diversity and the survival of all species of flora and fauna; observing optimum sustainable yield in the exploitation of living natural resources in the oceans; and preventing significant environmental pollution that almost never remains confined to one local area.[129]

In addition to highlighting the need for transnational cooperation to address envi-ronmental threats to human security, the proposed education program should also identify constructive proposals to explore and then aim at encouraging citizens' com-mitment to achieving a few basic goals. Foremost among these should be committing the United States to meet the Paris Agreement's temperature goal of holding global average temperature increase to "well below 2° C above preindustrial levels and pursu-ing efforts to limit the temperature increase to 1.5° C above preindustrial levels."[130]

Second, since totally *voluntary* environmental guidelines are unlikely to be sufficient to meet necessary goals in the forthcoming chapter of history, lawmaking needs to include some legally binding requirements on all states. Toward this end, the world needs to replace the existing United Nations Environment Program with a more pow-erful institution authorized to set binding guidelines and to help and ensure that states

---

[126] See Jared Diamond, *Collapse: How Societies Choose to Fail or Succeed* (New York: Penguin Books, 2011).

[127] President Trump claimed that climate change caused by global warming "is a hoax," after dismissing a landmark scientific report produced by the US government's own scientists. His administration sought to roll back key climate regulations at every turn. Justin Warland, "Donald Trump Called Climate Change a Hoax," *Time Magazine*, July 9, 2019, https://time.com/5622374/donald-trump-climate-change-hoax-event/. Calling global warming a "hoax" is easier than acknowledging that some global problems require global solutions.

[128] World Commission on Environment and Development, "Brundtland Report/Annexe 1. Summary of Proposed Legal Principles for Environmental Protection and Sustainable Development," https://en.wikisource.org/wiki/Brundtland_Report/Annexe_1._Summary_of_Proposed_Legal_Principles_for_Environmental_Protection_and_Sustainable_Development.

[129] World Commission on Environment and Development, "Brundtland Report," Annex 1.

[130] United Nations Climate Change, *The Paris Agreement*.

comply with them. Because of increased, conflictual pressures on the common heritage as tillable land, food, water, and other resources become scarcer, it is necessary to construct more reliable institutional mechanisms to negotiate or legislate agreements to protect the commons and address environmental conflicts that will arise.

Without some new institutional framework for decision-making, the world's people simply have no satisfactory way of addressing global environmental problems and their complicated connections with other economic, social, and security issues. The existing treaty-making process and balance-of-power dynamics are simply not capable of making necessary decisions. For example, the existing system has failed to deliver the cooperation needed to protect one-third of the world's 200 major international river basins that are not covered by any protective international agreement. Fewer than 30 of the 200 have established effective over-arching institutions.[131]

An effective environmental decision-making body might be established by building on experience of the UN Security Council, but by making an Environmental Security Council more fairly representative of the world's population and without any veto power, even though it should be authorized to render legally binding decisions to protect the biosphere.[132] In a new agency, representation in decision-making processes needs to include all stakeholders, not only national governments, and to increase the role of the scientific community and non-governmental organizations.[133] Corporate industry also needs to be present because industry deeply affects the environment.[134] Given governmental foot-dragging, additional transnational grassroots political pressures and international institutional strength are needed to move this idea toward fruition.

A third need, which cannot wait for the establishment of an Environmental Security Council, is to conclude a comprehensive treaty setting out states' rights and responsibilities in environmental management.[135] At present, there is not even a clear legal obligation for one country to inform a neighboring state if activity in its territory will affect the land, air, or water of its neighbor—an indication of how outmoded existing legal obligations are. They lag far behind rapid changes in human conduct from new technologies. Such a treaty should also follow up on the Brundtland Commission's suggestion that environmental disputes be handled in a systematic way. When a serious dispute arises, if it is not taken immediately to the International Court of Justice, states should be given up to 18 months to reach mutual agreement on a solution to the problem or on an agreed dispute-settlement arrangement. If they cannot reach

---

[131] World Commission on Environment and Development, *Our Common Future*, 316. Because the world's roughly 200 biogeographic zones seldom correspond with political boundaries, protecting the Earth's life-sustaining systems requires much trans-border cooperation to address desertification, acidification, and air, water, and soil conservation.

[132] See the suggestions by Schwartzberg, *Transforming*, 94–107; 287–293. See also Commission on Global Governance discussions of an economic security council, *Our Global Neighbourhood*, 153–158.

[133] World Commission on Environment and Development, *Our Common Future*, 326.

[134] World Commission on Environment and Development, *Our Common Future*, 329.

[135] World Commission on Environment and Development, *Our Common Future*, 332.

agreement, then the dispute should be submitted to conciliation at the request of any one of the concerned states and, if the issue remains unresolved, the parties should be required to submit the dispute to binding arbitration.[136] The possibility of invoking a required dispute settlement process at the request of a single state is a highly desirable step in the necessary direction of compulsory legal enforcement. Such a provision could provide a reasonable last resort before a major eco-catastrophe or international violence might occur.

Fourth, it would be helpful to establish a UN Common Heritage Council,[137] made up of reputable worldwide experts serving impartially in their individual capacities rather than as representatives of specific states, since the latter are often wedded to national sovereignty in ways that harm the global commons.[138] Such a council could at the outset help to govern the high seas, the underlying seabed, the Antarctic, outer space, and the moon, which are widely considered to be the "common heritage" of humankind. The council also would need to represent and engage in fruitful conversation with divergent parties such as indigenous and marginalized peoples, rich states as well as poor, exponents of private market solutions as well as of government planning, and those already negatively affected by global warming as well as those less affected. Bridging the necessary tasks would be difficult even with appropriate global architecture, but it has proven to be simply impossible to achieve when operating in today's antiquated political structures.

A fifth goal should be to obtain as many countries' commitments as possible to form an alliance built between countries with excess solar energy potential and those with insufficient energy resources. Surprisingly, substantial evidence shows that the world's entire electrical energy needs could be supplied by environmentally friendly solar panels placed in the desert regions of the world where the sun shines most consistently throughout the year. However, to exploit this presently unused energy, huge intercontinental electrical grids would be needed to connect the energy sources, near the equator, to the world's energy needs at other latitudes. The proposal for a global Green Grid Initiative[139] would connect the world's major urban and industrial centers, as Earth turns each day, with the planet's sunniest locations during the hours of highest demand, over the shortest transmission lines. However, to obtain the most energy at the least environmental and financial cost requires cooperative global decision-making which the world now lacks[140] but one can easily imagine creating. The payoffs would be enormous.

---

[136] World Commission on Environment and Development, *Our Common Future*, 334.

[137] Schwartzberg, *Transforming*, 274, 289.

[138] Schwartzberg, *Transforming*, 289–290.

[139] See Climate Parliament, *The Green Grid Initiative: Engineering A Climate Solution*, https://www.climate-parl.net/single-post/2018/12/20/High-level-discussion-on-regional-grids-for-renewables-in-Asia-to-be-held-at-Wilton-Park.

[140] This proposal is discussed in a documentary film, *The Energy Internet* (Empathy Media, 2019), which may be viewed on Amazon or from www.climateparl.net. Nicholas Dunlop, secretary-general of the World Climate Parliament, narrates. See also "Energy and Economic Growth," https://energyeconomicgrowth.org/news/wilton-park-dialogue-explores-cross-border-electricity-highways-harness-asias-vast-untapped.

Regardless of one's particular policy preferences, new international institutions are needed to conserve the environment and reduce risks of indecision or violent acts in future conflicts. Success in environmental peacebuilding, Joseph Schwartzberg suggests, will come to those willing "to recognize that all stakeholders deserve a meaningful voice in decision-making, to accept the policy implications of scientific evidence . . . , and to embrace an ethos that puts global welfare and intergenerational equity ahead of the near-term interests of particular nations and corporate giants."[141]

Although this chapter mentions a half dozen suggestions for new life-enhancing institutional architecture, this list is by no means exhaustive. This analysis contains only a few of many more innovations proposed by civil society organizations, UN agencies and expert panels, and government departments. Little doubt should remain that institutional innovation and structural changes can strengthen international law-making capacities and enforcement of desirable behavioral standards ranging from protecting human beings from genocide to decreasing the risks of armed conflict, from reducing poverty and unemployment to improving economic and environmental well-being, from monitoring officials' compliance with prohibitions of war crimes to enforcing law on people accused of mass murder, from effectively diminishing terrorist acts to enabling human-centered police enforcement ensuring compliance with laws upholding human dignity.

Although it is not possible to predict which of the preceding suggestions might turn out to bear the most fruit, policymakers and citizens should explore how to generate political support for moving forward in at least the following areas:

(1) to establish a more equitably representative and less easily blocked UN Security Council, or its replacement, with broader lawmaking and law-enforcing powers to enhance human security;

(2) to create an Environmental Security Council;

(3) to establish a Common Heritage Council;

(4) to build a global monitoring agency, with satellite and drone capabilities, and a world database containing evidence of compliance with laws prohibiting war crimes, genocide, crimes against humanity, and crimes against the peace;

(5) to create an individually recruited UN Emergency Police Force;

(6) to press for full participation by the United States and all national governments in the ICJ, including compulsory jurisdiction, and the ICC;

(7) to support the Treaty on Prohibition of Nuclear Weapons and the Kissinger et al. nuclear arms reduction proposal;

(8) to establish processes to increase compliance with the principle of civilian immunity;

(9) to meet the goal of 0.7 percent of GDP for development assistance;

(10) to support a full employment policy for all countries;

---

[141] Schwartzberg, *Transforming*, 288.

(11) to support universal public education everywhere in the world;

(12) to negotiate a comprehensive environmental treaty to define mutual responsibilities;

(13) to hold a world conference to discuss the Green Grid Initiative;

(14) to increase financial incentives for reducing poverty, unemployment, and greenhouse gas emissions; and

(15) to experiment with a virtual global parliamentary assembly and a global people's assembly.[142]

This chapter has showcased a variety of architectural innovations that would enable using sovereign living space more creatively to serve human beings' needs more effectively, to take advantage of the light from inclusive representation in decision-making, to shape institutions logically around functional needs by aligning form with function and resources with needs, to encourage open conversation and institutional experimentation to shape further building in the future, yet with all designs anchored in present realities. Although all carry some risk of failing, these risks are reasonable given the likely payoffs and the possibilities for remodeling the design which can occur as soon as the need for re-design becomes clear, as surely will happen after experience with the initial innovations matures and underutilized human potential comes more fully into view.

For these initiatives to be taken, nothing magical is required—only sustained insistence by many people that global processes be used to match the global extent of the problems to be addressed and that action be taken in order to realize equality in freedom and human security, the topics of the last two chapters.

---

[142] Many other desirable suggestions have been made by international study commissions and UN secretaries-general. See United Nations, General Assembly and Security Council, *The Future of United Nations Peace Operations: Implementation of the Recommendations of the High-Level Independent Panel on Peace Operations: Report of the Secretary-General*, A/70/95 S/2015/446, June 17, 2015, https://www.un.org/en/ga/search/view_doc.asp?symbol=S/2015/682. See also Schwartzberg, *Transforming*, 36–63.

8

Building Human Security

THE CASE PRESENTED in the preceding chapters for a global grand strategy nurturing human security depends for success not simply on the United States and like-minded governments but also on the aspirations and commitments of the governed, the citizens of the world. In this and the final chapter we explore how citizens may strive to live in ways that are both politically responsible and ethically conscientious while taking seriously all of today's frightening international realities. This chapter emphasizes policymakers' and citizens' responsibilities in the United States; the last chapter encourages readers to imagine how wise policy choices can be selected and then implemented globally.

The central question lurking behind this entire analysis is, How can a person express both ethical integrity *and* political responsibility when one's highest values are not implemented by one's own government? Those asking this question do not claim, of course, that anyone's life can be lived perfectly, either in ethical commitment or political action. Human beings are always imperfect and limited in understanding. The hope discussed here is that citizens can find a place to stand that makes clear their highest values while empowering them to speak out for a politically responsible way of living—and, when the time comes, a responsible way of dying. One's political-ethical stance can and should be clear. How others respond to it is largely out of one's control.

The formula for expressing ethical integrity and political responsibility is straightforward: Analyze problems and opportunities empirically and buttress objective analysis with human understanding informed by moral imagination and worldwide wisdom traditions in order to produce a vision of life-saving planetary architecture to which citizen-peacebuilders may devote their vocations and lives. Refuse to flinch from realities that are unpleasant or almost unbelievable if they are empirically true. For example, climate change is one of the most dangerous threats to human security, yet the four-year strategic plan of the United States Environmental Protection Agency (EPA) in the Trump administration did not even mention it![1] Stunningly, the EPA for four years did nothing to address it. Instead, it did much to *contribute* to that threat, such as weakening restrictions on how much carbon dioxide a car (or a country) may emit, and removing the United States from Kyoto and Paris guidelines being worked on by much of the rest of the world. This simple yet shocking reality demonstrates why concerned citizens must press their government (and all the world's governments) to do more to limit climate disruptions. They would be acting imprudently, irresponsibly, and immorally if they simply waited for policymakers or others citizens to advance responsible policies and make up for lost time.

More generally, governing officials have not been doing all that is needed for human security now, nor have they in the recent past, despite golden opportunities year after year since 1989. And there are few signs that they will do enough in the future—until pressed hard to do so. As philosopher Peter Singer concluded, well before Donald Trump became president: "It has to be said, in cool but plain language, that in recent years the international effort to build a global community has been hampered by the repeated failure of the United States to play its part."[2] The inclination of the US governing elite and many of its supporters to reject wise policies is why German Chancellor Angela Merkel offered the following advice after the United States withdrew from the Paris environmental agreement: those who understand what is happening "truly have to take our fate into our own hands" rather than wait for US leadership.[3] Concerned citizens in the United States and possibly everywhere need to be ready to act independently of their governments' tendencies to serve narrow interests; instead they need to prioritize acting in concert with like-minded citizens from every region of the world who are working for the good of all. Paying taxes and voting in elections are no longer sufficient to fulfill a citizen's responsibility for generating change. All able-bodied citizens should also devote, say, at least one hour every day to educating themselves and others about what should be done in public policy decision-making and then in political organizing to enable it to happen.

Citizens, with steady vision and unwavering commitment to save the United States and human civilization from impending catastrophes should mobilize locally, nationally, and globally in a diverse yet fundamentally united transnational social movement of global dimensions. A successful global grand strategy for human security depends on a "transnational social movement" that should include a broad coalition of cooperative national governments, municipal and state or provincial governments,

---

[1] Avery Anapol, "EPA's 4-Year Strategic Plan Does Not Mention 'Climate Change,'" *The Hill*, 11 October 2017.
[2] Singer, *One World*, 198.
[3] Giulia Paravicini, "Angela Merkel: Europe Must Take 'Our Fate' into Own Hands," *Politico*, May 28, 2017, https://www.politico.eu/singerarticle/angela-merkel-europe-cdu-must-take-its-fate-into-its-own-hands-elections-2017/.

human rights and other civil society organizations, religious groups, far-sighted corporations and labor unions, UN agencies and inter-governmental regional groupings, other international organizations, and activist groups of students, women and others willing to support a grand strategy for human security.[4] This analysis emphasizes the role of US citizens in bringing sustained energy and transnationality to a movement, but all parts of the coalition have important roles to play. A transnational movement also helps fulfill the conditions, noted in discussing a strategy for human security in Chapter 5, essential for encouraging identity expansions that become more inclusive and respectful of all human beings' rights. Ideally, the movement should include a wide diversity of people, from conservatives interested in preserving nature to progressives pressing for genuine equality of opportunity.[5]

This synthesis of research shows that the future does not need to be one of recurring violence and unending wars.[6] A rising transnational social movement can undertake widespread education, which would reflect the differences between identifying with exclusionary nationalism or with the global family to mount a full court press to construct institutions that are at once more democratic and effective, more powerful and accountable, more legitimate and global, and therefore more likely to succeed. In collaboration with like-minded governments and intergovernmental organizations, activists could build the kind of sustained pressure and transnational political coalition that established, for the first time in world history and to many people's surprise at the time, the innovations of the European Union and the International Criminal Court. Given the motivation, national governments could create new legal architecture to build transnational institutions with some supranational qualities.[7]

---

[4] Transnational social movements are discussed in Kenneth A. Gould and Tammy L. Lewis, *Transnational Social Movements* (Oxford: Oxford University Press, 2021, https://doi.org/10.1093/acrefore/9780190846626.013.491; and Jackie Smith, *Social Movements for Global Democracy* (Baltimore: Johns Hopkins University Press, 2008). Thomas Richard Davies surveys a wide diversity of research on social movements in *Transnational Social Movements*, https://www.oxfordbibliographies.com/view/document/obo-9780199743292/obo-9780199743292-0164.xml.

[5] US intelligence agencies indicate that existential threats catalyze bottom-up social movements, that an increasing number of movements are possible in coming years, and that social movements are becoming better equipped to agitate for social and political change. National Intelligence Council, *Global Trends*, 12, 107.

For suggestions about forming effective movements for better global governance, see Together First: A Global System That Works for All, https://together1st.org/; Global Governance Forum, https://globalgovernanceforum.org/about/; and Global Challenges Foundation (Stockholm), https://globalchallenges.org/.

For insight into local and transnational dimensions, see Sidney Tarrow, *The New Transnational Activism* (Cambridge: Cambridge University Press, 2005; Smith, *Social Movements for Global Democracy*; David Cortright, *Peace Works: The Citizen's Role in Ending the Cold War* (Boulder, CO: Westview, 1993; and Mark Engler and Paul Engler, *This Is an Uprising: How Nonviolent Revolt Is Shaping the Twenty-First Century* (New York: Nation Books, 2016).

[6] Wallensteen, *Understanding Conflict Resolution*; Senese and Vasquez, *The Steps to War: An Empirical Study*.

[7] For an instructive record of the sustained effort for structural change leading to the ICC, see the current reports and past chronicling of this pilgrimage on the website of the Coalition for the International Criminal Court, "Voices of Global Civil Society," http://www.coalitionfortheicc.org/fight/voices-global-civil-society.

Individuals need to act independently of foot-dragging governments bent on serving narrow interests, yet act together with many other people, groups, and governments to build consensus and bring about needed change. US citizens and a transnational social movement need each other for at least five reasons: (1) to strengthen democracy in the United States, (2) to change US policies until they serve broader human interests, (3) to bolster transnational democratic participation in decision-making on both sides of national borders, (4) to increase understanding of how best to universalize respect for human dignity and the global family, and (5) to empower like-minded leaders, institutions, and one another for implementing a global strategy for human security that would draw in part on US talent and resources. The first two of these topics are discussed in this chapter and the last three in the concluding chapter.

To be a responsible US citizen in the 21st century means one must also be a responsible global citizen. These two are inextricably linked because US interests cannot be met unless human interests are also met, and vice versa. US citizens can fulfill their destiny only if they operate within robustly democratic processes at home, something they can no longer take for granted, as is explored next.

8.1 BOLSTERING US DEMOCRACY

US political processes now lack some vital democratic underpinnings that are essential for building an effective transnational social movement. Some determined powerholders in US politics have succeeded in reducing the quality of US democratic political culture. Concerned citizens would be irresponsible if they acquiesced in letting a selfish political elite have its way, misleading the public and justifying inaction on global issues of grave importance. Deficiencies in US democracy can probably be overcome, but only with increased citizen vigilance and action, more objective civic education, more investigative reporting, and more concerted political pressure.[8]

The democratic principle is unfulfilled in US political processes in five primary ways:

(1) The Electoral College, although Constitutional, violates the democratic standard of a majority of voters electing the president.
(2) Gerrymandered congressional and statehouse districts deny fair democratic representation.
(3) Voter suppression compromises the principle of majority rule.

---

[8] Harms to US democracy are so severe that Joseph Nye concluded, "The most important challenge to the provision of world order in the twenty-first century comes not from without but from within." Nye, "Will the Liberal Order Survive?"

Better civic education is needed because it has become possible to elect someone as US president who is capable of "a chilling disregard for . . . cherished human rights." In the words of the executive director of Amnesty International, President Trump "exploited hatred, misogyny, racism and xenophobia and, in doing so, emboldened and empowered the most violent segments of our society." Margaret Huang, January 2018, letter on file with the author.

(4) Although important issues are usually decided in Washington in accord with legally prescribed procedures, some watershed decisions have been made without citizens being able to rely on transparent sources of information, without time or opportunity for informed public debate, and without majority opinion being influential in the legislative outcome.

(5) Some officials' chronic dishonesty, social media's amplification of false information, moneyed interests and large financial contributors' corrupting influences, foreign governments' pernicious impacts using cyber penetration, and undemocratic customs in Congress, which prevent issues from coming up for a vote, are suffocating democratic processes.

A brief examination of these democratic deficits in US political processes clarifies what citizens might do to bolster the democratic decision-making and social movement politics needed to save US democracy and to contribute to the next chapter of human civilization.

8.1.1 Surmounting the Electoral College

First, one of the primary flaws in US democracy is that the voting majority of US citizens does not always select the US president. In a recent span of only 16 years, the Electoral College has twice denied the presidency to the presidential candidate who indisputably won the most votes. It handed the keys to the White House to the candidate that more people voted against than voted for. The influence of many votes is lost in the presidential election because all those people beyond the bare 51 percent, which determine the electors in each state, exert no influence.[9] If decades ago Congress had simply required the Electoral College to cast electors proportionally in accord with the popular vote, there would have been no President George W. Bush and instead a President Al Gore, and no President Donald Trump and instead a President Hillary Clinton. The two presidencies that we did have, and their respective administrations, were not favored by a majority of voters but they brought some profoundly negative, lasting consequences for human security, US democracy, and US political culture, as well as unconscionable losses of life in unnecessary wars, environmental destruction, and hostility toward the growth of international law during two crucial periods, totaling 12 years, of history.

In such cases, the Electoral College unwisely inflicted minority rule on citizens when it selected the leader of US political culture, the chief architect of its international policies, the sole appointer of Supreme Court justices, and the orchestrator of major legislative initiatives in Congress. This causes huge impacts on the lives of every citizen of the United States and many throughout the world. A President Gore would have taken major strides to avert climate change at a time when initiatives could have succeeded

[9] Ester Fuchs, quoted by Paul Hond, "Faith in the System Is Fraying," *Columbia Magazine*, Fall 2018, 28–35.

at moderate cost, to take only one example. Regardless of whatever else President Hillary Clinton might have done in place of a President Trump, she would have stayed in the Paris environmental agreement, maintained the constraints on Iran's nuclear programs, advanced women's rights and racial understanding in the United States, and kept the Supreme Court ideologically more balanced. *Ten million* more people voted against Donald Trump than voted for him in 2016,[10] yet he governed as president and commander-in-chief for four enormously consequential years. One cannot honestly conclude that it does not matter who wins the Electoral College vote. This anachronism simply should no longer be accepted.[11]

8.1.2 *Reducing Gerrymandering*

US democracy is also compromised by the way that members of Congress and representatives in state governments are selected. Districts in many states are severely gerrymandered, undermining a fair connection between the number of citizens casting ballots for a party's candidates and the number of that party's representatives being seated in Congress and statehouses. Many more Republican members sit in the US House of Representatives and in state legislative chambers than their electoral totals would justify if the number elected were proportional to the number of votes they received. The overall consequences in recent years have magnified Republican influences far beyond what their number of votes would justify, simply because many electoral districts are gerrymandered. Of course, either political party may gerrymander if in power when redistricting occurs. Yet because both parties might gerrymander is not an argument for doing nothing to halt this unprincipled way of undermining constitutional guarantees for voters to have equal protection of the law.

Once gerrymandered, districts enable an unscrupulous party repeatedly to re-draw district lines to perpetuate themselves in office even though the overall vote tally in a state would not sustain their control of state legislatures or of congressional delegations in the US House of Representatives. For example, in 2010, Democrats received a 50.4 percent majority of votes for the Michigan state assembly, but Republicans received 57.3 percent of the seats. This empowered Republicans to legislate by themselves without needing to consult or compromise with Democrats to pass legislation. They passed a right-to-work law in this traditionally strong labor-union state, without a single Democratic vote. The right-to-work law further undermined Democratic electoral strength in the following years and enabled Republicans to sustain their unfair

---

[10] In a final tally, 10,699,000 more people voted for other candidates than for Trump, and 2,865,000 more voted for Clinton than for Trump. "Hillary Clinton Leads By 2.8 Million in Final Popular Vote Count," http://time.com/4608555/hillary-clinton-popular-vote-final/. See also former Senator Russ Feingold, "Our Legitimacy Crisis," *The Nation*, April 3, 2017, 4.

[11] "The Electoral College was designed by the Constitution's framers as a means of ensuring that a populist demagogue could not win the presidency. Instead, it handed the presidency to a demagogue that a majority of voters opposed." Howell and Moe, *Crisis of Democracy*, 74. In their view, "The Electoral College is an antidemocratic relic of the past, and it needs to go." Howell and Moe, *Crisis of Democracy*, 208.

advantage. The gap favoring Republicans increased again because of further redistricting controlled by Republicans. In both 2012 and 2014 Democrats received majorities of the votes cast for the state assembly, but again Republicans gained the majority of seats in the assembly, demonstrating that when one party gains control, it cannot be dislodged fairly in subsequent elections.[12] Those who have studied this problem say that gerrymandering "represents an unprecedented threat to our democracy."[13]

To deny democratic principles even more, a number of Supreme Court justices who were nominated for the bench by minority presidents have been responsible for many of the 5 to 4 decisions of the Court. One of these was the Court's decision in 2019 to do nothing about the practice of gerrymandering because the narrow Court majority incredulously claimed that they were unable to find an electoral formula that would be fairer in protecting citizens' constitutional rights than to allow gerrymandering. That Court decision will encourage more gerrymandering.

Electoral victories made possible by gerrymandered districts and the Electoral College, even though clearly undemocratic, have produced significant differences in law, politics, economics, environment, education, and public opinion formation that in turn have made needed international changes much more difficult to achieve in Congress and state legislatures. These consequences also make it more difficult to provide objective civic education in public schools, to select officials with majority support in subsequent elections, and to obtain fair judgments in the next case that comes to trial in courts with justices selected as a result of minority-tainted processes. Every year that passes without good educational opportunities for minorities, fair treatment for racially diverse populations, or improved job prospects for the poor, for example, destines more people to arise in a subculture that leaves them less able to function effectively in asserting their political rights at the polls or in the courts in the future. Subcultures of poverty and prejudice arise which become increasingly difficult to improve, yet relatively easy to exploit with predatory economics and politics.

8.1.3 Stopping Voter Suppression

In addition to these two major structural flaws, narrow nationalists also pursue disheartening efforts to suppress voters with darker skin color or higher educational levels.[14] Where state legislatures and governorships have been in the hands

---

[12] See Devin Caughey, Chris Tausanovitch, and Christopher Warshaw, "Partisan Gerrymandering and the Political Process: Effects on Roll-Call Voting and State Policies," *Election Law Journal*, https://www.liebertpub.com/doi/full/10.1089/elj.2017.0452; Cliff Sloan and Michael Waldman, "History Frowns on Partisan Gerrymandering," in *Democracy & Justice: Collected Writings*, ed. Jessica Katzen, Jim Lyons, Jeanine Plant-Chirlin, and Vivien Watts (New York: Brennan Center, New York University School of Law, 2017), 64–65; Tom Jacobs, "The Policy Consequences of Partisan Gerrymandering," *Pacific Standard*, October 4, 2017, https://psmag.com/news/the-policy-consequences-of-partisan-gerrymandering.

[13] See Sloan and Waldman, "History Frowns on Partisan Gerrymandering."

[14] Theodore Johnson and Max Feldman, *The New Voter Suppression* (New York: Brennan Center for Justice New York University School of Law, 2020); Feingold, "Our Legitimacy Crisis."

of narrow-minded or racially biased representatives, legislation has been shrewdly designed and judges appointed who are likely to discourage certain potential voters from casting ballots. Legally intricate initiatives are misleadingly written so that overturning or blocking them has been difficult in the limited times preceding elections. Voter suppression measures have advanced in many state legislatures with support from national Republican Party headquarters to discourage or prevent eligible voters from exercising their constitutional right to vote. The Department of Justice in the Trump administration added its weight on the side of discouraging citizens from voting by not challenging efforts by Republican state officials to keep people out of the polls who are unlikely to vote for Republican candidates.[15] Extensive efforts to suppress voters have included restricting voter registration, imposing restrictive voter identification laws, shortening voting periods, closing some polling places completely, increasing inconveniences for voters in certain districts, discouraging voting by mail, and intimidating voters from showing up at polling places. These efforts constitute a fundamental violation of democratic principles and human rights, causing racist consequences often imposed from generation to generation. In some states, temporary polling places were abolished because they enabled legal student voting to occur.[16]

These anti-democratic initiatives may be amplified by the common but dubious practice of allowing elections to be overseen by partisan officials in state political offices. That proved not to be a problem in the 2020 presidential election, as most state officials overseeing elections took professional pride in providing an exemplary non-partisan performance.[17] In other instances, if elections are administered by partisan people who do not perform as impartial electoral officials, truly fair elections and a welcoming invitation to vote may be questioned by some voters. To address this problem when it was overtly racial, a voting rights act was passed in 1965. This made a huge difference in increasing voter turnout. But today many benefits of that legislation are being eliminated. In 2013, the Supreme Court, by a 5 to 4 vote, decided that, because voting practices were no longer as heavily biased as previously, the law was no longer needed. The Supreme Court ruled that southern states with a long history of voting discrimination no longer needed to have their election changes approved by the federal government before taking effect, a practice called "preclearance." With this ruling, the Court destroyed the heart of the Voting Rights Act. Dissenting justice Ruth

---

[15] New York Times Editorial Board, "Partners in Voter Suppression." *New York Times*, August 11, 2017, A 20. "The Trump Justice Department takes the wrong side and backs Ohio's efforts to purge voters from the rolls."

[16] Michel Wines, "The Student Vote Is Surging. So Are Efforts to Suppress It," *New York Times*, October 24, 2019, https://www.nytimes.com/2019/10/24/us/voting-college-suppression.html?searchResultPosition=1.

[17] State officials in Georgia, for example, were resolutely honest and professional in carefully and accurately overseeing elections and ballot counting even though their personal preferences may have been different from the outcome of the tallied votes. They almost singlehandedly saved US democracy at one point when the president and others applied enormous pressure and asked them to subvert an honest reporting of voting results. "Transcript: President Trump's Phone Call with Georgia Election Officials," *New York Times*, January 4, 2021.

Bader Ginsburg aptly pointed out that "throwing out preclearance when it has worked and is continuing to work to stop discriminatory changes, is like throwing away your umbrella in a rainstorm because you are not getting wet."[18]

Suppressing voter turnout can produce significant shifts in some electoral outcomes. Manipulations to disempower legitimate expression of electoral preference lower citizen morale, even for those able and willing to vote, thereby further decreasing voter turnout while deepening divisions in US political culture. Suppression by persons with excluding identities who oppose human rights weakens the democratic body politic because the negative consequences of low voter participation multiply as they spread into many facets of legislatures, courts, school boards, law enforcement, and history—a major departure from the democratic belief that it is a patriotic duty of everyone to vote.

8.1.4 Encouraging Public Debate

A fourth limitation in US democratic processes is the failure of some important topics to receive adequate public discussion. As the eminent scholar of US democracy, Robert Dahl, has written, "No important area of public policy presents such a daunting challenge to the theory and practice of democracy as foreign policy. Not only does foreign policy virtually escape popular control, but it will be difficult, and perhaps even impossible, to rectify this enormous democratic failure."[19] Some important questions, such as "what should be US nuclear weapons strategy?" have never been vigorously debated by officials in public or by members of the public.[20] The United States is the only country on earth to have used nuclear weapons on other humans, yet US citizens have not discussed whether they prefer never again to use them first in battle. Although there never has been a serious public discussion about whether the US first-use policy is wise or moral, this continues to be the United States strategic position. The United States has prepared to use nuclear weapons first in battlefield situations rather than reserving them only to deter their use by others.

Even though US nuclear weapons policy since World War II, supported by leaders of both political parties, has not been a result of public debate and an expression of citizen preference, citizens have spent hundreds of billions of their dollars on policies which in practice keep alive the threat of first use. In addition to encouraging moral callousness as it prepares the US public and soldiers to accept initiating nuclear use, this US policy is arguably a violation of international law. First use denies civilians who would be affected by blast and radioactive fallout of their right to civilian immunity.[21]

---

[18] Ellen D. Katz, "Justice Ginsburg's Umbrella," University of Michigan Law School Scholarship Repository, (2015): 264, ekatz@umich.edu; https://repository.law.umich.edu/book_chapters/81.

[19] Robert Dahl, "Democracy Deficits and Foreign Policy," Dissent 46, no. 1 (Winter 1999): 110.

[20] See Robert A. Dahl, On Democracy (New Haven, CT: Yale University Press, 1998).

[21] In 1996, the ICJ ruled that the threat or use of nuclear weapons would generally be contrary to international law. The use of nuclear weapons in combat would be illegal because such weapons make

First use would also be unjustifiable if one followed a restrictive reading of just war standards. This policy can be destabilizing and dangerous because in a crisis it could encourage adversaries to launch their nuclear weapons when they first sense a warning of a US attack, without knowing for sure if an attack will occur and, if it does, whether it will be conventional or nuclear.

Why should the United States maintain a first-use policy when it has more than enough non-nuclear means of protecting itself and certainly far more than any other country? Citizens should ask for public discussion of a more constructive peacebuilding approach that would nurture customary international law against all uses of nuclear weapons, an ethic that the United States can hardly strengthen while maintaining a first-use policy itself.

The very nature of nuclear weapons, of course, also interferes with democratic decision-making about their use. Responses to threats, whether real or imagined, often must be given in a few minutes, which does not allow much time for discussion and for checking whether there is a real need or only a feared need to use nuclear weapons. To establish a no-first-use policy against an opponent that has not used them would at least provide a bulwark against irresponsible or premature decisions to use.

The possibility that an emotionally unstable or psychologically motivated president might launch an unnecessary war cries out for exercising more democratic control over decisions to use nuclear weapons. Citizens should debate whether the authority for sending massive destruction should be taken out of the hands of only one person[22]— the president—and shared at least among a small group of top elected officials[23] or put in the hands of Congress to arrange for the constitutionally required declaration of war.

---

distinctions between targeting soldiers and civilians extremely difficult. Exploding nuclear weapons causes indiscriminate harm, killing and wounding and exposing to radiation both civilians and soldiers.

The use of nuclear weapons would breach specific international laws, including the Declaration of St. Petersburg of 1868, because they would cause unnecessary suffering and prevent the avoidance and minimizing of loss of civilian life; the Hague Convention of 1907, because they would cause unnecessary suffering; the Universal Declaration of Human Rights of 1948, because widespread blast and radioactive contamination would interfere with innocent people's right to life, health, and peace; the Geneva Conventions of 1949, because protection of the wounded, sick, the infirm, expectant mothers, civilian hospitals, and health workers would not be ensured; and the Protocols to the Geneva Conventions of 1977, because there would be massive incidental losses of civilian lives and widespread, long-term damage to the environment. International Court of Justice, "Legality of the Threat or Use of Nuclear Weapons," https://www.icj-cij.org/en/case/95https://www.icj-cij.org/en/case/95; International Court of Justice, "Legality of the Use by a State of Nuclear Weapons in Armed Conflict," https://www.icj-cij.org/en/case/93.

[22] David Sanger, reporting how easily cyber tools might be used to manipulate strategic information, writes: "That a president could make snap decisions on which millions of lives depend, based on information that had been subtly manipulated, is sheer madness." Sanger, *Perfect Weapon*, 299. Howell and Moe declare: "Decisions about war are too important for one person to make," let alone decisions about nuclear war. *Crisis of Democracy*, 201.

[23] This group should probably include the vice president and the majority and minority leaders of both houses of Congress and perhaps others.

Even when some important topics do enter public debate, the quality of the discussion often is not helpful. In discussing US policy toward North Korea in 2019, for example, journalists spent more time and energy describing the threats and insults exchanged between the leaders of the two countries than informing the public about the values that were at stake at a deeper level than the superficial theatrics. A similar problem is that journalists often spend a disproportionate amount of time reporting on political partisanship in conflicts between the two US political parties or on the horse-race dimensions of whether a particular bill has the votes to pass, rather than devoting serious time to how the contents of pending legislation or policies will affect the common good. If US national security managers seldom promote thoughtful public discussion, and if citizens are not sufficiently informed by shallow journalism to know what to press leaders to do, then what are the prospects for governing wisely?

8.1.5 *Countering Threats to Democratic Integrity*

In addition to the four preceding democratic deficits, US citizens should help prepare one another to address rising anti-democratic influences, including

(1) officials in Congress and the executive branch who practice dishonesty, distort reality, and mislead others;
(2) citizens who are indifferent to or in favor of officials' falsehoods and the rise of anti-democratic populism;
(3) media that amplify dishonest propaganda for profit and power;
(4) national media policies that do not uphold democratic values, including giving insufficient attention to foreign governments trying to subvert democracy; and
(5) moneyed interests and wealthy partisans who distort and corrupt electoral processes.

First, citizens face difficulty obtaining an accurate understanding of what officials are really doing and why. Yet without full disclosure and truthful information they cannot make wise choices in self-government. Deliberate lying by officials and secrecy in decision-making may hide the truth or distort the real reasons for decisions. Campaign exaggerations and deceptions often lay the groundwork for dishonesty that continues after an election is over. Although dishonesty has not been practiced equally by all politicians or by both parties in recent years, it has been present for a long time and seems to be getting worse. To take an historical example, during his first campaign for the presidency, Richard Nixon set up a secret back channel to ask the South Vietnamese government secretly to scuttle an impending ceasefire that President Johnson was negotiating with the North Vietnamese. Nixon believed that if Johnson achieved peace before the election, it would be more likely that Nixon's opponent, Vice President Hubert Humphrey, would win the presidency. Of course, Nixon's secret initiative was completely illegal. Any private citizen is constitutionally prohibited from making any representation to foreign governments behind the back of US government officials.[24] The notes of H. R. Haldeman, a close Nixon aide, "show that Nixon committed a crime to win the presidential election."[25] It was nearly a half century after the fact that the public learned of Nixon's nefarious scheme in which he convinced top South Vietnamese officials not to support the peace agreement that President Johnson arranged. Although one cannot know with certainty that a peace settlement would have been signed before the election if Nixon had refrained from telling the South Vietnamese to wait for a ceasefire until he was president, it seems likely.[26]

Perhaps Nixon could be added to the list of people who would not have been in the White House if the democratic principle had been respected and someone would have been willing to expose his manipulation of peace negotiations to help him win the election. For this breach of democratic legal principles, the US public and servicemen and -women never received any restitution. Moreover, thousands of people were killed because the fighting was prolonged and the end of the war delayed. Many young people continued to fight and die without knowing that the war's extension had become a maneuver to help Nixon win the election. There were no discernible national benefits, then or subsequently, from subverting a negotiated peace agreement and prolonging the war.

Dishonesty had been present throughout the long war, presided over by four administrations (Kennedy, Johnson, Nixon, and Ford). Some of the secrecy seemed more for the purpose of insulating the war from criticism than for the purpose of enabling the operations to succeed. Early in the conflict President Johnson had distorted a Gulf of Tonkin incident between North Vietnamese and US naval vessels, making misleading claims that US ships had been attacked by North Vietnamese boats, in order to win congressional authorization and public support for the war. Later, officials assured the public "we seek no wider war" while secretly expanding US bombing into Cambodia and extending bombing of North Vietnam to its harbors.[27] In retrospect, it became clear that "successive White House administrations had intensified American involvement in the war while hiding their own doubts about the chances of success."[28] The recurring dishonesty enabled large expenditures of money on killing humans and plant life in Southeast Asia, which resulted in massive human and environmental destruction and unnecessary losses of US, Vietnamese, and Cambodian lives.

---

[24] President Johnson knew something about these illegal Republican efforts from internal intelligence reports. See Peter Baker, "Nixon Sought 'Monkey Wrench' in Vietnam Talks," *New York Times,* January 3, 2017, A1.

[25] Baker, "Nixon," A17.

[26] Baker, "Nixon," A17.

[27] This was investigated in the PBS documentary analysis, *The War in Vietnam,* by Ken Burns and Lynn Novick, https://www.pbs.org/show/vietnam-war/.

[28] Janny Scott, "Now It Can Be Told: How Neil Sheehan Got the Pentagon Papers," *New York Times,* January 7, 2021.

More recently, the illegal US attack[29] on Iraq and overthrow of the Iraqi govern-ment were justified by officials' false claim that Iraq possessed or soon would pos-sess nuclear weapons, a claim that was disputed at the time by independent observers and UN IAEA inspectors present in Iraq. A recent study of fighting in Afghanistan reported that US "officials routinely issue inflated assessments of progress that con-tradict what is actually happening there."[30] The US government "misleads the public on Afghanistan" to give the impression that the military is making progress when in fact since 2017 the Taliban had been making progress and holding "more Afghan territory than at any time since the American invasion."[31] The true story about Afghanistan had never come out until the *Washington Post* undertook a prolonged legal campaign, uti-lizing the Freedom of Information Act, to obtain thousands of pages of secret Defense Department communications in which US officials acknowledged routinely lying to the public and manipulating information to deceive other parts of the US government and the public.[32] Army General Douglas Lute, who helped the White House oversee the war during both the Bush and Obama administrations reported, "We didn't have the foggiest notion of what we were undertaking." Policymakers "were devoid of a fundamental understanding of Afghanistan—we didn't know what we were doing."[33] A senior National Security Council official reported that during the Obama years "the metrics were always manipulated."[34] The US mission eventually cut off outside access to US troops on the ground in an attempt to keep the mission as secret as possible to avoid criticism and objective analysis of what was going on.

The lack of honesty among key mid-range officials reporting on war or global warm-ing or tariff manipulations or Covid 19 transmissibility is magnified by misleading statements from political leaders at the highest level. Especially during the Trump administration, many officials apparently felt justified in making almost any self-serving claim that they thought they could get away with, no matter how untrue. Fact-checkers recorded more than 1,600 false or misleading statements made by President Trump during his first 300 days in office. During his first two and a half years, the US president spoke dishonestly to US citizens 12,019 times, an average of about 13 dishonest statements every day.[35] Such high-level, chronic dishonesty, which received

---

[29] The attack was illegal because it was not an act of self-defense and did not have authorization by the UN Security Council.

[30] Rod Nordland, Ash Ngu, and Fahim Abed, "How the US Government Misleads the Public on Afghanistan," *New York Times*, September 9, 2018, 12; Thomas Gibbons-Neff, "Documents Reveal Misleading Public Statements on War in Afghanistan," *New York Times*, December 9, 2019, https://www.nytimes.com/2019/12/09/world/asia/afghanistan-war-documents.html?smid=nytcore-ios-share.

[31] Nordland, Ngu, and Abed, "How the US Government Misleads," 12. Discrepancies are not merely a mat-ter of interpretation. Numerical data on Taliban strength, maternal mortality, and life expectancy show enormous disparity with independent sources and health researchers.

[32] See Thomas Gibbons-Neff, "Public Was Duped on Afghan War," *New York Times*, December 10, 2019, A1.

[33] Quoted by Gibbons-Neff, "Public Was Duped," A1.

[34] Quoted by Gibbons-Neff, "Public Was Duped," A9.

[35] Glenn Kessler, Salvador Rizzo, and Meg Kelly, "President Trump Has Made 12,019 False or Misleading Claims over 928 Days," *Washington Post*, August 12, 2019, https://www.washingtonpost.com/poli-tics/2019/08/12/president-trump-has-made-false-or-misleading-claims-over-days/?noredirect=on.

repeated and abundant support from most Republican members of the US Senate and House of Representatives, constitutes a grave threat to democracy,[36] smart decision-making, and respect for US citizens' rights.

Given inaccuracy in US discourse, citizens cannot make informed judgments about whether there is a reasonable prospect of success in a war effort. If there is not, then according to traditional just war standards, it is not a justifiable war. The misleading reasons for the US invasion of Iraq in 2003, during a pre-Trump mode of operation, confirm doubts about whether citizens can believe their own government's claims about fighting justifiable wars.[37] Even in non-war contexts, lying has frequently occurred about some other matters, such as related to testing and managing nuclear weapons.[38] Although problems of government dishonesty no doubt have been present since the first government, these have become more dangerous because of the larger destructiveness that current technologies bring and the widespread, often immediate consequences of government dishonesty on people's lives.

Second, the problem of dishonesty in governing is not simply the result of only one or a few emotionally impaired persons or a morally calloused political elite. In addition, tens of millions of citizens are indifferent to or enthusiastic about receiving meme-like falsehoods from officials and from digital and print media. President Trump was, according to some analysts, "a symptom" of a partly delusional society in which millions of citizens seem not to care about truthfulness.[39] People lose their perceptive and moral moorings when lies stream constantly from leaders and are repeated approvingly by party colleagues and by broadcasters on "news" programs. Timothy Egan pointed out that during the Trump administration "we have a White House of lies because a huge percentage of the population can't tell fact from fiction."[40] Over many years tens of millions have believed false stories, which could be easily laid to rest by checking the facts, such as that President Obama was not born in the United States. Citizens choose to watch popular media that amplify false information, act as propaganda agencies, and mislead voters who come not to care as much about the truth as about winning partisan battles. Often the outlets distort to increase profits

---

See also https://www.huffpost.com/entry/donald-trump-washington-post-fact-checker-figure_n_5d526ff0e4b0c63bcbecbbea.

[36] "Perhaps most harmful of all is his assault on the truth itself." These efforts "are supported at every step by the right-wing propaganda network, led by Fox." Howell and Moe, *Crisis of Democracy*, 109.

[37] A detailed description occurs in the PBS analysis, "The War in Vietnam." The US attack on Iraq was not an act of self-defense made in response to an Iraqi attack on the United States, nor was it carried out after a UN Security Council authorization. A preemptive attack could not be justified because the presence and freedom of movement of UN IAEA inspectors in Iraq at the time meant that no surprise attack on the United States would have been possible at that time.

[38] For example, when the United States lost a nuclear weapon at sea off the coast of Japan, this was not acknowledged for many years. It was "one of many cover-ups." David E. Sanger and Andrew E. Kramer, "U.S. Officials Suspect New Nuclear Missile in Explosion That Killed 7 Russians," *New York Times*, August 12, 2019.

[39] Timothy Egan, "Look in the Mirror: We're with Stupid," *New York Times*, November 18, 2017, A 18.

[40] Egan, "Mirror."

or market share. After observing the Trump administration from the inside, former secretary of state Rex Tillerson observed: "If our leaders seek to conceal the truth, or we as people become accepting of alternative realities that are no longer grounded in facts, then we as American citizens are on a pathway to relinquishing our freedom."[41]

Citizens easily adopt a post-truth political culture when the public has allowed or encouraged its educational systems "to become negligent in teaching the owner's manual of citizenship."[42] Another explanation for indifference to truth might be that "a society invested in real, tangible common projects needs objective truths," but "one organized around a desperate longing for a mythologized past does not."[43]

Experts on information warfare report that "a post-fact society emerges from despair and cynicism about the future."[44] In sharing these negative attitudes with others, many people gravitate toward "populism," which is sweeping across the United States and Europe, primarily because citizens feel frustrated by an absence of positive vision and political successes from their own governments. They sense they are being left behind. The rise of populism may be stimulated by fears of racial shifts in demographics, migratory competition, technological and environmental dislocations, and threatening socioeconomic forces from globalization. The problems facing US citizens "have gotten so severe, and government's responses have been so blatantly ineffective, that millions of Americans have embraced populism and a strongman style of leadership that threatens democracy itself."[45] The solution, in general terms, is more effective government, able to respond to people's grievances and concerns.

Third, although today's media may and some do provide accurate information and support democratic values with their excellent investigative reporting, other media have profited from amplifying people's intake of misleading, dishonest, extremist information. Because of the popularity of digitized information and the lack of sufficient public regulation, they have become a primary source for disinformation and its rapid, massive spread. Powerful domestic and secret foreign agencies using divisive, hateful messaging promote antagonisms among differing groups in the United States with a goal of causing havoc in US society as a viable democracy. Social media have also facilitated extremism in other countries, some of which has led to genocide. In 2018, people belatedly learned that military officials in Myanmar had used Facebook in a secret, elaborately designed "successful" effort to inflame their population against their own Rohingya population, using false identities and posing as popular sources within Myanmar. The military poured large amounts of money into and employed 700 people in this dishonest messaging operation that showed sham "news" photos of corpses from killings attributed to the Rohingya. Facebook spread thousands of

[41] Peter Baker, "Trump's Insults End a Brief Civil Interlude," *New York Times*, December 8, 2018, A 10.
[42] Egan, "Mirror."
[43] Michelle Goldberg, "Toxic Nostalgia Breeds Derangement," *New York Times*, August 19, 2019.
[44] Goldberg, "Toxic Nostalgia Breeds Derangement."
[45] Howell and Moe, *Crisis of Democracy*, 119.

messages depicting the Rohingya as terrorists,[46] which of course seemed to justify military crackdowns against them. It motivated public outcries for the Rohingya to leave the country of their birth. Government officials used Facebook and other social media secretly to manipulate their own people so they could commit genocide. Facebook should have taken stronger action "to avoid becoming an instigator of genocide."[47]

Facebook has been slow to take appropriate action in most cases because it profits from advertising geared to the number of people using it. The larger the number of users, the higher the advertising revenues. Often the more scandalous the message, the more people may tune in. Advertisers flock to heavily trafficked sites, yielding huge profits for the media platform. The United States has also been slow to regulate media. As a party to the genocide convention, the United States is obligated to do what it can to help prevent genocide by others. US officials and members of Congress should require all media, including Facebook, to use their communication privileges in ways that will not add to gross violations of human rights. Best practices should not enable media to profit from promoting hatred, facilitating killing, and hiding the truth.

Fourth, a deeply disconcerting aspect of the torrent of dishonesty and bigotry going to US citizens is the feeble US regulatory policy that allows it. Democracy cannot thrive as long as widely used communication platforms advance exclusivist, racist, xenophobic identities harboring prejudices rather than privileging factual information and helping users value truthful accounts that are respectful of human beings' fundamental rights. Even two years after there was widespread awareness that Russian intelligence services had been involved in far-reaching secret psychological warfare activities on social media to manipulate US electoral processes in 2016 to increase the electoral prospects for Donald Trump, Congress had not taken robust initiatives to guard against these practices. Instead, Congress allowed US groups to adapt the tactics of Russian intelligence operatives aimed at electing their preferred candidates by spreading false information about those whom they wanted to defeat.[48]

Because the airwaves belong to the whole citizenry, who are entitled to their being used for public benefit, the US government should regulate the use of airwaves for the common good. Heavily biased media have become a problem in recent years primarily as a result of conservatives' objections to establishing public guidelines for media. This was not always part of a conservative agenda. After radio was invented, President Herbert Hoover, a principled conservative, developed the first legislation to govern mass media, the Radio Act of 1927, based on the idea that, because airwaves belonged to the public, every broadcaster should serve the public interest. The same idea was used to regulate television when the Federal Communications Commission

---

[46] Paul Mozur, "A Genocide Incited on Facebook, with Posts from Myanmar's Military," *New York Times*, October 15, 2018.

[47] Mozur, "A Genocide." The U.S. National Intelligence Council anticipates that "Identity-based violence, including hate and political crimes, may increasingly be facilitated by social media." *Global Trends 2040*, 74.

[48] Mosur, "A Genocide."

established the Fairness Doctrine. This required a "reasonably balanced presentation of different political views."[49] Although conservatives supported this Republican initiative for several decades, by the time of Ronald Reagan they opposed fairness guidelines and repealed the Fairness Doctrine. The repeal allowed licensed broadcasters to ignore completely any obligation to serve the general public by representing opposing points of view. Soon there were more than 900 newly partisan radio talk shows enabling broadcasters to use public airwaves to propagandize directly for exclusivist causes without giving time to alternative views. This repeal also paved the way for Fox news.

Further deregulation of the communications industry removed most anti-monopoly provisions and enabled consolidation of media companies that served corporate elites and exclusivist causes at the expense of inclusive, democratic values. Most people no longer heard a fairly balanced diversity of opinions on their radios and TVs, to say nothing of internet sources. The failure to govern digital media in the interest of honest and balanced reporting has upended electoral processes, encouraged polarization, diminished democratic values, and misled voters. Social media in particular have amplified the voices of those eager to spread deceit by attracting viewers and advertisers to scandalous messages that "go viral." Threats to democracy are magnified by corporations eager to piggyback lucrative advertising on almost any message that might increase corporate sales or market share, even when the messages that attract the biggest viewership often are those carrying the most outrageous statements with no regard for truthfulness.

To prevent negative manipulations of public opinion and to safeguard honest elections, vigorous US governmental safeguards are required, but some officials in recent years have been lukewarm to taking needed initiatives, perhaps in part because they calculate that they may benefit from manipulations of public opinion. Even though substantial evidence indicates that foreign powers, such as Russia, Iran, and China have manipulated sentiment in the United States and other democracies, Washington officials and educators in public schools of many states need to do more to counter the spread of vicious information and to increase public vigilance for maintaining the integrity of democratic processes. Citizens need to exert more intentionality and obtain legislative help to amplify accurate information.[50]

Deliberate use of false information, whether by foreign governments engaged in cyber wars, unscrupulous corporations and citizens, or US public servants, poses a serious threat to democratic processes and outcomes. Social media have in practice become agents of surveillance and propaganda, gathering data about individual citizens and then exposing them to emotional appeals and misleading information to

---

[49] Quoted by Jill Lepore, "The Hacking of America," *New York Times*, September 14, 2018, IV, 1.

[50] The National Intelligence Council forecasts that "During the next 20 years, the algorithms and social media platforms that curate and distill massive amounts of data will produce content that could overtake expertise in shaping the political and social effects engendered by a hyperconnected information environment." *Global Trends 2040*, 71.

influence their values and conduct. These processes may be orchestrated by predators to play on citizens' weaknesses in order to increase prejudices, profits, or power, to promote divisiveness, to support authoritarian leaders, or to undermine democratic values.

If people's voting preferences are secretly manipulated and government decisions are justified with misleading information, an ethically sensitive person can hardly be confident that a policy is being carried out for legitimate reasons. If one does not want to be an unintentional accomplice to denying human rights or committing murder, then knowing whether a particular policy, drone attack, or war is justified becomes important. Citizens understandably need to know whether threats could have been addressed through strategic peacebuilding. To escape disinformation campaigns, which often arise from narrow nationalism, citizens and responsible journalists need to combine efforts to communicate accurate information to one another, at home and abroad, about the value consequences of what political leaders are doing. This is necessary to regain enough understanding to evaluate what government decisions to support or oppose.

As alluded to previously, the integrity of US democratic processes also has been compromised by hostile initiatives from other governments and very limited US responses. During the US electoral process in 2016, the Russian government attempted to sow misunderstanding, suspicion, discord, malice, prejudice, and even violence among US citizens in order to change the outcome of the election and destroy healthy democratic processes. US corporations inattentively helped to subsidize the dissemination of bigoted propaganda and lies about candidates by advertising on platforms that carried scandalous untruths. Facebook, for one, sent 126 million US citizens messages conjured up by Russians without informing US citizens of the origin of the messages which were presented as news reports. Russians secretly posted more than 1,000 videos on YouTube. Kathleen Hall Jamieson, who conducted extensive research into influences exerted in the 2016 presidential election, concluded that the many secret Russian interventions in public debate tilted the election in favor of Donald Trump and prevented a Hillary Clinton victory, even though the Russians were unable directly to fabricate false vote tallies.[51]

Fifth, although the consequences for democracy of the Supreme Court decision in 2010 to invalidate the Bipartisan Campaign Reform Act of 2002—also known as the McCain-Feingold Act—cannot be analyzed here, it is necessary to mention that the corrupting influence of money in electoral processes has become a significant threat to political egalitarianism among US citizens. The 5 to 4 Court decision opened corporate floodgates that enable special interests to use unlimited amounts of money to spread political advertising and propaganda throughout public airwaves.

---

[51] Kathleen Hall Jamieson, *Cyberwar: How Russian Hackers and Trolls Helped Elect a President* (Oxford: Oxford University Press, 2018).

The inequitable power of large monetary gifts from publicly unknown sources buys influence in elections and in legislative priorities afterward. This court-initiated change in campaign financial practices in 2010 enables a small number of people or corporations with an unusually large amount of money to exert more power in electoral and legislative politics than possessed by voting citizens of average means. This monetary influence, which may dwarf voters' influence in opinion formation, is not held to reasonable standards of honesty, transparency, or service to the commonweal. Those who wrote the US constitution could not have imagined the enormity of the influence gap between a citizen and a corporation that five justices on the Supreme Court would enable, because corporations did not even exist when the Constitution was written. An indirect yet extremely far-reaching result of this judicial overturn of congressional legislation is that now many pieces of congressional legislation favored by a majority of US citizens have no chance of even being brought to a vote, to say nothing of passing, because these newly empowered moneyed interests keep senators in power who control what is allowed to be put on the Senate's agenda to come up for a vote.

The influence of wealth, which is overwhelmingly concentrated in the hands of less than 10 percent of the population, has purchased favorable influence and violated democratic values at so many points that serious observers voice an urgent plea to save US democracy from capitalism's grasp of wealth to put power in the hands of a few. *The Economist* has warned that its Democracy Index has downgraded the United States from a "full democracy" to a "flawed" one because extreme US inequities mean the preferences of a majority of the US population are repeatedly ignored and the "will of the progressive majority subverted."[52] As a number of studies show, "the national agenda . . . is set by oligarchs and well-organized special interests." Democracy is in crisis not because the majority of citizens have become authoritarian but because economic elites, repeatedly financed by the wealthy to retain power, have little concern for the common good. Although Astra Taylor argues that "the primary threat facing democracy today is not one of populism but rather plutocracy,"[53] the two are strongly related. Populism arises from people feeling forgotten by elites, and plutocratic elites arise by benefiting from enablement by populists. An antidote to both plutocracy and populism requires implementing political and economic equality and disallowing large amounts of money to buy disproportionate influence to set the national legislative agenda, to influence officials' ascent to power or actions in office, or to employ former officials as corporate lobbyists after leaving office.

The control of the congressional agenda by moneyed interests can easily occur because the Senate majority leader can act almost as if he were an elected dictator in

---

[52] *The Economist*, "Global Democracy Has Another Bad Year," *The Economist*, January 22, 2020, http://www.eiu.com/topic/democracy-index; Astra Taylor, "Reimagine Democracy," *The Progressive* (February/March, 2020): 22.

[53] Taylor, "Reimagine Democracy," 25. See also Astra Taylor, *Democracy May Not Exist, But We'll Miss It When It's Gone* (New York: Metropolitan Books, Henry Holt, 2019); Feingold, "Our Legitimacy Crisis."

single-handedly being able to prevent legislation or presidential nominees from coming to the Senate floor for a vote. How can the will of a majority of citizens be respected if many important issues from pandemic relief to gun safety legislation, from a presidential court nominee by President Obama to Covid aid for states, from immigration legislation to relief for student loans be blocked by the majority leader, as Senator Mitch McConnell did at times between 2016 and 2021, so that the Senate did not even have an opportunity to vote on them?

Although many customs and institutions help to sustain democracy in the United States, democratic values are always vulnerable to dismissal and dismantlement. Although one violation of democratic principles in itself may not seem to do great harm, the combined consequences of all the above are cumulative, structural, and damaging over the long term. Democratic values are too often overridden by greed, prejudice, and oppressive political processes which together exert a negative systemic influence on all US politics and policies.

When all of the foregoing influences and democratic deficits are taken together, one can hardly escape the conclusion that the United States is beginning to look like an unhealthy quasi-democracy, requiring strong citizens' efforts to bring it closer to becoming a thoroughgoing democracy. Its democratic institutions are certainly not a failure, but the conduct of those now undermining them is deeply disappointing. If citizens find their government taking many actions that profoundly violate their commitment to human dignity, they need to call that government to greater accountability by taking bold, public stances on behalf of human freedom and dignity. If citizens feel that the US government repeatedly subordinates human dignity to less desirable goals, then perhaps the government has deserted those citizens; citizens have not deserted their government. Its legitimacy resides in serving its people's needs expressed in the values of human dignity. If US officials neglect these values, concerned citizens need to signal to other people in the United States and in all countries that they stand for human solidarity and dignity, even if their own government is, for the present, pursuing narrower interests.[54]

Unless concerned US citizens stand, with principled yet friendly firmness, against other citizens' or some officials' indifference to democracy, and unless they withhold support from the excessively militarized elements of US foreign policy and from unnecessary maintenance of an inequitable international system, constructive change will be unlikely. Pressures for ever higher levels of military preparedness and low attention to environmental needs, which are raised by both elitist and populist drives for economic gain and national power, will try to dampen public initiatives for human security. On the other hand, if support for unnecessarily high levels of military spending declines and for democratization based on economic equity and environmental

---

[54] Even without Donald Trump in the White House, the narrowly nationalist, populist threat is likely to continue. Howell and Moe, *Crisis of Democracy*, 112. Although normalcy may seem to return under a Biden presidency, the most serious challenge is to address the underlying sources of populism by building more effective governance, which will require a significant global governing capacity.

health rises, then policy planners will have increased incentives to bolster the rule of law to supplant military balancing with political and legal means of resolving conflict and promoting justice.

Even in the pre-Trump years, it was becoming clear that US democracy needed repair. Experts like William Howell and Terry Moe have offered suggestions for making the US government more effective to enable it to address fears and frustrations that drive people to populism.[55] Whether or not one agrees with their recommendations, US governmental reforms are needed to strengthen US democracy for its own survival as well as to contribute momentum to a grand strategy for human security. With help from science and social science, concerned citizens can strengthen US democracy and press for bringing congruency between the extent of grave problems, which is global, and the extent of the solutions which also must be global and addressed by global institutions undergirded by inclusive human identities in order to succeed.[56]

The four years of the Trump presidency were punctuated in January 2021 with what Republican Senator Mitt Romney described as an "insurrection incited by the President of the United States"[57] in which a mob invaded the Capitol and threatened Senators and Representatives at work in their chambers. Four years during which a majority of the Republican Party refused to call the president to accountability to the Constitution, the law, and time-honored democratic practices cast a lasting shadow over the depth and breadth of US citizens' commitment to democracy. Democracy's future is further threatened by insufficiently regulated social media that magnify dishonesty, prejudice, and conflict when they earn profits from doing so. The threats to democracy from populism and autocratic, demagogic political leaders all over the world, including the United States, underscore that more honest civic education and accurate, investigative journalism, coupled with citizens' commitment to acting independently and boldly to ensure officials' accountability at every level of governance are absolutely necessary to the future of self-government. Because the United States historically has been a reassuring example to democracies everywhere, and was a valuable influence in restoring democracy in Europe after fascism, Nazism, and World War II, the tarnished US image harms democracy everywhere. The US brush with antidemocratic forces may be a useful wake-up call to citizens, but it is a delusion for policymakers and citizens to think that the threats are over because Joe Biden was elected president. In addition to the improvements noted above, reforms of US laws and even the Constitution itself must occur to ensure that federal law enforcement and intelligence agencies possess unwavering independence and firm protection from presidential control and misuse. These reforms are not an option; they are necessary to maintain democracy in the United States.

---

[55] See especially chapter 4 in Howell and Moe, *Crisis of Democracy*.

[56] Congruence calls for correspondence between the scope of the problem and the inclusiveness of people in working out the solution.

[57] Senator Minority Leader Chuck Schumer used almost identical language to describe this event. "Biden's Win Is Confirmed, but Nation Is Shaken," *New York Times*, January 7, 2021.

The causes of malaise in US governance are the same as the causes of malaise in global governance—ineffective governance and insufficiently robust democratic processes and protections against abuse of power. The solutions are also the same for both domains, because each governing domain is part of one overall seamless domain. So the correlates of peace (Table 5.1) and the processes of peacebuilding need to be implemented for the benefit of US citizens and US democracy domestically, as well as for the benefit of citizens globally. In both domestic and global domains, not much can be accomplished by blaming others, as opposed to holding all powerful decision-makers accountable, whether blame is aimed at the left or the right, the populists or the socialists, the Montagues or the Capulets. It is necessary to examine everyone's conduct critically, of course, on the basis of principles of dignity, justice, and law to understand how to avoid repeating past mistakes and to identify the conduct to support or to oppose. Focus on principled conduct and misconduct is more helpful than stereotyping groups as inherently "bad people."

8.2 COSMOPOLITANIZING NATIONAL INTERESTS

Political mobilization is needed now, not only to enhance US democracy,[58] but also to press for broadening US national interests to embrace more inclusive human interests. Powerful decision-making elites *do* change—when enough underdogs insist that they change, but seldom much before, as the centuries-long, slow progress in the growth of human rights demonstrates.[59] The effort to save our earth's biosphere should focus our minds on the necessity for exerting more citizen pressure because that effort is now getting desperate. People in many countries accurately see themselves in a struggle on behalf of economic and environmental human rights to protect their own homes, their air and water, their parks, their climate, and their human dignity.[60]

Nathaniel Rich's depiction of our present situation is empirically accurate and stunning: "The world has warmed more than one degree Celsius since the Industrial Revolution. The Paris climate agreement . . . hoped to restrict warming to two degrees. The odds of succeeding . . . are one in 20. If by miracle we are able to limit warming to two degrees, we will only have to negotiate the extinction of the world's tropical

---

[58] Howell and Moe suggest applying the fast-track model for legislating international trade agreements to other legislation to enable at least the possibility of voting on legislation that might harmonize local or vested interests with the national interest, and the national interest with the human interest. Judicial and administrative appointments might also be covered by universal fast-track authority, so congressional gamesmanship can no longer block Senate decisions because a powerful Senate leader refuses to allow a vote. Howell and Moe, *Crisis of Democracy*, 177.

[59] This is well documented in Lauren, *International Human Rights*.

[60] This struggle may be animated by a sense of human destiny, although certainly not inevitability, in the outcome. Human networks have arisen across borders to serve common interests throughout history. The current proliferation of transnational interest groups, such as the coalition of environmentalists trying to restrain climate change, "is a natural outgrowth of the whole history of humankind." Wright, *Nonzero*, 223.

reefs, sea-level rise of several meters and the abandonment of the Persian Gulf. The climate scientist James Hansen has called two-degree warming 'a prescription for long-term disaster.' *Long-term disaster is now the best-case scenario.*"[61] Warming of three degrees would result in short-term disaster, including "the loss of most coastal cities." Robert Watson, the former director of the United Nations Intergovernmental Panel on Climate Change, has concluded that "three-degree warming is the realistic minimum. Four degrees: Europe in permanent drought: vast areas of China, India and Bangladesh claimed by desert; Polynesia swallowed by the sea; the Colorado River thinned to a trickle; the American Southwest largely uninhabitable. The prospect of a five-degree warming has prompted some of the world's leading climate scientists to warn of the end of human civilization."[62]

US citizens now must face the reality that the person for whom less than a majority of voters cast ballots for president in 2016, with the support of the Republican Party, tried to make America great by using means that have contributed to bringing the five-degree "end of human civilization." Those means include four years of denying United States robust participation in the international community's efforts to manage climate disruption. They also include the strong support for these self-destructive policies from most Republicans in the House and Senate and roughly 40 percent of US voters. Is increasing the risks for the "end of human civilization" a good bargain for US citizens, to say nothing of the rest of the world? The tragedy of the commons already is advancing at alarming speed while 18 million unnecessary deaths occur from poverty every year. If that number of people dying unnecessarily is insufficient to move today's powers that be, it is foolish to wait for those powers to be moved by adding the deaths of millions more. After all, the United States is focusing a trillion new dollars, with the applause of many duly elected members of Congress on both sides of the aisle, on purchasing more nuclear weapons rather than addressing poverty or racism at home, let alone worldwide environmental catastrophe. The people in the White House, the Senate, and the House who for three decades have fiercely opposed policies that serve the human interest rather than their narrow, selfish interests may mean well, but their consciousness seems numbed[63] beyond understanding and belief. Because the chain of responsibility between what they do and those they hurt is long, they feel absolved of wrongdoing even though they are directly implicated in harming millions of people because of their official actions and inactions.

If constructive measures had been taken in time, efforts to limit carbon emissions could have succeeded at easily managed costs: "If the world had adopted the proposal widely endorsed at the end of the '80s—a freezing of carbon emissions, with a reduction of 20 percent by 2005—warming could have been held to less than 1.5 degrees." Recall that as early as 1979, at the first World Climate Conference in Geneva, scientists

---

[61] Rich, "Losing Earth," 8.

[62] Rich, "Losing Earth," 8.

[63] The relevant concept of psychic numbing is developed by Robert Jay Lifton, "Beyond Psychic Numbing: A Call to Awareness," *American Journal of Orthopsychiatry* 52, no. 4 (1982): 619–629.

from 50 countries "agreed unanimously that it was 'urgently necessary' to act." Within a decade, 60 countries meeting in the Netherlands set a goal of holding a global summit meeting one year later to address the dangers of global warming. "Among scientists and world leaders, the sentiment was unanimous: Action had to be taken, and the United States would need to lead. It didn't."[64]

We must never let ourselves forget that the United States took this suicidal path long before Donald Trump became president. He probably would not have been able to become president except that many others had already endorsed such self-destructive steps.

Many US citizens could now join together within the United States to demand that the EPA acknowledge what science has confirmed about carbon emissions and act boldly to address the destruction of nature from greed and overconsumption.[65] But acting within the United States is insufficient. The necessary movement must be transnational because US citizens need help from citizens abroad to bring pressure on the US government and to identify the incentives needed to encourage positive change around the world. Also, citizens in other countries need help from partners in the United States to press their governments to make choices for human dignity, and to do it together. In this particular case, the United States became a major impediment to positive movement by never supporting the Kyoto ceiling and withdrawing for four years from the Paris accord even though the United States has been the world's all-time largest polluter. It needs to face positive and negative incentives of all sorts, from within the United States and from outside, until it genuinely tries to make up for lost time and leads the way to move far beyond the Paris agreement. As Muhammad Yunus concluded in discussing the need for new economic initiatives to provide jobs for all and bring net carbon emissions to zero: "The first, most important, and perhaps most difficult step is transforming our thinking," because existing thought patterns have unnecessarily "constrained the way we behave."[66] Is it possible that, by considering the Earth and the global family with whom we now share a common destiny, we might change our thinking and acting? That is the final question to which we now turn.

---

[64] Rich, "Losing Earth," 9.

[65] With the help of the Freedom of Information Act, the Union of Concerned Scientists has extensively documented that "the EPA was knowingly using a political ploy to try to undermine independent scientific analysis." Union of Concerned Scientists, "Political Motives Exposed at the EPA," *Catalyst*, 18, Summer 2018, 5, www.uscusa.org/EPA-FOIA.

[66] Yunus, *Three Zeros*, 229.

9

Where the Evidence Leads

TO FOLLOW WHERE the evidence leads, policymakers and citizens might explore how each of them can help implement the vision that this analysis has drawn from social science research, reinforced with understandings from history, and buttressed by cosmopolitan philosophical and religious insights. The evidence shows what is needed and suggests what is possible, but in itself produces nothing. For the empirical analysis to matter means choosing among alternative approaches and implementing preferred policies. Commitment is required to achieve sustainable security and peace. To move in the direction toward which the evidence points would turn us toward a human security paradigm and away from some traditional national security policies.

9.1 WEIGHING NATIONAL SECURITY AND HUMAN SECURITY

To assess how sensible that direction may be and to weigh the prospects for improving US security requires selecting thoughtfully among present and future policies that either follow existing US national security habits or change course to open new possibilities for human security. These possibilities could arise from implementing the correlates of peace to address all nations' security fears; to emphasize human security; to establish positive reciprocity and equity in all relationships; to expand the rule of law in the international community; and to build democratic global governance that enables formation and enforcement of laws essential for human security (summarized in Table 5.1).

Table 9.1 can help policymakers and citizens identify the choices that they find most promising. It admittedly oversimplifies in order to clarify differences that turn out to be quite instructive. It shows how the policies of officials pursuing *national* security mainly by maximizing US military power, in the left column, differ from policies of officials pursuing *human* security mainly by implementing the correlates of peace, in the right column. Keeping these two broad paradigms in mind while examining various grand strategies can contribute to making wise choices among specific policies.

TABLE 9.1

National Security and Human Security Paradigms

	National Security	Human Security
World Order	Maintain a militarized balance-of-power system, constituted by states competing militarily in a system of relative anarchy similar to the existing international system	Create a demilitarized balance-of-power system, constituted by states competing politically in a system of global governance capable of managing unified constraint on independent (mis)use of military power
Goal	Seek US military primacy and global dominance (including space) to maintain national security	Seek political, economic, and environmental security for all nations through equitable political and economic empowerment and collaborative constraint of national military action
Means	Use US resources to persuade or require others to accept US preferences, rules, and ways of thinking; accept recurring cold or hot wars against main strategic rivals and terrorist groups; threaten and fight wars to maintain primacy	Develop worldwide negotiations for a global legislative compact needed for survival; maintain order through law, advancing justice and human rights; use cosmopolitan enforcement of international laws for security and environmental protection
Methods	Rely on US military action when necessary; use alliances and international organizations if possible; maintain high US military preparedness, immoderate independence and separate sovereignty, narrow nationalism, US exceptionalism, overseas bases, possibly orbiting weapons	Orchestrate multilateral decision-making and enforcement; enforce law on individuals, including heads of government, and also on states; make the world safe for national differences by demilitarizing and complexifying balancing processes; welcome limited mutual vertical dispersal of sovereignty

(continued)

Table 9.1   Continued

	National Security	Human Security
Security Focus	Preserve US geopolitical and geo-economic advantages (in land, sea, air, and space) as far into the future as possible	Protect all nations against security threats; implement political, economic, and environmental human rights for all; establish cosmopolitan law enforcement
Security Institutions	Use the US military to maintain dominance and deterrence; use NATO and other alliances, the UN and other international organizations when convenient; refuse compulsory jurisdiction for the US in international courts dealing with political and security affairs; resist limits that multilateral institutions would impose on US unilateral use of force	Create global rule-of-law democratic institutions, arms control, UN police force, robust global monitoring and law-enforcing security agencies; democratize UN General Assembly and Security Council; create global people's assembly; use compulsory jurisdiction in the ICJ, ICC, and other courts
Leadership	Arises from narrow nationalism and populism, US self-reliance, and unilateralism spurred by shifting configurations of great-power dominance, rivalry, and alliance-building	Arises from dialogue among states and people of all nationalities committed to protection of human dignity; addresses conflicts through law-guided political processes to protect minority rights for all nations
Probable Outcomes	Recurring violence and threats to peace and survival of human civilization; environmental destruction; economic inequity and polarization; gross violations of human rights; zero-sum military competition for security; international anarchy; ensuring national survival will be unlikely to succeed for some nations	Deep-seated yet manageable political conflicts in sustaining peace; improved environmental health; elimination of poverty; curtailed violations of human rights; increased non-zero-sum relations for common security; sufficient bridling of anarchy to constrain the war-making function of sovereignty to ensure national survival for all nations

Table 9.1 suggests that, in a world with rising interdependence, maximizing the reliability of the correlates of peace will produce more US security and life-enhancing results than maximizing US military power. Paradoxically, a traditional national security paradigm is likely to yield less security for the United States than a human security paradigm. The human security column in Table 9.1 sketches attributes of a paradigm

shift that, if successful, could generate sustainable security and high-quality peace for the United States *folded in with human security*.[1] The shift in orientation brings necessary elements of national security policy within the human security framework. Policymakers and citizens who prefer to continue working within the traditional national security worldview (left column) certainly can try to do so, but they will be unlikely to achieve many long-term successes from that vantage point if the analysis of changes in international relations discussed in Chapter 1 is at all accurate. The days of diplomatic successes based on the old paradigm are fast disappearing. If human civilization is to survive, zero-sum or negative-sum relationships among competing national military organizations must give way to non-zero-sum or positive sum relationships that are mutually beneficial in security terms. Once again in human history, system change in the form of more inclusive governance, which could remain limited, may be able to replace war among former adversaries. A global grand strategy for human security, which of course includes US national security within it, is likely to produce more sustainable security for the United States than a singular focus on a US grand strategy for national security by itself.

The contrasting attributes that characterize the national security and human security paradigms can be associated with political realism and empirical realism, respectively, showing which version of "realism" is more empirically attuned to present realities and a positive future. Evidence shows that the human security column of empirical realism in Table 9.1 is comprehensive. It attends to everything necessary for security. It is coherent, addressing all problems together in their interconnected complexities, recognizing that one country's increased security should not exacerbate another country's insecurity. It takes seriously that all countries have needs, and that these will be recognized. All are represented in decision-making. All contribute to solutions. All benefit. All are likely to support changes, because it is the most effective way to hold each other accountable.

In contrast, the national security paradigm of political realism is uncomprehensive. It de-emphasizes or excludes almost everything related to security, save for the maximization of power for one's own state. It is incoherent, because when country A increases its security, this will increase country B's insecurity. Only the most powerful are well represented in the militarized balance-of-power system. Others are left out. It does not matter much to national security policymakers in country A if country B has needs unrelated to theirs. Self-help is mainly how states contribute to their security. If my country benefits, it does not matter that another country loses. Each state's accountability is primarily to itself, not to each other or to any international agency.

Empirical realists are unlikely to share with many of today's policymakers and political realists a number of their beliefs, such as that states react to each other like

---

[1] For a useful yet somewhat different comparison of national and global emphases, see Held, "Reframing Global Governance," 293–311.

billiard balls, that international anarchy is here to stay, that the international system, for practical purposes, is unchanging, and that international institutions make no significant difference in great power behavior.[2] Because empirical realists do not share these beliefs, they are more open to working for changes *within* states (through peaceful means) to encourage improved external behavior, to incentivizing constructive changes in the degree of anarchy in the international system, to utilizing benefits from variance in interstate relationships in order to institutionalize the best of this variance in changing the structure of the international system, and to nurturing ways that international institutions and great powers may work together to change the effective functioning of both.

Despite these contrasts, the concept of self-interest holds promise for finding some common ground between exponents of national security and human security, between political realists and empirical realists. Although many national governments and societies are not ready to embrace the proposed grand strategy for human security at this time, progressive states, corporations, and civil society groups inclined to endorse the six guidelines can teach and demonstrate for others that *self*-interest can be upheld by serving *common* interests, because the two interests converge in the long run, as do prudential and ethical concerns. Feelings of threat and insecurity may recede in a country *if* its security is dependably sustained while cross-boundary forms of cooperation weave a strengthening international social fabric. To achieve a positive outcome, one can even serve one's own self-interest by helping an adversary feel secure if it can be done in ways that do not enable the adversary to harm others.

As technology, communication, commerce, and interdependence naturally weave people into ever more inclusive and denser webs of interactions, US citizens may, if they choose, better equip themselves for meeting the future by

(1) reducing the exclusive focus on serving one national (US) group, and expanding willingness to share equitably in serving the human dignity of all;

(2) decreasing the almost exclusive focus on national governmental means and expanding attention to include upgrading representative international institutions;

(3) moderating the almost reverential service of capital interests while elevating the service of human needs and rights;

(4) encouraging leaders and practitioners of every religious tradition to review how their religious expressions might emphasize the universal-human-dignity dimensions of their faith traditions;

(5) moving negative externalities (e.g., air and water pollution) in environmental equations into inclusive assessments of all environmental costs and benefits;

---

[2] These four beliefs held by most political realists are documented in Chapter 2. See especially Mearsheimer, *The Great Delusion;* Mearsheimer, *The Tragedy of Great Power Politics;* Waltz, *Theory of International Politics;* and Korab-Karpowicz, "Political Realism in International Relations."

(6) imagining how to replace part of the role of military power with increased roles for legal, political, and economic power, thereby turning zero-sum military relations into non-zero-sum multidimensional relations, and complexifying simple-minded military competition in the balance-of-power system with more complex, multilateral governing processes;

(7) moderating emphasis on states' rights or national-sovereignty rights by increasing attention to popular sovereignty and universal human rights, with individuals taking more responsibility and insisting on increased accountability for states and all other powerful actors; and

(8) implementing as many elements of the human security paradigm as politically feasible while legitimate elements of the national security paradigm co-exist or gradually are absorbed in the human security framework.

On this suggestive path, people might imagine citizens of multiple races and ethnicities, from all nationalities and bioregions, expressing diverse cultures, religious faiths, and ways of life from within their own secure nations, addressing stubborn, serious differences through inclusive transnational political institutions while living in safety and peace in the international community.

In this final chapter, addressed to individual citizens and policymakers alike, we draw together the evidence from previous chapters that has shown why new human security peacebuilding policies and empirical realist theory may hold more promise than continuing past US policies, which often have been failing. At the margins between the old and the new, substantial historical experience in international relations offers hope that changes in international laws, organizations, and means of enforcement can address security problems more effectively than merely maximizing US power. Yet many policymakers in the United States and all the great powers have not allowed new thinking to carry much weight. To embrace it more fully as a way of achieving more US and human security will require robust efforts advanced by policymakers and citizens willing to act boldly with like-minded people transnationally to press for specific initiatives to increase security.

Because the remaining parts of this chapter discuss how transnational networks and coalitions of citizen advocates and social change organizations might work with intergovernmental organizations and like-minded governments to increase the possibility of implementing a global grand strategy for human security, it is written in a slightly different style than the preceding chapters. It is in part conjecture about the future and an invitation for readers to engage the evidence and consider action.

The following sections of this chapter illustrate only a few of the possibilities for change, which are vast in number. These suggest how concerned people may draw strength from and contribute strength to the value of human dignity, the gravitas of human rights, the attractiveness and challenge of transnational action by diverse peoples, the possibilities for citizen involvement in vital communication and even enforcement,[3] the pull of conscience in improving the quality of peace, the importance of system change, the challenge and nobility of honoring one's personal responsibilities, and the sometimes agonizing decisions about where to take a stand.

Discussion of these choices begins by noting the fundamental significance of human dignity followed by consideration of several intersecting factors that reinforce human dignity in society as they contribute to human security.

9.2 UNIVERSALIZING RESPECT FOR HUMAN DIGNITY

Human dignity is the bedrock on which human rights and human security stand.[4] As this analysis has demonstrated, human dignity can guide the direction of policies and shape new architectural structures to implement them. In this section we explore how it also can inspire support for initiatives. People's willingness to commit themselves to human dignity regardless of cultural background furnishes cohesive glue that can bind a diverse group of activists together in the United States and around the world, first, to implement correlates of peace and, second, to sustain security for people not part of one's nation. Human dignity also provides a solid basis for keeping one's identity grounded while it grows away from being narrowly national and toward becoming more universal. It can motivate sustained efforts by citizens locally, nationally, and globally to help implement durable initiatives that range widely from good civic education and political organizing to supporting human rights organizations and campaigning for eco-environmental reforms. Many people of all races and religions throughout the world, frustrated by violence, oppression, injustice, economic exploitation, environmental ruin, corruption, and indifference to truth all around them, stand ready to support a positive, unifying vision and to encourage one another in an honest, transnational social change movement to build more reliable security, if it is founded on human dignity rather than on nationally exclusionary, competitive, military power.[5]

Both the need (1) to broaden currently narrow national identities and interests and (2) to increase collaborative participation by people from many societies in a combined security effort can be advanced by strengthening people's commitment to human

---

[3] Citizen verification of police wrongdoing in the case of George Floyd's asphyxiation in Minneapolis in 2020 is an example that could be built on to make citizens' monitoring role even more extensive and reliable.

[4] The value of human dignity is explained in Chapter 2, section 2.

[5] For more on how to make transnational social movements effective, see Margaret Keck and Kathryn Sikkink, *Activists Beyond Borders* (Ithaca, NY: Cornell University Press, 1998); Kenneth Gould and Tammy Lewis, "Transnational Social Movements," in *Oxford Research Encyclopedia of International Studies* (Oxford: Oxford University Press, 2010), DOI 10.1093/acrefore/9780190846626.013.491; David A. Snow, Sarah A. Soule, Hanspeter Kriesi, and Holly McCammon, eds., *The Wiley Blackwell Companion to Social Movements* (Oxford: Wiley Blackwell, 2021); Peter B. Evans and Cesar Rodríguez-Garavito, *Transnational Advocacy Networks: Twenty Years of Evolving Theory and Practice* (Bogota, Colombia: Dejusticia, 2018); Jackie Smith and Dawn Wiest, *Social Movements in the World-System: The Politics of Crisis and Transformation* (New York: Russell Sage Foundation, 2012).

dignity and by encouraging moral imagination among US citizens and other nationalities around the ways that human dignity and human security are mutually reinforcing. Experienced mediators report that every person willing to exercise his or her moral imagination "has a capacity, even in moments of greatest pain, to understand that the welfare of my community is directly related to the welfare of your community."[6]

One benefit of a genuine commitment to respect human dignity in the present and future is that it enables one to acknowledge the truth about times when human dignity has not been respected in the past. Doing that increases one's honesty, credibility, and humility with others. Relinquishing any sense of superiority also reduces harsh rhetoric toward others, both of which interfere with cultivating common destiny. Truth telling is usually liberating; it establishes a foundation for communication conducive to working things out. It contributes to building a more inclusive and fruitful movement with additional people, especially among those who would be understandably skeptical of any claims to moral exceptionalism.

Identifying a problem in one's past enables one to use it as a building block in a non-zero-sum future. For example, US citizens understandably believe that the United States has been an exceptionally good country and unusually faithful in honoring freedom and liberty. To be sure, it has a rich history with countless pathbreaking, landmark laws and customs advancing freedom, economic growth, individual rights, and democratic values. Yet it also has suffered some violations of human dignity that citizens might benefit from recalling. American colonists and settlers were able, because of their superior firepower, to take land from people already dwelling in North America. They committed killings of native inhabitants that today would be called genocide. Over and above the land taken from the original inhabitants, the United States acquired nearly one-third of its contiguous continental territory from Mexico through the use of force. US citizens and leaders orchestrated two centuries of slavery and have not yet overcome racial discrimination. Although a wealthy country, the United States has perpetuated poverty as a subculture for millions of its own citizens.

Regardless of how one feels about valuing the distinctive history of a nationality, about suffering caused by historical actions that violate human dignity, about applying today's moral standards to yesterday's conduct, or about acknowledging national disappointments along with achievements, US policymakers and citizens can act more effectively throughout the world after relinquishing the idea that US leaders and citizens are morally exceptional or superior human beings.[7] In any case, to recall decisions to kill native inhabitants, to establish slavery and to delay addressing racism, to drop the second atomic bomb (if not also the first), to accept chronic inequity, to delay the franchise for women and African Americans, and to hold back international

---

[6] Lederach, *Moral Imagination*, 62.

[7] The long sweep of history seems to show that "the thesis of exceptionalism [is] a self-indulgent illusion." Wright, *Nonzero*, 172–173.

   For the first time, in their 2012 party platform, Republicans included a section extolling "American exceptionalism." Jett, "Republicans Are Blocking."

enforcement of the law against genocide can instill understanding of those who hold a different vision of human dignity than expressed in the preceding policies. Certainly, it is commendable to express genuine appreciation for courageous acts by many Americans over 300 years of living and dying to protect the United States and make it a democracy with abundant freedom, liberty, and prosperity. Emphasizing admirable deeds on behalf of human dignity is more helpful for building a movement than claiming superiority.

The value of human dignity is strengthened by the growing convergence between what seems necessary for protecting human security, on the one hand, and what is ethically desirable for upholding human dignity, on the other. This convergence is especially strong in the long run. Peace research has demonstrated that identities that treat all people as equals have great strategic value in peacebuilding.[8] A similar benefit flows from multiple centuries-old religious traditions that call for hospitality and compassion for strangers. Ethical leaders from Buddha through the Stoics, from the Hebrew prophets and Jesus to Mohammed, Gandhi, King, and many others point out that to increase moral sensitivity means to widen and ultimately universalize the group of people for whom one cares. Whether one is secular or religious, to be morally sensitive today means to care about people everywhere on Earth. Although ways of nurturing such attentiveness cannot be presented here, the compassionate elements of religious traditions can help universalize respect for all human beings, a security goal that governments have endorsed in secular language many years ago in the very first article of the Universal Declaration of Human Rights.

To be a citizen or government official answerable for human dignity means to exercise responsibilities both nationally and globally. The two domains of citizenship are functionally inseparable and increasingly one. This conclusion seems confirmed simply by recognizing all societies' common interest in a healthy biosphere and a reduction of threat from weapons of mass destruction. For that reason, if US citizens feel a sense of moral indignation at injustice on another continent or of grievance when realizable human rights are denied, this does not need to be interpreted as merely a negative feeling.[9] It may be recognized as or transformed into a positive experience of human solidarity. Similar sentiments arise in many people everywhere across cultural boundaries, suggesting that perhaps basic feelings of justifiable grievance or cross-border empathy may be "grounded in our genes."[10] Increasingly, scholars believe such feelings are a positive part of the emotional equipment designed by natural selection to incline human beings toward empathy, appreciation, or reciprocal altruism. Psychological research also supports the conclusion that the highest and most inclusive level of

---

[8] Lederach, *Moral Imagination*, 171–178; Lederach and Appleby, "Strategic Peacebuilding," 35–41; Oscar Schachter, "Relation of Peace and Human Rights," *International Legal Practitioner* 13 (September 1988), https://heinonline.org/HOL/LandingPage?handle=hein.journals/ilp13&div=30&id=&page=.

[9] Mohandas Gandhi observed that feelings of justifiable anger could be channeled constructively for positive changes. Mohandas Gandhi, *Gandhi's Autobiography* (Washington, DC: Public Affairs Press, 1954); Arun Gandhi, *The Gift of Anger* (New York: Simon and Schuster, 2018).

[10] Wright, *Nonzero*, 24; Christakis, *Blueprint: Evolutionary Origins*, 306–310.

human consciousness treats other human beings in general as ends rather than as means,[11] and that this consciousness extends both near and far. If nurtured constructively, such inclinations can encourage citizens to act cooperatively despite cultural differences, enliven them to more inclusive identities, and motivate them to work for human security because they have learned to care about fellow citizens as well as others far away.

Research findings from diverse academic disciplines in recent years show that human beings over millennia of history have demonstrated cooperative reciprocal tendencies as well as threatening competitive ones.[12] In the past, observers seem more frequently to have emphasized the latter. Nicholas Christakis, a physician, sociologist, and evolutionary biologist who has conducted research on human nature and compiled substantial research by others, reports that, in his view, humans "are fundamentally good and that . . . we are pre-wired to make societies that are filled with the sorts of things moral systems see as good."[13] Even if one remains agnostic about such findings, any discipline or school of thought that emphasizes only one human tendency or the other, cooperative or conflictual, inadvertently misses part of the human picture. Such a partial perspective should not guide major decisions about the alternatives to which human beings should limit themselves in the future, especially when it comes to decisions about killing and irredeemable destruction.

Increased attention to the long-term growth of cooperative, non-zero-sum relationships over millennia of human history has led some experts to conjecture about the possibility—not inevitability—that some units of governance may become larger and more inclusive than the Westphalian state has been since its origin in 1648. More widespread global governance could be an "outgrowth of the millennia-old expansion of non-zero-sumness among human beings."[14] Such statements are *not* a prediction or suggestion of inevitability. Human history simply seems to affirm that human beings have the possibility of creating enough worldwide non-zero-sum (cooperative) arrangements to allow more global governance. Alternatively, nations also have the option to destroy one another rather than to cooperate across boundaries. Of course, the possibility of destroying civilization is here now, well within the existing level of US military preparedness.

For our analytic purposes in this analysis, it is enough to know that the historical evolutionary record is clear: the total number of independent human groups has declined drastically over the long course of history; human groups have grown repeatedly to include larger numbers of people; larger groups have been characterized by more societal cooperation and complexity; and this process could progress further in

[11] Abraham Maslow, *The Farther Reaches of Human Nature* (New York: Viking, 1971), 279.
[12] Many of these are noted in Christakis, *Blueprint: Evolutionary Origins.*
[13] To the extent that this is confirmed, it could apply to global society as well, thereby improving prospects for survival. In his view, humanity's "social blueprint [from evolution] is a nontheological, human-independent source for the good things in life that we value." In brief, "a society is good when it enhances its members' happiness or survival." Christakis, *Blueprint: Evolutionary Origins*, 410–411.
[14] Wright, *Nonzero*, 210.

the future. Progression is not inevitable; it may be ours to choose or to ignore. To a limited degree, some indicative changes are under way in multiethnic states that are amalgamating diverse subnational groups into more inclusive national identities; in regional integration of the European Union; in more cooperative and inclusive international trade agreements; and in some international institution-building. But inter-group violence with widespread destruction remains possible, which is the challenge that this book and its readers are interested in addressing. Evolution cannot be counted on to save humanity from extinction of the human species. But evidence of some historical movement from competitive, zero-sum relationships to more cooperative, non-zero-sum relationships suggests that human beings might be able to choose an increased possibility of escaping extinction.

Because of the central concern with human survival in this analysis, when time-honored, widely shared specific moral preferences, whether found in religious traditions or evolutionary history, apparently contribute to human survival and when these preferences rationally dovetail with scientific findings of what contributes to survival, this coincidence is worthy of our notice. For some people it can become a multidimensional foundation on which to build strength and support for human security. For others it may be merely a curiosity. In either case, evidence accumulated across many disciplines suggests that if it is possible to love one's family and simultaneously to care for one's society or nation, it is also possible to love one's family, care for one's nation, and simultaneously express solidarity with one's global family or international society. Some citizens do this now and report joy in so doing.[15] This possibility seems fully consistent with both the value commitment to human dignity and the science of human security.

At times, some policies to uphold human dignity and to advance human security, such as to eliminate poverty, may arouse tension with national conduct. If one's nationalism is narrowly conceived, it will probably reduce one's sensitivity to nationals of other countries and result in policies such as not joining the Kyoto guidelines, pulling out of the Paris climate agreement, withdrawing from the Iran nuclear agreement, and never meeting the UN's 0.7 percent goal for reducing poverty, even though these actions do not serve US security more fully understood. A singularly national focus underestimates how "they" and "we" acting together can produce bigger mutual gains than each acting separately. Yet a combined multilateral secular and multi-faith ethical strategy, publicly announced, could enable concerned US citizens to support it and articulate their values more clearly and effectively than has been possible by merely voting periodically and writing to representatives in Congress. Norm entrepreneurs have shown that, even though universal values of human dignity have not been robustly expressed in some US policies,[16] many citizens believe that they *should* be.[17]

---

[15] Christakis, *Blueprint: Evolutionary Origins*, 272–422.

[16] Kim and Sikkink, "Explaining the Deterrence Effect of Human Rights Prosecutions," 939–963.

[17] See, for example, Steven Kull, *American Public Support for Foreign Aid in the Age of Trump* (Washington, DC: Brookings Report, July 31, 2017), https://www.brookings.edu/research/american-public-support-for-foreign-aid-in-the-age-of-trump/.

Keeping one's eye on human dignity and Nussbaum's 10 human capabilities does not resolve all questions, of course, but it assists citizens in evaluating policies more systematically and provides a basis for policymakers to respect human dignity, especially if even more evidence comes forth that doing so contributes to security.

9.3 FINDING EMPOWERMENT IN HUMAN RIGHTS

Commitment to human dignity inspires belief and action that all persons' human rights should be respected. To advance US and human security, concerned citizens could draw on the power of strong transnational human rights organizations[18] and commit themselves to educate themselves and other people about human rights— their own basic rights and the rights of others, along with concomitant duties to protect and implement all people's rights. These are the foundation of freedom, liberty, and it turns out, security in the long run. Such a commitment is widely needed because US civic education in schools and public education by journalists have been falling short in educating and empowering citizens with knowledge, skills, and motivation to influence life-and-death policies of their own government.[19] Governments already have underscored the importance of citizen education by declaring "that every individual and every organ of society shall strive by teaching and education to promote respect for human rights and fundamental freedoms."[20] Human rights education "should include peace, democracy, development and social justice," recognizing that these are "essential for the promotion of universal respect for and observance of all

---

[18] Some examples include Amnesty International, Human Rights Watch, Lawyers Committee for Human Rights, Office of the UN High Commissioner for Human Rights, and Office of the UN High Commissioner for Refugees. There are many others also doing good work.

[19] The breadth and depth of needed civic education are discussed in Rebecca Winthrop, "The Need for Civic Education in 21st-Century Schools," *Brookings Policy Big Ideas*, June 4, 2020, https://www.brookings.edu/ policy2020/bigideas/the-need-for-civic-education-in-21st-century-schools/; International Commission on Financing Global Education Opportunity, *The Learning Generation: Investing in Education for a Changing World*, https://report.educationcommission.org/report/; Parker J. Palmer, *Healing the Heart of Democracy: The Courage to Create a Politics Worthy of the Human Spirit* (San Francisco: Jossey-Bass, 2011), https://www.globalonenessproject.org/library/essays/five-habits-heal-heart-democracy; Matthew N. Atwell, John Bridgeland, and Peter Levine, *Civic Deserts: America's Civic Health Challenge*, https:// www.ncoc.org/wp-content/uploads/2017/10/2017CHIUpdate-FINAL-small.pdf; Robert D. Putnam, "Bowling Alone: America's Declining Social Capital," *Journal of Democracy* 6, no. 1 (1995): 65–78, doi:10.1353/jod.1995.0002; John K. Folger and Charles B. Nam, *Education of the American Population* (Washington: U.S. Department of Commerce, 1967); Kerry Kennedy, *Citizenship Education and the Modern State* (Washington, D.C.: Taylor & Francis, 1997); John Richardson and Richard C. Rowson, "For Democracy: Back Civic Education Worldwide," *International Herald Tribune*, December 6, 2002, https://www.nytimes.com/2002/12/06/opinion/IHT-for-democracy-back-civic-education-worldwide. html?searchResultPosition=1; and Jane Nelsen, *Positive Discipline* (New York: Ballatine Books, 1996).

[20] UN General Assembly, "United Nations Declaration on Human Rights Education and Training," General Assembly Resolution 66/137, December 19, 2011, https://www.ohchr.org/en/issues/education/training/ pages/undhreducationtraining.aspx.

human rights."[21] Citizens could encourage their governments to take their own rhetorical commitments more seriously.

An essential goal is to develop "a universal culture of human rights, in which everyone is aware of their own rights and responsibilities in respect of the rights of others, and promoting the development of the individual as a responsible member of a free, peaceful, pluralist and inclusive society."[22] Education for a human rights culture should "be based on the principles of equality, particularly between girls and boys and between women and men, human dignity, inclusion and non-discrimination." As an antidote to the divisive bigotry spread by anti-truth propagandists, a truth-telling transnational citizens' movement will "strengthen among all human beings the spirit of tolerance, dialogue, cooperation and solidarity."[23]

Human rights education might be aided by the growth of interdependence, because "interdependence has a way of breeding respect, or at least tolerance" for those with whom one interacts.[24] Although wider respect for people's basic humanity and awareness that all people are worthy of decent treatment has advanced with technological change, evolutionary psychologists believe it is also "rooted more fundamentally in human nature itself."[25] Even if viewing people as people may not extend much farther than practical interactions require, the deepening of interdependence seems to move citizens eventually closer to universal respect.

Not everyone can be an expert on human rights, but everyone can be a personal advocate for the rights to which he or she is committed and the duties that one is obligated to respect for others. Because every ethnicity and nationality on Earth is a minority in the context of the world's population, there should be widespread support for "the rights of persons belonging to national or ethnic, religious and linguistic minorities as an integral part of the development of a society as a whole and within a democratic framework based on the rule of law."[26]

A crucial part of human rights education is attending to *structural* impediments that cause existing problems to persist, that destroy hope, and that can lead to alienation

---

[21] *Official Records of the General Assembly*, Sixty-sixth Session, A/66/53, Supplement no. 53, chapter 1.

[22] United Nations, Office of the High Commissioner for Human Rights, "Declaration on the Right of Peoples to Peace," General Assembly Resolution 66/137, Annex 2, and A/Resolution 39/11, https://www. ohchr.org/EN/ProfessionalInterest/Pages/RightOfPeoplesToPeace.aspx#:~:text=The%20General%20 Assembly%20%2C,of%20international%20peace%20and%20security%2C&text=Solemnly%20 declares%20that%20othe%20preservation, 3.

[23] UN General Assembly Resolution 66/137, 3.

[24] Wright, *Nonzero*, 207.

[25] Wright, *Nonzero*, 208.

[26] United Nations Office of the High Commissioner for Human Rights, "Declaration on the Rights of Persons Belonging to National or Ethnic, Religious and Linguistic Minorities," General Assembly Resolution 47/135, December 18, 1992, https://www.ohchr.org/en/professionalinterest/pages/minorities.aspx; see also United Nations Office of the High Commissioner for Human Rights, "Declaration on the Right of Peoples to Peace," General Assembly Resolution 39/11, November 12, 1984, https://www. ohchr.org/EN/ProfessionalInterest/Pages/RightOfPeoplesToPeace.aspx#:~:text=The%20General%20 Assembly%20%2C,of%20international%20peace%20and%20security%2C&text=Solemnly%20 declares%20that%20othe%20preservation,3.

or even violent reactions. A benefit of initiatives to reform structures is that institutionalizing respect for human dignity within the United States will also contribute to similar goals internationally. Advancing essential rights does not require any ingredient that individuals do not already have within themselves—*if* they mindfully shed conditioning that they have received earlier in life that stifles uplifting changes in their own and others' lives.

Of course, there is enormous pluralism within the United States, and not everyone agrees that universal concern for human rights should be more highly valued than concern for US preeminence in national military power. Most US citizens value universal peace and justice to some degree, but some may value power for the United States and prosperity for themselves even more. Peace may be an instrument for enhancing power and prosperity rather than an end in itself. Such views need to be taken seriously and addressed. Many people oppose change in order to protect selfish interests or simply because fears may be psychologically immobilizing. Some are lethargic about abolishing poverty or ending global warming because they value personal consumption more than implementing human rights or protecting the Earth. Others may not think about the need for world law because they happily grew up with national law largely unbounded by international law.

All such views need to be invited into conversation, because US citizens should face the prospect that persistent resistance to adaptive change could result in massive death and destruction. Social change organizers need to take into account that, depending on the context, a minority of altruists leading wisely can bring a larger majority of otherwise seemingly uncaring individuals to cooperate for social uplift. Conversely, "a few egoists can induce a large number of altruists to defect."[27] These realities underscore the importance of exercising independent judgment and readying constructive plans for social change so they may be implemented whenever opportunities present themselves, often in times of crisis.

Another far-reaching problem is that many people are not prepared psychologically for life in global society.[28] Patterns of defensive behavior learned from ages 1 to 4 years often continue in adult life, even though those patterns may no longer be helpful or form a constructive response for adults in global society. Some citizens and political leaders have not developed mature personalities, remaining emotionally childish throughout their lives.[29] They may express authoritarian personality traits,[30] ignore inconvenient realities, and encourage others to support narrow identities by nurturing

---

[27] See Ernst Fehr and Urs Fischbacher, "The Nature of Human Altruism," *Nature* 425, no. 6960 (October 23, 2003), 785.

[28] For elaboration of this point, see the discussion in Chapter 4, section 4.7.2., "Narrow Nationalism Reinforces Systemic Dysfunction," especially the note reporting Darcia Narvaez's findings.

[29] While certainly making no claims of being a diagnostician, Secretary of Defense James Mattis reported that Donald Trump often "'acted like . . . a fifth or sixth grader.'" Philip Rucker and Robert Costa, "Bob Woodward's New Book Reveals a 'Nervous Breakdown' of Trump's Presidency," *Washington Post*, September 4, 2018; Bob Woodward, *Fear: Trump in the White House* (New York: Simon and Schuster, 2018).

[30] See Fromm, *Escape from Freedom*.

their fears through populist propaganda and demagogic distortions or lies. Citizens need to be prepared to stand against authoritarian impulses that may arise at almost any time and place. They are especially likely as crises deepen.

Students of the psychology of war and peace find substantial evidence that encouraging people to reduce reliance on war as the ultimate decider of political conflicts and to embrace some worldwide governance as a worthwhile goal should not be dismissed as merely a political long-shot. It can be an invitation to higher levels of psychological maturity and personality development.[31] Human health and human security reinforce each other. Even with strong identification with one's own nationality, it is possible to appreciate other nationalities at the same time—as long as national identification does not include feelings of fundamental superiority.[32]

9.4 INCREASING TRANSNATIONAL COOPERATION

US citizens who aim to serve legitimate US security interests by also acknowledging the security interests of others will support conversation and cooperation transnationally among potential political allies to develop a common grand strategy. Transnational coalitions are essential to build political strength, helpful for setting goals, and necessary for meeting challenges to security that do not end at the water's edge. For example, citizens active in competing nuclear weapons countries can simultaneously press their respective governments to halt further development of nuclear weapons. They can be more effective together than if they worked separately.

9.4.1 Expanding Democracy

To take an insufficiently addressed issue as illustration, transnational cooperation is needed to focus attention on every country's current democratic deficit: A democratic system confined to one country can no longer fulfill the democratic principle. For example, because many political decisions affecting US citizens are not made by the US government but are decided in other capitals, this condition constitutes a daily infraction of the democratic principle, and it is not going away. Of course, citizens living in less powerful countries bear the burden of even heavier democratic deficits than do US citizens, who have a powerful government to back them in international transactions.

Transnational citizens' groups are needed to redress, at least slightly, democratic deficits that exist in every country throughout the world. For example, if concerned US citizens inform people in other societies that they are less pugnacious, less ego-driven, and friendlier toward multilateral institutions than were US officials during

---

[31] Robert R. Holt, "Meeting Einstein's Challenge: New Thinking about Nuclear Weapons," *Bulletin of the Atomic Scientists* (April 3, 2015), https://thebulletin.org/2015/04/meeting-einsteins-challenge-new-thinking-about-nuclear-weapons/.

[32] Christakis, *Blueprint: Evolutionary Origins*, 275–276.

some recent administrations, they will strengthen common ground with like-minded people within and outside the United States. Similarly, Europeans struggling to hold a coalition of like-minded countries together to support the Paris climate accord or the International Criminal Court benefit from reminders that millions more US citizens voted for another presidential candidate than for Donald Trump in the election that brought him to the presidency, and that many US citizens have wanted to be environmentally and legally more responsible than many US policies have indicated, regardless of administration. In addition, poor countries need believable evidence that many in the United States want to abolish poverty and advance equity. Robust transnational social movement organizations can bolster democratic wisdom and decision-making in both national and global contexts.[33] Increased global communication among civil society actors creates new possibilities for advancing cosmopolitan principles and inclusive identities to build greater international understanding and political influence, as the Black Lives Matter movement experienced after social media spread video evidence around the world showing George Floyd's murder by police asphyxiation in May of 2020.

Democratic values legitimate the right of people everywhere to participate in major decisions that affect their lives, yet in today's interdependent world, there is serious neglect of the need for new international democratic institutions to enable more citizen participation in those decisions. Transnational social movements are not a sufficient measure to fulfill this need, but they are essential to empower people to participate in discourse across borders and to press for reducing global democratic deficits by helping to bring more globally representative institutions into being to set equitable standards and enforce law. If major catastrophes can be avoided, the centuries-old migration of governance from smaller to larger political units is likely to continue until the hyper-independence of states in the current international system is bridled and domesticated. Some political integration is likely to be driven by technological trends that go back millennia and have not slowed. Advances in military, transportation, communication, and other technologies make relations among countries more likely to benefit from mutually cooperative (non-zero-sum) relations,[34] and cross-border processes help bring these into being.

9.4.2 *Deepening and Broadening Social Movements*

To succeed in advancing democratic values and human security requires (1) social movements that aim to *broaden* participation with people across gender, racial, educational, class, and ideological boundaries within the United States and, additionally, across national and cultural boundaries with other countries; and (2) social movements

---

[33] The composition of a transnational social movement is described near the beginning of Chapter 8.
[34] Wright, *Nonzero*, 226.

that aim to *deepen* change to the structural level in political, economic, environmental, and human rights relationships.

Although a coalition of social movement organizations to broaden and deepen simultaneously faces big challenges, it also promises extensive achievements. A desire to include more people in a movement exists in tension with a commitment to deeper change. The transnational coalition proposed here needs to mediate between the broad inclusivity of people willing to work for the common good and a definition of goals that are deep enough to bring system change where possible. This combination of breadth and depth can succeed if the coalition defines widely attractive goals, rooted in the six guidelines for grand strategy, while remaining experimental as to the precise means for achieving these goals in local communities. It can succeed if it is transparent, democratic, free of corruption, and unwaveringly serves the dignity of every person on Earth.

One measure of benefit will be whether people can *feel* the difference that they are making, enabling them to experience camaraderie with like-minded people near and far. Although some changes must be structural and global, initiatives need to touch people locally and personally if they are to succeed. People's imaginations can "transcend what has been and is now, while still living in it,"[35] bringing the needs that imagination has revealed to the table of transformation. As recognition of inter-societal complexity and commitment to the long term are taken seriously, new political and economic mechanisms for relating, shaped by time-honored human rights, can gradually turn into changed attitudes and habits in people's daily lives.

Although an international movement advancing structural change faces daunting challenges, happily such a movement does not need to be organized by a handful of independent activists or their organizations. Enormous talent, experience, and resources exist in medium-sized and small democracies, some of which are prepared to lead. They can and sometimes will encourage action that is independent of foot-dragging governments and corporations. Looking at how other movements have succeeded demonstrates what is possible. Notice that, in creating the Treaty on the Prohibition of Nuclear Weapons, the Rome Statute establishing the International Criminal Court, or the Ottawa treaty banning land mines, the United States, China, Russia, and India did not bring these initiatives to life. Some officials wished them dead,[36] but so far they live. Of course, they will live more healthily when additional great powers join these positive initiatives for human security.

The countries most likely to implement the correlates of peace will be a group of like-minded national governments in which one would not be surprised to find Canada or Australia and New Zealand, the five Nordic countries or the Netherlands,

---

[35] Lederach, *Moral Imagination*, 59.

[36] This was John Bolton's carefully articulated preference for the ICC, noted in Chapter 3, and apparently shared by the George W. Bush administration. John Bolton, "No, No, No to the International Criminal Court," *Human Events* 54 (August 21, 1998), 2. Of course, opposition has been strong in the other three states as well.

Germany or other leaders in the EU, Japan or South Korea, South Africa or Mexico, or other forward-looking countries in Latin America, Africa, Asia, or elsewhere. Some of these like-minded governments, UN agencies, and other intergovernmental and non-governmental organizations have been building vital support for pioneering human security initiatives for several decades.

9.4.3 Increasing Communication and Enforcement

Although today's international community possesses relatively modest power, it possesses sufficient legitimacy to aid some work of social change groups, organizations, and supportive existing institutions when it chooses. As this happens, both governmental and non-governmental actors become more sensitive to one another's behavior and aware of mutually shared needs and goals within new institutions that may represent both public and private, for-profit and non-profit organizations in common deliberations.

Together, these groups should address the two greatest problems with present-day international anarchy: (1) the lack of communication and information about the intentions of other governments and of feared non-state actors, and (2) the inability to enforce agreements against cheaters. More effective international enforcement institutions, strengthened by detailed aerial surveillance and other new communication technologies, even as simple and omnipresent as smart phones, can help address both of these problems with assistance from international organizations. The latter, as neo-liberal institutionalists have long emphasized, are really "persistent and connected sets of rules (formal and informal) that prescribe behavioral roles, constrain activity, and shape expectations."[37]

Taking more creative initiatives with international institutions could produce multiple benefits: To reduce cheating on international agreements, they increase governments' and the international community's ability to monitor and verify agreements. They make it possible to impose agreed-on penalties if a state violates a collective agreement. To diminish the costs of negotiating agreements, they routinize meeting and talking together, establish procedures for "legislation," and enable short-cuts in implementation. To decrease fears and mistrust from lack of information, they provide access to more and better-quality evidence and communication; and they deliver knowledge of other governments' intentions and willingness to comply with agreements and long-term goals. To ease fear of uncertainties, they increase monitoring and transparency, encourage long-range planning, and add new dimensions of cooperation across related areas.[38] The international community can raise more hopeful

---

[37] Robert O. Keohane, *International Institutions and State Power: Essays in International Relations Theory* (Boulder, CO: Westview Press, 1989), 3. See also Stephen D. Krasner, *International Regimes* (Ithaca, NY: Cornell University Press, 1983).

[38] Robert O. Keohane and Lisa L. Martin, "The Promise of Institutionalist Theory," *International Security* 20, no. 1 (1995): 39–51.

institutions out of the relative anarchy of the old international system, moving sub-stantially beyond them when guided by astute understanding of common transna-tional interests of which an ever-growing number exists.

Skeptics about the feasibility of international system change might be encouraged by the reality that change does not need to occur all at once. In fact, it is preferable for it to occur gradually to obtain experience and build support along the way. Vertical dispersal of sovereignty, for example, as has happened to a limited degree in Europe, is likely to occur unevenly, with occasional reversals, repeated reviews, and constant refinements. In many cases, new system-changing architecture can be grafted onto familiar UN agencies that undergo reform or replacement. If change is gradual and experimental, it can include course correction if and when an initiative turns out to be unworkable.

The preferred architectural guideline for democratic governance is to enable all people to participate or be represented in decisions that affect their lives and to locate decisions as close to the people affected or as "low" in a governing hierarchy as pos-sible, following the principle of subsidiarity. Yet where laws are needed that everybody on Earth must obey, such as limiting nuclear weapons or global warming, these should be a product of as much global democratic process as feasible. Wherever substantive deficits exist, such as the absence of world law to enforce constraints on nuclear radio-activity or carbon emissions, the substantive deficit and the democratic deficit both need to be addressed simultaneously. The goal is to bring congruity between actors' inputs and substantive outputs, to make the amount of power and the inclusivity of the actors in decision-making congruent with the scope of the substantive content and location of the consequences on the output side of decision-making processes. If radioactive fallout or carbon emissions are to be limited worldwide, for example, estab-lishing those limits should include all national societies to help them succeed.

9.5 SEEKING QUALITY PEACE

An integral part of the quest for human security encompasses what Peter Wallensteen has concluded constitutes a "quality peace," which establishes and maintains the "con-ditions that make the inhabitants of a society (be it an area, a country, a region, a continent, or a planet) secure in life and dignity now and for the foreseeable future."[39] How one builds quality peace should be influenced by the area or areas that one has in mind, of course, yet mutual reinforcement in peacebuilding methods occurs across all dimensions from local to global. Striving for human security globally also serves the national security of US citizens in the long run. However, many citizens seem unaware of this or reluctant to sacrifice now in order to achieve quality peace for their own descendants and for all others in the long run. Often people appear to want power, wealth, recognition, and immediate egoistic satisfaction more than lasting peace,

---

[39] Wallensteen, *Quality Peace*, 205

justice, environmental balance, and respect for human dignity. Yet to prefer short-term egoistic gratification over long-term security undermines one's self-interest in survival or at least does not prioritize it reasonably.

Given these realities, advocates of human security need many people's diverse skills, ranging all the way from building personal psychological health to creating global institutions. To name only one example, upholding children's rights to psychological health could begin to address problems with authoritarian personalities and preda-tory nationalisms.[40] Improving psychological awareness of candidates' personalities can assist in selecting good leaders, in establishing more effective power-managing structures (e.g., checks and balances), and in supporting leaders inclined toward more equitable sharing of wealth and power while nurturing human solidarity. Many thoughtful professionals, policymakers, and parents, of course, are currently working to nurture healthy personalities and have been contributing to a wider movement for quality peace and human security.

Because the ethics of war and peace held by many citizens seem to be evolving in parallel with changing realities noted in Chapter 1, such as the inutility of war, it is instructive to examine these more closely for their contribution to upgrading the qual-ity of peace and advancing a strategy for human security. If the US government is slow to lead on issues of grave security importance, concerned policymakers and citizens can take a stance for positive change that they hope others will eventually endorse. For this to happen, they will need to consult their own sense of ethical responsibility. Traditionally, personal ethics would not be included in a book on international rela-tions because citizens normally would expect and would be expected by their govern-ment simply to follow whatever foreign policies US officials laid out.

Political realists have believed that personal ethics should not play a role in making foreign policy and that policymakers should not feel any moral obligations outside their own country as they pursue the national interest.[41] Even though many policy-makers and political realists still hold this familiar Machiavellian view, which separates public from private morality, many ethicists believe such thinking is no longer *pruden-tially* useful and never was *ethically* responsible.[42] For citizens and policymakers not to care ethically about people outside the United States does not enhance US security in any way, although it does make it much easier to inflict violence and poverty on others.

If citizens attempting to be morally responsible conclude that they cannot in good conscience always wait for the US government to act more wisely, then their personal ethics need exploration and implementation. The ethics of both citizens and US offi-cials influence the prospects for building peace and security. There is no responsible

---

[40] See Narváez, *Neurobiology and the Development of Human Morality*.

[41] George F. Kennan, *American Diplomacy 1900–1950* (Chicago: University of Chicago Press, 1951). Later in life, Kennan slightly amended his position on what he called the "legalistic-moralistic" approach in international relations. George F. Kennan, "Morality and Foreign Policy," *Foreign Affairs* 64, no. 2 (1985): 205–218.

[42] Charles Beitz, *Political Theory and International Relations* (Princeton, NJ: Princeton University Press, 1999).

way of segregating ethical concerns for local or national issues from global issues, as the following discussion demonstrates.

Well-known just war theory provides ethical standards for deciding whether a particular war is justifiable. A general presumption against war means that unless a war has a just cause and is waged using just means, it is unjustifiable. Any deliberately unjustifiable killing constitutes murder, not noble soldiering. A much newer theory, called "just peace," aims not only to prevent wars that are unjustifiable according to just war standards, but also to create improved social conditions that will take away circumstances that, if not removed, will lead toward the violence of oppression, rebellion, or war. Exponents of just peace thinking promote international cooperation to achieve greater justice and an end to human deprivation in order to make violence less likely and also to remove indirect or "structural violence" of unjust institutional structures.

If just war criteria for what constitutes a justifiable war are strictly applied, they clearly reduce people's and states' willingness to commit unwarranted violence. On the other hand, if loosely applied, they may justify one war (or one drone attack) after another, because the elasticity of the justifying standards can be stretched and are too easily met.[43] Just peace theorists try to overcome this problem by emphasizing cooperative actions to promote human well-being long before a war might occur. These are designed to keep war remote and out of bounds as a legitimate instrument of conflict resolution. As people find war less necessary because of greater consciousness of non-war ways of enforcing international law, fewer wars seem justifiable, even to just war exponents. And as additional scientific understanding reveals the ingredients for peacebuilding, just peace thinking and strategic peacebuilding become closely intertwined.

An indicator of changing attitudes toward whether *any* war can be justified is found in the World Council of Churches' call for national governments and religious organizations to shift focus from just war thinking to just peace thinking. The Council represents 349 Christian denominations with 600 million members living in 150 countries worldwide.[44] Although acknowledging that there are times when the United Nations may need to respond to threats to world peace with the use of military power within the constraints of international law, the World Council has found "justifications of armed conflict and war . . . increasingly implausible and unacceptable."[45] Indeed, "the Way of Just Peace is fundamentally different from the concept of 'just war' and much more than criteria for protecting people from the unjust use of force."[46] Although most

---

[43] John Mearsheimer, a political realist ready to employ war whenever necessary to protect national survival, has concluded that "just war theory produces a more bellicose orientation than realism." *Delusion*, Kindle, 4107.

[44] The Roman Catholic Church keeps informed of the work of the World Council but is not formally a member.

[45] Mathews George Chunakara, *Building Peace on Earth: Report of the International Ecumenical Peace Convocation* (Geneva, Switzerland: World Council of Churches, 2013), 180.

[46] Chunakara, *Building Peace*, 180.

of these churches have never been pacifist, they have declared, "We feel obliged as Christians to . . . challenge any . . . justifications of the use of military power and to consider reliance on the concept of a 'just war' and its customary use to be obsolete."[47]

Just peace theory can be summed up as a focus on interpersonal, intergroup, and international relations that advances peace, human security, and justice by treating others as you would have them treat you. It can appeal to people with spiritual sensitivities as well as to those without. Roots for just peace thinking can be found in Muslim traditions as well as Christian, and in Jewish traditions as well as Buddhist and Hindu. It is a process of continually expressing, establishing, and renewing shalom relationships, rather than attempting to establish a static end state.[48]

The changing ethics of war and peace may draw just war theorists away from their more zero-sum past, in which they judged whether a war is just from the perspective of one side of the conflict (their own), toward a more cooperative and inclusive non-zero-sum future that will judge both sides' justification in war from a single, inclusive "God's-eye perspective" that one associates with just peace thinking and aims at cooperative, win-win outcomes in which both sides benefit. Applying just war standards on all conflictual nations at once to produce a more cosmopolitan assessment of when war is justifiable places a state's actions in the context of global law enforcement, not merely national self-interest. This direction seems at once more faithfully Christian and more respectful toward and welcoming to people of all religious faiths, because it recognizes the preciousness of all human life and acknowledges that war-fighting has become questionable spiritually as well as of low utility prudentially, if not simply unnecessary and counter-productive.[49]

In addition, some theorists are moving beyond traditional just war acquiescence in the existing international system because they see compelling justification for concerned citizens to reduce their support for the killing practices and purposes of *any* system, domestic or international, regardless of the national context from which one looks at potential violence. This shift would facilitate re-design of global institutions gradually to replace existing enforcement through the militarized balance-of-power system with a worldwide rule of law, buttressed by international community policing or cosmopolitan law enforcement.[50]

A just peace perspective continuously seeks to minimize killing, even when law enforcement may require coercion. The World Council statement acknowledges the

---

[47] Chunakara, *Building Peace*, 182.

[48] The Hebrew concept of shalom means more than "peace." It includes physical, psychological, social, and spiritual well-being, flowing through all of one's relationships when they are made right.

[49] Chunakara, *Building Peace*, 182. In 2016 Pope Francis hosted an historic convocation focused on what he called "the active witness of nonviolence as a 'weapon' to achieve peace." The concluding document was entitled "An Appeal to the Catholic Church to Recommit to the Centrality of Gospel Nonviolence." Terrence J. Rynne, "Toward a New Theology of Peace," *Sojourners* 45, no 7 (July 2016), 9–10.

[50] For discussion, see Kaldor, *New and Old Wars*, Chapters 3, 4, and 5; Martin Shaw, "The Contemporary Mode of Warfare? Mary Kaldor's Theory of New Wars," *Review of International Political* Economy 7, no. 1 (2000): 171–180.

need for "just policing" to frame an ethic for the lawful use of force when UN peace-making, peacekeeping, or policing are necessary.[51] Just-police enforcement surely could replace just-war fighting in some situations, especially if the UN peace force, proposed in Chapter 7, were to be established. If just-police action came to enjoy high international legitimacy, and if police could be deployed in sufficiently large numbers and with appropriate technology and training, coercive enforcement might succeed in many contexts without combat.

Just peace theory emphasizes justice for all as an antidote to war formation and also as a building block for positive political cooperation by citizens and institutions working for sustainable peace. With progress in global peacebuilding, commitment to non-killing policies could become a serious aspiration, and, for perhaps the first time in world history, a realistic possibility, rather than merely following past assumptions that recurring wars will be justifiable. Could an intention to reduce killing in international relations become a constructive aspiration, just as it is imaginable that a national society might aspire to avoid intentional killing by police in domestic law enforcement? Perhaps stated more accurately, a goal within a country might be to minimize killing in law enforcement while recognizing that some killing may occur. Even in instances where police kill an accused person who may have resisted arrest and violently attacked the police, the overall goal in public law enforcement is not to kill. It is to apprehend the accused without killing. Because there seems to be no inherent reason that such an ideal goal could not also apply someday to much of international law enforcement, it gives imaginative room to those who want to commit themselves seamlessly to killing-avoidance, from local to global contexts.[52]

Those who aspire to non-killing, of course, should support strong attempts to investigate and stop wrongdoing wherever it might occur, by moving the locus of enforcement when possible from a battlefield to an international police action focused on apprehending the accused, or to a courtroom, a legislative agency, or a transformative dialogue with binding arbitration when necessary. Enforcement should not be downplayed, or the normative benefits of enforcement[53] and of respecting human security would be lost. Coercion must occur in quality peace, of course, when it is needed. Gradual movement away from traditional war-fighting might result from building on UN experience in peacemaking and peacekeeping. To achieve the benefit of US support for such initiatives could be enormously important, a topic to which we now turn.

---

[51] Chunakara, *Building Peace*, 182.

[52] The just peace perspective is broad enough to encompass a movement containing both those who aspire to international police enforcement and those who do not think that it is sufficient. Both may rely on armed enforcement of international law. If in the future all countries could be brought to limit their uses of armed force to law enforcement, this could be a significant step toward limiting illegitimate uses of armed force.

[53] These include both upholding justice and strengthening deterrence. On the latter, see Kim and Sikkink, "Deterrence Effect of Human Rights Prosecutions," 939–963.

9.6 EXERTING INFLUENCE FOR HUMAN SECURITY

To implement a more promising US security policy, which is to say a global grand strategy for human security, concerned US citizens can play a leadership role in the United States to enable healthy US participation in the much-needed transnational social movement described in Chapter 8. Many US citizens are painfully aware of living in a flawed or quasi-democratic society capable of electing dishonest or poorly informed people as leaders, who at times express belligerence and bigoted stereotyping of out-groups, with many members of Congress who repeatedly have applauded unhelpful executive branch behavior and directly rejected treaty ratifications that would have expanded the rule of law and strengthened arms control.

For citizens to wield dissenting power effectively requires their support for officials' preferred conduct to be dependable, and their withdrawal of support from officials' undesirable conduct to be tough-minded and unwavering. As argued in the Syrian case, supporting and incentivizing preferred *conduct* can be more effective than making ad hominem attacks and judging other *people* as evil or good. For example, political killings of civilians can be considered terrorist conduct that should always be opposed as a violation of civilian immunity, whether conducted by friend or foe, by a non-state actor or by one's own national government. "My country right or wrong" may show great loyalty to country (in the short run) but not great loyalty to the value of human dignity.

Concerned citizens also need to converse with those with whom they disagree to expand areas of understanding and possibly of common concern. Even if the need to pursue a path independent from the US government seems a judgment of US policies, it should not alienate citizens from policymakers or make citizens inefficacious in dealing with political opponents. Perhaps one's political opponents are doing the best they can with what they have been dealt. Some people have been trained to perpetuate diplomatic habits that impede innovative approaches to conflict rather than to transform conflict creatively. It can be difficult to know if a tit-for-tat diplomatic strategy that posits negative payback might produce acceptable results, at least in the short run. Moreover, some have not been psychologically prepared for change because they have a habit of projecting flaws in US policies onto others (and of course officials in other countries project their flaws on the United States). Nonetheless, better education and psychological health, combined with growing awareness of increasingly vexing global problems, as well as unused promising new opportunities, can open more positive vistas for many. Although it is not easy to find ways to develop a cooperative strategy to institutionalize peace among diverse national societies and to build human security, it is possible to do so, and without postulating any changes in human nature. Bold citizens' movements, tempered by open discussion of key questions with those with whom one disagrees, can help advance policies that are politically realistic and ethically desirable.

Nonviolent political initiatives against the forces resisting desirable changes will take many forms. One of the most important is for citizens to recognize that they need to think for themselves and strongly to support the US government when it upholds human dignity and to stand against US policies when they do not espouse international human rights and humanitarian law or implement the correlates of peace. Unthinking support undermines efforts to hold officials accountable. Citizens enjoy the freedom to support desirable policies and can shoulder the responsibility to say "no" to the state, as well as to any other actor, "whose behavior affronts conscience and fundamental moral precepts."[54] Many citizens recognize that "it's disturbing to have an administration . . . nakedly uninterested in our values,"[55] as US Ambassador David Rank reported when resigning his ambassadorial post to protest the US decision to pull out of the Paris climate agreement. Citizens need constantly to explore how to express support or opposition more effectively toward the policies of the US government, the main political parties, those running for office, private corporations, unions, other organizations that lobby government officials, school boards, communication and news media, social media, and any others exercising political power.

More specifically, citizens can firmly refuse to support any candidates or members of the House and Senate if they do not vote to meet international targets for foreign assistance and environmental protection, to ratify desirable treaties, to join the ICC, and more generally to implement the correlates of peace. On the other hand, support can be extended to those who act to implement these goals, even if they are based in distant districts, states, or countries. The unending challenges to democratic processes and human security call for concerned citizens to cooperate, insofar as possible, in supporting committed candidates and officials regardless of where they are located in electoral processes, parties, or geography. Concerned citizens' discussions about whom to support may encourage candidates to clarify their positions and offer more creative solutions to human security problems. Also, voting and helping to educate others on public policy issues are tasks that every person can do. Simply to have a very high percentage of all eligible voters better informed and going to the polls in every election could in itself transform US policies.

Citizens can offer support for or withdraw support from not only government officials, but also corporate executives, religious leaders, other civil society leaders, school board officials, or others if they are not working to implement the correlates of peace. Concerned citizens have a duty to assess the extent to which the purposes of major institutions align with the advancement of human security. If an organization does not radiate an inclusive identity with clear support for human rights, citizens' support can be shifted to one that does.

---

[54] For discussion of the context for taking such a stance, see Richard A. Falk, *Achieving Human Rights* (New York: Routledge, 2009), 206.

[55] He resigned in June 2017. Quoted by Roger Cohen, "The Desperation of Our Diplomats," *New York Times*, July 28, 20107, IV, 4, https://www.nytimes.com/2017/07/28/opinion/sunday/trump-tillerson-state-department-diplomats.html?searchResultPosition=3. See also Elise Labott, Zachary Cohen, and Michelle Kosinski, "Acting US Ambassador to China Quit over Trump Climate Decision," CNN News Alert, June 6, 2017, https://www.cnn.com/2017/06/05/politics/acting-ambassador-to-china-david-rank-resigns/index.html.

In addition to citizens wielding their political support more strictly, all of their purchases, charitable contributions, and volunteering could be reviewed to align them with the goals of implementing structural changes for human dignity. Citizens and their families could develop plans to reduce their energy consumption drawn from non-renewable sources. If as many of people's financial choices as possible would express human security preferences, citizens could exert a ripple effect on other political and economic decisions. These choices can be expressed every day—much more frequently than voting for president or a member of Congress. Preferential purchases even can be expressed by citizens in some countries where voting is suppressed or ineffective. By collecting necessary information to encourage aligning purchases with value preferences, journalists and citizens could influence some unscrupulous marketing that contributes to ecocide, reshape some corporate practices, and enable corporate officials to exert constructive influences on governing officials.

Because every adult on Earth makes some purchases, a transnational purchasing movement of millions of people could exert enough influence to move some corporate officials to support human security goals.[56] Some citizens have stopped purchasing gasoline, for example, from companies that engage in disinformation campaigns about global warming, and instead patronize those known for at least some "green" practices. Consumers are rewarding with purchases those manufacturers that make products that consume less electricity and fossil fuels. The possibilities for corporate influence are illustrated by Facebook changing its staunch refusal to limit hate speech. Mark Zuckerberg had frequently informed the public, Congress, and advertisers that Facebook would never back down on allowing all speech. Then advertisers, including Unilever, Coca-Cola, and Pfizer began criticizing Facebook for keeping hate speech on its pages. After more than 300 corporations began to withhold advertising, Facebook decided to reconsider.[57]

Of course, no provider of goods or services perfectly matches the goals of a movement for human security, but perfection is not necessary for citizens to exert significant influence *if* citizens act together. They simply need to articulate a fundamental goal that they want to advance, such as to limit global warming, and then identify a few companies that are environmentally more sensitive than others. Purchasing from the greenest companies while shunning the others can influence producers over time.[58] "Preferred providers" need not be perfect providers. They simply must be better at a specific value realization than others to enable consumers to support them while asking others to do at least as well.

---

[56] For suggestions for how to succeed, see Louis Hyman and Joseph Tohill, *Shopping for Change: Consumer Activism and the Possibilities of Purchasing Power* (Ithaca, NY: ILR Press and Cornell University Press, 2017).

[57] Tiffany Hsu and Mike Isaac, "Advertiser Exodus Snowballs as Facebook Struggles to Ease Concerns," *New York Times*, June 30, 2020, https://www.nytimes.com/2020/06/30/technology/facebook-advertising-boycott.html?searchResultPosition=2.

[58] See Ellis Jones, Ross Haenfler, and Brett Johnson with Brian Klocke, *The Better World Handbook: From Good Intentions to Everyday Actions* (Gabriola Island, Canada: New Society Publishers, 2001), betterworldhandbook.com.

Recognizing that positive change often rests on developing new habits, concerned citizens can continue imagining and implementing habits to expand influences for human security. Some already commit voluntary monthly contributions to support one or two exemplary organizations or candidates committed to implementing the correlates of peace. They volunteer regularly to support a human rights organization or global network devoted to generating truthful information about leaders and organizations worthy of support as well as about those from whom support might be withdrawn. Many find participating in such efforts to be fulfilling ways to promote change and diminish discouragement or alienation.[59]

In addition to the federal government and private corporations, municipal and state governmental institutions can also play influential roles in a transnational movement. Cooperation across international borders has sometimes occurred more easily among city or state governments in different countries facing similar needs than among national governments. Governors, mayors, and other local officials can sometimes be unusually effective in discovering ways to overcome partisan differences, perhaps because they may be less adversarially nationalistic and more focused on meeting daily needs of people in their communities. Inhabitants of cities know that human dignity may be wrenchingly denied if air or water pollution is not addressed or if law enforcement officials use excessive force, engage in discriminatory practices, or refuse to share police intelligence on suspected terrorists with other municipalities. California has at times influenced all auto and pickup truck manufacturers throughout the United States to improve their air pollution standards if they want to sell vehicles in California. This has also improved the quality of some vehicles marketed in other countries.

Individuals sometimes are discouraged from acting because they know that one person or one family is relatively powerless. But many citizens united, including both genders and every race, religion, class, and nationality, acting to domesticate the international system for the good of the global family, could generate sufficient force to produce new habits and genuine change. Any citizens prone to becoming discouraged by insufficient numbers in a coalition would do well to recall Lederach's observation that often the missing ingredient in change "is not the critical mass. The missing ingredient is the critical *yeast*."[60]

If deepened commitments and personal transformations are replicated widely, they could advance social transformation. Most people can be change-makers, yet they do

---

[59] Of course, smugness and self-righteousness have no place in effective activism even though change agents understandably hold fundamental convictions firmly. When successes occur, triumphalism also has no place because any success worthy of note would be a better manifestation of more people's rights based on deeper understanding of all people's realities, not a victory of one side over another. Cecelia Lynch offers excellent advice for avoiding elitist attitudes that may disempower human agency in "Neoliberal Ethics, the Humanitarian International, and Practices of Peacebuilding," in *Globalization, Social Movements, and Peacebuilding*, ed. Jackie Smith and Ernesto Verdeja (Syracuse, NY: Syracuse University Press, 2013), 47–68.

[60] Lederach, *Moral Imagination*, 91. Italics in original.

not know it. Columnist David Brooks once noted that "millions of people don't feel that they can take control of their own lives. If we could give everyone the chance to experience an agency moment, to express love and respect in action, the ramifications really would change the world."[61] Concerned citizens can provide some of the yeast required to move today's militarized international system toward a rule-of-law system if they recognize that they must act because simply waiting for the United States or other major powers to lead will be unlikely to produce enough helpful change soon enough to salvage our planet's climate or, perhaps, our civilization.[62] US citizens face a choice: Should they continue to accept the environmental destruction, denials of human rights, and recurring violence that are likely to accompany the existing anarchic international system, or should they accept the risks that would accompany initiatives to change the system in order to build a world of law and more democratic global institutions? Neither alternative is risk free, but the likely outcomes of one path seem far more promising than the likely outcomes of the other. The choices that US citizens make now are likely to determine whether subsequent generations will be able to avoid a world of extreme calamity.

To practice politics as usual seems likely to allow doors to close on many future possibilities for realizing human dignity. On the other hand, for those willing to accept the challenge of advancing human dignity, there is enough evidence to inspire hope and intensified efforts: Wide international support continues for human rights. Civil society organizations enjoy growing influence. Coalition efforts involving transnational social change groups, progressive states, and UN and other international organizations have had some successes (e.g., creating the ICC, achieving readiness from some states to strengthen the Paris agreement, completing treaties on the rights of children, nuclear weapons, land mines, and chlorofluorocarbons). Interest in holding leaders accountable for crimes against humanity continues. Growing numbers of citizens and policymakers acknowledge that ecological hazards and pandemics require collective action. International legal processes are slowly growing. Many state officials in the United States embodied professional integrity while serving voters in the 2020 elections even at personal risk to themselves. Early in the Biden administration, the United States re-joined the World Health Organization to help distribute COVID vaccine more equitably throughout the world.[63]

---

[61] David Brooks, "Everyone a Changemaker," *New York Times*, February 9, 2018, A 27.

[62] Joseph Nye has warned, "Washington's role in helping stabilize the world and underwrite its continued progress may be even more important now than ever. Americans and others may not notice the security and prosperity that the liberal order provides until they are gone—but by then, it may be too late." Nye, "Will the Liberal Order Survive?"

A chronic denial of empirical reality constitutes a form of mental illness when it occurs in individuals. In a collective mindset, it is delusion. It may be widely believed because it is consensually validated, but it is, nonetheless, delusion.

[63] Nick Cumming-Bruce and Sheryl Gay Stolberg, "Fauci Tells W.H.O. That US Stands Ready to Work with It," *New York Times*, January 21, 2021.

9.7 "WORKING TOWARD A WORLD WITHOUT WAR"

Some of the changes needed for human security today were already in John Kennedy's mind and heart as he returned to the United States after serving valiantly in the US Navy in the Pacific during World War II. As a returning veteran turned young journalist, Kennedy attended the San Francisco conference that was drafting the UN Charter. He was asked by one of his PT-boat friends what he thought of the conference. Kennedy reported that the diplomats from throughout the world meeting in San Francisco had been charged with the responsibility of building new global architecture to save future generations from a repetition of major war.[64] He went on: "When I think of how much this war has cost us, of the deaths of Cy and Peter and Orv and Gil and Demi and Joe and Billy and all of those thousands and millions who have died with them—when I think of all those gallant acts that I have seen or anyone has seen who has been to the war—it would be a very easy thing to feel disappointed and somewhat betrayed."[65]

Instead of achieving the goal to erect reliable war-preventing architecture in the international system, many nations came to San Francisco advancing their narrower selfish interests. He reflected on his wartime experience: "You have seen battlefields where sacrifice was the order of the day; to compare that sacrifice to the timidity and selfishness of the nations gathered at San Francisco must inevitably be disillusioning."[66]

He also listened to the arguments of Cord Meyer, another youthful returning veteran, who was about to start an organization favoring world federation as the best way to provide security while ending war. In one of his personal notebooks, Kennedy wrote, "Admittedly world organization with common obedience to law would be a solution," but it is "not that easy. If there is not the feeling that war is the ultimate evil, a feeling strong enough to drive . . . [nations] together, then you can't work out this internationalist plan." He knew such "things cannot be forced from the top."[67] Not only is it still true that there must be grassroots support for new architecture to rise, it is also true today, as then, that most people at the top in the great powers are slow to lead. Pathbreaking leadership can arise, but usually only with help from grassroots pressure below, because the "timidity and selfishness of the nations" hold them back. For these reasons, citizens across the United States and around the world constantly can benefit from empowering one another to think and act for human dignity if they want to avoid disillusionment from governments. Such a transnational movement might even possess an anti-war "feeling strong enough to drive . . . [nations] together" to work out a more creative "internationalist plan."

An encouraging and instructive example of planning for structural change also can be gleaned from Kennedy's experiences later as president. This occurred in a

---

[64] This goal was expressed in the Preamble to the Charter of the United Nations.

[65] Arthur Schlesinger, *A Thousand Days: John F. Kennedy in the White House* (Greenwich, CT: Fawcett, 1965), 88.

[66] Schlesinger, *Thousand Days*, 88.

[67] Schlesinger, *Thousand Days*, 88.

pathbreaking initiative pursued by Adlai Stevenson and President Kennedy in 1961. Stevenson, the former governor of Illinois, had been the Democratic Party's choice to run for US president in 1952 and again in 1956 against Dwight Eisenhower. Later, Stevenson was President Kennedy's choice for US representative to the United Nations, which was deeply engaged in far-reaching negotiations for disarmament at that time. Stevenson proposed a system-changing security approach in an address published by the US Department of State entitled, "Working Toward a World Without War." Aware of the dangers of nuclear cataclysm during the US-Soviet Cold War years, he acknowledged: "However difficult the vision of a world *without war* may be, it is not only a happier but an easier vision to imagine than one of a world *after war*."[68] President Kennedy had laid the foundation for these proposals when he told the General Assembly: "Every inhabitant of this planet must contemplate the day when this planet may no longer be habitable. Every man, woman, and child lives under a nuclear sword of Damocles, hanging by the slenderest of threads, capable of being cut at any moment by accident or miscalculation or by madness. The weapons of war must be abolished before they abolish us."[69]

The US plan "to create a world without war" entailed a series of steps, proceeding from the existing balance-of-power system through graduated arms reductions, leading eventually to the "ultimate goal" of internationally regulated constraints on the power and authority to make war and enforce peace. The plan reserved outer space exclusively for peaceful purposes and called for international programs for economic and social development as works of peacebuilding. It "insists especially upon the essential need to build up the machinery of peace while we tear down the machinery of war." The two "must go hand in hand." Indeed they "must be . . . two parts of a single program." Stevenson shared what this analysis earlier labeled the "empirical realist conclusion" that, because of nuclear dangers, system change was necessary and worth trying. This plan specified that as national armaments would be reduced, "we destroy an obsolete institution [war] for the settlement of disputes." Simultaneously, "we must create new institutions for the settlement of disputes." In the new world with no substantial national arsenals, "military power would be taken out of the hands of nations; but other forms of power would remain—and mostly in the hands of the same states which are the most powerful military states today."[70]

Stevenson sought to increase global governance to enable reducing national warmaking capacity: "If we travel the two roads together, if we build [governance] as we destroy [armaments], we can solve the technical problems of dismantling the vast apparatus of war." The US plan "would not usher in world government, but the world community would have the capacity to keep the peace." Significantly, "it would not

---

[68] Stevenson, "Working Toward a World Without War," 14. Italics in original. Stevenson delivered his address on November 15, 1961.

[69] President Kennedy speaking to the General Assembly, September 25, 1961, quoted by Stevenson, "Working Toward a World Without War," 17.

[70] Stevenson, "Working Toward a World Without War," 17.

end national sovereignty, but the sovereign right to commit national suicide would be yielded up forever."[71] In sum, "We do not hold the vision of a world without conflict. We do hold the vision of a world without war—and this inevitably requires an alternative system for coping with conflict. We cannot have one without the other."[72]

Stevenson wrote with a system-change signature. His anticipation of what an alternative system might do to manage the problem of nuclear weapons was a global parallel to regional thinking voiced in German foreign minister Fischer's statement about how Europe had solved its war problem by creating the European Union: system change in the form of more inclusive governance replaced war.[73] The Europeans' change in governance did free them from recurring wars on their continent.

For several reasons, before the US plan could be effectively negotiated, support for it waned in the United States itself. There were too many vested interests, both political and economic, pushing for higher levels of military preparedness. At the same time, the fascination with counter-insurgency warfare led some officials to focus efforts on moving militarily into Vietnam. Then President Kennedy was assassinated, leaving government under bureaucratic control inclined to follow past policies. There was insufficient grassroots public pressure supporting the idea of increasing global governance while diminishing armament under international legal control. The Cold War had weakened support for international institutions.[74]

Had it been possible to bring the thinking behind the Kennedy-Stevenson plan for a world without war into conversation with the later constitutive re-thinking of Gorbachev, and had there been more preparation for public understanding of what could be done, it might have been possible to have introduced some reforms to the international system after the Cold War and during the 1990s. More than 200 years earlier, Immanuel Kant confronted a similar problem of intellectual inertia impeding positive changes that he contemplated in his proposal for "Perpetual Peace." He urged citizens to become better informed and to think for themselves: "A large part of mankind gladly remain minors all their lives, long after nature has freed them from external guidance." Enlightenment, Kant wrote, is a person's "emergence from . . . self-imposed immaturity."[75] He urged: "Have the courage to use your own understanding."[76]

---

[71] Stevenson, "Working Toward a World Without War," 27.

[72] Stevenson, "Working Toward a World Without War," 18.

[73] Fischer's statement is discussed in Chapter 6, section 6.4.

[74] Cecelia Lynch's penetrating research provides a far-reaching analysis of how constructive citizen influences to reduce violence in international relations can be misconstrued and, as a result, used to sustain the old order. Rather than finding the inter-war peace movements in Britain and the United States responsible for appeasement and isolationist policies, they had in fact "legitimized . . . norms that underlay global international organization and, ultimately, the construction of the United Nations." Cecelia Lynch, *Beyond Appeasement: Interpreting Interwar Peace Movements in World Politics* (Ithaca, NY: Cornell University Press, 1999), 1–10.

[75] Avi Lifschitz, "The Enlightenment: Those Who Dare to Know," *History Today* 63, no. 9 (September 2013), https://www.historytoday.com/avi-lifschitz/enlightenment-those-who-dare-to-know.

[76] Immanuel Kant, "What Is Enlightenment?" trans. Mary C. Smith, http://www.columbia.edu/acis/ets/CCREAD/etscc/kant.html#note1.

Doing so could enable people to rise from their conditioning that now blocks deeply needed, empirically realistic national security planning.

Do today's national governments and international society have sufficient material and ideational capacity to change some aspects of the sovereign state system, which has been with us since the Peace of Westphalia? Sovereignty since medieval times has been shaped by the power of *ideas*, as Philpott has documented.[77] Ideas shape people's identities and beliefs about what constitutes legitimate political authority. Widely held ideas exert social power on elites who shape sovereign institutions, like the state, which has enjoyed legitimacy since 1648. Of course, states in turn constitute the international system and what might be called the "global constitution" more generally.

Two particularly large changes in ideas have played a key role, eventually causing the entire world to change how it was organized. First, new thinking about politics and religion brought the Protestant Reformation and religious wars in Europe. These ended medieval Christendom and made sovereign states the dominant political form in Europe from the peace settlement in 1648 until the present, although this has been somewhat qualified in recent years by the creation of the EU. Second, ideas about equality and nationalism later spread throughout the world and swept through colonial empires especially after World War II until, by the early 1960s, the states system expanded through the entire world. Colonialism was dismantled and independent states became the worldwide norm for political organization and legitimacy. In both major changes, "revolutions in ideas about [what constituted] legitimate political authority profoundly altered the 'constitution' that establishes basic authority in the international system."[78] A further modest change in sovereignty, to accommodate some more effective components of global governance to which George H. W. Bush referred, might have been possible after the end of the Cold War. But exclusionary nationalism and political realist assumptions impeded possible change. At that time and in this one respect, Washington might be said to have flown with the more old-fashioned sovereignty hawks in Moscow, Beijing, and elsewhere.

Recognizing the power of ideas to shape sovereignty and the de facto global constitution provides reason for some hope of system change in the midst of otherwise discouraging times for global governance. Perhaps scholars like Wendt, Deudney, and Philpott might agree that, because ideas constitute the basis for the prevailing global constitution, every person's new thinking, when added to millions of others, contributes to change (at least slightly). The ideas we hold, discuss with others, teach our children, and vote for can move the world closer to needed change, because our ideas collectively can amend the global constitution, even if at most times our influence seems imperceptible.[79]

---

[77] Philpott, *Revolutions in Sovereignty*.

[78] Philpott, *Revolutions in Sovereignty*, abstract, //press.princeton.edu/books/paperback/9780691057477/revolutions-in-sovereignty.

[79] "Revolutions in ideas bring revolutions in sovereignty." Philpott, *Revolutions in Sovereignty*, 6–7. Of course, changing ideas can be for good or ill, as the world discovered with the rise of populism in the United States.

People who want to live conscientiously despite their governing officials' short-sightedness and occasional inhumanity and dishonesty might find it useful to think of themselves as part of a group of concerned citizens who choose to walk a path toward an imagined global polity or community, respecting human dignity and seeking human security, even though some fellow nationals may not be on the same path. They could reasonably claim that (1) they are politically responsible, because they support practical measures to maximize peace and security for the United States and others, and (2) they are ethically sensitive, because they endorse means that pointedly nurture and protect human life rather than destroy it, including when coercive law enforcement is required. This twofold commitment to prudence and ethics, self-interest and altruism, can be the foundation on which sustainable peace can be built. The sense of not being aligned with everyone in the society in which one gratefully lives and works, while yearning for a polity that *could* be, might feel a bit like being on a pilgrimage to a better place.[80]

Individuals will experience good company in their pursuit of human security, because many others, perhaps most others, already seek a human-dignity future, even though everyone at times may feel lonely or discouraged when confronting bureaucratic power structures that seem unresponsive and yet shape people's understandings of truth. As has always been true of human rights movements, those who seek to implement a positive vision need to be in touch with like-minded people. Identifying with a community or polis that one can imagine and hold in one's mind even though it does not yet exist in political reality can make sense if it *could* exist, because such a vision can animate joy in another way of living in the present, a way that can draw society and government closer to the preferred world. Such a modest yet real achievement may be the most that an individual can expect at sobering moments in history when the "timidity and selfishness" of nations have not yet been sufficiently addressed by their citizens, and the values of human dignity are not as widely understood and upheld as many citizens earlier hoped.

9.8 REALIZING THE VISION

The synthesis of evidence found in peace and security research points to the conclusion that the best way for US policymakers and citizens to protect their own

---

[80] Richard Falk examines a pilgrimage metaphor in chapter 14 of *Achieving Human Rights*, 202–207.

    When faced with hard choices to counter German violence in World War II, French philosopher Simone Weil also urged people "to inhabit a space in which we live between the tasks of practicing genuine attention to what is and noting our longing for a set of goods for ourselves and our neighbours that might not right now be within our reach—whose vision might not yet be fully formed, but which confronted with these events we may wish to cry out for, and commit ourselves to securing as the basis for a human future worth believing in." Anna Rowlands, "Simone Weil and the Gift of Inarticulacy: How Not to Live in Lockdown," *Religion & Ethics* (May 6, 2020), https://www.abc.net.au/religion/anna-rowlands-simone-weil-lockdown-and-the-gift-of-inarticulacy/12220482.

long-range security is to implement a global grand strategy for human security, a strategy informed by six correlates of peace and security. To embark on this strategy, supportive governments and international organizations working with individuals and all willing groups in civil society could

(1) address all nations' security fears;
(2) emphasize human security no less than national security;
(3) establish reciprocity in international relationships and institutions;
(4) implement equity in all political, economic, and environmental processes and decisions;
(5) expand the rule of law in international relations; and
(6) build democratic global governance to enable formation and enforcement of laws essential for human security.

Replacing national grand strategy with global grand strategy can enable the militarized balance-of-power system to be gradually replaced with a web-like, more highly institutionalized balance-of-power system made up of legal, political, economic, and environmental balances, tempered by prudential checks on the most powerful agencies and actors in the system. To build a broad transnational coalition—including individuals, human rights organizations and other civil society groups, religious communities, far-sighted corporations, visionary political parties, municipal governments, progressive national governments, United Nations agencies, and other international organizations—to implement the correlates of peace should be doable, because the initial parts are already in place.[81]

Jackie Smith and Dawn Wiest point to transnational social networks that are beginning to "challenge states and other global actors as well as the interstate system itself."[82] In addition, they find that "the strengthening of international law and institutions has been shifting the bases of power and authority from claims of territorial sovereignty, backed by coercion, to normative claims based on persuasion. This has empowered new actors in the global political arena, including social movements and less powerful states."[83] In their view, we are moving toward a time when "movement-generated norms . . . will become more potent references and guides for action."[84] One may debate how strong the new influences of social movements and less powerful

---

[81] Although their purposes vary widely, many organizations are working across borders for more law-abiding global governance. During the 20th century, intergovernmental organizations grew to more than 7,300 and non-governmental organizations to 67,000. See Union of International Associations, *Yearbook of International Organizations 2003–04* (Munich: K. G. Saur Verlag, 2005), 2, appendix 3, 2914; *Yearbook of International Organizations*, https://www.uia.org/ybio/.

[82] Smith and Wiest, *Social Movements in the World-System*, 163.

[83] Smith and Wiest, *Social Movements in the World-System*, 163.

[84] Smith and Wiest, *Social Movements in the World-System*, 174.

states have become without doubting that these and other transnational influences are on the rise and have achieved some significant successes.[85]

Of course, merely hoping for more effective global governance will not make it happen. Falk reminds us that people's sense of citizenship needs to be embedded in a feeling of community "that binds at the level of emotion" in order to "lead to the construction of a new identity capable of addressing challenges of planetary scope."[86] To be sure, emotional support for world community would help to realize the grand strategy for human security. Yet this cautionary note is not a suggestion for inaction until a new, species-wide identity has taken root everywhere. On the contrary, it is a reminder that one should not acquiesce in accepting the status quo nor expect change without effort and struggle. Educating, organizing, and acting can build transnational emotional commitment where it did not exist before, as demonstrated, to a limited degree, in past international movements that assisted the achievements listed in Table 9.2. All these initiatives advanced with the help of pluralistic movements focused on a particular change at its time of establishment. Several of the most recent examples provide the best guides for what is required to mobilize support for a grand strategy for human security, but all provide useful lessons.

Despite many understandable grounds for pessimism about making progress toward a grand strategy for human security, a realistic appraisal of prospects should consider the following. First, some helpful international innovations probably could occur right now, without many changes in people's sense of global citizenship. Indeed, two positive steps toward human security already *were taken* by the United States and most other great powers, but then the United States *withdrew* from them both: the Paris climate accord and the Iran nuclear deal. Many positive initiatives are well within reach of the great powers right now, but policymakers do not grasp them because of the influence of vested interests in short-term wealth- and power-maximizing, the classic tragedy of the commons, about which it is possible to do something through political education and action.

Second, a sense of global citizenship may grow at the same time as institutional construction occurs. That sense does not need to *precede* it in all people, although of course it does in some. How much sense of global community was present for each of the positive lawmaking initiatives in Table 9.2? However one would measure it, the modest amount registered in most of those cases is presumably sufficient to implement additional initiatives if short-term foot-dragging and power-and-wealth maximizing policies could be tempered a bit more by concern for human dignity.

---

[85] See Thania Paffenholz, Christoph Spurk, Roberto Belloni, Sabine Kurtenbach, et al., "Enabling and Disenabling Factors for Civil Society Peacebuilding," in *Civil Society and Peacebuilding: A Critical Assessment*, ed. Thania Paffenholz (Boulder, CO: Lynne Rienner, 2010), 405–424.

[86] Falk, *Achieving Human Rights*, 203.

TABLE 9.2

Human Security Achievements Assisted by Transnational Social Movements

- Treaty on the Prohibition of Nuclear Weapons to delegitimize nuclear weapons 2017
- Paris agreement on climate protection 2016
- International Criminal Court to try leaders accused of crimes 2001
- UN Security Council Resolution 1325 emphasizing women's roles in peacebuilding 2000
- Ottawa Treaty to ban anti-personnel land mines 1997
- Kyoto guidelines for limiting atmospheric pollution 1997
- Comprehensive Nuclear-Test-Ban Treaty 1996
- Abolition of apartheid 1994
- International Criminal Tribunal for Rwanda to try leaders accused of crimes 1994
- International Criminal Tribunal for the Former Yugoslavia to try leaders accused of crimes 1993
- European Union 1993
- Convention on the Rights of the Child for protection of children 1989
- Montreal Protocol on Substances That Deplete the Ozone Layer 1987
- Convention on the Elimination of All Forms of Discrimination against Women 1979
- European Economic Community and Treaty of Rome 1957
- European Coal and Steel Community 1951
- Convention on the Prevention and Punishment of the Crime of Genocide 1948
- Universal Declaration of Human Rights 1948
- UN Charter and creation of the United Nations 1945

Third, governments do embrace internationalism when it satisfies their desires. People and governments may be attracted to global governance, if wisely and cautiously pursued, for the same reason that one of the first actions taken by every national government when it becomes independent, regardless of ideology, wealth, geography, or religious faith, is to join the United Nations. Why do all nations want to do this? Because the UN's modest degree of global governance offers them authoritative recognition and participation in worldwide decision-making that they cannot get anywhere else. The UN does not offer them wealth or even much security, the other two basic motivations for state behavior. Even though the UN is an imperfect institution, because it recognizes every state as worthy of being treated seriously and, in terms of formal legalities, more fairly than many were treated in the past, it attracts support. In return for obtaining worldwide recognition of the worth of their nationalities, a UN member agrees to grant equal value to other nationalities and not to inflict violence on others in return for not having violence inflicted on themselves. The United Nations was born in 1945, with a relatively low level of people's sense of international community, but it has survived because it recognizes the legitimacy of sub-universal (national) interests and folds those in with the customs and laws pre-scribing acceptable national behavior on the international stage, especially related to violence.[87]

How much depth of feeling about global citizenship is necessary to take the next steps in global governance? The short answer is this: No more is needed than now exists to implement the most obvious next steps. Much more is needed to take steps further down the road. Yet if the feasible next steps are taken now, more widespread and deeper feelings probably will arise to enable further steps later on. The complaint that global institutions cannot be built until after there is more sense of world commu-nity may be partly an excuse, often heard from governing elites in the great powers, for avoiding unwanted, yet obvious, next moves toward more genuine reciprocity, equity, and the rule of law.

Fourth, the recommendations flowing from this analysis apply to both the US gov-ernment and US citizens. Both influence prospects for achieving human security. Until US policymakers pursue a strategy closer to the one proposed here, concerned citizens may nevertheless draw on these recommendations to make clear where they stand on future security policy and where they want officials to head. Empirical realism can provide a continually updated place for concerned citizens to stand, not with self-righteousness, but with integrity and public witness, even if their own government is pursuing short-term benefits for itself and its supporters at the expense of human dignity. Standing up for a global grand strategy for human security shows citizens' eagerness to join hands with others throughout the world who believe that the com-mon good should have no less priority than the good for oneself. It lets the world know that these concerned citizens are committed to doing their utmost to implement the correlates of peace and security, to refuse support to any candidate for office who does not share their commitment, and to withhold discretionary business from corpora-tions or other groups that do not share it. When many citizens make this clear, gov-ernment and corporate changes will occur. In the meantime, such commitments are an exemplary way for citizens to live.

To make progress, concerned citizens might prepare to accept a struggle of lifelong duration, as has been necessary throughout history to bring about fundamental prog-ress in human rights.[88] Of course, concerned citizens might work in the short run to win the next election for a candidate worthy of support, because elections present opportunities to educate as well as to exercise power. At the same time, citizens also might designate part of their income and time to promote structural changes that may not occur for years, perhaps not until the next crisis galvanizes enough citizens' attention, consternation, or hope to arouse many more citizens to insist on the next institutional change for which scholars and activists will have previously drawn plans.

---

[87] Central among these is a renunciation of war except in self-defense or when authorized by the Security Council.

[88] See numerous examples of struggle over many years to make human rights gains, in Lauren, *International Human Rights*.

If these preparations are made, people will be less likely to "feel disappointed and somewhat betrayed"[89] by the timidity of governments as some returning veterans felt after World War II.

Citizens may be understandably skeptical about constructing more effective international institutions because they fear that such institutions might dominate, control, or subjugate national societies. Insisting on appropriate limits on all centers of power is one way of addressing that problem. This fear may arise in part because of an oversimplification that seems prevalent in political realism—that there are only two possibilities: international anarchy or unwanted hierarchy. But experience with democratic forms of governance suggests there is a third possibility in which a law-abiding and *limited* hierarchy can prevent and govern the violent excesses of anarchy with responsible governance, on the one hand, while avoiding the freedom-denying excesses of dictatorial hierarchy, on the other.[90] Morgenthau's "equality in freedom" offers genuine possibilities nationally, regionally, and globally.

It is not necessary for people of goodwill to agree with all aspects of this analysis in order to participate in a transnational coalition striving to implement the correlates of peace and to bring congruency between the global extent of problems and the group working on solutions.[91] The values of human dignity embedded in this grand strategy offer an intellectual, political, and, if wanted, even spiritual home for people seeking ways to be both politically responsible and ethically sensitive citizens.[92] This strategy embodying human dignity provides a road map for a journey that connects people everywhere with others struggling anywhere to live their fear-ridden lives in ways not determined by fears alone, with motivation rooted in a positive vision of human dignity for everyone on Earth, regardless of how far astray one's own government, sadly, may wander.

Concerned policymakers and citizens can move beyond the "timidity of nations" with confidence that upholding human dignity is a solid foundation for future political work. They also can moderate the "selfishness of nations" with a commitment to human rights and solidarity[93] in the service of human security for *all*. Hard-headed participation in such an effort encourages not only sober counting the costs of participation but also an uplifting feeling from honoring human connections that many instinctively sense are authentically life-giving.[94] There does not need to be a contradiction between

---

[89] The words are John Kennedy's, quoted in Schlesinger, *A Thousand Days*, 88.

[90] On this point, Deudney notes that "republican forms of governance, both within units and between them, are as different from hierarchy as they are from anarchy." See Deudney, "Regrounding Realism," 42.

[91] Congruence entails correspondence between the scope of the problem and the inclusiveness of people in working out the solution.

[92] Parker J. Palmer has discussed how to *Let Your Life Speak: Listening for the Voice of Vocation* (San Francisco: Jossey-Bass, 2000).

[93] The desired solidarity requires that states "envision the consequences of . . . action through others' eyes; that they hear the issues at stake debated from multiple perspectives; that they be required to confront evidence contrary to their own. Solidarity thus functions as both a value and a constraint." Slaughter, "Security, Solidarity, Sovereignty," 627.

[94] Examples of political practitioners with vision commensurate to the grand strategy proposed here include examples such as Nelson Mandela, South African president from 1994 to 1999; Gareth Evans,

self-interest and altruism if the "self" expands to include respect for all people and the "interest" expands toward the long term.

Resonating with the empirical research reflected in this book is a body of normative wisdom, symbolized by the Golden Rule and similar expressions in all major religious traditions[95] and in philosophical discourse such as Kant's categorical imperative: to treat others as we would like to have them treat us.[96] If we tried to imagine that our adversaries' past might have been our past, if their pain had been our pain, and if what animated their fears had aroused similar fears in us, then we would have a better understanding of how to treat each other. Recognizing similarities in our human natures and dissimilarities in our historical experiences can wisely inform a strategy for our common security and common destiny.

Empirical research and normative wisdom combine to help citizens identify a promising path toward security for the human family and to generate personal motivation to follow that path, perhaps even to experience a sense of joy for the peacebuilding opportunities that committed citizens hold in their minds, hearts, and hands, as well as a willingness to sacrifice when the path is difficult. This turns out not to be an easy path, nor a perfect peace, but the correlates of peace, informed by consciousness of inclusive human identity, do chart a helpful direction. No one can know if a coalition of concerned policymakers and citizens will succeed in saving the human species and the planet for future generations, but those who try at least will know that they have lived their lives to uphold human dignity.

Broadening one's identity and ethical sensitivities can make a difference, as philosopher Peter Singer has noted: "How well we come through the era of globalization (perhaps whether we come through at all) will depend on how we respond *ethically* to the idea that we live in one world. For the rich nations not to take a global ethical viewpoint has long been seriously morally wrong. Now it is also, in the long run, a danger to their security."[97] To live both prudently and ethically, citizens need to consider the diminishing moral significance of political boundaries, and, as Singer also suggests, to implement a "pragmatic, step-by-step approach to greater global governance."[98]

Rather than recurring wars, terrorism, economic and environmental calamities, cyberattacks, and runaway pandemics, the future can be brightened with more inclusive identities inspiring responsible governance able to establish sustainable peace

---

Australian foreign minister from 1988 to 1996 and participant in the Commission for Global Governance and the International Commission for Environment and Development; Lloyd Axworthy, Canadian foreign minister from 1996 to 2000; and, of course, others.

[95] See Brian D. Lepard, *Rethinking Humanitarian Intervention: A Fresh Legal Approach Based on Fundamental Ethical Principles in International Law and World Religions* (University Park: Pennsylvania State University Press, 2003).

[96] Kant's formulation is "Act only in accordance with that maxim through which you can at the same time will that it become a universal law." Immanuel Kant, *Grounding for the Metaphysics of Morals*, trans. James W. Ellington (Cambridge, MA: Hackett, 1993 [1785]), 30.

[97] Italics added. Singer, *One World*, 13.

[98] Singer, *One World*, 200.

with enhanced justice, human rights, economic well-being, and environmental health for all people. If the preceding statement is true, critics might ask, why has the world not already addressed people's basic needs and security fears by institutionalizing peace with augmented reciprocity, equity, rule of law, and global governance? The answer can be found in contemplating the reasons for the shortsighted, tragic habits evinced in the tragedy of the commons and the failed stag hunt.[99] Rather than perpetuate those self-destructive habits, the evidence now points us toward a realistic global grand strategy for peace and human security. By continually drawing on rigorous empirical analysis to inform action by concerned policymakers and citizens, it should be possible to engage underutilized human potential to implement "the things that make for peace" and together build dependable security and peace for all.[100]

---

[99] Both parables show actors motivated by the habit of apparent self-interest that, upon deeper reflection, contradicts an empirically realistic grasp of self-interest, which also is consonant with reciprocal altruism. Discouraging as those parables are, substantial evidence shows that their negative outcomes need not occur.

[100] Luke 19:42. The theory of empirical realism and the grand strategy proposed in this study remain open to changing human understandings arising from continuing syntheses of peace research, security studies, other social science research, and respect for the values of human dignity and peace expressed in the world's major religious and wisdom traditions as well as cosmopolitan philosophical explorations.

BIBLIOGRAPHY

Abramson, Jeff. Arms Control Association. *Issue Briefs* 10, no. 6 (June 7, 2018). https://www.armscontrol.org/taxonomy/term/31.

Abramson, Jeff. "States Link Efforts to Curb Arms Flows." *Arms Control Today* 46, no. 6 (2016): 25–26.

Abramson, Jeff. "UN General Assembly Adopts Arms Trade Treaty in Overwhelming Vote." *Arms Control Today* 43, no. 4 (2013): 15–21.

Acemoglu, Daron and James Robinson. *Why Nations Fail: The Origins of Power, Prosperity and Poverty*. New York: Crown, 2012.

Adams, Gordon. *The Iron Triangle: The Politics of Defense Contracting*. New York: Council on Economic Priorities, 1981.

Aleem, Zeeshan. "I Was Elected to Represent Pittsburgh, Not Paris." *Vox*, June 1 2017. https://www.vox.com/policy-and-politics/2017/6/1/15726656/pittsburgh-mayor-trump-paris.

Aloyo, Eamon. "Just War Theory and the Last of Last Resort." *Ethics & International Affairs* 29, no. 2 (2015): 187–201.

Alter, Karen J. *The New Terrain of International Law: Courts, Politics, Rights*. Princeton, NJ: Princeton University Press, 2014.

Alvarez, José E. *International Organizations as Law-Makers*. Oxford: Oxford University Press, 2006.

Amadeo, Kimberly. "U.S. Manufacturing, Statistics, and Outlook." https://www.thebalance.com/u-s-manufacturing-what-it-is-statistics-and-outlook-3305575.

Amis, Martin. *Einstein's Monsters*. London: Jonathan Cape, 1987.

Amstutz, Mark R. *International Ethics: Concepts, Theories, and Cases in Global Politics*. Lanham, MD: Rowman & Littlefield, 1999.

Anapol, Avery. "EPA's 4-Year Strategic Plan Does Not Mention 'Climate Change.'" October 11. //thehill.com/policy/energy-environment/354886-epas-four-year-strategic-plan-does-not-mention-climate-change.

Anderson, Benedict R. *Imagined Communities*. London: Verso, 2016.

Anderson, Elizabeth. "Economic Inequality and Human Development." *UN Development Report 2019: Beyond Income, Beyond Averages, Beyond Today: Inequalities in Human Development in the 21st Century Empowered Lives. Resilient Nations*. New York: United Nations, 2019.

Andreas, Peter and Ethan Avram Nadelmann. *Policing the Globe*. Oxford: Oxford University Press, 2006.

Anielski, Mark. "The Real Cost of Eliminating Poverty in 2016." http://www.anielski.com/real-cost-eliminating-poverty/.

Annex 1: "Johannesburg Declaration on Sustainable Development." *International Environmental Agreements: Politics, Law and Economics* 2, no. 4 (2002): 403.

Appiah, Anthony. *The Lies that Bind: Rethinking Identity, Creed, Country, Color, Class, Culture*. New York: W.W. Norton, 2018.

Appiah, Kwame Anthony. *Cosmopolitanism: Ethics in a World of Strangers*. New York: W.W. Norton, 2006.

Appleby, R. Scott, Atalia Omer, and David Little. *The Oxford Handbook of Religion, Conflict, and Peacebuilding*. New York: Oxford University Press, 2015.

Apsel, Joyce and Ernesto Verdeja. *Genocide Matters: Ongoing Issues and Emerging Perspectives*. New York: Routledge, 2013.

Arbour, Louise. "The Responsibility to Protect as a Duty of Care in International Law and Practice." *Review of International Studies* 34, no. 3 (2008): 445–458.

Arms Control Association. "Arms Control and Proliferation Profile: The United States." https://www.armscontrol.org/factsheets/unitedstatesprofile#bio.

Arms Control Association. "The Trillion (and a half) Dollar Triad?" *Arms Control Today* 9, no. 6 (August 18, 2017). https://www.armscontrol.org/issue-briefs/2017-08/trillion-half-dollar-triad.

Arms Control Association. "U.S. Fissile Material Ban Plan Fizzles." https://www.armscontrol.org/act/2004_10/Fissile_Material.

Art, Robert J. *A Grand Strategy for America*. Ithaca, NY: Cornell University Press, 2003.

Asku, Esref and Joseph A. Camilleri. *Democratizing Global Governance*. New York: Palgrave, 2002.

Associated Press. "Pentagon Official Says 9/11 Suspect Was Tortured." *Toronto Star*, January 14, 2009. https://www.thestar.com/news/world/2009/01/14/pentagon_official_says_911_suspect_was_tortured.html.

Associated Press. "Timeline of the Syrian Conflict as It Enters Its 8th Year," March 15, 2018, https://apnews.com/792a0bd7dd6a4006a78287f170165408.

Associated Press. "UN Says Civil War Has Cost Syria $388 Billion in Damage," August 9, 2018. https://apnews.com/article/aa0aaa2c44cd430196f572227b45c150.

Associated Press. "Trump on Kim Jong-un: 'We Fell in Love.'" *New York Times*, September 30, 2018. https://www.nytimes.com/video/us/100000006136380/trump-kim-jong-un-we-fell-in-love.html.

Astor, Maggie. "Want to Be Happy? Try Moving to Finland." *New York Times*, March 14, 2018. https://www.nytimes.com/2018/03/14/world/europe/worlds-happiest-countries.html.

"Atomic Education Urged by Einstein." *New York Times*, May 25, 1946, 11.

Atwell, Matthew N., John Bridgeland, and Peter Levine. *Civic Deserts: America's Civic Health Challenge.* https://www.ncoc.org/wp-content/uploads/2017/10/2017CHIUpdate-FINAL-small.pdf.

Australian Department of Foreign Affairs and Trade. Canberra Commission on the Elimination of Nuclear Weapons. *Report of the Canberra Commission on the Elimination of Nuclear Weapons.* Canberra: Australian Department of Foreign Affairs and Trade, 1996.

Avant, Deborah D., Martha Finnemore, and Susan K. Sell. *Who Governs the Globe?* New York: Cambridge University Press, 2010.

Axrmitage, J. A. "Should NATO Grow? A Dissent." *New York Review of Books* 42, no. 14 (1995): 74–75.

Bacevich, Andrew J. *American Empire: The Realities and Consequences of U.S. Diplomacy.* Cambridge, MA: Harvard University Press, 2002.

Bacevich, Andrew J. *America's War for the Greater Middle East: A Military History.* New York: Random House, 2016.

Bacevich, Andrew J. *The New American Militarism: How Americans Are Seduced by War.* Oxford: Oxford University Press, 2013.

Baker, Peter. "Nixon Sought 'Monkey Wrench' in Vietnam Talks." *New York Times,* January 3, 2017.

Baker, Peter. "Trump's Insults End a Brief Civil Interlude." *New York Times,* December 8, 2018.

Baker, Peter and Rick Gladstone. "Heralding 'America First' in Combative Speech, Trump Airs List of Threats." *New York Times,* September 20, 2017.

Baker, Peter and Michael Tackett. "Trump Says His 'Nuclear Button' Is 'Much Bigger' Than North Korea's." *New York Times,* January 2, 2018.

Bank for International Settlements. "Triennial Central Bank Survey: Foreign Exchange Turnover in April 2019." https://www.bis.org/statistics/rpfx19_fx.pdf.

Barber, Rebecca. "Uniting for Peace Not Aggression: Responding to Chemical Weapons in Syria Without Breaking the Law," *Journal of Conflict and Security Law* 24, no. 1 (2019): 71–110.

Barnett, Michael N. and Martha Finnemore. "The Politics, Power, and Pathologies of International Organizations." *International Organization* 53, no. 4 (1999): 699–732.

Barton, John and Barry Carter. "International Law and Institutions for a New Age." *Georgetown Law Journal* 81, no. 3 (1993): 535.

Baxi, Uphendra. "Public and Insurgent Reason: Adjudicatory Leadership in a Hyper-Globalizing World." In *Global Crises and the Crisis of Global Leadership,* edited by Stephen Gill, 161–178. Cambridge: Cambridge University Press, 2012.

Beardsworth, Richard. *Cosmopolitanism and International Relations Theory.* Cambridge: Polity, 2011.

Beck, Lewis White. *Immanuel Kant, On History.* Upper Saddle River, NJ: Prentice Hall, 2001.

Beck, Ulrich. *The Cosmopolitan Vision.* Cambridge: Polity Press, 2006.

Beck, Ulrich and Ciaran Cronin. "Cosmopolitan Vision." John Wiley. http://nbn-resolving.de/urn:nbn:de:101:1-201503074620.

Beckley, Michael. "Rogue Superpower: Why This Could Be an Illiberal American Century." *Foreign Affairs* 99, no. 6 (2020): 73–86.

Beers, Rand, Richard A. Clarke, Emilian Papadopoulos, Paul Salem, and John R. Allen. "Grand Strategy Versus Unending Extremism." *Annals of the American Academy of Political and Social Science* 668, no. 1 (2016): 82–92.

Beitz, Charles. *Political Theory and International Relations.* Princeton, NJ: Princeton University Press, 1999.

Bellamy, Alex J. *Massacres and Morality: Mass Atrocities in an Age of Civilian Immunity*. Oxford: Oxford University Press, 2012.

Bellamy, Alex J. and Edward C. Luck. *The Responsibility to Protect*. Newark, NJ: Polity Press, 2019.

Bellamy, Alex. "Ending Atrocity Crimes: The False Promise of Fatalism." *Ethics & International Affairs* 32, no. 3 (2018): 329–337.

Bellamy, Alex. "The Responsibility to Protect Turns Ten." *Ethics & International Affairs* 29, no. 2 (2015): 161–185.

Bellamy, Richard, Wolfgang Merkel, Rajeev Bhargava, Juliana Bidadanure, Thomas Christiano, Ulrike Felt, Colin Hay, et al. "Challenges of Inequality to Democracy." In *Rethinking Society for the 21st Century: Report of the International Panel on Social Progress: Political Regulation, Governance, and Societal Transformations*, vol. 2, 563–596. Cambridge: Cambridge University Press, 2018.

Benedick, Richard Elliot. *Ozone Diplomacy: New Directions in Safeguarding the Planet*. Cambridge, MA: Harvard University Press, 1991.

Benioff, Marc. "We Need a New Capitalism." *New York Times*, October 14, 2019.

Bergen, Peter L. "Warrior in Chief." *New York Times*, April 29, 2012.

Berger, Peter. *The Sacred Canopy: Elements of a Sociological Theory of Religion*. Garden City, NY: Doubleday, 1967.

Berry, Albert. "What Type of Global Governance Would Best Lower World Poverty and Inequality?" In *Global Governance, Poverty and Inequality*, edited by Jennifer Clapp and Rorden Wilkinson, 46–68. New York: Routledge, 2010.

Bertus, Ferreira. *The Use and Effectiveness of Community Policing in a Democracy*. Washington, DC: National Institute of Justice, 1996.

Betts, Richard K. *Conflict After the Cold War: Arguments on Causes of War and Peace*. New York: Macmillan, 1994.

Betz, David. "The American Way of Bombing: Changing Ethical and Legal Norms, from Flying Fortresses to Drones." *International Affairs* 91, no. 4 (2015): 927–928.

Bhutada, Govind. "The U.S. Share of the Global Economy over Time," January 14, 2021, https://www.visualcapitalist.com/u-s-share-of-global-economy-over-time/.

"Biden's Win Is Confirmed, but Nation Is Shaken." *New York Times*, January 7, 2021.

Blakeley, Ruth. "Drones, State Terrorism and International Law." *Critical Studies on Terrorism* 11, no. 2 (2018): 321–341. https://www-tandfonline-com.proxy.library.nd.edu/doi/full/10.1080/17539153.2018.1456722.

Bliddal, Henrik, Casper Sylvest, and Peter Wilson. *Classics of International Relations*. London: Routledge, 2013.

Bloomfield, Lincoln P., ed. *International Military Forces: The Question of Peacekeeping in an Armed and Disarming World*. Boston: Little, Brown, 1964.

Bohman, James and William Rehg. "Jurgen Habermas." In *Stanford Encyclopedia of Philosophy*. Stanford, CA: Stanford University Press, 2018.

Bolton, John R. "No, No, No to International Criminal Court." *Human Events* 54, no. 32 (1998): 1–2.

Booth, Ken and Nicholas J. Wheeler. *The Security Dilemma: Fear, Cooperation and Trust in World Politics*. New York: Palgrave Macmillan, 2010.

Borger, Julian, Saeed Kamali Dehghan, and Peter Beaumont. "Trump Threatens To Rip Up Iran Nuclear Deal." *The Guardian*, October 13, 2017. https://www.theguardian.com/us-news/2017/oct/13/trump-iran-nuclear-deal-congress.

Bosco, David L. *Rough Justice: The International Criminal Court in a World of Power Politics.* Oxford: Oxford University Press, 2014.

Boulding, Elise. *Building a Global Civic Culture: Education for an Interdependent World.* Syracuse, NY: Syracuse University Press, 1990.

Boulding, Elise. *Cultures of Peace: The Hidden Side of History.* Syracuse, NY: Syracuse University Press, 2000.

Boulding, Elise and Randall Forsberg. *Abolishing War: Cultures and Institutions.* Cambridge, MA: Boston Research Center for the 21st Century, 1998.

Boulding, Kenneth E. "Three Faces of Power." *Peace & Change* 16, no. 2 (1991): 220–223.

Boulding, Kenneth E. *Three Faces of Power.* Newbury Park, CA: Sage, 1989.

Boulding, Kenneth E. "Twelve Friendly Quarrels with Johan Galtung." *Journal of Peace Research* 14, no. 1 (1977): 75–86.

Bove, Laurence F. "Reflections on the Philosophy of Nonviolence and Peace Studies." In *Morality, Ethics, and Gifted Minds*, edited by Don Ambrose and Tracy Cross, 155–160. New York: Springer, 2009.

Bowcott, Owen, Oliver Holmes, and Erin Durkin. "John Bolton Threatens War Crimes Court with Sanctions in Virulent Attack." *The Guardian*, September 10, 2018. https://www.theguardian.com/us-news/2018/sep/10/john-bolton-castigate-icc-washington-speech.

Bowler, Tim. "Which Country Dominates the Global Arms Trade?" BBC report on SIPRI data, May 9, 2018. https://www.bbc.com/news/business-43873518#:~:text=And%20unsurprisingly%20it%20is%20a,Sipri)%2C%20tells%20the%20BBC.

Bowles, Samuel and Herbert Gintis. *A Cooperative Species: Human Reciprocity and Its Evolution.* Princeton, NJ: Princeton University Press, 2011.

Brands, Hal. *American Grand Strategy and the Liberal Order: Continuity, Change, and Options for the Future.* Santa Monica, CA: Rand, 2016.

Brands, Hal. *American Grand Strategy in the Age of Trump.* Washington, DC: Brookings Institution Press, 2018.

Brands, Hal. *The Promise and Pitfalls of Grand Strategy.* Carlisle, PA: Strategic Studies Institute, US Army War College, 2012.

Braut-Hegghammer, Malfrid. "Libya's Nuclear Turnaround: Perspectives from Tripoli." *Middle East Journal* 62, no. 1 (2008): 55.

Braut-Hegghammer, Malfrid. "Revisiting Osirak: Preventive Attacks and Nuclear Proliferation Risks." *International Security* 36, no. 1 (2011): 101.

Braut-Hegghammer, Malfrid. *Unclear Physics: Why Iraq and Libya Failed to Build Nuclear Weapons.* Ithaca, NY: Cornell University Press, 2016.

Braut-Hegghammer, Malfrid. "Why North Korea Succeeded at Getting Nuclear Weapons—When Iraq and Libya Failed." *Washington Post*, January 2, 2018.

Breslin, Shaun and George Christou. "Has the Human Security Agenda Come of Age? Definitions, Discourses and Debates." *Contemporary Politics* 21, no. 1 (2015): 1–10.

Brett, Judith and Anthony Moran. "Cosmopolitan Nationalism: Ordinary People Making Sense of Diversity." *Nations and Nationalism* 17, no. 1 (2011): 188–206.

Brodie, Janine. "Income Inequality and the Future of Global Governance." In *Critical Perspectives on the Crisis of Global Governance: Reimagining the Future*, edited by Stephen Gill, 45–88. New York: Palgrave Macmillan, 2016.

Brooks, David. "Everyone a Changemaker." *New York Times*, February 9, 2018.

Brooks, Rosa. "The Constitutional and Counterterrorism Implications of Targeted Killing." Hearing Before the Senate Judiciary Subcommittee on the Constitution, Civil Rights, and

Human Rights of the Senate Committee on the Judiciary, 113th Congress, April 23, 2013. www.judiciary.senate.gov/pdf/04-23-13BrooksTestimony.pdf.

Brooks, Rosa. "Drones and the International Rule of Law." *Ethics & International Affairs* 28, no. 1 (2014): 83–103.

Brooks, Stephen G. John Ikenberry, and William C. Wohlforth. "Don't Come Home, America: The Case against Retrenchment." *International Security* 37, no. 3 (Winter 2012/13): 7–51.

Brooks, Stephen G., G. John Ikenberry, and William C. Wohlforth. "Lean Forward: In Defense of American Engagement." *Foreign Affairs* 92 (2013): 130.

Brown, Garrett Wallace and David Held. *The Cosmopolitanism Reader*. Cambridge: Polity, 2010.

Brown, Seyom. *The Causes and Prevention of War*. New York: St. Martin's Press, 1994.

Brown, Seyom. *Higher Realism: A New Foreign Policy for the United States*. Boulder, CO: Paradigm, 2009.

Brown University. "Costs of War Project." http://watson.brown.edu/costsofwar/costs/economic.

Bull, Hedley and Adam Watson. *The Expansion of International Society*. Oxford: Oxford University Press, 1984.

Burke, Peter J. and Jan E. Stets. *Identity Theory*. New York: Oxford University Press, 2009.

Burroughs, John "How Reliance on Nuclear Weapons Erodes and Distorts International Law and Global Order." *Cadmus* 1, no. 5 (2012): 150–157.

Bush, George W. "Address Before a Joint Session of the Congress on the State of the Union," January 20, 2004. http://www.presidency.ucsb.edu/ws/?pid=29646.

Bush, George W. "State of the Union," January 29, 2002. https://georgewbush-whitehouse.archives.gov/news/releases/2002/01/20020129-11.html.

Bush, George H. W. "Address Before a Joint Session of Congress on the Persian Gulf Crisis and the Federal Budget Deficit." Washington, DC, September 11, 1990.

Butterfield, Herbert. "The Tragic Element in Modern International Conflict." *Review of Politics* 12, no. 2 (1950): 147–164.

Buzan, Barry. *People, States and Fear: An Agenda for International Security Studies in the Post–Cold War Era*. Colchester, UK: ECPR Press, 2007.

Caballero-Anthony, Mely. "Community Security: Human Security at 21." *Contemporary Politics* 21, no. 1 (2015): 53–69.

Cabrera, Lius. *Global Governance, Global Government: Institutional Visions for an Evolving World System*. Albany: State University of New York Press, 2011.

Callinicos, Alex. "Anti-War Protests Do Make a Difference." *Socialist Worker*, London (2005). https://socialistworker.co.uk/art/5932/Anti+war+protests+do+make+a+difference.

Cappellazzo, Natalie. "Mixing Oil and Water: The Role of Natural Resource Wealth in the Resolution of the Maritime Boundary Dispute Between Ghana and Cote D'Ivoire." *Boston College International and Comparative Law Review* 39 (2016): 1.

Caprioli, Mary. "Gendered Conflict." *Journal of Peace Research* 37, no. 1 (2000): 53–68.

Caprioli, Mary and Mark Boyer. "Gender, Violence, and International Crisis." *Journal of Conflict Resolution* 45 (August 2001): 503–518.

Carneiro, Robert. "Political Expansion as an Expression of the Principle of Competitive Exclusion." In *Origins of the State*, edited by Ronald Cohen and Elman Service, 205–223. Philadelphia: Institute for the Study of Human Issues, 1978.

Carpenter, R. C. *Innocent Women and Children: Gender, Norms and the Protection of Civilians*. Aldershot: Ashgate, 2006.

Carr, E. H. *The Twenty Years' Crisis, 1919–1939*. London: Palgrave Macmillan, 2016.

Caughey, Devin, Chris Tausanovitch, and Christopher Warshaw. "Partisan Gerrymandering and the Political Process: Effects on Roll-Call Voting and State Policies." *Election Law Journal: Rules, Politics, and Policy* 16, no. 4 (2017): 453–469.

Caves, John P. *Weapons of Mass Destruction: Challenges for the New Administration*. Washington, DC: Center for the Study of Weapons of Mass Destruction, 2016.

Chalecki, Elizabeth L. and Pacific Institute for Studies in Development, Environment, and Security. *Environmental Security: A Case Study of Climate Change*. Oakland, CA: Pacific Institute for Studies in Development, Environment, and Security, 2002.

Challenges Project. *Challenges of Peace Operations: Into the 21st Century, Concluding Report*. Stockholm: Elanders Gotab, 2002.

Chase-Lubitz, Jesse and Robbie Gramer. "Report: U.S. Ranks Near Bottom in Commitment to Global Development." *Foreign Policy* (September 6, 2017). https://foreignpolicy.com/2017/09/06/report-u-s-ranks-near-bottom-in-commitment-to-global-development-foreign-aid-diplomacy/.

Chayes, Abram and Antonia Handler Chayes. *The New Sovereignty: Compliance with International Regulatory Agreements*. Cambridge, MA: Harvard University Press, 1995.

Chemical Weapons Convention. https://www.opcw.org/fileadmin/OPCW/CWC/CWC_en.pdf.

Chen, Lung-chu, Harold D. Lasswell, Longzhi Chen, and Myres S. McDougal. *Human Rights and World Public Order: The Basic Policies of an International Law of Human Dignity*. New Haven, CT: Yale University Press, 1980.

Chenoweth, Erica and Maria J. Stephan. "Drop Your Weapons: When and Why Civil Resistance Works." *Foreign Affairs* 93, no. 4 (2014): 94–106.

Chenoweth, Erica and Maria J. Stephan, "Why Civil Resistance Works." *International Security* 33, no. 1 (2008): 7–44.

Chenoweth, Erica and Maria J. Stephan. *Why Civil Resistance Works: The Strategic Logic of Nonviolent Conflict*. New York: Columbia University Press, 2013.

Childress, Donald Earl. *The Role of Ethics in International Law*. New York: Cambridge University Press, 2012.

Chinkin, Christin. "International Law Framework with Respect to International Peace and Security." In *A Human Security Doctrine for Europe: Project, Principles, Practicalities*, edited by Marlies Glasius and Mary Kaldor. London: Routledge, 2006.

Christakis, Nicholas A. *Blueprint: The Evolutionary Origins of a Good Society*. New York: Little, Brown Spark, 2019.

Chunakara, Mathews George, ed. *Building Peace on Earth: Report of the International Ecumenical Peace Convocation*. Geneva: World Council of Churches, 2013.

Clausewitz, Carl von. *On War*, edited by Michel Howard and Peter Paret. Princeton, NJ: Princeton University Press, 1976.

Clapp, Jennifer and Rorden Wilkinson. *Global Governance, Poverty and Inequality*. New York: Routledge, 2010.

Clarke, Michael and Anthony Ricketts. "US Grand Strategy and National Security: The Dilemmas of Primacy, Decline and Denial." *Australian Journal of International Affairs* 71, no. 5 (2017): 479–498.

Climate Parliament. *The Energy Internet*. https://www.climateparl.net/copy-of-videos.

Climate Parliament. *The Green Grid Initiative: Engineering A Climate Solution*, https://www.climateparl.net/single-post/2018/12/20/High-level-discussion-on-regional-grids-for-renewables-in-Asia-to-be-held-at-Wilton-Park.

Clinton, David. "Rules for the World: International Organizations in Global Politics by Michael Barnett and Martha Finnemore." *Political Science Quarterly* 120, no. 3 (2005): 529–530.

CNN. "Senate Report: Rice, Cheney OK'd CIA Use of Waterboarding," April 23, 2009.

CNN. "Previously Secret Torture Memo Released." July 24, 2008.

Coalition for the International Criminal Court. "Voices of Global Civil Society." http://www.coalitionfortheicc.org/fight/voices-global-civil-society.

Cockburn, Andrew. "The Military-Industrial Virus: How Bloated Budgets Gut Our Defenses." *Harper's Magazine* 338, no. 2029 (June 2019): 61–67.

Cohen, Robert. "The Diplomats Can't Save Us." *New York Times*, July 30, 2017.

Cohen, Robert. "The Moral Rot Threatening America." *New York Times*, May 19, 2018.

Cohen, Roger. "The Desperation of Our Diplomats." *New York Times*, July 28, 2017.

Cohen, Ronald and Elman R. Service. *Origins of the State: The Anthropology of Political Evolution*. Philadelphia: Institute for the Study of Human Issues, 1978.

Cohn, Marjorie. "Introduction: A Frightening New Way of War." In *Drones and Targeted Killing: Legal, Moral, and Geopolitical Issues*, ed. Marjorie Cohn. Northampton, MA: Olive Branch Press, 2015.

Coleman, Peter. "Half the Peace: The Fear Challenge and the Case for Promoting Peace." *Courier* no. 93 (Summer, 2018): 7–11.

Collier, Paul. *The Bottom Billion*. Oxford: Oxford University Press, 2007.

Collier, Paul, Lani Elliott, Harvard Hegre, Anke Hoeffler, Marta Reynal-Querol, and Nicholas Sambanis. *Breaking the Conflict Trap: Civil War and Development Policy*. Washington, DC: World Bank, 2003.

Collier, Paul. *The Bottom Billion: Why the Poorest Countries Are Failing and What Can Be Done About It*. New York: Oxford University Press, 2007.

Commission on Global Governance. *Our Global Neighbourhood: The Report of the Commission on Global Governance*. Oxford: Oxford University Press, 1995.

Commission on Global Security, Justice and Governance. *Confronting the Crisis of Global Governance: Report of the Commission on Global Security, Justice and Governance*. The Hague and Washington, DC: Hague Institute for Global Justice and Stimson Center, 2015.

Conference of the United Nations on the Environment. "Report of the United Nations Conference on the Human Environment: Stockholm, 5–16 June 1972." New York: United Nations, 1973.

Confortini, Catia. "Violence Against Women, Masculinities, and the Global Economy." *Global Governance* 19, no. 2 (2013): 327–331.

Confortini, Catia. *Intelligent Compassion: The Women's International League for Peace and Freedom and Feminist Peace*. New York: Oxford University Press, 2012.

The Constitutional and "Counterterrorism Implications of Targeted Killing," *Hearing Before the Senate Judiciary Subcommittee on the Constitution, Civil Rights, and Human Rights of the Senate Committee on the Judiciary*, 113th Cong. 19–20, April. 23, 2013. www.judiciary.senate.gov/pdf/04-23-13BrooksTestimony.pdf.

Convention on the Elimination of All Forms of Discrimination Against Women. www.ohchr.org/EN/ProfessionalInterest/Pages/CEDAW.aspx.

Cooper, Helene. "Mattis Says North Korea Accelerating War Threats." *New York Times*, October 29, 2017.

Cortright, David. *Gandhi and Beyond: Nonviolence for a New Political Age*. Boulder, CO: Paradigm, 2009.

Cortright, David. *Peace Works: The Citizen's Role in Ending the Cold War*. Boulder, CO: Westview, 1993.

Cortright, David. *Truth Seekers: Voices of Peace and Nonviolence*. Maryknoll, NY: Orbis Books, 2020.

Cortright, David, Rachel Fairhurst, and Kristen Wall, eds. *Drones and the Future of Armed Conflict: Ethical, Legal, and Strategic Implications*. Chicago: University of Chicago Press, 2017.

Cortright, David and Rachel Fairhurst. "Winning Without War: Evaluating Military and Nonmilitary Strategies for Countering Terrorism." In *Drones and the Future of Armed Conflict*, edited by David Cortright, Rachel, and Kristen Wall. Chicago: University of Chicago Press, 2015.

Cortright, David and George A. Lopez, eds. *Uniting Against Terror: Cooperative Nonmilitary Responses to the Global Terrorist Threat*. Cambridge, MA: MIT Press, 2007.

Cortright, David, Conor Seyle, and Kristen Wall. *Governance for Peace: How Inclusive, Participatory and Accountable Institutions Promote Peace and Prosperity*. New York: Cambridge University Press, 2017.

Council on Foreign Relations, "Global Conflict Tracker," https://www.cfr.org/global-conflict-tracker/conflict/civil-war-syria.

Cox, Harvey. *Market as God*. Cambridge, MA: Harvard University Press, 2019.

Craig, Campbell. *Glimmer of a New Leviathan*. New York: Columbia University Press, 2003.

Craig, Campbell. "The Resurgent Idea of World Government." *Ethics and International Affairs* 22, no. 2 (Summer, 2008): 133–142.

Crawford, Neta C. "What Is War Good for? Background Ideas and Assumptions About the Legitimacy, Utility, and Costs of Offensive War." *British Journal of Politics and International Relations* 18, no. 2 (2016): 282–299.

Crawford, Neta. "United States Budgetary Costs of the Post-9/11 Wars through FY2019: $5.9 Trillion Spent and Obligated." (2018). https://watson.brown.edu/costsofwar/papers/2018/united-states-budgetary-costs-post-911-wars-through-fy2019-59-trillion-spent-and.

Crawford, Neta. *US Costs of Wars through 2014, $4.4 Trillion and Counting: Summary of Costs for the US Wars in Iraq, Afghanistan and Pakistan*. Providence, RI: Costs of War Project, 2014.

Credit Suisse Research Institute. "Global Wealth Report 2013." *Global Banking News (GBN)* (October, 2013): 1–63. https://web.archive.org/web/20150214155424/https:/publications.credit-suisse.com/tasks/render/file/?fileID=BCDB1364-A105-0560-1332EC9100FF5C83.

Crenshaw, Martha and Gary LaFree. *Countering Terrorism*. Washington, DC: Brookings Institution Press, 2017.

Crocker, Chester, Fen Hampson, and Pamela Aall. *Leashing the Dogs of War: Conflict Management in a Divided World*. Washington, DC: US Institute of Peace Press, 2007.

Crocker, Chester, Fen Osler Hampson, and Pamela Aall. *Turbulent Peace: The Challenges of Managing International Conflict*. Washington, DC: US Institute of Peace, 2001.

Cumming-Bruce, Nick and Sheryl Gay Stolberg. "Fauci Tells W.H.O. That U.S. Stands Ready to Work with It." *New York Times*, January 21, 2021.

Cutler, A. Claire. "New Constitutionalism, Democracy and the Future of Global Governance." In *Critical Perspectives on the Crisis of Global Governance: Reimagining the Future*, edited by Stephen Gill, 89–109. New York: Palgrave Macmillan, 2016.

Daalder, Ivo and Jan Lodal. "The Logic of Zero: Toward a World Without Nuclear Weapons." *Foreign Affairs* 87, no. 6 (2008): 80–95.

Dahl, Robert A. *On Democracy*. New Haven, CT: Yale University Press, 1998.

Dahl, Robert. "Democracy Deficits and Foreign Policy." *Dissent* 46, no. 1 (1999): 110–113.

d'Aquili, Eugene G. and Andrew B. Newberg. "The Neurophysiological Basis of Religions, or Why God Won't Go Away." *Zygon: Journal of Religion and Science* 33, no. 2 (1998): 187–201.

Darby, John and Roger MacGinty. *Contemporary Peacemaking: Conflict, Violence and Peace Processes*. New York: Palgrave, 2003.

Darby, John and Roger MacGinty. *Contemporary Peacemaking: Conflict, Peace Processes and Post-War Reconstruction*. New York: Springer, 2008.

Darwin, Charles. *The Descent of Man, and Selection in Relation to Sex*. New York: D. Appleton, 1878.

Davenport, Kelsey. "The NPT and the Origins of NATO's Nuclear Sharing Arrangements." *Arms Control Today* 47, no. 2 (2017): 41.

Davenport, Kelsey. "Trump's Cynical Gambit on the Iran Nuclear Deal." Arms Control Association, *Issue Briefs* 10, no. 2 (January 17, 2018). https://www.armscontrol.org/issue-briefs/2018-01/trumps-cynical-iran-nuclear-deal.

Davies, James B., Susanna Sandstrom, Anthony Shorrocks, and Edward N. Wolff. *The World Distribution of Household Wealth*. New York: United Nations University, World Institute for Development Economics Research, 2007.

Davies, Thomas Richard. *Transnational Social Movements*. https://www.oxfordbibliographies.com/view/document/obo-9780199743292/obo-9780199743292-0164.xml.

Davis, Julie Hirschfeld, Sheryl Gay Stolberg, and Thomas Kaplan. "Trump Alarms Lawmakers with Disparaging Words for Haiti and Africa." *New York Times*, January 11, 2018.

Dawsey, Josh. "Trump Derides Protections for Immigrants from 'Shithole' Countries." *Washington Post*, January 12, 2018.

"Declarations Recognizing as Compulsory the Jurisdiction of the International Court of Justice under Article 36, paragraph 2, of the Statute of the Court." https://treaties.un.org/doc/Publication/MTDSG/Volume%20I/Chapter%20I/I-4.en.pdf.

de Mello, Sergio Vieira, Maartje van Eerd, and Kaj Hofman. "Their Dignity Will Be Mine, as It Is Yours." In *The Role of the United Nations in Peace and Security, Global Development, and World Governance: An Assessment of the Evidence*, edited by Michaela Hordijk, 1–9. Lewiston, NY: Edwin Mellen Press, 2007.

De Silva, Joseph, Hugh Liebert, and Isaiah Wilson. *American Grand Strategy and the Future of U.S. Landpower*. Carlisle, PA: Strategic Studies Institute and US Army War College Press, 2014.

Demeritt, Jacqueline H. R., Angela D. Nichols, and Eliza G. Kelly. "Female Participation and Civil War Relapse." *Civil Wars* 16, no. 3 (2014): 346–368.

Deudney, Daniel. "Assessing Jonathan Schell's Nuclear Legacy: Theoretical Innovations and Political Impacts." International Studies Association Roundtable, San Francisco, April 4, 2018.

Deudney, Daniel. *Bounding Power: Republican Security Theory from the Polis to the Global Village*. Princeton, NJ: Princeton University Press, 2007.

Deudney, Daniel. *Dark Skies: Space Expansionism, Planetary Geopolitics, and the Ends of Humanity*. New York: Oxford University Press, 2020.

Deudney, Daniel H. "Going Critical: Toward a Modified Nuclear One Worldism." *Journal of International Political Theory* 15, no. 3 (2018): 367–385.

Deudney, Daniel. "Left Behind: Neorealism's Truncated Contextual Materialism and Republicanism." *International Relations* 23, no. 3 (2009): 341–371.

Deudney, Daniel. "Regrounding Realism: Anarchy, Security, and Changing Material Contexts." *Security Studies* 10, no. 1 (2000): 1–42.

Deudney, Daniel, and G. John Ikenberry. "Democratic Internationalism: An American Grand Strategy for a Post-Exceptionalist Era." *Council on Foreign Relations Working Paper*. New York: Council on Foreign Relations, 2012.

Deutsch, Karl W. *Political Community and the North American Area: International Organization in the Light of Historical Experience*. Princeton, NJ: Princeton University Press, 1968.

Diamond, Jared M. *Collapse: How Societies Choose to Fail or Succeed*. New York: Penguin, 2011.

Donnelly, Jack. *International Human Rights*. Boulder, CO: Westview Press, 2013.

Dovere, Edward-Isaac. "McCain, in Speech, Denounces 'Spurious Nationalism.'" *Politico*, October 16, 2017. https://www.politico.com/story/2017/10/16/john-mccain-nationalism-constitution-243848.

Downey, Thomas J. and Robert C. Johansen. "On Congress and U.S. Security." *World Policy Journal* 1, no. 2 (1984): 447–460.

Doyle, Michael W. "Kant, Liberal Legacies, and Foreign Affairs." *Philosophy & Public Affairs* 12, no. 3 (1983): 205–235.

Doyle, Michael W. and Nicholas Sambanis. *Making War and Building Peace: United Nations Peace Operations*. Princeton, NJ: Princeton University Press, 2006.

Drezner, Daniel W. "Military Primacy Doesn't Pay (Nearly as Much as You Think)." *International Security* 38, no. 1 (2013): 52–79.

Duncan, Mel. "Greater Than the Tread of Mighty Armies: Unarmed Civilian Protection Gaining Momentum Worldwide." *Courier*, no. 91 (Fall 2017): 3–7.

Dunoff, Jeffrey L. and Joel P. Trachtman. *Ruling the World? Constitutionalism, International Law, and Global Governance*. Cambridge: Cambridge University Press, 2009.

Durber, Susan and Fernando Enns, eds. *Walking Together*. Geneva: World Council of Churches, 2018.

Durch, William, J. *Discussion of the Report of the Panel on UN Peace Operations: The Brahimi Report*. Washington, DC: Stimson Center, 2000.

Durch, William J., Victoria K. Holt, Caroline R. Earle, and Moira K. Shanahan. *The Brahimi Report and the Future of UN Peace Operations*. Washington, DC: Henry L. Stimson Center Report, 2003.

Duxbury, Neil. "Golden Rule Reasoning, Moral Judgment, and Law." *Notre Dame Law Review* 84 (2008): 1529.

Economic Times. http://articles.economictimes.indiatimes.com/2013-10-10/news/42902947_1_world-bank-world-development-report-safety-net.

The Economist Democracy Index. "Global Democracy Has Another Bad Year." *The Economist*, January 22, 2020. https://Www.Economist.Com/Graphic-Detail/2020/01/22/Global-Democracy-has-another-Bad-Year.

Edsall, Thomas B. "Don't Feed the Troll in the Oval Office." *New York Times*, June 28, 2018.

Egan, Timothy. "Look in the Mirror: We're with Stupid." *New York Times*, November 18, 2017.

Einstein, Albert, P. A. Schilpp, and Philip Morrison. "The Proceedings of the American Philosophical Society; the Meaning of Relativity; Out of My Later Years and Albert Einstein: Philosopher-Scientist." *Physics Today* 3, no. 11 (1950): 30–32.

Einstein, Albert. *Out of My Later Years*. Secaucus, NJ: Citadel, 1956.

Eisenhower, Dwight D. "Farewell Address." Public Papers of the Presidents of the United States. Washington, DC: US Government Printing Office, 1960.

Elshtain, Jean Bethke. *Just War Theory*. New York: New York University Press, 1992.

"Energy and Economic Growth." https://energyeconomicgrowth.org/news/wilton-park-dialogue-explores-cross-border-electricity-highways-harness-asias-vast-untapped.

Engler, Mark and Paul Engler. *This Is an Uprising: How Nonviolent Revolt Is Shaping the Twenty-First Century*. New York: Nation Books, 2016.

Erikson, Erik H. *Gandhi's Truth: On the Origins of Militant Nonviolence*. New York: W.W. Norton, 1993.

Etzold, Thomas H. and John Lewis Gaddis. *Containment: Documents on American Policy and Strategy: 1945–1950*. New York: Columbia University, 1978.

Evangelista, Matthew, Henry Shue, and Tami Davis Biddle. *The American Way of Bombing: Changing Ethical and Legal Norms, from Flying Fortresses to Drones*. Ithaca, NY: Cornell University Press, 2014.

Evangelista, Matthew. "Is War Too Easy?" *Perspectives on Politics* 14, no. 1 (2016): 132–137.

Evangelista, Matthew. *Law, Ethics, and the War on Terror*. Cambridge: Polity Press, 2008.

Evans, Gareth J. and Mohamed Sahnoun. *The Responsibility to Protect: Report of the International Commission on Intervention and State Sovereignty*. Ottawa: International Development Research Centre, 2001.

Evans, Gareth J. *The Responsibility to Protect: Ending Mass Atrocity Crimes Once and for All*. Washington, DC: Brookings Institution Press, 2008.

Evans, Peter B. and Cesar Rodríguez-Garavito. *Transnational Advocacy Networks: Twenty Years of Evolving Theory and Practice*. Bogota, Colombia: Dejusticia, 2018.

Eveleth, Rose. *How Fake Images Change Our Memories and Behavior*. http://www.bbc.com/future/story/20121213-fake-pictures-make-real-memories.

Ewing, A. C. *The Individual, the State and World Government*. New York: Macmillan, 1947.

Ewing, A. C. "Individual, the State and World Government." http://www.heinonline.org.proxy.library.nd.edu/HOL/Index?collection=beal&index=beal/indvstwg.

Falk, Richard. "Ends and Means: Defining a Just War." *The Nation* 273, no. 13 (2001): 11.

Falk, Richard. "International Law and the Future." *Third World Quarterly* 27, no. 5 (2006): 727–737.

Falk, Richard. "Why Drones Are More Dangerous than Nuclear Weapons: Threats to International Law and World Order." In *Drones and Targeted Killing: Legal, Moral, and Geopolitical Issues*, edited by Majorie Cohn, 28–50. Northhampton, MA: Olive Branch Press, 2015.

Falk, Richard A. *Achieving Human Rights*. New York: Routledge, 2009.

Falk, Richard A. "Horizons of Global Governance." In *Critical Perspectives on the Crisis of Global Governance: Reimagining the Future*, edited by Stephen Gill, 24–44. New York: Palgrave Macmillan, 2016.

Falk, Richard A. *On Humane Governance: Toward a New Global Politics*. Cambridge: Polity, 1995.

Falk, Richard A. *Power Shift: On the New Global Order*. London: Zed Books, 2016.

Falk, Richard and Andrew Strauss. "On the Creation of a Global Peoples Assembly: Legitimacy and the Power of Popular Sovereignty." *Stanford Journal of International Law* 36, no. 2 (2000): 191–220.

Falk, Richard and Andrew Strauss. "Toward Global Parliament." *Foreign Affairs* 80, no. 1 (2001): 212–220.

Farer, Tom J. *Confronting Global Terrorism and American Neo-Conservatism: The Framework of a Liberal Grand Strategy*. Oxford: Oxford University Press, 2008.

Farer, Tom J. "Introduction." In *The International Bill of Human Rights*. Glen Ellen, CA: Entwistle Books, 1981.

Farrow, Ronan. *War on Peace: The End of Diplomacy and the Decline of American Influence.* New York: Norton, 2018.

Fassbender, Bardo, Anne Peters, Simone Peter, and Daniel Högger. *The Oxford Handbook of the History of International Law.* Oxford: Oxford University Press, 2012.

Fehr, Ernst and Urs Fischbacher. "The Nature of Human Altruism." *Nature* 425, no. 6960 (October 23, 2003): 785–791.

Fehr, Ernst and Simon Gachter. "Fairness and Retaliation: The Economics of Reciprocity." *Journal of Economic Perspectives* 14, no. 3 (2000): 159–182.

Fehr, Ernst, Alexander Klein, and Klaus Schmidt. "Fairness, Incentives and Contractual Incompleteness." *IDEAS Working Paper Series from RePEc*, 2001.

Feil, Scott. R. "Could 5,000 Peacekeepers Have Saved 500,000 Rwandans? Early Intervention Reconsidered." Institute for the Study of Diplomacy, *ISD Reports* (Walsh School of Foreign Service, Georgetown University) 3, no. 2 (April 1997).

Feingold, Russ. "Our Legitimacy Crisis." *The Nation*, April 3, 2017, 4.

Fellmeth, Aaron Xavier. "Questioning Civilian Immunity." *Texas International Law Journal* 43, no. 3 (2008): 453–501.

Fihn, Beatrice. "Women Against the Bomb." *The Nation* (December 3–10, 2018): 13–25.

Finnemore, Martha. "Dynamics of Global Governance: Building on What We Know." *International Studies Quarterly* 58, no. 1 (2014): 221–224.

Firmage, Edwin Brown. "The Treaty on the Non-Proliferation of Nuclear Weapons." *American Journal of International Law* 63, no. 4 (1969): 711–746.

Fischer, Joschka. "From Confederacy to Federation—Thoughts on the Finality of European Integration." https://ec.europa.eu/dorie/fileDownload.do?docId=192161&cardId=192161.

Fisher, Max. "Syria's Paradox: Why the War Only Ever Seems to Get Worse," *New York Times*, August 26, 2016, https://www.nytimes.com/2016/08/27/world/middleeast/syria-civil-war-why-get-worse.html?searchResultPosition=1.

Fisher, Max. "What Is Pulling Liberal Democracy Apart?" *New York Times*, November 2, 2018.

Fjelde, Hanne, Lisa Hultman, and Desirée Nilsson. "Protection through Presence: UN Peacekeeping and the Costs of Targeting Civilians." *International Organization* 73, no. 1 (2019): 103–131. https://dx.doi.org/10.1017/S0020818318000346.

Fletcher School, Tufts University. *Law of the Sea.* "LOSC Dispute Resolution Provisions." https://sites.tufts.edu/lawofthesea/chapter-nine/.

Fleurant, Aude, Nan Tian, Pieter D. Wezeman, Siemon T. Wezeman, and Alexandra Kuimova. *Trends in International Arms Transfers, 2017.* Stockholm: Stockholm International Peace Research Institute, 2018.

Flournoy, Michèle A., Shawn Brimley, Robert J. Art. *Finding Our Way: Debating American Grand Strategy.* Washington, DC: Center for a New American Security, 2008.

Flournoy, Michèle. "Q & A: U.S. Nuclear Weapons Policies: A Conversation with Michèle Flournoy." *Arms Control Today* 47, no. 6 (2017): 38–41.

The Fog of War: Eleven Lessons from the Life of Robert S. McNamara. https://movie.douban.com/review/5822451/#:~:text=Until%20then%2C%20we%20still%20can%20assert%20that%20McNamara%20was%20a%20realist.&text=But%20in%20the%20film%2C%20when,force%20in%20restricting%20the%20Military.

Folger, John K. and Charles B. Nam. *Education of the American Population.* Washington, DC: US Department of Commerce, 1967.

Food and Agricultural Organization of the United Nations. "1.02 Billion People Hungry." June 19, 2009. www.fao.org/news/story/en/item/20568/icode/.

"Forecasting Change in Military Technology, 2020–2040." *Military Technology* (2018): 204–224.

Ford, Christopher A. "Debating Disarmament: Interpreting Article VI of the Treaty on the Non-Proliferation of Nuclear Weapons." *Nonproliferation Review* 14, no. 3 (2007): 401–428.

Forest, Jim. *The Root of War Is Fear: Thomas Merton's Advice to Peacemakers*. Maryknoll, NY: Orbis, 2016.

Forsythe, David P. "International Relations—the Path Not Taken: Using International Law to Promote World Peace and Security." *CHOICE: Current Reviews for Academic Libraries* 44, no. 3 (2006): 559.

Forsythe David P. "United Nations Peacemaking." *Proceedings of the Academy of Political Science* 32, no. 4 (1977): 206–220.

Forsythe, David P. "United States Policy toward Enemy Detainees in the War on Terrorism." *Human Rights Quarterly* 28, no. 2 (2006): 465–491.

Fortna, Virginia Page. *Does Peacekeeping Work? Shaping Belligerents' Choices After Civil War*. Princeton. NJ: Princeton University Press, 2008. https://www.jstor.org/stable/j.ctt7sv7j.

Freedom House, "Freedom in the World: Report 2019." https://freedomhouse.org/report/freedom-world; https://freedomhouse.org/countries/freedom-world/scores.

Fried, John H. E. *Vietnam and International Law: The Illegality of United States Military Involvement*. Flanders, NJ: O'Hare Books, 1967.

Friedman, Thomas L. "Trump, Niger, and Connecting the Dots." *New York Times*, October 31, 2017.

Fromm, Erich. *Escape from Freedom*. New York: Farrar & Rinehart, 1941.

Fromm, Erich. *Man for Himself: An Inquiry into the Psychology of Ethics*. London: Routledge, 2003.

Fromm, Erich. *The Sane Society*. New York: Fawcett World Library, 1955.

Fry, Douglas P. *Beyond War: The Human Potential for Peace*. New York: Oxford, 2007.

Fry, Douglas P. "Cooperation for Survival: Creating a Global Peace System." In *War, Peace, and Human Nature*, edited by Douglas P. Fry, 544–558. New York: Oxford University Press, 2013.

Fry, Douglas P., ed. *War, Peace and Human Nature: The Convergence of Evolutionary and Cultural Views*. New York: Oxford University Press, 2013.

Fulbright, J. W. *The Arrogance of Power*. New York, Random House, 1966.

Gaddis, John Lewis. *On Grand Strategy*. New York: Penguin Press, 2018.

Galtung, Johan. *Peace by Peaceful Means: Peace and Conflict, Development and Civilization*. London: Sage, 1996.

Gandhi, Arun. *The Gift of Anger*. New York: Gallery, 2018.

Gandhi, Mohandas K. *Gandhi's Autobiography: The Story of My Experiments with Truth*. Washington, DC: Public Affairs Press, 1948.

Garrett-Peltier, Heidi. *Study Says Domestic, Not Military Spending, Fuels Job Growth*. Costs of War Project. Providence, RI: Watson Institute for International and Public Affairs, 2017.

Garwin, Richard L. "Report of an Independent Task Force Sponsored by the Council on Foreign Relations." *Nonlethal Technologies: Progress and Prospects*. New York: Council on Foreign Relations, 1999.

Gazis, Olivia. "In First Major Address, John Bolton Attacks Old Foes." CBS News, September 10, 2018. https://www.cbsnews.com/news/in-first-major-address-john-bolton-attacks-old-foe/.

Gibbons-Neff, Thomas. "Documents Reveal Misleading Public Statements on War in Afghanistan." *New York Times*, December 9, 2019.

Gibbons-Neff, Thomas. "Public Was Duped on Afghan War." *New York Times*, December 10, 2019.

Gibons-Neff, Thomas, Eric Schmitt, and Adam Goldman. "C.I.A. to Expand Its Covert Role in Afghanistan." *New York Times*, October 23, 2017.

Gill, Stephen. "At the Historical Crossroads—Radical Imaginaries and the Crisis of Global Governance." In *Critical Perspectives on the Crisis of Global Governance: Reimagining the Future*, edited by Stephen Gill, 181–199. New York: Palgrave Macmillan, 2016.

Gill, Stephen, ed. *Critical Perspectives on the Crisis of Global Governance: Reimagining the Future*. New York: Palgrave Macmillan, 2015.

Gill, Stephen, ed. *Global Crises and the Crisis of Global Leadership*. Cambridge: Cambridge University Press, 2012.

Gill, Stephen. "Reimagining the Future: Some Critical Reflections." In *Critical Perspectives on the Crisis of Global Governance: Reimagining the Future*, edited by Stephen Gill, 1–23. New York: Palgrave Macmillan, 2016.

Gill, Stephen and A. Claire Cutler. *New Constitutionalism and World Order*. Cambridge: Cambridge University Press, 2015.

Gintis, Herbert and Ernst Fehr. "The Social Structure of Cooperation and Punishment." *Behavioral and Brain Sciences* 35, no. 01 (2012): 28–29.

Gladstone, Rick. "Nobel Peace Prize Goes to Group Opposing Nuclear Weapons." *New York Times*, October 6, 2017.

Gladstone, Rick. "What Is the Iran Deal? Why Does Trump Hate It?" *New York Times*, October 5, 2017.

Glaser, Alexander, Zia Mian, and Frank Von Hippel. "Time to Ban Production of Nuclear Weapons Material." *Scientific American*, January 13, 2010. https://www.scientificamerican.com/article/time-to-ban-production-of-nuclear-weapons-material/.

Glaser, John. "NATO Expansion Is Unwise." *CATO at Liberty* (March 17, 2017). www.cato.org.

Glasius, Marlies and Mary Kaldor. "A Human Security Vision." In *A Human Security Doctrine for Europe: Project, Principles, Practicalities*, edited by Marlies Glasius and Mary Kaldor, 3–19. London: Routledge, 2006.

Glatz, Carol. "Pope: World Needs Nonviolent Responses to Social, Political Problems." Catholic News Service. December 15, 2016. https://www.ncronline.org/blogs/francis-chronicles/pope-world-needs-nonviolent-responses-social-political-problems; https://www.catholicnewsagency.com/news/pope-tells-ambassadors-to-make-courageous-choice-for-nonviolence-33375.

Glendon, Mary Ann. *A World Made New: Eleanor Roosevelt and the Universal Declaration of Human Rights*. New York: Random House, 2001.

Global Centre for the Responsibility to Protect. "Fulfilling the Responsibility to Protect: Strengthening Our Capacities to Prevent and Halt Mass Atrocities." September 24, 2010. https://reliefweb.int/report/rwanda/fulfilling-responsibility-protect-strengthening-our-capacities-prevent-and-halt-mass.

Global Challenges Foundation. Stockholm. https://globalchallenges.org/.

Global Governance Forum. https://globalgovernanceforum.org/about/.

Global Terrorism Index 2019. http://visionofhumanity.org/app/uploads/2019/11/GTI-2019web.pdf.

Goertz, Gary, Paul F. Diehl, and Alexandru Balas. *The Puzzle of Peace: The Evolution of Peace in the International System*. New York: Oxford University Press, 2016.

Goldberg, Michelle. "Toxic Nostalgia Breeds Derangement." *New York Times*, August 20, 2019.

Goldstein, Joshua S. *Winning the War on War: The Decline of Armed Conflict Worldwide*. New York: Dutton, 2011.

Gorius, Lea. "How Much Does It Cost to End Poverty?" The Borgen Project. https://borgen-project.org/how-much-does-it-cost-to-end-poverty/#:~:text=So%2C%20how%20much%20does%20it,per%20year%20for%2020%20years.

Gould, Kenneth A. and Tammy L. Lewis. *Transnational Social Movements.* Oxford: Oxford University Press, 2021. https://doi.org/10.1093/acrefore/9780190846626.013.491.

Government of Canada. *Towards a Rapid Reaction Capability for the United Nations: Report of the Government of Canada.* Ottawa: Government of Canada, 1995. https://s3.amazonaws.com/piquant/Langille/Towards+a+Rapid+Reaction+Capability+for+the+United+Nations.pdf.

Government of India, Ministry of Rural Development. *MGNREGA Sameeksha, An Anthology of Research Studies on the Mahatma Gandhi National Rural Employment Guarantee Act, 2005, 2006–2012, "Ministry of Rural Development."* New Delhi: Orient BlackSwan, 2012.

Grotius, Hugo. *Prolegomena to the Law of War and Peace.* Translated by Francis W. Kelsey. Indianapolis: Bobbs-Merrill, 1957.

Grovogui, Siba N'Zatioula. *Beyond Eurocentrism and Anarchy: Memories of International Order and Institutions.* New York: Palgrave Macmillan, 2006.

Guilhot, Nicolas. "Politics Between and Beyond Nations: Hans J. Morgenthau's Politics among Nations." In *Classics of International Relations: Essays in Criticism and Appreciation*, edited by Henrik Bliddal, Casper Sylvest, and Peter Wilson, 69–79. New York: Routledge, 2013.

Haakonssen, Knud and Adam Smith. *The Theory of Moral Sentiments.* New York: Cambridge University Press, 2002.

Haass, Richard and Dan Woren. *A World in Disarray: American Foreign Policy and the Crisis of the Old Order.* Books on Tape: Penguin Audio, 2017.

Haberman, Maggie and Michael S. Schmidt. "Trump Pardons Two Russia Inquiry Figures and Blackwater Guards." *New York Times*, December 22, 2020.

Habermas, Jürgen. "A Political Constitution for the Pluralist World Society?" In *The Cosmopolitanism Reader*, edited by Garrett W. Brown and David Held, 267–288. Cambridge: Polity Press, 2010.

Habermas, Jürgen. *Between Facts and Norms: Contribution to a Discourse Theory of Law and Democracy.* Translated by W. Rehg. Cambridge: Polity, 1996.

Hägel, Peter. *Global Governance.* Oxford: Oxford University Press, 2011.

Hägel, Peter. "Global Governance." *Oxford Bibliographies.* http://www.oxfordbibliographies.com.proxy.library.nd.edu/view/document/obo-9780199743292/obo-9780199743292-0015.xml?rskey=5hn11f&result=19&q=kant+perpetual+peace#firstMatch.

Haidt, Jonathan. *The Righteous Mind: Why Good People Are Divided by Politics and Religion.* New York: Pantheon Books, 2012.

Halpin, John. "Why We Need Inclusive Nationalism." *Democracy: A Journal of Ideas*, July 29, 2020. https://democracyjournal.org/arguments/why-we-need-inclusive-nationalism/.

Hammarskjöld, Dag. *Markings.* London: Faber & Faber, 1965.

Hampson, Fen Osler and Mark Raymond. "Human Security as a Global Public Good." In *International Organization and Global Governance*, edited by Thomas G. Weiss and Rorden Wilkinson, 524–534. New York: Routledge, 2013.

Hampson, Fen O. and Christopher K. Penny. "Human Security." In *The Oxford Handbook on the United Nations*, edited by Sam Daws and Thomas G. Weiss. http://www.oxfordhandbooks.com.proxy.library.nd.edu/view/10.1093/oxfordhb/9780199560103.001.0001/oxfordhb-9780199560103-e-031?rskey=BGlQXH&result=1.

Hanham, Melissa and Seiyeon Ji. "Advances in North Korea's Missile Program and What Comes Next." *Arms Control Today* 47, no. 7 (2017): 6–11.

Harbour, Frances V. "Reasonable Probability of Success as a Moral Criterion in the Western Just War Tradition." *Journal of Military Ethics* 10, no. 3 (2011): 230–241.

Hardin, Garrett. "The Tragedy of the Commons." *Science* 162, no. 3859 (1968): 1243–1248.

Hart, Julie Putnam and Anjel Stough-Hunter. *Pathways to Pacifism and Antiwar Activism Among U.S. Veterans: The Role of Moral Identity in Personal Transformation.* Lanham, MD: Lexington Books, 2017.

Hartung, William D. "The Costs of War." *The Nation* 307, no. 15 (December 17/24, 2018): 3–4.

Hartung, William D. "Eisenhower's Warning: The Military-Industrial Complex Forty Years Later." *World Policy Journal* 18, no. 1 (Spring 2001): 39–44.

Hashmi, Sohail H., ed. *Just Wars, Holy Wars, and Jihads: Christian, Jewish, and Muslim Encounters and Exchanges.* New York: Oxford University Press, 2012.

Hassan, Riffat. "On Human Rights and the Qur'anic Perspective." In *Human Rights in Religious Traditions,* edited by Arlene Swidler, 51–65. New York: Pilgrim Press, 1982.

Haydn, Patrick. *Cosmopolitan Global Politics.* Aldershot, UK: Ashgate, 2005.

Hazelton, Jacqueline L. "Drone Strikes and Grand Strategy: Toward a Political Understanding of the Uses of Unmanned Aerial Vehicle Attacks in US Security Policy." *Journal of Strategic Studies* 40, no. 1–2 (2017): 68–91.

Hegre, Håvard, Lisa Hultman, and Håvard Mokleiv Nygård. "Evaluating the Conflict-Reducing Effect of UN Peacekeeping Operations." *Journal of Politics* 81, no. 1 (2019): 215–232. https://search.datacite.org/works/10.1086/700203.

Hegre, Håvard, John R. Oneal, and Bruce Russett. "Trade Does Promote Peace: New Simultaneous Estimates of the Reciprocal Effects of Trade and Conflict." *Journal of Peace Research* 47, no. 6 (2010): 763–774.

Heidenrich, John G. "How to Prevent Genocide: A Guide for Policymakers, Scholars, and the Concerned Citizen." Westport, CT: Praeger, 2006.

Heilbroner, Robert L. *An Inquiry into the Human Prospect: Updated and Reconsidered for the 1980s.* New York: W.W. Norton, 1980.

Held, David. *Cosmopolitanism: Ideals and Realities.* Cambridge: Polity Press, 2010.

Held, David. *The Cosmopolitanism Reader.* Cambridge: Polity Press, 2010.

Held, David. *Democracy and the Global Order.* Cambridge: Polity Press, 1995.

Held, David. *Global Covenant: The Social Democratic Alternative to the Washington Consensus.* New York: John Wiley, 2013.

Held, David. "Reframing Global Governance: Apocalypse Soon or Reform!" In *The Cosmopolitan Reader,* edited by Garrett Wallace Brown and David Held, 293–311. Cambridge: Polity, 2010.

Held, David and Anthony McGrew. *Globalization/Anti-Globalization.* Cambridge: Polity, 2002.

Held, David and Mathias Koenig-Archibugi. *Taming Globalization Frontiers of Governance.* Cambridge: Polity, 2003.

Henkin, Louis. *How Nations Behave: Law and Foreign Policy.* New York: Columbia University Press, 1979.

Hentoff, Nat. *The Essays of A. J. Muste.* Indianapolis: Bobbs-Merrill, 1967.

Herbert, Bob. "Much of What Has Happened to the Military on Donald Rumsfeld's Watch Has Been Catastrophic." *New York Times,* May 23, 2005.

Herz, John H. "Idealist Internationalism and the Security Dilemma." *World Politics* 2, no. 2 (1950): 157–180.

Herz, John H. *Political Realism and Political Idealism: A Study in Theories and Realities.* Chicago: University of Chicago Press, 1973.

Heyns, Christof. "The International Law Framework Regulating the Use of Armed Drones." *International and Comparative Law Quarterly* 65 (2016): 791–827.

Hibbs, Mark. "Why Does the IAEA Do What It Does?" Carnegie Endowment for International Peace. https://carnegieendowment.org/2017/11/06/why-does-iaea-do-what-it-does-pub-74689.

"Hillary Clinton Leads by 2.8 Million in Final Popular Vote Count." http://time.com/4608555/hillary-clinton-popular-vote-final/.

Hillebrecht, Courtney, Tyler R. White, and Patrice McMahon. *State Responses to Human Security: At Home and Abroad*. New York: Routledge, 2014.

Hilpold, Peter. "Review Alex J. Bellamy, *Massacres and Morality: Mass Atrocities in an Age of Civilian Immunity*." *Austrian Review of International and European Law* 17, no. 1 (2015): 485–486.

Hobbes, Thomas. *Hobbes's Leviathan*. Oxford: Clarendon Press, 1958.

Hobbes, Thomas. *Leviathan, Or, the Matter, Form, and Power of a Commonwealth Ecclesiastical and Civil*. London: Printed for Andrew Crooke, 1651.

Hobson, John. *Europocentric Conception of World Politics*. Cambridge: Cambridge University Press, 2012.

Höglund, Kristine and Magnus Öberg. *Understanding Peace Research: Methods and Challenges*. New York: Routledge, 2011.

Holt, Robert. "Meeting Einstein's Challenge." *Bulletin of the Atomic Scientists*, April 3, 2015. https://thebulletin.org/2015/04/meeting-einsteins-challenge-new-thinking-about-nuclear-weapons/.

Hond, Paul. "Faith in the System Is Fraying." *Columbia Review* (Fall, 2018): 28–35.

Hordijk, Michaela, Maartje Van Eerd, and Kaj Hofman. *The Role of the United Nations in Peace and Security, Global Development, and World Governance: An Assessment of the Evidence*. Lewiston, NY: Edwin Mellen Press, 2007.

Howard-Hassmann, Rhoda. "Human Security: Undermining Human Rights?" *Human Rights Quarterly* 34, no. 1 (2012): 88–112.

Howell, William G. and Terry M. Moe. *Presidents, Populism, and the Crisis of Democracy*. Chicago: University of Chicago Press, 2020.

Hsu, Tiffany and Mike Isaac. "Advertiser Exodus Snowballs as Facebook Struggles to Ease Concerns." *New York Times*, June 30, 2020.

Huang, Margaret. January 2018. Letter on file with the author.

Hubbard, Ben. "German Court Convicts Former Syrian Official of Crimes Against Humanity." *New York Times*, February 24, 2021. https://www.nytimes.com/2021/02/24/world/middleeast/germany-court-syria-war-crimes.html.

Hudson, Valerie M., Bonnie Ballif-Spanvill, Mary Caprioli, and Chad F. Emmett. *Sex and World Peace*. New York: Columbia University, 2012.

Hughbank, Richard J. and Dave Grossman. "The Challenge of Getting Men to Kill." In *War, Peace, and Human Nature*, edited by David P. Fry, 495–513. New York: Oxford University Press, 2013.

Human Rights Watch. "Descriptions of Techniques Allegedly Authorized by the CIA." November 2005. https://www.hrw.org/report/2005/11/21/descriptions-techniques-allegedly-authorized-cia.

Human Rights Watch. "U.S.: Vice President Endorses Torture." October 26, 2006. https://www.hrw.org/news/2006/10/25/us-vice-president-endorses-torture.

Human Security Centre. "What Is Human Security?" In *The Human Security Report 2005: War and Peace in the 21st Century*. New York: Oxford University Press, 2005.

Human Security Report. *Human Security Report 2009/2010: The Causes of Peace and the Shrinking Costs of War*. New York: Oxford University Press, 2011.

Human Security Report. *Human Security Report 2013: The Decline in Global Violence: Evidence, Explanation, and Contestation*. Vancouver, British Columbia: Human Security Press, 2014.

Hyman, Louis and Joseph Tohill. *Shopping for Change: Consumer Activism and the Possibilities of Purchasing Power*. Ithaca, NY: Cornell University Press, 2017.

Hynek, Nik. *Human Security as Statecraft: Structural Conditions, Articulations and Unintended Consequences*. New York: Routledge, 2012.

Icelandic Human Rights Centre. "The Right to Equality and Nondiscrimination." http://www.humanrights.is/en/human-rights-education-project/human-rights-concepts-ideas-and-fora/substantive-human-rights/the-right-to-equality-and-non-discrimination.

Ikenberry, G. John. *After Victory: Institutions, Strategic Restraint, and the Rebuilding of Order After Major Wars*. Princeton, NJ: Princeton University Press, 2019.

Ikenberry, G. John. "America's Imperial Ambition." *Foreign Affairs* 81, no. 5 (2002): 44.

Ikenberry, G. John. "The End of Liberal International Order?" *International Affairs* 94, no. 1 (2018): 7–23.

Ikenberry, G. John. *Liberal Leviathan: The Origins, Crisis, and Transformation of the American World Order*. Princeton, NJ: Princeton University Press, 2011.

Ikenberry, G. John. *Liberal Order and Imperial Ambition*. Cambridge: Polity, 2006.

Ikenberry, G. John. *Power, Order, and Change in World Politics*. Cambridge: Cambridge University Press, 2014.

Ikenberry, G. John. *A World Safe for Democracy: Liberal Internationalism and the Crises of Global Order*. New Haven, CT: Yale University Press, 2020.

Independent Commission on Disarmament and Security Issues. *Common Security: A Programme for Disarmament*. London: Pan Books, 1982.

Independent Commission on International Development Issues. *North-South, a Programme for Survival: Report of the Independent Commission on International Development Issues*. Cambridge, MA: MIT Press, 1980.

Institute for Economics and Peace. *Global Peace Index 2020: Measuring Peace in a Complex World*. Sydney, Australia: 2020. https://www.visionofhumanity.org/wp-content/uploads/2020/10/GPI_2020_web.pdf.

Institute for Economics and Peace, annual report. *Global Terrorism Index 2020*. https://www.visionofhumanity.org/wp-content/uploads/2020/10/GPI_2020_web.pdf.

International Bar Association, Human Rights Institute. "The Legality of Armed Drones Under International Law." Background Paper, May 25, 2017. www.ibanet.org/Human_Rights_Institute/council-resolutions.aspx.

International Commission on Financing Global Education Opportunity. *The Learning Generation: Investing in Education for a Changing World*. https://report.educationcommission.org/report/.

International Court of Justice. "Legality of the Threat or Use of Nuclear Weapons." https://www.icj-cij.org/en/case/95https://www.icj-cij.org/en/case/95.

International Court of Justice. "Legality of the Use by a State of Nuclear Weapons in Armed Conflict." https://www.icj-cij.org/en/case/93.

International Court of Justice. "Military and Paramilitary Activities in and against Nicaragua." (Nicaragua v. United States of America). Merits, Judgment, I.C.J. Reports (1986).

International Criminal Court. "Situations Under Investigation." https://www.icc-cpi.int/pages/situation.aspx.

International Covenant on Civil and Political Rights. Article 7. https://www.ohchr.org/en/professionalinterest/pages/ccpr.aspx.

International Covenant on Civil and Political Rights (ICCPR). Article 26. https://www.ohchr.org/documents/professionalinterest/ccpr.pdf.

International Covenant on Economic, Social, and Cultural Rights. Articles 9, 11. Articles 12 and 13. https://www.ohchr.org/en/professionalinterest/pages/cescr.aspx.

International Human Rights and Conflict Resolution Clinic of Stanford Law School and Global Justice Clinic of New York University School of Law. *Living Under Drones: Death, Injury, and Trauma to Civilians from U.S. Drone Practices in Pakistan*. September 2012.

International Law Commission. "Draft Articles on the Responsibility of States for Internationally Wrongful Acts." http://untreaty.un.org/ilc/texts/instruments/english/commentaries/9_6_2001.pdf.

International Organization for Migration. *Migration and Climate Change*. Geneva: International Organization for Migration, 2008.

International Panel on Social Progress. *Rethinking Society for the 21st Century: Report of the International Panel on Social Progress*. Vol. 2, *Political Regulation, Governance, and Societal Transformations*. Cambridge: Cambridge University Press, 2018.

Interpol. "Wanted: International Criminal Court." https://www.interpol.int/Search-Page?search=international+criminal+court.

"International Police." *Police Practice & Research* 4, no. 2 (2003): 203–204. DOI 10.1080/15614260308014.

Intriligator, Michael D. "Global Security and Human Security." *International Journal of Development and Conflict* 1, no. 1 (2011): 1–10.

Jackson, Robert H. "Opening Statement before the International Military Tribunal, Nuremberg." https://www.roberthjackson.org/speech-and-writing/opening-statement-before-the-international-military-tribunal/.

Jacobs, Andrew. "U.S. Delegation Disrupts Accord on Breast Milk." *New York Times*, July 9, 2018.

Jacobs, Tom. "The Policy Consequences of Partisan Gerrymandering." *Pacific Standard*, October 4, 2017. https://psmag.com/news/the-policy-consequences-of-partisan-gerrymandering.

Jaffe, Gregg. "A Decade After the 9/11 Attacks, Americans Live in an Era of Endless War." *Washington Post*, September 4, 2011.

Jakes, Lara and Michael Crowley. "U.S. to Penalize War Crimes: Investigators Looking Into American Troops." *New York Times*, June 11, 2020. https://www.nytimes.com/2020/06/11/us/politics/international-criminal-court-troops-trump.html?searchResultPosition=3.

Jamieson, Kathleen Hall. *Cyberwar: How Russian Hackers and Trolls Helped Elect a President: What We Don't, Can't, and Do Know*. New York: Oxford University Press, 2018.

Jeong, Ho-Won. *Peacebuilding in Postconflict Societies: Strategy and Process*. Boulder, CO: L. Rienner, 2005.

Jepperson, Ronald L., Alexander Wendt, and Peter J. Katzenstein. "Norms, Identity, and Culture in National Security." In *The Culture of National Security*, edited by Peter J. Katzenstein, 58–60. New York: Columbia University Press, 1996.

Jett, Dennis. "Republicans Are Blocking Ratification of Even the Most Reasonable International Treaties." *New Republic*, December 26, 2014. https://newrepublic.com/article/120646/ratification-arms-trade-treaty-others-blocked-republicans.

Johansen, Robert C. "Developing a Grand Strategy for Peace and Human Security: Guidelines from Research, Theory, and Experience." *Global Governance* 23, no. 4 (2017): 525–536.

Johansen, Robert C. "The E-Parliament: Global Governance to Serve the Human Interest." *Widener Law Review* 13, no. 2 (2007): 319–345.

Johansen, Robert C. *The Future of Arms Control*. New York: World Policy Institute, 1988.

Johansen, Robert C. "The Future of United Nations Peacekeeping and Enforcement: A Framework for Policymaking." *Global Governance* 2, no. 3 (September–December 1996): 299–333.

Johansen, Robert C. "The Impact of U.S. Policy Toward the International Criminal Court on the Prevention of Genocide, War Crimes, and Crimes Against Humanity." *Human Rights Quarterly* 28, no. 2 (2006): 301–331.

Johansen, Robert C. *The National Interest and the Human Interest*. Princeton, NJ: Princeton University Press, 1980.

Johansen, Robert C. "Peace and Justice? The Contribution of International Judicial Processes to Peacebuilding." In *Strategies of Peace: Transforming Conflict in a Violent World*, edited by Daniel Philpott and Gerard F. Powers. New York: Oxford University Press, 2010.

Johansen, Robert C. "Proposal for a United Nations Emergency Peace Service." In *A United Nations Emergency Peace Service*, edited by Robert C. Johansen, 21–41. New York: Global Action to Prevent War, Nuclear Age Peace Foundation, and World Federalist Movement, 2006.

Johansen, Robert C., ed. *A United Nations Emergency Peace Service: To Prevent Genocide and Crimes Against Humanity*. New York: Global Action to Prevent War, Nuclear Age Peace Foundation, and World Federalist Movement, 2006.

Johansen, Robert C., Sherle R. Schwenninger, and Jerry W. Sanders. "Why World Policy." *World Policy Journal* 1, no. 1 (Fall 1983): v–vi.

Johnson, Jenna. "Trump Says 'Torture Works,' Backs Waterboarding and 'Much Worse.'" *Washington Post*, February 17, 2016.

Johnson, Theodore and Max Feldman. *The New Voter Suppression*. New York: Brennan Center for Justice New York University School of Law, 2020.

Johnstone, Ian. "The Power of Interpretative Communities." In *Power in Global Governance*, edited by Michael Barnett and Raymond Duvall. Cambridge: Cambridge University Press, 2005.

Jones, Brad. "The US Plans to Spend $1.2 Trillion on Nuclear Weapons over the Next 30 Years." https://futurism.com/us-plans-spend-trillion-nuclear-weapons-years.

Jones, Ellis, Ross Haenfler, and Brett Johnson, with Brian Klocke. *The Better World Handbook: From Good Intentions to Everyday Actions*. Gabriola Island, Canada: New Society Publishers, 2001.

Jones, Ellis. *The Better World Shopping Guide: Every Dollar Makes a Difference*. Gabriola Island, British Columbia: New Society Publishers, 2017.

Jones, Seth G. and Martin C. Libicki. *How Terrorist Groups End: Implications for Countering Al Qa'ida*. Santa Monica: Rand, 2008.

Juergensmeyer, Mark and Mona Kanwal Sheikh. "A Sociotheological Approach to Understanding Religious Violence." In *The Oxford Handbook of Religion and Violence*, edited by Michael Jerryson, Mark Juergensmeyer, and Margo Kitts, 619–642. Oxford: Oxford University Press, 2013.

Juergensmeyer, Mark, Margo Kitts, and Michael K. Jerryson. *The Oxford Handbook of Religion and Violence*. New York: Oxford University Press, 2013.

Judt, Tony. "What Have We Learned, if Anything?" *New York Review of Books*, May 1, 2008. http://www.nybooks.com/articles/21311.

Justenhoven, Heinz-Gerhard and Mary Ellen O'Connell. *Peace Through Law: Reflections on Pacem in Terris from Philosophy, Law, Theology, and Political Science*. Baden-Baden, Germany: Nomos, 2016.

Kagan, Donald. *On the Origins of War and the Preservation of Peace*. New York: Doubleday, 1995.

Kaldor, Mary. *Human Security: Reflections on Globalization and Intervention*. Cambridge: Polity, 2007.

Kaldor, Mary. *New and Old Wars*. Stanford, CA: Stanford University Press, 2012.

Kaldor, Mary and Shannon D. Beebe. *The Ultimate Weapon Is No Weapon: Human Security and the New Rules of War and Peace*. New York: Public Affairs, 2010.

Kalman, Izzy. "The Golden Rule." *Psychology Today*, May 11, 2011. https://www.psychologytoday.com/us/blog/resilience-bullying/201105/principle-number-three-the-golden-rule.

Kant, Immanuel. *Foundations of the Metaphysics of Morals and What Is Enlightenment*. New York: Macmillan, 1990.

Kant, Immanuel. *Grounding for the Metaphysics of Morals*, Translated by James W. Ellington. Cambridge: Hackett, 1993.

Kaplan, Robert. "Why John J. Mearsheimer Is Right (About Some Things)." *The Atlantic*, January/February 2012. https://www.theatlantic.com/magazine/archive/2012/01/why-john-j-mearsheimer-is-right-about-some-things/308839/.

Karasz, Palko. "Saudi Facilities Are Set Ablaze in Drone Strike." *New York Times*, September 15, 2019.

Kashiwagi, Akiko and Chico Harlan. "In Nagasaki and Hiroshima, Pope Francis Calls for Abolishing Nuclear Weapons." *Washington Post*, November 24, 2019.

Kaspersen, Anja. "Security by Design: Emerging Technologies Require New Approach to Oversight, Governance." *Courier* (Summer). Muscatine, IA: Stanley Foundation, 2017.

Katz, Ellen D. "Justice Ginsburg's Umbrella." University of Michigan Law School Scholarship Repository, 2015, 264, ekatz@umich.edu; https://repository.law.umich.edu/book_chapters/81.

Keck, Margaret and Kathryn Sikkink. *Activists Beyond Borders*. Ithaca, NY: Cornell University Press, 1998.

Kegley, Charles W. and Gregory A. Raymond. *How Nations Make Peace*. New York: St. Martin's, 1999.

Kelsen, Hans. "Is the Acheson Plan Constitutional?" *Western Political Quarterly* 3, no. 4 (1950): 512–527.

Kennan, George F. *American Diplomacy 1900–1950*. Chicago: University of Chicago Press, 1951.

Kennan, George F. "Morality and Foreign Policy." *Foreign Affairs* 64, no. 2 (1985): 205–218.

Kennedy, Kerry. *Citizenship Education and the Modern State*. Washington, DC: Taylor & Francis, 1997.

Kennedy, Paul. *The Rise and Fall of the Great Powers: Economic Change and Military Conflict from 1500 to 2000*. New York: Vintage, 1987.

Keohane, Robert O. *After Hegemony: Cooperation and Discord in the World Political Economy*. Princeton, NJ: Princeton University Press, 2005.

Keohane, Robert O. "Democracy-Enhancing Multilateralism." *International Organization* 63, no. 1 (2009): 1–31.

Keohane, Robert O. "Global Governance and Legitimacy." *Review of International Political Economy: Legitimacy and Global Governance* 18, no. 1 (2011): 99–109.

Keohane, Robert O., ed. *International Institutions and State Power: Essays in International Relations Theory*. Boulder, CO: Westview Press, 1989.

Keohane, Robert O. "Reciprocity in International Relations." *International Organization* 40, no. 1 (1986): 1–27.

Keohane, Robert O. and Lisa L. Martin. "The Promise of Institutionalist Theory." *International Security* 20, no. 1 (1995): 39–51.

Keohane, Robert O., Stephen Macedo, and Andrew Moravcsik. "Democracy-Enhancing Multilateralism." *International Organization* 63, no. 1 (2009): 1–31.

Kertzer, Joshua D., and Brian C. Rathbun. "Fair Is Fair: Social Preferences and Reciprocity in International Politics." *World Politics* 67, no. 4 (2015): 613–655.

Keshner, Andrew. "CEOs Are Paid 278 Times More than the Average U.S. Worker." *MarketWatch* (August 31, 2019). https://www.marketwatch.com/story/ceos-are-paid-278-times-more-than-the-average-us-worker-2019-08-15.

Kessler, Glenn and Colum Lynch. "Critic of U.N. Named Envoy." *Washington Post*, March 8, 2005.

Kessler, Glenn, Salvador Rizzo, and Meg Kelly. "President Trump Has Made 12,019 False or Misleading Claims over 928 Days." *Washington Post*, August 12, 2019.

Khan, Irene, David Petrasek, and Kofi A. Annan. *The Unheard Truth: Poverty and Human Rights*. New York: W.W. Norton, 2009.

Khlopkov, Anton V. "Roland Timerbaev: The Nuclear Nonproliferation Treaty Has Largely Achieved Its Goals." *Arms Control Today* 47, no. 7 (2017): 39–43.

Kim, Hunjoon and Kathryn Sikkink. "Explaining the Deterrence Effect of Human Rights Prosecutions for Transitional Countries." *International Studies Quarterly* 54, no. 4 (2010): 939–963.

Kimball, Daryl G. "Closing the Deal on a Robust Arms Trade Treaty." Arms Control Association, *Issue Briefs* 4, no. 3 (March 13, 2013). https://www.armscontrol.org/issuebriefs/Closing-the-Deal-on-a-Robust-Global-Arms-Trade-Treaty.

Kimball, Daryl and Kingston Reif. "Trump Questions U.S. Nuclear Policies." *Arms Control Today* 47, no. 2 (2017): 24–25.

Kimball, Daryl. "New Arms Race? No, Thanks." *Arms Control Today* 47, no. 1 (2017): 3.

Kinloch, Stephen P. "Utopian or Pragmatic? A UN Permanent Military Volunteer Force." *International Peacekeeping 3, no. 4* (Winter 1996).

Koh, Harold Hongju and Oona Anne Hathaway. *Foundations of International Law and Politics*. New York: Foundation Press Thomson West, 2005.

Kohn, Alfie. "Are Humans Innately Aggressive?" *Psychology Today*, June, 1988. http://www.alfiekohn.org/article/humans-innately-aggressive/.

Korab-Karpowicz, W. Julian. "Political Realism in International Relations." *Stanford Encyclopedia of Philosophy*. https://plato.stanford.edu/entries/realism-intl-relations/ (2010).

Koskenniemi, Martti. "Constitutionalism as Mindset: Reflections on Kantian Themes About International Law and Globalization." *Theoretical Inquiries in Law* 8, no. 1 (2006): 9–36.

Krasner, Stephen D. *International Regimes*. Ithaca, NY: Cornell University Press, 1983.

Krasno, Jean and Mitushi Das. "The Uniting for Peace Resolution and Other Ways of Circumventing the Authority of the Security Council." In *The UN Security Council and the Politics of International Authority*, edited by Bruce Cronin and Ian Hurd, 173–195. London: Routledge, 2008.

Kreiger, David. *Earth Citizenship*. Waging Peace Series. Santa Barbara: Nuclear Age Peace Foundation, 1989.

Kreps, Sarah and Christopher A. Preble. *The Power Problem: How American Military Dominance Makes Us Less Safe, Less Prosperous, and Less Free*. Cambridge: Perspectives on Politics, 2011. DOI: 10.1017/S1537592711001356.

Kristensen, Hans. "Why New START Is a Treaty Worth Keeping." *Arms Control Today* 47, no. 3 (2017): 36.

Krugman, Paul R. *Arguing with Zombies: Economics, Politics, and the Fight for a Better Future*. New York: W.W. Norton, 2020.

Krugman, Paul R. *End this Depression Now!* New York: W.W. Norton, 2013.

Ku, Charlotte. "The Evolution of International Law." In *International Organization and Global Governance*, edited by Thomas Weiss and Rorden Wilkinson, 35–48. London: Routledge, 2014. https://scholarship.law.tamu.edu/facscholar/1248.

Ku, Julian and John Yoo. "Taming Globalization: International Law, the U.S. Constitution, and the New World Order." New York: Oxford University Press, 2012.

Kuimova, Alexandra, Aude Fleurant, Nan Tian, et al. *Trends in International Arms Transfers*, 2017. https://www.sipri.org/sites/default/files/2018-03/fssipri_at2017_0.pdf.

Kull, Steven. *American Public Support for Foreign Aid in the Age of Trump*. Washington, DC: Brookings Report, July 31, 2017. https://www.brookings.edu/research/american-public-support-for-foreign-aid-in-the-age-of-trump/.

Kupchan, Charles A. *How Enemies Become Friends: The Sources of Stable Peace*. Princeton, NJ: Princeton University Press, 2010.

Kuper, Andrew. *Global Responsibilities: Who Must Deliver on Human Rights?* New York: Routledge, 2005.

Kwa, Aileen. *Power Politics in the WTO*. Bangkok: Focus on the Global South, 2003.

Labott, Elise, Zachary Cohen, and Michelle Kosinski. "Acting US Ambassador to China Quit over Trump Climate Decision." CNN News Alert, June 6, 2017.

Landler, Mark. "President Reshapes Vision for U.S. Role with Emphasis on One Word: Sovereignty." *New York Times*, September 20, 2017.

Landler, Mark. "Trump Abandons Iran Nuclear Deal He Long Scorned." *New York Times*, May 8, 2018. https://www.nytimes.com/2018/05/08/world/middleeast/trump-iran-nuclear-deal.html.

Lango, John W. *The Ethics of Armed Conflict: A Cosmopolitan Just War Theory*. Edinburgh: Edinburgh University Press, 2014.

Lauren, Paul Gordon. *The Evolution of International Human Rights: Visions Seen*. Philadelphia: University of Pennsylvania Press, 2011.

Lauterpacht, H. "The Grotian Tradition in International Law." *British Yearbook of International Law* 23, (1946): 1.

Layne, Christopher. *The Peace of Illusions: American Grand Strategy from 1940 to the Present*. Ithaca, NY: Cornell University Press, 2006.

Leakey, Richard E. and Roger Lewin. *People of the Lake: Man, His Origins, Nature and Future*. London: Collins, 1979.

Lebow, Richard Ned. "You Can't Keep a Bad Idea Down: Evolutionary Biology and International Relations." *International Politics Reviews* no. 1 (2013): 2–10.

Lederach, John Paul. *Building Peace: Sustainable Reconciliation in Divided Societies*. Washington, DC: United States Institute of Peace Press, 1997.

Lederach, John Paul. *The Moral Imagination: The Art and Soul of Building Peace*. Oxford: Oxford University Press, 2005.

Lederach, John Paul and R. Scott Appleby. "Strategic Peacebuilding: An Overview." In *Strategies of Peace: Transforming Conflict in a Violent World*, edited by Daniel Philpott and Gerard F. Powers, 19–44. New York: Oxford University Press, 2010.

Lee, Sally. "Losing at Monopoly." *Columbia Magazine*, Spring 2019.

Leon, Adriana and Chris Kraul. "Peru Wins Maritime Border Dispute with Chile over Key Fishing Grounds." *Los Angeles Times*, January 14, 2014. https://www.latimes.com/world/la-xpm-2014-jan-27-la-fg-wn-peru-territorial-dispute-chile-20140127-story.html.

Leon, Josh. "Poverty Capitalism: Interview with Ananya Roy." *Foreign Policy in Focus*, February 11, 2011. www-proquest-com.proxy.library.nd.edu/reports/poverty-capitalism-interview-with-ananya-roy/docview/855348073/se-2?accountid=12874.

Leonardi, Robert, Raffaella Nanetti, and Robert D. Putnam. *Making Democracy Work: Civic Traditions in Modern Italy*. Princeton, NJ: Princeton University Press, 1993.

Lepard, Brian D. *Rethinking Humanitarian Intervention: A Fresh Legal Approach Based on Fundamental Ethical Principles in International Law and World Religions*. University Park: Pennsylvania State University Press, 2003.

Lepore, Jill. "The Hacking of America." *New York Times*, September 14, 2018.

Levi, Werner. *Law and Politics in the International Society*. Beverly Hills, CA: Sage, 1976.

Lewis, Jeffrey. "Obama's Dream of a Nuclear-Free World Is Becoming a Nightmare." *Foreign Policy*, March 29, 2017. https://foreignpolicy.com/2017/03/29/obamas-dream-of-a-nuclear-free-world-is-becoming-a-nightmare/.

Libicki, Martin C. and Seth G. Jones. *How Terrorist Groups End: Lessons for Countering Al Qa'ida*. Santa Monica, CA: Rand, 2008.

Lieber, Robert J. *Power and Willpower in the American Future: Why the United States Is Not Destined to Decline*. Cambridge: Cambridge University Press, 2012.

Lifschitz, Avi. "The Enlightenment: Those Who Dare to Know." *History Today* 63, no. 9 (September 2013). https://www.historytoday.com/avi-lifschitz/enlightenment-those-who-dare-know.

Lifton, Robert Jay and Greg Mitchell. "The Age of Numbing (the Atomic Age at 50)." *Technology Review* 98, no. 6 (1995): 58.

Lifton, Robert Jay. "Beyond Psychic Numbing: A Call to Awareness." *American Journal of Orthopsychiatry* 52, no. 4 (1982): 619–629.

Linklater, Andrew. *Violence and Civilization in the Western States-Systems*. Cambridge: Cambridge University Press, 2017.

Lobell, Stephen E. *Structural Realism/Offensive and Defensive Realism*. New York: Oxford University Press, 2017.

Lopez-Claros, Augusto, Arthur L. Dahl, and Maja Groff. *Global Governance and the Emergence of Global Institutions for the 21st Century*. Cambridge: Cambridge University Press, 2020.

Louw, Lee-Ann and Johannes Lubbe Hendrik. "Threats to Security Posed by ISIS in Syria: A Human Security Approach." *Journal of Human Security* 13, no. 1 (2017): 16–21.

Lovell, Jeremy. "Climate Change to Make One Billion Refugees." Reuters, May 13, 2007. http://www.reuters.com/article/latestCrisis/idUSL10710325.

Lu, Catherine. "World Government." *Stanford Encyclopedia of Philosophy*. Stanford, CA: Stanford University Press, 2016. https://plato.stanford.edu/entries/world-government/.

Luck, Edward C. "The United Nations and the Responsibility to Protect." *Policy Analysis Brief*. Muscatine, IA: Stanley Foundation, August 2008. https://www.stanleyfoundation.org/publications/pab/LuckPAB808.pdf.

Lupel, Adam and Ernesto Verdeja. *Responding to Genocide: The Politics of International Action*. Boulder, CO: Lynne Rienner, 2013.

Luyster, Robert W. and Mary Pat Fisher. *Living Religions*. Englewood Cliffs, NJ: Prentice Hall, 1991.

Lynch, Cecelia. *Beyond Appeasement: Interpreting Interwar Peace Movements in World Politics*. Ithaca, NY: Cornell University Press, 1999.

Lynch, Cecelia. "Neoliberal Ethics, the Humanitarian International, and Practices of Peacebuilding." In *Globalization, Social Movements, and Peacebuilding*, edited by Jackie Smith and Ernesto Verdeja, 47–68. Syracuse, NY: Syracuse University Press, 2013. ⸌

Lynch, Cecelia. "Political Activism and the Social Origins of International Legal Norms." In *Law and Moral Action in World Politics*, edited by Cecelia Lynch and Michael Loriaux, 140–174. Minneapolis: University of Minnesota Press, 2000.

Lynch, Cecelia. *Wrestling with God: Ethical Precarity in Christianity and International Relations*. Cambridge: Cambridge University Press, 2020.

Lynch, Colum. "U.S. Allies Dispute Annan on Iraq War." *Washington Post*, September 17, 2004.

MacDonald, Paul K. and Joseph M. Parent. "Graceful Decline? The Surprising Success of Great Power Retrenchment." *International Security*, 35, no. 4 (Spring 2011): 7–44.

MacFarlane, S. N. and Yuen Foong Khong. *Human Security and the UN: A Critical History*. Bloomington: Indiana University Press, 2006.

Machiavelli, Niccolò. *The Prince*. Project Gutenberg, 2005. http://www.gutenberg.org/files/57037/57037-h/57037-h.htm.

Mamdani, Mahmood. "Responsibility to Protect or Right to Punish?" *Journal of Intervention and Statebuilding* 4, no. 1 (2010): 53–67.

Mann, Neelakshi and Varad Pande. *MGNREGA Sameeksha: An Anthology of Research Studies on the Mahatma Gandhi National Rural Employment Guarantee Act, 2005, 2006–2012*, New Delhi: India Ministry of Rural Development. 2012.

Mann, Thomas and Norman Ornstein. *It's Even Worse Than It Looks: How the American Constitutional System Collided with the New Politics of Extremism*. New York: Basic Books, 2016.

Mansbach, Richard W. and Kirsten L. Rafferty. *Introduction to Global Politics: A Journey from Yesterday to Tomorrow*. London: Routledge, 2008.

Mansfield, Edward D. and Jon C. Pevehouse. "Trade Blocs, Trade Blows, and International Conflict." *International Organization* 54 (2000): 775–808.

Manski, Ben and Jackie Smith. "Introduction: The Dynamics and Terrains of Local Democracy and Corporate Power in the 21st Century." In *Corporate Power and Local Democracy*, edited by Ben Manski and Jackie Smith. *Journal of World-Systems Research* 25, no. 1 (2019): 6–14. DOI: https://doi.org/10.5195/jwsr.2019.919.

Mansoor, Peter R. and Williamson Murray. *Grand Strategy and Military Alliances*. Cambridge: Cambridge University Press, 2016.

Manuel, Anja. *This Brave New World: India, China and the United States*. New York: Simon & Schuster, 2016.

Martel, William C. *Grand Strategy in Theory and Practice: The Need for an Effective American Foreign Policy*. New York: Cambridge University Press, 2015.

Martin, Adam, and Kristen Renwick Monroe. "Identity, Moral Choice, and the Moral Imagination: Is There a Neuroscientific Foundation for Altruism?" In *Morality, Ethics, and Gifted Minds*, edited by Don Ambrose and Tracy Cross, 73–88. New York: Springer, 2009.

Maslow, Abraham. *The Farther Reaches of Human Nature*. New York: Viking, 1971.

Matthieu, Ortiz. "Killer Robots." Arms Control Association *Issue Briefs* 10, no. 6 (June 7, 2018). https://www.armscontrol.org/taxonomy/term/31.

Mayer, Ann Elizabeth. *Islam and Human Rights*. London: Pinter, 1991.

Mayer, Jane. "Outsourcing Torture: The Secret History of America's 'Extraordinary Rendition' Program." *New Yorker*, February 14, 2005.

Maynard, Jonathan Leader. "Rethinking the Role of Ideology in Mass Atrocities." *Terrorism and Political Violence* 26, no. 5 (2014): 821–841.

Mazarr, Michael. "The Once and Future Order: What Comes After Hegemony?" *Foreign Affairs* 96, no. 1 (2017): 25–32.

Mazower, Mark. *Governing the World: The History of an Idea*. New York: Penguin Press, 2012.

McCain, John. "McCain Condemns 'Half-Baked, Spurious Nationalism' in Speech." *New York Times*, October 17, 2017. https://www.nytimes.com/aponline/2017/10/16/us/ap-us-liberty-medal-mccain.

McNeill, William H. *Arnold J. Toynbee: A Life*. New York: Oxford University Press, 1989.

Meaney, Thomas and Stephen Wertheim. "Trump's Foreign Policy Is Very American." *New York Times*, March 11, 2018.

Mearsheimer, John J. "America Unhinged." *National Interest* no. 129 (January/February 2014): 9–30.

Mearsheimer, John J. "The False Promise of International Institutions." *International Security* 19, no. 3 (1994): 5–49.

Mearsheimer, John J. *The Great Delusion: Liberal Dreams and International Realities*. New Haven, CT: Yale University Press, 2018. Kindle.

Mearsheimer, John J. *The Tragedy of Great Power Politics*. New York: W.W. Norton, 2014

Mearsheimer, John J. "Why the Ukraine Crisis Is the West's Fault: The Liberal Delusions that Provoked Putin." *Foreign Affairs* 93 (2014): 77–89.

Melander, Erik. "Gender Equality and Intrastate Armed Conflict." *International Studies Quarterly* 49, no. 4 (2005): 695–714.

Mello, Steven. "More COPS, Less Crime." *Journal of Public Economics* 172 (2019): 174–200.

Mellow, David. "Iraq: A Morally Justified Resort to War." *Journal of Applied Philosophy* 23, no. 3 (2006): 293–310.

Melman, Seymour. "Swordshares into Plowshares: Converting from Military to Civilian Production." *Technology Review* 89 (1986): 62.

Merton, Thomas. *New Seeds of Contemplation*. New York: New Directions, 2007.

Meyer, Cord. *Peace or Anarchy*. Boston: Little, Brown, 1947.

Mignolo, Walter D. "The Making and Closing of Eurocentric International Law: The Opening of a Multipolar World Order." *Comparative Studies of South Asia, Africa and the Middle East* 36, no. 1 (2016): 182–195.

Milanović, Branko. *Worlds Apart: Measuring International and Global Inequality*. Princeton, NJ: Princeton University Press, 2005.

Miller, Alice. "The Political Consequences of Child Abuse." *Journal of Psychohistory* 26, no. 2 (1998): 573.

Miller, Alice. "Poisonous Pedagogy." In *For Your Own Good*, edited by Alice Miller. New York: Farrar, Straus and Giroux, 1983.

Miller, Judith. "Sovereignty Isn't So Sacred Anymore." *New York Times*, April 18, 1999, IV, 4.

Mishel, Lawrence and Jori Kandra. *CEO Compensation Surged 14% in 2019 to $21.3 Million: CEOs Now Earn 320 Times as Much as a Typical Worker: Report*. Economic Policy Institute, 2020. https://files.epi.org/pdf/204513.pdf.

Monroe, Kristen Renwick. *The Heart of Altruism: Perceptions of a Common Humanity*. Princeton, NJ: Princeton University Press, 1996.

Monshipouri, Mahmood. "Islamic Thinking and the Internationalization of Human Rights." *Muslim World* 84, no. 3 (1994): 217.

Mora, Alberto J. *Ethical Considerations: Law, Foreign Policy, and the War on Terror*. New York: Carnegie Council for Ethics in International Affairs, 2007.

Morgenstern, Oskar and John Von Neumann. *Theory of Games and Economic Behavior*. Princeton, NJ: Princeton University Press, 1957.

Morgenthau, Hans J. "The Four Paradoxes of Nuclear Strategy." *American Political Science Review* 68, no. 1 (March 1964): 23–35.

Morgenthau, Hans J. *Politics Among Nations: The Struggle for Power and Peace*. New York: Knopf, 1967.

Morgenthau, Hans J. *The Purpose of American Politics*. New York: Knopf, 1960.

Morgenthau, Hans J. "What the Big Two Can, and Can't Negotiate." *New York Times*, September 20, 1959.

Mozur, Paul. "A Genocide Incited on Facebook, with Posts from Myanmar's Military." *New York Times*, October 15, 2018.

Murphy, Craig N. "The Last Two Centuries of Global Governance." *Global Governance*, 21, no. 2 (2015): 189–196.

Murphy, Craig. *Global Institutions, Marginalization, and Development*. New York: Routledge, 2005.

Murphy, Sean D. *The United States and the International Court of Justice: Coping with Antinomies*. http://scholarship.law.gwu.edu/cgi/viewcontent.cgi?article=1902&context=faculty_publications.

Naraghi-Anderlkini, Sanam. "21st Century Diplomacy: From Power Sharing to Responsibility Sharing." International Civil Society Action Network, *The Better Peace Tool* (2015): 3–28.

Nardin, Terry. "Middle-Ground Ethics: Can One Be Politically Realistic Without Being a Political Realist?" *Ethics and International Affairs* 25, no. 1 (March 1, 2011): 7–16.

Narváez, Darcia. *Neurobiology and the Development of Human Morality: Evolution, Culture, and Wisdom*. New York: W.W. Norton, 2014.

National Intelligence Council. *Global Trends 2040: A More Contested World*, March 2021. https://www.dni.gov/index.php/global-trends-home.

National Public Radio (NPR). "71 Soldiers Killed in Attack on Army Camp in Niger, December 12, 2019." www.npr.org/2019/12/12/787415274/71-soldiers-killed-in-attack-on-army-camp-in-niger.

Nelsen, Jane. *Positive Discipline*. New York: Ballantine Books, 1996.

Nepstad, Sharon Erickson. *Nonviolent Struggle: Theories, Strategies, and Dynamics*. Oxford: Oxford University Press, 2015.

"New CIA Docs Detail Brutal 'Extraordinary Rendition' Process." *Huffington Post*, August 28, 2009.

New York Times Editorial Board. "Partners in Voter Suppression." *New York Times*, August 11, 2017.

Nicholson, Simon and Paul Kevin Wapner. *Global Environmental Politics: From Person to Planet*. Boulder, CO: Paradigm, 2015.

Nicoles, Michelle. "U.N. Urges U.S., China, Others to Ratify Nuclear Test Ban Treaty." Reuters, September 23, 2016. http://www.reuters.com/article/us-un-nuclear-idUSKCN11T29J.

Niebuhr, Reinhold. *The Children of Light and the Children of Darkness: A Vindication of Democracy and a Critique of Its Traditional Defence*. New York: C. Scribner's Sons, 1944.

Niebuhr, Reinhold. "The Illusion of World Government." *Foreign Affairs* 27, no. 3 (1949): 379–388.

Niebuhr, Reinhold. *The Structure of Nations and Empires: A Study of the Recurring Patterns and Problems of the Political Order in Relation to the Unique Problems of the Nuclear Age*. New York: Scribner's, 1959.

Nielsen, Kai. "Cosmopolitan Nationalism." *Monist* 82, no. 3 (1999): 446–468.

Nilsson, Desirée. "Anchoring the Peace: Civil Society Actors in Peace Accords and Durable Peace." *International Interactions* 38, no. 2 (April 1, 2012): 243–266. http://www.tandfonline.com/doi/abs/10.1080/03050629.2012.659139.

Noack, Rick. "Why Does the Trump Administration Hate the International Criminal Court so Much?" *Washington Post*, April 5, 2019.

Noll, Douglas. *Peacemaking: Practicing at the Intersection of Law and Human Conflict*. Scottdale, PA: Herald Press, 2003.

Nordland, Rod, Ash Ngu, and Fahim Abed. "How the U.S. Government Misleads the Public on Afghanistan." *New York Times*, September 9, 2018.

Nordland, Rod. "U.N. Reports Rising Afghan Casualties." *New York Times*, August 10, 2010.

Nouwen, Henri J. *Lifesigns: Intimacy, Fecundity, and Ecstasy in Christian Perspective*. New York: Doubleday, 1996.

"Nuclear Weapons: Who Has What at a Glance." *Arms Control Today* 47, no. 2 (2017): 21–23.

Nussbaum, Martha C. *The Cosmopolitan Tradition: A Noble but Flawed Ideal*. Cambridge, MA: Belknap Press of Harvard University Press, 2019.

Nussbaum, Martha. "Patriotism and Cosmopolitanism." *Boston Review* 19, no. 5 (1994): 3.

Nussbaum, Martha C. "Toward a Globally Sensitive Patriotism." *Daedalus* 137, no. 3 (2008): 78–93.

Nye, Joseph S. "Will the Liberal Order Survive? The History of an Idea." *Foreign Affairs* 96, no. 1 (2017): 10.

O'Connell, Mary Ellen. *The Art of Law in the International Community*. Cambridge: Cambridge University Press, 2019. DOI:https://doi.org/10.1017/9781108551144.

O'Connell, Mary Ellen. "The Law on Lethal Force Begins with the Right to Life." *Journal on the Use of Force and International Law* 3, no. 2 (2016): 205–209.

O'Connell, Mary Ellen. *The Power and Purpose of International Law: Insights from the Theory and Practice of Enforcement*. New York: Oxford University Press, 2008.

O'Connell, Mary Ellen. "Reestablishing the Rule of Law as National Security." In *Reimagining the National Security State: Liberalism on the Brink*, edited by Karen J. Greenberg, 154–168. New York: Cambridge University Press, 2019.

O'Connell, Mary Ellen, Christian J. Tams, and Dire Tladi. *Self-Defence against Non-State Actors*. Cambridge: Cambridge University Press, 2019. DOI:https://doi.org/10.1017/9781108120173.

O'Connell, Mary Ellen and Lenore VanderZee. "The History of International Adjudication." In *The Oxford Handbook of International Adjudication*, edited by Cesare P. R. Romano, Karen J. Alter, and Yuval Shany. Oxford: Oxford University Press, 2013. DOI: 10.1093/law/9780199660681.003.0003.

O'Driscoll, Cian. "Book Review: *Massacres and Morality: Mass Atrocities in an Age of Civilian Immunity* by Alex J. Bellamy." *War in History* 20, no. 4 (2013): 563–564.

Office of the US Trade Representative. "Economy and Trade." https://ustr.gov/issue-areas/economy-trade.

Official Records of the UN General Assembly. Sixty-sixth Session, A/66/53, Supplement no. 53, chapter 1.

O'Gorman, Rick and A. Silke. *Terrorism as Altruism: An Evolutionary Model for Understanding Terrorist Psychology*. New York: Routledge, 2015.

O'Hanlon, Michael E. "Forecasting Change in Military Technology, 2020–2040." September 2018. https://www.brookings.edu/research/forecasting-change-in-military-technology-2020-2040/.

Omar, A. Rashied. *Islam Beyond Violent Extremism*. Cape Town, South Africa: Claremont Main Road Mosque, 2017.

O'Neill, Jacqueline and Jarad Ary. "Allies and Assets: Strengthening DDR and SSR Through Women's Inclusion." In *Monopoly of Force: The Nexus of DDR and SSR*. Washington, DC: National Defense University, 2010.

O'Reilly, Marie. "Inclusive Security and Peaceful Societies: Exploring the Evidence.." *Prism: A Journal of the Center for Complex Operations* 6, no. 1 (2016): 20–33.

O'Reilly, Marie. "Why Women? Inclusive Societies and Peaceful Societies." *Inclusive Security Report*, October, 2015, 1–16. https://www.inclusivesecurity.org/wp-content/uploads/2017/06/Why-Women-Report-2017.pdf.

Organization for Economic Cooperation and Development. *Divided We Stand: Why Inequality Keeps Rising*. Paris: OECD Publishing, 2011.

Organization for Economic Cooperation and Development. *In It Together: Why Less Inequality Benefits All*. Paris: OECD Publishing, 2015.

Otto, Dianne. "Rethinking the 'Universality' of Human Rights Law." *Columbia Human Rights Law Review* 29, no. 1 (1997): 1–46.

Oxfam Media Briefing. "The Cost of Inequality." January 18, 2013. https://oxfamilibrary.open-repository.com/bitstream/handle/10546/266321/mb-cost-of-inequality-180113-en.pdf;jsessionid=7F31C9518AF10A15A3E636EE726C666F?sequence=1.

Paffenholz, Thania. "Civil Society and Peacebuilding." In *Civil Society & Peacebuilding: A Critical Assessment*, edited by Thania Paffenholz, 43–64. Boulder, CO: Lynne Rienner, 2010.

Paffenholz, Thania, Christoph Spurk, Roberto Belloni, Sabine Kurtenbach, and Camilla Orjuela. "Enabling and Disenabling Factors for Civil Society Peacebuilding." In *Civil Society and Peacebuilding: A Critical Assessment*, edited by Thania Paffenholz, 405–424. Boulder, CO: Lynne Rienner, 2010.

Paige, Glenn D. *Nonkilling Global Political Science*. Honolulu, Hawaii: Center for Global Nonkilling, 2009.

Palmer, Parker J. *Let Your Life Speak: Listening for the Voice of Vocation*. San Francisco: Jossey-Bass, 2000.

Palmer, Parker J. *Healing the Heart of Democracy: The Courage to Create a Politics Worthy of the Human Spirit*. San Francisco: Jossey-Bass, 2011.

Pape, Robert Anthony. *Dying to Win: The Strategic Logic of Suicide Terrorism*. New York: Random House Trade Paperbacks, 2006.

Pape, Robert A. "It's the Occupation, Stupid." *Foreign Policy*, October 18, 2010. http://www.foreignpolicy.com/articles/2010.10/18/it_s_the_occupation-stupid.

Pape, Robert Anthony and James K. Feldman. *Cutting the Fuse: The Explosion of Global Suicide Terrorism and How to Stop It*. Chicago: University of Chicago Press, 2012.

Pardo, Matt. "German Military Bishop Says U.S. Wants to 'Hinder" International Criminal Court." *Catholic News Agency*, July 31, 2020. https://www.catholicnewsagency.com/news/german-military-bishop-says-us-wants-to-hinder-international-criminal-court-40895.

Paravicini, Giulia. "Angela Merkel: Europe Must Take 'Our Fate' into Own Hands." *Politico*, May 28, 2017. https://www.politico.eu/singerarticle/angela-merkel-europe-cdu-must-take-its-fate-into-its-own-hands-elections-2017.

Paris, Roland. "Human Security." *International Security* 26, no. 2 (2001): 87–102.

Paris, Roland. "International Peacebuilding and the 'Mission Civilisatrice.'" *Review of International Studies* 28, no. 4 (2002): 637–656.

Patomäki, Heikki. *Democratizing Globalization: The Leverage of the Tobin Tax*. New York: Zed Books/Palgrave, 2001.

Pattison, James. "The Ethics of Diplomatic Criticism: The Responsibility to Protect, Just War Theory and Presumptive Last Resort." *European Journal of International Relations* 21, no. 4 (2015): 935–957.

Pavlischek, Keith. "Proportionality in Warfare." *New Atlantis* no. 27 (2010): 21–34.

Paxton, Marie. *Agonistic Democracy*. New York: Taylor and Francis, 2019.

Payne, Rodger A. "Cooperative Security: Grand Strategy Meets Critical Theory?" *Millennium: Journal of International Studies* 40, no. 3 (June 2012): 604–624.

PBS analysis, "The War in Vietnam." http://www.pbs.org/kenburns/the-vietnam-war/episodes/.

Peou, Sorpong. *Human Security Studies: Theories, Methods, and Themes*. London: World Scientific, 2014.

Perry, Michael J. "A Global Political Morality: Human Rights, Democracy, and Constitutionalism." https://login.proxy.bib.uottawa.ca/login?url=.

Petriglieri, Gianpiero. "In Defense of Cosmopolitanism." *Harvard Business Review*, December 15, 2016. https://hbr.org/2016/12/in-defense-of-cosmopolitanism.

Pettersson, Thérése and Peter Wallensteen. "Armed Conflicts, 1946–2014." *Journal of Peace Research* 52, no. 4 (2015): 536–550. https://journals.sagepub.com/doi/10.1177/0022343315595927.

Pevehouse, Jon and Bruce Russett. "Democratic International Governmental Organizations Promote Peace." *International Organization* 60, no. 4 (2006): 969–1000.

Pfaff, William. *The Bullet's Song: Romantic Violence and Utopia*. New York: Simon & Schuster, 2004.

Phelps, Glenn and Steve Crabtree. *Gallup World*. "Richest 3% Hold One-Fifth of Collective Income." January 3, 2014. //news.gallup.com/poll/166721/worldwide-richest-hold-one-fifth-collective-income.aspx.

Philips, Amber. "'Half-Baked Spurious Nationalism': McCain's Most Biting Recent Criticisms of Trump." *Washington Post*, October 17, 2017.

Philpott, Daniel. *Revolutions in Sovereignty: How Ideas Shaped Modern International Relations*. Princeton, NJ: Princeton University Press, 2008.

Philpott, Daniel. *Revolutions in Sovereignty*. Abstract. //press.princeton.edu/books/paperback/9780691057477/revolutions-in-sovereignty.

Philpott, Daniel and Gerard F. Powers, eds. *Strategies of Peace: Transforming Conflict in a Violent World*. New York: Oxford University Press, 2010.

Pickering, Jeffrey and Mark Peceny. "Forging Democracy at Gunpoint." *International Studies Quarterly* 50, no. 3 (September 1, 2006): 539–559. https://www.jstor.org/stable/4092792.

Pickett, Kate and Richard G. Wilkinson. *The Spirit Level: Why Greater Equality Makes Societies Stronger*. New York: Bloomsbury Press, 2011.

Piketty, Thomas. *Capital in the Twenty-First Century*. Cambridge, MA: Harvard University Press, 2014.

Pillay, Sonya. "Bringing the CTBT into Force: Looking Back at the 2011 Article XIV Conference." VERTIC. http://www.vertic.org/media/assets/Publications/VB16.pdf.

Pincus, Walter. "The Dirty Secret of American Nuclear Arms in Korea." *New York Times*, March 19, 2018. https://www.nytimes.com/2018/03/19/opinion/korea-nuclear-arms-america.html.

Pinker, Steven. *The Better Angels of Our Nature: Why Violence Has Declined*. New York: Viking, 2011.

Plesch, Dan and Thomas G. Weiss. "1945's Lesson: 'Good Enough' Global Governance Ain't Good Enough." *Global Governance* 21 (2015): 203.

Pogge, Thomas. "Human Rights and Human Responsibilities." In *Global Responsibilities: Who Must Deliver on Human Rights?* edited by Andrew Kuper, 3–36. New York: Routledge, 2005.

Pogge, Thomas. *Politics as Usual*. London: Polity, 2010.

Pogge, Thomas. *World Poverty and Human Rights*. Cambridge: Polity, 2010.

Pope Francis. "Nonviolence: A Style of Politics for Peace." January 1, 2017. http://www.vatican.va/content/francesco/en/messages/peace/documents/papa-francesco_20161208_messaggio-l-giornata-mondiale-pace-2017.html.

Posen, Barry R. and Andrew L. Ross. "Competing Visions for U.S. Grand Strategy." *International Security* 21, no. 3 (1996): 5–53.

Posen, Barry. *Restraint: A New Foundation for U.S. Grand Strategy*. Ithaca, NY: Cornell University Press, 2014.

Porter, Patrick. "A World Imagined: Nostalgia and Liberal Order." CATO Institute. *Policy Analysis*, no. 843, June 5, 2018.

Posen, Barry R. "A Grand Strategy of Restraint." In *Finding Our Way: Debating American Strategy*, edited by Michele A. Flournoy and Shawn Brimley. Washington, DC: Center for a New American Security, 2008.

Powers, Gerard F. "From an Ethics of War to an Ethics of Peace." In *From Just War to Modern Peace Ethics*, edited by Heinz-Gerhard Justenhoven and William A. Barbieri Jr. Berlin: De Gruyter, 2012.

Prasad, Aarathi. "The Benevolent Power of Other People." *New York Times Book Review*, May 10, 2019. https://www.nytimes.com/2019/05/10/books/review/nicholas-christakis-blueprint-origins-society.html.

"Preamble." Chemical Weapons Convention. https://www.opcw.org/chemical-weapons-convention.

Preble, Christopher. "Adapting to American Decline." *New York Times*, April 22, 2018.

Preble, Christopher A. "The Power Problem: How American Military Dominance Makes Us Less Safe, Less Prosperous, and Less Free." https://doi-org.proxy.library.nd.edu/10.7591/9780801459153.

Priest, Dana and Barton Gellman. "U.S. Decries Abuse but Defends Interrogations." *Washington Post*, December 26, 2002.

Pritchard, Ambrose Evans. "IMF Raises Spectre of Civil Wars as Global Inequalities Worsen." *The Telegraph*, February 1, 2011. http://www.telegraph.co.uk/finance/globalbusiness/8296987/IMF-raises-spectre-of-civil-wars-as-global-inequalities-worsen.html.

Putnam, Robert D. "Bowling Alone: America's Declining Social Capital." *Journal of Democracy* 6, no. 1 (1995): 65–78. doi:10.1353/jod.1995.0002.

Quish, Ed. "Pragmatism, Social Democracy, and the Politics of Democratic Association." *European Journal of Pragmatism and American Philosophy*. https://journals.openedition.org/ejpap/1987.

Rabin, Roni Caryn. "Trump Stance on Breast-Feeding and Formula Criticized by Medical Experts." *New York Times*, July 9, 2018.

Ramsden, Michael. "'Uniting for Peace' and Humanitarian Intervention: The Authorizing Function of the U.N. General Assembly." *Washington International Law Journal* 25 (2016): 267–304.

Rees, Martin J. *Our Final Century: Will Civilisation Survive the Twenty-First Century?* London: Arrow, 2003.

Reeve, Zoey. "Islamist Terrorism as Parochial Altruism." *Terrorism and Political Violence* 32, no. 1 (2020): 38–56.

Regan, Patrick M. and Aida Paskeviciute. "Women's Access to Politics and Peaceful States." *Journal of Peace Research* 40, no. 3 (2003): 287–302.

Reich, Robert B. *Beyond Outrage: What Has Gone Wrong with Our Economy and Our Democracy, and How to Fix It.* New York: Vintage Books, 2012.

Reif, Kingston. "Trump Nuclear Tweet Sparks Controversy." *Arms Control Today* 47, no. 1 (2017): 35–36.

Renteln, Alison Dundes. *International Human Rights: Universalism Versus Relativism.* Newbury Park, CA: Sage, 1990.

Reus-Smit, Christian and Duncan Snidal. "Reuniting Ethics and Social Science: The Oxford Handbook of International Relations." *Ethics & International Affairs* 22, no. 3 (2008): 261–271.

Reuters and Iraq News. "Casualties by Country and Year." http://www.icasualties.org/.

Rice, Susan E. "John Bolton: Tough Love or Tough Luck?" Brookings Institution, March 8, 2005. https://www.brookings.edu/opinions/john-bolton-tough-love-or-tough-luck/.

Rich, Nathaniel. "Losing Earth: The Decade We Almost Stopped Climate Change." *New York Times Magazine*, August 5, 2018, 7–70.

Richardson, John and Richard C. Rowson. "For Democracy: Back Civic Education Worldwide." *International Herald Tribune*, December 6, 2002. https://www.nytimes.com/2002/12/06/opinion/IHT-for-democracy-back-civic-education-worldwide.html?searchResultPosition=1.

Ridley, Matt. *The Origins of Virtue: Human Instincts and the Evolution of Cooperation.* New York: Penguin Books, 1998.

Rieff, David. *A Bed for the Night: Humanitarianism in Crisis.* New York: Simon & Schuster, 2002.

"Right to Peace." A/RES/71/189, L. 29, 4. https://documents-dds-ny.un.org/doc/UNDOC/GEN/N16/454/62/pdf/N1645462.pdf?OpenElement.

Rokeach, Milton. "Inducing Change and Stability in Belief Systems and Personality Structures." *Journal of Social Issues* 41, no. 1 (1985): 153–171.

Rokeach, Milton. *The Nature of Human Values.* New York: Free Press, 1973.

Rokeach, Milton. *Understanding Human Values: Individual and Societal.* New York: Free Press, 1979.

Ronis, Sheila R. *Forging an American Grand Strategy: Securing a Path through a Complex Future: Selected Presentations from a Symposium at the National Defense University.* Carlisle, PA: Strategic Studies Institute and US Army War College Press, 2013.

Roper Center for Public Opinion Research. "Seventy Years of U.S. Public Opinion on the United Nations." 2015. https://ropercenter.cornell.edu/blog/seventy-years-us-public-opinion-united-nations.

Roscoe, Paul. "Social Signaling, Conflict Management, the Construction of Peace." In *War, Peace, and Human Nature*, edited by Douglas P. Fry, 475–494. New York: Oxford University Press, 2013.

Rose, Frank. "Emerging Threats: Outer Space, Cyberspace, and Undersea Cables." *Arms Control Today* 47, no. 1 (2017): 52.

Rosecrance, Richard. "The One World of Hans Morgenthau." *Social Research* 48, no. 4 (Winter 1981): 749–765.

Rosenau, James N. "Governance in the Twenty-First Century." *Global Governance* 1, no. 1 (1995): 13–43.

Rostow, Nicholas. *Grand Strategy and International Law*. Washington, DC: Institute for National Strategic Studies, National Defense University, 2012.

Rousseau, Jean-Jacques. *A Discourse on the Origin of Inequality*. New York: Penguin, 1984.

Rowlands, Anna. "Simone Weil and the Gift of Inarticulacy: How Not to Live in Lockdown." *Religion & Ethics*, May 6, 2020. https://www.abc.net.au/religion/anna-rowlands-simone-weil-lockdown-and-the-gift-of-inarticulacy/12220482.

Roy, Ananya. *Poverty Capital: Micro Finance and the Making of Development*. New York: Routledge, 2010.

Rozpedowski, Joanna K. "Just Peace at War's End: The *Jus Post Bellum* Principles as National and Human Security Imperatives—Lessons of Iraq and Kosovo." *Global Jurist* 15, no. 3 (2015): 491–517.

Rucker, Philip and Robert Costa. "Bob Woodward's New Book Reveals a 'Nervous Breakdown' of Trump's Presidency." *Washington Post*, September 4, 2018.

Ruger, William. "A Realist's Guide to Grand Strategy." *American Conservative*, August 26, 2014. https://www.theamericanconservative.com/articles/a-realists-guide-to-grand-strategy/.

Ruggie, John. "Taking Embedded Liberalism Global: The Corporate Connection." In *Taming Globalization*, edited by David Held and Mathias Koenig-Archibugi. Cambridge: Polity, 2003.

Russbach, Olibier. "The Citizen's Right to International Law." In *Law and Moral Action in World Politics*, edited by Cecelia Lynch and Michael Loriaux, 253–269. Minneapolis: University of Minnesota Press, 2000.

Russett, Bruce M. *Grasping the Democratic Peace: Principles for a Post-Cold War World*. Princeton, NJ: Princeton University Press, 1993.

Russett, Bruce, Christopher Layne, David Spiro, and Michael Doyle. "The Democratic Peace." *International Security* 19, no. 4 (1995): 164–184.

Russett, Bruce M. and John R. Oneal. *Triangulating Peace: Democracy, Interdependence, and International Organizations*. New York: W.W. Norton, 2001.

Russett, Bruce, John Oneal, and Michael Berbaum. "Causes of Peace: Democracy, Interdependence, and International Organizations, 1886–1992." *International Studies Quarterly* 47, no. 3 (September 2003): 371–393.

Ryngaert, Cedric and Math Noortmann. *Human Security and International Law: The Challenge of Non-State Actors*. Cambridge: Intersentia, 2014.

Rynne, Terrence J. "Toward a New Theology of Peace." *Sojourners* 45, no 7 (July 2016): 9–10.

Sachs, Jeffrey. *The Price of Civilization: Economics and Ethics After the Fall*. London: Vintage, 2012.

Santos, Boaventura de Sousa. *Toward a New Legal Common Sense: Law, Globalization, and Emancipation*. London: Butterworths, 2002.

Saunders, Rebecca. *Plausible Legality: Legal Culture and Political Imperative in the Global War on Terror*. New York: Oxford University Press, 2018.

Sanders-Zakre, Alicia. "Nuclear Weapons Ban Treaty Adopted." *Arms Control Today* 47, no. 6 (2017): 21–22.

Sanders-Zakre, Alicia. "States Hesitate to Sign Nuclear Ban Treaty." *Arms Control Today* 47, no. 7 (2017): 31–32.

Sanger, David E. *The Perfect Weapon: War, Sabotage, and Fear in the Cyber Age*. New York: Broadway Books, 2019.

Sanger, David E. and Andrew E. Kramer. "U.S. Officials Suspect New Nuclear Missile in Explosion That Killed 7 Russians." *New York Times*, August 12, 2019.

Sanger, David E., Nicole Perlroth, and Julian E. Barnes. "As Understanding of Russian Hacking Grows, So Does Alarm." *New York Times*, January 2, 2021.

Sanger, David E., Choe Sang-Hun, and Motoko Rich. "Allies Weighing Nuclear Options as Threat Looms." *New York Times*, October 29, 2017.

Satariano, Adam. "Will There Be a Ban on Killer Robots?" *New York Times*, October 19, 2018.

Schacter, Daniel L. *The Seven Sins of Memory: How the Mind Forgets and Remembers*. Boston: Houghton Mifflin, 2001.

Schachter, Oscar. "Relation of Peace and Human Rights." *International Legal Practitioner* 13 (September 1988). https://heinonline.org/HOL/LandingPage?handle=hein.journals/ilp13&div=30&id=&page=.

Schaffner, Brian F. *The Acceptance and Expression of Prejudice During the Trump Era*. Cambridge: Cambridge University Press, 2020.

Schaffner, Brian F. "Follow the Racist? The Consequences of Trump's Expressions of Prejudice for Mass Rhetoric." Tufts University Report. https://tufts.app.box.com/s/zhpop8u1sjw6g7y4zx81074ugl9ord1i.

Schell, Jonathan. *The Seventh Decade: The New Shape of Nuclear Danger*. New York: Holt, 2008.

Schelling, Thomas C. *The Strategy of Conflict*. New York: Oxford University Press, 1963.

Scheuerman, William E. "The (Classical) Realist Vision of Global Reform." *International Theory* 2, no. 2 (2010): 246–282.

Scheuerman, William E. *The Realist Case for Global Reform*. Cambridge: Polity Press, 2011.

Schlabach, Gerald W., ed. *Just Policing, Not War: An Alternative Response to World Violence*. Collegeville, MN: Liturgical Press, 2007.

Schlesinger, Arthur M. *A Thousand Days: John F. Kennedy in the White House*. Greenwich, CT: Fawcett, 1965.

Schoenbaum, Thomas J. *International Relations: The Path Not Taken: Using International Law to Promote World Peace and Security*. New York: Cambridge University Press, 2006.

Schrijver, Nico. "September 11 and Challenges to International Law." In *The Role of the United Nations in Peace and Security, Global Development, and World Governance: An Assessment of the Evidence*, edited by Michaela Horkijk, Maartje van Eerd, and Kaj Hofman, 55–76. Lewiston, NY: Edwin Mellen Press, 2007.

Schwartzberg, Joseph E. *Transforming the United Nations System: Designs for a Workable World*. Tokyo: United Nations University Press, 2013.

Scott, Janny. "Now It Can Be Told: How Neil Sheehan Got the Pentagon Papers." *New York Times*, January 7, 2021. https://www.nytimes.com/2021/01/07/us/pentagon-papers-neil-sheehan.html?searchResultPosition=3.

Security Assistance Monitor. *Arms Sales Dashboard*. https://securityassistance.org/contentnn/arms-sales-dashboard.

Sen, Amartya. *Development as Freedom*. New York: Alfred Knopf, 2000.

Sen, Amartya. "Global Justice and Beyond." In *Global Public Goods*, edited by Inge Kaul, Isabelle Grunbert, and Marc A. Stern. New York: United Nations Development Program, 1999.

"Senator Tim Kaine Questions Legality of US Led Airstrikes." *All Things Considered with Michel Martin*. National Public Radio, April 14, 2018.

Senese, Paul Domenic and John A. Vasquez. *The Steps to War: An Empirical Study*. Princeton, NJ: Princeton University Press, 2008.

Sengupta, Somini and Rick Gladstone. "United States and Allies Protest U.N. Talks to Ban Nuclear Weapons." *New York Times*, March 27, 2017.

Sethi, Rajiv and Eswaran Somanathan. "Understanding Reciprocity." *Journal of Economic Behavior & Organization* 50, no. 1 (2003): 1–27.

Seville Statement, UNESCO General Conference. Culture of Peace Programme, November 16, 1989. http://www.unesco.org/cpp/uk/declarations/seville.pdf.

Sharp, Gene. *The Politics of Nonviolent Action*. Boston: P. Sargent, 1973.

Shaw, Martin. "The Contemporary Mode of Warfare? Mary Kaldor's Theory of New Wars." *Review of International Political Economy* 7, no. 1 (2000): 171–180.

Shawcross, William. *Deliver Us from Evil: Peacekeepers, Warlords, and a World of Endless Conflict*. New York: Simon & Schuster, 2000.

Sheikh, Mona K. "Guardians of God: Understanding the Religious Violence of Pakistan's Taliban." University of Copenhagen, Department of Political Science, PhD Dissertation, 2011.

Shultz, George P., William J. Perry, Henry A. Kissinger, and Sam Nunn. "A World Free of Nuclear Weapons." *Wall Street Journal*, January 4, 2007.

Sides, John, Michael Tesler, and Lynn Vavreck. *Identity Crisis: The 2016 Presidential Campaign and the Battle for the Meaning of America*. Princeton, NJ: Princeton University Press, 2017.

Singer, Peter. *One World: The Ethics of Globalization*. New Haven, CT: Yale University Press, 2008.

Singer, Peter. *Practical Ethics*. Cambridge: Cambridge University Press, 2011.

Slaughter, Anne-Marie. *A New World Order*. Princeton, NJ: Princeton University Press, 2004.

Slaughter, Anne-Marie. "Security, Solidarity, and Sovereignty: The Grand Themes of UN Reform." *American Journal of International Law* 99, no. 3 (2005): 619–631.

Smith, Adam. *The Theory of Moral Sentiments, Or, an Essay Towards an Analysis of the Principles, by which Men Naturally Judge Concerning the Conduct and Character, First of their Neighbours, and Afterwards of Themselves*. Boston: Wells and Lilly, 1817.

Smith, Huston. *The Religions of Man*. New York: Harper & Row, 1958.

Smith, Jackie. *Social Movements for Global Democracy*. Baltimore: Johns Hopkins University Press, 2008.

Smith, Jackie and Dawn Wiest. *Social Movements in the World-System: The Politics of Crisis and Transformation*. New York: Russell Sage Foundation, 2012.

Smith, Jackie and Ernesto Verdeja. *Globalization, Social Movements, and Peacebuilding*. Syracuse, NY: Syracuse University Press, 2013.

Smith, Michael E. "A Liberal Grand Strategy in a Realist World? Power, Purpose and the EU's Changing Global Role." *Journal of European Public Policy* 18, no. 2 (2011): 144–163.

Smith, Rupert. *The Utility of Force: The Art of War in the Modern World*. New York: Vintage, 2008.

Snow, David A, Sarah A. Soule, Hanspeter Kriesi, and Holly McCammon, eds. *The Wiley Blackwell Companion to Social Movements*. Oxford: Wiley Blackwell, 2021.

Soan, Cliff and Michael Waldman. "History Frowns on Partisan Gerrymandering." *Washington Post*, October 1, 2017.

Sohn, Louis B. and Grenville Clark. *World Peace Through World Law: Two Alternative Plans*. Cambridge, MA: Harvard University Press, 1966.

Spaniel, William. "Here's What Could Happen if a President Trump Tore Up the Iran Nuclear Deal." *Washington Post*, July 11, 2016. https://www.washingtonpost.com/news/monkey-cage/wp/2016/07/11/heres-what-could-happen-if-a-president-trump-tore-up-the-iran-nuclear-deal/.

Speer, James. "Hans Morgenthau and the World State." *World Politics* 20, no. 2 (1968): 207.

Springs, Jason A. "Healthy Conflict in an Era of Intractability: Reply to Four Critical Responses." *Journal of Religious Ethics* 48, no. 2 (2020): 316–341.

Springs, Jason A. *Healthy Conflict in Contemporary American Society: From Enemy to Adversary*. Cambridge: Cambridge University Press, 2018.

Stahn, Carsten and Henning Melber. *Peace Diplomacy, Global Justice and International Agency Rethinking Human Security and Ethics in the Spirit of Dag Hammarskjöld*. Cambridge: Cambridge University Press, 2014.

Stanlick, Nancy, Daniel P. Collette, and Thomas Hobbes. *The Essential Leviathan: A Modernized Edition*. Cambridge, MA: Hackett, 2016.

Stapleton, Bradford Ian. "The Problem with the Light Footprint: Shifting Tactics in Lieu of Strategy." *Policy Analysis* 792. Washington, DC: Cato Institute, 2016.

Stassen, Glen Harold, ed. *Just Peacemaking: The New Paradigm for the Ethics of Peace and War*. Cleveland, OH: Pilgrim Press, 2008.

Statista. "The Syrian Civil War—Statistics & Facts." November 20, 2020. https://www.statista.com/topics/4216/the-syrian-civil-war/.

Steinfels, Peter. "The War Against Just War: Enough Already." *Commonweal* 144, no. 11 (2017): 15.

Sterba, James P. "Freedom from Poverty as a Human Right: Who Owes What to the Very Poor?" *Ethics and International Affairs* 22, no. 2 (Summer, 2008): 227–229.

Stets, Jan E. and Michael J. Carter. "A Theory of the Self for the Sociology of Morality." *American Sociological Review* 77, no. 1 (2012): 120–140.

Stets, Jan E. and Michael J. Carter. "The Moral Self: Applying Identity Theory." *Social Psychology Quarterly* 74, no. 2 (2011): 192–215.

Stevenson, Adlai E. "Working Toward a World without War." In *Disarmament: The New U.S. Initiative*, edited by United States Arms Control and Disarmament Agency, 13–28. Washington, DC: US Government Printing Office, 1962.

Stewart, Frances. *Horizontal Inequalities as a Cause of Conflict: Understanding Group Violence in Multiethnic Societies*. New York: Palgrave Macmillan, 2008.

Stewart, Frances. "Global Aspects and Implications of Horizontal Inequalities: Inequalities Experienced by Muslims Worldwide." In *Global Governance, Poverty and Inequality*, edited by Rorden Wilkinson, 265–294. New York: Routledge, 2010.

Stewart, Frances. "Root Causes of Violent Conflict in Developing Countries." *BMJ (British Medical Journal)* 324, no. 7333 (2002): 342.

Stiglitz, Joseph E. "The End of Neo-Liberalism?" *Project Syndicate*, July 7, 2008. https://www.project-syndicate.org/commentary/the-end-of-neo-liberalism?barrier=accesspaylog.

Stiglitz, Joseph E. *The Price of Inequality: How Today's Divided Society Endangers Our Future*. New York: W.W. Norton, 2012.

Stockholm International Peace Research Institute. "SIPRI Military Expenditure Database." https://www.sipri.org/databases/milex; https://www.sipri.org/research/armament-and-disarmament/arms-transfers-and-military-spending/military-expenditure.

Stockholm International Peace Research Institute. *Trends in International Arms Transfer, 2014*. www.sipri.org; https://www.sipri.org/research/armament-and-disarmament/arms-transfers-and-military-spending/international-arms-transfers.

Stockholm International Peace Research Institute "USA and France Dramatically Increase Major Arms Exports," March 9, 2020. https://www.sipri.org/media/press-release/2020/usa-and-france-dramatically-increase-major-arms-exports-saudi-arabia-largest-arms-importer-says.

Tams, Christian J. "World Peace Through International Adjudication?" In *Peace Through Law: Reflections on Pacem in Terris from Philosophy, Law, Theology, and Political Science*, edited by Heinz-Gerhard Justenhoven and Mary Ellen O'Connell, 215–254. Baden-Baden, Germany: Nomos, 2016.

Tarnas, Richard. *Cosmos and Psyche: Intimations of a New World View*. New York: Viking, 2006.

Tarrow, Sidney. *The New Transnational Activism*. Cambridge: Cambridge University Press, 2005.

Tarrow, Sid and David S. Meyer, eds. *The Resistance: The Dawn of the Anti-Trump Opposition Movement*. New York: Oxford University Press, 2018.

Task Force on Systemic Pesticides. *Worldwide Integrated Assessment of the Impact of Systemic Pesticides on Biodiversity and Ecosystems*, 2014. https://oaq.qc.ca/wp-content/uploads/2016/03/TaskForce_Pesticide.pdf; https://link.springer.com/article/10.1007/s11356-014-3220-1.

Taub, Amanda. "The Rise of American Authoritarianism." *Vox*, 2016. https://www.vox.com/2016/3/1/11127424/trump-authoritarianism.

Taylor, Astra. *Democracy May Not Exist, but We'll Miss It When It's Gone*. New York: Metropolitan Books, Henry Holt, 2019.

Taylor, Astra. "Reimagine Democracy." *The Progressive*, February/March, 2020, 22–25.

Taylor, Max, Ken Pease, and Jason Roach. *Evolutionary Psychology and Terrorism*. London: Taylor & Francis, 2015.

Taylor, Stuart. "U.S. Plans to Quit World Court Case on Nicaragua Suit." *New York Times*, January 19, 1985.

Tennis, Maggie. "Republicans Aim to Produce Banned Missile." *Arms Control Today* 47, no. 7 (2017): 24–25.

Terkel, Amanda. "Lindsey Graham: Drone Strikes Have Killed 4,700 People." *New York Times*, February 21, 2013.

Thakur, Ramesh. *The United Nations, Peace and Security: From Collective Security to the Responsibility to Protect*. Cambridge: Cambridge University Press, 2006.

Thayer, Bradley A. *Darwin and International Relations: On the Evolutionary Origins of War and Ethnic Conflict*. Lexington: University of Kentucky, 2009.

Thrall, A. Trevor and Caroline Dorminey. "Risky Business: The Role of Arms Sales in U.S. Foreign Policy." Policy Analysis. Washington, DC: CATO Institute, 2018.

Tickner, J. Ann. *A Feminist Voyage Through International Relations*. New York: Oxford University Press, 2014.

Tingbergen, Jan. "Financing for Sustainable Development." http://www.oecd.org/dac/stats/the07odagnitarget-ahistory.htm.

Tinbergen, Jan. "Global Governance for the 21st Century." In United Nations Human Development Programme. *Human Development Report 1994: New Dimensions of Human Security*. New York: Oxford University Press, 1994, 98.

Together First: A Global System That Works for All. "Bringing New Voices into Global Governance." https://together1st.org/.

Tran, Mark. "FBI Files Detail Guantánamo Torture Tactic." *The Guardian*, January 3, 2007.

"Transcript: President Trump's Phone Call with Georgia Election Officials." *New York Times*, January 4, 2021.

Treaty on European Union. Article 3 (5). https://eur-lex.europa.eu/legal-content/EN/TXT/HTML/?uri=CELEX:12008M003&from=EN.

Treaty on the Non-Proliferation of Nuclear Weapons. Article VI. https://www.un.org/disarmament/wmd/nuclear/npt/.

Trotta, Daniel. "Iraq War Costs U.S. More Than $2 Trillion." Reuters. https://www.reuters.com/article/us-iraq-war-anniversary-idUSBRE92D0PG20130314.

Turner, Bryan S. "Cosmopolitan Virtue, Globalization and Patriotism." *Theory, Culture & Society* 19, no. 1–2 (2002): 45–63.

Turpen, Elizabeth. "Achieving Nonproliferation Goals: Moving from Denial to Technology Governance." Policy Analysis Brief for the Stanley Foundation. Washington, DC: Stimson

Center, 2009. https://www.stimson.org/2009/achieving-nonproliferation-goals-moving-denial-technology-governance/.

Tveit, Olav Fykse. *Just Peace: Ecumenical, Intercultural, and Interdisciplinary Perspectives.* Eugene: Wipf and Stock, 2013.

Tyler, Patrick. "A New Power in the Streets." *New York Times,* February 17, 2003.

UNESCO General Conference, November 16, 1989. "Culture of Peace Programme." http://www.unesco.org/cpp/uk/declarations/seville.pdf.

UNESCO. Institute for Statistics. "Literacy Topic," 2008. www.uis.unesco.org/ev.php?

UN General Assembly. "Declaration on the Right to Peace." Resolution A/C.3/71/L.29, October 31, 2016.

UN General Assembly. "Declaration on the Right to Peace." Resolution A/71/189, February 2, 2017.

UN General Assembly, "United Nations Declaration on Human Rights Education and Training," General Assembly Resolution 66/137, December 19, 2011. https://www.ohchr.org/en/issues/education/training/pages/undhreducationtraining.aspx.

UN Security Council Resolutions Referencing R2P: Global Centre for the Responsibility to Protect. www.globalr2p.org.

Union of Concerned Scientists. "Political Motives Exposed at the EPA." *Catalyst* 18 Summer 2018, 5, www.uscusa.org/EPA-FOIA.

Union of Concerned Scientists. "Global Warming." https://www.ucsusa.org/global-warming#. WleVlq6nEdU.

Union of International Associations. *Yearbook of International Organizations, 2020–21.* https://uia.org/sites/uia.org/files/misc_pdfs/pubs/yb_2020_vol2_lookinside.pdf.

Union of International Associations. *Yearbook of International Organizations 2003–04.* Munich: K. G. Saur Verlag, 2005.

United Nations. Charter. Article 2 (4). https://www.un.org/en/about-us/un-charter/full-text.

United Nations Convention on the Law of the Sea. Article 1. https://www.un.org/depts/los/convention_agreements/convention_overview_convention.htm.

United Nations Convention on the Law of the Sea. "Preamble," 1833 *U.N.T.S.* 397. http://www.un.org/depts/los/convention_agreements/texts/unclos/preamble.htm.

United Nations Climate Change. *The Paris Agreement.* https://www.un.org/en/climatechange/paris-agreement.

United Nations Department for Disarmament Affairs. *The Implications of Establishing an International Satellite Monitoring Agency. Report of the Secretary-General.* New York: United Nations, 1983.

United Nations Department of Peacekeeping Operations: Department of Field Support. *Guidelines: The Role of United Nations Police in Protection of Civilians.* New York: United Nations, 2017.

United Nations Development Programme. *Human Development Report 1992: Global Dimensions of Human Development.* New York: Oxford University Press, 1992.

United Nations Development Programme. *Human Development Report 1999: Globalization with a Human Face.* http://www.hdr.undp.org/en/content/human-development-report-1999.

United Nations Development Programme. *Human Development Report 1994: New Dimensions of Human Security.* New York: Oxford University Press, 1994.

United Nations Development Programme. *Human Development Report 2018: Statistical Update: Human Development Indices and Indicators.* http://hdr.undp.org/en/content/human-development-indices-indicators-2018.

United Nations Development Programme. "A World Social Charter." *Human Development Report 1994*, 6. New York: Oxford University Press, 1994.

United Nations Division for Ocean Affairs and the Law of the Sea. *United Nations Convention on the Law of the Sea.* New York: United Nations,1982.

United Nations General Assembly. Convention on the Prevention and Punishment of the Crime of Genocide. https:// www.un.org/ en/genocideprevention/ documents/ atrocity-crimes/ Doc.1_ Convention%20on%20the%20. Prevention%20and%20Punishment%20 of%20the%20Crime%20of%20Genocide.pdf.

United Nations General Assembly. *Declaration of the Right of Peoples to Peace*, November 12, 1984. https://www.ohchr.org/EN/ProfessionalInterest/Pages/RightOfPeoplesToPeace. aspx.

United Nations General Assembly. Resolution A/RES/377(V), November 3, 1950.

United Nations General Assembly. United Nations Trust Fund for Human Security. Res 66/ 290. https://www.un.org/humansecurity/what-is-human-security/.

United Nations General Assembly. *United Nations Declaration on Human Rights Education and Training.* https://www.ohchr.org/en/issues/education/training/pages/undhreducation-training.aspx.

United Nations General Assembly & Security Council. *The Future of United Nations Peace Operations: Implementation of the Recommendations of the High-Level Independent Panel on Peace Operations: Report of the Secretary-General*, A/70/95 S/2015/446, June 17, 2015. New York: United Nations, 2015.

United Nations High Commissioner for Human Rights. *Good Governance Practices for the Protection of Human Rights.* New York: United Nations Office of the High Commissioner for Human Rights, 2007.

United Nations High Commissioner for Refugees. "Figures at a Glance." https://www. unhcr.org/en-us/figures-at-a-glance.html#:~:text=How%20many%20refugees%20are%20 there,under%20the%20age%20of%2018.

United Nations High-Level Panel of Eminent Persons on the Post 2015 Development Agenda. *A New Global Partnership: Eradicate Poverty and Transform Economies through Sustainable Development: Report.* New York: United Nations, 2013.

United Nations High-Level Panel on Threats, Challenges, and Change. *A More Secure World: Our Shared Responsibility: Report of the High-Level Panel on Threats, Challenges, and Change.* New York: United Nations, 2004.

United Nations News. Global Perspective Human Stories. "Syria: The Tragedy Is Deepening: Nearly 5 Million Children Have Known Nothing but War." March 14, 2020. https://news. un.org/en/story/2020/03/1059471.

United Nations News. "U.S. Sanctions Against International Court Staff a 'Direct Attack' on Judicial Independence." June 25, 2020. https://news.un.org/en/story/2020/06/1067142.

United Nations Office for the Coordination of Humanitarian Affairs, OCHA Services. "Women's Participation in Peace Negotiations: Connections between Presence and Influence." October 2012, 3. https://reliefweb.int/report/world/women%E2%80%99s-participation-peace-negotiations-connections-between-presence-and-influence.

United Nations Office for Disarmament Affairs. *The Biological Weapons Convention.* New York: United Nations, 2014.

United Nations Office of the High Commissioner for Human Rights. "Declaration on the Right of Peoples to Peace," General Assembly Resolution 39/11, November 12, 1984. https://www.ohchr.org/EN/ProfessionalInterest/Pages/RightOfPeoplesToPeace.

aspx#:~:text=The%20General%20Assembly%20%2C,of%20international%20peace%20
and%20security%2C&text=Solemnly%20declares%20that%20the%20preservation,3.

United Nations Office of the High Commissioner for Human Rights. "Declaration on the Rights of Persons Belonging to National or Ethnic, Religious and Linguistic Minorities." General Assembly Resolution 47/135, December 18, 1992. https://www.ohchr.org/en/professionalinterest/pages/minorities.aspx.

United Nations Secretary-General Kofi Annan. *The Rule of Law and Transitional Justice in Conflict and Post-Conflict Societies: Report of the Secretary-General.* New York: United Nations, 2004.   https://www.un.org/ruleoflaw/blog/document/the-rule-of-law-and-transitional-justice-in-conflict-and-post-conflict-societies-report-of-the-secretary-general/.

United Nations Secretary-General Kofi Annan. "Secretary-General Presents His Annual Report to General Assembly," SG/SM/7136, GA/9596, September 20, 1999. https://www.un.org/press/en/1999/19990920.sgsm7136.html.

United Nations Secretary-General Kofi Annan. "Secretary-General Salutes International Workshop of Human Security in Mongolia," Press Release SG/SM/7382 (May 8, 2000): 103, https://www.un.org/press/en/2000/20000508.sgsm7382.doc.html.

United Nations Secretary-General Kofi Annan. "Statement by UN Secretary-General Kofi Annan." President Jacques Chirac of France and Secretary-General Kofi Annan, September 19, 2001. //www.un.org/News/Press/docs/2001/sgsm7964.doc.htm.United Nations Secretary-General Kofi Annan. UN High-Level Panel Report. *In Larger Freedom: Towards Development, Security and Human Rights for All.* Report of the Secretary-General, UN Doc. A/59/2005 & annex (2005), 58, para 6(h). http://www.un.org/largerfreedom/contents.htm.

United Nations Special Session of the General Assembly Devoted to Disarmament. "Study on the Implications of Establishing an International Satellite Monitoring Agency." UN Document no. A/AC 206/14. New York: United Nations, 1981.

United States Army. *Law of Land Warfare* (Field Manual 27–10). https://web.archive.org/web/20041015013450/http://www.afsc.army.mil/gc/files/FM27-10.pdf.

United States Joint Forces Command. *Joint Operating Environment 2010: US National Security Posture Statement.* http://www.fas.org/man/eprint/joe2010.pdf.

Universal Declaration of Human Rights. https://www.un.org/en/about-us/universal-declaration-of-human-rights.

Urquhart, Brian and Francois Heisbourg. "Prospects for a Rapid Response Capability." In *Peacemaking and Peacekeeping for the New Century*, edited by Olara Otunnu and Michael W. Doyle. Lanham, MD: Rowman & Littlefield, 1998.

"U.S. and European Catholic Bishops Call for Strategy to Eliminate Nuclear Weapons Globally." July 6, 2017. http://www.usccb.org/news/2017/17-121.cfm.

US Arms Control and Disarmament Agency. "U.S. Nuclear Modernization Programs." *Arms Control Today*, August 2017. https://www.armscontrol.org/factsheets/USNuclear Modernization.

US Army. *Law of Land Warfare.* Field Manual 27–10: 85, 271, 378, A-5, A-24, A-41, A-70, A-118. https://web.archive.org/web/20041015013450/http://www.afsc.army.mil/gc/files/FM27-10.pdf.

Van Dijk, Jan. "Human Security: A New Agenda for Integrated, Global Action, International Conference on Space and Water: Towards Sustainable Development and Human Security." Santiago, Chile, April 1, 2004. hhttp://www.unodc.org/speech_2004-04-01_1.html.

Varshney, Ashutosh. *Ethnic Conflict and Civic Life: Hindus and Muslims in India.* New Haven, CT: Yale University Press, 2003.

Vasquez, John A. "The Steps to War: Toward a Scientific Explanation of Correlates of War Findings." *World Politics* 40 (1987): 108–145.

Vasquez, John A. *What Do We Know About War?* Lanham, MD: Rowan & Littlefield, 2012.

Vatican News. "The Pope: Not Using or Possessing Nuclear Arms Will Be Added to the Catechism." *Vatican News*. https://www.vaticannews.va/en/pope/news/2019-11/pope-francis-press-conference-japan-airplane.

Verdeja, Ernesto. *Unchopping a Tree: Reconciliation in the Aftermath of Political Violence*. Philadelphia: Temple University Press, 2009.

Verwimp, Philip, Patricia Justino, Tilman Brück, and Patricia Justino. "Poverty and Violent Conflict: A Micro-Level Perspective on the Causes and Duration of Warfare." *Journal of Peace Research* 46, no. 3 (2009): 315–333.

Vidal, John. "UN Environment Programme: 200 Species Extinct Every Day, Unlike Anything Since Dinosaurs Disappeared 65 Million Years Ago." *Huffington Post* May 25, 2011. http://www.huffingtonpost.com/2010/08/17/un-environment-programme-_n_684562.html.

Vitalis, Robert. *White World Order, Black Power Politics: The Birth of American International Relations*. Ithaca, NY: Cornell University Press, 2015.

Vitoria, Francisco de. "On the Law of War." In *Morality of War: A Reader*, edited by David Kinsell and Craig L. Carr, 70–79. Boulder, CO: Lynn Rienner, 2007.

Vogel, Gretchen. "Behavioral Evolution: The Evolution of the Golden Rule." *Science* 303, no. 5661 (2004): 1128–1131.

Volker, Kurt. "What the U.S. Risks by Relying on Drones." *Washington Post*, October 26, 2012.

Voronkova, Anastasia. "Are Nationalism and Cosmopolitanism Compatible?" https://www.e-ir.info/2010/11/25/are-nationalism-and-cosmopolitanism-compatible/.

Wallach, Lori. "The World Trade Organization Is Dying. What Should Replace It?" *New York Times*, November 28, 2019.

Wallensteen, Peter. *Preventing Violent Conflicts: Past Record and Future Challenges*. Uppsala, Sweden: Uppsala University Department of Peace and Conflict Research, 1998.

Wallensteen, Peter. *Quality Peace: Peacebuilding, Victory, and World Order*. New York: Oxford University Press, 2015.

Wallensteen, Peter. *Understanding Conflict Resolution*. Los Angeles: Sage, 2015.

Wallensteen, Peter. "Universalism vs. Particularism: On the Limits of Major Power Order." *Journal of Peace Research* 21, no. 3 (1984): 243–257.

Wallensteen, Peter. "War in Peace Research." In *Peace Research: Theory and Practice*, edited by Peter Wallensteen. New York: Routledge, 2011.

Wallensteen, Peter and Isak Svensson. "Talking Peace: International Mediation in Armed Conflicts." *Journal of Peace Research* 51, no. 2 (2014): 315–327.

Wallensteen, Peter, Michel Wieviorka, Itty Abraham, Karin Aggestam, Alexander Bellamy, Lars-Erik Cederman, Jerôme Ferret, et al. "Violence, Wars, Peace, Security." In *Rethinking Society for the 21st Century: Report of the International Panel on Social Progress: Political Regulation, Governance, and Societal Transformations*, vol. 2, 411–456. International Panel on Social Progress, 2018. doi:10.1017/9781108399661.

Walls, Laura Dassow. *Henry David Thoreau: A Life*. Chicago: University of Chicago Press, 2017.

Walt, Stephen M. *The Hell of Good Intentions: America's Foreign Policy Elite and the Decline of U.S. Primacy*. New York: Farrar, Straus and Giroux, 2018.

Waltz, Kenneth N. *Man, the State and War. A Theoretical Analysis*. New York: Columbia University Press, 1959.

Waltz, Kenneth. *Theory of International Politics*. Reading, MA: Addison-Wesley, 1979.

Walzer, Michael. *Arguing about War*. New Haven, CT: Yale University Press, 2004.

Walzer, Michael. *Just and Unjust Wars: A Moral Argument with Historical Illustrations*. New York: Basic Books, 1977.

Walzer, Michael. "Responsibility and Proportionality in State and Nonstate Wars." *Parameters* 39, no. 1 (2009): 40–52.

Wapner, Paul Kevin, Lester Edwin J. Ruiz, and Richard A. Falk. *Principled World Politics: The Challenge of Normative International Relations*. Lanham, MD: Rowman & Littlefield, 2000.

The War in Vietnam. By Ken Burns and Lynn Novick. https://www.pbs.org/show/vietnam-war/.

Warland, Justin. "Donald Trump Called Climate Change a Hoax." *Time Magazine*, July 9, 2019. https://time.com/5622374/donald-trump-climate-change-hoax-event/.

Warrick, Joby. "CIA Tactics Endorsed in Secret Memos." *Washington Post*, October 15, 2008.

Watson Institute, "Costs of War," November 30, 2020, https://watson.brown.edu/costsofwar/figures/2019/direct-war-death-toll-2001-801000.

Webel, Charles P. and Jorgen Johansen, eds. *Peace and Conflict Studies: A Reader*. New York: Routledge, 2012.

Weeramantry, Christopher Gregory. *Universalising International Law*. Leiden: Nijhoff, 2004.

Weiner, Tim and Barbara Crossette. "George F. Kennan Dies at 101; Leading Strategist of Cold War." *New York Times*, March 18, 2005.

Weiss, Thomas G. *Global Governance: Why? What? Whither?* Cambridge: Polity, 2013.

Weiss, Thomas G. "Pollyanna Is Not a Role Model—Humanitarian Business and Consequentialist Ethics." *Development Dialogue* 2014, no. 62 (2014): 98–101.

Weiss, Thomas G., David P. Forsythe, Roger A. Coate, and Kelly-Kate Pease. *The United Nations and Changing World Politics*. Boulder, CO: Westview, 2014.

Weiss, Thomas G. and Ramesh Thakur. *Global Governance and the UN: An Unfinished Journey*. United Nations Intellectual History Project Series. Bloomington: Indiana University Press, 2010.

Weiss, Thomas G., Conor Seyle, and Kelsey Collidge. *Non-State Actors and Global Governance: A Look at the Numbers*. Broomfield, CO: One Earth Future Foundation, 2013.

Weiss, Thomas G., D. Conor Seyle, and Kelsey Coolidge. *The Rise of Non-State Actors in Global Governance: Opportunities and Limitations*. Broomfield, CO: One Earth Future Foundation, 2013. https://acuns.org/wp-content/uploads/2013/11/gg-weiss.pdf; www.oneearthfuture.org.

Weiss, Thomas and Rorden Wilkinson. "Change and Continuity in Global Governance." *Ethics & International Affairs* 29, no. 4 (2015): 397–406.

Weiss, Thomas and Rorden Wilkinson. "Global Governance to the Rescue: Saving International Relations?" *Global Governance* 20, no. 1 (2014): 19–36.

Weiss, Thomas G. and Rorden Wilkinson. "The Globally Governed-Everyday Global Governance." *Global Governance* 24, no. 2 (2018): 193–210.

Weiss, Thomas G. and Rorden Wilkinson. *International Organization and Global Governance*. New York: Routledge, 2014.

Weiss, Thomas G. and Rorden Wilkinson. "Rethinking Global Governance? Complexity, Authority, Power, Change." *International Studies Quarterly* 58, no. 1 (2014): 207–215.

Wellman, James K. and Clark B. Lombardi. *Religion and Human Security: A Global Perspective*. New York: Oxford University Press, 2012.

Wendt, Alexander. "Anarchy Is What States Make of It: The Social Construction of Power Politics." *International Organization* 46, no. 2 (1992): 391–425.

Wendt, Alexander. "On Constitution and Causation in International Relations." *Review of International Studies* 24 (1998): 101–117.

Wendt, Alexander. *Social Theory of International Politics*. Cambridge: Cambridge University Press, 1999.

Wendt, Alexander. "Why a World State Is Inevitable." *European Journal of International Relations* 9, no. 4 (December 2003): 491–542.

Wendt, Alexander and Raymond Duvall. "Sovereignty and the UFO." *Political Theory* 36, no. 4 (August 1, 2008): 607–633.

Wertheim, Stephen. "The Only Way to End 'Endless War.'" *New York Times*, September 14, 2019.

West, Darrell M. and Christian Lansang. "Global Manufacturing Scorecard: How the US Compares to 18 Other Nations," July 10, 2018. https://www.brookings.edu/research/global-manufacturing-scorecard-how-the-us-compares-to-18-other-nations/.

Whippman, David. "Introduction: Do New Wars Call for New Laws?" In *New Wars, New Laws? Applying the Laws of War in 21st Century Conflicts*, edited by David Whippman and Matthew Evangelista. Ardsley, NY: Transnational, 2005.

White, Ralph K. *Fearful Warriors: A Psychological Profile of U.S.-Soviet Relations*. New York: Free Press, 1984.

WHO and UNICEF. *Progress on Drinking Water and Sanitation*. 2017, 7, 30. https://www.unicef.org/reports/progress-on-drinking-water-sanitation-and-hygiene-2019.

Wikipedia. "Nuclear Weapons Testing." https://en.wikipedia.org/wiki/Nuclear_weapons_testing.

Wilson, Edward O. *Genesis: The Deep Origin of Societies*. New York: W.W. Norton, 2019.

Wines, Michael. "The Student Vote Is Surging. So Are Efforts to Suppress It." *New York Times*, October 24, 2019.

Winright, Tobias. "Community Policing as a Paradigm for International Relations." In *Just Policing, Not War: An Alternative Response to World Violence*, edited by Gerald W. Schlabach, 130–152. Collegeville, MN: Liturgical Press, 2007.

Winslow, Donna J. "Human Security." In *The Role of the United Nations in Peace and Security, Global Development, and World Governance: An Assessment of the Evidence*, edited by Michaela Hordijk, Maartje van Eerd, and Kau Hofman, 103–124. Lewiston: Edwin Mellen Press, 2007.

Winthrop, Rebecca. "The Need for Civic Education in 21st-Century Schools." *Brookings Policy Big Ideas*, June 4, 2020. https://www.brookings.edu/policy2020/bigideas/the-need-for-civic-education-in-21st-century-schools/.

Wong, Edward. "Hacking U.S. Secrets, China Pushes for Drones." *New York Times*, September 21, 2013.

Woodward, Bob. *Fear: Trump in the White House*. New York: Simon and Schuster, 2018.

World Commission on Environment and Development. "Brundtland Report/Annexe 1. Summary of Proposed Legal Principles for Environmental Protection and Sustainable Development." https://en.wikisource.org/wiki/Brundtland_Report/Annexe_1._Summary_of_Proposed_Legal_Principles_for_Environmental_Protection_and_Sustainable_Development.

World Commission on Environment, and Development. *Our Common Future: From One Earth to One World*. New York: Oxford University Press, 1987.

World Happiness Report 2019. https://worldhappiness.report/ed/2019/.

World Markets Research Centre. *Global Terrorism Index*. https://www.visionofhumanity.org/wp-content/uploads/2020/11/GTI-2019-web.pdf.

Wright, Quincy. *A Study of War*. Chicago: University of Chicago Press, 1965.

Wright, Quincy. *The Role of International Law in the Elimination of War*. Dobbs Ferry, NY: Oceana, 1961.

Wright, Robert. *The Moral Animal: Evolutionary Psychology and Everyday Life*. New York: Pantheon Books, 1994.

Wright, Robert. *NonZero: The Logic of Human Destiny*. New York: Vintage Books, 2001.

Yearbook of International Organizations, https://www.uia.org/ybio/.

Yetiv, Steven A. *The Absence of Grand Strategy: The United States in the Persian Gulf, 1972–2005*. Baltimore: Johns Hopkins University Press, 2008.

Yoder, John Howard. *When War Is Unjust: Being Honest in Just-War Thinking*. Eugene, OR: Wipf and Stock, 2001.

Yunus, Muhammad. *A World of Three Zeroes: The New Economics of Zero Poverty, Zero Unemployment, and Zero Carbon Emissions*. London: Scribe, 2017.

Zartman, I. William, ed. *Peacemaking in International Conflict: Methods and Techniques*. Washington, DC: US Institute of Peace Press, 2007.

Zaum, Dominik. "The Security Council, the General Assembly and War: The Uniting for Peace Resolution." In *The United Nations Security Council and War: The Evolution of Thought and Practice since 1945*, edited by Vaughan Lowe, Adam Roberts, Jennifer Welsh, and Dominik Zaum, 154–174. Oxford: Oxford University Press, 2008.

Zenko, Micah. *Reforming U.S. Drone Strike Policies*. Council on Foreign Relations. Council Special Report no. 65, January 2013. i.cfr.org/content/publications/attachments/Drones_CSR65.pdf.

Zinn, Howard. *The Power of Nonviolence: Writings by Advocates of Peace*. Boston: Beacon Press, 2002.

Zoller, Elizabeth. *Peacetime Unilateral Remedies*. Dobbs Ferry, NY: Transnational, 1984.

Zughni, Farrah and Jeff Abramson. "At Mine Ban Meeting, U.S. Still Mum on Policy." *Arms Control Today* 41, no. 1 (2011): 49.

Index

For the benefit of digital users, indexed terms that span two pages (e.g., 52–53) may, on occasion, appear on only one of those pages.

Tables and figures are indicated by *t* and *f* following the page number

'